WHO BUILT AMERICA?

WHO
WORKING PEOPLE

AMERICAN SOCIAL HISTORY PROJECT
CITY UNIVERSITY OF NEW YORK
under the direction of
HERBERT G. GUTMAN

BUILT AMERICA?

AND THE NATION'S ECONOMY, POLITICS, CULTURE, AND SOCIETY

VOLUME ONE: FROM CONQUEST AND COLONIZATION
THROUGH RECONSTRUCTION AND THE GREAT UPRISING OF 1877

BRUCE LEVINE

STEPHEN BRIER

DAVID BRUNDAGE

EDWARD COUNTRYMAN

DOROTHY FENNELL

MARCUS REDIKER

JOSHUA BROWN, *Visual Editor*

Eric Foner and Alfred Young, *Consulting Editors*

PANTHEON BOOKS | NEW YORK

Library of Congress Cataloging-in-Publication Data

Who built America? : working people and the nation's economy,
politics, culture, and society / Bruce Levine . . . [et al.].
p. cm.
Contents: From conquest and colonization through Reconstruction
and the great uprising of 1877.
Result of work of the American Social History Project.
Includes bibliographical references.
ISBN 0-394-54663-6 (v. 1).—ISBN 0-679-72699-3 (pbk. : v. 1)
1. Working class—United States—History. 2. United States—
Social conditions. 3. United States—History. I. Levine, Bruce C., 1949–
II. American Social History Project.
HD8066.W47 1990
305.5′62′0973—dc20   89-43240

Permissions and credits are given on pages 583–88.

Interior design by Robert Bull Design.

Manufactured in the United States of America

First Edition

CONTENTS

PREFACE xi

PART ONE: **COLONIZATION AND REVOLUTION: 1607–1790** **3**

1 EUROPE COLONIZES THE AMERICAS: The Meeting of Three Worlds 7

The Peoples of the New World 9
Crisis in Europe 15
West Africa and the International Slave Trade 19
Capitalism and Colonization 27

2 SLAVERY AND THE GROWTH OF THE SOUTHERN COLONIES **39**

Colonizing the Chesapeake 40
The Labor "Problem" 48
Conflict and Slavery 54
Slavery Spreads 60
African-American Culture 65
The South on the Eve of Revolution 71

3 FREE LABOR AND THE GROWTH OF THE NORTHERN COLONIES **79**

The Great Invasion 81
Conquest and Resistance 85
Patterns on the Land 91
Cities by the Sea 97
Women's Worlds 109
The Rulers and the Ruled 115
The North on the Eve of Revolution 117

4 "THE GREATNESS OF THIS REVOLUTION" **127**

The Imperial Crisis 129
The Sons and Daughters of Liberty 136
Resistance Becomes Revolution 146

A People's War 151
People's Government 156
The Grand Federal Edifice 166
The Legacy of the Revolution 175

PART TWO: **FREE LABOR AND SLAVERY, 1790–1860**   **179**

5 THE GROWTH OF THE SLAVE SOUTH   **183**

Birth of the Cotton Kingdom 185
A New South Emerges 189
The Slave South 195
   The Slaveowners 195
   The Yeomen 201
   The Slaves 204
Industrial and Urban Growth 213

6 THE FREE-LABOR NORTH   **221**

Merchant Capital and the Transportation Revolution 224
Indians in the Northwest 228
Crops and Commerce 231
Paths to Wage Labor 238
   The Unskilled Laborer 240
   The Artisan 242
   The Outworker 249
   The Factory Worker 251
Depression, Recovery, Expansion 256
Immigrants and the Social Structure 264

7 CHANGING PATTERNS OF SOCIAL LIFE   **269**

The Middle-Class Ideal 271
Plebeian Realities 277
Southern Families 284
Barbecues, Barn-Raisings, and Bees 289
Commercial Amusements 291
Leisure in the Slave Quarters 299
Evangelical Protestantism 301
Roman Catholicism 308
Freethinkers 310
Evangelicals and Slavery 311

8 THE FIGHT FOR FREE LABOR IN THE NORTH   **319**

Journeymen Unite 321
The Workingmen's Parties Oppose Monopoly 325

Solidarity or Conspiracy?   331
Women Workers Mobilize   335
Unskilled Labor Organizes   340
Depression Takes Its Toll   342
The Search for Solutions   346
The Labor Movement after the Depression   354
On the Eve of War   360

9 THE STRUGGLE OVER SLAVE LABOR   **365**

Slaves Resist and Adapt   366
Dissent and Democracy in the South   372
Slavery and Sectional Conflict   375
Abolition and Reaction   377
Northern Workers and the Antislavery Movement   383
Slavery and Westward Expansion   386
The Compromise of 1850   393
A New Party Alignment   403
Toward a Showdown   407

PART THREE: **WAR, RECONSTRUCTION, AND LABOR, 1860–1877**   **413**

10 THE CIVIL WAR: America's Second Revolution   **417**

The South Secedes   418
For Union—or Against Slavery?   424
Soldiers' Lives   435
War Transforms the North   440
African-Americans in the War   448
War Transforms the South   455
The War's End   460

11 EMANCIPATION AND RECONSTRUCTION   **465**

Rehearsals for Reconstruction   466
Emancipation and the Meaning of Freedom   473
Legislating Reconstruction   481
Radical Reconstruction in the South   490
Retreat from Reconstruction   500
The End of Reconstruction   511

12 INDUSTRIAL LABOR AFTER THE WAR   **515**

Railroads and the West   516
Industry and Workers   523
Workers' Struggles   531
The National Labor Union   538

Depression and Conflict   545
The Great Uprising of 1877   553

CONCLUSION: A New Phase in American History   559

SOURCES   563

CREDITS   583

CONTRIBUTORS   589

INDEX   591

To Herbert Gutman,
   who taught us new ways to look at the working class.

To Harry Brier,
   who taught us never to lose faith in its possibilities.

To Isidor Levine,
   who knew what was what.

PREFACE

Who built the seven towers of Thebes?
The books are filled with the names of kings.
Was it kings who hauled the craggy blocks of stone? . . .
In the evening when the Chinese wall was finished,
Where did the masons go?

—Bertolt Brecht,
"Questions from a Worker Who Reads" (1935)

WHO BUILT AMERICA? surveys the nation's past from an important but often neglected perspective—the experiences of ordinary men and women and the role they played in the making of modern America. As recently as thirty years ago, such a focus would have been virtually impossible. The research and writing (as well as teaching) of most U.S. historians remained focused on presidents, politics, wars, and the life and values of the nation's elite—the familiar framework their profession had consistently favored. Moreover, most historians accepted the notion that there had been little fundamental social and economic conflict in America's past, that a broad consensus about the nation's basic values and its extraordinary prosperity had united the vast majority of its citizens.

In the past three decades, much has changed. The social and political upheavals of the 1960s and early 1970s prompted a number of historians—including all of the authors of this book—to expand their inquiries into America's past. They made dramatic discoveries about the behavior and beliefs of groups traditionally slighted by the older historical synthesis: craftsmen, Indians, women, slaves, small farmers, factory workers, and myriad immigrant groups. They also helped unearth a long and sustained history of conflict among Americans of different classes, races, national origins, and genders over the meaning of American ideals of liberty and equality and the distribution of the nation's enormous material wealth. Their discoveries allowed these historians to think and write differently about familiar topics, including the American Revolution, westward expansion, slavery, the rise of industrial capitalism, and the Civil War and Reconstruction. It also led to the emergence of entire new fields of inquiry, especially working-class and social history, and the dramatic expansion of older areas of scholarly interest, including women's, African-American, and immigrant history.

Despite the enormous ferment in the profession, however, mainstream American history writing remained essentially unaffected by the new scholarship and the insights that it offered. Moreover, debates about the significance of the new scholarship were bottled up in the narrow confines of the profession, where only academics contested over the issues.

The late Herbert G. Gutman—who inspired, collaborated in, and oversaw the American Social History Project until his death in 1985—was one of the first American historians to identify these problems and call for their correction. Gutman suggested that there was a pressing need to overcome the "balkanization" that characterized historical analysis. He called in 1982 for "a new national synthesis" that would use the social and labor history he played so large a role in launching to recast the older economic and political analysis that continued to dominate writing and teaching about American history. This new synthesis would have much to tell ordinary citizens about their country and about the values and traditions that shaped and sustained it. Gutman also forcefully argued for making the new synthesis accessible to a broad audience that encompassed general readers as well as students and teachers in any setting.

The American Social History Project was created to realize these ambitious ends. The idea for the Project grew out of a series of National Endowment for the Humanities (NEH) seminars on social history for labor leaders that Herbert Gutman and Stephen Brier conducted at the City University of New York (CUNY) in the late 1970s. The extraordinary excitement generated by social history among these working adults led Gutman and Brier to found the ASHP in 1981. Supported by major grants from the NEH, the Ford Foundation, CUNY, and others, the ASHP staff—numbering at times as many as a dozen researchers, writers, teachers, artists, and filmmakers—set out to produce a wide range of accessible educational materials, including books, videos, and viewer guides, and to train college, high-school, and adult- and labor-education teachers to use them effectively. *Who Built America?* serves as the intellectual keystone of the Project's work.

Who Built America? thus offers a uniquely cast history of the United States. Its central focus and organizing theme are the changing nature of the work that built, sustained, and transformed American society over the course of almost four centuries and the changing conditions, experiences, outlooks, and conduct of the people who performed that essential labor. This focus permits the integration of the history of community, family, gender roles, race, and ethnicity into the more familiar history of politics and economic development. Exploring the history of the nation's laboring majority, moreover, also renders more intelligible the beliefs and actions of the nation's economic, political, and intellectual elites.

For the purposes of this book, we have defined the category of "working people" broadly. Throughout much of its history, the nation's actual workforce embraced a wide spectrum of people laboring in very different conditions and settings—free and unfree; small proprietor and propertyless; agricultural and domestic as well as industrial, commercial, clerical, and service. Answering the question "Who built America?" therefore requires attention not only to wage-earning industrial employees but also indentured servants, slaves, tenants, sharecroppers, independent farm families, artisans, day laborers, clerks, domestic workers, outworkers, and women and children performing unpaid family labor—in short, the great majority of the American population at every phase of the country's development. Ignoring such people would thus not only fail to answer the question posed by our title. It would also miss the protracted, recurring, and complex processes out of which a modern working class emerged.

We have divided this study into two volumes. The principal theme of the first volume is the rise and subsequent decline of various precapitalist labor systems, especially racial slavery, and the parallel development and ultimate dominance of capitalism and its system of wage labor. The volume's twelve chapters are divided into three parts:

- Part One covers the three centuries from the chronic crisis of European feudal and mercantile society that led to the colonization of North America and examines the different peoples (European, African, and Amerindian) brought together in the process, through the establishment and evolution of the northern and southern colonies, to the colonists' successful war for independence.
- Part Two covers the seven decades following the creation of a national government, through profound economic, social, and political changes, including the industrial revolution, the growth of the cotton kingdom, the dramatic expansion westward, and the growing conflict between the free-labor system in the North and the system of racial slavery in the South that culminated in the Civil War.
- Part Three recounts that war—America's Second Revolution—on the battlefield and homefront, the northern victory and the emancipation of the slaves, the hopes and fears engendered during the Reconstruction era, ending with the

celebration in 1876 of the nation's centenary, the formal end of Reconstruction, and the explosive nationwide strike wave of 1877. Together the dramatic events of 1876–77 signal the end of one major epoch in American social, economic, and political history, and the beginning of another.

The second volume carries the narrative and analysis to the present day. It considers the increasing significance of industrial capitalism and wage labor for the country's economy, social relations, domestic politics, foreign policy, popular culture, and intellectual life during the nation's second century, and focuses on the corresponding growth and continual recomposition of the American working class.

We have supplemented the text of each chapter with excerpts from numerous historical documents (letters, diaries, autobiographies, poems, songs, journalism, fiction, official testimony, and oral histories). These "first-person" sidebars convey the experience and often the voice of working people during the various historical periods covered in the book. In the interest of clarity, we have sometimes modernized spelling, punctuation, and (especially in the case of the earliest documents) language. Much of the oral testimony of African-Americans, which was largely recorded and published by whites, originally appeared in a form of exaggerated and stereotyped dialect. Following the lead of others, we have rendered that testimony into standard English.

Each chapter also has drawings, paintings, prints, and photographs that derive from the historical periods covered. Most of the illustrations in this book are images that were reproduced and sold in their period, including pictures in books, pamphlets, newspapers, and magazines, individually published broadsides and lithographs, and paired photographs sold as "stereoscopic views." These images and their captions present some of the ways the topics of each chapter were portrayed and interpreted, as well as how people received information. The visual record of the past—particularly regarding the lives of working men and women, immigrants, and people of color—requires careful consideration: our captions often alert the reader to distortions and gaps that pock the visual roadway. Pictures that were produced and viewed in specific historical eras can teach us a lot about working peoples' lives, but it is equally important to understand there is much that these pictures obscure or fail to show.

A book of this size and scope is, of necessity, the result of a team effort. The conception, structure, thematic and analytical emphases, outlining, drafting, and illustration of *Who Built America?* all involved interaction among the authors, other members of the ASHP staff, and our advisors. That process began in 1982. Research and Writing Director Bruce Levine, working closely with Herbert Gutman, drafted memos outlining the two volumes' basic conceptual and chronological focus and describing the content and broad themes of each chapter. The ASHP staff discussed these ideas at length, after which particular authors drafted individual chapters. These first drafts were critiqued and revised, as were later drafts—a process of collaboration that shaped this volume.

Not all of the Project staff who participated in this process are named on the title page. Josh Brown, Kate Pfordresher, and Bret Eynon, the Project's audiovisual staff, contributed to the book's conceptual and historiographical development. They also insisted that questions of teaching receive as much attention as those of historical interpretation. Joshua Freeman, who joined the staff in 1984 to work on the second volume, was a gracious and insightful colleague and critic. Research assistants Michael Hyman and Michael Musuraca also provided historiographical and theoretical insights.

However collaborative this process, though, in the end the chapters were the product of the work of individuals. ASHP staff writer Dorothy Fennell wrote preliminary drafts of the volume's first four chapters. Herbert Gutman and Fennell then substantially recast chapter 2 and also drafted chapter 5. Bruce Levine drafted and revised chapters 6 through 9, edited the accompanying documents, and prepared the chapters for publication. He also rewrote chapters 1 and 5, preparing the latter for publication. Contributing author Edward Countryman wrote new drafts of chapters 3 and 4, which were edited and prepared for publication by contributing author Marcus Rediker, who also completed the final editing and preparation of chapters 1 and 2. Staff writer David Brundage drafted and revised chapters 10 through 12. Project Director Stephen Brier rewrote chapters 10, 11, and 12 and prepared them for publication, edited the documents for those chapters as well as for chapters 1 through 4, and drafted the volume's introductions.

The writers were ably assisted over the years by a corps of research assistants, including Annie Chamberlain, Elisa Krause, Phil Leahy, Michael Musuraca, and especially Michael Hyman, who was responsible for collecting many of the volume's first-person documents, and David Osborn, who ordered the pictures. Project administrators Nancy Hoch, Allyson Purpura, Thea Martinez, and especially Elizabeth Sheehan (who did two separate tours of duty), endured endless requests for printed drafts of the chapters.

A number of colleagues read and criticized some or all of the chapters. We would like to thank Jon Amsden, Carol Berkin, Ira Berlin, Jeanne Chase, Thomas Dublin, Stanley Engerman, Carol Groneman,

Steven Hahn, Alice Kessler-Harris, Gary Kulik, James McPherson, Joanne Meyerowitz, Nell Painter, Roger Ransom, Mary Ryan, Herb Sloan, Sean Wilentz, and Eric Wolf for their thoughtful responses.

The illustrations in *Who Built America?* are part of an archive of historical pictures gathered since 1982 by the American Social History Project's audiovisual staff. Kate Pfordresher's aesthetic and critical judgment was crucial to the construction of the collection. Bret Eynon's ability to find just the right image for the *Who Built America?* video series contributed greatly to the illustration of this volume as well. We also would like to thank a number of friends and colleagues for their help. Peter Buckley, Susan Davis, Herb Sloan, Irene Wamsler, and Al Young generously directed us to picture sources and suggested approaches to captioning. Finally, we want to thank the staffs of research libraries (in particular, the New York Public Library), collections, and archives, as well as private collectors who assisted us in securing the illustrations. The contributions of other individuals and institutions to the illustration of *Who Built America?*, too numerous to list here, are acknowledged in the picture credits.

We are indebted to the Project's board of directors—Peter Almond, Ira Berlin, Eric Foner, Carol Groneman, Leon Litwack, and Roy Rosenzweig for their continuing support and encouragement.

We especially want to acknowledge Eric Foner and Alfred Young, the volume's consulting editors. Both felt an obligation to help finish the work started by their friend and colleague, Herb Gutman. Eric Foner read the entire manuscript twice. And he was generous about allowing us to freely use his important study on Reconstruction as we shaped the final version of our own chapter on that subject. Al Young's commitment to and involvement with this book never wavered over the course of four years. He continually pushed us to make the text, the documents, and the illustrations in Part One better.

We are grateful to the institutions that provided financial support to the Project, and thus made possible the writing of this book. The substantial original grant awards from the National Endowment for the Humanities and the Ford Foundation allowed us to bring the Project staff together and sustained our labors through 1986. We want to thank Len Oliver and James Dougherty of the NEH and Susan Berresford, Sheila Biddle, Alison Bernstein, and Gladys Hardy of the Ford Foundation for their good advice and their patience. Without the support of Chancellor Joseph Murphy of the City University of New York, the Project would never have survived after 1986. This book has been made possible in large measure by Joe Murphy's abiding commitment to working-class education. We also want to thank President Harold Proshansky and the support staff of the CUNY Graduate Center, where we were based until 1989, and President Paul

LeClerc and the faculty of Hunter College, where the Project now resides.

Finally, we want to acknowledge our colleagues at Pantheon Books. André Schiffrin, the managing director, and James Peck, our acquisitions editor, kept the faith, even after Herb Gutman's death. Wendy Wolf's sharp humor and good sense made the production process more stimulating and palatable than it might have been. Designer Bob Bull, art director Fearn Cutler, and production manager Kathy Grasso expertly rendered a book from a foreboding pile of typescript and photographs, and assured that the appearance of *Who Built America?* not only appeals to the eye but also conveys critical information. And David Frederickson, our style and copy editor, always was willing and able to cut through the thickets of our prose to the heart of the arguments we wanted to make. David was as much our collaborator in the end as our editor.

In acknowledging the contributions to this volume, it would be difficult to exaggerate the role of Herbert Gutman. The impact of Herb's wide-ranging knowledge of American history—conveyed to us in four years of meetings, memos, chapter critiques, individual consultations, and writing and rewriting of text—was central to the conception of our task and the evolution of the manuscript. Our collective and individual debt to Herb is, quite simply, immeasurable. In completing and publishing *Who Built America?*, it is our hope that we have succeeded in meeting the high standards he set for himself throughout his rich but too-brief career.

WHO BUILT AMERICA?

John Speed, Map of America, 1626.

PART ONE

COLONIZATION AND REVOLUTION

1607 – 1790

MODERN AMERICA had its beginnings in a crisis-ridden feudal Europe. In the fifteenth century, rulers and men of commerce began a frantic worldwide search for new sources of wealth. They created a vast new Atlantic system of expropriation and exchange which, over the next three centuries, linked together and dramatically transformed Africa, America, and even Europe itself. The violent seizure of New World land from its Indian inhabitants, the settlement and growth of Europe's New World societies, and the transportation of millions of enslaved Africans made possible a massive accumulation of wealth in Europe. In the process, capitalism—a new economic system with accompanying social values and political ideologies—emerged in Europe and subsequently in North America.

We shall see how this process worked itself out on the east coast of North America. In the seventeenth century, very different ways of life emerged in Britain's northern and southern colonies. In the North—in particular in New England—the aspirations of the migrants and the stony soil they encountered led to limited small-scale farming, maritime trade, and urban craft production based on a system of family and free labor, along with some use of indentured servants. In the South, more favorable soil and climate and the single-minded pursuit of wealth led to a system of large-scale plantation

The United States, prior to the Treaty of Peace, 1783.

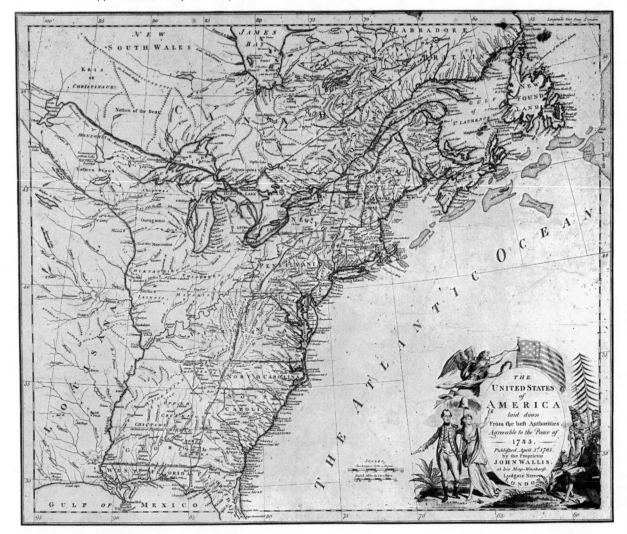

agriculture sustained originally by the labor of indentured servants and later by African slaves. Distinct labor systems—free and unfree—increasingly defined the ways of life of the two regions.

Colonial America was wracked by political, economic, religious, and racial conflict. The colonists fought with the Indians as they expanded westward and displaced them. They struggled with Africans, who proved unwilling laborers. And colonists fought with each other over who would own the land, who would govern society, and how religion would be practiced.

In the next century, America evolved from a diverse group of colonies toward nationhood. Beginning in the 1760s, internal conflicts merged with the larger conflict over America's imperial relationship to the "mother country." Colonists sought at first to secure their rights as subjects of the English empire and ended by demanding complete independence from British rule. This movement for independence was supported by a broad coalition of Americans—rich, middling, and poor; northern and southern; men and women. The climax was reached in 1775 when war erupted, leading finally to victory in 1783—the first successful colonial revolution in modern history—and the creation in 1787 of a national government with a Constitution based on republican principles.

Much of this story of America's birth is familiar. How we interpret what happened and from whose perspective we will tell the story is not.

Familiar historical figures—Washington, Adams, Jefferson—were major actors on the Revolutionary stage. So too were the vast majority of "ordinary" Americans—slaves and free people; farmers, artisans, laborers, and seamen. These people did not merely participate in events; they shaped the outcome in fundamental ways, sometimes in conflict, at other times by cooperating with elite leaders. Working Americans also attached distinct meanings of their own to the republican ideals embodied in the Declaration of Independence and the Bill of Rights.

Revolutionary-era America expressed a profound tension between ideals of liberty and equality on the one hand, and, on the other, the plunder of Indian land, the enslavement of African peoples, the exploitation of European-born workers, and the political and social inequality suffered by women. We shall see how these contradictions shaped America's colonial experience and how they defined the limits of its revolutionary heritage.

"America." The natural bounty of the New World on display in a seventeenth-century Flemish painting. On the left of the central panel, America is represented by Indians who lounge alongside the favored object of European desire, a collection of gold weights.

1 EUROPE COLONIZES THE AMERICAS

THE MEETING OF THREE WORLDS

IN 1492, after two stormy months crossing a treacherous Atlantic, Christopher Columbus, a Genoese mariner of humble origins and great ambition, stepped ashore on a tiny island in the Caribbean. He was met by a group of the native Americans who had lived there for centuries. This encounter marked the beginning of a fundamental transformation of both America and Europe—and, within a century, of Africa as well.

Columbus and his handful of sailors were the first of a swelling stream of Europeans who, with increasing confidence, crossed and recrossed a once-formidable ocean. These first travelers to the New World exchanged gifts with their hosts as equals, but before long, the visitors, with their superior weapons, fell upon the people of the

Americas and took almost anything they wanted. Hundreds of European adventurers followed Columbus across the Atlantic, bringing men and guns in an effort to take control of America's native societies. Everywhere they went, they carried deadly European diseases unknown to the peoples of the New World, which made the work of plunder and domination much easier. Against the Aztecs of Mexico, one of the mightiest societies of the New World, the conquerers had the additional advantage of having been mistaken for the gods whose arrival had been foretold in ancient prophecies. The Aztecs did not realize their mistake until it was too late: ruins soon marked the spots where once had stood cities and temples as great as any in Europe.

Millions of Europeans and Africans crossed the Atlantic over the next three centuries. Most of the former came willingly, determined either to find gold and return home as rich as kings, or to claim land and begin life over again in the New World. Others came as indentured servants or, worse yet, as victims who had been kidnapped to be sold into slavery. Virtually all of the Africans came unwillingly, first in Portuguese ships bound for the sugar plantations hacked out of the jungles of Brazil in the sixteenth century, and in the next century in Dutch and English vessels bound for the sugar fields of the Caribbean and the tobacco fields of Virginia.

Before Columbus, Indian society in the Americas was immensely diverse, ranging from small egalitarian bands of nomadic hunters and gatherers who eked out a bare subsistence, to populous and complex societies with elaborate hierarchies and stores of glittering riches. West Africa, too, had a mixture of smaller societies and more developed kingdoms, many of which would soon be transformed or obliterated by the burgeoning slave trade.

But the most dynamic source of change lay in Europe, where the search for more revenue and power led rulers to colonize the Americas. In Central and South America, Spanish and Portuguese operations began as glorified pirate expeditions, plundering gold, silver, and other valuables produced by native populations. But later, when the mere plunder of existing wealth proved inadequate, the form of colonialism began to change. Stable European settlements now forced American Indian and African laborers to produce not only precious metals, but also agricultural products that brought huge profits in a developing world market. To acquire and discipline its labor force, Europeans utilized (and radically changed) forms of coerced labor that already existed in parts of West Africa and America.

North of Mexico, the major influence came from England, where the transition from feudalism to capitalism had opened the way to momentous social and economic changes. Old feudal forms of obligatory labor, as well as the more cooperative economy of the peasant

The New Chronicle and Good Government. A drawing by a seventeenth-century Andean nobleman, Felipe Guamán Poma de Ayala, depicts the Incan view of the world. The kingdom of Peru, the capital city of Cuzco in its center, is situated at the top of the world, overshadowing Spain below. Guamán Poma's 1200-page *Nueva corónica y buen gobierno,* illustrated with 400 quill drawings, was written between 1587 and 1615. It comprises a unique Andean interpretation of Peruvian history from the Creation through the Spanish conquest.

village, gradually dissolved. In their place arose a new capitalist system—production for profit based primarily upon wage labor. The rise of capitalism brought intense conflict and, in its wake, a powerful popular tradition that frequently resisted the new order, enshrining ideas of freedom from subservience and dependence, and of the political and economic rights necessary to maintain independence. The English thus brought both capitalist practices and a popular democratic tradition to North America. Here, as in Europe, the two coexisted dynamically—sometimes in harmony, sometimes in conflict.

The origins of American society—and the dramatic, unparalleled encounter among the red, white, and black people of the Atlantic world—lay in the imperial expansion of a crisis-ridden Europe. In exploring these origins, we shall survey the early histories of native American and African societies, as well as those of the European societies that would lead the exploration and colonization of America. The English, like many who came before them, built their settlements in North America around systems of labor that necessarily linked the peoples of several continents. The interactions of native Americans, Africans, and Europeans shaped the evolution of the Americas and have had profound effects throughout the world down to the present day.

THE PEOPLES OF THE NEW WORLD

The "New World" discovered by Columbus was not new, nor was it a "virgin land" that beckoned European settlement. For thousands of years North and South America had been inhabited, in many areas as densely as Europe. When Columbus began his westward voyage, perhaps seventy million people lived in the New World, more than seven million of them north of Mexico. The Europeans who encountered these millions thought at first that they had landed in India (an ill-defined area that then included much of East Asia) and hence they called these people "Indians." Archaeologists today believe that these people were indeed descended from Asians—more specifically, from Siberian migrants who probably reached North America around 9000 B.C. Crossing over to the Alaskan peninsula, these nomadic pioneers and their offspring slowly drifted southward and eastward in search of the wildlife and vegetation necessary to sustain them. Eventually, they covered much of North and South America.

As the migrants fanned out over the two continents, groups branched off in different directions. Adapting in relative isolation to their local environments, they slowly evolved distinct ways of life and forms of communication. New World natives lived in a wide variety of ways and spoke an extraordinary array of languages—by the year

MAIO
HATVNCVSQVI·AI
MORAI quilla

A drawing from Guamán Poma's *Nueva corónica* depicts Incans gathering the annual May harvest before the Spanish came.

1500, they spoke some two thousand languages, making the New World the richest and most diverse linguistic region in the world.

Between 8000 and 1500 B.C., several of these groups had begun to move beyond hunting and gathering to the deliberate cultivation of plants, which brought a major increase in the supply of food. The same epoch witnessed important improvements in hunting methods: the bow and arrow, which originated in Asia, crossed the Bering Strait into North America.

With increasingly reliable food supplies, populations increased and human energies that had gone into acquiring food were freed for other activities. Indian society itself grew more complex, though more in some parts of the hemisphere than in others; as some groups moved slowly toward tillage, many hunters and gatherers continued to live off the earth's natural bounty. But those who cultivated their food became more stable geographically and socially, and they usually grew more powerful than their neighbors.

In the fifteenth century, the most highly developed Indian societies of this kind were the Aztecs (in today's Mexico and Guatemala) and the Incas (centered in today's Peru and Bolivia). The Inca empire had expanded in the fifteenth century; by the time of the Spanish conquest, it stretched far down the Andes and the western coast of South America, from north of modern Quito, Ecuador, to southern Chile. A royal family was surrounded by aristocrats and other notables (including regional rulers whose realms had been absorbed into the empire), all of whom were supported by the obligatory labor of the common people. Women wove cloth that was highly valued in commerce and religious ceremony. Men worked the fields and built the roads and canals that united the empire and irrigated the arid land.

North of the isthmus, the Aztecs—a loosely confederated empire in central Mexico that built upon the accomplishments of the earlier Olmec, Mayan, and Toltec empires—were fifteen to twenty million strong when Cortez and his *conquistadores* arrived in 1519. They lived in a complex society that boasted impressive achievements in metallurgy and urbanization. Gold and silver graced their temples, many of which were in Tenochtitlán, a capital city of three hundred thousand. Aztec society was based on a clan system through which land was distributed and farming organized, much of it on communal lands. At the top of the social structure sat the emperor (the "chief of men"), who was selected from the royal line by the highest nobility. Other important social groups included priests, war chiefs, and wealthy merchants. The commoners, the vast bulk of Aztec society, consisted of craftsmen, farmers, soldiers, laborers, and slaves. The Aztecs, who exacted tribute from the many outlying tribes they had subordinated, were themselves subjected to the control of Spain by 1521.

To the north, the population was sparser and the tribes were smaller. Among the most complex and geographically stable of the North American Indians were the Hopi and Zuni in the highlands north of Mexico. Like the Incas and Aztecs, though on a smaller scale, they had evolved an agricultural economy dependent upon an elaborate irrigation system. From the continental plains eastward to the Atlantic coast, other Indian groups sustained themselves through varying combinations of agriculture, hunting, gathering, and trade. The denser populations and more complex societies tended to be in the Southeast and Gulf region.

The Woodland Indians of the Northeast—the ones the English settlers first encountered—were made up of distinct groups that shared a number of characteristics. The region that would later be called New England may have contained between seventy thousand and a hundred thousand Indians at the beginning of the seventeenth century. They lived in villages whose few hundred inhabitants were strongly linked by ties of kinship. Shelters were simple, temporary, and easily moved. The villages themselves were relocated according to seasonal and ecological changes.

North of Maine's Kennebec River, where the land was not very hospitable, agriculture played no role in the Indians' economies. The men usually fished and hunted for large game, while the women gathered nuts, berries, and other plants, trapped smaller animals (including birds), saw to the camps, raised the children, made clothing, and prepared food. But farther south, agriculture was important: Indians cultivated grains for as much as half to two-thirds of their food. Women did most of the agricultural work; the fields were close enough to the village so that they could be worked without interfering with the women's other responsibilities.

Perhaps the most striking characteristic of the North American Indians was the strength of the kinship and tribal ties that bound the individual to the group as a whole. Among both agriculturalists and hunter-gatherers, these ties were stronger than among contemporaneous Europeans, Asians, or Africans. At a time when most English peasants had already lost access to lands once owned by the village in common, all lands (and waters) cultivated, hunted, fished, or otherwise used by Indian villages were still deemed the common property of all village members. Even when a family was allotted a plot of land for its crops, that grant was always temporary and did not bar other villagers from using it for other purposes, such as gathering wild berries or felling trees for canoes.

Group possession of the land implied group rights to its bounty. All had a claim to the harvest, just as all partook of the yield of the hunt. Of course, small items that a person produced independently usually belonged to that individual alone. But this rule, too, was applied

"Yes, We Eat It." Guamán Poma's version of a meeting between an Incan king and one of the Spaniards left behind by Pizarro after his first voyage to Peru. Curious about the Spanish obsession with gold, the Incan used sign language to ask his visitor if the Spaniards ate the metal. "Yes," the Spaniard answered, misunderstanding, "we eat it." According to Guamán Poma, to satisfy this strange diet, the Indians began to offer gold to the Spaniards.

loosely, for possessions were often given away as tokens of mutual obligation. "Although every proprietor knows his own," one Englishman noted, "yet all things (so long as they will last) are used in common amongst them: a bisket cake given to one; that one breaks it equally into so many parts, as there be persons in his company, and distributes it." This cultural trait shocked European observers, who had grown accustomed to the possessive ways and values of early capitalist society. A French cleric reported that the Micmac Indians of Nova Scotia were "so generous and liberal towards one another that they seem not to have any attachment to the little they possess, for they deprive themselves thereof very willingly and in very good spirit the very moment they know that their friends have need of it." Another Jesuit discovered that in Iroquois territory (including much of the land stretching from northern New York down to Pennsylvania, from the Adirondacks to the Great Lakes), there were no poorhouses "because there are neither mendicants nor paupers as long as there are any rich people among them. Their kindness, humanity, and courtesy not only make them liberal with what they have but cause them to possess hardly anything except in common. A whole village must be without corn before any individual can be obliged to endure privation."

These customs were sustained by religious views that saw human beings as but temporary custodians of the world and everything in it. A century later, another European missionary described the belief among the Delaware Indians that God "made the Earth and all it contains for the common good of mankind. . . . Whatever liveth on the land, whatsoever groweth out of the earth, and all that is in the rivers and waters . . . was given jointly to all, and everyone is entitled to his share."

The very organization of Indian society guaranteed that the distribution of wealth would be roughly but strenuously egalitarian. This economic equality reinforced the individual's sense of group identity and the utter necessity of group membership. The tribe could therefore shape personal conduct without recourse to elaborate legislative, judicial, or executive regulation. Behavior dangerous or unacceptable to the society was quite effectively limited by public disapproval, denunciation, ridicule, or—most dramatically—by expulsion from the group itself.

Peace and equality within the tribe did not, of course, guarantee similar relations with other tribes. Since only membership in a group conferred the rights described above, conflicts between groups over access to land and resources often produced war. During the fifteenth century, five Indian groups (the Mohawk, Oneida, Cayuga, Onondaga, and Seneca) formed the Iroquois Confederacy, apparently to minimize precisely such conflicts. Yet while the confederation eliminated armed conflict among those groups, it by no means guaranteed peace between the Iroquois and other nearby tribes. In fact, so highly prized was martial prowess that Iroquois tribal leadership commonly passed to those who boasted the greatest reputations in battle. Among other Indian communities, individuals gained authority in other ways.

In all cases, though, leadership was collective, and firm limits curbed the rulers' power. Without an army or police force separate from the tribe as a whole, individuals remained leaders only as long as they retained widespread allegiance. In the 1670s, missionary Daniel Gookin noted of such leaders that "very frequently their men will leave them upon distaste or harsh dealings, and go and live among other [leaders] that can protect them: so that their princes endeavor to carry it obligingly and lovingly unto their people, lest they should desert them, and thereby their strength, power, and tribute would be diminished."

Europeans were sometimes shocked to discover that Indian leadership was not restricted simply to men. At a time when most European women experienced strict subordination to men, women in many Indian tribes seem to have enjoyed a remarkable degree of personal independence and group power. Iroquois families, for example, were both matrilineal and matrilocal: that is, they traced descent through the female line and lived in the residence of the wife or mother. Iroquois women controlled their own homes and fields, exercised the right of divorce at will, and retained the right to appoint leaders. They also closely supervised the deliberations and decisions of their appointees; tribal leaders whose performance displeased the women could be demoted.

Many Indian social and political institutions experienced cataclysmic change when the Europeans came, largely because they brought diseases such as smallpox, malaria, and measles, against which the Indians had developed no immunity. The natives died (in the words of one

"THE WOMEN . . . JOIN TOGETHER FOR THE HEAVY WORK"

Many Indian tribes depended on the labor of women for agricultural production. In this description of the Iroquois, a Jesuit missionary details the collective process employed by the tribe's women in planting and harvesting maize (corn), the staple crop of most North American Indian tribes.

THE FIRST WORK done in the fields is gathering and burning the stubble. Then the ground is ploughed to make it ready to receive the grain which they . . . throw there. . . .

All the women of the village join together for the heavy work. They make numerous different bands according to the different quarters where they have their fields and pass from one field to the other helping each other. . . .

The mistress of the field where they are working distributes to each one of the workers the grain or seed for sowing, which they receive in little *mannes* or baskets four or five fingers high and as wide, so that they can calculate the number of grains given out. . . .

They keep their fields very clean. . . . There is also a set time for this [task] when they work all in common. Then each one carries with her a bundle of little sticks . . . with her individual mark and gaily decorated with vermilion. They use these to mark their accomplishments and to make their work show up. . . .

The festival of binding together corn shocks . . . takes place at night in the fields and is the only occasion when the men, who do no work either in the fields or with the harvest, are called upon by the women to help.

~PREGVNTA·EL·AVTOR
MAVILLAVAI·ACHAMITAMA

Oral history. Guamán Poma presents himself consulting older Indians to learn the history of pre-Inca and Inca Peru.

Spanish observer) "like fish in a bucket." In the century after Columbus's first voyage, the million-strong Indian population of Hispaniola (today's Haiti and Dominican Republic) was virtually extinguished. From the Caribbean, the epidemics soon spread throughout the Americas, first to the lowlands and then into the highland centers of the great Indian empires. Massive numbers—probably the majority—of the native population of Central and South America succumbed to wave after wave of epidemics. It was, according to an Aztec villager, as if "the course of humanity" had been altered. Before the Europeans arrived there had been "no sickness . . . , no aching bones . . . , no high fever . . . , no burning chest . . . , no abdominal pain . . . , no consumption . . . [and] no headache. The foreigners made it otherwise when they arrived here."

The "great dying" was immediately caused by European germs. Just as in Europe, however, epidemics also had social causes. Spanish and Portuguese deportation of enslaved Indians to other lands, the brutal and exhausting conditions of labor imposed by the conquerors upon those remaining behind, and malnutrition due to the disruption of established systems of agriculture and food distribution—these and other aspects of European colonialism played major roles in weakening the Indians and boosting mortality among them. Death rates were highest where Indian-European contact had been strongest. More than two-thirds of the Eastern Abenaki Indians in Maine, for example, died in just the first decade of the seventeenth century after contact with European fishermen. Throughout the hemisphere, this devastation of the native population made it much easier for the conquerors to reorganize economic, social, and political life to serve colonial goals.

Indian society was also transformed by the subtler powers of European commerce. During the fifteenth and sixteenth centuries, ships from Portugal, France, and England appeared with growing frequency off Newfoundland and in the Gulf of St. Lawrence. The first came in search of fish to supply a growing market and replace a shrinking supply in European waters. Soon the fishing crews set up base camps along the Canadian shore and began bartering with the Algonkian-speaking residents, at first for food. The Indians envied the newcomers their more sophisticated manufactures, but had little to offer in the way of gold, silver, or gems in return. Beaver, on the other hand, was plentiful—and its fur was valued by Europeans in making clothing and hats. The terms of the exchange were soon set. Eventually, the French, Dutch, and English made the North American fur trade a major commercial venture.

This trade laid the foundation for the much more numerous and permanent European settlements to come. But even in the short run, the fur trade fostered irreversible changes in North American Indian life. Those Indians hardy enough to survive European microbes grew increasingly dependent upon European goods and therefore on the fur trade. This had many results: As the beaver population near the Atlantic was hunted down, quickly diminishing, Indian hunters moved inland in search of fresh supplies, soon colliding with other Indian groups. The need for the prized pelts set tribe against tribe, and competing groups of Europeans were usually pleased to sell arms to the rivals. War not only caused many deaths, but shaped and reshaped the territories and alliances of many tribes. Meanwhile, the growing importance of hunting and warfare widened the gap between male and female roles, strengthening the power of men at the expense of that of women, and enhancing the claims of hunters and warriors to village and tribal leadership. By depriving many native American peoples of their traditional methods of sustaining and governing themselves, these developments left the Indians a set of stark alternatives: to labor under the control and for the benefit of their conquerors or to move west and seek assimilation into other, more powerful Indian groups that might carry on the resistance against European encroachment.

CRISIS IN EUROPE

The European side of the story—the "discovery," conquest, and settlement of the Americas in the fifteenth, sixteenth, and seventeenth centuries—is studded with references to gold. Even when Europeans discussed their religious or political motives, gold (and later silver) always forced its way into the conversation. Christopher Columbus, the first European "hero" of the tale, announced that "the best thing in the world is gold. It can even send souls to heaven." A Spaniard who followed in his footsteps expressed similar views. "We came here," he said, "to serve God and the king and also to get rich."

The single-minded hunt for gold animated the original European conquest of Central and South America. In 1519, as Hernán Cortés and his band advanced on the Aztec capital of Tenochtitlán, the emperor Montezuma sent out envoys bearing gifts, hoping to ingratiate himself with the strange visitors. But his generosity served merely to whet the foreigners' immense appetites. "When they were given these presents," one Aztec later told a missionary, "the Spaniards burst into smiles; their eyes shone with pleasure." They "picked up the gold and fingered it like monkeys; they seemed to be transported by joy, as if their hearts were illumined and made new." Indeed, the Indian recalled, "their bodies swelled with greed, and their hunger was ravenous; they hungered like pigs for that gold." Cortés himself explained this ravenous appetite to the Aztecs. "We Spaniards suffer from a disease of the heart," he told them, "the specific remedy for which is gold."

This "disease"—gold-hunger—drove many Europeans to conquer and colonize the Americas. What kind of illness was it? What were its origins? To answer these questions, we must take a closer look at the Old World before Columbus's voyage.

In 1492, Spain, like Europe as a whole, was an agrarian society. After centuries of decline and decay since the collapse of the western Roman Empire in the fifth century, Spain began to grow again as trade revived in the tenth and eleventh centuries. The merchants who organized this commerce made their homes in cities and towns (Seville and its outports), where skilled artisans produced both luxury goods for trade and the everyday items needed by the urban population. But the center of popular life and the sources of economic and political power still lay in the countryside. The great majority of people—eight or nine out of ten—eked out a subsistence by tilling the soil. Their labor supported a feudal ruling class of a monarch, aristocrats, and church officials who lived in relative luxury.

Over the centuries, feudal society had become mired in a profound contradiction. During the second millennium, as long-distance trade expanded and the costs of warfare increased, feudal rulers found that they could not squeeze enough wealth out of peasants and urban producers to satisfy their military needs and their increasingly exotic and expensive tastes. By bleeding the peasantry—and by pumping so much wealth into unproductive expenditures—they inhibited agricultural improvement. Just as important, peasants themselves resisted their rulers' demands, striving to retain as much of their produce as possible. This enduring conflict between lord and peasant exploded in periodic economic, social, and political crises of huge proportions, most notably in the fourteenth century and again in the seventeenth.

The nobility of Europe tried to solve their financial problems not only by tightening their grip on peasants and townspeople but by grasping at the lands and riches of other rulers. The first solution led to peasant and urban revolts, as in Flanders in 1302 and 1323–28, Thessalonica in the 1340s, France in 1358, Florence in 1378, and England, where Wat Tyler's peasant revolt in 1381 took control of the city of London. (It was no accident that the legend of Robin Hood—who stole from the rich and gave to the poor—took firm root during the fourteenth century.) Internal crises coexisted with external aggression as rivalry among Europe's rulers produced a seemingly endless cycle of wars that raged from one end of the continent to the other.

Wartime destruction and agricultural stagnation, combined with

Columbus discovers . . . ? A plate from a 1493 edition of Columbus's letters depicts an explorer landing somewhere—but not in America. The galley ship in the foreground could never endure an ocean voyage and bears no resemblance to Columbus's vessels. The illustration probably derived from an older publication about Mediterranean exploration.

A New World beast. Illustrations that appeared in sixteenth-century accounts of European exploration of the Americas often showed exotic wildlife that owed as much to imagination as to observation. This woodcut, from a book by a French Franciscan friar whose two-month visit to Brazil in 1555 was largely spent in a sickbed, probably represents an American bison.

Implanting a new faith. A sixteenth-century Spanish drawing approvingly documents the destruction of Aztec temples in Tlaxcala, Mexico.

natural population growth and changes in climate, made for deadly results. Famine struck northern Europe in 1317 and the south thirty years later. In Silesia it was reported that the poor were reduced to eating the corpses of executed criminals. An impoverished and malnourished population thus fell easy prey to disease, and plague ravaged the continent repeatedly after midcentury. Between 1300 and 1400, Europe's population had fallen by about 40 percent. Trade contracted and banking houses collapsed; feudal incomes declined accordingly.

If Europe's rulers were to shore up their power, it seemed that some reorganization of society would be needed. In most cases, this involved greater centralization of power. In one country after another, internal struggles—among the nobility and between nobles and peasants—facilitated (even required) the rise of a more powerful monarch capable of arbitrating among the combatants, imposing his or her will, and thereby limiting the damage to society as a whole.

Yet even strengthened monarchies could not solve the underlying problem of inadequate revenues. New sources of wealth were needed. Ships and sailors might bring luxury goods from Asia (exotic spices, dyes, and jewels) as slaves mined the precious metals (gold and silver) necessary to purchase these luxuries. The hunt for such wealth appealed not only to monarchs and aristocrats, but equally to merchants, intrigued by tales of Asian riches like those told by Marco Polo at the end of the thirteenth century.

But there were obstacles to long-distance trade: Venice, Genoa, Byzantium, and Turkey controlled the familiar Mediterranean routes to the East. In an effort to bypass these powers, merchant adventurers underwritten by Portugal, Spain, France, the Netherlands, and England sought new ways to reach the wealth of India, China, and the Spice Islands. The Portuguese concentrated on finding an eastern sea route to Asia, gradually working their way down the African coast. Their project finally paid off in 1497, when Vasco da Gama rounded the Cape of Good Hope and then (with the aid of a noted Arab navigator) sailed on to the shores of India.

Acting for Spain, Columbus hoped to find a more direct westerly route to the same destination. His search unexpectedly brought him to the "New World" of America, where he and his successors continued their search for booty. It took adventurers from Spain and Portugal less than fifty years to conquer Central and South America and to overrun the surrounding lands and peoples. "Those lands do not produce bread or wine," observed one Spanish writer early in the sixteenth century, "but they do produce large quantities of gold, in which lordship consists."

Between 1500 and 1650 Spain extracted staggering quantities from

Central and South America—more than 180 tons of gold and 16,000 tons of silver. At first the Spaniards obtained the coveted metals simply by melting down Indian possessions. As soon as they exhausted this source, they put Indians to work prospecting for gold in streams and then mining for silver.

Of course, the Americas yielded other riches besides gold and silver, notably dyestuffs (from the cochineal insect and the indigo plant), cacao, and various gems. Eventually, the Europeans did organize the production of bread and other food to support themselves in their conquered lands. The piecemeal and pragmatic shift by Iberian colonizers from the simple plunder of existing Indian riches to the systematic production of new wealth launched a new phase of European colonialism, with far-reaching consequences.

In the early sixteenth century, the Portuguese initiated the "new colonialism" in their colony of Brazil. There they introduced a novel and ominous system of plantation agriculture, in which Indian and African slaves labored to produce sugar and tobacco crops for sale in Europe. Plantation regimes would soon be established in Latin America, the Caribbean, and North America. Slavery had taken root in the New World.

Slavery was an ancient system with independent roots all over the globe, in ancient Greece and Rome, in Africa and Byzantium, under Islam and Christianity. In western Europe, outright slavery eventually had died out by the fourteenth century, giving way to the less extreme form of bondage known as serfdom. Slavery survived longer in Africa, where most slaves were outsiders captured in battle or locals reduced to slavery through indebtedness or as punishment for crime. But unlike the form that evolved in the New World, slavery in the Old World was rarely permanent or heritable. Nor was it as extreme: slaves themselves retained many personal rights. Most importantly, it was not based on race.

As a way of obtaining and disciplining a large agricultural labor force, slavery began to flourish only with the expansion of the world market. In the early modern era, Europeans were unable to conquer the African mainland, so Portugal turned to the Americas in order to realize its agricultural and commercial ambitions. There the demand for laborers increased rapidly as lucrative European markets for sugar and tobacco made the plantation system extremely profitable. But in the Americas, problems arose in finding a suitable workforce. Disease continued to ravage the native labor supply, and those who survived—still surrounded by their own people and natural habitats—proved too difficult to control and discipline. Portuguese planters therefore turned back to Africa in search of the slave laborers they desired; Spain and ultimately France and England followed suit. By the turn of the seventeenth century, Africa's involuntary immigrants to the

New World already numbered more than a quarter million. In fact, from the fifteenth through the eighteenth century, fully six out of every seven people who arrived in the Americas were African slaves.

WEST AFRICA AND THE INTERNATIONAL SLAVE TRADE

At the time of Columbus's voyage, the total population of Africa may have exceeded eighty million—about the same as Europe's. An extraordinary diversity of cultures and economies characterized the continent, from the Islamic-influenced Berber society on the Mediterranean and the Muslim merchant-traders of Mombassa on the Indian Ocean, to the Bantu farmers in the fertile agricultural region that is now Nigeria, to the food-collecting San and pastoral Khoi-Khoi in what is now South Africa. Four-fifths of Africa's people lived below the vast Sahara Desert.

West Africa. A 1606 Venetian map.

The population of West Africa, the area ultimately most important to the slave trade with the New World, totaled about eleven million in 1500. West Africa stretched from Guinea and Senegal on Africa's western Atlantic coast, to the rich farmlands west of the Niger River, to the trading societies in the Niger River delta in the East. Sixteenth-century West Africa, like the rest of the continent, encompassed an acute diversity of social, economic, and cultural systems.

Most West Africans traditionally lived and worked in the country-side in groups organized around family or kinship networks. Polygyny—a marriage system where one man has several wives—was the dominant mode of family organization in West Africa. Each wife and her children usually lived in a separate household, although cooperation in the production and distribution of food was common.

An engraving from a seventeenth-century Dutch survey of Africa. The royal court of Benin is shown in the foreground, while the expansive city stretches into the distance.

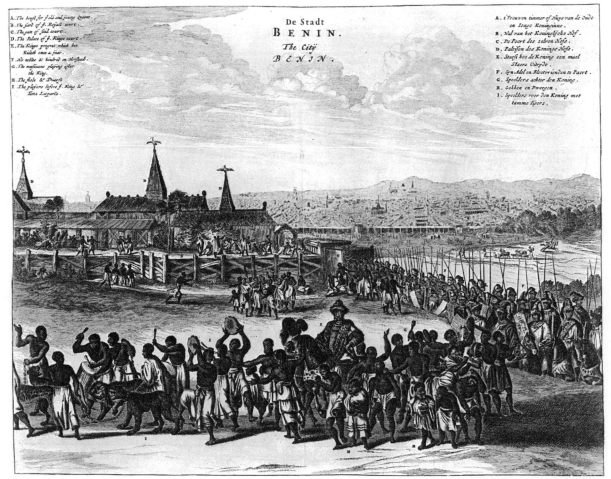

West African families sustained themselves through highly successful tropical farming of tubers, bananas, millet, and rice, using iron tools (they had mined iron ore and manufactured iron implements since Roman times). They also raised livestock, including cattle, sheep, goats, and fowl. There was little call to grow more than the family needed, although whatever surplus was produced provided the basis of a vigorous barter economy. Women were as active in such trade as men, particularly in local marketplaces.

Women and children also worked alongside men in farming and in tending livestock. The labor of slaves often supplemented that of family members. Slavery in West African societies was widespread before 1500. But it took the form of domestic servitude: slaves were attached to kinship or family groups; their enslavement was not heritable; and they could work off their enslavement rather than be bound for life.

Family and kin groups owned the land communally, living within what one commentator described as "a vigorous egalitarianism." Family and clan leaders exercised power and authority beyond their individual groups in the collective leadership of villages and larger political confederations. Religious practices were diverse and local, stressing the individual's ties to a larger spiritual world that was shaped by the legacy of ancestors, the cycles of nature, and the existence of a great and all-knowing Creator.

These village societies and kin groups grew increasingly dependent on West Africa's kingdoms, whose kings, like their European counterparts, helped guarantee the peace and encouraged the region's expanding commerce. Between the eighth and sixteenth centuries, the most powerful of these political leaders was the ruler of the Kingdom of Ghana, a "divine" king who dominated all the land in west-central Africa from the great Sahara Desert to the Gulf of Guinea and from the Niger River to the Atlantic coast. Ghana's power was further enhanced by the region's sizable gold production. Eventually weakened by external warfare, Ghana's rule gave way in the fourteenth century to the Mali Empire, which probably was the world's largest empire at the time. To the south of Mali lay the smaller but nonetheless powerful kingdoms of Benin, Dahomey, and Congo, which came to prominence in the sixteenth and seventeenth centuries.

The growing power and significance of West Africa's princes encouraged a vital commercial economy centered in the region's thriving trading cities. Important market-centers—including Benin, Timbuktu, and Gao—housed craftsmen, traders, priests, and scholars, and promoted the growth of handicrafts and arts, schools, and sophisticated legal systems. Timbuktu, for example, possessed a university that rivaled any in Europe; Benin's artists created a style of royal sculpture and decorative art that was coveted around the world. A

Dutchman, visiting Benin in 1602, favorably compared the city's size and character to his native Amsterdam.

The trading cities also stood at the center of West Africa's vast export trade that included gold, ivory, cotton stuffs, leather, and spices. Such "exotic" West African goods had penetrated markets in North Africa, the Middle East, and even Europe as early as the Ghanaian and Mali empires. A small group of merchants and traders were enriched by this trade, allowing them, by the middle of the sixteenth century, to exercise significant economic and political power. On the eve of European contact, then, West Africa boasted a highly developed economy and society, dense with agricultural settlements and trading centers that were involved in networks of exchange that crossed Africa and reached markets well beyond.

Early in the fifteenth century, Portugal established Europe's first trading ties with West Africa. The Portugese came in search of ivory and, most importantly, gold, nine tons of which were produced each year by West African miners. Portugal shipped 170,000 gold coins annually from West Africa early in the sixteenth century in exchange for textiles, wheat, and metal utensils. A Portuguese visitor reported in 1506 that excellent cotton goods could also be obtained all along the Guinea coast. Around 1550, the English sea captain William Towerson marveled at the "fine iron goods" available there, including "spears, fish-hooks, farming

"OUR LAND IS UNCOMMONLY RICH AND FRUITFUL . . ."

Olaudah Equiano was kidnapped at age ten from his home in the Benin Empire on the Guinea coast in southern Nigeria. He was sold into slavery and brought to the New World. Equiano was able to buy his freedom within ten years of his capture, from wages earned as a servant to an English naval officer. He then wrote an autobiography, The Interesting Narrative of the Life of Olaudah Equiano, *published in New York in 1791, which includes this description of the West African world out of which he came.*

THE KINGDOM of Benin . . . is divided into many provinces or districts, in one of the most remote and fertile of which I was born, in the year 1745, situated in a charming, fruitful vale named Essaka. The distance of this province from the capital of Benin and the seacoast must be very considerable; for I had never heard of white men or Europeans, nor of the sea; and our subjection to the king of Benin was little more than nominal. . . .

We are almost a nation of dancers, musicians, and poets. Thus every great event, such as a triumphant return from battle, or other cause of public rejoicing, is celebrated in public dances, which are accompanied with songs and music suited to the occasion. The assembly is separated into four divisions [or age grades] . . . . Each represents some interesting scene of real life, such as a great achievement, domestic employment, a pathetic story, or some rural sport. . . . This gives our dances a spirit and variety which I have scarcely seen elsewhere. We have many musical instruments, particularly drums of different kinds, a piece of music which resembles a guitar, and another much like a stickado [xylophone].

Our manner of living is entirely plain; for as yet the natives are unacquainted with those refinements in cookery which debauch the taste: bullocks, goats, and poultry supply the greatest part of their food. These constitute likewise the principal wealth of the country, and the chief articles of its commerce. The flesh is usually stewed in a pan. To make it savory we sometimes use also pepper and other spices; and we have salt made of wood ashes. Our vegetables are mostly plantains [bananas], yams, beans, and Indian corn. The head of the family usually eats alone; his wives and slaves have also their separate tables. . . .

Our land is uncommonly rich and fruitful, and produces all kinds of vegetables in great abundance. We have plenty of Indian corn, and vast quantities of cotton and tobacco. . . . All our industry is exerted to improve those blessings of nature. Agriculture is our chief employment; and every one, even the children and women, are engaged in it. Thus we are all habituated to labor from our earliest years. Every one contributes something to the common stock; and, as we are unacquainted with idleness, we have no beggars. The benefits of such a mode of living are obvious.

tools, and swords that are exceedingly sharp on both edges." In 1589, a European visitor to Benin described the bewildering array of goods in its thriving marketplace:

> Pepper and elephant teeth, oil of palm, cloth made of cotton wool very curiously woven, and cloth made of the bark of palm trees were procured in exchange for cloth, both linen and woolen, iron works of sundry sorts, Manillos or bracelets of copper, glass beads and coral. . . . They have good store of soap . . . also many pretty fine mats and baskets that they make, and spoons of elephant's teeth very curiously wrought with divers proportions of fowls and beasts made upon them.

But gold, iron, and exotic goods were not all that Europeans coveted in West Africa. As early as 1444, the Portugese had opened a small but thriving market for African slaves, who were transported back to Portugal to work as lifelong domestic servants. West African

Mbanza, the capital city of the Kingdom of Congo, represented in a seventeenth-century Dutch print.

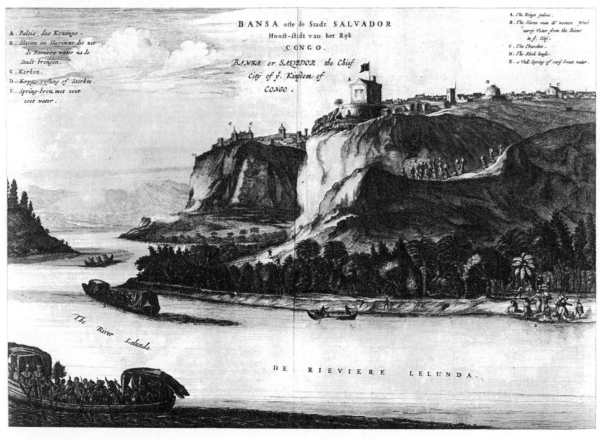

"The Spanish Treatment of Fugitive Black Slaves." An engraving from the Frankfurt edition of Girolamo Benzoni's widely read sixteenth-century history of America, *Historia del mondo nuovo*. The Milanese author denounced Spanish treatment of Indians and, more unusual, of African slaves in the New World.

princes and merchants saw such commerce as consistent with their own notions of domestic slavery and, more importantly, as a logical extension of the long-distance trade that already allowed West African products to reach the Mediterranean and beyond.

As the European demand for bound labor increased in the sixteenth and early seventeenth centuries, however, the structure of the slave trade changed dramatically. Europeans needed a large labor force—first to work in the metal mines of South and Central America and then to cultivate their thriving sugar and tobacco plantations in the West Indies and in North and South America. West African slaves offered the ideal solution to Europeans' New World labor problems. In 1510 the Spanish crown legalized the sale of Africans in the Americas. Eight years later a Spanish ship carried the first full cargo of Africans directly from the Guinea coast to the Americas. Portugal's modest domestic market for bound servants in the fifteenth century had changed by the middle of the sixteenth century into an international thirst for labor that Spain, Holland, Portugal, and England could quench only by permanently enslaving huge numbers of Africans. The international slave trade, which would span the next three centuries of African, European, and American history, had begun. Before it was over, ten to twelve million Africans would be transported to the New World. Only about 5 percent went to British North America; most ended up in Brazil, the West Indies, and Central America.

Many West African kings and wealthy merchants were willing and able participants in the international slave trade, joining hands with Europeans in the capture, delivery, and ultimate enslavement of Africans. In response to increased European demand, the West African ruling elite stepped up the hunt for suitable human merchandise, which meant increased—and increasingly lethal—regional warfare carried out with imported European firearms. The victors (especially Johnny Kabes, the main middleman between the English and the Ashanti people on the Guinea coast in the late seventeenth century) expanded their wealth and power, sometimes creating new kingdoms.

But the slave trade also destabilized the region as a whole. Large numbers of coastal West Africans fled to the interior as the hunt for slaves intensified in the seventeenth century. Simultaneously, the influx of inexpensive European trade goods drove local iron and textile artisans out of business, further undermining the African economy and increasing its dependence upon the European connection. As in the New World, this combination of demographic, military, and economic pressures facilitated the eventual European colonization of the continent, although in the case of West Africa actual colonization would not come until the nineteenth century. Perhaps most importantly, the international slave trade resulted in the loss to African societies of millions of their youngest and strongest producers.

". . . OUR COUNTRY IS BEING COMPLETELY DEPOPULATED"

The slave trade had a profound effect not only on the people enslaved, but also on the African societies they came from. In a 1526 letter from King Nzinga Mbemba of the Congo (baptized King Affonso I) to King João III of Portugal, the African ruler condemned the impact of the slave trade on his own people, an impact that would intensify in the next century.

SIR, YOUR HIGHNESS should know how our Kingdom is being lost in so many ways. . . . We cannot reckon how great the damage is, since [your Portuguese] merchants are taking every day our natives, sons of the land and the sons of our noblemen and vassals and our relatives. . . . So great, Sir, is the corruption and licentiousness that our country is being completely depopulated, and Your Highness should not agree with this or accept it as in your service. . . . That is why we beg of Your Highness to help and assist us in this matter, commanding your factors [representatives] that they should not send here either merchants or wares, because it is our will that in these Kingdoms there should not be any trade of slaves nor outlet for them. . . .

Moreover, Sir, in our Kingdoms there is another great inconvenience which is of little service to God, and this is that many of our people [are] keenly desirous . . . of the wares and things of your Kingdoms, which are brought here by your people. In order to satisfy their voracious appetite, [they] seize many of our people, freed and exempt men, and very often it happens that they kidnap even noblemen and the sons of noblemen, and our relatives, and take them to be sold to the white men who are in our Kingdoms. . . .

Europeans organized the international slave trade with great inge-
nuity and determination. They armed the soldiers of West African
princes and rich merchants and provided the economic incentive that
led to the capture of tens of thousands of Africans each year. Most
were seized in the interior as far away as Angola and transported in
chains to the "Slave Coast" near Benin on the Gulf of Guinea. Many
captives died en route; those that survived were placed in stockades.
Jean Barbot, a French trade representative in West Africa in the late
seventeenth century, described the slave pens that held captured
slaves ready for the "Middle Passage"—the brutal voyage to enslavement in the New World:

> As the slaves come down to Ouidah from the inland coun-
> try they are put into a booth or prison, built for that pur-
> pose near the beach, all of them together; and when the
> Europeans are to receive them, they are brought out into a
> large plain, where the ships' surgeons examine every part
> of every one of them, to the smallest member, men and
> women being all stark naked. Such as are allowed [judged]
> good and sound are set on one side . . . ; [each] is marked
> on the breast with a red-hot iron, imprinting the mark of
> the French, English, or Dutch companies so that each na-
> tion may distinguish their own property, and so as to pre-
> vent their being changed by the sellers for others that are
> worse. . . . In this particular, care is taken that the women,
> as the tenderest, are not burnt too hard.

Capture and transport to these coastal holding pens were but the
first steps in a long and often violent process of turning African men
and women into slaves, a process that met with much individual and
some collective resistance at every turn. Once purchased and appro-
priately marked by their new European owners, Africans were packed
belowdecks in wooden sailing ships. Slave ships were designed to
carry the largest number of human beings in the smallest possible
space. Slavers accepted the fact that some number of the Africans—
probably one in six—would die en route to the New World. They died
from malnutrition, disease, and suicide and occasionally in shipboard
revolts that were brutally suppressed by the European crews.

Ships that plied the slave trade between Europe, Africa, and America rarely sailed empty. They carried cheap European goods—cottons,
alcohol, metalwork, and firearms—to the West African coast. These
were traded for slaves, who were then transported on the same ships
to the West Indies and America and exchanged for sugar and tobacco.
These products, grown by slave labor, were then carried back to Europe to satisfy a growing appetite for New World products. This tri-

angular trade helped assure maximum profits for all involved—in particular for the Europeans who began and sustained it, but also for the trade's African beneficiaries, those who supplied its human cargo.

The enslaved African men, women, and children transported to the New World came from different parts of the continent, from distinct societies and cultures. They spoke an array of languages and carried with them a variety of customs and beliefs. But many enslaved Africans also shared common skills and fundamental assumptions about the nature of religion, culture, kinship, and social life. They built upon these commonalities as they began the long and painful transition to a new, specifically African-American culture, as we shall see. This process, so crucial to the history of the New World, commenced the moment they boarded the slave ships, as they began out of necessity to overcome their differences, as they cooperated toward the common end of survival in a strange land.

CAPITALISM AND COLONIZATION

England was a relative latecomer in the history of European colonization. Until the end of the sixteenth century, Spain dominated the Atlantic and discouraged other European initiatives. The English opted for hit-and-run raids on convoys sailing colonial booty back to Spain.

But after England defeated the Armada, the great Spanish war fleet, in 1588, Spain could no longer keep the nations of northwestern Europe out of the New World. In North America, the French and Dutch quickly took advantage of Spanish weakness, the former founding Quebec (1608) and the latter, Albany (1614) and New Amsterdam (1624). The English established colonies at Jamestown (1607), New Plymouth (1620), and Massachusetts Bay (1630). In the two decades after the planting of New Plymouth, almost eighty thousand men and women left the British Isles to settle in North America.

Among these British colonists, some—especially the merchants who organized and financed the colonial expeditions—hoped to make their fortune by taking advantage of new opportunities in production and trade. But probably most of those who staked their lives on a dangerous ocean and an alien continent did so simply to retain (or regain) the precious economic independence and political freedom that increasingly eluded them at home. Both groups were propelled by the crisis of European feudalism.

As in Spain and elsewhere in Europe, England's old landed aristocrats found themselves in a major crisis by the early fourteenth century. And they too sought to extricate themselves by squeezing their serfs harder than ever. The lords demanded that the peasants devote longer hours to compulsory labor on the demesnes, the landlords' own lands. Especially after midcentury, the peasants resisted this pressure: Some fled their villages, escaping to the comparative freedom and security of nearby towns. Others stayed behind but simply refused to meet the new obligations.

When the nobility responded with brutal repression, they touched off one of the greatest popular revolts of English history, the peasant war of 1381. Although the revolt was ultimately defeated, its scope and ferocity frightened the landlords and discouraged further attempts to squeeze more from the peasants. It also encouraged the peasants to fight against both their unfree status as serfs and their obligation to pay rent in the form of labor.

Beginning in the middle of the fourteenth century, therefore, serfdom itself withered, as did the whole system of demesne cultivation. Unable to compel peasants to work the demesnes, landlords divided them into smaller plots, parceled them out, and began to live on the rents they collected. While rent payments and other obligations thus survived, their level declined significantly. Even hired laborers benefited, as the shrinking supply of workers—reduced by plagues and almost constant warfare—improved real wages and conditions.

This did not mean, of course, that the late medieval period was a golden age for working people. In the household, women and children remained subservient to the father. The low level of productivity kept society very poor and condemned most people to a life that was, in the words of English philosopher Thomas Hobbes, "poor, nasty, brutish, and short." Disease, accidents, and high mortality rates for infants and mothers kept life unpredictable and brief, on average less than forty years. Even among the aristocrats, far better off than the common villagers, two in five children died before reaching maturity, nor was it uncommon for childbirth to result in the death of the mother.

Still, compared to both earlier and later periods, English peasants of the late fourteenth and early fifteenth centuries enjoyed a remarkable degree of freedom from landlord domination. The same bonds that successfully united peasants against lords also limited conflicts among villagers. Although money already played a significant role in village relations, so did voluntary cooperation. Stability was maintained by a web of mutual obligations, services, and rights, which included access to common land, where peasants could graze livestock, cultivate a garden, forage for firewood, or perhaps cut timber and sell it for a modest profit. For the poorest, such rights could spell the difference between survival and ruin. The village did not tolerate individual profiteering from others' need, limiting the prices that could be charged for certain necessities like bread.

Villagers frowned on an overlarge accumulation of land by any individual, though some were certainly better off than others. The tensions that arose between richer and poorer peasants and between peasants and their hired laborers were not, however, especially severe. Members of the oldest and best-off peasant families often controlled village affairs, although usually with the guidance of the lords' representatives. These village councils formulated rules (as one Warwickshire council put it) "for the common profit [and] with the consent of all," and any breach of these rules was a crime against the whole community.

Though serfdom disappeared, the concessions that the peasants won from the nobility were limited. Most importantly, few villagers enjoyed outright ownership of the land they cultivated—instead of becoming independent small farmers, most merely leased plots from their landlord. Nor could they renew those leases at will or pass them on automatically to their children. At first, the limitations of tenancy had little impact. But after the middle of the fifteenth century, changing economic conditions—especially agricultural "improvements," including the redivision and reallotment of common lands and the growth of pasture farming, as well as the resurgence of commerce— undermined the security of these peasant leaseholders.

Such changes had already altered England's social structure in other important ways. Conflicts within the medieval military aristocracy, culminating in the late-fifteenth-century Wars of the Roses, thinned its ranks. This carnage permitted a new group of men known as the gentry, who held more modern, market-oriented values, to increase their wealth and political influence. Their ascent was further aided by the clash between the English monarchy and the Roman Catholic Church. Chafing at the power wielded within England by the pope, King Henry VIII broke with Rome in the 1530s, made himself head of an independent Church of England, and proceeded to confiscate and then sell vast quantities of Church lands.

Members of the gentry were well placed to buy those and other lands, thereby adding to their status, landed wealth, and power while supplying ideological, economic, and political support to both the monarchy and English Protestantism. The monarchy, in turn, looked with growing favor upon these upstarts, listening with care to their many commercial propositions. Some even received noble titles, entering the depleted ranks of the aristocracy and thereby altering its complexion; more than a few aristocratic heirs began to follow the capitalistic lead of these businessmen-turned-noblemen. Most of the gentry, however, remained outside the House of Lords, exerting their considerable influence nationally through the House of Commons and locally through the powerful office of justice of the peace.

The fortunes of the large urban merchants rose as well, especially those linked to the expanding textile industry. As trade grew—both within Britain and with foreign lands—these merchants prospered; they then allied with the rural gentry in support of commercial policies and the crown. The monarchy reciprocated by granting them special privileges, including royal monopolies of trading rights to specific parts of the world. Early beneficiaries included the founders of the Muscovy Company (1553), the Spanish Company (1577), the Senegal Adventurers (1588), the East India Company (1600), the Virginia Company (1607), and the Massachusetts Bay Company (1629). By the end of the sixteenth century, some merchants had grown as wealthy as the landed aristocrats.

The reorganization of the English upper classes—and the expansion of trade—brought with them the massive dispossession of rural tenants who had worked their lands for generations. By the end of the fifteenth century, landlords were again demanding higher rents, now increasingly in the form of cash. Those unable to pay were replaced with others more amenable to commercial agriculture.

Landlords also began to take over land for sheep. The growth of textile exports made wool-growing more and more profitable. But sheep needed extensive fields for grazing, so landlords evicted tenants from leased land and enclosed (fenced) the common lands that tenants had traditionally used to supplement their diets, and, in hard times, simply to survive—the "patrimony of the poor." Forty percent of the English population worked for wages of some kind by the end of the seventeenth century. Thousands of tenants were driven into a tenuous existence as farmhands, miners, weavers, soldiers, and sailors. Many single women were forced to spin wool into thread in isolated drudgery; the word "spinster" eventually became synonymous with "lonely, unmarried female."

Hordes of "masterless men and women," the victims of dispossession and increased population growth, strolled the countryside trying to sell the one thing they had left in life: their labor. Their plight was worsened by a series of harvest failures, rising food prices, and inflation. Many were reduced to begging and sometimes stealing to survive. The growing number of beggars, paupers, and criminals so alarmed the better-off that Parliament hastened to lock up the wanderers in poorhouses and workhouses. In 1563 Parliament passed the Statute of Artificers, which compelled people to work and mandated low wages, long hours, and harsh working conditions for millions of impoverished English men, women, and children. "Idleness," or unwillingness to work, became a serious crime, to be punished by imprisonment or public whipping.

The statute, and the numerous amendments added over the next century, assumed that propertyless people were not legally free and that they had a duty to work for their betters. Servants, for example, could not leave their employers without first buying a "ticket of re-

"They Live Like Beasts, Voide of Lawe and All Good Order." England's subjugation of Ireland during the reign of Elizabeth I served as a rehearsal for the colonization of Virginia in the seventeenth century. As in the later New World colony, the crown licensed private individuals and companies to undertake conquest and settlement for their own profit. Colonists expropriated Irish lands and rationalized their violence against the Irish by viewing them as savage pagans. In this sixteenth-century woodcut, English soldiers return to their camp carrying a grisly trophy of conquest.

lease" from the local justice of the peace. This was not the same notion of labor service that lords had demanded from their tenants for the right to work the land, but rather a bold effort to provide a source of cheap, dependent labor for a new class of commercial farmers, merchants, and textile manufacturers. According to these new laws, children inherited the occupations of their parents, thus ensuring a ready supply of destitute wage laborers. The same gentry who now needed so many laborers to tend their sheep, crops, and looms were also the justices of the peace who legally controlled local wage rates—and, not surprisingly, kept them extremely low. Wages remained low between 1530 and 1640, despite a fivefold increase in the price of food, rent, and fuel.

Other evicted tenants moved to the cities, swelling the population and adding to the demand for food and goods. Migrants also came from Scotland, Ireland, Wales, and the European continent. By 1600, London's population was at least 200,000—four times as large as in 1500. The demand for life's necessities—among urban wage laborers and artisans, and among a growing part of the rural population that no longer grew its own food but instead worked for wages—caused prices to rise. In the cities as in the countryside, the cost of food, clothing, and fuel rose much faster than income.

Peasants and laborers objected to radical changes in the customary practices. When bakers tried to ignore traditional price ceilings on bread—designed to prevent starvation among the poor—crowds, generally led by women, rose in furious protest. These confrontations ended peaceably if the baker agreed to lower the price. But if not, the crowd often took the bread and left on the counter only enough coins to cover the "just price." Even more widespread was opposition to wholesale dispossession. One bitter response to enclosure was this verse:

> They hang the man and flog the woman
> Who steals the goose from off the Common;
> But let the greater criminal loose
> Who steals the Common from the goose.

Peasant families had held rights to the commons and to the land they had worked "by our times and by all time beyond the memory of man," as the tenants of Bushey Manor argued in 1563; they demanded continuation of these rights. Sixteen years later, outraged Southampton tenants protested attacks on their customary rights to the common land: "We think it our duty in conscience to keep, uphold, and maintain [the common land] as we found it for our posterity to come, without diminishing any part or parcel from it, but rather to augment more to it if may be."

Many of these protests blossomed into full-scale riots, usually precipitated by food shortages or enclosure. In Oxfordshire in 1596, one popular leader claimed, "It wold never be merrye till some of the gentlemen were knocked down." Some of the risings were led by women, who, the rioters believed, "were lawlesse, and not subject to the lawes of the realm as men are."

The years 1580–1640 were, then, a period of wrenching social and economic change. The distance between rich and poor grew wider as the wealthy seized new economic opportunities, while the common folk suffered through some of the hardest years in all of English history.

The poor were not the only ones distressed by the changes. Many among the middling sort —especially Puritans, who were ardent religious reformers and soon would become revolutionaries—thought that society itself was coming apart. The breakdown of village life, rising social disorder, and what they saw as increasingly flagrant sin and corruption moved many to join utopian projects bound for New Plymouth or Massachusetts Bay. In the New World, Puritans hoped to rebuild the community and restore the discipline they saw disintegrating in England. Their "city upon a hill" would shine like a beacon back to the worldly and degenerate mother country.

Emigration to the New World was but one response to the turmoil. A confluence of other factors led to the English Revolution, the first revolution in the modern Atlantic world. The revolution, which began after 1640, exploded from the combustible

"THE POOREST HE THAT IS IN ENGLAND HAS A LIFE TO LIVE . . ."

English revolutionaries heatedly debated the principles of popular government. In 1647, the "Agreement of the People" was presented to the General Council of the revolutionary Army, meeting in the town of Putney. The ensuing Putney Debates revealed sharp divisions among the revolutionaries. Commissary-General Ireton, a close ally of Oliver Cromwell, argued that ownership of property was a necessary qualification for the franchise. Colonel Rainborough and Mr. Petty, leaders of the radical Levelers, asserted that all freeborn Englishmen should be allowed to vote for representatives to the new Parliament. The terms of this debate would reverberate a century and a half later in America's own revolution.

MR. PETTY: We judge that all inhabitants that have not lost their birthright should have an equal voice in elections.

COLONEL RAINBOROUGH: . . . For really I think that the poorest he that is in England has a life to live, as the greatest he; and therefore truly, sir, I think it's clear, that every man that is to live under a government ought first by his own consent to put himself under that government, and I do think that the poorest man in England is not at all bound in a strict sense to that government that he hath not had a voice to put himself under. . . .

COMMISSARY-GENERAL IRETON: I think that no person has a right to an interest or share in the disposing of the affairs of the kingdom, and in determining or choosing those that shall determine what laws we shall be ruled by here—no person hath a right to this, that hath not a permanent fixed interest in the kingdom. . . . But that by a man's being born here he shall have a share in that power that shall dispose of the lands here, and of all things here, I do not think it is sufficient ground. . . . Those that choose the representatives for the making of laws by which this state and kingdom are to be governed are the persons who, taken together, do comprehend the local interest of this kingdom; that is, the persons in whom all land lies, and those in corporations in whom all trading lies. . . .

COLONEL RAINBOROUGH: I do not find anything in the Law of God, that a lord shall choose twenty burgesses and a gentleman but two, or a poor man shall choose none. I . . . am still of the opinion that every man born in England cannot, ought not, neither by the Law of God nor the Law of Nature, to be exempted from the choice of those who are to make laws for him to live under, and for him, for aught I know, to lose his life under. . . .

mix of wrenching social change, economic dislocation, and political instability that had characterized the country since 1580.

Both sides in the conflict, grouped loosely around the crown and Parliament, could count supporters at all levels—lower, middling, and upper—of English society. In 1640 the monarchy under King Charles I faced a worsening crisis: funds were short, and Parliament was proving most uncooperative. The king's effort to impose church government by Anglican bishops on the churches of Presbyterian Scotland had met with armed resistance, which could not be overcome without funds for an army. An even deeper crisis lay in the split among English landlords and merchants—who were divided over economic matters, foreign policy, and religion—and in the deepening dissatisfaction among many of the country's middling and poor folk. A constitutional crisis, beginning with the king insisting on his power to tax without Parliament's consent, ensued; but by 1642 the struggle had moved beyond king and Parliament to involve London crowds and others who had never played major roles in the nation's politics. England was soon engulfed in civil war (1642–46 and 1648–49), the king was beheaded (1649), and a republican commonwealth under Oliver Cromwell was installed (1649–60). Constitutional limitations imposed by Parliament assured that royal absolutism had been decisively curtailed in England.

One of the most momentous developments within the Revolution was the emergence of a diverse lot of religious radicals, who frightened the propertied classes to their depths. The breakdown of the old order meant a breakdown in the traditional censorship, and after 1642 almost every heretical idea imaginable was being preached and printed. Poor and middling men and women, styling themselves Levelers, Ranters, Diggers, and Seekers, met together to question almost every tenet of the established order, religious and otherwise. They wondered aloud if heaven and hell weren't simply inventions of the rich to discipline the poor; if the church had any right to extract tithes; if more people ought not to have the vote; if free love wasn't truly godly; if enclosure, wage labor, and even private property itself were morally right. Such ideas scared the ruling class into a renewed unity and the restoration of the monarchy in 1660, but they also expanded the boundaries of political thought and action, providing an extraordinary legacy to any in later generations who would find fault either with monarchy or with the rule of rich men.

The turbulent 1640s and 1650s produced other results crucial to the later history of England, Europe, and the New World. The Revolution, itself made possible by the social and economic changes of 1580 to 1640, confirmed and consolidated the increasing social polarization of England and further facilitated the rise of capitalism. The revolutionaries abolished the whole structure of feudal landownership, thus protecting their own property in land, limiting the monarch's taxing power, effectively transforming land into a commodity, and thereby accelerating the trend toward agricultural improvement. All legal obstacles to enclosure were removed; landlords who prior to the Revolution had been censured were now encouraged. The Revolution also strengthened ties between agriculture and commerce, between landed and monied interests, especially after the propertied classes closed ranks in 1660 against the anarchy and radicalism of the civil-war years. The Revolution also unleashed a new, vigorous, more aggressive foreign policy concerned with renewed commercial and colonial development. The nation's men of property thus drastically weakened the king's control of land, commerce, and foreign policy. Although these men would not bring the monarch completely to heel until the Glorious Revolution in 1688, they had at least secured their own power, and with it the promise of unfettered capitalist expansion. They had also established the principle, best expressed by philosopher John Locke in 1690 in his *Two Treatises of Government*, that a people had the right to depose a ruler who had betrayed their trust.

"STAND UP NOW, DIGGERS ALL!"

The Diggers, a radical sect that emerged at the same time as the Levelers during the English Revolution, condemned the social and economic inequalities of seventeenth-century England in biblical terms. The Diggers' leader, Gerrard Winstanley, usually issued formal written tracts to communicate his ideas. In 1649, Winstanley (perhaps aided by his colleague, the poet Robert Coster) penned "The Digger's Song," which attacked the authority of the king, the gentry, the clergy, and the law. Such beliefs were shared by many poor English men and women who migrated to North America in search of a better life.

You noble Diggers all, stand up now, stand up now.
You noble Diggers all, stand up now;
   The waste land to maintain, seeing Cavaliers by name
   Your digging do disdain and persons all defame.
Stand up now, stand up now!

Your houses they pull down, stand up now, stand up now,
Your houses they pull down, stand up now;
   Your houses they pull down to fright poor men in town
   But the gentry must come down, and the poor shall wear the crown.
Stand up now, Diggers all!

With spades and hoes and ploughs, stand up now, stand up now,
With spades and hoes and ploughs stand up now;
   Your freedom to uphold, seeing Cavaliers are bold

England experienced wracking social change, dispossession, population growth, and popular protest at precisely the moment when it began to found and people its colonies overseas. As more peasants found themselves uprooted from the soil than could be employed in industry, colonization seemed to offer a solution. As the poor flocked to the cities in search of jobs, they met promoters who offered passage to the New World in exchange for a few years' labor as indentured servants. Colonization appealed to John Donne, for example, because it would "sweep your streets, and wash your doors, from idle persons, and the children of idle persons, and employ them." In 1622 a preacher described London's laboring poor to the Virginia Company as "people who rose early, worked all day and went late to bed, yet were scarce able to put bread in their mouths at week's end and clothes on their back at year's end." Here, he said, were prospective colonists. In 1628, Sir Francis Bacon saw in colonization a cure for the "rebellions of the belly" brought on by the reorganization of agriculture.

But popular attachment to traditional rights survived, especially in the stubborn belief that people had a right not only to survive, but to live in dignity and respect as economically independent members of their communities. Complete dependence on wage-labor was not an acceptable substitute for that right. Many thousands of English men and women who shared these attitudes took passage to North America in search of a new start.

The chance for that new start was a different product of the same economic forces that had uprooted them in the first place, for the transition from feudalism to capitalism involved not only changes within English society but also a radical extension of England's ambitions overseas. Henry VIII's declaration in 1534 that England was no longer under the authority of the Church of Rome marked the beginning of a two-hundred-year effort to make England richer

To kill you if they could, and right from you to hold.
Stand up now, Diggers all! . . .

The gentry are all round, stand up now, stand up now,
The gentry are all round, stand up now;
   The gentry are all round, on each side they are found,
   Their wisdom's so profound to cheat us of the ground.
Stand up now, stand up now! . . .

The clergy they come in, stand up now, stand up now.
The clergy they come in, stand up now;
   The clergy they come in and say it is a sin
   That we should now begin our freedom for to win.
Stand up now, Diggers all! . . .

'Gainst lawyers and 'gainst priests stand up now, stand up now,
'Gainst lawyers and 'gainst priests stand up now;
   For tyrants are they both, even flat against their oath,
   To grant us they are loath free meat and drink and cloth.
Stand up now, Diggers all! . . .

To conquer them by love, come in now, come in now,
To conquer them by love, come in now;
   To conquer them by love, as it does you behove,
   For He is King above, no power is like to love.
Glory *here*, Diggers all!

and mightier than her continental rivals. The effort was ultimately successful: by 1763, English ships dominated the seas and England was the most powerful nation in the world.

The arsenal of economic policies employed in this effort are known as "mercantilism"—a system, not of free trade, but of strictly regulated economic activity, aimed at enriching the state. Mercantilists accepted the medieval view that the total amount of wealth in the world remained more or less fixed. Therefore, prosperity required maintaining one's own share of that wealth—and, if possible, increasing it. Riches could best be obtained, in Locke's words, by taking it "from our neighbors." Francis Bacon explained that the burden of increasing one's wealth "must be [placed] upon the foreigner, for whatsoever is somewhere gotten is somewhere lost."

To accomplish this shift of wealth, the state had to be active. State control of commerce, often by means of granting monopolies, remained central to all economic thought and policy. As a colonial empire became more and more central to England's economic ambitions, these mercantilist principles came to shape colonial policy. At each step, policy aimed to expand England's share of colonial raw materials and (somewhat later) colonial markets for English goods. Parliamentary acts therefore protected royal trading monopolies from foreign (and domestic) competition, and the king favored his friends with economic privileges, including grants of land, and occasionally of entire colonies. Indeed, relations between these colonies and the mother country were defined by a web of such monopolies, restrictions, subsidies, and tariffs, all aimed at keeping the colonies firmly and profitably linked to England.

"... WHY ARE YOU THUS JEALOUS OF OUR LOVES?"

The following statement by Powhatan, leader of the Algonquin people in colonial Virginia, speaks eloquently about the rapidly deteriorating relations between the first colonists and the Indians upon whom the English were so dependent in the colony's early years. Powhatan's statement was addressed to Captain John Smith, governor of the Virginia colony, in 1612 (only five years after the colony's founding), and was taken down by two of Smith's associates.

CAPTAIN SMITH, YOU may understand that I . . . know the difference of peace and war better than any in my Country. But now I am old, and ere long must die. My brethren, namely Opichapam, Opechankanough, and Kekataugh, my two sisters, and their two daughters, are distinctly each other's successors. I wish their experiences no less than mine, and your love of them, no less than mine to you: but this bruit [noise] from Nansamund, that you are come to destroy my Country, so much affrighteth all my people, as they dare not visit you. What will it avail you to take [by force] that you may quietly have with love, or to destroy them that provide you food? What can you get by war, when we can hide our provisions and fly to the woods, whereby you must famish, by wronging us your friends? And why are you thus jealous of our loves, seeing us unarmed . . . and are willing still to feed you with that [which] you cannot get but by our labors? Think you I am so simple not to know it is better to eat good meat, lie well, and sleep quietly with my women and children, laugh, and be merry with you, have copper, hatchets, or what I want being your friend; than be forced to fly . . . , and thus with miserable fear end my miserable life, leaving my pleasures to such youths as you? . . . Let this therefore assure you of our loves, and every year our friendly trade shall furnish you with corn; and now also if you would come in friendly manner to see us, and not thus with your guns and swords, as [if] to invade your foes.

But first came the business of conquering North America. When the English arrived in the early seventeenth century, they encountered the Indians of northeastern America, who lived chiefly in egalitarian tribes and subsisted on different combinations of hunting, fishing, food-gathering, and farming. The earliest English colonists relied heavily upon aid from and trade with these native peoples. But gradually disease and trade undermined the patterns and institutions of Indian society.

The English built agricultural settlements that rested initially on various combinations of free and indentured labor. Northern society would evolve in the direction of yeoman farming and urban craft production based on family and free labor. In the South, the tobacco and rice plantations at first relied on the unfree labor of indentured servants and eventually depended on the labor of enslaved Africans and their progeny. The expansion of farming in both regions brought a change in English-Indian relations. Once anxious for Indian help and commerce, the colonists now came more and more to covet Indian land, resulting in an unequal, centuries-long conflict for control of the northern part of the continent.

The settlement of British North America was part of a global process by which Europe established imperial dominance. The driving force in the creation of new societies was a series of national and social struggles in Europe that, on the one hand, caused frustrated European rulers to look for new sources of wealth and, on the other, caused enough discontent among their common folk that many were willing to venture their all in a gamble of settling in a strange land. The actual process and outcome of colonization depended upon a complex array of social, political, and economic developments in America, Africa, and Europe. We can now turn our attention to the evolution of society in the English colonies—northern and southern—and the United States that supplanted them.

Belowdecks. The interior of a Spanish slave ship bound for the West Indies. After a British naval frigate captured the slaver, one of its officers descended belowdecks to record the horrible conditions of the Africans' Middle Passage.

2 SLAVERY AND THE GROWTH OF THE SOUTHERN COLONIES

DURING the pioneer decades, English colonists in the region surrounding Chesapeake Bay confronted and overcame major obstacles to establish permanent settlements in the New World. In these decisive years, men and women from England learned to survive on a continent that many peoples already called home, to make the first southern colonies in Virginia, and later in Maryland, economically viable, to organize local governments, and most important of all, to adapt their Old World values, habits, and expectations to New World realities. The decisions they made in the earliest years were the first steps in forming a distinctly southern society that was vastly different from both the old one they had left in England and the new one their countrymen were creating in the North.

Tobacco Plant. The first published illustration of the plant. A woodcut in *Stirpium Adversaria Nova*, a botanical study published in 1570.

By 1700, Virginians had pushed far to the west the native American tribes that had originally occupied the land. English settlers now used that land to grow tobacco, the crop around which the entire economy revolved. Tobacco was a "poor-man's crop" that could be produced on small holdings with a limited supply of labor, and indeed most tobacco farmers were men of modest but independent means. Some cultivators of the "sotweed," however, were tenants, whose labor developed the holdings of larger landholders, and a few were indentured servants who hoped eventually to acquire land of their own.

But by the turn of the century, the two most important social groups were the African slaves, who toiled in the tobacco fields, and the master class—slaveowners of power, privilege, and position—that employed them. As the wealthiest Virginians bought more and more slaves to replace the indentured servants whose labor had built the plantation system but whose later rebellious ways had produced deep social instability, these big planters in turn grew increasingly wealthy on their new bondsmen's labor. The emergence of a class of African slaves and a slaveowning aristocracy—first in Virginia, and then throughout the American South—is the single most important development in the early history of this region.

Yet the power of the slaveowning class, great as it was, was not safe from popular challenge, as the bewigged and ruffled gentlemen of the South discovered in the course of the eighteenth century. Indeed, by the 1760s they were confronted in various and maddening ways by their own unhappy slaves, by discontented small farmers from the western counties of their colonies, and by poorer followers of evangelical religion who considered them to be hopelessly mired in corrupt and sinful ways. As imperial conflict loomed with Great Britain, and as America entered the revolutionary era, the southern ruling class had so many internal problems that they could not be sure what the future would hold.

COLONIZING THE CHESAPEAKE

A plan to colonize Virginia was devised in 1606, when a group of merchants joined together to form the Virginia Company of London. James I had given them exclusive title to the territory between present-day North Carolina and New York—a vast, unexplored expanse about which these men knew practically nothing. But based on the experience of the Spanish in South America and the reports of the English adventurer Arthur Barlowe, who had explored the area south of Virginia in 1584, they expected to make money. Virginia, the promoters hoped, would contain the precious metals that would enrich the stockholders quickly; failing that, it would at least have the capacity to produce such modest valuables as glass, lead, and medicinal plants that would bring a reasonable return on their investment. Barlowe had reported that sassafras grew in abundance; it was thought to cure syphilis, so it had an assured market. Based on such speculation, the company attracted hundreds of petty investors to finance the first expedition to Virginia.

Nothing went right for the hundred and five men and boys who arrived to found Jamestown in May 1607. Only thirty-eight survived the next eight months, and throughout the first decade of settlement half to two-thirds of all immigrants died within a year of their arrival. Part of the reason lay in the unhealthy climate of the Chesapeake marshlands. But the first colonists also suffered from their own inexperience and naïve expectations. Reports of earlier explorers had led them to expect a Garden of Eden where food could be plucked without effort, where clothes and shelter would hardly be needed, where the docile native people would do whatever work had to be done.

But Virginia was not Eden, and those who came to this strange new land were particularly ill-suited to the task of survival. Among three hundred men and women who came to Jamestown from 1607 through 1609 were nearly sixty aristocrats, who considered labor far beneath them. These "gentlemen" knew nothing of planting crops, building shelters, or any other work basic to survival. The rest of the settlers were mostly unskilled laborers, military recruits, and servants. The few craftsman among them included such specialists as clockmakers, jewelers, and gentlemen's perfumers. Overwhelmingly male, single, and young, these early colonists had no idea how to build permanent farming communities in Virginia. And in any case, that was not their intention. They had come, as employees of the Virginia Company, to exploit the colony's natural wealth, and to return home richer.

Disappointed in their expectations, they faced the choice of starving or stealing from the native people. When they chose the latter, any hope for a peaceful and productive coexistence with American Indians began to dwindle. For the next sixty years, nearly constant guerrilla warfare characterized Indian-English relations. During these decades, full-fledged war erupted twice between colonists and a confederation of tribes named after their leader, Chief Powhatan. Opechancanough, Powhatan's brother and successor, led both campaigns against the settlers. In 1622, his men killed 347 colonists, nearly one-third of the white population, before English authorities agreed to prevent settlers from encroaching on Indian lands and to stop missionary work among the tribes. By 1644 the colony had grown to 8,000 settlers, and once again encroachment led to war. This time more than 500 colonists died before Opechancanough was captured and killed. Two years later the Powhatans signed a treaty that ac-

The title page of a 1609 pamphlet published in London promoting investment in the Virginia Company.

knowledged English authority and established cordial but fragile trading relations between the two peoples.

No one who had seen early Jamestown would have predicted such a complete victory for the English. In the beginning, Jamestown's starving gentlemen bowled in the streets while precious supplies dwindled, fields remained uncultivated, and skeptical Indians waited patiently for the intruders to die. To bring order to this chaos, the officers of the Virginia Company took several steps to correct the mistakes of the first expedition. First they tried to replace soldiers and adventurers with what they hoped would be morally superior men. After 1609, for example, the company paid special attention to the religious beliefs of prospective colonists. Recruiters rejected any man who could not "bring or render some good testimony of his relationship to God." For the next ten years, the colonists had to attend daily religious services in which company ministers led them in prayer for both social harmony and a "sevenfold return" on the shareholders' investment. The company gave equal attention to finding a new group of leaders who could be counted upon to wrest obedience from the men and women under their command.

Anticipating the possibility that God might ignore these prayers and that colonists might disobey even these more determined leaders, the company also imposed a harsh, militaristic code of law on the

"A Festive Dance." John White drew a "green corn" celebration in the Indian village of Secoton sometime around 1585. The Indians in his drawings appear exotic, yet also reassuringly familiar. Their poses, resembling figures in classical antiquity, and their discreetly draped clothes may have been intended to calm British fears of Indian violence and immorality.

"Village of Pomeiooc." White, who painted this watercolor sketch of a Chesapeake Indian village, was appointed governor of the unsuccessful Virginia colony of Raleigh in 1587. His concern for recruiting colonists for the Virginia Company led him to underplay or omit many aspects of Indian life that would disturb British sensibilities and deter potential colonists.

struggling settlement. The so-called Lawes Divine, Morall, and Martiall gave these leaders the authority to set the colonists to work under a strict "militarie discipline" harsher than any known in England. They began by dividing the colonists into labor gangs that could be easily supervised. Each morning "the beating of the Drum" summoned them to labor; at the end of the long workday, another drum beat them to church. From here they marched home to a fitful night on the dirt floor of a vermin-infested barracks.

Every aspect of the settlers' regimented and bleak existence came under the scrutiny of the Virginia Company. Colonists could not return to England without permission, and censors read their often pitiful letters to relatives and friends at home. The laws imposed the death penalty upon anyone who "shall dare to detract, slaunder, calumniate, or utter unseemly, and unfitting speeches" against the company, its officers, or its publications; who killed a domestic animal without the company's permission; or who ran away, as some did, to live with the Indians. But the method of punishment varied according to rank: gentlemen convicted of capital crimes were hanged or shot in a dignified manner, while servants were often mutilated before and after execution. For lesser crimes, wealthy men paid fines while inferiors suffered the lash, the branding iron, or the loss of an ear, nose, tongue, or limb.

The brutal, militaristic approach to labor and discipline flowed directly from the Virginia Company's goal of making money in the New World. It financed the expedition to Jamestown for profit, not in the Puritan hope of establishing a more perfect society, morally and politically superior to England. The company's method of coercing labor did succeed, but at the same time it established a social precedent that helped pave the way for the most extreme form of coerced labor, chattel slavery.

Coerced labor under the company laws was at first aimed only at growing the food and constructing the shelters needed to survive. Having barely achieved these goals, the company set the colonists to work making money. In 1611 the company began to grow tobacco, increasingly popular in England, where it was thought to have medicinal properties. While some men now labored in the tobacco fields, a few women, such as Ann Leyden and June Wright, stitched shirts for other colonists. When these shirts did not meet company standards, the women were, according to one eyewitness, "whipped, and Ann Leyden being then with child, the same night thereof miscarried."

Within a few years, the Virginia Company and all those men who had acquired land from it had turned, heart and soul, to the cultivation of tobacco. For the first time Virginia proved hospitable. Its fertile soil and long growing season were well suited to tobacco, and its tidal rivers made the vast interior accessible to the ocean-going English vessels that carried the crop across the Atlantic.

". . . TO BE IN ENGLAND AGAIN"

The dangers posed by disease and hostile Indians, the pain of separation from home, and the persistent problem of securing adequate food left many new settlers in a state of despair. This letter, dated March 20, 1623, is from Richard Frethorne, an indentured servant, to his parents in England. Frethorne had landed in Virginia three months earlier. Two-thirds of his fellow ship passengers had died since arriving in the colony. Frethorne asks his parents to "redeem," that is, buy out, his indenture.

LOVING AND KIND father and mother . . . this is to let you understand that I your child am in a most heavy case by reason of the nature of the country [which] is such that it causeth much sickness, [such] as the scurvy and the bloody flux, and diverse other diseases, which maketh the body very poor and weak. And when we are sick there is nothing to comfort us, for since I came out of the ship, I never ate anything but peas and lobiollie (that is water gruel); as for deer or venison I never saw any since I came into this land; there is indeed some fowl, but we are not allowed to go and get it, but must work hard both early and late for a mess of water gruel, and a mouthful of bread and beef. A mouthful of bread, for a penny loaf must serve for 4 men which is most pitiful if you did know as much as I, when people cry out day and night— Oh! that they were in England without their limbs—and would [sacrifice] any limb to be in England again. . . .

We live in fear of the enemy every hour, yet we have had to combat with them . . . and we took two alive, and make slaves of them . . . for we are in great danger, for our Plantation is very weak, by reason of the dearth, and sickness, of our company. . . .

But I am not half, a quarter so strong as I was in England, and all is for want of victuals, for I do protest unto you that I have eaten more in a day at home then I have allowed me here for a week. . . . If you love me you will redeem me suddenly, for which I do entreat and beg, and if you cannot get the merchants to redeem me for some little money then for God's sake get a gathering or entreat some good folks to lay out some little sum of money, in meal, and cheese and butter, and beef. . . .

Good father do not forget me, but have mercy and pity my miserable case. I know if you did but see me you would weep to see me, for I have but one suit, but it is a strange one, . . . and as for my part I have set down my resolution that . . . the answer of this letter will be life or death to me, therefore good father send as soon as you can . . .

The colony boomed; tobacco exports rose from 2,000 pounds in 1615 to 1.5 million pounds a mere fifteen years later.

Tobacco saved the Virginia colony from rapid demise. Even if the colonists could have survived without tobacco, the company had no interest in a colony that merely survived, and had planned to abandon Virginia as a hopeless failure. Tobacco alone offered the spectacular profits that revitalized interest in the colonial endeavor. Thus the Virginia Company turned to the task of enticing more people to go there to grow ever-larger quantities of tobacco.

To induce prospective colonists to sign up, the company offered land in exchange for labor or other services. Skilled artisans would receive "a house and four acres as long as they plied their trades" in Virginia. A man could receive fifty acres for himself and another fifty for every man, woman, and child he brought to the colony. The company also promised land to anyone who would serve a term as a bonded servant. And any planter who could pay 120 pounds of "the best leaf tobacco" could buy a wife from the Virginia Company.

There were reforms in the government of the colony as well. Martial law was softened, and in 1619, an independent governing body, the House of Burgesses, was set up. Nearly all adult English freemen now had the right to elect representatives who shared the responsibilities of governing the colony with officials chosen by the company.

These concessions worked, and between 1619 and 1625 nearly 5,000 settlers came to Virginia. But its very success spelled the death of the company, as the rapidly expanding colony simply outgrew the military organization the company had imposed to turn disaster into a goldmine. In 1624 King James I dissolved the Virginia Company and made Virginia a royal colony under his direct supervision.

But even by 1630, daily life in the royal colony still had little in common with that of the English village. Instead of building towns or villages, tobacco planters had scattered along the vast network of navigable rivers. The most successful planters owned hundreds of acres, but few of these plantations afforded their owners more comfort than the meanest dwelling of an English laborer: planters and servants alike lived in crude one-room shacks. In the swampy woodlands of the Chesapeake, most planters lived lonely lives, miles from neighbors or friends, surrounded by workers who labored within easy striking distance of disgruntled Indians. Men scrambling for wealth had little time for public spirit or civic cooperation. Hardly a community, early Virginia was an armed camp where individualism, competition, and fear prevailed. Tobacco planters abused their servants with "intolerable oppression and hard usage." One servant claimed that he was treated "like a damn'd slave."

Over the next thirty years, the tobacco economy expanded, and thousands of English immigrants flocked to Virginia and to the new

John Smith and the Indians. Smith, one of the first governing councillors of the Virginia colony, took a less benevolent view of the Indians than John White. This engraving from his *Generall Historie of Virginia*, published in 1624, shows the Chesapeake tribes as threatening giants. Smith recommended repression: "bring them to be tractable, civil, and industrious . . . that the fruit of their labor might make us some recompense."

colony of Maryland, established by the Catholic Lord Baltimore in 1634. Their lives revolved so fully around a competitive scuffle for tobacco and money that they had little energy for anything else. Religion, for example, was used primarily to coerce laborers, and little time or money could be found for schools. Some planters could not even be persuaded to organize, much less to participate in, a militia. One member of the House of Burgesses was so busy getting rich off tobacco that he attended only one session in eight years.

At the top of this fragile new society were the men who had been most successful at wringing wealth out of the fertile soil and the wretched lives of their servants. Those sitting in the House of Burgesses and on the colonial bench had scratched their way to the top.

Ætatis suæ 21. A°. 1616.

Matoaks als Rebecka daughter to the mighty Prince
Powhatan Emperour of Attanoughkomouck als Virginia
converted and baptized in the Christian faith, and
Wife to the wor.ll M.r Tho: Rolff.

A portrait of Pocahontas, the daughter of Chief Powhatan, at the age of twenty-one, soon after her arrival in London. According to John Smith, Pocahontas saved him from execution when he was captured by the Algonquins in 1607. She subsequently married an English gentleman and became the first Indian of "royal blood" to be brought to England for the edification and entertainment of the nobility—and the first to succumb to Great Britain's inhospitable climate, probably dying of tuberculosis sometime after 1616.

These shrewd and often ruthless survivors had married the widows of wealthy planters, made the best deals, or paid the highest bribes to force other men to do their bidding. By midcentury, many such men had acquired thousands of acres apiece. Their exercise of power through government and law was an undisguised attempt to use the tools of civil authority to keep an upper hand in the intense battle for profit.

What had residents in the Chesapeake achieved in the first five decades of settlement? The Virginia Company had given way to a colony, albeit one conducted along the rigid lines and for the limited purpose first established by the company. The disease and malnutrition of the first years had been largely overcome; the life expectancy of the next generation of American-born colonists was at least as good as the forty years their English counterparts enjoyed. Many Indian tribes had been wiped out or pushed westward, where they maintained an uneasy truce with English traders and the few isolated colonists who lived nearby. Most important of all, the colony had become a financial success, attractive both to the crown for the tobacco taxes it provided and to the English immigrants who came in search of opportunities that had eluded them in England.

But measured by other standards, society in the Chesapeake in about 1660 had failed. It looked nothing like the ideal rural society of small family farms that an earlier generation of English writers had thought possible in the New World. To a shocking extent, the quest for tobacco profits justified an individualistic adventurism that was unknown in most stable English communities. With few exceptions, colonists were either landowners or the servants they employed. Neither group enjoyed much in the way of community or family life, in part because the Virginia Company and the planter elite had focused on attracting young male laborers—men outnumbered women by at least three to one, in some areas by as much as six to one. Throughout the Chesapeake, immigrants had been separated from their parents, and the children of immigrants were often orphaned before reaching adulthood. All these factors made Chesapeake society seem unstable—even crude and amoral.

THE LABOR "PROBLEM"

Of all the problems Virginia's employers faced in the first five decades of colonization, the organization of labor proved the hardest to solve. Once it became clear that fortunes could be made growing tobacco, landowners saw nothing but missed opportunities in the vast lands they could not work without the labor of others. No planter, no matter how hard he worked, could accumulate great riches without employing others to till his fields. Thus it happened that the first two generations of planters, rich in land but poor in workers, had to find and discipline a labor force to make their land yield its wealth. It was their central preoccupation and their hardest task.

The need to enlarge the workforce did not impel the Chesapeake planters to improve the conditions of employment. Indeed, like most English employers in this age, they drew quite the opposite conclusion from the labor shortage: they sought to exploit to the full those they did entice or force to come to the tobacco fields of Virginia. Building upon the dehumanizing model of labor discipline pioneered by the Virginia Company, the big planters worked steadily to reduce

THE INCONVENIENCIES
THAT HAVE HAPPENED TO SOME PERSONS WHICH HAVE TRANSPORTED THEMSELVES

from *England* to *Virginia*, vvithout prouisions necessary to sustaine themselues, hath greatly hindred the *Progresse of that noble Plantation*: For preuention of the like disorders heereafter, that no man suffer, either through ignorance or misinformation; it is thought requisite to publish this short declaration: wherein is contained a particular of such necessaries, as either priuate families or single persons shall haue cause to furnish themselues with, for their better support at their first landing in Virginia; whereby also greater numbers may receiue in part, directions how to prouide themselues.

Apparrell.

ApparrEll for one man, and so after the rate for more.

	li.	s.	d.
One Monmouth Cap	00	01	10
Three falling bands		01	03
Three shirts		07	06
One waste-coate		02	02
One suite of Canuase		07	06
One suite of Frize		10	00
One suite of Cloth		15	00
Three paire of Irish stockins		04	
Foure paire of shooes		08	08
One paire of garters		00	10
One doozen of points		00	03
One paire of Canuase sheets		08	00
Seuen ells of Canuase, to make a bed and boulster, to be filled in *Virginia* 8.s.		08	00
One Rug for a bed 8. s. which with the bed seruing for two men, halfe is			
Fiue ells coorse Canuase, to make a bed at Sea for two men, to be filled with straw, iiij.s.		05	00
One coorse Rug at Sea for two men, will cost vj.s. is for one			
	04	00	00

Victuall.

For a whole yeere for one man, and so for more after the rate.

	li.	s.	d.
Eight bushels of Meale	02	00	00
Two bushels of peafe at 3.s.		06	00
Two bushels of Oatemeale 4.s. 6.d.		09	00
One gallon of *Aquauitae*		02	06
One gallon of Oyle		03	06
Two gallons of Vineger 1. s.		02	00
	03	03	00

Armes.

For one man, but if halfe of your men haue armour it is sufficient so that all haue Peeces and swords.

	li.	s.	d.
One Armour compleat, light		17	00
One long Peece, fiue foot or fiue and a halfe, neere Musket bore	01	02	
One sword		05	
One belt		01	
One bandaleere		01	06
Twenty pound of powder		18	00
Sixty pound of shot or lead, Pistoll and Goose shot		05	00
	03	09	06

Tooles.

For a family of 6. persons and so after the rate for more.

	li.	s.	d.
Fiue broad howes at 2.s. a piece		10	
Fiue narrow howes at 16.d. a piece		06	08
Two broad Axes at 3.s. 8.d. a piece		07	04
Fiue felling Axes at 18.d. a piece		07	06
Two steele hand sawes at 16.d. a piece		02	08
Two two-hand-sawes at 5. s. a piece		10	
One whip-saw, set and filed with box, file, and wrest		10	
Two hammers 12.d. a piece		02	00
Three shouels 18.d. a piece		04	06
Two spades at 18.d. a piece		03	
Two augers 6.d. a piece		01	00
Sixe chissels 6.d. a piece		03	00
Two percers stocked 4.d. a piece		00	08
Three gimlets 2.d. a piece		00	06
Two hatchets 21.d. a piece		03	06
Two froues to cleaue pale 18.d.		03	00
Two hand-bills 20. a piece		03	04
One grindlestone 4.s.		04	00
Nailes of all sorts to the value of		02	00
Two Pickaxes		03	
	06	02	08

Houshold Implements.

For a family of 6. persons, and so for more or lesse after the rate.

	li.	s.	d.
One Iron Pot		07	
One kettle		06	
One large frying-pan		02	06
One gridiron		01	06
Two skillets		05	
One spit		02	
Platters, dishes, spoones of wood		04	
	01	08	00

	li.	s.	d.
For Suger, Spice, and fruit, and at Sea for 6.men.	00	12	06
So the full charge of Apparrell, Victuall, Armes, Tooles, and houshold stuffe, and after this rate for each person, will amount vnto about the summe of	12	10	00
The passage of each man is	06	00	00
The fraight of these prouisions for a man, will bee about halfe a Tun, which is	01	10	00
So the whole charge will amount to about	20	00	00

Nets, hookes, lines, and a tent must be added, if the number of people be greater, as also some kine. And thus is the vsuall proportion that the Virginia *Company* doe bestow vpon their *Tenants* which they send.

Whosoeuer transports himselfe or any other at his owne charge vnto *Virginia*, shall for each person so transported before Midsummer 1625. haue to him and his heires for euer fifty Acres of Land vpon a first, and fifty Acres vpon a second diuision.

Imprinted at London by FELIX KYNGSTON. 1622.

A 1622 notice directed to British free men and their families lists the necessities to be obtained by prospective *voluntary* immigrants before embarking for Virginia.

the other colonists to a condition of servile dependency. This degradation of labor in Virginia produced profound social tensions, and after decades of experimentation with a variety of coercive labor arrangements, the colony stood on the verge of civil war in the 1670s. Ultimately, after decades of uncertainty and conflict, the planters sought to solve their labor problems by permanently enslaving Africans and their Chesapeake-born descendants.

The first Virginians, as we have seen, expected American Indians to be the colony's labor force. Mercantilist theorists had encouraged such beliefs long before anyone sailed for Virginia. Settlers sincerely believed that English goods and civility would seduce and domesticate a native population they thought to be inferior to the English in every way. When the Powhatan Indians refused to play their assigned role, the planters considered enslaving them. But for several decades after 1607, the Chesapeake tribes were too well armed, too numerous, and too familiar with the countryside to be easily enslaved. After the war of 1622, the planters resolved instead to remove the Indians—a decision implemented with increasing severity throughout the seventeenth century.

The planters looked elsewhere for laborers. English authorities offered a helping hand by forcibly transporting some of London's orphans to work in the tobacco fields. Between 1617 and 1624 several hundred orphans, including scores who had vigorously protested "their unwillingness to go to Virginia," were turned over to planters to work until they reached the age of twenty-one. By then, these orphans could be set free, having been "brought to goodness under severe Masters." Crown and planters alike applauded this arrangement, since it turned troublesome or financially burdensome orphans into productive assets. Only the involuntary child migrants objected, for in reality all they could expect was several months or years of hard labor and a premature death.

With equal enthusiasm the crown also advocated the forced migration of English convicts, but planters opposed the plan; they had no desire to employ men and women who had already demonstrated a readiness to break the law. They successfully limited the number of convicts transported to Virginia until later in the century.

Intractable Indians and an inadequate supply of orphans left planters little choice but to recruit young adults. These recruits signed an indenture, agreeing to work for four to seven years in exchange for passage to the New World; at the end of the period, they would get their freedom, a new set of clothes, a few tools, and fifty acres of land. For many who chose indentured servitude, this was their best, and possibly their only, chance to acquire that much land. Thus it is not surprising that during the seventeenth century, 75 to 85 percent of the estimated 130,000 people who journeyed from England to the Chesapeake came as indentured servants. Single men, between the ages of fifteen and twenty-four, accounted for three-fourths of them. Most worked with one or two other indentured servants on tobacco farms at the delicate but routine tasks of sprouting, transplanting,

A British engraving represents a fictional colonial success story. Polly Haycock, pregnant and unmarried, is sentenced to transportation to Virginia as an indentured servant. Brutalized by her master, Polly is released from her servitude by a Virginia magistrate. She marries her rescuer and the tale ends with Polly rich, a plantation mistress who mistreats her own servants.

and curing tobacco. During the growing season the fields had to be hoed often, and much additional labor was needed to eke out a subsistence through gardening, hunting, and foraging.

Indentured women, who accounted for nearly all unmarried female immigrants, comprised but a small percentage of the population. Only a few hundred, for example, went to Maryland, where in the seventeenth century men outnumbered women six to one. Women's work depended on the social status of their employers. If indentured to marginal planters, women labored in the fields, which Englishwomen did not do at home. Indeed, such work contradicted the ideal division between men's labor outside the home and women's labor inside it, considered by English authorities on the family to be essential to maintaining the father's position as master of the family. Wealthier planters and merchants employed their female servants at domestic tasks such as washing clothes, sewing, "dressing the victuals," "righting up the home," and childrearing.

Some planters also bought slaves and set them to work alongside English indentured servants. Nearly all were English-speaking male

Africans who had already worked as slaves for several years on the tobacco or sugar plantations of the West Indies. The first group arrived in a Dutch man-of-war in 1619, but even by 1660, when the English population of the Chesapeake had reached thirty thousand, there were probably fewer than fifteen hundred Afro-Caribbeans in the region. We know very little about their status, but the available evidence indicates that most labored as slaves for life. Some, however, worked as indentured servants. By midcentury a few slaves had been able to buy their freedom and find employment as craftsmen, laborers, tenants, or independent farmers. Anthony Johnson, a black yeoman farmer of Pungoteague Creek in Virginia, died too soon to know that his grandson in 1677 had named his farm Angola.

Indentured servants faced such terrible working conditions that nearly two-thirds of them died before their terms expired. Neither escaped the virtually limitless authority that colonial law gave to their masters. Indentured servants generally served four to seven years, though blacks served longer than whites. But inexact terms, unregulated by law or custom as they were in England, added to the servants' misery. In Virginia, the court officials and local magistrates to whom abused servants might appeal were the very men who employed and mistreated them. Servants accused of insubordination could be fined, branded, or whipped. More serious offenders faced execution, usually at a public ceremony attended by fellow servants and staged to set a vivid example for all the discontented in their ranks. Unmarried women servants who became pregnant, as did an estimated 20 percent, received special punishment. All had to serve additional years; some had their children taken from them and sold, for a few pounds of tobacco, to another master. Masters permitted these female servants to marry only if the father of the child reimbursed the master for the loss of his servant, a financial obligation well beyond the means of most.

Indentured servants did not enjoy the full customary rights or legal protections of their English counterparts. The Elizabethan Statute of Artificers kept English laborers, both at home and abroad, at work ten to fourteen hours a day, six days a week. But in the Chesapeake, labor discipline was maintained largely by brute force rather than the subtler constraints of law and civil society. Virginia servants lacked the right of all other freeborn Englishmen to hold their masters criminally liable for mistreatment or breach of contract. Furthermore, only Chesapeake servants could be repeatedly bought and sold. These conditions, combined with the fact that most servants had no family in the Chesapeake, usually resulted in lives of abject misery. "So the truth is," the servant Edward Hill complained to his brother in England, "we live in the fearfullest age that ever Christians lived in."

This system of labor satisfied the planters' needs for several decades. During this time most servants died before their terms expired, so the planters usually did not have to make good on their promise of land, which would have created competitors who might have driven the price of tobacco down. After 1650, however, improvements in diet and living conditions produced a higher survival rate among indentured servants, even though the long hours and harsh conditions of labor remained. Life for former servants who became landowners in Virginia and Maryland was far from easy. But for a time it was possible for them to aspire to minor political offices, and to secure the right to vote for those prominent planters who filled nearly all important public positions.

The planter elite continued to protect its own interests. New laws in Virginia and Maryland lengthened the years of service, and other steps were taken to deny freedmen the promised fifty acres and to narrow the economic and political opportunities of smallholders.

Wealthy planters reserved the most desirable land in the Chesapeake for themselves and their children. Territory most accessible to ex-servants was marginal—either controlled by local Indian tribes or too far removed from the rivers to allow its owners to market their tobacco. Those smallholders close enough to the waterways were at the mercy of wealthier planters, whose control over the ships that carried the tobacco to market enabled them to gouge their more marginal competitors. Those who overcame this obstacle were all too vulnerable to the high taxes and fees arbitrarily imposed by the planter-dominated House of Burgesses. By 1672 all of these conditions had combined to produce a large group of frustrated, debt-ridden landowners. Their violently expressed anger and discontent, Virginia Governor William Berkeley told the London Privy Council, set a bad example for servants.

The system of indentured servitude itself began to lose its original appeal for planters as soon as the majority of servants survived their terms and clamored for the land they had been promised. When the planters refused to share wealth and power with their former servants, this group of free but unlanded people grew increasingly large and rebellious. The planters' geographical isolation and unrelenting drive for profit increased their vulnerability. As late as 1681, Lord Culpepper, Governor of Virginia, was noting, "Masters have guns. Servants not trusted." The fear of social disorder increased as the population of unlanded former servants grew larger and more discontented. By 1660 it was not at all apparent how to keep servants on the job and keep free men and women in their place. But something had to be done. Here was a problem that the next generation of Virginians would have to solve.

CONFLICT AND SLAVERY

Between 1660 and 1710, planters slowly abandoned the system of indentured servitude in favor of a labor force made up almost exclusively of slaves from Africa. Social tensions that had accompanied the labor problem erupted, first in scattered violence and then, in 1676, in a full-scale insurrection known as Bacon's Rebellion. This was a key moment in the process whereby southern planters created a society in which whites were free, if politically and socially unequal, and blacks were permanently enslaved. In this society, white farmers, artisans, tenants, and laborers won the civil rights and economic opportunity that came in time to constitute American freedom, while tobacco planters turned to the new source and system of labor that became American slavery.

Beginning in the 1650s, the earliest planters, who had achieved success through the use of indentured servants, had been partially replaced in the House of Burgesses and all other important places by more recent immigrants who were richer, better connected, and more typical of the seventeenth-century English aristocracy. Once it became clear that it was possible to survive and prosper in the southern colonies, the younger sons of England's gentry began to come to America. Some had inherited thousands of acres long since bought from the Virginia Company. Others simply came with enough cash to buy plantations or unimproved land. In England, primogeniture —the law by which the eldest son inherited his father's whole estate—barred younger sons from the status and wealth their fathers commanded. In America, however, they could begin at the top.

In the tumultuous 1660s and 1670s, these men became the new ruling elite of Virginia. At first they took over the county offices that an earlier generation had set up to wrest political control from the Virginia Company and the Cromwellian government that had beheaded Charles I. The new magistrates and county officers created additional political offices, which they soon filled with their relatives. Then they took over the House of Burgesses. By the end of the seventeenth century, blood or marriage connected 90 percent of Virginia's burgesses; they created an aristocracy whose heirs could be found among the South's leading families more than a century later.

This changing of the guard began at a time of tremendous turmoil in England; between 1640 and 1660 the English were too preoccupied with civil war at home to pay much attention to what was going on in the colonies. Virginia planters turned to Dutch merchants to carry their tobacco to Europe and their cattle to the Caribbean. Access to the latter market encouraged landowners to shift more of their land from tobacco to cattle and cereal grains, which they traded for rum, sugar, and Afro-Caribbean slaves. And they could trade without paying duties to the government.

When Charles II gained the restored throne in 1660, he declared war on the Dutch and reasserted the authority of the crown over the colonists, who had come to think of free trade as a political right and to regard any English law as invalid unless ratified by their own assemblies. But neither principle withstood direct challenge from the crown, and planters grumbled but obeyed new trade regulations imposed in the 1660s: All colonial products had to be shipped in English vessels—built, owned, and manned by Englishmen. All tobacco had to be shipped first to England or Ireland, or to another English colony,

"The Voyage of the Sable Venus from Angola to the West Indies." A 1794 British engraving attempts to ennoble the slave trade by mimicking Sandro Botticelli's celebrated fifteenth-century painting, *The Birth of Venus*.

where it was assessed an import duty. If the cargo was transshipped there, it now cost the planter an export duty as well. Such regulations greatly enriched the crown and London merchants, but burdened the Chesapeake planters. To make matters worse, overproduction in the 1660s and 1670s drove the price of tobacco to an all-time low, just as the English-Dutch wars disrupted trade and obliged colonists to raise taxes to pay for forts and troops. Even nature turned ugly—bad weather caused crops to rot in the fields, and disease killed fifty thousand cattle.

To make sure the planters paid their taxes despite these difficulties, Charles II relied on his friend and loyal supporter Governor William Berkeley. Berkeley and those he chose to favor with office composed Virginia's royal officialdom, which was often at loggerheads with the House of Burgesses. Though these two ruling groups overlapped somewhat in goals and personnel, they were divided by a fundamental conflict. The amount of revenue the crown collected depended solely upon how much tobacco was shipped, not how much it sold for. Thus the crown had little interest in diversified agriculture or any effort to limit tobacco production. The fortunes of the planters, however, rose and fell with the price of tobacco; overproduction, which drove the price down, was a major concern.

But all well-to-do Virginians faced a more immediate problem— the increasing discontent among ex-servants, who clamored for land, and among indebted planters, who fought skirmishes with the Indians who lived near their hard-won marginal lands. Neither group supported the Virginia government, and during the English-Dutch wars, Governor Berkeley feared that if Dutch forces invaded Virginia, "at least one-third" of the single freemen "would revolt . . . in hopes of bettering their condition by sharing the Plunder of the Country with them." Others feared that these rowdy and desperate men, who were "Poor Endebted Discontented and Armed," might rebel at any time, even without outside provocation.

These misgivings intensified as indentured servants—the other large, unruly group in the Chesapeake—actually rebelled. After midcentury the number of runaway servants increased steadily, and in 1661 and 1663, servants in two separate counties took up arms and demanded freedom. The first episode occurred in York County, where servants complained of "hard usage" and poor diets. Isaac Friend, their leader, planned to bring together about forty servants. They would then "get arms" and march through the country, raising recruits by urging servants "who would be for liberty, and free from bondage," to join them. Once a large enough force had been aroused, the rebels "would go through the Country and kill those that made any opposition, and they would either be free or die for it." An informer enabled officials to nip this plot in the bud; they put Friend under constant surveillance. A far harsher punishment was meted out to the servants who rebelled in Gloucester County in 1663—several of them were executed for their "villainous Plot to destroy their Masters, and afterwards to set up for themselves."

Indentured servants and discontented freemen saw two groups keeping them from getting the land they wanted—the propertied elites who ruled them, and the Indians, whom they viewed as heathens who had no just claim to the land. Nearly all colonists, not just the dispossessed, shared this self-serving contempt for American Indians; in 1676 Governor Berkeley conspired with the powerful planters to enslave all Indians in Virginia. Before he could act, though, Nathaniel Bacon, a well-to-do young planter who thought Berkeley too lenient with local Indians, took matters into his own hands. In May 1676, he led a mixed band of prosperous neighbors from the north bank of the James River and indebted farmers from the south in an unauthorized assault on a village of friendly Indians.

With this attack, all hell broke loose in Virginia. Middling farmers—and even larger numbers of poor freemen, indentured servants, and slaves—formed a rebel army. Berkeley's militia captured Bacon in June. The governor made him write a confession and then pardoned him, in a move to conciliate Bacon's followers and reestablish the authority of the ruling elite. But Bacon, who "heard what an incredible Number of the meanest [poorest] of People were everywhere Armed to assist him and his cause," soon renewed his attacks. Over the summer and into the fall of 1676, Bacon's forces drove Berkeley out of the colony, attempted to capture the governor of Maryland, plundered the estates of their prosperous

---

"THE DECLARATION OF THE PEOPLE"

In announcing the rebellion in 1676, Nathaniel Bacon issued "The Declaration of the People," in which he detailed a set of grievances of the common people against Governor Berkeley's administration and argued the revolutionary notion that Berkeley's authority could not be considered legitimate without the consent of the people.

FOR HAVING UPON specious pretenses of Public works raised unjust Taxes upon the Commonality for the advancement of private Favorites and other sinister ends. . . .

For having abused and rendered Contemptible the Majesty of Justice, [by] advancing to places of judicature scandalous and Ignorant favorites.

For having wronged his Majesty's Prerogative and Interest by assuming the monopoly of the Beaver Trade.

By having in that unjust gaine Bartered and sold his Majesty's Country and the lives of his Loyal Subjects to the Barbarous Heathen [the Indians].

For having protected, favored, and Imboldened the Indians against his Majesty's most Loyal subjects, never contriving, requiring, or appointing any due or proper means [to prevent] their many Invasions, Murders, and Robberies Committed upon us. . . .

For having . . . forged a Commission by we know not what hand, not only without but against the Consent of the People, for raising and effecting of Civil Wars and distractions. . . .

Of these the aforesaid Articles we accuse Sir William Berkeley, as guilty of each and every one of the same, and as one, who has Traitorously attempted, violated and Injured his Majesty's Interest here. . . .

These are therefore in his Majesty's name, to Command you forthwith to seize the Persons above mentioned as Traitors to your King and Country, . . . and if you want any other Assistance, you are forthwith to demand it in the Name of the People of all the Counties of Virginia.

NATH. BACON, Gen'l *By the Consent of the People.*

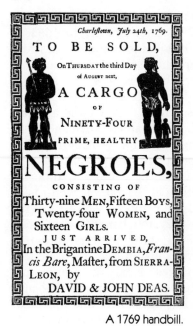

A 1769 handbill.

adversaries, and massacred hundreds of Indians. In September, when Berkeley tried to reassert his authority in Virginia, Bacon and his men burned Jamestown to the ground. His forces had been swollen by the servants and slaves of Berkeley loyalists, who joined the campaign in exchange for their freedom. For the next four weeks, Bacon and his men looted the estates of Berkeley's backers and collected tribute from other wealthy planters. Bacon died of dysentery on October 26; when armed vessels arrived from England two weeks later, the rebellious mood of Bacon's more prosperous converts cooled, but hundreds of armed slaves, indentured servants, and "Freemen that had but lately crept out of the condition of Servants" fought on until they were captured or killed. The rebellion was over by the end of January 1677.

Bacon's Rebellion had given the most oppressed whites and blacks in the Chesapeake an unprecedented opportunity to turn the world upside down. According to its critics, this "Rabble of the basest sort of People" had sought "the subversion of the Laws and to Levell all." Bacon's rhetoric had drawn no distinction between whites and blacks, freemen and slaves. He had spoken only of the "common people," united by poverty and their oppression at the hands of wealthy planters, "unworthy favourites and juggling parasites." The power of Bacon's combination of freemen, servants, and slaves—and the interracial solidarity they displayed—so alarmed the leading planters that they quickly took steps to prevent a recurrence.

Efforts focused first on reducing social tensions among whites in the Chesapeake. Disagreements between local and royal authorities became less heated as Charles II limited the power of his council in Virginia and extended that of the House of Burgesses. Both parties worked together to appease the frustrated freemen, who wanted, more than anything else, land. New legislation curbed wild and often illegal speculation in land—such as that practiced by the king himself when he gave two friends all the public lands in Virginia. Access to land was further eased by a campaign to drive the Indians over the mountains into present-day Kentucky and Tennessee. Finally, Parliament began investigating the treatment of indentured servants and began to prosecute recruiters who used such illegal tactics as kidnapping, misrepresentation, and fraud.

The ultimate achievement of social order in the Chesapeake, however, depended upon a new distinction in the way the ruling elite treated whites and blacks. Whites were guaranteed their freedom—and taught to fear and despise blacks, who lost what little freedom they had. Through laws that placed all whites above and separate from blacks, Virginia's elites created racial bonds among whites that withstood the strains of economic and political inequality, and made

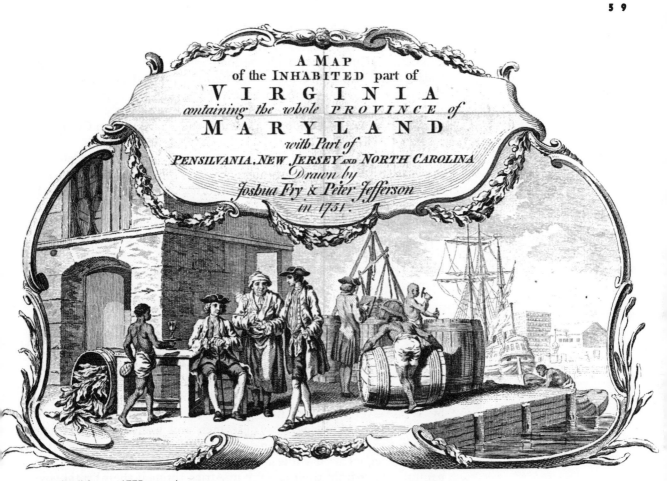

A detail from a 1775 map shows slaves packing tobacco in barrels on a Virginia wharf for shipment abroad.

it unlikely that poor whites would join blacks against the rulers. By importing thousands of African slaves and by guaranteeing that they would never become free, the planters solved their labor problem and drove a wedge between the two halves of the South's most dependent population, thereby ensuring their own continued dominance.

For generations, Chesapeake planters had searched for a labor force that could be exploited to the fullest. Only slaves, the colony's experience had demonstrated, could fulfill this need, and it seemed easiest to enslave African men and women, who could be uprooted from their homeland, stripped of all rights, and treated as property. For the first three-quarters of the seventeenth century, most captured Africans had been sold in the Caribbean, where the high sugar profits justified buying slaves, despite high mortality rates, and where the work was so strenuous that English indentured servants finally refused to do it. By 1660, many Chesapeake tobacco planters could also afford slaves, and they bought as many slaves as carriers, legal and illegal, were willing to bring to Virginia. The Navigation Acts had cut them off from the Dutch slavers; after that, the legal supply was not fully adequate until the eighteenth century, despite the expansion of the English slaving monopoly known as the Royal African Company in 1672.

Slavery had existed in Virginia since 1619, but it gained official sanction in colonial law only in 1660. Soon more laws declared that a child's status followed that of the mother and that baptism "doth not make a man free." Other laws, even more restrictive, followed Bacon's Rebellion. Legislation banned interracial marriage, severely punished white women who bore racially mixed children, and it stripped free blacks of their property and rights. In 1699, the courts held that masters could not be prosecuted for murder if slaves died from injuries sustained while being punished for insubordination. By 1705, the contempt earlier generations of planters had shown for American Indians and English indentured servants had reached its logical culmination in a slave code that gave masters unrestricted power over a labor force that would never be free.

The African population grew enormously. Only about 2,000 slaves lived in Virginia in 1670, most brought from the Caribbean. After 1680, most came directly from Africa; their number swelled to 20,000 by 1700. Over the next fifty years some 100,000 Africans were brought to the Chesapeake. These men and women, unlike their predecessors, did not speak English, nor did they have any opportunity to be equal with whites. They were slaves for life, a fact made painfully clear from their capture in Africa through their brutal voyage to their arrival in Virginia—where, said one observer at the turn of the century, "They can be selected according to pleasure, young and old, men and women. They are entirely naked when they arrive, having only corals of different colors around their necks and arms."

SLAVERY SPREADS

As the new tobacco aristocrats of the Chesapeake region in the upper South solved their labor problem with permanent racial slavery, immigrants began to colonize the lower South, settling in the areas that would later be the Carolinas and Georgia. Early on, migrants from Virginia brought tobacco and slavery in the Albermarle region that became North Carolina, but the first South Carolinians and Georgians rejected both tobacco and an exclusively slave labor system. They grew a variety of crops with a workforce that included family members, indentured servants, and wage laborers, as well as slaves.

Establishing the Colony of Georgia. An illustration from a 1733 book advocating colonization depicts Georgia as an idyllic, bountiful land—the perfect setting for the creation of a well-ordered, hierarchical society. Note the gentleman in the right corner supervising the work.

The history of the lower South differed from that of the Chesapeake in many ways. Carolina's Fundamental Principles of government were drafted not by profit-seeking investors, but by the English political philosopher John Locke, whose subsequent writings helped to inspire among a later generation of Americans the belief that all men were created equal. Locke envisioned a harmonious agricultural society with an economy based upon mixed farming, cattle-raising, and an Indian trade in deerskins. The colony's proprietors planned to recruit only "seasoned" colonists from the West Indies who would pay their own passage. They would be offered land at low prices and encouraged to form communities of self-sufficient family farms. The crown granted all colonists political and religious freedom, and adult white males were promised the right to vote for assemblymen who were to govern the colony with the help of noblemen drawn from England.

Migrants from the West Indies flocked to Carolina. Many were Barbadians who owned too few slaves and too little land to make a successful transition from the traditional tobacco to sugar; by the 1650s, they had few prospects on their already overpopulated, overcultivated island. These migrants were generally older than the first Chesapeake colonists; many had families. Immigrants from Scotland, Germany, and Ireland also turned to mixed family farming. The children of some of the richest planters of the sugar islands also came to Carolina, bringing hundreds of slaves, along with the customs of the West Indian gentry. Nonetheless, in the beginning, independent, non-slaveowning white farmers outnumbered slaveowners, indentured servants, unlanded laborers, and slaves.

The colony, however, failed to fulfill its promoters' expectations. Few English nobles actually migrated to the colony; the tiny minority of wealthy migrants accumulated thousands of acres and quickly seized political control. Many of these leading families settled in Charleston, which soon became the largest port city in the South. Most colonists lived on modest farms, close to the coast, where they grew their own food and raised cattle for export to the West Indies, according to the original mercantilist plan. But this mixed subsistence farming generated little revenue for the crown.

On their own initiative, other colonists organized a slave trade with the West Indies, exchanging American Indians—captured from the tribes that did not supply the lucrative deerskins—for rum and sugar. These traders, along with the most successful farmers, employed Afro-Caribbean slaves, indentured servants from England and Ireland, and some white native Americans. Prior to 1705 the leading families of Charleston, not farmers, owned most of the slaves.

During the colony's pioneer decades, neither indentured servants nor slaves faced conditions as brutal as in the Chesapeake. Here everyone, not just laborers, suffered from semitropical diseases, poor nutrition, and inadequate shelter, but survival rates improved with each generation—after 1750, births began to outnumber deaths among freemen and slaves. Everyone worked hard, but few laborers were treated as badly as the indentured servants in the Chesapeake. After 1680, indentured servants no longer flocked to the South, and those who came refused to accept terms of more than five years. Both the availability of land in other colonies and the restrictions imposed on the masters after 1676 enhanced the bargaining power of prospective indentured servants.

Other differences between the two regions made it difficult for slaveowners to mimic the rigid and brutal slave system of the Chesapeake. Defending the colony from hostile foreign troops in Florida and Louisiana sometimes required that slaves be mobilized and armed—a policy fraught with danger. Even more important, commercial cattle growers, unlike tobacco planters, required a mobile, self-reliant labor force. The slaves' skill at raising cattle in a subtropical climate—a skill brought from Africa—was recognized. Since the cattle were not fenced, the slaves who tended them had to move with the herds and run down strays.

All in all, then, the slaves and other laborers of seventeenth-century Carolina enjoyed a degree of freedom their counterparts in early Virginia never knew. In 1706, for example, several petitioners from Craven and Berkeley counties complained that in "the last election Jews, Strangers, Sailors, Servants, Negroes, and almost every French Man" in the two counties "came down to elect, and their votes were taken." Thomas Nairne, a Carolina Indian agent, noted in 1710 that "enrolled in our Militia [are] a considerable Number of active, able, Negro Slaves; and Law gives everyone of those his freedom, who in Time of an Invasion kills an Enemy." Those Afro-Caribbean slaves who were not offered this chance for freedom took advantage of the loose supervision on cattle farms and the sparse settlement of frontier society to escape slavery altogether. Many fled into the swampy interior and established independent communities with anti-English Indians. Such opportunities to escape slavery disappeared, though, when the Yamassee Indians were virtually wiped out in 1720 and white settlers began to migrate inland.

Throughout the Carolina low country, slavery became more rigid as rice became the main export in the eighteenth century and economic opportunities for mixed farming declined. Determined to reap the riches that only staple production could provide, the wealthy planters of Barbadian ancestry banished the white yeomanry to the hinterland and consolidated their farms into vast rice plantations of several thousand acres, turning almost exclusively to African slaves for their workforce. By 1708 blacks outnumbered whites for the first time in any colony on the North American continent. Many of these same Africans, as free men and women, had grown rice at home. In eighteenth-century Carolina they could expect nothing but lifelong slavery as the rice economy spread and frontier conditions gave way to a more settled, structured, race-bound society.

By the middle of the eighteenth century, Georgia had much in common with the Carolinas (which became separate royal colonies in 1729), even though neither rice nor slavery had been part of its original

"SLAVES, TO ALL INTENTS AND PURPOSES"

Carolina's Slave Code, enacted in 1712, was one of the first comprehensive acts regulating slave life in the North American colonies. Note the racist arguments used explicitly to justify the permanent enslavement of "negroes, mulattoes, mestizoes [mixed Indian and European people], and Indians" and their children.

WHEREAS, THE PLANTATIONS and estates of this province cannot be well and sufficiently managed and brought into use, without the labor and service of negroes and other slaves; and forasmuch as the said negroes and other slaves brought into the people of this Province for that purpose, are of barbarous, wild, savage natures, and such as renders them wholly unqualified to be governed by the laws, customs, and practices of this Province; but that it is absolutely necessary, that such other constitutions, laws and orders, should in this Province be made and enacted, for the good regulating and ordering of them, as may restrain the disorders, rapines and inhumanity, to which they are naturally prone and inclined, and may also tend to the safety and security of the people of this Province and their estates; to which purpose,

BE IT THEREFORE ENACTED ... that all negroes, mulattoes, mestizoes or Indians, which at any time heretofore have been sold, or now are held or taken to be, or hereafter shall be bought and sold for slaves, are hereby declared slaves; and they, and their children, are hereby made and declared slaves, to all intents and purposes. ...

settlement plan. Founded in 1732 as a military buffer between South Carolina and Spanish Florida, Georgia was settled by Englishmen who had avoided debtors' prison by signing up for the colony's militia. Georgia's promoters wanted to develop a silk industry, for which they recruited skilled workers from Italy and unskilled laborers from Germany, Scotland, and Ireland. The original plan did not call for women or children, because they could play no role in the colony's defense. The defensive purpose of the colony also precluded slavery, which was banned in 1735. Unlike most other white southerners, a small group of Georgia residents actually objected to slavery on moral grounds; in 1738 they petitioned the king to ignore requests by other Georgians to admit slaves. These petitioners found "perpetual slavery" to be "shocking to human Nature," and worried that someday whites would pay a heavy price for enslaving men and women who held freedom as "dear" as they did.

But rice culture spread to Georgia, and in 1749 the colony rescinded its ban on slavery; a plantation economy soon developed. The profit motive undoubtedly helped to break down whatever military, economic, or moral objections to slavery the colony's original proprietors had had. Equally important was the hostility of slaveowners in neighboring colonies, who viewed a ban on slavery in Georgia as a possible enticement to their own slaves—who, none doubted, yearned to be free.

Rice culture, however, still lacked the closely supervised and highly regimented labor of the tobacco economy. Rice required none of the daily attention of tobacco, so slaves not engaged in the backbreaking and unhealthy work of planting and harvesting rice in water-

"View of Mulberry House and Grounds." A painting of a rice plantation near Charleston in the 1770s. The master's house is framed by the slave quarters. The size of the slave cabins is probably inaccurate, suggesting a height and spaciousness that the one-room cabins did not possess.

filled trenches spent the day repairing dams, building canals, and mending fences. Many had done similar work in Africa, and their experience helped both to shape the system of labor and to enhance their bargaining position with English masters who did not know how to grow rice.

Even so, conditions were brutal. Masters had unrestricted authority over their slaves and did not hesitate to use it. Hard work, poor diet, and ill usage contributed to high mortality. Everywhere brute force maintained discipline. In South Carolina, recaptured runaway slaves received no mercy—the law called for the amputation of the testicles of a male runaway and the ears of a female.

While rice plantations spread in the low country, yet another slave system developed in bustling Charleston, the largest port in the South. Beginning in the 1720s, the most successful rice planters left overseers in charge of their plantations and moved to Charleston, where the climate was healthier and the society more stimulating. There they formed an aristocracy at least as wealthy and elegant as that of Virginia. Many slaves in Charleston were hired out to work for master craftsmen as shipbuilders, ropemakers, stevedores, leatherworkers, and carpenters. Unlike plantation slaves, many urban slaves were skilled, literate, and of mixed English and African origin. By 1776, half of Charleston's twelve thousand inhabitants were blacks. They had more cultural and physical interaction with their masters than did the plantation slaves in either the low country or the Chesapeake. This integration had many consequences, not the least of which was the occasional opportunity either to buy or be granted freedom.

AFRICAN-AMERICAN CULTURE

By 1765, the American slave system that would last another century was firmly in place. That system defined blacks as white men's property, yet within its confines, blacks created fragile institutions of their own through which they asserted their dignity and their humanity. They established family, kinship, and community networks that extended beyond the limits of any one plantation and survived the slave sales that separated husband from wife and parent from child. African-Americans also practiced their own religion, composed songs, created dances, devised ceremonies, and established ways of living and thinking that distinguished them from both their masters and their African ancestors. This rich African-American culture evolved over two centuries as some 500,000 transported Africans and their descendants learned to resist the degradation and oppression of their enslavement and to assert some control over their day-to-day existence. This culture was neither English nor African, neither imposed by the master class nor imported as a mere relic of an irretrievably lost past. It was instead a blend, adapted to the peculiar needs of a people in bondage. The slaves retained what they could of their African heritage and reconciled it with what they were forced to do and what they had learned to do to survive in America.

Masters, of course, defined the context of daily life and limited the ways in which the slaves could act. Masters determined working conditions, enforced dehumanizing slave codes, and ultimately held the power of life and death. Yet, if the system was to work, they had to be able to depend on their slaves' ability to act in ways that only human beings can. Slaves had to be able to take care of each other and to raise children. They had to learn English, to perform a variety of tasks, and, in some cases, to manage other slaves. Slaves did all of these things, and they taught their children to do likewise.

No distinctive new culture emerged, however, among the first two generations of blacks in the Chesapeake. Less than 1,500 slaves were brought to Virginia and Maryland before 1680, and contact among them was limited by their dispersal among the much larger English population. Nearly all slaves performed dull, repetitive work, closely supervised by their masters; they had little time for themselves. There were few women or children among them, and families were almost nonexistent. Most important, there were as yet no rigid barriers dividing white and black laborers. Most of these African-Caribbean blacks already spoke English, and some could expect to gain their freedom. Under these circumstances they adopted the culture of their English fellow servants fairly easily. Black and white servants conspired, drank, ran away, and "frolicked" together. According to Reverend James Blair of Virginia, some blacks even converted to Christianity in the misguided belief "that some time or other Christianity will help them to their freedom."

But a distinctly African-American culture did evolve when the number of Africans increased and racial laws restricted their contact with whites—first in the Chesapeake and then in the lower South. The number of blacks in the South increased dramatically after 1680; most came directly from West Africa rather than the Caribbean.

When the captive Africans were taken aboard the ships for the trip to America, the men were separated from the women and children, and all were chained in the holds in groups of three or four. They had no idea where they were going, nor what awaited them. One slaver reported that his captives from Guinea believed they were being "carried like sheep to the slaughter, and that Europeans [were] fond of their flesh." When many of his slaves tried to commit suicide by not eating, another trader knocked out their teeth and force-fed them. Ships were so crowded that an individual could hardly turn around; the "loathsome smells" of sweat and excrement often "brought on a

sickness among the slaves." As the voyage progressed, "the shrieks of the women and groans of the dying reduced the whole to a scene of horror almost inconceivable."

No single common language, religion, trade, or set of customs united these unwilling passengers. There were princesses, ironworkers, and farmers robbed of their realms, tools, and land. In America, they could not speak their many native languages, ply their trades, play their assigned kinship roles, practice their religions—some of the many things that distinguished them as coming from diverse African villages and regions. But there were similarities among them, and out of the most tenuous similarities—in social practices, religious beliefs, and new work experiences—they began to form bonds. They consoled each other, cooperated to survive, and began to give order, as best they could, to social interaction in the New World. Cooperative action of any sort would have been impossible unless slaves who spoke many different languages learned to communicate with each other. They learned English, of course, but in South Carolina they combined it with several African tongues to form Gullah, which served as the common and unifying language.

Slaves did in fact have some opportunity to practice old customs, because nearly half of them lived together in groups of ten or more. We know very little about what they actually retained from their African past, but English observers noted their non-Christian beliefs, as well as their African dances, songs, and "revels." Masters, intent on destroying any remnant of their chattels' free identities, discouraged African customs and languages generally; the work habits, family arrangements, and religious beliefs that

". . . A WORLD OF BAD SPIRITS"

In Chapter 1, Olaudah Equiano described his West African homeland. Here he recounts the horrors of the Atlantic crossing in his 1791 autobiography. He had been enslaved in Africa and transported to North America as a boy of ten in 1765.

THE FIRST OBJECT which saluted my eyes when I arrived on the coast was the sea, and a slave ship which was then riding at anchor and waiting for its cargo. These filled me with astonishment, which was soon converted into terror when I was carried on board. I was immediately handled and tossed up to see if I were sound by some of the crew, and I was now persuaded that I had gotten into a world of bad spirits and that they were going to kill me. Indeed such were the horrors of my views and fears at that moment that, if ten thousand worlds had been my own, I would have freely parted with them all to have exchanged my condition with that of the meanest slave in my own country. . . .

I was soon put down under the decks, and there I received such a salutation in my nostrils as I had never experienced in my life: so that with the loathsomeness of the stench and crying together, I became so sick and low that I was not able to eat. . . . I now wished for the last friend, death, to relieve me; but soon, to my grief, two of the white men offered me eatables, and on my refusing to eat, one of them held me fast by the hands . . . and tied my feet while the other flogged me severely. I had never experienced anything of this kind before, and although, not being used to the water, I naturally feared that element the first time I saw it, yet nevertheless could I have got over the nettings I would have jumped over the side. . . .

One day, when we had a smooth sea and moderate wind, two of my wearied countrymen, . . . preferring death to such a life of misery, somehow made through the nettings and jumped into the sea: immediately another quite dejected fellow, who on account of his illness, was suffered to be out of irons, also followed their example; and I believe many more would very soon have done the same if they had not been prevented by the ship's crew who were instantly alarmed. . . . Two of the wretches were drowned, but they got the other, and afterwards flogged him unmercifully for thus attempting to prefer death to slavery.

"The Old Plantation." This unusual late-eighteenth-century painting by an unknown artist indicates the blending of cultural influences in the slaves' quarters. African and American culture merge in the slaves' dress, dance, and musical instruments (a drum and banjo). The ceremony is probably a wedding where, by African custom, the bride and groom jump over a stick.

were most similar to English practices were the ones most likely to survive.

The strong emphasis African societies placed on kinship, and especially on ties between brothers and sisters, helped these uprooted people to survive their enslavement. Although kinship systems varied among African tribes and nations, and slavery in any case prevented any African system from being recreated, such bonds were universal. As such, they provided an important context in which an African-American culture could unfold. Observers noted, for example, that unrelated captives on slave ships began to refer to each other as brothers and sisters, and that sexual intercourse between such "siblings" was forbidden. Those slaves who survived taught their children to call former shipmates aunts and uncles. In America, these sibling ties entailed serious responsibilities, imposed and accepted. Over several generations, these kinship practices helped slaves from diverse backgrounds to order their lives and maintain connections that extended beyond a single slave quarter, plantation, or county.

Even after 1680, it was not easy to develop these bonds. The constant arrival of new immigrants strained the resources of whatever collective institutions already existed. Slaves were frequently sent from one plantation to another, fracturing their communities. High death rates and an unbalanced sex ratio led to competition over women, further destabilizing slave communities. After 1720 in the Chesapeake and 1760 in the low country, however, these remaining impediments largely disappeared: the number of men and women equalized, and fewer and fewer blacks were imported from Africa as American slaves formed families. As a result, young American blacks were raised by African-American parents in an emerging African-American culture, not "seasoned" by white masters as their predecessors had been. In Maryland and Virginia the majority of slaves were native-born by the 1740s; this was true throughout the South by the end of the century.

As a sense of community developed among the growing numbers of slaves, they worked together to resist slavery and reduce the harshness of labor. They conspired to break tools, feign illness, and avoid learning new tasks. Some had brought a knowledge of poisons from Africa, and now used it against their masters.

On a few occasions, slaves also rose up against their masters in desperate bids for freedom. In the Stono Rebellion of 1739, for example, about twenty slaves recently arrived in South Carolina from Angola, joined by other slaves from surrounding plantations, tried to fight their way to Spanish Florida. After stealing arms and killing several planter families, they got as far as the Stono River, where a white militia overtook them.

Other runaways, in a striking adaptation of their African heritage, formed fugitive backwoods communities. Near present-day Lexington, Virginia, one group in 1728 created a village, building homes like those they had known in Africa, establishing a tribal government under a chief who had been a prince in Africa,

"BARNS BEING BURNT . . ."

Slaves' resistance took many forms. In South Carolina, slaves involved in rice production often burned down the barns where the harvested rice was stored. This October 14, 1732, letter, printed in the South Carolina Gazette, *reveals how common the slave "custom" of barn-burning had become in one part of the colony.*

I HAVE TAKEN Notice for Several Years past, that there has not one Winter elapsed, without one or more Barns being burnt, and two Winters since, there was no less than five. Whether it is owing to Accident, Carelessness, or Severity, I will not pretend to determine; but am afraid, chiefly to the [latter two causes]. I desire therefore, as a Friend to the Planters, that you'll insert the following Account from Pon Pon, which, I hope, will forewarn the Planters of their Danger, and make them for the future, more careful and human:

About 3 Weeks since, Mr. James Gray worked his Negroes late in his Barn at Night, and the next Morning before Day, hurried them out again, and when they came to it, found it burnt down to the Ground, and all that was in it.

". . . A BLOODY TRAGEDY"

Full-scale rebellion was rare, but the very possibility of such insurrection terrified southern whites, as this letter, printed in the October 22, 1730, issue of the Boston Weekly News-Letter, *reveals. A slave uprising planned to begin in Charleston, South Carolina, on August 15, 1730, was uncovered in advance. This report hints at how slaves planned to spread their actions out of the city into the countryside.*

I SHALL GIVE an Account of a bloody Tragedy which was to have been executed here last Saturday night (the 15th Inst.) by the Negroes, who had conspired to Rise and destroy us, and had almost brought it to pass: but it pleased God to appear for us, and confound their Councils. For some of them proposed that the Negroes of every Plantation should destroy their own Masters; but others were for Rising in a Body, and giving the blow at once on surprise; and thus they differed. They soon made a great Body at the back of the Town, and had a great Dance, and expected the Country Negroes to come & join them; and had not an overruling Providence discovered their Intrigues, we had been all in Blood. . . . The Chief of them, with the others, is apprehended and in Irons, in order to a Tryal, and we are in Hopes to find out the whole Affair.

"An Overseer Doing His Duty." A relaxed overseer watches two slave women at work in a Virginia scene sketched by Benjamin Henry Latrobe in 1798. Latrobe (who would become one of the most influential architects in nineteenth-century America) had been in the United States only two years, but during that brief time he grew to detest slavery (suggested in the sarcastic title of the sketch).

and using African farming techniques (and stolen implements) to grow crops. It was a year before whites destroyed the village, killed the chief, and returned the residents to their masters.

By 1760, African-Americans accounted for more than one-third of the South's total population; in South Carolina they were the majority, and in the Chesapeake they constituted about 40 percent of the population. The statistics we have are imprecise, but probably half of all blacks lived on large plantations in groups of twenty or more. Perhaps as many as one-third, though, lived in groups of five or less, had close contact with whites, and worked for masters who had neither large brick mansions nor genteel manners.

Most African-Americans probably lived in dwellings shared only with their immediate families. Within the family cabin blacks enjoyed a space that was mostly theirs, where to some extent they could shape their own lives. Here they determined the range of their kinship group, provided for "outsiders"—unrelated slaves acquired by the master—and even sheltered runaways from other plantations. Within this private sphere, they took last names different from their masters', and bestowed the names of grandparents and great-grandparents—Cuffee, Quash—upon their children, linking them to an African past and to the memory of freedom.

Slaveowners, by reducing men and women to property, tried to deny the humanity of their slaves. African-Americans, by creating their own institutions and social practices, reasserted the humanity that their masters tried to circumscribe. By exercising daily resistance, by building bonds of family and kinship, and by preserving their African culture, slaves fashioned a social identity that enabled them to maintain their dignity despite their captivity and their oppression.

THE SOUTH ON THE EVE OF REVOLUTION

By the middle of the eighteenth century, the population of the southern colonies numbered just over 300,000 whites and about 200,000 black slaves. Nearly two-thirds of all southerners lived in Virginia and Maryland and a third in the two Carolinas; only about 5,000 people had settled in Georgia.

In Virginia, a significant number of settlers had moved inland along the many navigable rivers; by 1750, Virginia farmers were cultivating fields two hundred miles from the Atlantic. Elsewhere, except for a few isolated outposts, the colonists stayed within a hundred miles of the coast, where Indians no longer lived and where farmers, planters, and merchants had easier access to British markets, credit, and manufactured goods. Such were the meager inroads that five generations had made into the vast continent of North America.

In the more densely settled coastal areas, life was no longer a fierce struggle for survival. Slavery and the plantation economy were securely in place. Chesapeake farmers and planters exchanged their tobacco, cattle, and grain for English and European manufactures, African slaves, and Caribbean rum. From the Carolinas and Georgia, the exports were rice, indigo, and naval stores such as pitch, tar, and tim-

Charleston entertainment, 1760. Having served supper and then after-dinner drinks, a young slave dozes while members of Charleston's merchant-planter elite carouse around the dining-room table. The drawing is set in the home of Peter Manigault (seated at the left center), scion of one of the wealthiest families in colonial Carolina.

ber. Each of the five southern colonies had a colonial assembly and system of courts that governed in accordance with English political and legal precedents. The king's representatives in each colony included a royal governor, customs collectors, and a host of other officials charged with overseeing colonial trade.

Southern customs and lifestyles no longer horrified English visitors as they had in earlier decades. Though few of the increasing numbers born in the South would ever see England, many shared an English cultural identity, and to the extent that they could, they duplicated the social norms of their English peers. Men no longer outnumbered women in the colonies, and the family became the center of social life. Most southern white women contributed to the family income by spinning, weaving, gardening, and selling dairy products, as did their counterparts in England. For all, the Anglican Church was the only official church, and individual communities throughout the South levied taxes to pay the salaries of a clergy often educated and ordained in England. As in England, the common folk often deferred to the wealthy in matters of state, religion, and law.

Though life at midcentury was less precarious for all free southerners, dramatic distinctions existed between rich and poor. Tobacco and rice, speculation in western land, slave-trading, and shipping had made a few southerners very wealthy. The richest 10 percent owned half of all the South's wealth—including one-seventh of its people. Along with the Crown's official representatives, the wealthy controlled the government, the courts, and the church. This aristocracy

"Nondescripts . . . near Oaks, Virginia." "A family of poor White children," Latrobe noted in his sketchbook, "observed from the Stage carrying peaches to a neighboring Barbecue for Sale." The woman and children in this 1796 sketch wear large, stiff bonnets common to that part of Virginia.

mimicked the style of the English gentry, building spacious mansions, importing elaborate furnishings, and maintaining large numbers of servants. Gentlemen planters, renowned for their drinking, gambling, and horse-racing, set the cultural standards of the day. The emergence of a self-confident and self-conscious slaveowning aristocracy by midcentury was one of the most important developments of the era.

Most white southerners lived in more humble surroundings, without servants, slaves, or silverware. Land was easier to acquire in the South than in England and few European visitors failed to note the abundance of food and the prevalence of landownership. In Virginia, for example, about 70 percent of the white families farmed their own land in 1750, consuming roughly 60 percent of what they produced and bartering the surplus for tools and other goods they could not make. But those at the lower end of the scale slipped easily into poverty, and at least another 20 percent of the white population owned little more than the clothes they wore. Many landless men worked as tenants on the large estates or as wage laborers in agriculture, shipping, or the crafts. These men, along with another 10 to 30 percent of the population who could not meet the property qualification, were denied the vote, as were all blacks and women.

By 1770 a large portion of the South's white population lived in the least settled areas, away from the coast. This back country attracted both the children of poor to middling native-born southerners and the most recent immigrants from Ireland, Scotland, and Germany. Frontier dwellers were generally poorer than their coastal counterparts, and society itself was less structured, authority less established.

"PITY YOUR DISTRESSED DAUGHTER"

Well into the eighteenth century, many women committed themselves to indentured servitude in exchange for passage to the North American colonies. In this 1756 letter to her parents in England, Elizabeth Sprigs, a female servant in Maryland, describes her life and labor.

Honored Father

My being forever banished from your sight will I hope pardon the boldness I now take of troubling you with these [words]. . . . O Dear Father, believe that I am going to relate the words of truth and sincerity, and balance my former bad conduct [to] my sufferings here, and then I am sure you'll pity your distressed daughter. What we unfortunate English people suffer here is beyond the probability of you in England to conceive. Let it suffice that I, one of the unhappy number, am toiling almost day and night, and very often in the horses' drudgery, with only this comfort that "you bitch you do not half enough," and then tied up and whipped to that degree that you'd not serve an animal. Scarce anything but Indian corn and salt to eat and that even begrudged nay many Negroes are better used, almost naked no shoes nor stockings to wear, and the comfort after slaving during Master's pleasure, what rest we can get is to wrap ourselves up in a blanket and lay upon the ground. This is the deplorable condition your poor Betty endures, and now I beg if you have any bowels of compassion left show it by sending me some relief, clothing is the principal thing wanting, which if you should condescend to, may easily send them to me by any ships bound to Baltimore Town, Patapsco River, Maryland, and give me leave to conclude in duty to you and Uncles and Aunts, and respect to all friends, Honored Father

Your undutiful and
disobedient child
ELIZABETH SPRIGS

There were few great plantations here or large concentrations of slaves. In the western countries of North Carolina, for example, only about 12 percent of the white population owned slaves, and very few owned more than five.

Land on the frontier was cheaper than on the coast, and thousands obtained legal title through squatter's rights—that is, by building a cabin, clearing a number of acres, and planting a crop. By this device, colonial governments bolstered their claims to the interior against the counterclaims of other colonies, American Indians, and English speculators. Though few of these modest settlers achieved more than a decent subsistence, they established communities in which a rough frontier equality prevailed among a determined people.

Yet such stabilizing factors as widespread landownership, frontier opportunity, an expanding export economy, and suffrage for white male propertyholders did not eliminate all sources of social conflict in the South. The starkest and most brutal conflicts existed between slaves and masters, and between native Americans and colonists; but even within white society, sharp conflicts arose over access to land. Those who owned no land struggled to get it, while the landed fought to keep and increase their holdings. Such struggles often pitted large landowners and speculators against middling and poorer whites who worked the land to survive. Disputes also erupted over religion, politics, and other economic issues.

Even the top of southern society was not immune to friction. Wealthy planters and representatives of the king vied for power and the spoils of office. Planters complained about the "exorbitant" salaries they had to pay governors and other Crown officials, and thought them too eager to exploit the region and its public lands for quick profit and speculative gains, regardless of the long-term effect on the economy. Such infighting caused political instability and opened new opportunities for challenges from below.

People in the back country of the lower South seriously challenged the coastal elite in the 1760s. Grievances varied from one colony to another, but most concerned access to the land and representation in the colonial assemblies. Complaints readily escalated into violent confrontations, because frontier dwellers were already organized into armed—usually democratic—militias for defense against Indians.

Though coastal authorities in the Carolinas and Georgia accused frontier-dwellers of living "out of the bounds of the law," these people were not overly violent or reckless. They were simply less deferential, more irreverent, and more egalitarian than their low-country peers. Settlers on the frontier, as elsewhere, also drew a distinction between legitimate and illegitimate authority, and claimed the right of all free-born Englishmen to oppose the latter. People expected the wealthy to rule, but also to protect the larger interests of the community. When they didn't, ordinary men and women claimed the right to take collective action on behalf of the community.

In the 1760s, South Carolina's back-country farmers and slaveowning planters took up arms after the legislature failed to respond to their grievances. This general problem had taken a concrete form when a crime wave swept the back country and local officials failed to pursue bandits who threatened life and property. Appeals to the coastal elite fell on deaf ears. So between 1767 and 1769, groups of vigilantes calling themselves Regulators took control. Though the leaders came from the small minority of ambitious, commercially oriented slaveowners, thousands of small farmers supported them. The Regulators burned the homes of suspected thieves and punished others by whipping them or banishing them from the country. The groups disbanded in 1769 when the assembly passed the Circuit Court Act, giving settlers the courts, jails, and sheriffs they wanted. Other concessions included additional representatives and the creation of two new parishes, complete with legal and political institutions.

In North Carolina, a more dramatic and protracted struggle occurred between 1765 and 1771, when another band of Regulators resorted to force after their legal pleas had been rejected. A group of lawyers and land speculators had recently moved to the frontier and had begun taking over local offices and accumulating large tracts of land, much as the new elite of Virginia had done a century earlier. Until their arrival, it had been possible for middling and poor whites to acquire land in the back country and hold local political office. When the new

"HAVE NOT YOUR PURSES BEEN PILLAGED . . . ?"

Regulators of the North Carolina back country circulated open letters to their fellow citizens, setting forth their grievances against the ruling planters and the local men who were profiting at their expense. The following tract, written by an anonymous Regulator in September 1769, is addressed "To the INHABITANTS *of the Province of North-Carolina." The tract appeals to farmers to vote for representatives of their own kind.*

Dear Brethren,

Nothing is more common for Persons who look upon themselves to be injured than to resent and complain. These are sounded aloud, and plain in Proportion to the Apprehension of it. . . .

The late Commotions and crying Dissatisfactions among the common People of this Province, is not unknown nor unfelt by any thinking Person. No Person among you could be at a Loss to find out the true Cause. I dare venture to assert you all advised [as] to the Application of the Public Money; these you saw misapplied to the enriching of Individuals, or at least embezzled in some way without defraying the public Expenses. Have not your Purses been pillaged by the exorbitant and unlawful Fees taken by Officers, Clerks, &c? . . .

The Exorbitant, not to say unlawful Fees, required and assumed by Officers; the unnecessary, not to say destructive Abridgement of a Court's Jurisdiction; the enormous Encrease of the provincial Tax unnecessary; these are Evils of which no Person can be insensible, and which I doubt not has been lamented by each of you. . . .

I need not inform you that a Majority of our Assembly is composed of Lawyers, Clerks, and others in Connection with them, while by our own Voice we have excluded the Planter. . . . We have not the least Reason to expect the Good of the Farmer, and consequently of the Community, will be consulted by those who hang on Favour, or depend on the Intricacies of the Laws. . . .

But you will say, What is the Remedy against this malignant Disease?

I will venture to prescribe a sovereign one if duly applied; that is, as you have now a fit Opportunity, choose for your Representatives or Burgesses such Men as have given you the strongest Reason to believe they are truly honest: Such as are disinterested, publick spirited, who will not allow their private Advantage once to stand in Competition with the public Good. . . .

migrants—with their close ties to slavery, the plantation economy, and the coastal elite—threatened this opportunity, backwoods farmers, laborers, and tenants rose in rebellion. The Regulators were ultimately defeated in a violent confrontation in May 1771 known as the Battle of the Alamance.

Armed conflict in the Carolinas posed a serious challenge to the ruling elite, but it remained isolated and contained. A broader challenge emerged in the 1740s, when poor and politically disenfranchised whites throughout the South joined an evangelical religious movement known as the Great Awakening. Before 1720, the clergy and other well-educated colonists had begun to take the "enlightened" view, then current in Europe and England, that God was rational and kind. The evangelicals rejected the increasingly refined, polite, and philosophical religious discourse of the rationalists. Their God was wrathful and disgusted with the sinfulness of mankind. Individuals could be saved only by recognizing their own helplessness and depravity in the face of an almighty God. Salvation was available only to those who surrendered to God, through an emotional conversion, and asked for his forgiveness.

Evangelicalism smoldered among the less prosperous orders of southern society and erupted with a vengeance in the 1760s. The eruption was particularly intense in Virginia, where the colony's yeomen farmers enthusiastically participated in a powerful evangelical challenge to the wealthy planters' way of life and social values. Ordinary men and women in Virginia and across the South increasingly relied on vivid religious imagery and language in confrontations with their elite antagonists. Evangelicalism became a major source of egalitarian attitudes and engendered numerous demands that challenged

"Bunn, the Blacksmith, at a Campmeeting near Georgetown." In 1809, Latrobe attended a Virginia Methodist revival meeting, where he sketched the effective performance of a self-educated, artisan preacher. "A general groaning was going on," Latrobe wrote in his journal, "in several parts of the Camp, women were shrieking, and just under the stage there was an uncommon bustle, and cry, which I understood arose from some persons who were under conversion."

planter control. Poorly educated itinerant preachers, steeped in the oral traditions of the poorest people in the South, taught their growing flocks that ordinary men and women were more likely candidates for divine inspiration than the less humble aristocrats and educated clergymen who led them. And many of these evangelicals—considered by Virginia's well-to-do "continual fomenters of discord"—held the extremely radical belief that before God, all men and women, black and white, were equal. All could surrender to God and be saved. By democratizing salvation in this way, evangelical preachers helped to erode some of the deference in colonial society, even before the Revolution uprooted it in a deeper way.

Equally important, the evangelical movement helped to popularize the belief that government was merely the human mechanism through which God guaranteed equality among individuals from various classes. In this belief, illiterate mechanics and backwoods farmers found salvation for themselves and for society. This optimism, along with the evangelical focus on the evils of material wealth, gambling, and horse-racing, frontally challenged the planters. By looking down on the planters' worldly comforts and pleasures, evangelicals also questioned the legitimacy of their rule and the superiority of their culture. This simple challenge helped to sharpen already acute tensions between rich and poor, master and slave.

Racism provided the glue that kept white southern society from flying apart. Through the Civil War and even beyond, wealthy southern landowners were able to convince many poor whites that the division between white and black meant more than that between rich and poor. Nonetheless, profound tensions divided southern society and undermined established authority on the eve of the American Revolution. Dispossessed Indians fought with the now-dominant Europeans and their offspring, as did enslaved Africans. Settlers of European descent often fought bitterly among themselves. The well-to-do might snarl at each other as they jockeyed for power and position in the colonial assemblies, then make peace to battle middling and poor folk over land rights. Conflict over the land erupted into violence because there was so little room for compromise. What tenants and landless laborers gained, speculators and landlords lost. The stakes were high, and each side marshaled its forces as the political compromise between rich and poor whites in the aftermath of Bacon's Rebellion ceased to satisfy the men and women who had extended southern settlement to the west. Virginia, founded a century and a half earlier by a company of adventurers in search of profits, had become a prosperous, if troubled, society based on the commercial agriculture of the slave plantation. It stood in stark contrast to its colonial neighbors to the north.

Colonial trades. Illustrations from the American edition of *The Book of Trades,* a British survey of crafts that were practiced in the colonies.

A Bricklayer? WR fc.

A Carpenter. WR fc.

A Cooper WR fc.

Shipwright WR fc.

Spinner. WR fc.

Straw Hat Maker. WR fc.

3 FREE LABOR AND THE GROWTH OF THE NORTHERN COLONIES

Hat-maker. W.R. sc.

Type Founder. W.R. sc.

IN THE Massachusetts House of Representatives hangs a gilded image of a codfish. Its purpose is to acknowledge that Massachusetts drew its first prosperity from the sea. New York City's official seal displays the sails of a windmill, two barrels, a beaver, a white man, and an Indian. They, too, teach a history lesson: New York grew wealthy from furs that Indians trapped and from grain grown by farmers and ground by millers, all shipped in barrels made by coopers. Here, then, were the bases of northern colonial society. There would be no mines, as in Mexico and Peru, no tobacco or rice plantations, as in Virginia or South Carolina. Rather than plundering their way to great riches, most northern colonists achieved a "decent competency" or more by patient, steady toil on the land or at sea.

Originally, the land of New England and the middle Atlantic colonies had belonged to a variety of native American tribes, but by the late seventeenth century a combination of disease, war, and trading dependency had killed many Indians and subjugated others to the control of European settlers and their offspring. Yet others, whose power could not be ignored, still controlled their own lives, but they lived considerably west of the thriving European settlements.

By 1700, most Euro-Americans in the northern colonies lived in the countryside, the vast majority supporting themselves reasonably well on the bounty of small, independent farms. Farm families formed the very backbone of northern colonial society. A few men of privilege and ambition were assembling great estates on which hired tenants enriched them, but such developments seemed exceptional. Large cities were unknown: Boston, New York, and Philadelphia were only overgrown villages in 1700, with a few thousand inhabitants. But the citizens of these towns did live very differently from their rural counterparts. There were merchants who owned ships and there were seamen who sailed before the mast, master artisans and apprentices, professionals and day laborers. And in both the towns and the countryside, there were unfree people, some of them whites bound for a time as indentured servants, others blacks bound for life as slaves.

The northern colonies grew impressively over the course of the eighteenth century, but their expansion came at a price. The increasing power and wealth of large landlords threatened the survival of those who labored as tenants on gigantic estates. A dramatic increase in domestic and international trade resulted in the growth of Boston, New York, and Philadelphia, whose populations mushroomed to 20,000 and more by midcentury. But at the same time, class and political tensions intensified in these crucial port cities. As the northern economy expanded, colonists—both rural and urban, rich and poor, and even the vast majority of "a middling sort"—found themselves drawn ever tighter into England's colonial web.

The squires and tenants of New York and New Jersey, the independent farm families of Massachusetts and Pennsylvania, the urban craftsmen and the churchgoing women—these northern colonists argued endlessly about the kind of society they wanted even as they fought to protect their various social, economic, and political interests. Their disputes went on in churches, in town meetings and provincial assemblies, in newspapers and pamphlets, and in the streets and marketplaces. They argued and fought in the towns and across the countryside, both of which seethed with discontent after 1750. Some disputes were merely verbal, while others led to destruction, bloodshed, and death. The specific ways in which these diverse, hardworking, contentious Europeans built their outposts in the New

World would, over time, transform their relationships to one another—and eventually to Great Britain itself.

THE GREAT INVASION

For well over a century before the first settlers came to America, Europeans had turned up here and there, now and then—some as adventurers whose names we remember even now, such as John Cabot, Giovanni da Verrazano, and Henry Hudson, others as the common sailors who crewed such men's ships. Some were would-be colonizers like Sir Humphrey Gilbert, who led an expedition to Newfoundland in 1583. Most, however, were fishermen, drawn to the great fishing grounds that lie off northern New England and maritime Canada.

None of them stayed. At most, a few fishermen built racks for drying their catch and shacks for wintering over. Early in the seventeenth century, however, Europeans began to cross the Atlantic with a view to settling, and once they launched their invasion their numbers swelled and swelled. The French arrived first, establishing Québec in 1608. The Dutch founded Fort Orange (Albany) in 1614. Sweden's short-lived colonizing venture in the Delaware Valley began in 1638 at Fort Christina (Wilmington).

The English came relatively late, but once their migration began, wave after wave followed. The Pilgrims, religious dissenters who had first tried to settle in Holland, arrived at what became Plymouth, Massachusetts, in 1620. In 1630 the first Puritan fleet sailed into Massachusetts Bay, inaugurating an operation that brought twenty thousand people to Massachusetts within a decade. They began by establishing Boston and a ring of towns around it. Pushing down the coast, they eventually founded Rhode Island and the port towns of the Connecticut shore. Some settlers entered the rich, open valley of the Connecticut River; by the end of the 1630s they had established the towns of Springfield, Hartford, and Windsor. Northeast of Boston lay ramshackle fishing camps that became the basis of such settlements as Gloucester, Marblehead, Newburyport, and Salem.

But the Puritan exodus was over by 1640, for England itself was by then verging on civil war and revolution. The Puritans had been driven out by their deep dislike of what England was becoming under the first two Stuart kings, James I and Charles I. Much of their complaint was the intense persecution by Charles and his Archbishop of Canterbury, William Laud, that plagued their meetings and ministers. But many Puritans also loathed the kind of society taking shape in England, especially its rising disorder and increasing extremes of wealth and poverty. Puritanism attracted hardworking people, bent on improving themselves in the world. It also drew many people whose ideal society revolved around cooperation and community, rather than

Mr. Richard Mather.

A 1670 portrait of the Puritan leader, the first woodcut printed in the colonies.

individualism and materialism. Such beliefs offered a sharp contrast between the early northern colonists and their southern counterparts.

When the crisis broke in England, most Puritans stopped thinking of emigration and turned instead to reshaping their own society, attempting to build a commonwealth in which they might live without a monarchy and a House of Lords. Their attempt failed in the long run, and both king and lords returned in 1660.

With the return of the monarchy under Charles II, the English began to look westward again, a matter now of high politics and imperial adventure. Great men in London, such as the king's brother James, Duke of York, made up their minds to build an American empire, and they looked first to the Dutch settlements. Twice they sent expeditions to conquer the New Netherlands, first in 1664 and again a decade later. King Charles eventually won the battle and gave the province to his brother, who promptly renamed it New York in honor of himself. The king gave him New Jersey as well. Neither Charles nor James, of course, ever saw the dominions that passed between their hands.

The duke, in turn, gave New Jersey to two of his close associates, Lord John Berkeley and Sir George Carteret, and in 1676 William Penn and three other Quaker gentlemen acquired Carteret's share. By the early 1680s Quakers had acquired control of a large mass of land, which they named Pennsylvania. Penn, who had extremely lofty connections, launched a grand scheme of settlement. The king owed him £16,000, and Penn agreed to forgive the debt in return for what is now Pennsylvania. The Penns thus became hereditary proprietors of their new province, and until the Revolution its governorship would descend in their line. In an era when titled aristocrats in England no longer enjoyed the right to rule that had been theirs in the Middle Ages, the Penns, who never took an actual peerage, had created an American feudal lordship on the grandest scale. William Penn advertised for colonists in 1681, and a year later his first party arrived on the Delaware River and founded Philadelphia.

But matters were not as simple as this familiar chronology of settlement might imply. Movement to the New World involved both intense excitement and deep uncertainty. It also involved confrontation with Indians, who had their own names for all these places and who saw no reason why distant kings and dukes—or any Europeans at all, for that matter—should be claiming ownership. Further, colonization involved intense international rivalry: between the Swedes and the Dutch, between the Dutch and the English, and eventually, for almost a century, between the English and the French. Even the English themselves were gripped by dispute and anxiety. It took most of the colonial period to work out the boundaries between the provinces. New York and New Hampshire, for example, quarreled over what is now Vermont until 1764. More was at stake than lines on a map; the issue affected the lives of individuals and entire communities.

The colonies attracted diverse people. From the British Isles came not just English but Highland Scots, Scotch-Irish, Welsh, and even a few Catholic Irish. Many left depressed textile regions in search of a new start. From mainland Europe came Huguenot (Protestant) French and many Protestant Germans. A few Sephardic Jews made their way to America from the Mediterranean. Most of these people were of the "industrious sort"—craftsmen, yeomen farmers, and small merchants—who came more or less willingly, though for indentured servants the immediate prospect was several years of labor for someone else. Pennsylvania and the northern Chesapeake drew large numbers of such servants, who were still coming as late as the Revolution, though by then their numbers were dwindling. The European migrants were joined by Africans who came in chains. New York, in particular, imported sizable numbers, and from 1730 to the end of the century, roughly 15 percent of New York City's population was of African origin.

Many came with the hope of becoming landholders, a status denied them in England; others came to secure independence as craftsmen. Some migrants came to satisfy their greed, some to escape from what others' greed was doing to Europe. The Massachusetts Bay Puritans wanted to build a "City upon a Hill" that would be a "Model of Christian Charity" for the world to behold. Others, like the original Pilgrims of the *Mayflower* and Pennsylvania's Amish people, simply wanted the world to leave them alone. Some people came to convert the Indians, while others came to exploit them. Some wanted to do both; others could not tell the difference.

Many of these settlers were pushed westward by the explosive transformation of life in early modern Europe that was fueled by the emergence of capitalism. Massachusetts was founded by the Massachusetts Bay Company, and from the arrival of the first fleet in 1630 until 1684, the company's charter remained the province's legal basis. The company was formed by ambitious men who pooled their surplus capital, but the company's charter conferred political power as well as economic rights. A clause in the charter allowed the company to hold business meetings wherever it chose, and in 1629 a group of men led by John Winthrop decided to take advantage of that technicality. They wanted to move both charter and company to the New World and establish a better way of life. Winthrop was a Cambridge-educated East Anglian gentleman. He had much in common with Oliver Cromwell, who would lead the Puritan revolution against King

Charles a decade later. Many New Englanders would return to England to aid Cromwell and his forces.

In Massachusetts, Winthrop's people abandoned all plans to make profits for the company. The Massachusetts governor and representatives of the general court became the province's political leaders. "Freemanship" (membership) in the company would no longer be open to investors; instead, it became the exclusive privilege of male members of an organized Puritan church.

Other provinces were founded in different ways, but Massachusetts best illustrates the complex response of the earliest English settlers to the world of capitalist endeavor. Its most basic institution was a direct product of that world, but the founders put it to a use of their own, divorced from the profit motive. Similar complexities and contradictions would characterize the colonial and revolutionary eras.

Feudalism (as well as capitalism) made its way across the Atlantic, and the Penns were not its only direct beneficiaries. The Calvert family, who held the hereditary title Baron Baltimore, were granted Maryland from Charles I on terms very similar to the ones enjoyed by the Penns, and there were shorter-lived proprietorships in New Jersey and in both Carolinas. In New York, both the Dutch and the English governments granted large tracts of land on what amounted to feudal terms, with hereditary manor lords who enjoyed the right to hold court and sit in judgment over their tenants. None of them ever exercised that right, but three of those manorial families had what amounted to private seats in colonial New York's legislature. Like the uncertain provincial boundaries, this hangover from the Middle Ages would provoke a great deal of social strife.

Most New Englanders, however, wanted nothing to do with feudalism. When two Puritan peers inquired in 1635 about migrating to Massachusetts, they were told that they would be welcome but that they would enjoy no special privileges. Neither came. But the Puritans brought other elements of English civilization: their faith, their sense of what a farming community ought to look like and how its people ought to act, and an intense devotion to family life. They brought great respect for learning, not just among the lucky few who went to Harvard College after its founding in 1636, but among the many of both sexes who learned to read.

The northern and southern colonies were European transplants, but from the beginning they developed in distinctive ways. One major difference was that migrants to the northern colonies never had to live within a social and economic system whose basis was outright exploitation. Moreover, as we have seen, the earliest migrants to the southern colonies on the Chesapeake found themselves living in frightful conditions and they died at an appalling rate. The northern colonies proved far healthier for Europeans. In Massachusetts the first generation enjoyed life expectancies far higher than any in Europe. People who might have died in middle age were now living to be elderly. Children survived the hazards of infancy at an unprecedented rate. As Indians died from white men's diseases, white men and women themselves began to multiply rapidly, their population doubling every twenty years.

Puritans or not, English settlers were heirs to the popular upheaval of the civil war. In England as in America, Puritans, Presbyterians, Quakers, and Baptists were adherents of revolutionary beliefs. And like many ardent revolutionaries, they found it almost impossible to agree among themselves: they could be as harsh to one another as to any common enemy. Nonetheless, they presented radical alternatives to the social visions of the Church of England and Roman Catholicism. New Englanders showed it by honoring the name of Cromwell almost as much as that of Winthrop. They proved the point again by offering refuge to the "regicides," the executioners of Charles I, when his son's ascension to the throne put their own lives in danger. Almost all the colonists proved it by living for a century and a half without lords and bishops, most of that time under a monarch who was so distant as to make little real difference, usually, in their lives.

The invaders' goal, then, was to build a new Europe in the American wilderness. They brought with them an ancient knowledge, not just capitalism and the feudal husk that still surrounded it, not just Christianity and English political culture, but ways of farming and building and weaving and spinning that seemed timeless. But from the very beginning they were creating a new world, not simply transplanting an old one. What they built was as fresh and unprecedented as it was old and hallowed. They knew what they owed to Europe, and indeed many of them still called England "home" at the time of the American Revolution. But they slowly began to realize that living on the Atlantic's western shore meant that their world was not just distant from the Europe they had left behind; it was becoming something fundamentally different as well.

CONQUEST AND RESISTANCE

For native Americans in the North as in the South, the problems of life were different from those faced by European settlers. Once the Europeans made contact, the Indians' world started to change in ways they found difficult even to understand, let alone to control. There had been some 500,000 Indians in eastern North America when the English came; now diseases they had never known thinned their ranks, in some areas killing as much as 90 percent of the population. Their enemies brought weapons and trade goods that rendered their own ancient ways suddenly obsolete. Traders offered them huge supplies of potent rum; they had never known alcohol, and many succumbed. They found themselves in great wars that were not of their making. Their whole material environment—animals, plants, and even climate—began to change.

It was a time of torment such as few peoples have ever known. As the Mohegans of Connecticut put it long after their defeat:

> Yea the Times have turn'd everything Upside down, or rather we have changed the good Times, Chiefly by the help of the White People. For in Times past our Fore-Fathers lived in Peace . . . and had everything in Great plenty . . . and now we plainly see that . . . poor Widows and Orphans Must be pushed one side and there they Must set a-Crying, Starving, and die.

Northern colonists, like those in the South, confronted the Indians with all the arrogance of a people bent on conquest. The English in particular decided that native Americans did not, according to English law, actually own their land; they merely occupied it. Indians, after all, built no houses or churches of brick and stone. They used no draft animals. Their men lazed about all day while their women scratched away in fields where corn, beans, and squash grew wildly. There were no fences and hedges to indicate where one person's property ended and another's began. When the Indian men did bestir themselves, it was to hunt, and to English eyes this was an occupation fit only for idle aristocrats and ne'er-do-well poachers.

With such a perspective, the invaders quickly convinced themselves that the Indians' only real task was to get out of their way. Puritans knew, well before they embarked for Massachusetts Bay, that an epidemic had already wiped out most of the Indians there. They decided that it was simply God's way of clearing the ground for His chosen people. In 1636 those same Puritans waged a war of outright extermination against the Pequot tribe of Connecticut. "We must burn them!" cried one captain. In the course of the "battle" that followed, some four hundred Pequots died by fire and the sword. The Pequots simply ceased to exist as a people.

In the aftermath of contact with European diseases, the natives of Nantucket Island, off Cape Cod, found their position indefensible. They were some twenty-five hundred strong in 1600; two centuries later only twenty-two survivors remained. Diseases carried by early traders caused their numbers to dwindle even before the first settlers arrived. And yet Indians made the newcomers welcome. Puritan traders advanced coveted goods to the Indians, who swiftly fell into debt to their guests. Merchants forced them to pay off their debts by going to sea as crewmen on whaleboats, but the Indians found that they

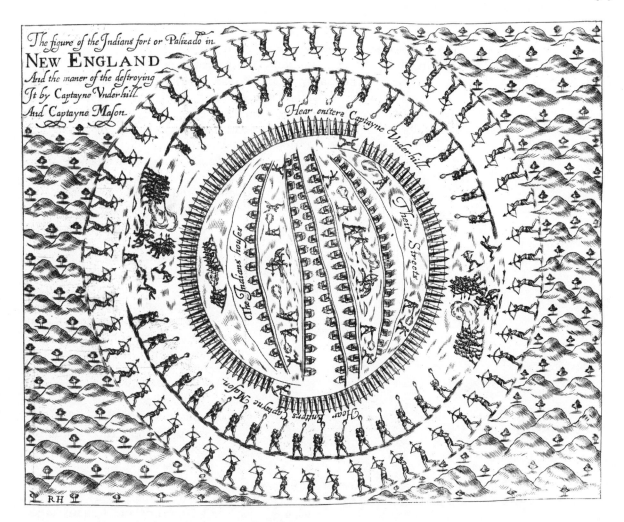

The figure of the Indians fort or Palizado in
NEW ENGLAND
And the maner of the destroying
It by Captayne Vnderhill
And Captayne Mason

Hear entera Captayne Vnderhill

Their Streets

The Indians howses

Hear Enters Captayne Mason

RH

"We Must Burn Them." An engraving from a contemporary account of the Pequot war shows the dawn raid on the Pequot fort at Mystic, Connecticut, on May 26, 1637. "Many were burnt in the fort, both men, women, and children. Others forced out, . . . twenty and thirty at a time, which our soldiers received and entertained with the point of the sword. Down fell men, women, and children; those that scaped us fell into the hands of the Indians that were in the rear of us."

could never earn enough to settle their accounts. They ended up trapped in a cycle of debt and forced labor from which there was no escape.

The Micmacs of Nova Scotia were trapped in a different way. Like the Nantucket Indians, they wanted the goods the European traders offered, and they found that traders would readily exchange them for furs. The Micmacs lived too far north for agriculture, so they depended on animals, fish, and birds for survival. Traditionally they had maintained a balance with their prey, treating them with a respect that was almost religious in nature. They hunted only what they actually needed. But Europe was hungry for furs.

When the Micmacs found that pelts brought them all the guns, cloth, ironware, and drink they wanted, they embarked on an orgy of animal destruction. Within a few years their beaver were gone and the fur frontier moved west, leaving the Micmacs to live in a world in which they could no longer support themselves.

The pressures of invasion, disease, drink, and warfare were enormous, but native Americans were not simply victims. Rather, they also were active agents in shaping the history of the early northern colonies. Some resisted European encroachment. In 1675 and 1676 the New England interior broke out in open warfare, remembered as King Philip's War after the English name of one of the major sachems involved, whose real name was Metacom. The Puritans provoked the war, but Metacom made it his own grand struggle, uniting all the surviving New England tribes. He won the Abenaki, the Pennacocks, and the Sokoki to his cause, and even some of the Nipmucks, who had converted to Christianity and largely accepted English ways. But he could not win the Narragansetts until a series of Puritan atrocities convinced them that war was their only possible recourse.

But Metacom was unable to win allies outside New England. When Governor Edmund Andros of New York brought his province's troops and even the Mohawk nation into the fray, Metacom's movement was doomed, and the price of defeat was heavy. Those who did not flee or die were captured and sold into slavery. As in 1636, the Puritan policy was to "kill and destroy them, according to the utmost power God shall give."

But where the smaller tribes of New England Indians failed, the Iroquois of western New York succeeded. They enjoyed a number of advantages. One was their location, for they straddled the Mohawk Valley and the Lake Ontario plain, which gave them control of both the fur-rich Adirondack Mountains and the only route to the deep interior. As long as they could hold that land, both the French at Montreal and the Dutch and the English at Albany had to court them.

"... THE INDIANS IN OLD TIMES ..."

The survival of Canada's Micmac tribe depended on the abundance of the animals they hunted. These animals—moose, beaver, and elk—provided the tribe with food and clothing. A French traveler, Nicholas Denys, described the Micmacs' hunting methods in a book first published in 1672.

AFTER THEY HAVE lived for some time in one place, which they have beaten [for animals] all around their camp, they go and camp fifteen or twenty leagues [about fifty miles] away. Then the women and girls must carry the wigwam, their dishes, their bags, their skins, their robes, and everything they can take, for the men and the boys carry nothing....

The hunting by the Indians in old times was easy for them. They killed animals only in proportion as they had need of them. When they were tired of eating one sort, they killed some of another. If they did not wish longer to eat meat, they caught some fish. They never made an accumulation of skins of Moose, Beaver, Otter, or others, but only so far as they need them for personal use.

... The hunting of the Beaver took place in summer with arrows, when they were taken in the woods, or else in lakes or ponds.... But the commonest and most certain way was to break their dam, and make them lose the water. Then the Beavers found themselves without water...; their houses showed everywhere. The Indians took them with blow of arrows and of spears; and, having a sufficiency, they left all the rest.

But their greatest resource was their numbers, estimated at ten thousand at the beginning of the seventeenth century. The Mohawks, Senecas, Onondagas, Oneidas, and Cayugas formed their great confederacy just before the first whites arrived, and thanks to it they prospered. By the time the Europeans first encountered them they had achieved internal peace and had consolidated a powerful position among their neighbors. They lived in palisaded villages surrounded by sprawling fields. By the time of their first contact with Europeans, the Iroquois had already grasped many of the lessons taught by the history of other tribes. They knew how the "praying Indians" of Massachusetts had been thoroughly crushed by the Puritan missionaries, who converted them to Christianity and changed their entire way of life. French Jesuits, who respected Indian culture, had more success among the Iroquois. But when a Yankee preacher named Samuel Kirkland approached the Senecas, an Indian named Onoogwandikha told his fellows: "Brethren attend! . . . If we Senecas . . . receive this white man, and attend to the Book which was made solely for white people, we shall become a *miserable abject people* . . . we shall soon lose the spirit of true men."

The Iroquois could be fierce fighters if the Europeans provoked their ire. But they could also be open and receptive. A male prisoner taken in war might be tortured terribly, and if he proved brave his captors might consume his body so as to take on his courage. But he might also be adopted into the tribe, within which he could rise to the highest rank. The very name Old White Chief bespoke one leader's origins. Female prisoners were not molested sexually, and one who accepted adoption sometimes became an honored matriarch in a society in which women wielded unusually great power. In 1716 the Iroquois Confederacy even adopted a whole tribe, the Tuscaroras, who spoke a related language and who had migrated north after Europeans drove them from their original home in North Carolina.

The Iroquois also became masters of diplomacy, as subtle as any European power. During the first century and a half of contact, they balanced first the Dutch against the French, then the French against the English, and the English against their colonists. While their strategy lasted, it enabled the Iroquois to stay above the great European struggle for empire in North America. Different tribes might lean in different directions, but the confederacy never split. Only when the American Revolution fundamentally altered the balance of power did Iroquois diplomacy finally fail.

Whatever their tribe, the northern Indians were the area's first—and its real—pioneers. They were the masters of the New World environment. They knew its geography, its climate, its plants, and its animals. Most of what the Europeans learned, the Indians taught

A

NARRATIVE

OF THE

CAPTIVITY, SUFFERINGS AND REMOVES

OF

Mrs. *Mary Rowlandson*,

Who was taken Prisoner by the INDIANS with several others,
and treated in the most barbarous and cruel Manner by those
vile Savages : With many other remarkable Events during her
TRAVELS.

Written by her own Hand, for her private Use, and now made
public at the earnest Desire of some Friends, and for the Benefit of the afflicted.

BOSTON

Printed and Sold at JOHN BOYLE's Printing-Office, next Door
to the *Three Doves* in Marlborough-Street. 1773.

Captivity. In 1676, during King Philip's War, Mary Rowlandson was captured by Indians raiding Lancaster, Massachusetts; after being held for three months, she was ransomed and freed. She later wrote *The Sovereignty and Goodness of God: A Narrative . . .*, which was published in 1682 and often reprinted (here in a 1773 edition). It was the first of many "captivity" narratives, which portrayed captivity as a test of the protagonists' Puritan faith.

them, and without that knowledge survival would have been much more difficult, and in many cases utterly impossible. The familiar story of Squanto teaching the Pilgrims how to plant corn and thus saving them from starvation is the best illustration. But, as in the South, the Europeans' arrival in New England ultimately made a cataclysmic difference to Indian life. Any Indian who let himself be drawn into the fur trade entered a web of commerce that stretched from the deepest forests to the capitals of Europe. As the case of the Micmacs showed, to enter that web was to change the conditions of life forever.

The Indians, of course, did not ask the Europeans to come, with their guns, their blankets, their drink, and their microbes. They did not ask for wars whose causes usually lay across the great Atlantic. They did not ask to fight those wars to the point of extermination, rather than according to either the "civilized" rules by which Europeans fought among themselves or the traditional ways of precontact

Indian life. In one large sense they were victims, driven further and further back in a retreat that would not end until they had lost the whole continent. Increasingly, they, not the Europeans and their descendants, were the ones who found themselves confronting a new world, for the Europeans knew exactly what they wanted and they set out to get it on their own terms. But in another large sense the woodland tribes held the whites off remarkably well. In the 150 years between early settlement and the Revolution, the boundary of white settlement moved inland by at most a few hundred miles. Holding it back for so long was a major achievement, not least because the delay allowed inland tribes like the Iroquois to prepare themselves for their own meetings with the invaders from beyond the seas. The contrast with the swiftness of the Indian collapse in parts of Central and South America was very great.

PATTERNS ON THE LAND

Settlements in the northern colonies in the seventeenth century were small and scattered. Roads were no more than tracks, and rain or the runoff from melting snow easily turned them into mud wallows. Only the smallest streams were bridged. Most of the land remained covered in forest. To the eyes of European settlers it seemed a "howling wilderness."

The first goal of the British invaders was to change the land. They wanted to clear the forest, fence in their fields, build houses and barns and churches and stores, and plant European crops. They wanted to raise sheep and cattle and fowl rather than hunt deer and wild turkeys. They wanted, in short, to make America look like Europe.

Even so small a matter as the introduction of pigs made a huge difference in economic life. Following European custom, colonists let the animals roam free in the woods, to be rounded up when they were needed. They built fences to keep them away from their own crops. But the pigs were aggressive, invading Indians' unfenced fields and driving their animals off, which deeply annoyed the Indians. Roger Williams, father both of the province of Rhode Island and of the American tradition of free conscience, was one of the few first-generation colonists who took the Indians seriously as the real owners of the land. He watched how hogs destroyed clam beds that the Narragansetts prized and he described the Indians' feelings: "Of all English Cattell, the Swine . . . are most hateful to all Natives, and they call them filthy cutthroats."

Indians and Europeans, as we have seen, had very different understandings of what it meant to possess the land. For Indians a title was collective and relative: all members of a tribe owned the land; there was no such thing as rent or purchase. For Europeans, ownership was individual and absolute: the holder of a legally recognized title had the right to forbid any use of the land by anyone else. The result of this difference in understanding was tragic. For Europeans, land that the Indians had not actually cleared was not really theirs. For Indians, "selling" the land to Europeans meant no more than allowing them some right to use it. A conflict developed not simply over ownership, but between two completely different ways of understanding human-kind's place in the landscape.

Differences developed among the European settlers as well. In early Massachusetts the province usually made grants to whole towns, not to separate individuals. Dedham, just west of Boston, was founded when a small group of heads of families petitioned the General Court in 1636 for a grant in common. They had spent months working out a town covenant that would establish the terms on which they would live. Their basic premises were that the town and the family were more important than the individual, and that social peace was more important than personal gain. Initially they even planned to call their town Contentment. The name of nearby Concord still recalls the value such people placed on quiet harmony.

The provincial government responded generously to such requests. The founders of Andover received a grant of some sixty square miles—more than 38,000 acres—for a population that numbered only forty families as late as 1662. Townsmen themselves decided their collective fate after that, sometimes through meetings of the whole town and sometimes through special committees. Initially they held the land in reserve. When the town of Sudbury made its first division, it handed out only 751 acres in all. The largest single grant was 76 acres; the smallest was 4.

At first these people divided the land into large open fields rather than separate enclosed farms, a longstanding pattern familiar in England. People lived together in central villages, offering one another mutual support and defense. Each townperson had individual strips in the different fields, but people worked together as a group, from the first plowing to the harvest. Which field to use and which crops to plant were to be decided by the whole community. Individuals received their strips on the basis of the whole town's judgment about how much they needed. A man's prestige (being the minister or having a good name from England), community need (for a miller or a blacksmith), and individual necessity (the number of children in a given family) all influenced the outcome of the decision.

These places have been called "closed, corporate, Christian utopian communities." Their people emphatically rejected feudalism. Until the American Revolution their greatest social fear was that landlordism and tenantry would rear their ugly heads among them.

But they also rejected free, competitive individualism, preferring instead to shape every aspect of their lives to achieve their goal of grace and harmony. They "gathered" their independent Congregational churches in roughly the same way they created their towns. Like the town, each separate Puritan church rested on a carefully worked-out covenant. Town membership and church membership were never identical, but Puritans expected their churches to be the "heart" of their brave attempt to create human perfection. Male heads of families created mechanisms of patriarchal control that governed their children's lives well into adulthood. Personal freedom was not at a premium, but this way of life did give social peace and stability to much of New England for a whole century. In an epoch marked by great disruption, this was "the Puritans' greatest achievement."

But not all New England towns developed this way. The ports and fishing camps that lay northeast of Boston settled down only slowly. Springfield, in the Connecticut Valley in western Massachusetts, lay amid rich bottomlands along the river and good meadows on the hills above. But most of that land fell into the hands of a single father and son, William and John Pynchon. By 1685 the younger Pynchon held eighteen hundred acres, almost five times as much as the next-largest landowner. Almost everyone in Springfield fell into John Pynchon's debt at one time or another. Pynchon never hesitated to call in a debt if it suited him, even if the debtor lost his land. Springfield, therefore, was no utopia, except perhaps for the Pynchons, whose successful pursuit of wealth and power dominated the town and its life. Springfield was ruled not by an association of patriarchs, but rather by a squire.

John Pynchon was not the only such figure. Until the Revolution, the whole Connecticut Valley in western Massachusetts was dominated by men whose standing earned them the title "River Gods." They dominated its delegation to the provincial assembly. They hobnobbed with the provincial governor. They became the colonels of the militia and the judges of the county court. But on the whole, the New England ethos ran against them. It proved impossible to maintain the religious intensity of the early settlements of Dedham or Andover, but the founders' vision of a society in which people concentrated on living together in peace and harmony persisted long after open fields had been forgotten. Even the wild fishing ports became places where men and women valued harmony and worked hard to achieve it. New Englanders never fully agreed that a whole community should become dependent on a single man, as Springfield did on John Pynchon.

Outside New England, would-be squires found that they had it much easier. By the middle of the eighteenth century, the most prom-

J U L Y.

Harvesting. A farm family at work in the fields. A woodcut from a Pennsylvania almanac published in the 1760s.

inent social feature on the map of New York were the great estates of the Hudson and Mohawk valleys. The result was a society sharply divided along class lines, for families like the Van Rensselaers, the Johnsons, the Livingstons, the Schuylers, the Philipses, and the Morrises lived in one way and their tenants in quite another. This was a world in which a poor, cringing tenant might seek permission to sell his leasehold "provided your Honnour consents." It was a world in which a landlord's daughter might marry "under a crimson canopy emblazoned with the family crest in gold" while, "as on rent day, the tenants gathered before the manor hall." It was a world in which Sir William Johnson, the eighteenth-century "Mohawk Baronet," actually owned the local courthouse, jail, and Anglican church.

At first, when their land was empty, landlords made tenancy attractive so as to secure scarce labor. Mills, roads, help with livestock, years of free rent for new arrivals: all of these were used to lure people to do the hard work necessary to transform a simple grant of land into a great and productive estate. But such benefits came at a high price. A tenant who wanted to sell out could expect the landlord to pay him for whatever "improvements" he had made, but sell he must and move on if he wanted to own his own farm. If he did sell, the landlord could demand one-third of the purchase price. Tenants had to give the landlord first option to buy their crops and to grind their grain at his mill. The landlord could insist that they plant certain kinds of fruit trees or build certain kinds of houses; he, not they, would be the long-term beneficiary. The result was often the creation of immense wealth. By the time of the Revolution the value of the freehold of Philipse Manor, near New York City, was estimated at £500,000. Frederick Philipse, lord of the manor, enjoyed far more of that wealth than the fifteen hundred people who made up his tenant force.

Some landlords, such as Philipse and Sir William Johnson, tried to create stable, paternalistic communities guided by good relations between landlords and tenants. When Philipse inherited his manor in 1760, he raised rents but promised that he would never do it again, and he stuck to his word. But others were out to gain all they could. His brother-in-law, Colonel Beverly Robinson, raised rents three times as Philipse held his steady. Not surprisingly, Philipse's tenants proved loyal to him; Robinson's did not. Moreover, tenants knew that some of the estates rested on very shaky legal bases. Livingston Manor, about forty miles south of Albany, occupied 160,000 acres of prime Hudson Valley farmland. But the original grant to the first manor lord had been intended to total no more than 6,000 acres. Ill-drawn surveys and outright fraud had contributed the rest, and the tenants knew it.

On the western bank of the Hudson River and throughout Pennsylvania a different pattern emerged. The Penn family never set up lesser lordships in their fief. Instead, they sold land directly to the settlers who applied for it. Some purchasers became landlords in their own right, but they never enjoyed the power of a New York manor lord or even a John Pynchon, which is one reason why eighteenth-century Pennsylvania acquired a reputation as "the best poor man's country." Neither closed to outsiders like most of New England nor riven by deep class differences like New York, it attracted far more migrants than either. As of 1770 New York's population stood at approximately 162,000, but that of Pennsylvania, founded decades later, had already surpassed 240,000.

Pennsylvania's people were a diverse lot. Its English Quakers were of the "middling sort," many of them skilled artisans who came to the colony to ply their trades and live in religious harmony. Germans of peasant origins, often members of religious sects, came to found utopian communities on Pennsylvania's rich farmland. Many Germans and Scotch-Irish, who arrived in large numbers by the middle of the eighteenth century, came as indentured servants. Some ser-

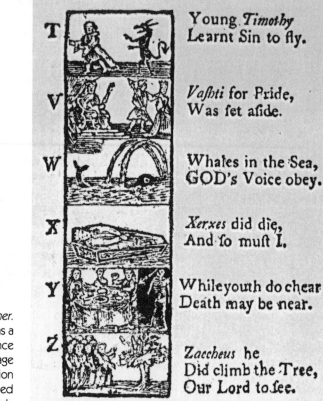

T   Young *Timothy*
Learnt Sin to fly.

V   *Vashti* for Pride,
Was set aside.

W   Whales in the Sea,
GOD's Voice obey.

X   *Xerxes* did die,
And so must I.

Y   While youth do chear
Death may be near.

Z   *Zaccheus* he
Did climb the Tree,
Our Lord to see.

New England Primer.
The alphabet as a
lesson in obedience
and restraint: a page
from a 1767 edition
of the widely used
schoolbook.

vants from the British Isles were convicts in search of a new start.
Both the Quakers and the German sectarians were pacifists; the
Scotch-Irish, on the other hand, were deeply accustomed to conflict.
They had known it in Ireland, both with the English overlords who
brought them there from Scotland in the first place, and with the
Gaelic Irish, who did not want them. As they migrated to the colonial
frontier, trouble always seemed to follow. But virtually all Pennsylvanians held in common a reputation for sturdy independence. When
a gentleman-pamphleteer named John Dickinson wanted to drama-
tize that trait during one of the early debates on the Revolution,
he could think of no better way than to style himself "a farmer in
Pennsylvania."

Whether they were New England villagers, New York tenants, or
Pennsylvania yeomen, eighteenth-century farmers had a complex relationship to the world of commerce and trade. Some farmers were
largely self-sufficient, either growing or making virtually everything

they needed. As one writer put it: "What should we American farmers be without the distinct possession of that soil? It feeds us, it clothes us, from it we draw even a great exuberancy, our best meat, our richest drink; the very honey of our bees comes from this privileged spot."

But most country people grew surpluses, and they needed to market them at the best price they could find. By the third quarter of the eighteenth century, wheat from New York, Pennsylvania, and the northern Chesapeake fed people all around the Atlantic basin. Even more than the Indians who hunted furs, the farmers who grew the wheat were enmeshed in an almost global market governed by supply and demand, profit and loss. Nonetheless, these farmers also grew mixed food crops to give their families as much autonomy as possible. They built local networks of barter and mutual exchange, in which a tradesman might accept "wheat, rye, Indian corn, as well as cash, or anything that is good to eat," in return for his services.

These same people bought and sold land constantly. But for the most part they did it to build holdings large enough to provide for their children, not because of insatiable greed. For every John Pynchon or Robert Livingston who plunged into a single-minded pursuit of wealth, there were many people who held a different, more modest idea of the good life. These ordinary folk wanted to stand together in communities and to stand individually on land of their own, not to run as fast as they could in an endless race for wealth.

CITIES BY THE SEA

From the very beginning, the people of Boston, New York, and Philadelphia lived differently. Each town quickly established itself as a place where trade and manufacturing, rather than farming, formed the essential basis of life. Lesser centers, such as Newport, Albany, and Baltimore, gradually developed in the same direction.

In the seventeenth century, these towns were nothing more than overgrown villages. Until well after independence, Boston occupied no more than the peninsula that jutted into Massachusetts Bay, linked to the mainland by a narrow spit called Boston Neck. The town grew steadily for a century, but around 1750 it began to stagnate, and its population leveled off at about 15,000. Legally it was not a city at all, for it governed itself by the same open town meetings that were used in the tiniest backwoods villages. Ordinary Bostonians valued those open meetings highly. As early as 1708 a proposal was made to abandon them and create a mayor and a board of aldermen, but it was resoundingly defeated, not least because people objected to the requirement of £1,000 to qualify for the new offices. As one pamphleteer put it, "The rich will exert that right of Dominion, which they

Shipbuilding. A late-eighteenth-century engraving depicts in unusual detail work in a Philadelphia shipyard.

think they have exclusive of all others . . . and then the Great Men will no more have the Dissatisfaction of seeing their Poorer Neighbours stand up for equal Privileges with them."

New York and Philadelphia were cities in the legal sense. In the former, the mayor was picked by the governor but the aldermen were chosen by election. In the latter the corporation was, as in many an English borough, "closed," which allowed its officials to pick their own successors. New York and Philadelphia outpaced Boston, but not by much. As late as 1770, New York filled only the southernmost part of Manhattan Island, where the financial district now stands, and it boasted a mere 21,000 inhabitants. Philadelphia was North America's fastest-growing city, reaching a total of 25,000 by the same year. But its people occupied little more than the modern downtown area. Only about 7 percent of all colonists lived in places with populations over 2,500 in 1770. All of these, even the largest, were "walking towns" easily crossed on foot, full of what their residents saw as familiar places and faces.

Small though they were, the towns were far more complex than the countryside. They were political capitals where men with a claim to rule gathered to do the province's business. They were centers of commerce, dispatching and receiving ships over thousands of miles. Increasingly they were centers of wealth. By the eve of independence, some of their merchants enjoyed fortunes that were respectable even by lofty British standards. The ports were centers of upper-class culture, with colleges, playhouses, concerts, and artists that imitated Europe's best. Two of those artists, the Philadelphian Benjamin West and the Bostonian John Singleton Copley, made original contributions that influenced the course of eighteenth-century art.

As the gilded cod of Massachusetts suggests, Boston began to develop as soon as its fishermen went to sea. "Here is good store of fish," one of the earliest migrants said, "if we had boates to go 8 or 10 leagues to sea to fish in." Fishermen knew that if they salted and dried their cod, they could market it far away. But fishing boats and the larger vessels needed to transport the dried fish meant that Boston needed shipyards, ropewalks, iron foundries, and sailmaking shops. These, in turn, required skilled artisans to run them. One change opened up the need and the possibility of others.

The towns quickly developed their own social order, with different classes living in distinctly different ways. The richest were likely to be merchants, some of them trading across the Atlantic, and others, usually less wealthy, along the American coast and in the Caribbean. Voyages in the transatlantic trade took ships to Britain, mainland Europe, Africa, or the Azores. They carried fish from the Grand Banks, flour from Pennsylvania, barrel staves from New York's forests, flaxseed for Irish linen growers, lemons, salt, oil, and wine. They also carried slaves: "Don't forget the Guinea voyage!" was a common instruction from shipowners to their captains. On occasion the captain might also be told to sell the ship itself overseas and get home any way possible, for American shipyards had a good reputation that brought high prices for their vessels.

As colonial merchants built their fortunes, they became part of a transatlantic elite, acquiring connections that linked them to the highest circles in England. By 1750 a daughter of New York's DeLancey family had married a knighted British admiral, and one of its sons was close to the Archbishop of Canterbury. Such families had correspondents and partners in faraway ports. They lived in a

Clothes make the man. In colonial New England, merchants commissioned paintings that would display not only their faces but their place in society as well. Boston merchant Joseph Sherburne ostentatiously indicated his rank and wealth in this portrait by John Singleton Copley painted in the late 1760s.

sprawling cosmopolitan world, in which events thousands of miles away were just as important as what was happening to the neighbors next door.

A professional class also began to take shape in the cities, beginning with the Protestant ministry. In the eighteenth century, lawyers emerged as a separate group, serving landowners and merchants with their specialized skills as they imitated the customs of the English bar. Ministers and lawyers formed the core of a colonial intellectual elite, producing the bulk of early America's writing and scholarship.

Commerce makes the man. Other merchants, such as James Tilley in this 1757 painting attributed to Copley, preferred to emphasize the source of their wealth in their portraits.

Most townspeople, however, were not merchants or ministers or lawyers. They belonged instead to the "laboring classes," and they worked with their hands and their muscle. Dress set working men apart from the elite. Leather work aprons, plain hair, and long trousers clearly signaled that their wearers did not belong in a world where men wore satin coats, powdered wigs, and knee breeches. Various groups of workingmen inhabited the colonial cities, many of them associated with maritime commerce. Shipwrights and ironmakers were employed in the largest manufacturing establishments. Their skill and status gave them considerable freedom and control of their own time. Sailors lived in a world with its own special dangers and customs. Inhabitants of the sea itself as much as any port town, they developed friendships that spanned distances as great as those of the merchants who employed them. Danger from storms and shipwreck, the fear that the British navy might impress them into service for the king, or that a privateer or enemy man-of-war might capture them, the tough physical discipline that a captain could impose, low pay, and constant discomfort: these were the conditions of their lives. They knew that if they did not stick together they might not survive. "One and all" became their motto.

The goal of most laboring townsmen was to become a master "mechanic" or artisan, which meant serving several years as an apprentice, learning the secrets and skills of a trade while legally bound to serve one's master. Upon completion of apprenticeship, the laborer became a journeyman, hired for a time as he saved to open a shop of his own. If a man did become a master in his own right, he had to be many things: a producer, using his own tools to turn out goods; a businessman, buying raw materials and selling finished products; a teacher, training apprentices; and an employer, hiring journeymen as perhaps he himself had once been hired. "Mastery" meant the ownership of a shop and the command of a respected set of skills. Most of all, it meant independence and control of one's working environment.

Some master artisans, like the Boston silversmith Paul Revere, achieved considerable comfort. Revere's North End house, still standing, was no Beacon

". . . STONES AND BRICKBATS"

To supply men for its navy, the British government regularly employed "press gangs" to seize colonial merchant seamen. Boston was plagued by such impressment in the 1740s; trade suffered as colonial seamen fled the port. On November 16, 1747, several hundred Boston sailors and laborers, white and black, tried to halt an impressment by taking British officers hostage. The following account is taken from a December 1, 1747, letter written by Massachusetts governor William Shirley to the Lords of Trade.

THE MOB NOW increased and joined by some inhabitants came to the Town House (just after candle light) and armed as in the morning, assaulted the Council Chamber . . . by throwing stones and brickbats in at the windows, and having broke all the windows of the lower floor . . . forcibly entered into it. . . .

In this confusion . . . the Speaker of the House and others of the Assembly pressed me much to speak two or three words to the mob . . . ; and in this parley one of the mob, an inhabitant of the town, called upon me to deliver up the Lieutenant of the *Lark*, which I refused to do; after which among other things, he demanded of me why a boy, one Warren now under sentence of death in jail for being [involved] in a press gang which killed two sailors in this town in the act of impressing, was not executed; and I acquainted 'em his execution was suspended by his Majesty's order till his pleasure shall be known upon it; whereupon the same person, who was the mob's spokesman, asked me "if I did not remember Porteous's case who was hanged upon a sign post in Edinburgh." I told 'em very well, and that I hoped they remembered what the consequence of that proceeding was to the inhabitants of the city; after which I thought it high time to make an end of parleying with the mob, and retired into the Council Chamber. . . .

In the evening the mob forcibly searched the Navy Hospital upon the Town Common in order to let out what seamen they could find there belonging to the King's ships; and [searched] seven or eight private houses for [British] officers, and took four or five petty officers; but soon released 'em without any ill usage . . . their chief intent appearing to be, from the beginning, not to use the officers ill any otherwise than by detaining 'em, in hopes of obliging [British commodore Charles] Knowles to give up the impressed men.

Crafts make the man. Boston silver-smith Paul Revere was one of the few colonial craftsmen painted by Copley. In this painting, dating from about 1770, Revere posed at his workbench, wearing the artisan's plain linen shirt and vest, and displaying his engraving tools and an unfinished teapot.

Hill mansion, but clearly he did not live in poverty. Under special circumstances an artisan might claim international fame: the Phila-delphia printer Benjamin Franklin became one of the foremost figures of the age. But much more typical of an artisan's course was the one followed by the Boston shoemaker George Robert Twelves Hewes, who never grew wealthy. He did win fame, but only in his very old age, as one of the last survivors of the American Revolution.

Men like Franklin and Revere were relentless self-improvers. The mottos and slogans Franklin printed in *Poor Richard's Almanac* showed his belief that hard work and self-discipline would carry a man far in the world. Franklin's own life seemed to prove the point. Revere expressed his pride by having Copley paint him in his ordinary work clothes with his tools in front of him while he fingered a silver teapot he had made. Poorer working Bostonians like Hewes expressed many of their concerns every November 5, when they gathered on "Pope's Day" to commemorate the discovery in 1605 of the Gunpowder Plot, in which a group of English Catholics were caught planting explosives beneath the House of Commons.

Bostonians like Hewes paraded effigies of Guy Fawkes, the pope, and the devil during the Pope's Day celebrations. Separate "companies" from the town's north and south ends brawled, the victors casting the losers' effigies into the flames of a bonfire. On one level these cobblers, apprentices, and mariners were showing how strongly they believed that the Protestant Reformation had made the world a better place. On another they were reminding themselves of the seventeenth-century upheavals that had generated their own "English liberty." Still more, they were celebrating a day of misrule when the streets were theirs, a brief carnival when people like themselves took control of the streets of Boston.

The goal of most artisans was to acquire a "decent competency"—enough property and skill to stand on their own two feet. But many could not be sure that they ever would. By the third quarter of the eighteenth century, real poverty wracked the colonial cities, as demonstrated by poor-relief figures: in 1775 Boston spent seven times as much per capita on the poor as it had at the beginning of the century. Figures for property ownership showed the same problem. In Philadelphia the share of property held by the bottom 30 percent of taxpayers slid from 2.6 percent in 1687 to barely 1 percent in 1774, while the share held by the top 5 percent climbed from 30 percent to 55 percent.

Such problems did not bother

"... PLOUGH DEEP, WHILE SLUGGARDS SLEEP"

Benjamin Franklin's Poor Richard's Almanack *was perhaps the most popular advice book published in colonial America. Although many of Franklin's proverbs and homilies are now clichés, at the time they reflected the abiding belief of farmers and skilled artisans in the dignity and importance of their labor in northern colonial society.*

INDUSTRY NEED NOT wish, as Poor Richard says, and he that lives upon Hope will die fasting. There are no Gains without Pains; then Help Hands, for I have no Lands, or if I have, they are smartly taxed. And, as Poor Richard likewise observes, He that hath a Trade hath an Estate; and he that hath a Calling, hath an Office of Profit and Honour; but then the Trade must be worked at, and Calling well followed, or neither the Estate nor the Office will enable us to pay our taxes. If we are industrious, we shall never starve; for, as Poor Richard says, At the working Man's House Hunger looks in, but dares not enter. Nor will the Bailiff or the Constable enter, for Industry pays Debts, while Despair encreaseth them, says Poor Richard. What though you have no Treasure, nor has any rich Relation left you a Legacy, Diligence is the Mother of Goodluck, as Poor Richard says, and God gives all Things to Industry. Then plough deep, while Sluggards sleep, and you shall have Corn to sell and to keep, says Poor Dick.... If you were a Servant, would you not be ashamed that a good Master should catch you idle? Are you then your own Master, be ashamed to catch yourself idle, as Poor Dick says. When there is so much to be done for yourself, your Family, your Country, and your gracious King, be up by Peep of Day; Let not the Sun look down and say, Inglorious here he lies.

Revere or Franklin, at least not directly. But they were very real for someone like Hewes, for whom one bad year meant the humiliation of debtors' prison, the poorhouse, or out-relief. Such difficulties were worse still for the ordinary laborers who loaded and unloaded ships, carted goods, and sold their labor from day to day. But at least such people could console themselves that they were free. At the bottom of the cities' social scale there were many people, both white and black, indentured servants and slaves, who were not free at all.

Indentured servants came to the middle colonies, as they did in the South, throughout the colonial period. Most were single males who came from the south of England and London; they entered America through colonial ports like Philadelphia, where they worked off their indentures and tended to stay on. More than half were artisans and craftsmen, and another quarter were laborers and personal servants. The colonial iron and construction industries were hungry for such skilled workers, and occasionally servants bargained themselves into good situations. Young families also came as indentured servants, typically hailing from rural areas in the north of England, Scotland, and other parts of Europe. These families tended to work off their indentures in agricultural areas at the edges of colonial settlement, such as western New York, after which they hoped to find a piece of land to farm on their own. These were people whose plight in Britain was so hard that they were willing to sell a large portion of their adult lives to escape it. They knew that in America they faced the prospect of being sold to a complete stranger who would govern their lives for four to seven years. They went nonetheless, but it is not surprising that their "fondness for freedom" often plagued their masters.

Slaves in the northern colonies experienced far worse. Slave labor did not become the basis of northern society, as it did in the south and the Caribbean. But a slave's term of service was for life, not just for a few years. Although black slaves could be found on some northern farms, particularly larger estates in

"FORTY SHILLINGS REWARD"

The lot of indentured servants was extremely difficult in colonial America, as evidenced by the number of servants who ran away from their masters. Masters often were reduced to placing advertisements in local newspapers to announce the disappearance of their servants, as these notices—from a shipmaster in New York in 1737, and from a merchant in Albany in 1761—suggest.

RUN AWAY FROM the Brigantine Joanna . . . an Irish Servant man, named Charles McCammel, aged about 25 Years, a tall lusty Man, wearing his own black Hair. . . . N.B. The Servant having been offr'd 8 shillings for his Hair, it's suppos'd he may have cut it off. He speaks very good English.

FORTY SHILLINGS REWARD. For taking up and securing Mary Brown, alias Edwards, a Pennsylvania born indented Servant, who ran away from the Service of . . . her Master a few days ago: She is a so-so-sort of a looking Woman, inclinable to Clumsiness, much Pock pitted, which gives her an hard Favour and a frosty Look, wants several of her Teeth, yet speaks good English and Dutch, about 26 or 28 Years old, perhaps 30. Had on and about her when she went off a red quilted Pettycoat, a crossbarr'd brown and white Josey [jersey], a sorry red Cloak and the making of a new stuff Wrapper, supposed to be gone towards Philadelphia, via New York.—James Crofton, Albany

New York, most ended up in northern port cities. Boston merchants and master artisans began acquiring large numbers of African slaves after 1710. By 1740, thirteen hundred slaves lived in Boston, nearly 10 percent of the population; slaves in Philadelphia and New York represented a comparable percentage. Mostly men, slaves performed menial city jobs, working as porters, cartmen, dockworkers, stockmen, and day laborers. Most urban slaves lived alone in a back room or attic of their master's house. A few blacks also lived as freemen in northern cities, although they could neither vote nor own property. All African-Americans in the North—slave and free alike—had extensive contact with whites at workplaces, taverns, cockfights, and fairs.

Many northern whites were hostile toward this small African-American population, reflecting fears of slave revolts and insurrections. In 1712, for example, a group of white New Yorkers was fired upon by a band of twenty black slaves when they attempted to put out a fire the slaves had set. The white militia quickly routed the armed slaves, initiating several weeks of arrests, trials, suicides, and executions. The governor later boasted that judges had found "the most exemplary punishments that could possibly be thought of" in sentencing the convicted men to be burned alive at the stake, drawn and quartered, or gibbeted (hanged). In all, nineteen slaves were executed. Although such punishments were swift and brutal, they did little to quell the fear of slave revolts among New York's white population. In 1741, slaves accused of arson and theft were also charged with conspiring to kill the white residents of New York. Eighteen more blacks were either burned to death or hanged; so were four whites who were implicated in the conspiracy.

Despite such treatment, African-American slaves in the North found ways to affirm their dignity and define and maintain their own communities and culture. Like their southern counterparts, African slaves in the north carried with them remnants of African rituals and cultural forms, which they adapted to the North American environment. Every spring in New York City and Albany, for example, slaves celebrated the festival they called Pinkster. They derived the name from the Jewish and Christian feast of Pentecost, but they made the festival all their own. Albany slaves performed "the original Congo dances as danced in their native Africa. They had a chief, old King Charley . . . a prince in his old country. . . . The music consisted of a sort of drum . . . upon which Old Charley did most of the beating, accompanied by singing some queer African air."

By the middle of the eighteenth century, slaves in a number of New England cities had initiated "Negro Election Day," an annual event at which the slave community "elected" its own governors, judges, sheriffs, and magistrates. Although these black leaders did not exercise official political power, they were able to represent the interests

An Exhortation to young and old to be cautious of small Crimes, left they become habitual, and lead them before they are aware into those of the most heinous Nature. Occasioned by the unhappy Case of *Levi Ames*, Executed on *Boston*-Neck, *October* 21st, 1773, for the Crime of Burglary.

Colonial justice. Public executions were occasions for common people to express approval of the punishment of those who broke the moral code. This broadside, printed and distributed in Boston in 1773, tells the story of a twenty-one-year-old convicted burglar, Levi Ames. The ritual of execution extended over a period of two months: on Sundays, Ames was conveyed in shackles through the streets of Boston, followed by crowds of men, women, and children. Each Sabbath journey ended at a different church, where Ames stood while the minister delivered a moralizing sermon.

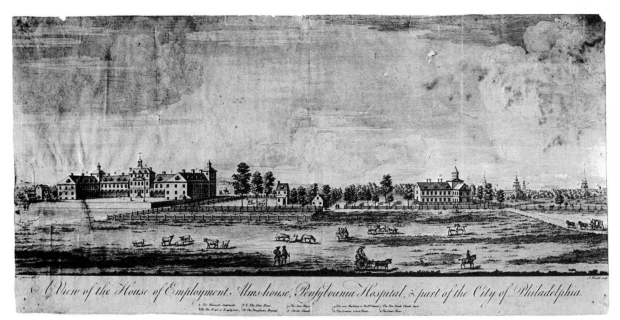

A View of the House of Employment, Alms-house, Pensylvania Hospital, & part of the City of Philadelphia.

The increasing numbers of urban poor taxed the resources of colonial cities. Many were incarcerated in almshouses and workhouses, but these institutions grew overcrowded. This 1767 engraving commemorates the opening of new facilities on the outskirts of Philadelphia. Typically, the print emphasizes the institution's bucolic setting rather than the less picturesque activities within its walls.

of the African-American community in moments of conflict or controversy. Negro Election Day was usually celebrated with elaborate parades, community feasts, and games and dances, many of the latter based on African rituals and traditions. Events like Pinkster and Negro Election Day, which lasted in some towns well into the nineteenth century, offered an institutionalized release from the everyday pressures of slavery and encouraged a sense of continuity and solidarity within the slave community. Like the Boston craftsmen and journeymen on Pope's Day, northern urban slaves were able to find ways to maintain important traditions and establish enduring institutions in the midst of slavery's oppression.

Almost all urban dwellers, from the poorest slave to the wealthiest merchant, depended in one way or another on commerce, which was the heartbeat of early American cities. But colonists were not free to organize their commerce as they saw fit. As early as the mid-seventeenth century, Parliament began to organize the provincial economies for the mother country's own benefit. With the passage of the Navigation Acts, foreign vessels could not enter colonial ports; colonial goods bound for the European mainland had to be shipped via England; "enumerated" goods, such as tobacco, rice, and naval stores, could be marketed only there. Parliament also acted against American manufactures, in 1732 prohibiting the marketing of hats across provincial boundaries. Eighteen years later, colonials were forbidden to refine the crude iron that they smelted in great abundance. Instead, they were to ship it to England for finishing. These restrictions were serious, but their actual enforcement was lax. Moreover, the Navigation Acts did bring real benefits, especially to shipbuilding, for colonial ships were defined within its terms as British. By 1770 one-third of the "British" merchant fleet had in fact been built with America's abundant timber.

Commerce within the towns was restricted as well. Throughout the years of colonial development, European thinkers debated the advantages of letting an open market dictate supplies and prices. The foremost proponent of the market was the Scottish economist Adam Smith, who published his free-trade manifesto, *The Wealth of Nations*, in 1776. In its time, what Smith had to say was, at least to some, profoundly liberating; it helped generate the enormous explosion of creative capitalist energy that transformed the whole world in the nineteenth century. But in Europe and America alike, many people clung to an older way of conducting trade, believing that society's rulers had an obligation to see that the market provided what people needed, at a quality they would accept, and at a price they could afford.

The "assize of bread" illustrated these older arrangements. The assize was a decree issued by town authorities to establish the price and the weight of the ordinary brown loaf. The goal was to balance the need of consumers for a good, cheap supply of bread with the need of farmers and bakers for a decent return on their work. New York City still used the system as late as the nineteenth century. Both Dutch and English authorities in New York set up controlled markets, in which it was illegal to "forestall" (buy provisions on their way to market), "regrate" (buy in the market in order to sell again), and "engross" (buy a crop that was still in the fields). In times of crisis, the authorities took even stronger measures. In 1748 the mayor and aldermen of New York asked the provincial government to lay an embargo on wheat. "Great and unusual exportations," they said, had made it "most excessive dear, to the very great oppression of all degrees of people, but more especially to the industrious poor."

When the authorities refused to act, ordinary people sometimes did, drawing on traditional notions of justice carried with them to the New World. In 1713 a Boston merchant named Andrew Belcher learned that grain was short in the West Indies. He began to plan some "great and unusual exportations" of his own to take advantage of the scarcity, and he refused to listen when the selectmen begged him to take a more modest profit at home. When it became clear that he intended to go ahead with his plan, a crowd of two hundred people broke into his stores and seized his grain. When the lieutenant-governor tried to stop them, someone shot him, though the wound was not fatal. Such actions were common in the eighteenth century. They happened in the British colonies, in South America, in continental Europe, and, as we have seen, most significantly in England.

Crowd actions, often approved by the highest colonial officials, came in many shapes and sizes and in support of a wide variety of causes. "Mobs, a sort of them at least, are constitutional [i.e., legal]," observed Thomas Hutchinson, who became both governor of Massachusetts and the victim of one of the century's most violent risings. After the sacking of his elegant house by a Stamp Act crowd in 1765, Hutchinson might have thought otherwise.

But crowd risings were not the only way ordinary people took part in northern public life. The Boston town meeting debated whatever issues it chose. In Philadelphia and New York, assembly elections could be raucous, even violent affairs, with candidates treating the voters to strong drink, and brickbats and heated language filling the air. Militia units, sheriff's posses, and volunteer fire companies were simply crowds that had been organized and given official sanction. Master craftsmen soon began to act collectively to control their trades. Philadelphia's builders founded their "Carpenters' Company" in 1724, which began as simply a friendly society. But such organizations sought increasingly to regulate prices, to decide who could enter the trade, and to set the rules for apprenticeship. Organizations set up for one purpose spilled over into others. By 1760 a Philadelphian whose house was in flames had his choice of companies to put them out. Among them were the Hibernia Fire Company, whose members were wholly Irish, and the Cordwainers' Fire Company, made up exclusively of shoemakers.

Townspeople had an importance far out of proportion to their numbers. They animated the hubs of social, economic, and political power, the centers of communication and intellectual life, the major points of connection between North America, the British Empire, and the wider world. In the 1760s and 1770s townspeople took the lead in the movement that cut America's political ties to the Old World.

WOMEN'S WORLDS

Indians and blacks, farmers and landlords, artisans and merchants: all of these groups, of course, included women. But the women of each group usually had more in common with their men than they did with the women of the other groups. An early view of New Amsterdam illustrates the point, for the black woman slave it depicts is distinguished from the male slaves around her only by the shape of her body. She and they are doing exactly the same work.

Almost all northern women shared the near-certainty of spending their adulthood as wives. With the blessing of the church and the protection of the government, women of European descent pursued marriage as life's normal course. Indians and Africans enjoyed neither the blessing nor the protection. But they did share the prospect of permanent commitment to marriage, "the important crisis upon which our fate depends." Some women, of course, remained unmarried, but in most colonists' eyes these were sad cases. Free, independent women were uncommon, at least until after the Revolution, when bold women began to regard "liberty" as "a better husband."

In this precontraceptive age, almost every married woman spent a large part of her life pregnant and caring for children. The women of Andover, Massachusetts, experienced more than five births per marriage in every decade between 1650 and 1720, and between 1690 and

A late-eighteenth-century anonymous painting of a woman sewing.

Farm work. An engraving from a 1760 New York almanac shows one woman milking a cow and another churning butter.

1710 the rate was higher than seven. Such women had good reason to fear childbirth, for roughly one in thirty deliveries caused the mother's death. The seventeenth-century Massachusetts poet Anne Bradstreet described to her husband how she felt as she neared the end of one of her pregnancies: "How soon, my dear, death may my steps attend, / How soon it may be thy lot to lose thy friend." Yet New England women's chances of survival were much better than those of their sisters in England or in the southern colonies, and were almost as good as those of men in the same age groups. In four out of every five early New England marriages, both partners survived to the end of their childbearing years.

By modern standards, colonial women married relatively late, but regardless of age, this action had great consequences. For second-generation Andover brides, the average age at marriage was 22.3 years; for third-generation brides it jumped to 24.5 years. In strictly legal terms, a colonial woman ceased to exist as an independent being when she married. Unless she made special arrangements, a wife did not control her own property, nor was she able to make a binding contract. Her husband was the head of the family, and both church and government insisted that she obey him. He controlled the family's property, whether he had earned it, inherited it, or acquired it through her. The common usage "Goodman Brown, his wife" expressed the married woman's status.

Untimely deaths. The graveyards of colonial New England testified to the hazards of childbirth for colonial women and their babies.

In reality if not in law, a wife was her husband's partner. Households, not individuals, were the basic units of economic and social life, and women were utterly essential to their operation. Sex-role differentiation was real, as was the sense that a man's work was more important than a women's. The way northern colonists dismissed the significance of the field labor done by Indian women is illustrative; had men done it instead, they might have realized that Indians did not live by hunting alone.

But roles sometimes overlapped. During the harvest, northern farmwives frequently joined in getting the crops in. The wife of an artisan was almost certain to acquire some of her husband's skills and to take a hand in production. A woman's work in the kitchen and its garden, in the dairy, or at the spinning wheel was just as essential to the family's well-being as what a man did in the fields or the shop. Women made cheese and butter, which were vital sources of cash income. Women produced the soap that kept the family clean and the beer, the cider, and much of the food that sustained its members.

Women's work was hard. The minister and poet Edward Taylor (1642–1729) tried to romanticize it in his poem "Huswifery":

> Make me, O Lord, thy Spinning wheele Compleat
> Thy Holy Worde my Distaff make for mee.

In his borrowed female voice, Taylor used the familiar Christian image of the church as the bride of Christ. But in 1782 Ruth Belknap of Dover, New Hampshire, replied with verses that possessed quite a different tone:

> Up in the morning I must rise
> Before I've time to rub my eyes.
> With half-pin'd gown, unbuckled shoe,
> I haste to milk my lowing cow.
> But, Oh! it makes my heart to ake,
> I have no bread till I can bake,
> And then, alas! it makes me sputter,
> For I must churn or have no butter.
> The hogs with swill too I must serve;
> For hogs must eat or men will starve.

Belknap was a minister's wife, as much a Christian as Taylor. But for her, "huswifery" was less a matter of metaphysics than the here-and-now misery on butchery day of looking "like ten thousand sluts, /My kitchen spread with grease and guts."

Some women did as much as they could on their own, daring to be "as independent as circumstances will admit." But to be an unmarried woman in a farming community was a wretched fate. The best that could be hoped for was to have a room in the house of some relative, paid for by the performance of household chores. Widows also often found life trying. The law guaranteed the "widow's portion" of her husband's estate, but only in life tenancy, not as a freehold property to do with as she chose. In working her estate, she was frequently as dependent on her son or son-in-law as she once had been on her husband, and before him on her father. Virtually the only other possibility (and then only for a woman who was literate) was to open a "dame school," where she could teach village children in return for a pittance.

Life was somewhat easier for women, single and married, in the northern towns, for there they found more options. Women took in lodgers; they ran taverns; they made fashionable clothes for other women more fortunate than themselves. They sewed, did housework, nursed, and practiced midwifery. Some worked as prostitutes. It was not unusual for widows of artisans to take charge of their husbands' shops: Elizabeth Holt succeeded her husband as the publisher of the *New York Journal*, and she became New York State's official printer during the Revolution.

Some women became "she-merchants," most of whom ran corner stores. A few prospered as long-distance traders. Perhaps the most notable was the Bostonian Elizabeth Murray Smith, who was so prosperous that she was able, as she proudly put it, "to live and act as I please." Like Paul Revere, she celebrated herself by commissioning a portrait from John Singleton Copley. Unlike Revere, she posed in elegant costume, and Copley painted her in a conventional feminine mode, with a bunch of fruit in her hands. But her bearing and assertive expression belie any thought that this woman was either submissive or decorative.

Elizabeth Murray Smith was an unusually strong and self-willed woman. Most colonial women, however, lacked her confidence. Phrases like "the foolishness of us women" and "the natural timidity of our sex" cropped up again and again in their letters and their diaries, so often that "female" almost became a synonym for "inferior" in their usage. But even those women who occasionally doubted themselves sometimes left their mark on the world. The women of Marblehead took out their anger about King Philip's War on two Indian prisoners in 1676 by literally tearing them to pieces. In 1704 Boston women showed what they thought of soldiers who had just returned from a disastrous expedition by sousing them with their chamberpots. In the 1730s women took the lead when Bostonians campaigned successfully against a plan for a controlled market; unlike New Yorkers, they saw no benefit in it. Occasionally men disguised themselves "in women's Cloaths" before taking collective action of their own. In Exeter, New Hampshire, in 1719, such a crowd prevented a sheriff from serving a writ. Like real women's participation in popular risings, this ritual masquerade was a transplant from Europe, where it was an accepted part of social and political occasions in which working people had the customary right to "turn the world upside down."

Women found their best arena for public involvement in the church. The radical sects of seventeenth-century England had flirted boldly with the idea of sexual equality, and even some mainstream Puritans leaned toward the idea. Puritan women were occasionally members of a church while their husbands were not. Unlike men, they had no formal voice in church affairs, but they still enjoyed the prestige of being "visible saints." By the eighteenth century, New England church membership was far more common among women than among men.

Some women went even further in their religious activities. Mistress Anne Hutchinson, who arrived in Boston in 1634 full of Puritan zeal, was a midwife and a community leader who began to invite her patients and friends to gather at her house to discuss weekly sermons. Such meetings were not unusual, but her sharp criticisms of some of the Puritan ministers and magistrates were. Hutchinson brought to Massachusetts the very same radical antinomian spirit that exploded into public visibility with the outbreak of the English Revolution. Her vision proved attractive: men began to join her gatherings, including the youthful Sir Henry Vane, whose prestige as a knight won him the governorship of the province in 1635.

The movement burst into open dissidence as Hutchinson and her followers began to disrupt the services conducted by ministers of whom they did not approve. In 1636 the clergy and the authorities retaliated, expelling Hutchinson from the church. During her trial for heresy she traded biblical quotations ably with her persecutors, but they refused to accept an untutored woman as an equal. Hutchinson was pregnant during her ordeal, and the authorities allowed her to remain in the colony until she gave birth. When the infant proved to be horribly deformed, they took it as a sure sign that she had been doing the devil's work. She was banished from the colony.

Throughout the colonial period northern women like Hutchinson, who dared to directly challenge the power men wielded, were rare. But by the end of the first century of settlement, rigid patriarchal controls were beginning to weaken. One sign can be seen in women's personal behavior. In the 1720s and the 1730s the probability that a Massachusetts bride would be pregnant at the time of her wedding was between one in three and one in two. The father of the child was almost certainly her prospective husband, and together the couple challenged their own parents' considerable authority. For two gener-

Witchcraft. Women were accused, prosecuted, and occasionally executed for the crime of witchcraft in seventeenth-century New England. Although Anne Hutchinson was never accused outright of being a witch, the delivery of a deformed, stillborn infant to one of her female associates in 1638 was interpreted by the Puritan fathers as the Devil's work. This illustration from an eighteenth-century chapbook (a cheaply printed pamphlet) presents a "monstrous" birth as a sign of witchcraft.

ations aging heads of families had been using their control of the land to control their own children's lives. But now young couples were both seizing their own independence and loosening the bonds that had held New England communities together since the beginning.

Women were present in the northern settlements from the start, which distinguished the area from the provinces farther south. The founders of Virginia came to the New World to get rich and get out. They built a society where there were far fewer women than men through most of the seventeenth century. But the founders of New England and Pennsylvania intended to build lasting communities, and women were necessary parts of the task. The early settlers built patriarchal social orders; their subordination of women was only one aspect of a world dominated by white, property-owning adult males. Whether colonial women knew it or not, their subsequent stirrings toward independence from that patriarchy had much in common with the yearning of African-Americans for freedom from their slavery and with the growing discontent that ordinary white men felt toward the increasingly galling inequalities of class.

THE RULERS AND THE RULED

By modern standards, the colonial North was not a democratic place. The vast majority had no part in public life. Slaves, servants, women, youths, and adult males who did not meet the minimum property requirement were denied the rights to vote and hold public office. The last group amounted to perhaps half the free adult male population; together, these groups constituted as much as 80 to 90 percent of the population. Moreover, a great deal of power in the northern colonies lay with people who had not been elected to anything: royal governors in most provinces, whichever Penn occupied the Pennsylvania proprietorship, members of the governors' councils (except in Massachusetts, Connecticut, and Rhode Island), mayors, judges, sheriffs, and the members of Philadelphia's closed corporation.

Voters frequently "deferred" to their social "betters"—the merchants, planters, lawyers, and large landowners who sat in the colonial assemblies. Rarely did genuine farmers or artisans enter the charmed circle where real political power was wielded. Farmers did frequently become assembly members in New England, where each organized town normally chose its own delegate, but even there the voices that counted most belonged to great merchants, to graduates of Harvard and Yale, and to the "River Gods" of the Connecticut Valley. In New York, where the assembly had fewer than thirty seats in all (with three effectively hereditary), there was no pretense of democracy. A shoemaker-turned-lawyer named Abraham Yates learned that in no uncertain terms in 1761 when he tried to win a seat. He was roundly defeated by no less a figure than Sir Willliam Johnson, and he was bitter ever afterward.

Yet in another sense the northern colonies were among the most democratic places on earth. In the eighteenth century, after New England's suffrage was no longer tied exclusively to church membership, eligibility for the vote was determined by the same basic rule that held in England. A man had to have a freehold worth £40 or a renthold valued at forty shillings per year. In England that was enough to keep most people from the polls, but in America, where land was more easily obtained, upward of half the free adult males could vote. This number included most of the tenants on New York's great estates, although voice voting meant that the landlord's candidate rarely lost. There were other ways to the vote as well: the "freemanship" of New York and Albany, which was open to most craftsmen, was an important means of political expression among urban workingmen.

The colonists governed themselves under their own version of the British constitution. A governor represented the king, and in all the colonies except Rhode Island and Connecticut (where he was elected) and Pennsylvania (where the Penns chose him), the king actually named his representative. Usually he was a fortune-hunter mainly intent on improving his own estate. But he found himself having to placate both his royal master, who issued detailed instructions, and the leading figures of the province, who often had distinct interests of their own. The other main political institutions were the council, a pale imitation of the House of Lords, and the assembly, whose members liked to compare themselves to the House of Commons. The governor had an absolute veto on laws, as did the crown (a power it did not have in England itself). He also had great patronage in matters of office-holding and land distribution, but wily colonial politicians frequently outwitted him about such matters.

Throughout the eighteenth century, popular politics was noisy and tumultuous, especially in the major northern port cities. In Boston, politics grew more popular despite the fact that the official town meeting was much smaller than the town's adult male population. After 1750, economic decline kept many former property-holders from voting. Yet twice a major political figure arose whose appeal was explicitly popular. The first was Elisha Cooke, Jr., early in the century. The second was Samuel Adams, who would become a leading radical figure during the revolution. Both were educated, privileged men, but each owed his power to his support of popular measures, including protection of the domestic economy and endorsement of cheap paper money.

New York had no town meeting, but public life there was more open than in any other American city. It had the highest proportion of men able to vote, and unlike Philadelphians or Bostonians, these voters often elected workingmen. Fully 30 percent of the councilmen chosen in New York in the early 1760s were mechanics—three times the proportion in Boston. Laboring men exercised a powerful presence at election time. "Jack Bowline and Tom Hatchway" and "Mr. Axe and Mr. Hammer" appeared as signatures on handbills. Every gentleman thought it "an honour to receive a visit from the meanest freeholder, nay condescend to shake hands with the dirtiest mechanic in the country." Popular politics was an old tradition. As early as 1734 "Timothy Wheelwright" was warning in print that "a poor honest man is preferable to a rich knave."

The "tone" of political life in each of the three major cities, as in each of the separate northern colonies, was distinctive, but the basic facts were similar. A sizable group of men found themselves neither wholly in nor wholly out of the political arena. They might well be courted at election time by popular politicians like Cooke and Adams or Pennsylvania's David Lloyd and Sir William Keith, but also by rich men like New York's many Morrises, DeLanceys, and Livingstons. "Mobs, Bonfires, . . . Huzzas," and parades "not of ye wise, ye Rich the learned [but] mostly of Rabble Butchers, porters & Tagrags" often accompanied elections. A politician who scorned the popular element, such as Boston's Thomas Hutchinson, might find himself despised. "Let it burn," a crowd shouted when his house caught fire in 1750. Popular politics was on the rise, but ascent to the commanding heights of public life remained essentially a privilege of class, not a right of citizenship.

THE NORTH ON THE EVE OF REVOLUTION

By 1750 the colonies were becoming mature societies. Their populations were multiplying rapidly. Noticing that the number of Americans was doubling every twenty years, the astute Benjamin Franklin took it as the surest sign of America's rising glory. Two of the great ports, New York and Philadelphia, grew increasingly prosperous. A colonial elite had emerged and was busily consolidating its power. Its members—landlords, lawyers, and merchants—began to treat themselves to elegant houses, fine furniture, and imported carriages as they founded new colleges—Princeton, Brown, the College of Philadelphia, King's College in New York—in which to educate their sons. Colonial writers began to tell the world that America was a good place to live, and Europeans started to believe them.

But maturity brought in its wake not only prosperity but tension. Part of the problem was war: the great struggle between Britain and France for mastery of the eighteenth-century world was under way, and the colonists, northern and southern, found themselves repeatedly embroiled in conflict. Another part of the tension emerged from their own societies, for some ordinary folk saw that wartime suffering was not shared equally, that some grew rich—or richer—in war years, and that some of the achievements of the elite were at the people's expense. Those tensions expressed themselves in religious and cultural dispute, in political squabbling, and in open combat, sometimes between armed men. In the years before the Revolution, America was an exciting, tense, and sometimes dangerous place.

War was a fact of colonial life in the eighteenth century, and usually it was not of the colonials' making. Again and again, events that had nothing to do with them forced them to fight and to raise taxes to pay for armies and fleets. King William's War (1689–97), Queen Anne's War (1702–13), the War of Jenkins' Ear (1739–44), King George's War (1744–48), and the great French and Indian War (1754–63) are the names they gave to the separate chapters in a seemingly endless European struggle. Only the last of these actually began in America, when a young Virginia militia colonel by the name of George Washington blundered into an engagement with French troops in western Pennsylvania.

Colonial merchants grew very rich if they could win wartime government contracts. During the last colonial war, the New Yorker Oliver DeLancey boosted his fortune to well over £100,000, a vast sum for the age. He had the advantage of extremely good political connections in the city the British made their American headquarters. But some lesser men also prospered during wartime. Farmers found that the military needed their crops; gunsmiths made weapons; blacksmiths fashioned ironware; shipyard workers produced vessels; carpenters built barracks and fortresses. Even draymen and porters gained, for the army needed their muscle and carts to transport its supplies. But as New York gained, Boston entered a long stagnation. New England as a whole had been unable to feed itself for decades, and now its principal town was losing the trade that had always fueled its prosperity.

War had other consequences, one of which was to build the self-confidence of the presumably "inferior" colonists. In 1755 British general Edward Braddock led a major expedition into western Pennsylvania to drive the French from Fort Duquesne. The British marched with all the pomp and noise of an eighteenth-century army; the French and their Indian allies merely hid behind trees and rocks, waiting for their moment. When the two sides ultimately met, Braddock's command was wiped out—except for a Virginia militia detachment under the same George Washington whose blunder the year before had ignited the hostilities in the first place. The reputation Washington won then would serve him well when it came time in 1775 for the colonies to choose a commander to lead their forces against the British.

The armies sent to America reflected Britain's social order. Officers were aristocrats and gentlemen who bought their commissions; men in the ranks were often society's poorest and most disadvantaged. The militias fielded by colonial governments in turn reflected the quite different social order of Britain's New World settlements. New England units were usually made up of the community's young men. As Thomas Pownall, governor of Massachusetts, put it in 1758, "most of these soldiers . . . are Freeholders, who pay taxes, [or] are the sons of some of our Militia colonels, and the sons of many of our Field Officers, now doing duty as Privates." For the British regulars, soldiering was a dead end, but for the colonists it was a stepping-stone toward personal independence, a way to earn prestige as they saw a bit of the world. They took it for granted that the captain who gave them orders on training day might well have been the storekeeper who regularly sold them goods or even the blacksmith who shod their horses.

To British officers such attitudes seemed incredible nonsense or, worse, uppity presumption—either one a sign of unreliability. Consequently they treated the Americans as mere auxiliaries in military affairs. They came to think that anything the Americans accomplished did not amount to much. In 1745 a Massachusetts expedition captured the mighty French fortress of Louisbourg on Cape Breton Island in Nova Scotia. It was a tremendous victory, which should have ended New Englanders' long-standing fear of their Catholic neighbors to the north. But when the war ended, the British negotiators simply traded it back to France, as if it were only a pawn. After the final French defeat and withdrawal in 1763, British statesmen would take the same attitude toward the whole American war effort.

Meanwhile, a domestic crisis was brewing, largely because of the surging growth of the northern colonial population and the emergence of an increasingly commercial way of life. In eastern New England, population densities neared English levels,

> ## ". . . WE ARE DEBARRED ENGLISHMEN'S LIBERTY"
>
> *Colonists who served as soldiers in England's wars in North America often complained about the hardships and arbitrariness of army life. When members of a Massachusetts regiment were not allowed to go home at what they understood to be the end of their tour of duty during the Seven Years' War, they refused to serve. Writing in his diary, a Massachusetts soldier notes that his rights as a free-born Englishman had been trampled on by such English actions.*
>
> [SEPTEMBER 30, 1759.] Cold weather is coming on apace, which will make us look round about us and put [on] our winter clothing, and we shall stand in need of good liquors [in order] to keep our spirits on cold winter's days. And we, being here within stone walls, are not likely to get liquors or clothes at this time of the year; and though we be Englishmen born, we are debarred Englishmen's liberty. Therefore we now see what it is to be under martial law and to be with the [British] regulars, who are but little better than slaves to their officers. And when I get out of their [power] I shall take care of how I get in again.
>
> [October] 31. And so now our time has come to an end according to enlistment, but we are not yet [allowed to go] home. . . .
>
> November 1. The regiment was ordered out . . . to hear what the colonel had to say to them as our time was out and we all swore that we would do no more duty here. So it was a day of much confusion with the regiment.

and the agricultural system could not support all the inhabitants. Farming techniques had never been especially efficient, and, except for places like the Connecticut Valley, the soil was stony and thin. The fourth generation of New Englanders came to maturity with the dawning recognition that they, unlike their parents and grandparents, had no prospect of living their lives in the towns where they had been born. The tiny, worn-out farms some would inherit would not permit it. Many had not even an exhausted plot of land to call their own.

New Englanders had been a relatively settled people, but now they had to move. They opened up new town sites in the Massachusetts and Connecticut highlands. They trekked northward to New Hampshire. They wandered into an ill-defined region, claimed by New Hampshire and New York alike, that lay between the upper Connecticut Valley and Lake George and Lake Champlain. Moving helped to solve some of their problems, for they found land in abundance, but mobility created new problems of its own.

Whether they moved or stayed, New Englanders found that the quality of life was changing around them. In the seventeenth century and the early decades of the eighteenth, they had established and conducted their town meetings on the premise that they valued consensus above all else. But now meetings grew contentious, even bitter. Selectmen who had held office for years, even decades, were unseated. Hamlets remote from the village centers petitioned the General Court to become towns on their own. New Englanders still wanted their villages to be "peaceable kingdoms," but the founders' project of building a "modell of Christian charitie" for the world to see, admire, and imitate now began to look like an unrealizable dream.

One result of such changes was the profound cultural crisis known as the Great Awakening. As noted above, this wave of evangelical religious fervor swept like a firestorm through the colonies from Georgia to New Hampshire in the late 1730s and the early 1740s. In the North, its flames billowed highest in New England. One of its key figures was Jonathan Edwards, pastor of Northampton, Massachusetts, whose famous sermon "Sinners in the Hands of an Angry God" is one of the masterpieces of American preaching. Edwards, along with men such as the Englishman George Whitefield and the Americans Gilbert Tennent and James Davenport, abandoned the dry, logical, rationalistic arguments of the traditional Puritan style and reached straight for the heart. Their message was simple: only sinners who cast themselves on God's mercy would be saved. To people who were unhappily convinced of their own selfishness, who knew that they did not measure up to their parents' standards, the message was profoundly appealing. Perhaps equally comforting was the intense, if brief, emotional community the Great Awakening offered to people whose kingdoms were no longer peaceable.

SCHUYLKILL

"Baptism on the Schuylkill." The frontispiece to *Materials Towards a History of the American Baptists,* published in Philadelphia in 1770, shows the ritual immersion of adults baptized into the church.

Jonathan Edwards stayed in his own pulpit until his congregation fired him. But Whitefield, Tennent, Davenport, and many others were "itinerants," wandering preachers who went where the spirit—and the anxious multitudes—called. They attracted huge audiences: at Whitefield's last Boston appearance in 1740 he preached to twenty thousand people on the common. Initially the colonial authorities of church and state welcomed the spiritual renewal promised by White-field. But where the itinerants went, disruption almost always followed. Congregations refused to honor and support their old pastors, and, in response to this attack on established authority, Connecticut elites actually passed a law against wandering preachers. When Tennent and then Davenport followed Whitefield to Boston, their preaching revived the ecstatic visions of equality that had fired the poor of revolutionary England a century before. Their sermons began to address hard political and economic questions, especially whether Massachusetts should set up a land bank, serving ordinary people, or a silver bank, serving the rich. Calvinist culture and social developments intersected to produce a call for a renewal of community and social obligation in a time when individualism and self-interest were gaining strength. The result was to move the poor to a greater awareness of their situation and to leave many communities deeply divided.

The Awakening resolved emotional tensions for some, but it could not solve the deeper social and economic problems people faced. The last decades of the colonial period witnessed upheaval in the American countryside, from the South Carolina interior to the mountains of northern New England. The Paxton Boys of western Pennsylvania marched on Philadelphia in 1763. In northern New Jersey and the

Hudson Valley, land rioters set out at midcentury to end the dominion of great landlords, and in 1766 the Hudson Valley erupted in an insurrection that spread from New York City to Albany. The Green Mountains, the disputed area between New York and New Hampshire, was a hot spot of outright guerrilla warfare after 1764, pitting the Green Mountain Boys, who had settled there under New Hampshire title, against the full authority of the province of New York.

There were many reasons for these conflicts. For the Scotch-Irish Paxton Boys (as for Bacon's rebels in late-seventeenth-century Virginia) it was Indians, whose land they wanted and whom they killed whenever they could. In New Jersey, New York, and the Green Mountains, land was again the basic problem. But in these cases rebellion erupted as small farmers, who believed they had the right to freeholds of their own, confronted landowners who, as one of them put it, wanted a world where they could lord it over "amiable and innocent tenants."

In New Jersey the problem was the "East Jersey Proprietors," who claimed for themselves a huge area around present-day Newark. In the Hudson Valley it was the great manors and estates. In the Green Mountains the problem was whether the whole region would be organized along the lines of New York or New England. The claimants of the vast tracts of land enjoyed powerful backing. The title of the Jersey Proprietors reached back to a seventeenth-century grant by the duke of York. The New York manors and estates had been bestowed on their owners by both the Dutch and English governments. And the Privy Council itself, the king's closest advisers, decided in 1764 that New York, not New Hampshire, should have the Green Mountains. Small wonder that William Prendergast, leader of the Hudson Valley rising of 1766, complained that "there was no law for poor men" and that the Green Mountain Boys said they were "out of the bounds of the law."

Against the landlords and their powerful backing, the small farmers claimed that moral right was on their side. In New Jersey they invoked an Indian title to disputed land and denied that either the king of England or the duke of York had ever enjoyed the right to grant American land without the Indians' consent. Angry Hudson Valley tenants knew that the bases of some of the great estates, most notably Livingston Manor, were fraudulent. They knew as well that the boundary between New York and Massachusetts had never been fixed and that New York landholders were straining to expand their estates eastward. The holders of New Hampshire grants in the Green Mountains claimed that they they had bought their land in good faith, with the intention of actually farming it themselves, whereas their New York rivals had only gain by speculation in mind.

The small farmers were angry and they said so. Hudson Valley

A contemporary engraving satirizes Quaker Philadelphia's military preparations
as the Paxton Boys neared the city in 1763.
An accompanying poem concludes:

To kill the Paxtonians, they then did Advance,
With Guns on their Shoulders, but how did they Prance;
When a troop of Dutch Butchers came to help them to fight,
Some down with their Guns, ran away in a Fright.

Their Cannon they drew up to the Court House,
For fear that the Paxtons the Meeting would force,
When the Orator mounted upon the Court Steps
And very Gently the Mob he dismis'd.

leader William Prendergast declared that "it was hard they were not allowed to have any property." Green Mountain leader Ethan Allen, confronted by a hostile New Yorker, told him, "God Damn your Governour, Laws, King, Council, and Assembly." One Jerseyman was quoted in 1749 as saying he wished the authorities had "fired upon them the said Rioters, for if they had they never should have seen such work, for if they would have destroy'd them all and drove them into the sea." And the small farmers did more than talk. They tore down fences and houses that belonged to people who accepted titles

". . . ALWAYS OPPRESSED BY THE RICH"

William Prendergast and his fellow Hudson Valley tenants took direct action against their landlords in the spring of 1766. More than two thousand armed tenants, calling themselves "Levelers" after the English civil war radicals a century earlier, battled landlords, sheriffs, and even a British army regiment dispatched from Albany. The tenant army finally was dispersed in June and its leaders, including Prendergast, were arrested and put on trial for riotous assault and "high treason." The excerpt that follows comes from the record of Prendergast's trial in August 1766. Convicted, Prendergast ultimately was pardoned by the king and returned home a hero.

Attorney General opens:

1. That . . . there was a discontent [among] some Tenants in the County on Account of the Tenure of their farms. . . .
2. That [the landlords] having sued a Number of their Tenants in Eject-ment, the prisoner [Prendergast], with a great number of others, com-bined to put out those who had been sent in by the landlords and restored the [original tenants to] possession [of the land]. . . .
6. That accordingly they armed themselves in a Great Multitude under the prisoner's Command, and did proceed to deliver [free] some prisoners in the Jail of New York [City]. . . .
7. That they assumed regal power by Erecting Courts and Laws and trying and punishing a Justice of the Peace for doing the duty of his office. . . .
9. [That they] came to a Resolution to oppose the King's Troops, did in two instances by firing on them and wounding [several]. One of the wounded [soldiers] dead. . . .

[Prosecution witness] Moss Kent sworn:

The occasion of the Mob was discontent with their Landlord's Terms and would not cease till Terms altered which they were willing to submit to arbi-tration. Some of the Mob declared that they would defend the Tenants against prosecution for Rent. If they were [convicted] they would rescue them out of Jail as they also would if any committed [to jail] on Account of the Mob['s actions] and that they would stand by each other with Lives and fortunes . . . and would maintain those in possession [of land who] were put in by the Mob . . . because they were poor and therefore [the Mob] were determined to do them justice, that poor Men were always oppressed by the rich.

The persons that might properly be called Mob Men were about 300; the rest only Spectators. . . . [Witness Kent] understood their Design was to [open up] all Jails in which any of the Mob Men should be committed. That when they went to New York [City], they expected to be assisted by the poor people there.

from the great owners. They broke open jails and freed pris-oners. The Green Mountain Boys made it impossible for courts to open under New York authority, and they and the Jer-seymen opened courts of their own in which they tried their enemies. The Jerseymen had their own jail "back in the woods." Land-rioters also col-lected taxes from their support-ers and formed themselves into militia companies. In the Green Mountains they erected the en-tire structure of New England–style town governments.

The colonial authorities took these rural rioters with deadly seriousness. When the Paxton Boys marched on Philadelphia, pacifist Quakers suddenly de-cided that it was time to learn how to fire a musket. When the Hudson Valley tenants rose three years later, New York's rul-ers sent two regiments of British troops, who subsequently sup-pressed the movement and sentenced their leader to a grue-some death. New Jersey land-lords called for a law modeled on Parliament's response to the Scottish Jacobite rising of 1715, to sentence men to death by name. New York actually passed such a law to deal with the Green Mountain rebels. The reb-els called it the Bloody Act for the way it "destines men to aw-ful fate, and hangs and damns without a trial." These were not short-lived, sporadic affairs like the risings in the towns, in which the rioters merely asked for a just price for bread. The questions at stake were fundamental in a society in which land was the most important form of property and source of wealth.

The land-rioters, whether protesting against specific landlords or eastern domination, were only a small percentage of the people of the northern colonies. But so, numerically, were those who made up the crowds of the great ports, the "awakened" who thronged to hear Whitefield and others rail against pride and avarice, the discontented in the New England town meetings, the citizen-soldiers who returned home from colonial wars to face rising poverty in the cities, and the slaves and indentured servants who longed for freedom. Despite their many differences, together these people contributed to a rising sense of crisis in the northern colonies. They also helped to spread the belief that ordinary people and popular politics would have to be part of the solution to that crisis.

Two of the northern colonies, Massachusetts Bay and Pennsylvania, had begun as utopian experiments in religious community. But by the 1760s they, like the rest of the North, had been transformed into something quite different. Prosperous, but plagued with social and political tensions, many of which were caused by the unequal sharing of the spoils of prosperity, the northern colonies, like those to the South, entered a period of conflict in the last third of the eighteenth century. That conflict would take many forms: between landlords and tenants; between urban elites and artisans, journeymen, and the poor; and, of greatest significance, between the needs of imperial England and the demands of an emerging movement for American independence.

As war with France approached, this woodcut appeared in a 1754 edition of Benjamin Franklin's *Pennsylvania Gazette* as a call to Britain's colonies to form a unified defense. Eleven years later Britain attempted to enforce the Stamp Act, and Paul Revere, looking for an effective image for resistance, appropriated the old symbol.

4 "THE GREATNESS OF THIS REVOLUTION"

E.

IN 1763 Britain stood triumphant in the Western world. After half a century of war, it had finally defeated France, and the Union Jack flew proudly from Detroit to Calcutta. All of North America east of the Mississippi and north of Florida was now British, and the thirteen original colonies were as jubilant in victory as Britain itself. Colonists gloried in George III, their youthful "best of kings"; they celebrated the victories of his armies and the wisdom of his ministers; they rejoiced that, like Britons "at home," they were the heirs to a tradition of freedom unique in all of human history.

Yet twenty years later, in 1783, those who had once been colonists faced humiliated British negotiators in Paris, signing a treaty that acknowledged the Americans' revolutionary victory and the end of the first British Empire. The former colonies now called themselves the United States of America; their people now called themselves citizens of a republic. American trade was suddenly much freer to go where American merchants desired. A generation of gifted political leaders had emerged: Benjamin Franklin, the wise Philadelphia printer whose name much of the Atlantic world now knew; Thomas Jefferson, author of the stirring document that declared American independence; John Adams of Massachusetts, who would be second president of the United States; and, most of all, George Washington, who seemed to Americans and Europeans alike to be the perfect symbol of republican virtue.

The story of the American Revolution is often told in terms of such men, whose achievements were undeniably great. Adams, in a fit of jealousy, once wondered if future historians would reduce the Revolution to a scenario in which Franklin, the inventor of the lightning rod, smites the earth with his invention, Washington springs out, Franklin electrifies him, and the two of them accomplish the whole Revolution on their own. Adams was worried that he himself would be forgotten. His fears, of course, proved groundless, for his name is prominent in the histories of the Revolution.

Yet many other revolutionaries have been forgotten, as if Adams, Franklin, Washington, and other leaders accomplished the Revolution by themselves. In truth, the American Revolution was the work of a generation—rich, middling, and poor, men and women. A few members of this generation won fame and prominence, but most did not. The vast majority of the revolutionaries, who were farmers, artisans, laborers, and other common folk of the day, expressed earnest patriotism and made many sacrifices; thousands gave their lives to secure American independence. Yet the goals, actions, and accomplishments of the ordinary men and women who called themselves patriots have largely been obscured by the sheer brilliance and eloquence of their famous leaders. This is unfortunate because it is only by understanding their efforts that we can grasp the sudden, unprecedented death of a transatlantic empire and the simultaneous birth of the world's first modern republic. These common men and women helped to change the world and changed themselves in the process. This chapter tells their story.

The Revolutionary War forced this generation to confront a question they had never wanted to ask: were they Americans or were they Britons who lived in America? A sizable minority decided that they were the latter and declared their loyalty to the British crown. Many more tried to stay neutral, though events did not always permit them to do so. Many others chose independence, but for a dazzling array of reasons. The Revolution was never a single, unified movement whose members agreed on what they wanted. It was instead a series of coalitions—forming, dissolving, and forming again under the pressure of events and the strain of differences among the revolutionaries.

George Washington was catapulted from the comfortable obscurity of his Virginia plantation to world fame, but his was not the only life transformed. Helping to make the Revolution made a huge difference to the Boston shoemaker George Robert Twelves Hewes, who trembled and scraped before his "betters" beforehand, but who took off his hat for no man at its end. Hewes and many men like him had come to value their "equal rights," the foremost of which was their right to a share in the government. The Revolution likewise made an immense difference to the way the New Jersey farmwife Mary Hay Burn saw the world. "Should I not have liberty," she wrote to her soldier husband, "whilst you strive for liberty?" Other American women shared her way of thinking, as did the thousands of African-Americans held in bondage. In 1760 American slavery was simply a fact of life that many whites took for granted and that blacks were forced to endure. But by 1800 slavery was on the way out in most northern states, and under attack in others. Fortified by the growing community of free blacks in the revolutionary era, slaves would intensify their own struggle for freedom.

The Revolution, in short, did more than simply secure independence for Britain's colonies. It transformed people's lives and, in so doing, it created a popular, democratic legacy that remains powerful today. How did the Revolution happen? Most of all, how did ordinary colonists—George Washington's foot soldiers, Thomas Jefferson's slaves, and John Adams's wife—attempt to make the Revolution their own?

THE IMPERIAL CRISIS

Although the colonists were tense and troubled at the end of the French and Indian War in 1763, they did not speak of revolution. Now that the French were gone, most colonials wanted to resume the lives they had led before the war. But both long-term trends and short-term developments made that impossible.

Part of the problem was the nature of the empire. British statesmen had begun to realize that the colonies, especially in the North, were potential rivals. The Hat Act of 1732 and the Iron Act of 1750 had attempted to limit the development of the colonial economy. So had Britain's decision in 1752 not to allow the New England colonies to make their paper currency a "legal tender" in payment of debts. In 1764 Parliament extended that prohibition to all of its North American dominions.

Taken by themselves, the Hat Act and the Iron Act were relatively unimportant, if only because the British made no serious effort to enforce them. Despite the Iron Act, the colonial iron industry was by 1776 producing one-seventh of the world's output. The Currency Act of 1764 was more serious. The provincial economies were chronically starved for coin, and the provincial governments had tried to remedy the situation by issuing paper currency. Some had kept their issues under control, but others let them inflate. Controlled or not, the colonial currencies were resented by traders in Britain, who wanted payment in sterling. The act was a clear sign that Parliament put the vital interests of the colonial economies second. That point had been demonstrated long before, in 1733, when Parliament decided that the need of West Indian sugar planters for a guaranteed North American market was more important than the need of North American importers for the cheaper goods that the French and Spanish islands could produce. The result was the Molasses Act, which tried to exclude French and Spanish molasses by stiff taxation. That act, too, went largely unenforced. But in the decade after 1764, Parliament embarked on a determined campaign to make the colonies serve British interests.

Britain had its reasons for the campaign, for beneath its triumph lay exhaustion. The government of William Pitt had spent lavishly on the struggle with France, and Prime Minister George Grenville faced an enormous national debt. He saw no way to pay it, and furthermore he knew that the cost of maintaining what had recently been won would be high. An empire required a ready fleet and army, and well-paid officials. Otherwise it would all come apart, much faster than it had been put together.

Grenville looked west for an answer. The colonists had gained more than anyone else from the French defeat. Their historic enemy was gone. The whole seaboard, along with unimpeded access to the interior and the fur trade, was theirs. And Grenville was not the only British statesman who thought the Americans had won these great benefits at little cost to themselves.

Everyone knew that the separate provinces had cooperated badly, if at all, during the colonial wars. They had held back both men and resources. They had brazenly traded with the enemy, under flags of truce and by simple smuggling. Assemblies had refused to pay governors their salaries. The White Pine Act, intended to preserve America's best timber for the Royal Navy, could not be enforced, despite its patriotic purpose. The colonial customs service cost more to administer than it produced.

Any solution to these problems had to come through Parliament. Most European monarchs might do as they pleased, but the British crown could tax and make laws only with Parliament's consent. This was the heart of Britain's unwritten constitution and the great safeguard of British liberty. As far as Grenville was concerned, the colonists were fully subject to the constitution, and hence to Parliament. Their provincial assemblies were mere conveniences, much like the boards of aldermen that ran the boroughs and towns of England. Only Parliament spoke for the general good. The general good now required that the colonists acknowledge their subordination and start paying their own way within the empire.

The colonists, Grenville and Parliament soon discovered, were not eager to comply. Parliamentary initiatives and colonial resistance would result in three major imperial crises between 1765 and 1775. As we shall see, in each crisis the stakes would escalate, involving growing numbers of colonists from all levels of American society in a struggle that ultimately would lead to independence. These dissaffected English subjects formed an expanding revolutionary coalition that by 1776 stood ready to overthrow British power by force of arms and to proclaim a new nation.

But in 1764, before any of this transpired, the British government rightly assumed its ability to control its colonial subjects. In that year, Grenville proposed a three-step plan of action against the American colonists. He took the first two steps with the passage of the Revenue (or Sugar) Act of 1764. Grenville first sought to end the notorious inefficiency of the Navigation Acts. New officials would be sent to America to combat smuggling, and as an incentive they would receive one-third of the value of every cargo and vessel they helped to condemn. To ensure success, their cases would be heard in "courts of vice-admiralty," where a judge alone would render the verdict. There would be no juries, full of the defendant's friends and neighbors, to interfere with imperial justice.

Grenville's second step was to raise revenues directly from the colonies. Previously all customs duties had been designed simply to keep the colonists within the economic boundaries of the empire, making them, for example, buy their molasses from Jamaica rather than from Haiti or Santo Domingo. But the Sugar Act abandoned the old principle of a high tax on foreign molasses and none on British. Now the same duty would be paid no matter where the molasses came from; the purpose of the innovation was to raise money.

Grenville's next action—passage of the Stamp Act of 1765—precipitated the first imperial crisis. The act's principle was simple. An appropriate stamp had to be bought for any object or to carry out any action specified in the act. Legal, church, political, and commercial documents, passports, dice and playing cards, books and newspapers, even advertisements—all were subject to duty. Furthermore, the tax had to be paid in hard currency. Like the Sugar Act, the act was to be enforced in the vice-admiralty courts. The money raised was to stay in the colonies, to help pay for colonial administration. But it would not be subject to colonial control. Now the king's governors would be

Britannia, surrounded by her amputated limbs—marked Virginia, Pennsylvania, New York, and New England—contemplates the decline of her empire in this 1767 engraving published in Great Britain. The cartoon, attributed to Benjamin Franklin, warned of the consequences of alienating the colonies through enforcement of the Stamp Act. Franklin, who was in England representing the colonists' claims, arranged to have the image printed on cards that he distributed to members of Parliament.

freed to do his bidding, no longer fearing that if they did, local assemblies would withhold their salaries.

The Stamp Act had something to make virtually every colonist angry. From newspaper readers to young people getting married and old people making out their wills, from apprentices signing indentures to merchants signing contracts, from pious folk going to church to drinkers going to the tavern, everyone would feel the effects of the new tax. The Stamp Act struck with particular force at the power of the colonial elite. For decades they had controlled the taxation and administration of their own societies. In their assemblies they imitated the precedents and the practices of the House of Commons, telling themselves and their people that for all local purposes they, not the Commons, were the guardians of British liberty. The elite had grown used to acting as a ruling class, and they made a compelling argument that their rule was in everyone's best interest. But if they lost their control of taxation, they knew they would be rulers no more. They began to resist parliamentary initiatives.

In England, ministers and laws came and went, but from 1765 onward, Parliament grew increasingly determined to enforce its will and to make the colonists acknowledge their inferior place in the imperial order. Parliament repealed the Stamp Act in 1766, but simultaneously passed a Declaratory Act, asserting that it could "make laws and statutes . . . to bind the colonies and people of America . . . in all cases whatsoever." It was an empty gesture, but it paved the way for two future imperial crises.

The second imperial crisis commenced in 1767, when Parliament and Charles Townshend, chancellor of the exchequer, sought to tax the colonies again. Townshend had always been suspicious of the colonists, and now he saw a chance both to raise money and to reassert parliamentary supremacy. Townshend thought that the colonists had rejected the Stamp Act because it was an "internal" tax, collected within the colonies themselves, but that they would accept an "external" tax, collected at their ports. They had, after all, complied with the Sugar Act of 1764, even though some of them had grumbled about it. Townshend considered the distinction between internal and external illogical, and in fact it was a distinction the colonists themselves had not made. Parliament accepted the logic, though, and passed a bill to tax paint, paper, lead, glass, and tea as they arrived in colonial ports.

Meanwhile the British government was taking other steps. It suspended New York's assembly for refusing to vote supplies for troops stationed in the province. It set up a special board of commissioners in Boston to run the American customs service. And a year later, it sent two regiments of troops to Boston to protect the commissioners and their hirelings.

A small detachment of redcoats had always been stationed in New York, but Boston had never had a garrison. A large force remained in New York at the end of the colonial wars, and now the people of both ports had to put up with what amounted to military occupation. Off-duty soldiers competed with civilians for work, while noisy military parades disturbed weekday business and Sunday prayer. In New York members of the garrison made it a point of honor to destroy every "liberty pole" the colonists set up. In Boston a guardpost was placed at the Neck to catch the army's deserters; everyone entering or leaving town was forced to submit to the sentries' orders. The colonists' resentment was fueled by the long-standing English belief that a standing army constituted a dangerous threat to liberty.

Meanwhile the customs service had declared war on the American economy. The tidewaiters, inspectors, and other minor officials who went over to enforce the Navigation Acts saw the Americans as disloyal at best, criminal at worst. These officials wanted their share of the rich rewards that came from catching smugglers. They had at their command a set of laws so complex that virtually every intercolonial traveler, every ship leaving or entering port, violated some technicality. Even the discovery of a small private venture that a sailor had stashed in a corner of a ship's hold was enough to bring a condemnation of the whole ship and its cargo if the proper paperwork had not been done. Everyone, from the greatest merchant, such as John Hancock of Boston, to the most ordinary seaman, could find himself a victim.

From 1768 to 1770 the colonists opposed the Townshend duties by refusing to import British goods. Pamphleteers debated Parliament's power to tax and to shut down colonial assemblies. Crowds befouled the houses of customs men and sometimes tarred and feathered the officials themselves. Relations between civilians and soldiers grew increasingly strained and volatile. It finally came to bloodshed, as we shall see, on the "Fatal Fifth of March," 1770, in the Boston Massacre. Soldiers guarding the customs house in Boston opened fire on civilians who were taunting them, killing five. Parliament decided that it had had enough conflict for the moment. It repealed all the Townshend duties except for the one on tea. Nonimportation collapsed, the Boston troops were withdrawn to Castle Island in the harbor, and the second imperial crisis was over.

The third and last crisis began late in 1773. For reasons that had nothing to do with America, the British East India Company was in severe financial trouble. The company was too important to be allowed to fail, and Parliament came to the rescue by allowing only its chosen agents to market the tea sold in each port. Even with the Townshend duty paid, the company would still undercut American merchants who, as John Adams put it, had "honestly smuggled" their tea from Holland. Everyone would be happy, for Parliament would get its tax, the company would get its revenue, and the colonists would get cheap tea.

But the Americans refused the bribe. Philadelphia and New York did not let even the first tea ships anchor in their harbors. In Boston, however, a tea ship did dock at the end of November 1773. Governor Thomas Hutchinson, whose sons would profit as the company's Boston agents, refused to let it leave without unloading the tea and paying the tax on it. The governor began to negotiate with leaders chosen by "the whole Body of the People," gathered in daylong meetings. Finally the negotiations failed and some "Mohawks" boarded the ship on the night of December 17 and dumped the tea overboard. Of course they were not real Indians but a few patriot leaders and many workingmen who knew how to rig a block and tackle and how to find their way around in a ship's dark hold.

Britain responded to Boston's "tea party" by passing four "coercive" or "intolerable" acts, as they came to be known. The first closed Boston's harbor until the town paid for the tea. The second act permanently altered the government of Massachusetts, revoking the charter that the king had granted in 1691. It ended the colony's unique privilege of electing its own council; it also limited town meetings to one per year, and then only to elect local officers. The third act allowed British officials accused of wrongdoing to be tried in another province or in Britain itself, away from the inflamed passions of the port. The fourth made it easy for the authorities to billet troops in colonial homes. To cap it all, General Thomas Gage, the supreme British commander in America, replaced Hutchinson as governor. This time there would be no humiliating British retreat.

Britain's original purpose was simply to solve its own problems, but questions of high principle emerged on both sides of the Atlantic as the conflict escalated. The basic premise in Britain was that, according to its revered unwritten constitution, Parliament and the crown together were supreme. In practice Parliament occasionally admitted mistakes; in theory it always asserted its full authority. That is why it passed the Declaratory Act when it repealed the Stamp Act, and why it left the tea duty in force in 1770.

Until very late in the third crisis, most colonists accepted Parliament's right to legislate for them, to command them to do some things and forbid them to do others. Imperial interest required that there be some supreme authority, and the only alternative to Parliament was to have the crown act by itself. No one wanted that. But taxing for revenue was another matter. Supposedly a tax was not a "law" in the strict sense, but rather the people's free gift to the king, which is why a tax bill could originate only in the House of Commons. Its members alone were the people's representatives, qualified to make that "free gift" in their name. No one disputed the point, not George Grenville, not Charles Townshend, and certainly not King George III.

The colonists elected no members of Parliament, but as far as the rulers of Britain were concerned that posed no problem, for most people in Britain itself could not vote either. As one parliamentary spokesman put it, no Briton was actually represented, but "all are virtually represented . . . for every Member sits not as Representative of his own Constituents, but as one of that august Assembly by which all the Commons of Great Britain are represented." The colonists saw it differently. As the Virginia House of Burgesses pointed out at the time of the Stamp Act, "the taxation of the People by themselves or by persons chosen by themselves . . . is the distinguishing Characteristick of British Freedom." For the burgesses, the "persons chosen" by Virginians could only be the members of their own House, the only people for whom any Virginians at all had a vote. Colonial pamphleteers picked up the point and developed it so well that the British never tried to use the argument again.

Alongside the constitutional argument lay a related problem, Britain's need to make the rest of the empire economically subordinate to itself. The colonies produced raw materials, and some colonists got rich in the process. But Britain had to be the center of commerce and manufacturing, and its wealth was paramount. Any movement toward economic autonomy and independent development—such as the proposal of a group of Philadelphia "gentlemen" in 1775 to establish "an *American* Manufactory" for textiles—had to be limited.

The Caribbean and the southern mainland colonies presented no great challenge to British economic dominance, because their staple export crops—especially tobacco, sugar, and rice—fit well into the imperial economy. But the northern colonies were another matter. Every year they became more like—and hence more dangerous to—Britain. The Hat Act and the Iron Act were deliberate attempts to check their economic development, as was the Currency Act of 1764. The Sugar Act, the Stamp Act, and the Townshend taxes were not only constitutional issues but also direct interventions in the American economy for Britain's benefit. The tea crisis was a clear sign that the fortunes of the East India Company were considered more important to Britain than the economic health of the colonial cities and their class of merchants. From the British point of view, the initiatives made perfect sense; by their own logic, they would have been foolish to pursue any other course. But from the colonial point of view, it would have been foolish not to resist the British actions.

THE SONS AND DAUGHTERS OF LIBERTY

American resistance to British policies intensified in each of the three imperial crises that erupted in the decade before the revolution. Diverse groups of colonists with very different desires and interests came together to oppose British rule. A coalition that included ordinary men and women—urban artisans and common laborers, servants, sailors, and farmers—as well as merchants, professionals, and slaveowners emerged well before 1775. This revolutionary coalition would first resist British policies, then move toward independence from Britain, and finally conceive of a new political and social order to replace colonial status.

The first revolutionary coalition prevented the implementation of the Stamp Act in 1765. It was led by the colonial elite, many of whose members sat alone in their book-lined studies and gathered together in institutions like the Virginia House of Burgesses. The burgesses passed strongly worded resolutions against the Stamp Act in June 1765, and over the next few months eight other colonial assemblies followed their example. In October, nine official colonial delegations gathered in New York City for a Stamp Act Congress, which adopted fourteen equally strong resolutions and sent petitions to Parliament and an address to the king.

Meanwhile colonial pamphleteers were beginning a decade-long campaign that would undermine virtually everything colonists had believed about themselves and the mother country. At first the pamphleteers were hesitant, fully aware that they were toying with dangerous ideas. As elite lawyers, merchants, and gentlemen, they wrote for their own kind in the language that privileged, educated men easily understood. But by the mid-1770s hesitancy gave way to open outrage, and fear of dangerous ideas to a defiant proclamation of revolutionary ideals. Thomas Jefferson, writing in 1774, had no qualms about declaring that even the Navigation Acts were "void" on the ground that "the British Parliament has no right to exercise authority over us." Jefferson boldly chose to advise the king rather than to cringe before him. "Let those flatter who fear," Jefferson wrote; "it is not an American art."

The greatest pamphleteer of all, however, did not come from the American elite. He was Thomas Paine, who migrated from England to Philadelphia in 1774. When Paine published his *Common Sense* in January 1776, it won such tremendous acclaim that Paine modestly called it "the greatest sale that any performance ever had since the use of letters." As many as 150,000 copies rolled off printing presses throughout the colonies, and people from New Hampshire to Georgia cheered Paine's powerful advocacy of full independence. But Paine's

affix the STAMP.

This is the Place to

Printed in the bottom right-hand corner of the October 24, 1765, *Pennsylvania Journal and Weekly Advertiser.*

popularity also owed much to the way he wrote. Paine did not aim *Common Sense* at the educated; he wrote in plain language for ordinary artisans and farmers, people who could read but who were not bookish. *Common Sense* invited them to join the high-level political discussion. Indeed, its publication was a sign of how important ordinary people had become in the American independence movement. How and why did such people decide that the imperial crisis involved not only the great men who had always ruled them, but also themselves? How did they become the heart of the revolutionary coalition? How did they come to embrace Tom Paine's democratic message?

From the Stamp Act in 1765 to the Boston Tea Party in 1773, the major seaports were the bulwarks of popular resistance. Though their people comprised only a small minority of all colonists, Boston, New York, and Philadelphia formed the revolution's "urban crucible." A small group who called themselves the Loyal Nine initiated Boston's resistance in the summer of 1765. These small traders and artisans knew that resisting the Stamp Act would require more than resolutions and pamphlets. They decided to make August 14 a day of open-air political theater to show Bostonians what the act would mean when it went into effect in November. They began the day by hanging effigies on a tree near Boston Neck, the first of the many Liberty Trees around which Americans would rally. The effigies represented George Grenville and Lord Bute, a thoroughly hated Scot who had been the king's tutor and briefly

---

"IN PRAISE OF LIBERTY"

Colonists' protests against the Stamp Act took many forms, including hanging and burning effigies of British officials, and destroying the offices and houses of Stamp Act commissioners and royal officials. The following account—from the patriot newspaper, the Boston Gazette, August 19, 1765— of an attack on Andrew Oliver, appointed Boston's stamp collector, shows how effective such dramatic crowd actions could be.

EARLY ON WEDNESDAY morning last, the effigy of a gentleman sustaining a very unpopular office, viz, that of Stamp Master, was found hanging on a tree in the most public part of the town, together with a boot, wherein was concealed a young imp of the Devil represented as peeping out of the top. On the breast of the effigy was a label, "IN PRAISE OF LIBERTY," and announcing vengeance on the subverters of it. And underneath was the following words: He That Takes This Down Is an Enemy to His Country. The owner of the tree ... endeavored to take it down; but being advised to the contrary by the populace, lest it should occasion the demolition of his windows, if not worse, desisted from the attempt. The diversion it occasioned among the multitude of spectators who continually assembled the whole day, is surprising: not a peasant was suffered to pass down to the market ... till he had stopped and got his articles stamped by the effigy. Towards dark some thousands repaired to the said place of rendezvous, and having taken down the pageantry, they proceeded with it along the main street to the town house, thru which they carried it, and continued their route thru Tilby Street to Oliver's dock, where there was a new brick building just finished; and they imagining it to be designed for a Stamp Office, instantly set about demolishing of it, which they thoroughly effected in about half an hour. . . .

The next day the transactions of the preceding night was of course the general topic of conversation; when the Stamp Master, in order to appease the sensations which seemed to possess the breasts of everyone at the prospect of a future stamp duty, sent a card to several gentlemen, acquainting them that he had absolutely declined having any concern in that office, which being publically read ... it was thought all uneasiness would subside. But the evening following [the crowd] again assembled, erected a number of stages with tar barrels, etc., in the form of a pyramid, in the center of which was a flag staff, and a Union flag hoisted; whereupon 'tis said, the Stamp Master sent them a letter with the aforementioned resolution of non-acceptance, and assurance of endeavors to serve the province, etc. Upon which they thought proper to demolish the bonfire and retire. . . .

Resistance to the Stamp Act. A generation after the event, an etching in a 1784 German pocket almanac imaginatively celebrated the Boston crowd (including women, African-Americans, and leather-aproned artisans) burning stamped papers.

his prime minister. Another was Andrew Oliver, the Boston merchant who had accepted the office of stamp distributor. The familiar Pope's Day imagery had a new political content.

All that day the Nine ran a mock stamp office under the Liberty Tree. Carters with loads of goods, farmers coming to town with their crops, people on foot and on horseback all had their goods ceremoniously stamped as they passed by. The Nine had already made contact with shoemaker Ebenezer MacIntosh, leader of one of the two Pope's Day crowds. Later in the evening MacIntosh appeared, with both crowds behind him. They paraded with the effigies in traditional style and burned them. Then some searched out a small building they assumed to be Oliver's stamp office and leveled it, while others marched on to his house, where they smashed some windows, tore down fencing, and built a bonfire. The next day, Oliver announced that he was resigning his office.

Crowds had long been a major institution in colonial life. In the decade that followed this first Stamp Act rising, they became an independent political force. In the province of New York alone, fifty-seven risings erupted between 1764 and 1775. Crowds intimidated stamp distributors and forced them to resign their posts, with the result that only in Georgia was the act ever enforced. Crowds also tore down buildings: not only was Andrew Oliver's suspected stamp office leveled, so too was the elegant mansion of his kinsman Thomas Hutchinson only twelve days later. An equally lovely New York City house called Vauxhall was sacked at the beginning of November. So too was a New York playhouse that a crowd demolished on opening night in May 1766, when its members became outraged at the ostentatious dress and carriages of the theater's wealthy audience. Crowds tarred and feathered customs men and defaced their property with the contents of privies. A crowd in Providence even burned a government revenue cutter, the *Gaspée,* when it was run aground in Narragansett Bay. Crowds erected Liberty Poles, in imitation of the Tree of Liberty sanctified by Boston patriots. They brawled with British soldiers on the streets of both New York and Boston. A crowd disguised as Indians, as we have seen, dumped the East India Company's tea into Boston Harbor at the end of 1773. When a ship arrived at New York a few months later with more tea, another group of "Mohawks" began to prepare themselves. But as they donned their warpaint, people at quayside surged onto the ship and destroyed the tea themselves. Then they paraded to "the Fields" beyond the city walls with the empty casks and burned them. New Yorkers had staged the same parade almost a decade earlier after they tore down the playhouse in 1766. Then, too, they had shouted, "Liberty! Liberty!" as they marched.

Disguises, effigies, parades, bonfires, razings, confrontations with the British military and governmental authority: such popular tactics were perfectly familiar to eighteenth-century Americans. But now matters were given new political meaning and gravity by the looming imperial crisis and by the increasingly bitter class divisions within the colonies themselves. Boston's economy was stagnant by 1750, and at the end of the colonial wars, depression struck the other port towns as well. A verse in a New York newspaper in 1767 began,

The times grow hard,
poor people cry,
for want of money,
corn to buy.

Another important development was the unprecedented degree of political organization that began to appear among the colonists, the emergence of groups usually lumped together under the generic name the Sons of Liberty. As formal organizations, the Sons of Liberty lasted only as long as the Stamp Act crisis. But the members became the Revolution's popular leadership, and in effect their influence lasted through the imperial crisis and into the first years of the new nation.

They began with Boston's Loyal Nine. A list drawn up by John Adams after a visit showed the kind of men they were: "John Smith the Brazier, Thomas Crofts the Painter, [Benjamin] Edes the Printer, Stephen Claverly the Brazier, ... George Trott Jeweller." These men were artisans; they were joined in the Sons of Liberty by two other types of men.

There were men like Samuel Adams of Boston and Dr. Thomas Young, who turned up in Albany, Boston, Newport, and finally Tom Paine's Philadel-

"LET EVERY MAN DO HIS DUTY . . ."

The Boston Tea Party is described by George Robert Twelves Hewes, a poor shoemaker who was a participant in the dramatic actions. Hewes had been at the scene of the Boston Massacre three years earlier. In this memoir, taken down by James Hawkes in 1834, Hewes describes the meeting of "the Whole body of the People" that deliberated on the action and then describes the disciplined destruction of the tea.

ON THE DAY preceding the seventeenth [of December], there was a meeting of the citizens of the county of Suffolk, convened at one of the churches in Boston, for the purpose of consulting on what measures might be considered expedient to prevent the landing of the tea, or secure the people from the collection of the duty. At that meeting a committee was appointed to wait on Governor Hutchinson, and [to ask] whether he would take any measures to satisfy the people on the object of the meeting.... When the committee returned and informed the meeting of the absence of the Governor, there was a confused murmur among the members, and the meeting was immediately dissolved, many of them crying out, "Let every man do his duty, and be true to his country"; and there was a general huzza for Griffin's wharf....

When we arrived at the wharf, there were three of our number who assumed an authority to direct our operations, to which we readily submitted. They divided us into three parties, for the purpose of boarding the three [tea] ships.... We were immediately ordered by the respective commanders to board all the ships at the same time, which we promptly obeyed. The commander of the division to which I belonged, as soon as we were aboard the ship, appointed me boatswain, and ordered me to go the [ship's] captain and demand of him the keys to the hatches and a dozen candles. I made the demand accordingly, and the captain promptly ... delivered the articles; but requested me at the same time to do no damage to the ship or rigging. We then were ordered by our commander to open the hatches and take out all the chests of tea and throw them overboard, and we immediately proceeded to execute his orders, first cutting and splitting the chests with our tomahawks, so as thoroughly to expose them to the effects of the water.

In about three hours from the time we went on board, we had thus broken and thrown overboard every tea chest to be found in the ship, while those on the other ships were disposing of the tea in the same way, at the same time. We were surrounded by British armed ships, but no attempt was made to resist us.

phia. Adams, Young, and Paine made their livings with their minds rather than their muscles. Adams was a Harvard graduate who dreamed of turning America into a Christian commonwealth and who courted popular support in the Boston town meeting. Young, on the other hand, was a religious freethinker (a deist) and self-taught physician who found most of his patients among the poor. Paine was an artisan, shopkeeper, and tax-collector; he held liberal views on religion. But religious differences did not stop the three from working together. Other key figures were men like New York's Isaac Sears, the son of a Cape Cod oysterman, who went to sea early in life. Eventually he became a captain of merchant ships and privateers and finally he settled down ashore as a trader in his own right. He did business with other colonies, not with Britain, and the greater traders looked down on him, addressing him as "Captain" rather than the more prestigious "Mr." or "Esq." or "Gent." Sears well knew the ordinary sailors who drank in his father-in-law's waterfront tavern.

The third major type in the Sons of Liberty were wealthy merchants, who made up an important wing of the revolutionary leadership. The most famous of these men was the eminent merchant and smuggler John Hancock of Boston. Before the advent of the revolutionary movement, great social distance stood between Hancock and ordinary people, but that distance lessened after 1770 as Hancock showed his colors as a virtuous patriot. The transition was revealed in the attitudes of George Hewes, who early in his life stood quaking before Hancock for a New Year's toast; after 1773 Hewes saw the wealthy merchant as but another fellow patriot who labored with him in the cause of freedom. Men such as Hancock thus earned their status within the movement as they learned how to be genuinely popular leaders.

The organized Sons of Liberty depended on their contacts with people like MacIntosh and Hewes, or Tony and Daly, two New York carpenters who could "raise or suppress a mob instantly." They also depended on popular memories that reached back to the English civil war. In 1774, "Joyce, Jun." appeared as the "Captain" of the "Committee for Tarring and Feathering." Every Bostonian knew that this referred to the minor officer who had captured the fugitive King Charles I, and thus assured his execution. The Sons depended on high principle, as did New Yorker Alexander McDougall in his angry broadside of 1779, "To the Betrayed Inhabitants of the City and Colony of New York." And they depended on appeals to direct economic interest: Like McDougall, the New Yorker John Lamb was angry about the presence of British troops in his city. But whereas McDougall claimed constitutional wrongs, Lamb claimed that the troops wrongfully took colonists' jobs.

In the end, the resistance movement developed because the imperial crisis intersected with crises in the lives of all colonists, rich, middling, and poor, as an account of the events in Boston in the early months of 1770 graphically demonstrates. For almost five years the popular leadership had told Bostonians to keep their private and local concerns out of the discussion of public events. Their newspaper, the Boston *Gazette*, blasted away at Britain, its policies, and its minions. Unlike New York's radical paper, the *Journal*, it said nothing about rents, prices, and employment. But Bostonians nonetheless had severe worries at home.

Trouble began in February, with a series of demonstrations against violators of the intercolonial nonimportation agreement against the Townshend duties. On February 22 a customs official named Ebenezer Richardson tried to break up a picket line in front of an importer's shop. When some boys pelted Richardson with stones, he retreated to his own house. He poked his gun barrel through one of his windows and fired, killing eleven-year-old Christopher Seider. The boy's funeral became a day of mourning for the whole town. Richardson was lucky to escape with his life.

A few days later an off-duty soldier named Patrick Walker wandered into a rope walk seeking casual work. It was nothing unusual for an ill-paid soldier to try to supplement his wage. But jobs were scarce. Less than two months before, similar job-seeking had provoked several days of street brawls in New York City. Perhaps Boston's ropemakers knew about that. Perhaps they thought of Christopher Seider's funeral, or recalled how parades by the troops had disrupted their Sunday church services. Perhaps they remembered how sentries posted at Boston Neck had harassed them, or how a professional army was an instrument of tyranny. Whatever their thoughts, one of the ropemakers summed up their feelings by telling the soldier that if he wanted a job, he could go clean "my shithouse."

The soldier was insulted, which is precisely what the ropemaker intended. The redcoat went back to his barracks to round up his friends, and soon a brawl broke out. A few nights later, on March 5, soldiers from Walker's regiment were on guard duty outside the King Street customs house. A large crowd, some of them ropemakers, gathered and began to throw snowballs and brickbats. They were angry at those who seemed to be the cause of all the pain and sorrow of the past month. For their part, the soldiers were frightened by those who seemed to be a vicious, bloodthirsty mob, and they opened fire. A few minutes later four Bostonians lay dead; a fifth would die later. All five were men of the laboring classes: Crispus Attucks, a half-Indian, half-African sailor; James Caldwell, a ship's mate; Patrick Carr, an Irish-born journeyman leathermaker; Samuel Gray, a ropemaker; and

Samuel Maverick, an apprentice to an ivory turner. The coming revolution had witnessed its first bloodshed. The fact that the blood spilled had been that of laboring men helped solidify the support of that critical segment of colonial society for the expanding revolutionary coalition.

Bostonians were outraged, and for the next thirteen years they observed March 5 as a day of public mourning. But the Boston Massacre nonetheless marked an end, not a beginning. Over the next few months the second wave of American resistance collapsed, thanks to Britain's repeal of four of the Townshend duties, to its evacuation of the troops from Boston to Castle Island, and, not least, to Boston's slowly returning economic prosperity. But the collapse itself brought renewed debate and argument.

Paul Revere issued his version of the Boston Massacre three weeks after the incident. The print (which Revere plagiarized from a fellow Boston engraver) was widely circulated and repeatedly copied (over twenty-five times). The print was the official Patriot version of the incident: British soldiers actually did not fire a well-disciplined volley; white men were not the sole actors in the incident; and the Bostonians provoked the soldiers with taunts and thrown objects.

For two years the centerpiece of resistance had been the nonimportation of British goods—a strategy that had never been popular with merchants and never fully enforceable. Boston loyalists scored a major propaganda victory against the town's radicals during the boycott by simply publishing the imports made by self-proclaimed patriotic traders. By 1770 most patriot-merchants were jockeying for position: no one wanted to be first, but everyone wanted to get their orders off to London as quickly as possible when nonimportation ended.

But artisans thought they ought to have a voice in the decision to end nonimportation. The repeal of four of the duties left one in force, and the aftermath of the Declaratory Act in 1766 was evidence enough that Britain still meant business. Artisans also realized that the boycott had helped rather than hurt them. Nonimportation meant orders for work at home, especially for craftsmen, which helped immensely in a time of economic distress. In Philadelphia a

The Boston Massacre, ca. 1858. Artists continued to redraw, repaint, and reinterpret the Boston Massacre. This engraving based on a painting by Alonzo Chappel still omits Crispus Attucks, but shows the chaos of the confrontation and captures the horror of soldiers shooting down unarmed citizens.

pamphleteer who signed himself "A Tradesman" asked "the majority of the Tradesmen, Farmers, and other Freemen" what ending the boycott would mean for them. Were they willing to "suffer the Credit and Liberties of the Province . . . to be sacrificed to the interests of a few Merchants?" Had most people gained or lost? More than simple self-interest was involved; as a New York writer put it, nothing could be "more flagrantly wrong, than the assertion of some of our mercantile dons, that the Mechanics have no right to give their Sentiments." By the end of 1770 the issue had spilled over into the colonies' larger political life. "Brother Chip" said to his fellow Philadelphia mechanics that if they did not have "the Liberty of nominating such persons whom we approve," their "Freedom of Voting" was "at an end."

Women, too, began to find that the resistance movement changed their lives and expanded their prospects. The "Sons of Liberty" appealed to the "Daughters of Liberty" to uphold the boycott of British goods. These women met to make homespun cloth as a substitute for British textiles. One report of a spinning bee, in which political education enhanced solidarity, expressed the hope that "the Ladies . . . may vie with the men in contributions to the preservation . . . of their country." The refusal of tea became a powerful sign of women's commitment. They "rejected the poisonous Bohea" (in Rhode Island), "made their breakfast upon Rye Coffee" (New Hampshire), and "totally

---

"REMEMBER THE LADIES . . ."

Some American women were fired by the possibilities of the revolution, among them Abigail Adams, wife of John Adams, a Boston lawyer who was attending the Continental Congress in Philadelphia. Abigail Adams read Paine's Common Sense and agreed with its plea for independence; she wrote to her husband, raising the question of revising laws affecting the status of women. John Adams's response shows the fears of elite patriots that subordinate people of all sorts were throwing off their deference to their social "betters."

ABIGAIL ADAMS TO John Adams, Braintree [Mass.], March 31, 1776
I long to hear that you have declared an independency—and by the way in the new Code of Laws, which I suppose it will be necessary for you to make, I desire you would Remember the Ladies, and be more generous and favorable to them than your ancestors. Do not put such unlimited power into the hand of the Husbands. Remember all Men would be tyrants if they could. If particular care and attention is not paid to the Ladies we are determined to foment a Rebellion, and will not hold ourselves bound by any Laws in which we have no voice, or Representation.

That your Sex are Naturally Tyrannical is a Truth so thoroughly established as to admit of no dispute, but such of you as wish to be happy willingly give up the harsh title of Master for the more tender and endearing one of Friend. Why then, not put it out of the power of the vicious and the Lawless to use us with cruelty and indignity with impunity? Men of Sense in all Ages abhor those customs which treat us only as the vassals of your Sex. Regard us then as Beings placed by providence under your protection and in imitation of the Supreme Being make use of that power only for our happiness.

JOHN ADAMS TO Abigail Adams, Philadelphia, April 14, 1776
As to your extraordinary Code of Laws. I cannot but laugh. We have been told that our Struggle has loosened the bands of Government everywhere. That Children and Apprentices were disobedient—that schools and Colleges were grown turbulent—that Indians slighted their Guardians and Negroes grew insolent to their Masters. But your Letter was the first Intimation that another Tribe more numerous and powerful than all the rest were grown discontented. This is rather too coarse a Compliment but you are so saucy, I won't blot it out.

Depend upon it, We know better than to repeal our Masculine systems. . . . Rather than give up this, which would completely subject Us to the Despotism of the Petticoat, I hope General Washington, and all our brave Heroes would fight.

abstained" (Massachusetts). These women had "commenced perfect citizens," taking on a public role to which many were unaccustomed. Before long, many thought of themselves as "persons of consequence" rather than the "poor females" they had been before.

Early in 1774 an astute young gentleman named Gouverneur Morris found himself standing on a balcony as a New York City meeting debated how to respond to the Intolerable Acts. On one side were the merchants and property-owners, men like Morris himself. On the other were "all the tradesmen, etc., who thought it worthwhile to leave daily labor for the good of the country." "The mob begin to think and to reason," he wrote. "Poor reptiles," he called them, but "with fear and with trembling" he predicted that "ere noon they will bite." Morris was always a bit melodramatic, but he understood what he saw. Nine years of activity in the resistance movement had given these people a new political identity and a voice that would not be stilled.

"A Society of Patriotic Ladies." Cheap prints depicting current events were in great demand in both England and the colonies. This 1775 British print presented a scene in Edenton, North Carolina. Fifty-one women signed a declaration in support of nonimportation, swearing not to drink tea or purchase other British imports. The artist treats the women with scorn, portraying them as ugly, impressionable, and neglectful of their children.

RESISTANCE BECOMES REVOLUTION

The overwhelming majority of colonists were rural people, and independence would never have been achieved without their support. Their entry pushed a movement of resistance toward revolution. In the first crisis, the initial American coalition had created a movement that joined the colonial elite with angry townspeople. Together they successfully resisted the Stamp Act and, in the second crisis, the Townshend taxes. But they could do little more. In the third and final crisis, farmers entered the fray.

Like the earlier movement in the towns, the new coalition began in Massachusetts. In 1772 the Boston town meeting appointed a Committee of Correspondence to rouse the interior. Initially its efforts met with apathy and sometimes suspicion. Farmers lived in a smaller, more isolated world than townspeople, and even the greatest events sometimes passed them by. Some of the people to whom the Boston committee wrote thought that the whole matter of imperial relations was beyond their ken. Others feared that the real purpose of the movement was to let overstocked Boston merchants get rid of their surplus goods in the countryside. As late as 1773 the people of Ashfield, Massachusetts, were more worried about splits in their church than about high politics. But in 1774, country people began to respond, and they did so with increasing vigor.

In August 1774, the Worcester County Court was ready to open for the first time since the passage of the coercive Massachusetts Government Act. Its judges bore new commissions, issued by Governor Gage according to the act's provisions. All Massachusetts patriots agreed that the courts themselves were unconstitutional. They also agreed that the opening of the courts would set a deadly precedent.

The Worcester court never opened, nor did its counterparts in other counties throughout the province. When the judges arrived at the town of Worcester they found virtually the whole male populace of the county armed and assembled in their militia units, town by town. The crowd was orderly but determined, and by the day's end the judges had undergone the humiliating ritual of walking bareheaded through the throng, reading aloud their statements resigning their posts. In one sense this was nothing new, for stamp distributors had been forced to do the same several years earlier. But the previous effort had only prevented one act from going into effect, while the newly forced resignation of judges, recently appointed royal councilors, and lesser officials all over the province went considerably further. By the end of the summer the provincial government had collapsed and the governor's writ went no further than his troops could march. The general court met in Salem in defiance of his order

"The Able Doctor, or America Swallowing the Bitter Draught." Many British prints sympathized with the colonists' claims. In this engraving published in the April 1774 *London Magazine,* America (depicted as an Indian woman) is assaulted by several recognizable British statesmen—principally Lord North, the Prime Minister, who forces tea down her throat (only to have it spat back into his face)—while France and Spain look on and Britannia averts her eyes in shame. By June 1775, the engraving reached the colonies, where it was copied and reproduced by Paul Revere.

that dissolved it. Militia units drilled under officers who did not acknowledge the governor's authority, and town meetings and county conventions took charge of local affairs. The countryside had moved beyond mere resistance to revolution.

The constitutional issue was important, but more was at stake than the legality of the Massachusetts Government Act. Massachusetts farmers may have been isolated, but they had long-standing memories and fears of their own. One reason their ancestors had fled seventeenth-century England was to escape the remnants of feudalism; they wanted no lords over them. In the mid-1680s, when Massachusetts lost its first charter, farmers had briefly been forced to endure the despotic rule of royal officials who sought to use legal technicalities to strip them of their land. When word came of England's expulsion of James II in 1688, farmers united enthusiastically to depose the official usurpers. In the 1740s Massachusetts farmers wanted a land bank in order to lessen the possibility of losing their farms because of debts and taxes. The Stamp Act, with its insistence on payment in hard coin that farmers did not have, raised the specter of losing their land once again. The farmers knew perfectly well that the judges of the county courts were the governor's men long before new commissions were issued, and they did not like it. In 1772 a Boston committee cut to the heart of rural fears when it argued, "If the breath of a British house of commons can originate an act for taking away our money, our lands will go next or be subject to rack rents from haughty and relentless landlords who will ride at ease, while we are trodden in the dirt."

Country folk themselves said little before 1774. But farm families christened newborn boys Oliver, after Cromwell, showing what they were thinking. The Massachusetts Government Act alone did not bring the farmers of Worcester County to their courthouse green. They were moved by their deepest fears, nourished by a century and a half of history.

By the end of 1774, New England was effectively united. So was white Virginia, where, despite the evangelical challenge to their ways, the planter class remained firmly in control. Popular leaders such as Patrick Henry bridged the gap between the "gentle" and "simple" parts of the population as they denounced "luxury" and extolled the "virtue" of the patriot cause. Over the next year and a half the strange combination of stern Puritans and Virginia gentlemen constituted a driving force for strong measures and eventually for independence.

The Virginia and New England leaders found their forum in two successive Continental Congresses. The first met for six weeks at Philadelphia in the autumn of 1774; its successor convened there in April 1775. By the time the second met, war had broken out in Massachusetts, and the Congress found itself a revolutionary government. It adjourned and moved and changed members many times, but it never fully dissolved until it was replaced by the government established by the Constitutional Convention more than a decade later.

When the first Congress met, its radical members sought to make the rest of America see that they shared Boston's problems. The eventual result was the Continental Association, which decreed a complete boycott of European commerce and which called for the creation of popular committees everywhere to enforce it. The task of the Second Congress was more complex. Initially it faced the problem of organizing a war effort. But by early 1776 its members had realized that they would have to face the question of independence. They understood that there was a great deal of opposition to it, for although New England and Virginia were effectively united, most of the rest of America was not.

Prior to independence, the worst disunity and the greatest doubts about militancy came from New York and Pennsylvania, where the colonial elite split sharply. The political group that formed around New York City's DeLancey family chose loyalism early on. In Pennsylvania, Joseph Galloway, longtime political associate of Benjamin

"The Bostonians Paying the Excise-Man, or Tarring and Feathering." A 1774 British print depicts the tarring and feathering of Boston Commissioner of Customs John Malcolm. Tarring and feathering was a ritual of humiliation and public warning that stopped just short of serious injury. In this print, Malcolm is attacked under the Liberty Tree by several Patriots, including a leather-aproned artisan, while the Boston Tea Party occurs in the background (it actually took place four weeks earlier). This anti-Patriot print may have been a response to the sympathetic "The Able Doctor" engraving (see page 147) published earlier the same year.

Franklin, led a sizable portion of the Philadelphia elite in the same direction. These men decided that the dangers posed by the gathering revolutionary movement were greater than those posed by the British themselves. Many others, such as Pennsylvania's John Dickinson and most of the rest of New York's upper class, stood trembling at the brink long after Virginians like Washington and Jefferson and Massachusetts men like John Adams and John Hancock had made up their minds. Until 1776 most moderates did their best to stave off independence. Thereafter they did all they could to achieve a political order in which their own class would be safe and secure.

They had good reason to worry about disorder, for the people of their provinces were not united behind them or anybody else. In New York and Pennsylvania, both intense radicalism and strongly felt popular loyalty to the king were developing. Philadelphia and New York City witnessed the emergence of a new popular political movement made up of mechanics and the old Sons of Liberty. As early as 1773 New York artisans were meeting in taverns in order "to concert matters" and in 1774 they bought a building of their own and named it Liberty Hall. Mechanics organized New York's tea party in March 1774; they were the "poor reptiles" described by Gouverneur Morris as he watched the city's first committee election.

Between 1774 and 1776 these "reptiles" found a new political forum in the popular committee movement. The first step, taken even before Congress's call for committees to enforce the association, was the election of Committees of Correspondence. Their founders deliberately based them as broadly as possible; thus New York City's Committee of Fifty included both fiery radicals and men who would shortly declare their loyalty to the crown. But the election of new committees to enforce the association, and newer ones to coordinate the war effort once fighting broke out, brought marked change. By early 1776 the urban committees were dominated by the same kind of men who had been Sons of Liberty a decade before; the country committees were controlled by obscure farmers. In New York the artisans formed a committee of their own, and in Philadelphia a committee represented the privates in the city's militia. A dramatic alteration had taken place both in how public life was run and in who was running it. The most radical political force of the revolution had been unleashed.

But others held back. Loyalism, the decision to stand with the king rather than with Congress, proved a stubborn problem for the revolutionaries. In a few places, like the prosperous farming country around New York City, loyalists constituted a strong majority. In others, including New York's Hudson and Mohawk valleys, parts of New Jersey, Maryland's eastern shore, and much of the Carolina back-country, they were numerous enough to turn the struggle between Britain and the colonies into a veritable civil war.

People had their reasons for choosing sides. The people on the islands around Manhattan—in present-day Queens and Brooklyn, and on Staten Island—knew that they were vulnerable to Britain's military might. Further, they had never thought that the struggle with Britain involved them. Some Hudson Valley tenants simply followed their loyalist landlords. Poor white Marylanders were deeply suspi-

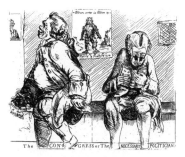

A particularly derisive comment on colonial demands, this 1775 British etching shows two Tory politicians evaluating Patriot documents in a privy (or "necessary" house). A tarred-and-feathered figure decorates the outhouse wall.

cious of the planter elite. As one wheelmaker put it, "The gentlemen were intending to make us all fight [the British to protect] their land and Negroes. . . . If I had a few more white people to join me I could get all the Negroes to back us, and they would do more good in the night than the white people could do in the day." Some Virginia blacks rallied to the king because he promised them freedom in exchange for fighting in the royal forces. Back-country Carolina whites did so because the low-country revolutionary leaders were the same men who had put down their own Regulator movements only a few years before. Most Indians likewise chose the crown. They knew perfectly well that only British restraint stood between them and a land-hungry American people whose hatred of Indians had deep roots in the colonial experience.

Americans entered the final crisis with Britain, then, as a divided people, not a united one. In one sense a nation was in birth. Among the merchants, slaveholders, farmers, and urban artisans and laborers who made up the revolutionary coalition there was a powerful feeling that they were part of a truly grand cause and a sudden realization that this was their moment to remake their world as they wanted it to be. But what some felt as exhilarating possibility others experienced as reason for fear. Some swallowed their fear and decided to make the best of what they could not avoid, "swimming with a stream," as one elite New Yorker put it, that "it is impossible to stem." But others decided that without a king and what he stood for, life as they knew it would be impossible.

The choice was not often easy. As a man named John Commons said to a clandestine meeting of upstate New York farmers, "Those who thought the Congress was in the right should go, and those who thought the king was right should stay." But Commons himself "did not know who was right." His voice was not as loud nor nearly as eloquent as those of Tom Paine and Thomas Jefferson, but Commons's ambivalence suggests the uncertainty some Americans felt at the moment of independence.

A PEOPLE'S WAR

War finally broke out in April 1775. Over the winter since the closing of the Massachusetts courts, New Englanders had prepared for combat. In occupied Boston, a committee of artisans watched troop movements closely, knowing that sooner or later General Gage would act. In the villages people gathered supplies while the militias drilled in earnest. A Massachusetts provincial congress met to replace the old general court and began to plan for an army of up to fifteen thousand men. But that army existed only on paper when Gage dispatched a midnight expedition to Concord to capture supplies hidden there.

The Boston artisans' committee dispatched Paul Revere and several other riders to warn the interior, but the march of Gage's troops could not have been kept secret in any case. When the British detachment arrived at Lexington, the local militia was arrayed on the green with their muskets drawn. They intended no more than a symbolic confrontation, but someone fired. A few minutes later eight villagers were dead. The expedition marched on toward its goal.

The outward march was easy, but the return to Boston was not. Along the entire route, farmers and mechanics sniped at Gage's men from behind trees and rocks. Their fire was pitiless. These citizen-soldiers, without uniforms, ill-equipped, and barely trained, threw up siege lines around Boston, and in June they showed again how well they could fight. Gage decided to dislodge them from Breed's (Bunker) Hill, overlooking Charlestown. In the end the British succeeded, but only at so great a price that they did not try to take any more emplacements.

"The Battle of Lexington." One of four prints based on drawings sketched shortly after the battle at Lexington, by Amos Doolittle, a twenty-one-year-old engraver who visited the site as a member of the Connecticut militia. Although the location is rendered with accuracy, the drawing misrepresents the behavior of British troops, whose discipline was less than perfect. The four prints, on sale by December 1775, were the first American illustrations of warfare during the Revolution.

The Continental Congress had many reasons to name George Washington to command its ragtag army. One was his reputation as a military leader in the French and Indian War; another was his availability, which he signaled by wearing his militia uniform when he took his seat in Congress in Philadelphia. But most of the reasons were political. Washington was a southerner, and the appointment of someone like him was necessary if the war was to be more than a New England affair. Most of all, he was a wealthy member of Virginia's ruling class, and he would bring prestige and support to his position.

From the start Washington's goal was to command "a respectable army." As he consolidated his command, conditions in the army became ever more like those of the redcoats his troops were fighting. The rude, often dirty democracy of the war's initial months gave way to harsh discipline. Washington and his ideas about discipline perfectly symbolized the hopes of many members of Congress for independent America. The departure of the British, when it came, would lead to an ordered society under the control of an American elite.

During the six long years between the first shots and the final American victory, the Continental Army campaigned in New York,

A print, possibly made in America, presents the plundering retreat of British troops on April 19, 1775. The unknown artist chose to portray the King's soldiers as donkeys, and the advancing Massachusetts troops in disciplined ranks (in fact, they fought as guerrillas, harassing the British from the shelter of houses, trees, and rocks).

The Retreat

From Concord to Lexington of the Army of Wild Irish Asses Defeated by the Brave American Militia

Mr Deacon Mr Loeings Mr Mulikens Mr Bonds Houses and Barn all Plunder'd and Burnt on April 19th

...d according to Act June 12 1775

New Jersey, Pennsylvania, and the South. Its finest moments came with the victories at Saratoga, in upstate New York, in 1777 and at Yorktown, Virginia, in 1781. The first victory, in which Washington had no direct part, ended a major British attempt to cut off New England from the rest of America. One consequence of the patriot victory at Saratoga was to bring France into the war on the American side. The second victory, at Yorktown, was masterminded by Washington. The American forces trapped a major British regiment that had marched north from the Carolinas under Lord Cornwallis. For years Washington's essential strategy had been to demonstrate that the British could not win the war, and here was the final proof. But there were also many bad times. One of the worst was the loss of Long Island and New York City in August 1776. Washington's retreat was brilliant, thanks largely to the fleet of fishermen who ferried his army across the East River just when the British were in a position to crush it. But New York City remained in British hands until 1783.

Throughout the war, service was dangerous, conditions often appalling, and supplies frequently so scarce that soldiers froze and starved. The terrible winter at Valley Forge, outside Philadelphia, was not the army's worst trial by cold; that came in 1779–80, when it spent six weeks at Morristown, New Jersey, on one-eighth rations, with pay five months in arrears. As that ordeal was nearing its end, two Connecticut regiments "paraded under arms" to demand better conditions, but were eventually dispersed by Pennsylvania units. The following January the Pennsylvanians themselves, together with Jerseymen, broke into open mutiny, which was crushed only by the executions of the leaders. As a private named Joseph Plumb Martin said in 1780, the soldiers were cursing themselves for their "imbecility in staying there and starving . . . for an ungrateful people." Nor did the agony end

". . . I TOOK MY STAND"

Sarah Osborne was a servant in the household of a blacksmith in Albany, New York, when she met and married Aaron Osborne, a blacksmith and Revolutionary War veteran. Without Sarah's knowledge, Aaron reenlisted in the Continental Army and insisted that his wife travel with him. Sarah ultimately agreed to "volunteer" for the duration of the war. A selection from her diary provides a rare glimpse at the role women played in winning the war for independence.

WE . . . MARCHED IMMEDIATELY for a place called Williamsburg, [Virginia,] myself alternately on horseback and on foot. There arrived, we remained two days till the army all came in by land and then marched for Yorktown, or Little York as it was then called. The [New] York troops were posted at the right, the Connecticut troops next, and the French to the left. In about one day, we reached the place of encampment about one mile from Yorktown. I was on foot as were the other females. My attention was arrested by the appearance of a large plain between us and Yorktown and an entrenchment thrown up. I saw a number of dead Negroes lying round, whom I was told the British had driven out of the town and left to starve, or were first starved and then thrown out. I took my stand just back of the American tents, say about a mile from the town, and busied myself washing, mending, and cooking for the soldiers, in which I was assisted by the other females; some men washed their own clothing. I heard the roar of the artillery for a number of days, and the last night the Americans threw up entrenchments; it was a misty, foggy night, rather wet but not rainy. Every soldier [built] for himself, and I afterwards went into the entrenchments. My husband was there throwing up entrenchments, and I cooked and carried in beef, and bread, and coffee (in a gallon pot) to the soldiers in the entrenchment.

"The Bucks of America." The flag carried by Boston's black militia unit, one of three African-American companies that served in the Continental Army.

with the ultimate victory at Yorktown. For almost two years the army encamped at Newburgh, New York, awaiting its final payment of wages. Disgruntled officers seriously considered a coup against Congress; Washington foiled them with an effective speech rather than with the firing squads he used against the enlisted men. The soldiers finally disbanded with no more than a token settlement for what they were owed.

The war effort mobilized many kinds of labor. Most of the soldiers were young, poor people who had been apprentices, laborers, landless farm boys, and slaves. Some had been drafted; some had volunteered; some had gone as paid substitutes for richer men. Some were African-Americans (from the northern colonies), perhaps serving in place of

Thayendanegea. Guy Johnson, who succeeded his father-in-law Sir William Johnson as British superintendent of Indian affairs, is the ostensible subject of Benjamin West's painting, but it is the shadowy figure of Thayendanegea, or Joseph Brant, that characterizes the picture. This Mohawk chief, educated at New Hampshire's Indian School (later Dartmouth College), saw the war as an opportunity to gain Indian independence; he sided with the British in exchange for specific concessions. After a brief visit to Great Britain in 1775–76 (where this picture was painted), Thayendanegea returned to the colonies. Throughout the war, he led Iroquois raids on New York frontier settlements.

A detail from an English printed handkerchief represents the contributions of three American sisters to the struggle for independence: while their husbands fight, they run the farm—milling, baking, and, here, plowing.

their masters, more likely having run away in search of their freedom. When a whole British army surrendered at Saratoga, revolutionary leaders tried their best to recruit prisoners of war. Among them were many Hessian mercenaries, from the German state of Hesse, whose deployment by George III was one of the major grievances listed in the Declaration of Independence. Several thousand women traveled with the army. Most were "on the ration" as cooks, nurses, laundresses, orderlies, and gravediggers. They performed services that the army needed desperately, and they endured everything the soldiers did except battle itself.

Without this motley crew of poor whites, slaves, foreigners, and women, the British would have triumphed easily. The citizen-soldiers, the artisans who dropped their tools and the farmers who stepped from behind their plows to join their militia units on short-term duty, made a vital contribution, but their enthusiasm did not always last. As Washington himself fully understood, America's greatest military need was for an army that could stay together, however much it retreated, however often it was defeated, and however much its soldiers suffered. As long as such an army survived, the British could not conquer America.

PEOPLE'S GOVERNMENT

The Declaration of Independence, penned by Thomas Jefferson, has long been regarded as the classical expression of American revolutionary ideology. The document not only stated that "these United Colonies are, and of right ought to be, Free and Independent States," but did so in language that was, in its day, as radical as it was eloquent. The Declaration insisted that "the history of the present King of Great Britain is a history of repeated injuries and usurpations, all having in direct object the establishment of an absolute Tyranny over these States." The ultimate source of sovereignty lay not in government, and certainly not in kingship, but rather in "the consent of the governed," that is, the American people. And according to the Declaration, "It is their right, it is their duty, to throw off" oppressive government. Americans were exercising their right of revolution.

But the Declaration went even further, boldly proclaiming at the outset, "We hold these truths to be self-evident, that all men are created equal, that they are endowed by their Creator with certain unalienable rights, that among these are Life, Liberty, and the pursuit of Happiness." These lines argued that the proper foundation of government was a universal truth evident not simply to an expensively educated political elite, but to the common sense of all men; that these men, by their very existence, embody—and hence, in political terms, fully deserve—"unalienable rights"; and that the purpose of society and government is the fulfillment and protection of the needs of its citizens—their lives, liberties, and pursuit of happiness.

The Declaration was more than an abstract philosophical statement. It was a political document designed to bring unity to the revolutionary coalition—the farmers, artisans, laborers, slaveholders, professionals, and merchants who in 1776 made up the revolutionary movement. The emphasis on equality, self-evident truths, and broadly held rights had special appeal for the recently mobilized popular elements, and in fact that language would not have been in the Declaration if not for the political importance of common folk in the movement. But there were limits to the democratic thrust of the Declaration. Jefferson, despite his ownership of a number of African-American slaves, sought, in an early draft, to attack the slave trade as oppressive to "the sacred rights of life and liberty," of "human nature itself." These words were deleted, however, by other members of the Continental Congress, whose economic interests severely limited their vision of equality, liberty, freedom, and rights.

When the Declaration was finally signed, it symbolized the final collapse of the old political order. A ramshackle system of local committees and state conventions, culminating in the Continental Congress itself, took the place of royal institutions. The congressmen tended to be people of prominence and position, such as the Adams cousins, Samuel and John, or the New York landowner Robert R. Livingston, or Benjamin Franklin, or, until his appointment as commander-in-chief, George Washington. But the town and county committees and the state conventions were full of lesser lights, men who found in the Revolution their chance to leap to political prominence. Abraham Yates, the ambitious cobbler-turned-lawyer from Albany, New York, was one such man. Until the Albany committee made him its chairman, his ambitions had been thwarted, as we have seen, by the great men whom he scorned as "high flyers."

By the summer of 1775, the committees, and not the remnants of royal government, held real power, transacting "all such matters as they shall conceive may tend to the welfare of the American cause." Committees raised militia units, organized supplies, tried and jailed the Revolution's enemies, and began to control goods and prices. They called mass meetings "to take the sense of the citizens." When New York's royal governor, who had fled to a British warship for his own safety, tried to counter the movement by calling an election for the provincial assembly, the committees frustrated him by seeing that radicals won. In any case, the provincial congress was ready to keep the assembly from interfering "with political subjects."

The movement started slowest—but ultimately went farthest—in Philadelphia. In the beginning, moderates controlled both the city government and the provincial assembly, not daring to choose either outright loyalism or open commitment to the Revolution. But opposition to their hesitation mounted, culminating in June 1776, when the popular committee pushed the old assembly to final collapse and inaugurated the Revolution's boldest experiment in popular democracy. The committee had the support of people like the city's militia privates, who organized a committee of their own in order to express their demands. The privates wanted to elect their own officers (as was sometimes done in frontier militias) rather than have them appointed from on high. They wanted to end the legal right that allowed the well-heeled to buy their way out of military service by providing substitutes. The privilege was originally a gesture to Quaker pacifism, but to the privates it seemed mere class advantage. They also wanted the militia to abandon fancy uniforms and wear plain hunting shirts, officers and men alike.

Amid this popular ferment, Tom Paine produced *Common Sense* in January 1776. His great pamphlet was an impassioned attack on the British monarchy and everything it stood for. King George was "the royal brute of England." The history of the crown he wore could not "bear examining," for William the Conqueror was no more than "a French Bastard landing with an armed Banditti and establishing himself King." Paine attacked the whole principle of monarchy and succession that "everywhere . . . have laid (not this or that Kingdom only) but the world in blood and ashes." Being part of the British Empire brought no benefit to the colonies, for "England consults the good of this country no farther than it answers for her own purpose." Paine turned what had begun as a family quarrel about taxes into an issue of importance for all humanity: "Freedom hath been hunted round the Globe. . . . O! receive the fugitive, and prepare in time an asylum for mankind."

Paine was a republican who believed that people could govern themselves without the artificial distinctions of monarchy and nobility: " 'Tis the Republican and not the Monarchical part of the Constitution of England which Englishmen glory

". . . COMMON SENSE AND A PLAIN UNDERSTANDING"

When a convention was called in 1776 to frame a constitution for the state of Pennsylvania, James Cannon, a radical patriot leader, advised ordinary Pennsylvanians to be certain to select delegates who would respect the rights and authority of the people. Cannon addressed the following broadside to the members of the Philadelphia militia, setting forth the qualities —including "common Sense and a plain Understanding"— he thought such delegates should possess.

A GOVERNMENT MADE for the common Good should be framed by Men who can have no Interest besides the common Interest of Mankind. It is the Happiness of America that there is no Rank above that of Freeman existing in it; and much of our future welfare and Tranquillity will depend on its remaining so forever; for this Reason, great and over-grown rich Men will be improper to be trusted, they will be too apt to be framing Distinctions in Society, because they will reap the Benefits of all such Distinctions. . . . Honesty, common Sense, and a plain Understanding, when unbiased by sinister Motives, are fully equal to the Task—Men of like Passions and Interests with ourselves are most likely to frame us a good Constitution. . . . Some who have been very backward in declaring you a free People, will be very forward in offering themselves to frame your Constitution; but trust them not, however well recommended.

in." He wanted his republic to be simple. There was no need for elaborate institutions to balance one social interest against another. Instead, "let the assemblies be annual, with a President only." Paine had made himself the voice of the artisans and farmers whom the revolution had roused, as his pamphlet's enormous sale showed. His call for independence and simple republican government reverberated across the continent. In the words of one enthusiastic pamphlet, "the people" themselves would make "the best governors."

In the summer of 1776 many who shared Paine's ideas came to power in Pennsylvania and fashioned their own state constitution. It established a single-chamber state legislature, elected annually by all taxpaying adult males. There were no property requirements for holding office. Abandoning the idea of a powerful governorship, the new constitution lodged executive power in a president and council, whose job would simply be to serve the legislature. Except on "occasions of special necessity," every bill that came before the legislature was to be "printed for the consideration of the people" before it became law.

People elsewhere felt the same exhilarating sense that the ways of the old order could simply be abandoned. Like Pennsylvania, the states of Delaware, New Hampshire, and South Carolina all chose the title "president" for their chief executive. It bore none of the connotations of arbitrary, quasi-royal power that "governor" had acquired. Vermont, tearing itself free of New York at the beginning of 1777, simply copied Pennsylvania's radical constitution. Vermont's Green Mountain Boys had for a decade waged a guerrilla struggle against New York and its oppressive land system. They had a great deal in common with other rural rebels: the New Jersey and Hudson Valley land-rioters, the Regulators of North and South Carolina, the Massachusetts farmers who revolted against their state government in 1786, and the back-country Pennsylvanians who rebelled against the federal government in 1794. But unlike every other rural insurgency, the Vermonters succeeded. They learned about the Pennsylvania constitution from Dr. Thomas Young, former Son of Liberty, member of Tom Paine's circle, lifelong enemy of landlordism, and close friend of their own leader, Ethan Allen. That they modeled their state on his suggestions demonstrated how much farmers like themselves and the urban artisans who surrounded Paine had in common.

But other Americans were horrified rather than elated by these democratic possibilities. John Adams, as enthusiastic for independence as Paine himself, wrote a major pamphlet, *Thoughts on Government*, to counter Paine's simple republicanism. To his mind, it was impossible to live without "balanced" institutions, especially an upper legislative house that would be the preserve of the rich. The state constitutions adopted by Maryland, New York, and Massachusetts owed a great deal more to Adams than to Paine. Maryland put as much distance as possible between its people and rulers, with stiff property requirements for voting, stiffer ones for holding office, and long intervals between elections. New York and Massachusetts both created state senates that were essentially intended to represent property, not people. They established strong governorships, whose holders would be independent of the legislature rather than servants of it. In Adams's phrase, their goal was to "glide insensibly" from a colonial society in which people knew their place to a republican society founded on the principles of hierarchy and order.

The debate on the state constitutions revealed the lines of stress within the coalition that had won independence. The same essential groups and forces were present everywhere, but the balance varied from state to state. In Pennsylvania the men of moderation panicked at the moment of independence, leaving those who supported Paine's radical ideas in control. In New York, moderates kept their heads and used "well-timed delays, indefatigable industry, and minute . . . attention to every favourable circumstance" to maintain their position. In Maryland the planter class took fright and built a fortress of institutions around itself. In Virginia, where slavery limited the political threat of the lower orders, the elite nonetheless created a constitution that kept their own kind firmly in control. The ideological question at issue was whether public-spirited citizens could govern themselves directly, through the simplest of political institutions. The social question was what sort of people would rule—"the better sort," who had long held sway, or the artisans and farmers and small-scale traders for whom Tom Paine spoke in Common Sense.

The war for independence opened yet another fissure, this one over economic problems. In order to finance the war, Congress and the separate state governments had to print ever larger quantities of paper money, and the result was the worst inflation America had ever known. Congress resolved the worst of the problem in 1779 by drastically devaluing its currency. But even that did not end the chronic shortage of goods brought about by the British blockade of American ports and by the huge demands of the American, French, and British armies.

People who were trapped by inflation and shortage—later, as we shall see, by glut and depression—tried to make sense of what was happening and to find a way to deal with it. Many of them, especially those who had read Paine so avidly in 1776, turned to ancient tradition, claiming that in a good society, the public interest ought to come before private gain. If supplies were scarce, it was because "hoarders" were holding them back. If prices were rising, it was the fault of "speculators." These circumstances entitled people to act for themselves, and they did. Crowds, often made up of women, fought wartime inflation with the rituals of popular price-setting. News that a trader had a supply of tea or salt often earned him a visit from a crowd, who offered a "just price" before taking what they wanted. It happened in the Hudson Valley, in the New England interior, and in seacoast Massachusetts towns. Soldiers in the Continental Army sometimes protected the mobs of women. In Boston "Joyce, Jun." led the crowds that carted monopolizers out of town.

In 1779 people all over the North revived their revolutionary committees to deal with the crisis. As early as 1776 a few people had wanted to make popular committees a permanent part of the new order; New York City's mechanics even sent a strongly worded message to the provincial congress demanding that citizens be able to revive their committees whenever they wanted. But many people probably expected them to disappear. The constitution that New York finally adopted in 1777 even called them "temporary expedients . . . to exist no longer than the grievances of the people should remain without redress."

Now "the people" had decided that the economy was a major problem and that their republican governments were doing nothing about it. In 1774 and 1775, the problem had been the British. By 1779 it was "overbearing merchants, a swarm of monopolizers, an infernal gang of Tories." To blame distress on monopolizers was nothing new, but to try to eliminate it through popular committees was. Americans fused an ancient tradition of economic corporatism and an immediate revolutionary experience of direct political involvement.

But not everyone favored regulation by revolutionary committee. Businessmen responded to the Continental Association by defending their "undoubted . . . liberty, in eating, drinking, buying, selling, communing, and acting what, with whom, and as we please." By 1779 critics of regulation included Tom Paine, who, like his fellow Briton Adam Smith, had concluded that a free market would be liberating and that it need not lead to the rich trampling the poor. Some artisans, such as the Philadelphia tanners, attacked

". . . WE CANNOT LIVE WITHOUT BREAD"

In December 1778 a Philadelphia resident, styling himself Mobility, wrote the following letter to a local newspaper, attacking monopolizers and calling, in no uncertain terms, for strong measures by crowds to guarantee the distribution of bread, "the Staff of Life."

THIS COUNTRY HAS been reduced to the brink of ruin by the infamous practices of Monopolizers and Forestallers. Not satisfied with monopolizing European and West-Indian goods, they have lately monopolized the Staff of Life. Hence, the universal cry of the scarcity and high price of Flour. It has been found in Britain and France, that the People have always done themselves justice when the scarcity of bread has arisen from the avarice of forestallers. They have broken open magazines [warehouses]—appropriated stores to their own use without paying for them—and in some instances have hung up the culprits who have created their distress, without judge or jury. Hear this and tremble, ye enemies to the freedom and happiness of your country. We can live without sugar, molasses, and rum—but we cannot live without bread. Hunger will break through stone walls, and the resentment excited by it may end in your destruction.

the committee revival and declared that trade ought to "be as free as air, uninterrupted as the tide." The most vocal critics were great merchants like Philadelphian Robert Morris and the small storekeepers who had to deal with the angry men and women who demanded tea and other commodities at a just price.

These merchants already knew that to get what they wanted, they had to act together as a political force. Despite the popular radicalism of 1776, they had won major victories in the writing of the constitutions of many states. In Pennsylvania, where they had been routed in 1776, they founded a "Republican Society" dedicated to the twin goals of promoting a free market and abolishing the state's radical constitution. But they accomplished relatively little. Even in Maryland, where men of wealth virtually monopolized office, they were forced to recognize "the wisdom of sacrifice" and to give in to popular demands.

Only in Massachusetts did the forces of hard money, free trade, and balanced political institutions get their way fully, with disastrous results for inland debtor farmers. The state took until 1780 to adopt its constitution, and when the new government took effect, the men of commerce took control of it. They adopted firm policies. Unlike its neighbors, Massachusetts would have no legal-tender paper currency; it would give no protection to debtors, whether their creditors were American, loyalist, or British. If farmers and artisans were ruined because they could not pay their debts or their taxes, it was regrettable, but no less a necessity.

When peace and victory finally came with the signing of the Treaty of Paris in 1783, they brought even more problems in their wake. American ports reopened to British commerce, resulting in an immediate burst of consumption, for people with money were hungry for luxuries that British merchants were delighted to supply. But boom turned rapidly to glut and glut to depression. The slump lasted through 1784, 1785, and 1786.

When the postwar depression struck, British creditors called in debts from their American trading partners, who in turn passed on the demand: from Boston to the county towns like Worcester and Springfield; from there to small villages, where country storekeepers faced the choice of going bankrupt themselves or making their farmer customers pay up. The depression was bad everywhere, but in some states the laws offered some protection to debtors. But not in Massachusetts. The government itself made matters worse by its tax demands, insisting on the same hard currency that merchants wanted. Of course the farmers had none, and once again they found themselves haunted by their worst fear, that they would lose their land and suffer degradation to the status of tenant or hired laborer.

The result, in 1786, was Shays's Rebellion, named for the former

Shays's Rebellion. The portraits of Daniel Shays and Job Shattuck, leaders of the Massachusetts "Regulators," appeared on the cover of *Bickerstaff's Boston Almanack* in 1787.

captain in the Continental Army who became its leader. From the farmers' perspective the problem in 1786 was much the same as 1774, as was their response: they gathered under arms and closed the courts. But in 1774 they had worked in concert with Boston radicals. Now some of those Bostonians, allied with conservative merchants, controlled the state government, and as far as they were concerned, the courts now under attack were wholly legitimate, for they were created by a constitution that was the work of the people of Massachusetts. Bostonians also considered the courts utterly necessary, for without known laws and courts to enforce them, commerce could not be carried on.

The government responded by sending General Benjamin Lincoln and a force of well-organized militiamen to the west to put down the growing insurrection. Shays and his ragtag army of farmers proved no match, and they scattered. Shays and a few others fled the state into exile. Four leaders were condemned to death, then were reprieved just as they were about to be hanged. Chief Justice William Cushing, who tried the case, branded them the worst offenders imaginable. They were men who had tried "to overturn all government and order, to shake off all restraints, human and divine," men who had given themselves up "wholly to the power of the most restless, malevolent, destructive, tormenting passions." This was public theater, intended to show the farmers of Massachusetts who was in control. It had the desired effect, as individuals and whole towns soon dropped to their knees to beg forgiveness. "'Tis true that I have been a committeeman," wrote one, but "I am sincerely sorry . . . and hope it will be overlooked and pardoned."

Although the Shaysite rebels had tasted victory over Britain only a dozen years before, they now suffered defeat at the hands of men who had once been their revolutionary comrades-in-arms. In their defeat they began to learn the most basic lesson of the politics of the new order: The old notion of small communities defending themselves against outsiders was dead. Only people with common interests who organized themselves and formally entered the political arena had a chance. The farmers showed that they had learned this lesson in state elections held the very next year. The hard-money governor James Bowdoin lost his seat to the popular John Hancock. New men flooded into the legislature, most of them from western towns that for years had not bothered to send delegates. Hancock, like Bowdoin, was both a Bostonian and a man of commerce. But he was a well-practiced, popular politician, and he, like his counterparts in other states, did recognize "the wisdom of sacrifice" and "the genius of the people." Massachusetts had changed: symbolically, at least, the elite made concessions to the demands of ordinary people.

Massachusetts was the only state that exploded in the late 1780s, but there were "combustibles in every state," for the revolution had raised more questions than it had answered. One of these was slavery. For a white Virginian of the early eighteenth century, such as the diarist William Byrd II, owning other human beings was simply a fact of life. But for many planters of the revolutionary generation, including both Washington and Jefferson, it was a problem, one that they agonized over but could not resolve. For a few southerners, including the Virginia lawyer George Wythe, who tried as a judge to rule slavery illegal, it had become an abomination.

A swelling number of northerners agreed. They included notables such as Alexander Hamilton, who freed the slaves that his marriage brought him and helped found the New York Manumission Society. They also included many ordinary people. As one obscure New Yorker commented in 1785, slavery was "cruelty in the extreme" and "the severest reproach" to the new nation. One of its most effective enemies was the same Massachusetts justice who condemned the Shaysite leaders. In 1780 he handed down a ruling that abolished slavery in his state.

But the most important abolitionists were African-Americans themselves, who seized the revolutionary moment to take their own first steps toward liberation. Before the revolution, free blacks were rare, only a few thousand strong, but by the end of the revolutionary era (1820) their numbers had swelled to nearly two hundred thousand. Some won their freedom by fighting with the British, beginning with the few who answered the call of Lord Dunmore, the royal governor of Virginia who promised freedom to slaves who rallied to him in 1775, and ending with the many who fled with the last British forces when they finally evacuated. Several thousand more won it by fighting on the American side. Jehu Grant, a New England slave, fled his master and enlisted in the Continental Army "when I saw liberty

"... INALIENABLE RIGHT TO FREEDOM"

Throughout the revolutionary era, scores of slaves signed petitions that linked their demands for freedom with the cause of American independence. Below is the text of one such petition presented to the Massachusetts legislature.

TO THE HONORABLE Counsel and House of Representatives for the State of Massachusetts in General Court Assembled, January 13, 1777:
The petition of a great number of blacks detained in a state of slavery in the bowels of a free and Christian country humbly show that your petitioners [state] that they have in common with all other men a natural and inalienable right to that freedom which the Great Parent of the heavens has bestowed equally on all mankind and which they have never forfeited by any compact or agreement whatever. They were unjustly dragged by the hand of cruel power from their dearest friends and some of them even torn from the embraces of their tender parents—from a populous, pleasant, and plentiful country, and in violation of laws of nature and of nations, and in defiance of all the tender feelings of humanity brought here to be sold like beasts of burden and like them condemned to slavery for life....

Every principle from which America has acted in the course of their unhappy difficulties with Great Britain pleads stronger than a thousand arguments in favor of your petitioners, and they, therefore, humbly request that your honors give this petition its due weight and consideration and cause an act of the Legislature to be passed whereby they may be restored to the enjoyments of that which is the natural right of all men—and their children who were born in this land of liberty—not to be held as slaves.

poles and the people all engaged for the support of freedom; I could not but like and be pleased with such a thing." A few brought lawsuits, one of which led to Justice Cushing's decision that if Massachusetts was to be part of a virtuous republic, it could not tolerate slavery. Many thousands literally seized their liberty by running away from their masters in the chaos of war, usually along "the Philadelphia Road," to the city where the abolitionist movement was strongest.

Economic and ideological changes propelled the movement toward freedom. The decreasing importance of slavery in the northern economies increased the frequency of manumission, as did the transition in the upper South from tobacco to grain. These changes—along with the staying power of the egalitarian and libertarian rhetoric of the Revolution, and the emphasis on the equal brotherhood of believers within a surging evangelical movement—strengthened abolitionism and the political will of the African-American community to gain and secure their freedom. Slaves turned the rhetoric of the revolution to their own ends. Although Jefferson and other leaders obviously did not have their own slaves in mind when they adopted the Declaration of Independence, holding that "all men are created equal," a few years later a group of New Hampshire slaves had themselves firmly in mind when they claimed that freedom was "an inherent right of the human species, not to be surrendered but by consent."

Moreover, a growing unity came to characterize African-American life, for both slave and free alike. In the urban north, the recently emancipated built families, households, and neighborhoods; they organized their own churches and schools; they formed voluntary associations like the African Union Society of Newport, Rhode Island, and the Free African Society of Philadelphia. They created the institutional foundation, the scaffolding of freedom, of African-American society itself, for both themselves and their descendents.

Among whites rich, middling, and poor, among blacks, among women as well as men, the Revolution encouraged people to think that it was both possible and necessary to take control of their own livelihoods. Merchants and commercial farmers gained greater access to commercial markets, and more farmers gained greater access to land made available through confiscation of loyalist and royal property and through the opening of vast new western territories now in the federal public domain. Some Americans took the logic even further and saw that they could take control of their societies, even though this meant certain conflict with people whose interests and ideas were different from their own. No group understood this more fully than the American elite. In 1787 and 1788 they went on the offensive in the last great struggle of the era, intending to resolve the question of what kind of place an independent America would be. The result was the Federal Constitution.

THE GRAND FEDERAL EDIFICE

One year after the suppression of Shays' Rebellion, a group of the self-selected elite met in a special convention in Philadelphia in the summer of 1787 to draft the Constitution of the United States. The document went into effect in 1788, after more special conventions in nine of the thirteen states had ratified it. Two more of the original states ratified the document before the year was out, and the two holdouts, Rhode Island and North Carolina, finally entered the union early in George Washington's presidency. The political revolution was over.

The Philadelphia convention was very much an elite affair. Most of the delegates were merchants, lawyers, landholders, and southern planters. Among them were Robert Morris of Philadelphia, the "financier" of the Revolution, and New York's Alexander Hamilton, who had climbed from obscurity to fame as Washington's aide-de-camp, to wealth as the son-in-law of a great New York landlord, and to power as an essayist, lawyer, and politician. James Madison of Virginia—who had already written a private essay, "The Vices of the Political System of the United States," which outlined most of the changes the Constitution would make—was a leading figure. In the chair of the convention sat the stately George Washington.

Almost all of the delegates had experienced the Revolution at the center of the storm. They had been army officers, large-scale traders, members of the Continental Congress, and ambassadors. They had seen firsthand the troubles of organizing a full-scale war. They had been embarrassed time and again by America's inability to deal straightforwardly with foreign diplomats and generals. They had seen the states make a mockery of the clauses in the peace treaty that pledged no further harassment of loyalists. They had watched the states pass postwar laws to protect debtors, heedless of the interests of creditors and the international reputation of America's merchants.

What they had not seen, or at least had not experienced with any great sympathy, was the radical democratic possibilities that the Revolution had opened for men unlike themselves. For most of the nabobs who gathered in the City of Brotherly Love, a crowd was nothing but a vicious mob, a popular committee was democracy gone mad, price controls were a device for the poor to rob the rich, and the presence of farmers and artisans in major public office was an absurdity. Their basic conviction was that something had gone profoundly wrong in the states, especially when the supporters of paper money began to get out of hand. Shays' Rebellion was merely the most striking evidence of this widespread trend. The convention delegates were

Solid and Pure. The flag carried by master, journeymen, and apprentice pewterers in the July 1788 parade in New York City celebrating ratification of the Constitution.

republicans, committed to the belief that a government must rest on its people's consent. But for the most part they were not democrats: they had little faith that ordinary people could run society wisely or well.

History has called them "the founding fathers" or "the framers"; they themselves chose the word "federalists." They were groping toward a new understanding of republicanism. The idea of a republic was of course nothing new, but after the experience of the ancient Greeks and Romans, virtually all thinkers had agreed that a republic was possible only under special circumstances. A republic had to be small, both in size and in population. Its people had to be virtuous, thinking of the common good rather than private interests. They had to be bound together by a single economic interest. A republic might be commercial, like the Renaissance city-state of Venice, or it might be agrarian, like the cantons of Switzerland. But put the two interests together, many believed, and they would clash until tyranny arose. The Massachusetts experience seemed to prove it. By 1787, republicanism had a long history of failure. It seemed to those who met in Philadelphia that America might yet prove another tragic example.

But some of the federalists took a new point of departure. James Madison articulated it most clearly in the tenth and fifty-first of the

Federalist papers that he, Hamilton, and John Jay published in New York during the ratification campaign. Madison abandoned many of the traditional notions: instead of a small republic, he saw possibilities for an extensive one; instead of a single virtuous public interest, he hoped for many private interests, all jostling and competing. If enough interests were present in a large enough arena, Madison reasoned, none would be powerful enough to oppress the others. "Extend the sphere," he wrote, "and you take in a greater variety of parties and interests; you make it less probable that a majority . . . will have a common motive to invade the rights of other citizens."

It was a major breakthrough in political thought. But it was no less a complete repudiation of many of the values and ideas that had guided colonial development and even the Revolution itself. Madison's political thought initiated a long transition from classical republicanism to modern liberalism, from an emphasis on public virtue and a certain equality of condition to a new stress on self-interest and equality of opportunity. His political notions had a great deal in common with the economic ideas developed a decade earlier by Adam Smith in *The Wealth of Nations*. Though unaware of the fact, Madison had fixed the cornerstone of American liberalism—the ideology of free trade and competitive individualism under which both the American republic and American capitalism would develop in the century that followed.

The framers' first solution, then, was a large republic that dwarfed all previous attempts to live without a monarch. Their second was to give that republic a much stronger government. Since 1781 the United States in Congress Assembled (as the country called itself) had operated under the Articles of Confederation, the first American constitution. Congress could make war, peace, and foreign policy, and it could create an army, a navy, and a state bureaucracy. It controlled the western lands ceded by the British in the peace treaty. But it could not tax. It had no executive to do its will and no courts to enforce its laws and treaties. Each state had a single vote, regardless of its size. A measure of the success of government under the Articles was its ability to win the war and negotiate an extremely favorable peace. A measure of its failure was its inability to pay its debts, enforce the terms of the peace treaty, or even resolve the issue of Vermont's independence from New York.

Virtually everyone agreed that the Articles needed to be changed, if only so Congress could pay its foreign debts and win financial credibility. But this was no easy matter, because changing the Articles required the consent of the legislatures of all thirteen original states. Further, Hamilton and Madison wanted more than a few additional powers. Since 1782 Hamilton had campaigned for a stronger central government run by men "whose principles are not of the *leveling kind.*" He pressed his argument relentlessly in his court cases, essays, correspondence, and activities as a New York assemblyman. One of his major goals was to end the dominance of a coalition of New York's farmers and artisans. One of his major achievements was to convince his state's squabbling landlords and merchants to unite in their own class interest as a coherent political force. His goal during the constitutional convention was a stronger and more elitist government that would guarantee opportunity for ambitious men like himself and security for people who had "anything to lose."

Madison's great contribution was to set the agenda at the Philadelphia meeting. The stated purpose of the convention was to propose amendments to the Articles of Confederation. But at Madison's prodding, another Virginian proposed "amendments" that completely abolished the original document and offered a fresh start. The most drastic change was that special conventions, not the state legislatures, would decide the issue of ratification. According to the terms of the Articles of Confederation—the duly constituted basis of American government—these amendments, like the new Constitution as a whole, were illegal.

Hamilton and Madison both would have been glad to see the states reduced to simple administrative units, but that proved impossible to achieve. The final compromise was the present American system of "dual federalism," in which federal and state governments were legally the creatures of the people, the real sovereign power. One "great difficulty," in Madison's words, was "the affair of representation; and if this could be adjusted, all others would be surmounted." The institutional answer to Madison's question was to replace the single-chamber congress with one made up of two houses. In the Senate, all the states would be equal, while in the House of Representatives, representation would be based proportionally on population. Yet by themselves both the federal and the state governments were empty shells. The real question was the relationship between the central government and American society as a whole.

Slavery remained a vexing problem, North and South. Though some of the southerners at the convention, including Washington, had qualms about it, most of the planter class did not. But slavery still posed problems of representation—for, legally, slaves were defined as both people and things. As people they were moral, responsible beings, members of society deemed by the law to have both obligations and rights, however limited. As things they were living extensions of the will of their masters, deemed by the same law to be no better than horses or cattle. Were they, then, to be counted as part of the southern population for the purpose of deciding the size of delegations to the House of Representatives?

Southern delegates, including Madison, wanted to have it both

In the frontispiece from a 1792 Philadelphia publication (left), *The Lady's Magazine and Repository of Entertaining Knowledge,* Columbia is presented with a petition for the "Rights of Woman." In contrast, an engraving published sometime after 1785 (right) prescribes the limits beyond which no virtuous woman's aspirations should go.

ways. Counting the slaves would greatly increase the South's influence; they made up, after all, 40 percent of all Virginians. But as slaves they had no vote for the "representatives" their numbers earned. Northern delegates saw through the ruse. Gouverneur Morris, speaking for Pennsylvania, pointed out that slavery was just one of many special interests, and that if it won representation, others should as well. Morris was no abolitionist, but he disliked slavery and he spoke for many of his fellow northerners. The great fault line in American society lay exposed for the whole convention to see.

The result was compromise, the first of many between North and South. Slaves would be counted for political representation, but five slaves would count as three free persons. Southerners won two more points. One was that until 1808 there could be no restriction by Congress on "the Migration or Importation of such Persons as any of the States now existing shall think proper to admit." In other words, the slave trade would continue, at least for a while. Meanwhile, northerners succeeded in banning slavery in the western territories with the passage by the Continental Congress of the Northwest Ordinance. The other southern success was the inclusion of clause stating that "No Person held to Service or Labour in one State ... escaping into another, shall be discharged from such Service or Labour." Fugitive slaves would have to be returned to their owners. The Constitution never used the word "slavery," but nevertheless gave it legitimacy and powerful institutional support at precisely the time when large numbers of Americans were finally doubting its rightfulness.

The Constitution also suited the needs of northern commerce. It created a vast common market, organized on the principle that uniform law and the needs of long-distance trade were more important than local custom and the needs of particular communities. Congress was awarded the power to regulate interstate and foreign commerce. It was also to establish a uniform bankruptcy law, mint coin and regulate money, "fix the standard of Weights and Measures," register patents and copyrights, and create a postal service. "Full faith and credit" would be "given in each state" to other states' court decisions. States were forbidden to "emit Bills of Credit, make anything but Gold or Silver Coin a Tender in Payment of Debts" or "pass any ... Law impairing the obligation of Contracts."

Although the Constitution was the work of an elite with its own interests fully in mind, it proved to have popular appeal as well. Indeed, only if voters elected convention delegates who favored ratification would it go into effect. But the opposition was powerful too: two states refused to ratify, and in four more the contest was extremely close. The Anti-Federalists included state-level politicians who feared the loss of their influence. They also included many popular radicals who distrusted the schemes of the great men in Philadelphia. Farmers of the interior expressed the strongest opposition. In fact, so strong was their opposition that the Constitution might not have been ratified at all without some clever political maneuvering. In Pennsylvania the ratifying convention was called on short notice, in order to foreclose the back country from organizing its opposition. In New York Anti-Federalists won a massive majority, and it took the threat that New York City would secede and ratify the Constitution on its own to bring the state around to consent.

But in the major towns, the crucibles of the Revolution, support for the constitution was overwhelming. From the beginning, urban working people, especially artisans, had wanted public policies to protect their own interests from outside competition, which is why they had opposed ending nonimportation in 1770 and why so many had wanted economic controls to limit wartime inflation. Now they saw in a strong national government their own best chance for prosperity. They had had little hand in the Constitution's actual making, but they had a great deal to do with its ratification, especially in the crucial states of Massachusetts, New York, and Pennsylvania.

By the time the Massachusetts convention met in early January 1788, it was clear that the contest would be tough, and that if the state refused to ratify, the constitution itself might fail. Western and Shaysite farmers understood perfectly well that part of the Constitution's purpose was to end forever the power of custom and community solidarity on which their rebellion had been based, and consequently their delegates strongly opposed ratification. Even a few Boston radicals mistrusted the whole project. "I confess, as I enter the Building, I stumble at the threshold" was how Samuel Adams put it.

But Adams's political base lay among Boston mechanics, and they wanted the Constitution. Paul Revere presided over some four hundred such workers who announced their support for the Constitution, hoping to influence Samuel Adams and the convention delegates who would follow him. Adams came around to support ratification, and the convention voted to accept. When it did, Boston's artisans celebrated with a parade in which forty different groups of tradesmen marched. One newspaper called it "an exhibition to which America has never witnessed an equal."

As state after state ratified, artisans elsewhere marched in similar parades. The biggest was Philadelphia's, held on July 4, 1788, with eighty-six units in the line of march. At the center were two elaborate floats, both of them metaphors for what the artisans thought the Revolution had wrought. One showed the "New Roof," or "Grand Federal Edifice." Behind it came the

---

"THIS FEDERAL SHIP WILL OUR COMMERCE REVIVE"

The following account of the New York City parade commemorating the ratification of the Constitution—taken from the New York Packet, *August 5, 1788—includes descriptions of the floats constructed by each artisan group and the banners they carried. The slogans and mottoes reveal the reasons for their support of a stronger federal government.*

ABOUT TEN O'CLOCK, 13 guns were fired from the Federal Ship, *Hamilton,* being the signal for the procession to move, the different bodies of which it was composed having already collected from their various places of meeting. It now set out from the Fields [a public park] proceeding down Broadway....

First Division ... A Band of Music. Tailors. A flag 10 by 11 feet, field sky blue, a fine landscape—Adam and Eve represented naked excepting fig leaves for aprons, nearly in full stature in a sitting posture—motto "And they sewed fig leaves together." ...

Second Division ... Tanners and Curriers ... Skinners, Breeches Makers and Glovers ... a flag of cream-colored silk ... the motto, "Americans encourage your own manufacturing." ...

Fourth Division. Carpenters ... Representing under the standard of the United States a portraiture of his Excellency General Washington, the motto, "Freedom's favorite son!" ... a motto on the frieze "The love of our country prevails" ... 392 rank and file....

Fifth Division ... Windsor and Rush Chair Makers ... 60 men with Green and Red cockades in their hats, emblematical of their business ... the motto:

The Federal States in union bound
O'er all the world our chairs are found

Sixth Division. Black Smiths and Nailors ... 120 in order ... Ship joiners. Motto:

Our Merchants may venture to ship without fear
For Pilots of skill shall the Hamilton steer
This federal ship will our commerce revive
And merchants and ship wrights and joiners shall thrive....

city's construction trades: architects, carpenters, sawmakers, and filemakers. The other was the Federal Ship *Union* with a crew of twenty-five sailors. Pilots, boatbuilders, sailmakers, ship carpenters, ropemakers, and finally "merchants and traders" followed it. Then came the rest of the tradesmen, some on floats working at their crafts, and all of them waving proud banners. Blacksmiths beat swords into sickles and plowshares beneath the motto "By Hammer and Hand All Arts Do Stand." Bricklayers proudly asserted that "Both Buildings and Rulers Are the Work of Our Hands."

Thirty years earlier, no American would have dared to make such a statement. Like all British subjects, these former colonists had revered a distant, superior monarch who sat atop a huge social pyramid. Their former idea of an official parade was a coronation procession, in which a society of unequal people displayed itself, from the lowest level to the highest. But now a new social vision had been born. As they marched, they celebrated the history of the revolution they had helped to make. They celebrated the prospect of a prosperous republican society. And they celebrated themselves, productive working men whose rights and dignity equaled anyone's.

Yet despite the outpouring of urban support, the Constitution remained extremely controversial in the new nation as a whole. Fears of the stronger, more centralized national government promised by the Constitution naturally ran deep among a people that had just fought a very bitter revolution against a "tyrannical" British government of great centralized power. The ultimate key to the popular acceptance of the Constitution was the Bill of Rights.

The Founding Fathers in Philadelphia had scarcely considered the need for a Bill of Rights. George Mason of Virginia had raised the matter, but the dele-

". . . MONEYED MEN, THAT TALK SO FINELY"

Many rural Americans opposed the ratification of the Constitution, contending that the new federal government would be controlled by "aristocrats" and wealthy men. In the debates at the convention held in Massachusetts in 1788 to consider how the state should vote on ratification, Amos Singletary, a farmer from the interior, who claimed never to have had a day of schooling in his life, expressed these fears.

HON. MR. SINGLETARY: Mr. President, I should not have troubled the Convention again, if some gentlemen had not called on them that were on the stage in the beginning of our troubles, in the year 1775. I was one of them. I have had the honor to be a member of the court all the time, Mr. President, and I say that, if any body had proposed such a Constitution as this in that day, it would have been thrown away at once. It would not have been looked at. We contended with Great Britain, some said for a threepenny duty on tea; but it was not that; it was because they claimed a right to tax us and bind us in all cases whatever. And does not this Constitution do the same? Does it not take away all we have—all our property? Does it not lay *all* taxes, duties, imposts [import fees], and excises? And what more have we to give? They tell us Congress won't lay dry taxes upon us, but collect all the money they want by impost. . . . They won't be able to raise money enough by impost, and then they will lay it on the land, and take all we have got. These lawyers, and men of learning, and moneyed men, that talk so finely, and gloss over matters so smoothly, to make us poor illiterate people swallow down the pill, expect to get into Congress themselves; they expect to be the managers of this Constitution, and get all the power and all the money into their own hands, and then they will swallow up all us little folks, like the great *Leviathan*, Mr. President; yes, just as the whale swallowed up *Jonah*.

gations of every state voted against him. The Anti-Federalists, who distrusted the schemes of the Philadelphia convention, raised a loud cry of indignation over the Constitution's granting of major powers to the federal government, as well as the absence of a guarantee of popular liberties. The Anti-Federalists pressed their concerns in the state ratifying conventions, where they saw that the popular demand for a Bill of Rights was strong, especially in the rural areas. The result of this widespread demand was that five states, including three of the most powerful (Massachusetts, New York, and Virginia), ratified the Constitution on the understanding that a Bill of Rights would quickly be added.

Federalist leaders gave ground to popular wisdom. Congress, under Madison's leadership, drafted twelve amendments that had originally been suggested by the state ratifying conventions. These were submitted to the states, which subsequently ratified ten of the amendments, officially appended to the Constitution as the Bill of Rights on December 15, 1791.

The first amendment guaranteed the freedoms of speech, press, religion, and assembly. The rights to petition government for redress of grievances, to trial by jury, and to punishment that was neither cruel nor unusual, as well as such rights of due process as freedom from unwarranted searches and seizures of property, were also assured. The guarantee of these rights had particular meaning to the large numbers of Americans who, in the tumultuous decade before the Revolution, had exercised the freedoms of speech, assembly, and press and resisted unlawful searches and impressment by the British army. The Bill of Rights also guaranteed Americans' right to bear arms for purposes of establishing local militias, which would make a standing army unnecessary. Although the Anti-Federalists lost the struggle to reduce overcentralized national powers, they and others who shared their libertarian concerns won a major and lasting victory in securing a Bill of Rights that protected the rights of citizens against government.

In the end, the Constitution and the Bill of Rights represented many things to many people. For northern men of commerce it was the necessary underpinning for both commercial wealth and class advantage. For southern planters it was a bulwark for the perpetuation of slavery. For urban artisans, the new powers of the federal government could encourage both the commerce and the manufacturing through which their crafts might be encouraged to flourish and grow.

Small farmers, although initially opposed to the Constitution, quickly learned that the new federal system had made possible a society in which people could organize around their common interests. Some women began to grasp that point as well. Only in one state, New Jersey, could they vote (and they would lose that right shortly).

But in other ways the Revolution had brought women into public affairs and enabled them to question the subordination that their mothers and grandmothers had taken for granted. For more than a century the great question in American political culture had been the relationship of different orders of men. Now, formally at least, that was resolved, with the principle that all white male citizens were legally equal. For the next full century one of the republic's major questions would be whether that equality ought to extend to people who were not white and not male.

For African-Americans, the Constitution represented a major blow to their desire for emancipation. The Constitution lent new legitimacy to slavery and helped to create the conditions by which it would spread across the South in the next century. The Bill of Rights, which guaranteed that citizens were able to organize politically to protect their rights and interests, offered nothing to slaves. Such possibilities for African-Americans would have to await another revolutionary moment in the next century finally to be realized.

For Indians, the first Americans, the Revolution and the Constitution constituted an unqualified disaster. Until 1776 they had been able to play different groups of European invaders off against each other. Now the United States stood supreme. The Senecas of New York, once the proud "keepers of the western gate" of the Iroquois Confederacy, were a beaten, demoralized people who huddled in rural slums. Many of the Mohawks, who had fought so valiantly on the British side, fled to Canada. Further south the Cherokees pathetically tried to adopt the ways of the Europeans in America. But they and the rest of the Indians who lived east of the Mississippi quickly learned that they were bereft of protection. Settlers who wanted their land usually got it. Each black, at least, counted for three-fifths of a human being according to the Constitution; Indians counted for nothing. They paid the highest price of all for the success of the American Revolution. They found no place under the Federalists' "New Roof."

THE LEGACY OF THE REVOLUTION

The last great coalition of the Revolution, which created and ratified the Constitution, consisted of plantation slaveowners, commercial farmers, northern businessmen and merchants, and urban workingmen. Almost all of them agreed that the Revolution had been for the good. There would be no permanent restoration of monarchy, as in seventeenth-century England. There would be no political party strong enough to attempt it.

When urban working people, who had so great a hand in both destroying the power of Britain and creating the United States, marched to celebrate the new Constitution, they were joined by men whom

GENERAL GEORGE WASHINGTON. Reviewing the Western army at Fort Cumberland the 18th of Octobr 1794

Washington suppresses a rebellion. Faced with a primitive transportation system, western Pennsylvania farmers distilled whiskey from grain as the best means to get their produce to eastern markets. In 1794, after a new federal liquor tax disrupted their livelihood, the farmers rebelled. In this painting President Washington is shown at Fort Cumberland, Virginia, reviewing the vanguard of the fifteen-thousand troops he dispatched to suppress the Whiskey Rebellion.

they had bitterly opposed not long before. In Philadelphia the celebration concluded with a speech by James Wilson, a conservative jurist, an enemy of Pennsylvania's radical constitution of 1776, and a man whose fortified house had actually been besieged by mechanics and militiamen during the economic crisis of 1779. In New York, artisans marched behind a "federal ship" named the *Hamilton*, in honor of Alexander Hamilton, a man who had always been hostile to the expanded political role working people had won for themselves during the Revolution.

But this newfound harmony did not mean that working people meekly accepted the authority assumed by their longtime elite antagonists. The Revolution had dealt a decisive blow to the deferential habits of many of America's working people, and indeed this liberation was also a powerful part of the revolutionary legacy. The wealthy could no longer be sure that their lofty station entitled them to rule, that their pretensions to authority would go unchallenged. John Adams, as we have seen, feared as early as 1776 that "our struggle has loosened the bands of government everywhere." The "bands" between generations, classes, races, and sexes had indeed been stretched by the disobedience, turbulence, and insolence ordinary Americans demonstrated during the revolutionary upheaval. Such behavior helped assure that future generations of working people would no longer simply defer to their social "betters" on public matters.

"The Rights of Man: or Tommy Paine, the Little American Taylor, Taking the Measure of the Crown, for a New Pair of Revolution Breeches." British conservatives had little love for the author of *Common Sense*—especially after he returned to England in 1787 and pressed for radical republican goals in the land of his birth. Caricaturist James Gillray lampooned Paine in this 1791 cartoon, which appeared soon after the publication of his *The Rights of Man*. But the British establishment took Paine more seriously; within the year, Paine fled to revolutionary France to avoid imprisonment.

In a broader sense, the Revolution also revealed the capacity of ordinary people to alter the very process of history. As Tom Paine cautioned in *Common Sense*, "Kings are not taken away by miracles, neither are changes in governments brought about by any other means than such as are common and human; and such as we are using now." As the opening act in the cataclysmic "Age of Revolution" that would quickly spread to France and beyond, the American Revolution—the first successful colonial war for liberation—demonstrated for subsequent generations the growing power of popular movements literally to make history.

The United States, c. 1857.

FREE LABOR AND SLAVERY

1790-1860

BETWEEN 1790 and 1860, America was transformed from a small agrarian society on the Atlantic coast to a wealthy country with a diverse economy that reached across the continent to the Pacific. Twenty new states joined the original thirteen, and the nation's population swelled from four million to over thirty-one million. But this period of unparalleled growth and prosperity also produced deepening divisions in the population—divisions of class, gender, nationality, and race. By 1860, the most divisive issue—whether America would be a society based on free labor or slavery—had brought the nation to the verge of civil war.

In 1790, however, the issue of slavery seemed secondary, at least to Americans of European descent. The new nation was confidently launching an unprecedented experiment in national republican government, backed by a seemingly limitless supply of land and natural resources. Most white Americans were justifiably optimistic about their own and the new nation's future.

A new economic system, industrial capitalism, took root. In the North, revolutions in transportation and then manufacturing accelerated markedly after 1800, undermining the older system of local craft production and family farming. By the 1830s and 1840s, New England capitalists had brought workers together in the nation's first factories to weave cloth. Other workers—in some cases whole families, in others women alone—labored in their homes to make shoes and clothing for market. An expanding network of roads and canals carried such consumer goods from the Northeast to the new settlements in Ohio, Indiana, and Illinois and brought raw materials and foodstuffs from the West to the East. As in the colonial era, one result of this expansion was that Indian peoples faced the choice of moving west again or being exterminated.

In the South, the manufacturing and transportation systems remained largely undeveloped. But the region nonetheless felt the profound changes wrought by an industrial revolution international in scope. Cotton replaced tobacco as the South's principal cash crop. A thriving plantation economy spread dramatically after 1820 from the upper South to Alabama, Mississippi, Louisiana, and, by the 1840s, Texas, bringing with it a burgeoning system of slave labor. Hundreds of thousands of African-American slaves were transported to these new areas to produce cotton for the expanding domestic and international markets. As in the North, Indian tribes in the South faced white settlers' insatiable greed for land.

By midcentury, the industrial revolution had drawn millions of Americans—including artisans, factory hands, domestic servants, and day laborers, as well as small farmers—into a market economy where they sold their labor or their products. In the process, the ideal of the self-sufficient, independent farm or artisan family came under attack as large numbers of Americans became dependent upon wages. At several points in this era, wage workers—by now two out of every five Americans—experienced the full meaning of that dependency, as manufacturing ground to a halt and tens of thousands were thrown out of work.

The industrial revolution changed more than patterns of labor. It also helped reshape centuries-old family structures and gender roles and fostered the growth of cities and a new urban culture. Industrialization also transformed the population, as a massive wave of immigrants from northern and western Europe flooded the cities and the countryside in the 1840s and 1850s. Most of these new immigrants—many of whom came to escape economic, social, and political misery at home—became wage laborers, contributing to the formation of a growing and distinctly multinational working class. They also intro-

PART TWO

duced radical theories and practices, including socialism, to American politics and broadened the base of American Catholicism. Their contributions were not always well received. In the 1840s and 1850s, many Americans tried to exclude new immigrants, blaming them for causing the wrenching changes evident in the emerging industrial society.

Industrialization, and the demographic and cultural changes that went with it, profoundly affected the nation's political life, touching off an intense debate over what sort of society America was becoming. The commercial and industrial elite embraced a liberal capitalist interpretation of the revolutionary legacy, emphasizing the role of self-interest and the marketplace in governing social and economic relations. Many working people, especially those who did well in the new order, were attracted to the idea that liberty meant individual upward mobility and improved living standards. Others—including many of the working people dislocated by industrialization—criticized the emerging order as antithetical to the ideals of the Revolution and celebrated instead the Revolution's republican traditions of independence, mutuality, and citizen participation.

Working Americans—men and women, free-born and slave—resisted the dependent status that came with industrial development, insisting that America had not been created to make a few men rich and powerful at the expense of all others. They attacked the "tyranny" of their employers and masters, condemning them as "Tories in disguise," in the words of women textile workers in the 1830s, and argued for liberty and equality by drawing upon "the Spirit of our Patriotic ancestors." And working people undertook to defend their interests and restore the nation to republican virtue, through local workingmen's parties and trade unions, cooperative workshops and utopian communities, and slave rebellions and strikes. Women's-suffrage and abolition societies also pressed the fight to extend the boundaries of freedom and equality.

Of all the diverse claims for "equal rights" raised in these years, one—the demand for the end of slavery—became the central political issue of the day. Over the decades, the country divided between those who desired an America whose labor was legally free, as in the North, and those who believed that only a system based on slave labor could guarantee a harmonious social order in the South. A basic question emerged as America expanded westward and new territories sought statehood: should these new states be free or slave?

As we will see in Part Two, this question affected America's politics, moral values, and ultimately even its very survival as a nation. Although a number of political compromises after 1820 maintained an uneasy peace between the two systems, by 1860 this conflict had set the stage for a second and even bloodier revolution.

5 THE GROWTH OF THE SLAVE SOUTH

"Five Generations on Smith's Plantation, Beaufort, South Carolina." An African-American family photographed in 1862.

IN 1824, the year John Quincy Adams became the sixth president of the United States, a baby girl was born at Cedar Vale, a plantation in Nansemond County, Virginia, some fifty miles from the lower Chesapeake Bay. Huldah, the infant—like her parents, Margaret and Tom, and her six brothers and sisters—was the property of the up-and-coming farmer and slaveowner John Cowper Cohoon, Jr.

Cohoon's power over his human property set the contours of their lives. He sold Huldah's younger sister Amy before she reached adulthood. When Huldah came of age, Cohoon chose to let her marry Lewis Orton, who was owned by a neighbor. One of their four children, named after Lewis, died in infancy; the other three lived apart from their father but with their mother—and, like her, became Cohoon's property. Eventually, Cohoon gave Huldah and her children to one of his own sons, and her sister Adeline to another.

The chattel slavery of the American South was a novel hybrid of ancient and modern. It harnessed one of the earliest forms of unfree labor, slavery, to a decidedly modern purpose—the large-scale production of commodities such as sugar and tobacco for a capitalist world market. And with the rise of King Cotton, American slaves produced the most important raw material in the new Industrial Revolution. Both aspects of this institution, the precapitalist and the capitalist, shaped the lives of the people caught up in it.

For seven decades after the ratification of the federal Constitution, from 1790 to 1860, chattel slavery remained the distinctive institution of the American South. The society was far from static: it was a time of rapid economic growth, physical expansion, and social change. At the center of these developments was cotton, a crop that came to dominate the region's life. Under King Cotton's reign, the number of slave states grew from just six to fifteen, while the region's population multiplied more than five times.

It was by working his slaves and adding to their number—through marriage, purchase, and natural reproduction—that John Cowper Cohoon and thousands like him grew rich. By the time he died in 1863, Cohoon had increased his slave property from the one man given him by his father to a total of forty-seven, making him one of the biggest planters in the county. And it was her status as a chattel that defined Huldah's life, separating her from two sisters and preventing her and her children from living with her husband and their father.

When Huldah was born in 1824, the South was caught up in a cotton-growing boom that would last another three decades and more. All other crops were quickly eclipsed in importance. Rice exports hardly increased between 1790 and 1860. The value of tobacco exports doubled, but this crop dropped from 15 percent of the value of all U.S. exports in 1820 to only 6 percent by 1845. Sugar fared better. Based almost entirely in Louisiana, the commercial production of cane sugar multiplied about five times between 1800 and the Civil War. But cotton became the South's chief money crop: production doubled every ten years between 1800 and 1860; cotton already made up more than half the value of the nation's total exports by 1820.

Living in Virginia, Huldah did not labor in the cotton fields that came to dominate the landscape of the lower South and the more recently settled Southwest. Yet the cotton boom and the southwestward expansion of slavery touched her life and the lives of all southerners. From 1790 to 1860, perhaps a million slaves—possibly including members of Huldah's family—were forcibly transported to the new Southwest, especially to Mississippi, Alabama, Louisiana, Arkansas, and Texas. They provided the labor force that enabled planters to grow wealthy satisfying the British textile manufacturers' seemingly insatiable demand for cotton. The ownership of labor was the key to a cotton planter's fortune.

Throughout this period, a growing majority of all white southerners owned no slaves, and many white farmers grew little or no cotton at all as late as 1860. Yet slavery and cotton affected the lives of even those whose main crops were the foods they ate, and who grew those crops with their own labor. Over time, the great profits to be made in slave-produced cotton pushed up the price of slaves and land, retarded the growth of industry, towns, and cities, and affected all other aspects of economic life in the South.

The commands of King Cotton affected the South's American Indian population as well. Once again, western expansion put whites on a collision course with Indians. In 1790, American Indians occupied villages throughout the twenty-five million acres of the later cotton-growing states. Many of these people were herded onto reservations. Others moved west, voluntarily or not, while still others tried to survive in the South by adopting the agricultural practices of white farmers. They bought land, farmed it, and sent their children to public schools. But such efforts at integration ultimately failed, and these Indians joined others in the forced march west that President Andrew Jackson ordered in the 1830s. They were displaced, just as the coastal tribes—including the Nansemonds, who gave their name to Huldah's birthplace—had been, long before.

BIRTH OF THE COTTON KINGDOM

Not counting the Indian population, just under two million people lived in the U.S. South in 1790, roughly a third of them black and two-thirds white. Most lived on the coastal plain and the piedmont— the foothills of the Appalachian Mountains. More than a third of all southerners still lived and worked in Virginia, and more than half lived in Virginia and Maryland combined. Of the region's nearly 700,000 blacks, 95 percent were slaves; most of the 33,000 free blacks lived in towns and cities. Only about one-third of the whites owned slaves; those who owned twenty or more were the elite classified as planters in the U.S. Census.

By 1790, Nansemond County, like the rest of the South, had recovered from the economic disruption and devastation wrought by the American Revolution. During the next decade, tobacco production in Virginia and Maryland finally returned to pre-revolutionary levels, and those who grew rice in the Carolinas and Georgia did better than ever. Tobacco and rice were still the major products of slave-based commercial agriculture. But other planters in the sea-island districts of the Carolinas and Georgia were turning to a new commercial crop,

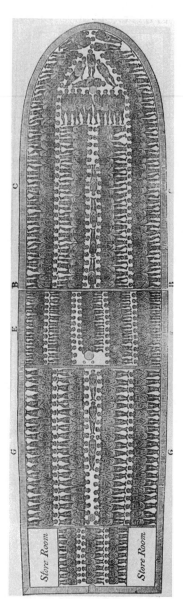

Strange cargo. A diagram of the interior of a "slaver," from an 1808 report on the African slave trade.

long-staple cotton; in 1791 they already produced some 2 million pounds. And soon there was a growing demand for the sugar cane of Louisiana (an area purchased by the United States in 1803). Although many Americans abhorred the institution of slavery and the northern states moved toward gradual emancipation beginning in the 1770s, independence from Britain and then the new U.S. Constitution left slavery's legal and institutional supports secure.

The South's system of slave-based agriculture had its problems—exhausted soil, declining demand, and low prices, for instance, threatened the tobacco economy. Nonetheless, slaves remained the area's most valuable assets, and success rewarded planters who used their human capital productively. Doing so meant making the right decisions—about what to grow, where to grow it, and how to market it. Planters had to respond to a changing world economy, led by an industrializing England. The key raw material in this new economy was cotton, and those who could supply it were sure to profit.

It was becoming less and less profitable to grow tobacco with slaves, but the flourishing rice economy in South Carolina and Georgia, expanding sugar production in Louisiana, and, ultimately, the spread of cotton throughout the lower South all guaranteed the continued vitality of the slave system. Southern planters imported more than eighty thousand Africans between 1790 and 1808, the year Congress outlawed further importation.

From the start, cotton was clearly a promising crop—slaves could grow it, and England's demand would continue to drive the price of cotton up. But until the mid-1790s, only sea-island cotton, which grew well along the coast of Georgia and the Carolinas, was profitable. Attempts to grow it elsewhere in the South had failed, though planters quickly found that another variety—short-staple, green-seed cotton—could be grown much more widely.

This type of cotton, however, presented problems. It contained sticky seeds that were hard to separate from the cotton fibers—and the high cost of having slaves remove the seeds by hand made the entire enterprise unprofitable. Obviously, growers needed a device that could remove the cotton seeds quickly and cheaply. In 1793, the Massachusetts-born Eli Whitney, who had gone to Georgia as a tutor, devised just such a simple gin. His invention meant that cotton could now be grown profitably almost anywhere south of Virginia, Kentucky, and Missouri.

By the turn of the century, southerners had begun the westward migration that was to change the face of the South. The migrants included both small cotton farmers and pioneers who subsisted on livestock herding, hunting, and small-scale farming. Later came big planters attracted by the richer soil of the new southwestern land;

whenever cotton prices rose, purchases of government land there increased.

The earliest migrants settled in empty land, but all too soon the westward expansion brought settlers into open conflict with some of the sixty thousand American Indians of the area. Among the largest tribes were the Cherokee and Creeks, who occupied the western Carolinas and Georgia and eastern Alabama and Tennessee. Their neighbors, the Choctaws, Chickasaws, and Seminoles, occupied parts of western Alabama and northern Mississippi and Florida. These "Five Civilized Tribes," as the whites called them, all lived in stable agrarian societies.

Some of these groups had allied with England in the American Revolution in hopes of securing title to their land. This calculated risk had failed, and before long the new U.S. government set out to "Christianize" and "civilize" the Indian nations. This policy soon proved to mean replacing tribal social structures and values with those more proper to a market-oriented society. In particular, it meant weakening the ties connecting the individual Indian to the community and binding the community as a whole to its land. "Unless some system is marked out by which there shall be a separate allotment of land to each individual," as a U.S. commissioner of Indian affairs later put it, "you will look in vain for any general casting off of savagism." He concluded, "Common property and civilization cannot coexist."

Of course, dividing communal tribal land into the private plots belonging to individuals also made it easier for whites to acquire legal title to that land. One method was already tried and true: First, merchants drew the Indians into debt, often through questionable bookkeeping. This debt then became a tool with which to dispossess the debtors. As President Thomas Jefferson wrote, "When these debts get beyond what the individuals can pay, they become willing to lop them off by a cession of lands." Informed that their debts had grown because of accumulating interest, Creek leaders vainly responded that "there was no word for it [interest] in their language."

Government policy also helped create a new class of culturally assimilated Indians, many of mixed Indian and white parentage. Some of them became substantial slaveholding cotton farmers. With white backing, the assimilated Indians acquired growing political power within the Indian councils and used it to promote the transformation of local Indian society into an approximation of white America. Finally, the Indian tribes—supposedly treated as independent nations—were made subject to federal and state laws.

Resistance to this whole process flared early. In 1809–1811 the Shawnee leaders Tecumseh and his brother Tenskwatawa tried to rally the tribes of present-day Mississippi, Alabama, and Georgia to

Methought the souls of all that I had murder'd, came to my tent Act 5 Sc 3.

RICHARD III.

Andrew Jackson's role in the First Seminole War is resurrected in this anti-Democratic cartoon published during the 1828 presidential campaign. Whig caricaturist David Claypoole Johnston fashioned the Democratic candidate's head and shoulders out of a military tent, cannons, swords, and the bodies of dead Indians. The cartoon was captioned with a line from Shakespeare's play about the treacherous, despotic king: "Methought the souls of all that I had murder'd, came to my tent."

united and armed resistance alongside tribes of the upper Midwest. More culturally assimilated, the main body of the southern tribes refused. But some of the younger Upper Creek males—already angered by mounting U.S. pressures on their land and society—had rallied to Tecumseh's standard. These militants, known as Red Sticks, became increasingly estranged from Lower Creek leaders, who favoring accommodating to U.S. power. In 1813, a bloody war erupted, pitting the Red Sticks against thousands of white southern militiamen, as well as Lower Creek, Cherokee, Choctaw, and Chickasaw warriors who hoped for greater leniency from whites in exchange for this alliance. The fierce but unequal combat ended in March 1814 at the battle of Horseshoe Bend, where more than a thousand Indians died and Andrew Jackson (commanding the West Tennessee militia) added to his military reputation. The Treaty of Fort Jackson transferred fourteen million acres (more than half the land in Alabama) from the defeated Creeks to U.S. control. Among the losers in this deal were the Lower Creeks, who had allied with Jackson.

The defeat at Horseshoe Bend opened the floodgates to southern white migrants, who soon itched to complete the Indians' removal. The Creeks of Georgia were driven westward in 1826. Hoping to avoid similar treatment, most other southeastern Indians tried to adapt to the white society that was surrounding them. The Cherokees, who had embarked on this path years earlier, went as far as to adopt a formal constitution modeled on that of the United States, complete with distinct legislative, executive, and judicial branches.

". . . BEYOND THE GREAT RIVER"

In this 1832 petition to Congress, leaders of the Creek nation protested their forcible expulsion from the Gulf coast region onto lands beyond the Mississippi River, in present-day Oklahoma.

IT HAS BEEN . . . with alarm and consternation that we find ourselves assailed in these our last retreats. Though our possessions have shrunk to a narrow compass, they contain all that endears itself to our heart. Beneath the soil which we inhabit, lie the frail remnants of what heretofore composed the bodies of our fathers and of our children, our wives and our kindred. Their value was enhanced as their extent was curtailed. Yet we are now menaced with being driven from these narrow limits, and compelled to seek an asylum from the craving desires of the white man, beyond the great river. If the alternative offered us—if the lands offered us be, as we are told, of greater value than those which we derived from our ancestors, and they from God, we freely relinquish all the advantages which they possess, and will be satisfied with that which we already have. If they are inferior in value, we submit it to the justice of our white brethren, whether they will compel us to a disadvantageous exchange. If there be any particular inducements either to individuals or communities which render our lands particularly valuable, why should not we, the rightful proprietors, be suffered to enjoy them? Can any adventitious value enhance them more in the eyes of the white man, than the solemn associations to which we have adverted, do in our own?

We are assured that, beyond the Mississippi, we shall be exempted from further exaction; that no State authority can there reach us; that we shall be secure and happy in these distant abodes. Can we obtain, or can our white brethren give assurances more distinct and positive, than those we have already received and trusted? Can their power exempt us from intrusion in our promised borders, if they are incompetent to our protection where we are? Can we feel secure when farther removed from our father's [the president's] eye than now, when he hears our remonstrances and listens to our complaints? We have heretofore received every assurance and every guarantee that our imperfect knowledge could desire; we confided in it as ample for all our purposes; and we know not what to require which would obviate further embarrassments.

Seminoles. George Catlin's 1838 sketch shows seven of the 250 Seminoles imprisoned at Fort Moultrie, Charleston, South Carolina. They were captured with Seminole leader Osceola near St. Augustine, Florida, after U.S. troops violated a truce agreement.

But before long the whites made clear that they wanted less to transform the Indians than to remove them entirely from the region and its valuable land.

During the decade of the 1830s, the federal government set out to relocate all southeastern tribes onto lands west of the Mississippi. Twenty-three thousand Choctaws and some Cherokees were pressured into moving on in 1831–32. Others who refused were transported by force—the Alabama Creeks in 1836, the Chickasaws the next year. In 1837–38, federal troops uprooted fifteen to twenty thousand Cherokees and herded them across the eight-hundred-mile "Trail of Tears" to present-day Oklahoma; one in four died on the way. Most of the Seminoles were removed between 1832 and 1835, but for the next seven years, a Seminole minority led by Osceola fought the U.S. Army to a stalemate, successfully resisting attempts to uproot them. This, however, was the exception to the rule; by the 1840s, only fragments of the original tribal population remained in the Gulf region.

A NEW SOUTH EMERGES

Between 1816 and 1840, as whites completed the removal of the southeastern tribes, a true cotton kingdom arose on the foundations laid during the earlier era. In 1816, southern slaves were already producing about 125 million pounds of cotton a year, mostly in South Carolina and Georgia. So big an output soon made the South the world's leading producer of cotton. But by 1840, production had climbed to over 834 million pounds, and the center of cotton production had shifted decisively westward into the new Gulf states of Alabama, Mississippi, and Louisiana. In general, the rural areas of these lower-South states had fewer free blacks than other areas of the South, and their white population seemed to be more firmly committed to slavery than any other group of Americans.

As the cotton belt shifted west, so did many of the South's people. Although Virginia remained the single most populous state, the Gulf states as a whole contained the majority of both free and slave populations. Here, too, were the largest slave plantations in the South outside the rice counties of the South Carolina and Georgia coast.

Migrants to the new South came from all over the old. In particular, droves left the piedmont region of the Carolinas and Georgia. Other migrants moved from Virginia into Kentucky, Tennessee, and Missouri. About half of the North Carolina migrants headed for the same states, while the other half ventured further south. Still other southerners went from eastern Tennessee into western Tennessee and Arkansas and from Kentucky into Missouri.

Their migration was facilitated by the invention of the steamboat in the 1780s. In 1817, the steamboats were already plying the western rivers, and the port of New Orleans welcomed some seventeen of them, full of migrants and freight. Just three decades later, more than five hundred steamboats arrived each year.

Steamboats and the new railroads made it possible for southern migrants to exchange products with people back East and with other migrants then settling the Northwest—Ohio, Indiana, and Illinois. With the aid of the steamboat, especially, northwesterners could market their surplus grain and livestock in the new South, just as new planters in Louisiana, Mississippi, Arkansas, and Tennessee could sell some tobacco, sugar, rice, and cotton in the Northwest. Towns and cities along this route—including Pittsburgh and Cincinnati on the Ohio River, and New Orleans and St. Louis on the Mississippi—flourished.

In this manner the new West and South became temporarily linked in an economic partnership that helped make them political allies during the 1820s and 1830s, despite the ban on slavery in the Northwest Territory. In both sections of the nation, most people still remained largely outside this new national market economy, living instead on small farms that produced enough for the family to survive and little else. But those who had the land and labor to produce a surplus also had a market, and thus a chance to expand production and prosper. Nonetheless, while the planters in the Gulf region could

Slave trader, Sold to Tennessee,

Arise! Arise! and weep no more dry up your tears, we shall part no more, Come rose we go to Tennessee, that happy shore. To old virginia never — never — return.

the Company going to Tennessee from Staunton. Augusta County, — the law of virginia Suffered them to go on. I was Astonished at this boldness, the Carrier Stopped a moment. then Ordered the march, I Saw the plan it is Commonly in this State, with the negro's in droves Sold,

Lewis Miller, a sometime artist and carpenter whose work often took him to Virginia, observed this "cottle" of slaves on their way to new owners in Tennessee. Miller sketched the scene and transcribed the words of the slaves' song.

buy enough food from northwestern farmers to feed their slaves, they could not expect to sell much cotton in the Northwest; English textile manufacturers were their biggest customers.

Other key players in the cotton economy were the commission merchants, usually from the North or England, though based in the South. These factors made loans and sold insurance to farmers and planters, warehoused their cotton in port, and arranged to ship it to buyers abroad. In exchange, they got a hefty share of the sale price—

up to a fifth. They also brought manufactured goods from Europe and the Northeast to the South. By the 1850s, factor commissions were siphoning somewhere between $100 and $150 million a year from the South into the North. Thus the entire nation developed a substantial stake in cotton and slavery.

Factors also lent migrants the money to start new plantations or

King Cotton. The South's staple, packed into bales and awaiting transport up the Mississippi River, fills a New Orleans wharf.

"Woodcutter's Cabin on the Mississippi." French artist August Hervieu sketched a poor white family in 1827. The drawing later appeared as an illustration in British author Frances Trollope's acerbic and very popular account of a stay in the United States, *Domestic Manners of the Americans,* published in 1832.

to buy more land and slaves. Such loans were necessary; it took a new planter four or five years to get started. During this time his slaves cleared and plowed the land, built shelters, and planted the first cotton crop. These were years of exhausting labor that brought in no money. Thus the planter had to live on borrowed money until his plantation became productive in cotton and self-sufficient in food.

But though commercial production of staples, especially cotton, was already the cornerstone of the economy of the South, most southern whites in this era nevertheless remained on the fringes of that economy. In 1830, two-thirds of all southern white families owned no slaves. Some owned small farms near the large plantations, working in close cooperation with them. Many of them grew cotton and hoped one day to become planters themselves. In the meantime, they depended upon wealthy, powerful planters for a broad range of economic, social, and political services.

A second and larger group of small farmers lived in the hills, away from the plantation belt. Few of them participated in the export economy or shared in its ample profits. These southerners prized economic and social independence as highly as their eighteenth-century forebears had, and they ran their farms accordingly. They knew that staking everything on cotton was too risky for them: a sudden drop

A "model" plantation. Oak Lawn, a large Louisiana sugar plantation on the Bayou Teche. Its slave quarters included forty-two cabins.

in prices could land them in debt, even strip them of their land. These farm families therefore concentrated on producing the food, tools, and clothing they themselves needed, aiming first at self-sufficiency. If they produced more than they needed, they could sell or exchange the surplus locally for such necessities as sugar, coffee, molasses, nails, needles, tableware, and cooking utensils. Corn was the preferred crop, because it was useful regardless of its market price; it could be eaten by family members and by livestock, and it could easily be bartered for other goods. Not until a record rise in the price of cotton during the 1850s would large numbers of these small landowners begin to change their cautious farm strategy.

THE SLAVE SOUTH

In the last two decades before the Civil War, the South continued to expand and change. Its total population grew by over half (from 7 to 11 million), and the cotton kingdom, which in 1845 already extended from the Carolinas southwestward to eastern Texas and from Tennessee down to Florida, now pushed farther, into Arkansas and the Texas plain. Frontier settlements in western Missouri and Arkansas, which contained but a tiny number of settlers in 1840, experienced the most rapid growth. In the old upper South, though, and most clearly in Maryland, the southwestern migration weakened chattel slavery's position in the economy.

But in southern agriculture as a whole, the dominant role of cotton was now clearer than ever. On a map showing where the major southern crops were grown in 1860, the sugar parishes of Louisiana, the rice counties of the Mississippi delta and the coast of South Carolina and Georgia, and the tobacco counties of inland Virginia, Kentucky, and Tennessee are mere islands in a vast sea of cotton. Encouraged by rising cotton prices in the 1850s, small farmers in the upland South began allotting more and more of their land and labor to cotton, thereby becoming enmeshed in the export economy. The South now produced two-thirds of all the cotton grown in the world. Three-quarters of this crop, some five million bales (1 bale = 500 pounds), went to England, where textile workers turned it into fabric that eventually clothed not only the British but also millions of other Europeans, Americans, East Indians, and Africans.

The Slaveowners

The slaveowning population was still expanding steadily in these years. Between 1830 and 1860, their numbers increased from about 225,000 to almost 400,000. Many of the new owners came from the ranks of previously slaveless small farmers.

But though the absolute number of slaveowners grew, the total white population grew faster. Slaves were becoming more expensive, and only a shrinking proportion of all southern whites owned them: 36 percent in 1830, 31 percent in 1850, and only 26 percent by 1860. Nonetheless, slavery was the source of economic power in the antebellum South, so a smaller portion of the total white population controlled the great bulk of the region's wealth.

By the 1850s, the wealthiest of all were a small group of planters who owned the best cropland best served by river transportation. At the top of the slaveholding pyramid stood the planter aristocracy, made up in 1860 of roughly ten thousand families—fewer than 3 percent of all slaveowners. Each of these families owned more than fifty slaves, and together they owned about a fourth of all the slaves in the nation. (Three thousand of these families each owned a hundred slaves or more—some 10 percent of the nation's slaves.)

Next was a more numerous but less wealthy layer of middling planters who owned between fifteen and fifty slaves; Huldah's master, John Cowper Cohoon, belongs in this category.

At the lower end of this scale were to be found most of the slaveholders in the country. For though the large and middling planters owned the majority of the slaves, the average slaveholder was not the lord of a plantation. Rather he was a male forty-four-year-old southern-born farmer. He owned five or six slaves and land valued at about $3,000. Even that much property made him many times wealthier than the average northerner, but dependence on the export economy still left him quite vulnerable to sharp drops in crop prices

"The Old Plantation Home." The slave quarters as a carefree world, basking in the glow of the planter's benevolence. The plantation as the perfect extended family was a common theme of pro-slavery prints before the Civil War—and after. This lithograph by the popular firm of Currier and Ives was published in 1872.

or jumps in the price of slaves, land, and transport. Debt and economic uncertainty affected such people much more than they did the planter aristocracy.

We know the planter elite best from its self-descriptions and later from novels and films that romanticized its life as elegant, cultured, leisurely, removed from the hectic pace and pressures of commerce or industry. Four years before the Civil War, the governor of Virginia described his state's planters as people who are "civilized in the solicitude, gracious in the amenities of life, and refined and conservative in social habits . . . who have leisure for the cultivation of morals, manners, philosophy, and politics."

Planters liked to see themselves in the role of stern but loving fathers guiding the lives of their plantation families—especially their slave "children"—with paternal wisdom and justice. The slave, wrote Virginian George Fitzhugh, "is but a grown-up child, and must be governed as a child. . . . The master occupies toward him the place of parent or guardian." Fitzhugh contrasted this supposed paternal guardianship with the reckless individualism he saw in the "free society" of the North. There, he declared scornfully,

> none but the selfish virtues are in repute, because none other help a man in the race of competition. . . . Selfishness is almost the only motive of human conduct in free society, where every man is taught that it is his first duty to change and better his pecuniary situation.

A map of servitude. The back of a Louisiana slave named Gordon, photographed in 1863 after he escaped to the Union forces.

Southern planters were undoubtedly different from northern merchants and manufacturers, distinguished especially by the experiences, expectations, and values that went along with owning a laborer's body instead of hiring part of his time for wages. But the southern slaveowners were no less deeply enmeshed in the international market economy, no less subject to its demands. Large-scale commercial production of cotton, sugar, rice, and tobacco was a business run for profit. And slavery was first and foremost a way of controlling the labor that produced those profits. As North Carolina's Supreme Court observed approvingly in 1829, the purpose of slavery "is the profit of the Master," and the purpose of the slave is "to toil that another may reap the fruits." For those masters who behaved accordingly, chattel slavery could fulfill this purpose well. An enterprising and lucky individual like John Cowper Cohoon could parlay a small holding into a substantial estate. On the other hand, a slaveowner who ignored the requirements of profit-making and labor control in order to live up to some abstract standard of unselfish behavior risked business failure and ruin.

These business requirements were felt by both slaveholder and slave. Because slave labor yielded their wealth, power, and leisure, successful farmers and planters felt compelled to accumulate more slaves—not unlike northern industrialists accumulating machinery, but without the same increase in productivity. "To sell cotton in order to buy negroes," one observer noted in Mississippi, "to make more cotton to buy more negroes, *ad infinitum*, is the aim and direct tendency of all the operations of the thoroughgoing cotton planter." As eastern land wore out, even elite planter families were compelled to uproot themselves, join the southwestern migration, and submit to the ruder life on the cotton frontier. In Jasper County, Georgia, for example, almost six out of every ten slaveholders moved on between 1850 and 1860. Having moved from North Carolina to Alabama with her slaveholder husband, May Drake expressed her discontent in letters to her family: "To a female who has once been blest with every comfort, and even every luxury, blest with the society of a large and respectable circle of relations and friends . . . to such people Mississippi and Alabama are but a dreary waste." Another wrote, "The farmers in this country [Alabama] live in a miserable manner. They think only of making money, and their houses are hardly fit to live in."

All the economic pressures and calculations left their clearest imprint on the relationship between masters and slaves—contrary to the hopes of people like Fitzhugh. The paternalist ethos claimed to value people and the proper relationships among them higher than concerns about dollars and cents. According to Fitzhugh himself, one of the principal beneficiaries of this attitude was "the sanctity and purity of the family circle." Indeed, he asserted, "slavery, marriage, religion" existed in "intimate connection and dependence" with each other. "The Slave Institution at the South," enthused another writer, "increases the tendency to dignify the family." But the actual workings of the South's slave-labor system constantly contradicted and discredited such claims.

This contradiction revealed itself with particular cruelty in the way slavery continually broke up African-American families. Upon the death of a master, the slave families he owned were often divided up among heirs and creditors. And though some tried to avoid it, owners with economic problems often sold off individual slaves, separating family members. Former slave Elizabeth Keckley remembered a Virginia master who purchased more hogs than he could pay for. "To escape from his embarrassment," she wrote, "it was necessary to sell one of the slaves." He selected the son of his cook. That mother was forced to ready her son and send him to the master's house, where the boy was "placed in the scales, and was sold, like the hogs, at so much per pound." If the method of determining the boy's price was not typical, the fact of and reason for his sale were.

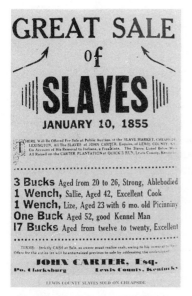

Slaves for sale, 1855. The twenty-three slaves to be sold belonged to a Kentucky planter, John Carter, who decided to "liquidate his assets" before moving to the free state of Indiana.

As slavery's heartland moved southwestward, the forced migration of hundreds of thousands of African-Americans caused the massive destruction of families. This happened most obviously when masters stayed put but sold individual slaves into the deep South. But even migrating masters who took all their slaves with them regularly broke up slave families, since slave marriages (like the one between Huldah and Lewis Orton) often joined people belonging to different masters, especially on the smaller farms most common in the upper South. The migration of one master's chattel meant separation from family members belonging to others. Masters forcibly broke up somewhere between a fifth and a third of all slave marriages.

Masters also sold slaves away from their family as a punishment for various infractions of the rules. (Huldah's master, John Cohoon, sold two slaves for such reasons.) But the threat of sale was only one way to control slave behavior; both rewards and punishments were used. Owners often gave extra food or clothing, preferred work assignments, and (much more rarely) small amounts of cash to those slaves who picked the most cotton or bore the largest number of children. And the task system of labor organization (discussed below) common in rice cultivation offered its own inducements.

Not surprisingly, though, punishment was used more often than reward. Whipping was the most common. In the rice districts of South Carolina, slaves were most often punished for failing to complete tasks assigned to them. Former slave Hagar Brown remembered, "Don't do your task, driver wave that whip, put you over a barrel, beat you so blood run down." An overseer employed by a prominent rice planter, Robert Allson, gave twelve lashes to eight women for "hoeing bad corn." On the Louisiana cotton plantation of Bennett Barrow, similarly, some three-quarters of the incidents that led to physical punishments were work-related: for "not picking cotton," "for not picking as well as he can," for picking "very trashy cotton," "for not bringing her cotton up," etc. On average, Barrow whipped one of his slaves every four days. Others were im-

"MY MASTER HAS SOLD ALBERT TO A TRADER . . ."

In the following letter, a slave woman named Maria Perkins writes to her husband, Richard, about the sale of their children and the possibility of being sold herself.

Charlottesville, Oct. 8th, 1852

Dear Husband

I write you a letter to let you know my distress. My master has sold Albert to a trader on Monday court day and myself and [our] other child is for sale also and I want [to] . . . hear from you very soon before next court [day] if you can. . . . I don't want you to wait till Christmas. I want you to tell Dr. Hamelton and your master if either will buy me they can attend to it now and then I can go afterwards. I don't want a trader to get me. They asked me if I had got any person to buy me and I told them no. They took me to the courthouse too [but] they never put me up [for sale]. A man [by] the name of Brady bought Albert and [he] is gone. I don't know where. They say he lives in Scottesville. My things is in several places some is in Staunton and if I should be sold I don't know what will become of them. I don't expect to meet with the luck to get that way till I am quite heartsick. Nothing more.

I am and ever will be your kind wife,
Maria Perkins.

"The Slave Auction." Slavery, and particularly slave auctions, left an indelible impression on many visitors to the antebellum South. One of them was a British artist, Eyre Crowe, who sketched a Richmond slave sale in 1853.

prisoned, chained, beaten, shot, or maimed in other ways. And with all this, his biographer tells us, Barrow treated slaves better than did many of his neighbors. "It is not the fault of the slaveholder that he is so cruel," wrote the former slave Solomon Northup, "so much as it is the fault of the system under which he lives." "Talk not about kind and Christian masters," agreed James Pennington, another former slave. "They are not masters of the system. The system is master of them."

Ironically, the profit motive sometimes also set limits on a master's cruelty. Compared with slaves in the Caribbean and South America, North American slaves were generally punished less brutally and fed and clothed more adequately. One reason was economic: the rising price of slaves in North America—especially after the ban on the Atlantic slave trade—put a premium on keeping one's slaves alive as long as possible and encouraging them to reproduce. (A field hand cost $600 at the turn of the century and three times that in 1860.) Slave children, after all, added to an owner's assets, whether as additional labor or valuable goods to sell. The former Georgia planter John C. Reed reported that "the greatest profit of all was what the master thought of and talked of all the day long—the natural increase of his slaves as he called it," which required "keeping slaves healthy and rapidly multiplying." A South Carolina planter kept his slaves' cabins whitewashed because he believed doing so "makes the slave prolific," adding, "I have, at this time, a hundred and fifty of these people; and their annual increase may be estimated as adding as much to my income as arises from all other sources."

Economic considerations also led large cotton plantations to become more self-sufficient in food between 1840 and 1860. With their plantations at last established, southwestern planters set their slaves to work raising the animals and food crops (especially corn) previously bought from northwestern farmers. This made economic sense because the growing and harvesting seasons of cotton and corn did not conflict and because growing food with cheap cheap slave labor cost less than buying it from the free farmers of the Northwest. And as the trade between the Northwest and Southwest decreased, economic ties between the Northwest and Northeast grew stronger. This economic realignment would prove politically important as sectional animosity deepened in the 1850s.

The Yeomen

Planters were not the only southerners to alter their economic behavior in the1850s. The cotton boom now led more small farmers into cotton cultivation. Those nearest to transportation, like up-country Georgia farmers near the new Western and Atlantic Railroad, found it easiest to take this step. By the end of the decade, about half of all slaveless farmers in the cotton kingdom were growing cotton for market; in fact, more southerners grew more cotton during the 1850s than at any other time.

A free man of color. A form issued by a Virginia county court in 1858 to Richard Cogbill, certifying his claim to be a free-born African-American.

High cotton prices were not the only reason. Many subsistence farmers were beginning to suffer the negative effects of economic growth. Land was becoming more expensive and less available—just when the practice of partible inheritance (dividing property among one's children) left many southern landowners with farms too small to support a family.

This situation was most acute in the oldest southern communities. Many small farmers sold their land to wealthy neighbors (who thus grew wealthier still). Some took the cash and set out to try their luck further south and west. Others (like Abraham Lincoln's family, who moved from Kentucky to Indiana to Illinois) migrated into the free and border states and territories. Twice as many Americans made this trek as moved from free states to slave. Still others joined the growing ranks of southern tenants, farmhands, and textile workers. In 1856, the *Southern Cultivator* decried the "large number [of whites] at the South who have no legal right nor interest in the soil [and] no homes of their own." Indeed, by 1860 a third of the South's white population was propertyless.

For many small farmers struggling to hold on to their land, rising cotton prices looked like a godsend. By growing a little cotton they could earn the cash to buy what they could no longer produce for themselves. In the short run, the spread of the cotton economy helped to unify southerners at opposite ends of the economic ladder. Especially in the lower South, formerly self-sufficient farmers turning to cotton became most dependent on their slaveowning planter neighbors. Marginal and even middling cotton producers often looked to wealthy planters to rent them slaves, to employ their sons—as plantation overseers, for example—and to gin, transport, and market their cotton. For similar services, farmers in the North had to deal with merchants and brokers, who often used their middleman position to squeeze small farmers. In the South, planters shielded yeomen from such pressures, apparently helping to shore up small-scale white farming in the region.

The strengthening of slavery in the society of the new South coincided with its erosion in the upper South. As tobacco cultivation moved inland in search of better soil, the Chesapeake area turned to mixed farming, especially of wheat and other cereals. In Nansemond County, for example, grain and livestock came to dominate the economy. This change in crops brought with it a change in the labor system: tobacco required a year-round work force, while wheat needed large numbers of hands only at harvest, so maintaining many slaves (who had to be fed and clothed all year long, even when idle) was uneconomical.

Slave quarters. A row of rude cabins comprised the slave quarters of
a plantation on Fort George Island,
Florida.

Some masters—especially in Virginia—managed to adapt to the changing reality without abandoning slavery. The 1808 constitutional ban on importing slaves and the suppression of the international slave trade came just when demand in the deep South was growing; this made the domestic slave trade very profitable. When sold to an Alabama cotton planter, a Louisiana sugar baron, or a Carolina rice grower, a slave born and raised in Maryland or Virginia fetched his or her master a handsome return on his investment.

Nevertheless, the decline of tobacco in the upper South meant the eventual decline of slavery there, too. Maryland moved steadily toward a free-labor economy. In 1790, four out of every ten white Maryland families had owned slaves; by 1850, fewer than two out of ten did so. The impact of all this on black life in Maryland was even more dramatic. As a result of the revolutionary era's libertarian spirit and economic and political disruptions, the Chesapeake's free black population grew tenfold (to sixty thousand) by 1810. In that year, one out of five Maryland blacks was free. By 1860, about half the state's black residents were out of slavery. Many sought the greater freedom and diversity of the towns, especially Baltimore. In other cases, white masters who emancipated their slaves then either hired them as wage laborers or took them on as tenant farmers working small parcels of land.

Slaveowning in Virginia was also declining, but more slowly. Along the Virginia coast, larger masters began renting slaves to small white farmers early in the century. And unlike Maryland, Virginia had a great expanse of inland territory into which slave-based staple production could be moved as conditions near the coast deteriorated. Still, 10 percent of Virginia's blacks were free by 1850, compared to less than 1 percent in Mississippi, Texas, Alabama, and Georgia. In Missouri and Kentucky, two other states of the upper South, the fortunes of slavery by the 1850s also seemed in doubt.

The Slaves

Just under four million unfree men, women, and children lived and labored in the South in 1860—about a third of the total southern population. Nine out of ten lived in the countryside, most in a broad belt stretching from coastal South Carolina inland through central Georgia, Alabama, and Mississippi and then bending southward down the lower Mississippi Valley to New Orleans.

Ten percent of all enslaved laborers in the South worked in industry, transportation, construction, lumbering, or mining. Another 15 percent were domestic servants or performed other types of nonagricultural labor. The rest—fully three-quarters of the total slave labor force—worked directly on the land: 55 percent in cotton, 10 percent in tobacco, and 10 percent in sugar, rice, or hemp. Their labor supported the South's entire agrarian economy, producing more than half its tobacco, three-quarters of its cotton, and almost all of the rice, sugar, and hemp.

The slave agriculture of this new and bigger South rested on larger units than in the past. More than half of all slaves now belonged to owners of at least twenty slaves each. And for every slave who worked on a farm with fewer than ten slaves, there was another who worked on a plantation with more than fifty slaves. Nearly half of all slave laborers in the cotton kingdom worked on plantations boasting more

RATION DAY.

A master distributes provisions in an illustration from a weekly newspaper report on the operations of a plantation around 1860. The engraving suggests that this planter provided his slaves with a varied and nutritious diet, which was not typically the case. It fails to show the gardens and other methods slaves used to supplement often meager or boring fare.

than four hundred acres of cultivated land; together they produced about half the nation's cotton. (In contrast, the typical farm family of the Northwest lived and worked, usually unaided, on fifty acres of land.)

In the seventeenth and eighteenth centuries, competition from Caribbean sugar planters bid up the price North Americans had to

"Family Worship in a Plantation in South Carolina." An engraving from a British illustrated weekly depicts the scene in a "rude chapel" of a Port Royal, South Carolina, plantation, where the master and mistress are "engaged in Divine worship, surrounded by [their] slaves, in a state of almost patriarchal simplicity." Virtually all published illustrations of slavery are either apologist images of planter benevolence such as this, or critical views of slavery's brutality.

pay for their slaves. Congress's 1808 prohibition against the importation of Africans further constricted the supply, which boosted prices even higher. These high prices led owners to place a premium on the survival and natural reproduction of the slaves they already owned. The fact that their owners could not afford to work them to death gave blacks greater leverage—backed up with often subtle forms of day-to-day resistance—in alleviating their conditions. As the living standards of the North American population as a whole improved during the early nineteenth century, this complex interplay of planter self-interest and slave assertiveness helped the black population improve its conditions as well. One ex-slave later recalled that his owner "fed us regular on good, substantial food, just like you'd tend to your horse, if you had a real good one."

Of course, their improved living standards did not raise the slaves' conditions to that of whites—or even of free blacks. Owners extracted as much labor from their slaves as they could and spent as

"THE BARGAIN WAS AGREED UPON . . ."

In 1841, Solomon Northup, a free African-American living in New York, was kidnapped while visiting Washington, D.C., and sold into slavery. He spent the next twelve years of his life working on plantations in Louisiana, finally attaining freedom in 1853. His book, Twelve Years a Slave, *presented a stark, detailed account of day-to-day slave life, including this depiction of a sale run by a slave-dealer named Freeman.*

NEXT DAY MANY customers called to examine Freeman's "new lot." The latter gentleman was very loquacious, dwelling at much length upon our several good points and qualities. He would make us hold up our heads, walk briskly back and forth, while customers would feel of our hands and arms and bodies, turn us about, ask us what we could do, make us open our mouths and show our teeth, precisely as a jockey examines a horse which he is about to barter for or purchase. Sometimes a man or woman was taken back to the small house in the yard, stripped, and inspected more minutely. Scars upon a slave's back were considered evidence of a rebellious or unruly spirit, and hurt his sale. . . .

During the day, however, a number of sales were made. David and Caroline were purchased together by a Natchez planter. They left us, grinning broadly, and in a most happy state of mind, caused by the fact of their not being separated. Sethe was sold to a planter of Baton Rouge, her eyes flashing with anger as she was led away.

The same man also purchased Randall. The little fellow was made to jump, and run across the floor, and perform many other feats exhibiting his activity

little as possible. This led to what former slave Frederick Douglass remembered as "the close-fisted stinginess that fed the poor slave on coarse cornmeal and tainted meat, that clothed him in [coarse] tow-linen and hurried him on to toil through the field in all weathers, with wind and rain beating through his tattered garments." A typical field hand received a weekly food ration of just three and a half pounds of salt pork or bacon and a quarter-bushel of cornmeal. While high in the calories needed for heavy labor, that diet was seriously deficient nutritionally, even when slaves themselves supplemented it by hunting, fishing, or cultivating small garden plots. Slaves' shelter and clothing were also far inferior to that of the worst-paid northern laborer. By one estimate the cost of feeding, clothing, and housing slaves added up to less than a quarter of the value of the crops they produced. White farmers working their own land kept a far higher portion of their own output.

Slaves worked much harder and longer hours than whites. Twelve to fifteen hours per day, often at backbreaking work, was the norm. While most free married women worked only in the home, both female and male slaves, as well as young children, worked for the master. As Emily Burke (a white schoolteacher from the North who worked near Savannah, Georgia, in the 1830s and 1840s) observed, "During the greater part of the winter season, the negro women are busy in picking, ginning, and packing the cotton for market." Thus under the South's slave system of labor, a slaveowner could profit from the productivity of an entire family in ways that most employers of free people could not.

Even as the physical conditions of slave life improved during the early nineteenth century, other burdens of slavery increased. Perhaps nothing symbolized the human cost of bondage so vividly as the wholesale destruction of slave families in

and condition. All the time the trade was going on, Eliza was crying aloud, and wringing her hands. She besought the man not to buy him, unless he also bought herself and Emily. She promised, in that case, to be the most faithful slave that ever lived. The man answered that he could not afford it, and then Eliza burst into a paroxysm of grief, weeping plaintively. Freeman turned round to her, savagely, with his whip in his uplifted hand, ordering her to stop her noise, or . . . he would take her to the yard and give her a hundred lashes. Yes, he would take the nonsense out of her pretty quick—if he didn't, might he be d——d. Eliza shrunk before him, and tried to wipe away her tears, but it was all in vain. She wanted to be with her children, she said, the little time she had to live.

All the frowns and threats of Freeman could not wholly silence the afflicted mother. She kept on begging and beseeching them, most piteously, not to separate the three. Over and over again she told them how she loved her boy. A great many times she repeated her former promises—how very faithful and obedient she would be; how hard she would labor day and night, to the last moment of her life; if he would only buy them all together. But it was of no avail; the man could not afford it. The bargain was agreed upon, and Randall must go alone. Then Eliza ran to him; embraced him passionately; kissed him again and again; told him to remember her—all the while her tears falling in the boy's face like rain. . . .

The planter from Baton Rouge, with his new purchase, was ready to depart.

"Don't cry, mama. I will be a good boy. Don't cry," said Randall, looking back, as they passed out the door.

What has become of the lad, God knows. It was a mournful scene indeed. I would have cried myself if I had dared.

these years. In 1863, a former Virginia slave woman encountered the husband from whom she had been forcibly separated years earlier. Both had since remarried. Seeing her former spouse "was like a stroke of death to me. We threw ourselves into each other's arms and cried," she said. "White folks got a heap to answer for the way they've done to colored folks! So much they wouldn't never pray it away!" The loss of children was even more painful. "When they took from me the last little girl," recalled another woman, "oh, I believed I never should have got over it! It almost broke my heart!" A poem of the 1850s, entitled "The Slave-Mother's Reply," portrayed the sentiments of slave women from North Carolina:

> Georgia's rice-fields show the care
> Of my boys who labor there;
> Alabama claims the three
> Last who settled on my knee;
> Children seven, seven masters hold
> By their cursed power of gold.

During these decades, a combination of factors—including the increasing market value of slaves and white fear of free blacks—steadily foreclosed the blacks' chances of escaping slavery. The modest emancipationist sentiment of the 1780s and 1790s soon gave way to a state-by-state campaign to make even individual emancipation more and more difficult. It became a crime to teach a slave to read and write. Free blacks found themselves hounded, had their rights limited, their movements restricted, their very presence in southern states assailed and sometimes banned. An 1831 petition to Virginia's legislature explained the white fear of black freedom. Once "indulged with the hope of freedom," otherwise "submissive and easily controlled" slaves "reject restraint and become almost wholly un-

"THE COLORED MAN HAS NO REDRESS . . ."

Uneasy about the existence of a free black population in the South, lawmakers passed strict measures restricting the rights of nonslave blacks in their states, as described below by a black Kentuckian named Washington Spaulding.

OUR PRINCIPAL DIFFICULTY here grows out of the police laws, which are very stringent. For instance, a police officer may go [to] a house at night, without any search warrant, and, if the door is not opened when he knocks, force it in, and ransack the house, and the colored man has no redress. At other times, they come and say they are hunting for stolen goods or runaway slaves, and, some of them being great scoundrels, if they see a piece of goods, which may have been purchased, they will take it and carry it off. If I go out of the state, I cannot come back to it again. The penalty is imprisonment in the penitentiary. . . . If a freeman comes here (perhaps he may have been born free), he cannot get free papers, and if the police find out that he has got no free papers, they snap him up, and put him in jail. Sometimes they remain in jail three, four, and five months before they are brought to trial. My children are just tied down here. If they go to Louisiana, there is no chance for them, unless I can get some white man to go to New Orleans and swear they belong to him, and claim them as his slaves. . . . There are many cases of assault and battery in which we can have no redress. I have known a case here where a man bought himself three times. The last time, he was chained on board a boat, to be sent South, when a gentleman who now lives in New York saw him, and bought him, and gave him his free papers.

From dawn to dusk. Men, women, and children pick cotton under the watchful eye of an overseer.

manageable." The petition added, "It is by the expectation of liberty, and by that alone, that they can be rendered a dangerous population."

Though slaves used in agriculture had much in common, the specific types of labor and working conditions varied greatly from place to place. Much of this variation in work stemmed from the crop itself. All agricultural labor involved weeks of plowing and planting followed by months of hoeing the fields and tending the growing crops. The busy weeks of harvesting that usually began in August did not end until each crop had been cut, weighed, prepared for export, and stored. Then came the miscellaneous chores of winter. There were fences to build and mend, hogs to slaughter, and wood to chop, stack, and haul. Slaves also performed the carpentry and blacksmithing that kept a plantation productive and in good repair.

Dawn signaled the start of a working day that often extended far into the night. Most fieldwork ended at dusk, but there might be cotton to gin, sugar to mill, corn to grind, or any number of other tasks that could be done indoors by the light of a lantern. Even after the master or overseer ended this segment of the working day, there were meals to prepare and children to feed, wash, and put to bed. Many slaves also grew food in small gardens near their quarters. Slaves also had to clean their cabins, wash and mend their clothes, and do all the other chores of daily life.

Some crops demanded the care and attention of highly skilled individuals, while others could be cultivated by slaves organized into gangs that worked systematically and rapidly across a field. Rice cultivation required skilled and precise labor. In March women generally had the responsibility for planting rice. It was never just scattered about a plowed field like other grains; each seed had to be carefully placed in a single row along the deep trenches that had been plowed and shaped earlier. Over the next five months, the fields had to be alternately flooded, left to dry in the sun, and hoed; delay in any of these steps could ruin an entire crop. The harvest began in August and kept every able-bodied slave in the fields until October. Men cut the rice plants with sickles while women followed, bundling them. Later the plants had to be flailed by hand to separate the grain from the stalk. Rice cultivation involved intricate systems of dams and dikes to flood and drain the land; they were usually built and repaired after the harvest and before the spring planting.

Much of the work on the rice plantations of the Georgia and South Carolina low country was organized according to the task system. Here each slave was assigned a particular task each day. Those who worked slowly might find themselves working longer hours than usual, but if the task was completed early, the rest of the day belonged to the individual. This arrangement was intended to encourage slaves to do their work quickly even without close supervision. George Gould later remembered that his master "used to come in the field, and tell the overseers not to balk [us], if we got done soon to let us alone and do our own work as we pleased." The task system also permitted a degree of personal autonomy and even modest economic well-being unknown under gang labor. Those finishing their tasks early might spend their free time producing or acquiring things—fish, game, handicrafts, crops, even livestock—for personal use, barter, and sale. Thus Mary Jess, a low-country South Carolina slave, would later recall how she "worked and earned money outside her regular task work," and Adam LeCount tended to his "own field" after completing his task. Owners permitted these activities both to speed up work in the rice fields and to shift responsibility for feeding their laborers onto the laborers themselves.

Rice cultivation also involved special perils. Work in those fields exposed slaves to malaria, pneumonia, and tuberculosis. One visitor attributed the high number of deaths among slaves to the "constant moisture and heat of the atmosphere, together with the alternate

An engraving from abolitionist George Bourne's *Slavery Illustrated in Its Effects upon Women,* published in 1837.

floodings and dryings of the fields, on which the negroes are perpetually at work, often ankle-deep in mud, with their bare heads exposed to the fierce rays of the sun." This visitor also observed that "at such seasons every white man leaves the spot, as a matter of course, and proceeds inland to the high grounds; or, if he can afford it, he travels northward to the springs of Saratoga, or the lakes of Canada."

Charles Ball had been a slave in both Maryland and Georgia. In a memoir written after winning his freedom, Ball contrasted rice cultivation to the work on a tobacco plantation. Two differences he emphasized were the lower mortality rates among slaves who grew tobacco and the seasonal slack periods that followed the weeks of hard labor on the tobacco plantations.

On tobacco plantations, plowing began in April. In May the tobacco plants that had been growing indoors since March were transplanted to the fields. For the next several months, gangs of slaves periodically worked in the fields, weeding, hoeing, and pruning the lower leaves of the tobacco plants. The plants were harvested in August and September, then hung to dry. Slaves then stripped the stalks and prepared the leaves for export or manufacturing. After the hard weeks of harvesting, this work seemed comparatively easy to Ball. In the winter, which Ball found to be "some sort of respite from the toils of the year," slaves chopped wood, "repaired fences, split rails for new fences, slaughtered hogs, cleared new land, [and] raised tobacco plants for the next planting."

Cotton was another story altogether. Since it required none of the skill or delicacy demanded by rice, cotton could be cultivated by large gangs of laborers, a system that forced planters to emphasize supervision and discipline. Working side by side through most of the year, men and women swept across one field after another, plowing, planting, hoeing, and picking at an unrelenting pace set by a leader. Solomon Northup, a free New York black who was kidnapped and sold to a Louisiana cotton planter, wrote that the fastest worker took "the lead row," and anyone who fell behind or was "a moment idle [was] whipped."

Through the heat of August, September, and October, all able-bodied men and women picked the cotton, walking stooped over, pulling the bolls from the prickly pods, which cut their hands. This unrelenting labor kept them in the fields from sunrise until it was, Northup wrote, "too dark to see, and when the moon is full, they oftentimes labor till the middle of the night." No one would stop, "even at dinner time, nor return to the quarters, however late it be, until the order to halt" was heard.

"An ordinary day's work," for Northup and the other slaves who worked Master Epps's plantation, was two hundred pounds of cotton. Some slaves, including Northup, picked less, while one woman named Patsy earned a reputation as the fastest and most skillful field-worker in the area for the five hundred pounds she could pick in a day. Skills, of course, varied from one individual to another, and no slave had much incentive to work as hard as possible. Thus the master relied on force both to determine how hard an individual could work and to maintain productivity.

Epps, like most slaveowners, used the whip to get his slaves to work as hard as possible. Northup recalled that when someone "new and unaccustomed to picking" went to the field for the first time, he or she was "whipped up smartly, and made for that day to pick as fast" as possible. However much cotton was picked that day became the standard amount the master expected from that individual. Each day ended at the scales where an overseer weighed the cotton each slave had picked; those who fell short of their quota were whipped.

Despite the whip, Northup never picked cotton fast enough to satisfy Epps, who therefore rented him out to a nearby sugar planter for a dollar a day. Masters often rented out slaves whose labor they did not immediately need or whom they wanted to punish, but the consequences were complex. Rented slaves were exposed to other masters, who might treat them even worse than their owners had—punishment indeed. But a slave exposed to a number of bosses might more readily measure (and perhaps condemn) the treatment received at the hands of his own master. A rented slave, cut off from family and friends, might find disobedience or resistance of any kind all the more difficult. On the other hand, a rented slave working in a series of locales could acquire a knowledge of the countryside that might be useful in escape attempts.

In this case, Solomon Northup welcomed being rented because he proved more "suited" to cutting sugarcane. Like cotton, sugar was cultivated and harvested by gangs of slaves laboring in unison. They planted and hoed between January and April. Harvesting began in October. At the Hawkins plantation, Northup was soon leading a gang of fifty to a hundred cutters. By January, the slaves were preparing for another crop.

Some slaves, both male and female, worked as servants in

"WE WEREN'T ALLOWED TO SIT DOWN"

As young female slaves grew old enough, most went to work in the fields. But some became personal servants to their owners, an experience one of them later recalled:

WHEN I WAS nine years old, they took me from my mother and sold me. Massa Tinsley made me the house girl. I had to make the beds, clean the house, and other things. After I finished my regular work, I would go to the mistress's room, bow to her, and stand there till she noticed me. Then she would say, "Martha, are you through with your work?" I'd say, "Yes mam." She'd say, "No you ain't; you haven't lowered the shades." I'd then lower the shades, fill the water pitcher, arrange the towels on the washstand, and anything else mistress wanted me to do. Then she'd tell me that was about all to do in there. Then I would go to the other rooms in the house and do the same things. We weren't allowed to sit down. We had to be doing something all day. Whenever we were in the presence of any of the white folks, we had to stand up.

the homes of the plantation owners. Frederick Douglass remembered that servants were "carefully selected, not only with a view to their capacity and adeptness, but with especial regard to their personal appearance, their graceful agility, and pleasing address." These slaves, he wrote, "constituted a sort of black aristocracy" who "resembled the field hands in nothing except their color." Douglass concluded, "In dress, as well as in form and feature, in manner and speech, in tastes and habits, the distance between these favored few and the sorrow and hunger-smitten multitudes of the . . . field were immense."

But the house slaves, though privileged, still worked hard. Black women worked at such demanding domestic tasks as washing clothes, cleaning, child-care, and cooking. The white teacher Emily Burke considered this last responsibility the most demanding of all, involving both long hours and heavy labor. "After having cooked the supper and washed the dishes," Burke observed of one slave cook, "she goes about making preparations for the next morning's meal. In the first place she goes into the woods to gather sticks and dried limbs of trees, which she ties in bundles and brings to the kitchen on her head, with which to kindle the morning fire." The woman completed her night's work by grinding all the corn needed for the next day's hominy and bread. The next morning she must rise early, "for she has every article of food that comes on to the table to cook."

INDUSTRIAL AND URBAN GROWTH

According to the census, about one out of every ten slave laborers in 1860 produced nonagricultural goods. This statistic includes slaves working under widely varied conditions—those employed on the farm or plantation as blacksmiths, barrel-makers, or carpenters, for example, as well as those who did their work in towns or cities. But even in the cities, the majority of slaves performed domestic duties in private homes, hotels, and restaurants; only somewhere between an eighth and a tenth performed industrial labor, whatever the level of skill. They worked in textile mills, tobacco factories, and ironworks, built roads and railroads, moved goods on steamships and docks and as teamsters and cartmen.

Most southern factories were located in the upper South. At the famous Tredegar ironworks in Richmond, Virginia, slaves chopped wood for the furnaces, smelted ore, and forged metal. But there were also industrial slaves in the lower South. At a cotton mill in Athens, Georgia, more than a hundred slaves worked alongside an equal number of whites at such tasks as spinning and weaving. Two other types of work that were done almost exclusively by slaves were roadbuilding and teamstering. Road crews were often made up of slaves rented from local masters.

The small proportion of slaves engaged in industrial work reflected an important characteristic of the antebellum southern economy. By 1850, cotton and slavery had brought prosperity and expansion to the South, but not significant industrial or urban development, though both had occurred throughout the rest of the nation.

True, exports did stimulate some urban growth. New Orleans, through which much of the cotton crop was shipped to England, throve. So did Baltimore, Mobile, Charleston, Savannah, Norfolk, and Richmond. But except for these ocean and river ports, the South remained overwhelmingly agricultural. Most towns were little more than isolated trading villages where nearby farmers and planters took their cotton to be shipped to the major ports. This did not seem unusual early in the century, when the North's own development was just beginning. But by 1850, the contrast between North and South was stark.

Partly because of a slump in cotton prices during the 1830s and 1840s, partly to reduce the North's economic power over the South, some southern leaders displayed greater interest in their region's urban, commercial, and industrial development during the 1850s. "At present," an Alabama newspaper editor grumbled in 1851, "the North fattens and grows rich upon the South. . . . Northerners abuse and denounce slavery and slaveholders, yet our slaves are clothed with Northern manufactured goods, have Northern hats and shoes, work with Northern hoes, plows, and other implements" while "the slaveholder dresses in Northern goods, rides in a Northern saddle . . . sports his Northern carriage . . . reads Northern books."

The Southern Commercial Convention—founded in the 1830s—was now revived to encourage and publicize regional development. And in fact, some of the wealthiest planters did begin to invest more of their cotton profits in other sectors of the economy. They established banks, thereby increasing the ability of southerners to finance their own economic expansion. They also built more railroads. In Alabama alone, 610 additional miles of track were laid in the 1850s. Cities grew. Industrial output increased, too, as more southerners built sawmills and gristmills, which employed a quarter of Alabama's industrial labor force in 1860. Planters also began to finance the development of a textile industry.

The South's urban working population expanded as well, though it was still small in comparison with that in the North. But the preference among southern-born whites for agriculture meant that much of this labor force had to be recruited from among the black and foreign-born population. Irish, free blacks, and slaves performed most of the cities' unskilled work. And while southern-born whites clustered in piloting, printing, and the building trades, German and British workers held many of the remaining skilled jobs.

All this was too little too late to change the basic shape of the southern economy, as textiles had changed both England and the American Northeast. The railroads eased the movement of cotton from farm to port but did little to diversify the economy. By 1860, the entire South still produced only 6 percent of the nation's cotton textiles. Lowell, Massachusetts, alone contained as many spindles as could be found throughout the entire southern textile industry. Other ways of measuring tell the same story. While 60 percent of the North's labor force worked outside agriculture by 1860, only 16 percent of the South's labor force did. And though more than one out of every three northeasterners already lived in towns and cities, in the Southeast the corresponding proportion was still only one in eight.

What caused the lag in southern urban and industrial development? Although the point is still debated, the slave-labor system itself appears principally responsible. Specifically, the system's most important precapitalist characteristic—the fact that the laborer was owned by another as personal property—retarded development in a number of ways. For one thing, the rural population, overwhelmingly composed of impoverished slaves and poor white farmers, constituted a weak market for all but the coarsest consumer goods.

Equally important, slavery discouraged efforts to raise the productivity of labor technologically, the basis of economic development and social progress. Slaveowners bought few of the labor-saving farm implements so popular among northwestern family farmers at midcentury, whose manufacture underpinned northwestern industry and indirectly stimulated the production of coal and iron. Slaveowners could expand production by simply buying more slaves and moving onto richer land. Despite the urgings of the Southern Commercial Convention, therefore, the 1850s brought a sharp decline in the value of farm implements manufactured in the booming Southwest.

Problems also arose in trying to base urban industry on slave labor. The high profits to be made in raising cotton tended to keep not only investment capital but also slave laborers on the land. Especially in the late 1840s and the 1850s, the same high cotton prices that enriched southern slaveowners led them to withdraw slaves from the cities and transport them into the countryside—including large numbers of skilled artisans, who were now used to start new plantations.

Insofar as the South's economy did diversify, expanding its urban and industrial sectors, it did so at the expense of slavery itself. The experience of the upper South—Delaware and Maryland in particular—testifies eloquently to this trend. When a slave worked in a town or city, the bonds of slavery were loosened in a number of ways. Urban work brought a slave into close touch with free blacks and the world outside the South. That exposure encouraged and assisted attempts to escape slavery altogether. Two Irish longshoremen working alongside the slave Frederick Douglass in Baltimore, for example, "expressed the deepest sympathy for me, and the most dedicated hatred of slavery. They went so far as to tell me that I ought to run away and go to the North, that I should find friends there, and that I should then be as free as anybody." Douglass "remembered their words and their advice, and looked forward to an escape to the North as a possible means of gaining the liberty for which my heart panted." By passing as a free black sailor, an impersonation aided by his experience in the shipyard and the assistance of real free blacks, Douglass did escape to the North a few years later. Others simply took advantage of the relative anonymity of cities and disappeared into the South's urban free black population.

Naturally, planters found the side-effects of urbanization and industrialization very threatening. Slave flight was by no means the only problem. The greater freedom (especially freedom of movement) that generally went with urban employment tended to erode the slaveowners' power. "The ties which bound together the master and the slave," the New Orleans *Daily Picayune* complained, were being "gradually severed" in that city, as slave workers "become intemperate, disorderly, and lose the respect which the servant should entertain for the master." Even worse was the fact that "their example is contagious upon those [slaves] who do not possess these dangerous privileges." Industrial slaves, warned Senator James H. Hammond of South Carolina, "were more than half freed" and destined to become "the most corrupt and turbulent" sector of

---

". . . HE HAD BEEN TOO FREE WITH THE NIGGERS"

Frederick Law Olmsted, later known as the co-designer of New York's Central Park, made several extended tours of the South for the New York Times *in the 1850s. Here Olmsted describes a coalmine operated by a workforce composed of slaves and white immigrants. His description suggests that although slaves doing industrial work in cities were granted a certain amount of autonomy, social relationships between blacks and whites remained severely regimented.*

YESTERDAY I VISITED a coal-pit: the majority of the mining laborers are slaves, and commonly athletic and fine-looking Negroes; but a considerable number of white hands are also employed, and they occupy all the responsible posts. The slaves are, some of them, owned by the Mining Company; but the most are hired of their owners, at from $120 to $200 a year, the company boarding and clothing them. (I have the impression that I heard it was customary to give them a certain allowance of money and let them find their own board.)

The whites are mostly English or Welshmen. One of them, with whom I conversed, told me that he had been here several years; he had previously lived some years at the North. He got better wages here than he had earned at the North, but he was not contented, and did not intend to remain. On pressing him for the reason of his discontent, he said, after some hesitation, that he had rather live where he could be more free; a man had to be too "*discreet*" here: if one happened to say anything that gave offense, they thought no more of drawing a pistol or a knife upon him, than they would of kicking a dog that was in their way. Not long since, a young English fellow came to the pit, and was put to work along with a gang of Negroes. One morning, about a week afterwards, twenty or thirty men called on him, and told him that they would allow him fifteen minutes to get out of sight, and if they ever saw him in those parts again, they would "give him hell." They were all armed, and there was nothing for the young fellow to do but to move "right off."

"What reason did they give him for it?"

"They did not give him any reason."

"But what had he done?"

"Why I believe they thought he had been too free with the niggers; he wasn't used to them, you see, sir, and he talked to 'em free like, and they thought he'd make 'em think too much of themselves."

the South's slave labor force. "It is not to be denied," concluded a Savannah grand jury in 1845, that such freedoms were "striking directly at the existence of our institutions, and unless broken up in time, will result in the total prostration of existing relations." "The cities," another white Southerner typically concluded, "is no place for niggers! They get strange notions into their heads and grow discontented. They ought, every one of them, [to] be sent back onto the plantations."

Slavery was ill suited to industrial work, and it impeded the formation of a free labor force. Competition from cheap slave laborers—whether direct or indirect, immediate or potential—tended to depress the status, conditions, and pay rates of free workers as well. More generally, a society based on slavery regarded working for others as particularly degraded. A leading advocate of southern economic development, Senator George Mason of Virginia, complained that "slavery discourages arts and manufactures. The poor despise labor when performed by slaves." The stigma thereby attached to wage labor further discouraged whites from undertaking such work. Given the choice, therefore, most white wage-earners (including the overwhelming majority of Irish and German immigrants of the 1830s through the 1850s) preferred to take their chances in the urban North.

Moreover, the conflicts and insecurities bred by slave society led most owners to both fear and despise the social classes, institutions, and values that went along with widespread manufacturing and free wage labor. "We have no cities. We don't want them," typically exclaimed one white Alabaman. "We want no manufactures; we desire no trading, no mechanical or manufacturing classes. As long as we have our rice, our sugar, our tobacco, and our cotton, we can command wealth to purchase all we want."

Most of all, slaveowners worried that free wage-earners and their employers would seek first to limit the use of slave labor and eventually collide with the whole slave-labor system. Incidents like Frederick Douglass's beating and physical ejection, while still a slave, from a Baltimore shipyard seemed to justify the first fear. A pitched battle waged in a small town across the Chesapeake Bay twenty years later, in 1858, symbolized the second fear. That conflict pitted ardent proslavery forces against an outspoken foe of slavery, James L. Bowers, and his defenders. As ominous as the fight itself was a reporter's estimate that "at least three-quarters of the people are on Bowers's side," including "nearly all the laboring class." The fact that the South's urban working class was growing increasingly top-heavy with immigrants—who seemed to have little loyalty to or even respect for the South's deeply rooted system of chattel slavery—only deepened planter anxiety. The Charleston *Standard* therefore spoke for many slaveowners when it branded the growing ranks of foreign-born workers "a curse rather than a blessing to our peculiar institution."

From the first, chattel slavery arose and throve in North America in response to and as part of the important economic changes that gradually transformed Europe and its colonies. A fusion of ancient and modern economic arrangements, this labor system succeeded as a way to compel people to perform difficult, unrewarding work that they would have avoided if they had been free.

In its early stages, the capitalist industrial revolution of the eighteenth and nineteenth centuries made slavery more profitable than ever. In both Great Britain and the United States, industrialism at first was based largely on the mass production of textiles. During the first half of the nineteenth century, African-American slaves supplied the overwhelming bulk of the raw cotton that fed the textile factories on both continents. Three major developments made this possible: the invention of the cotton gin, the expulsion of most Indian residents of the Gulf region, and the westward movement of free whites and unfree blacks.

A cartoon in an 1857 edition of *Harper's New Monthly Magazine* satirizes the planting techniques espoused by "Squire Broadacre," a Virginia farmer. With access to slave labor, many southern planters resisted technical innovations, mechanical and otherwise, that would improve agricultural output.

OLD VIRGINIA LABOR-SAVING MACHINE.

This chapter has focused on the economic system as a whole and the hardships and limitations it imposed on the slave population. This was the world in which Afro-Americans were compelled to live and work. But despite the extremely repressive nature of this system, the slaves were far more than passive victims. As we shall see in later chapters, they created and defended a culture and institutions that bound them to one another and asserted their own human dignity. In turn, those efforts influenced the development of slavery and southern society. And when conditions made it possible, Afro-Americans played a critical role in destroying that system and bringing about their own emancipation.

New Hampshire textile-mill workers, c. 1854. Framed portraits of workers of the Amoskeag Manufacturing Company in Manchester.

6 THE FREE-LABOR NORTH

THE EXPANSION of the slave-labor South was part of a larger, national process of growth. During the first half of the nineteenth century, the Louisiana Purchase (1803), the acquisition of Florida (1819), the annexation of Texas (1845), the acquisition of Oregon (1846), and cessions after the war with Mexico (1848) more than tripled the territory of the United States. More dramatic still was the growth of population. As a result of natural increase, immigration, and the absorption of people already living in the acquired territories, there were six times as many people (31.4 million) in the United States in 1860 as in 1800.

Together with this sheer physical growth went an even more important economic development. But while population grew throughout the expanding nation, there was more economic development in the states and territories of the North. Between the Revolution and the Civil War, America's industrial revolution began in earnest there. First in New England and then in the mid-Atlantic and midwestern states, old methods of producing and transporting goods underwent basic and far-reaching changes. This momentous process, in turn, transformed the ways men and women worked as well as what they wore, what they ate, and where they lived. The same changes also affected how northerners thought about themselves and other citizens. Finally, this whole transformation redefined the central issues that shaped nineteenth-century American politics.

Daniel Webster, a prominent senator from Massachusetts, enthusiastically embraced America's industrial revolution. "It is an extraordinary era in which we live," he exulted in 1847. "It is altogether new. The world has seen nothing like it before." An era "remarkable for scientific research into the heavens, the earth, and what is beneath the earth" was "more remarkable still for the application of this scientific research to the pursuits of life."

Webster cheered for good reason. The productivity of labor rose impressively, increasing almost 30 percent during the two decades prior to the Civil War; in 1860 one person could produce twice as much wheat as in 1800, twice as much pig iron, and more than four times as much cotton cloth. Increased productivity combined with the soaring population to produce a staggering increase in national wealth. Indeed, between 1840 and 1860 alone, the nation's agricultural output more than doubled in value, and that of its construction, mining, and manufacturing industries grew three times or more.

Such rapid growth and change would have startled the Founding Fathers, most of whom had seen formidable obstacles to industrial development in America. In 1780 John Adams had predicted that the country would not supply its own manufactures for a thousand years; the society's basic structure and values—the way ordinary citizens lived, worked, and thought—inhibited manufacturing. In 1810, Albert Gallatin, the secretary of the treasury, specified some of the obstacles: "the superior attractions of agricultural pursuits" over industrial ones and "the abundance of land compared with the population, the high price of labor, and the want of sufficient capital." He could also have cited the small domestic market for manufactured goods.

The items on Gallatin's list reflected the survival of an older way of life and work. Most Americans in 1810 still worked the land, and wished to continue to do so. Moreover, there seemed to be plenty of new land available for anyone who wanted it. But who, in that case, would perform the industrial and factory work? And who would work for less than what Gallatin considered a "high price"? The "want of sufficient capital" reflected the cautious conservatism of American merchants, whose experiences and preferences disposed them to seek their profits in trade—the business of buying and selling—and not to invest in production itself. Where, then, would the country find the capital needed to develop its industry? Finally, most Americans—especially farm families—made with their own hands nearly all the things they needed. So long as this pattern persisted, there was little market for manufactured goods, and thus little reason for industry to expand.

In short, the industrial growth that so delighted men like Daniel Webster required a radical reorganization of society and popular beliefs. Settled ways of living and working had to be abandoned. Traditional values and assumptions had to be either redefined or replaced.

That is exactly what happened in the free states—if often in unexpected ways—during the first half of the nineteenth century. This overall transformation generally occurred in three stages.

First, commerce expanded, a trend already well under way in the colonial era. Stepped-up trade meant that the number of items people made for their own use steadily declined. Increasingly they produced goods such as wheat, corn, cloth, and shoes to sell in distant markets. The money they earned allowed them to buy other goods.

Second, social and class relations changed in response to these economic developments. Stepped-up commerce and competition further widened inequalities of wealth within the North's broad layer of independent, self-employed small farmers and artisans. Some prospered, accumulated wealth, expanded their farms and workshops, and became employers. At the same time, others declined, some of them losing their farms and workshops entirely; those unable to start anew had little choice but to hire out to their more fortunate neighbors. The growing class of wage-earners swelled dramatically during the 1840s and 1850s, when millions of foreigners—mostly farmers, laborers, and artisans from Ireland, Germany, and Britain—made their way to America's industrializing North.

Finally, changing class relations affected the pace of mechanization, the introduction into the production process of new types of tools driven by nonhuman power sources (such as water and steam). Extensive mechanization began only during the 1840s and 1850s, once the growth of commerce and the creation of an industrial wage-labor force made such new innovations practical and profitable. Along with the simple division of labor, such mechanization made possible much of the dramatic increase in human productivity usually associated with the industrial revolution.

MERCHANT CAPITAL AND THE TRANSPORTATION REVOLUTION

Although both North and South were overwhelmingly agricultural in 1800, they already differed from each other in fundamental ways. Southern planters had already built an economy that used large work-forces to produce commodities, but in the North, neither lifelong work for others nor production for the market was nearly as common or central to the economy. Most northern whites belonged to small-farm families that consumed most of what they produced. And what trade there was tended to be exchange among neighbors; as late as 1820, only a fifth of the North's total farm crop found its way beyond the local community into the nation's small urban markets. Farm families, moreover, bought comparatively little: about two-thirds of the clothing Americans wore between 1810 and 1820 was homemade.

A primitive transportation system kept northern rural and urban producers apart and blocked a brisker commerce. The major rivers ran north-south, not east-west, the route required to link the Atlantic coast with the hinterland. In 1800, the region's few roads and bridges were poorly constructed and maintained. The entire country had only about a hundred miles of canals, few more than a mile or so in length. Inland transportation therefore was slow, difficult, and expensive. Shipping a ton of goods three thousand miles from Europe to the North American coast cost $9—but $9 would move the same cargo only thirty miles overland. Poor transportation discouraged trade between isolated communities and protected those producing for limited local markets from faraway competitors.

The wealthy and powerful northern merchant elite lived and conducted business largely at the country's physical and social periphery in 1800. Unlike southern planters, they generally did not concern themselves with production. Their wealth came largely from trade— the profits from "buying cheap and selling dear"—which brought them into contact primarily with the small fraction of Americans (fewer than one in twenty) who lived in or near seaport cities.

Even the urban markets were limited. The biggest mercantile profits went to Yankee traders involved in the transatlantic and coastal trade, carrying European manufactures (especially luxury goods) to the Americas, and American and Caribbean plantation produce to Europe. By remaining neutral in the wars that preoccupied Europe in the 1790s and early 1800s, America's northeastern merchants virtually monopolized trade routes closed to others. Trade with China also offered substantial rewards.

Mercantile success brought great wealth to some and gave employment to many others, especially smaller merchants and artisans con-

"The Lackawanna Valley." George Inness's panoramic painting, commissioned by the Delaware, Lackawanna, and Western Railroad in 1855, placed the symbol of industrialization in a bucolic setting. The railroad's president paid Inness $75 to paint a scene showing three locomotives. The artist gave him only one train, but obliged the president's zeal for advertising by painting three tracks leading into the new Scranton roundhouse, instead of the one that actually existed.

nected with shipping, such as sailmakers, ropemakers, carpenters, caulkers, and barrelmakers. But it did not substantially improve the North's position in world production. "Our catalogue of merchants," the Philadelphia congressman and statistician Adam Seybert wrote of these years, "was swelled much beyond what it was entitled to from the state of our population. . . . The brilliant prospects held out by commerce caused our citizens to neglect the mechanical and manufacturing branches of industry." Between 1795 and 1815, the United States imported 20 percent more than it exported, creating a trade deficit of about $350 million. Worse still, nearly half of American exports were really only re-exports—goods produced abroad, which were purchased by American merchants, and resold abroad. Although this kind of trade amassed profits, it did not directly stimulate the growth of domestic commercial agriculture or industry.

In the end, changing patterns of world trade forced many American merchant capitalists out of maritime commerce. After the European peace settlement in 1815, England, France, and other major maritime powers quickly resumed their trading roles. The resulting competition was fierce, and freight rates fell by half. Northern merchants retained only a declining share of the decreasingly profitable commerce, both in the Atlantic and in the Pacific. A prominent Bostonian, John M. Forbes, found himself steadily forced out of the China trade, finally retiring in 1837. "Competition," he explained, "is so sharp here that money must be made by the most penurious saving in fitting or storing goods . . . , or by being constantly on the lookout and giving up body and soul to managing business."

Some of the more farsighted merchants turned their eyes away from international trade toward the American continent. A handful put their capital directly into manufacturing, especially textiles. But in the first decades of the nineteenth century, most of the investments went into internal commerce and the necessary improvements in transportation: the construction and maintenance of roads, canals, and bridges, and, later, steamboats and railroads.

Anxious to share in the prosperity anticipated from rising commerce, state and local governments encouraged such investments

Building the Erie Canal. Building the canal took heavy physical labor. A contemporary lithograph by Anthony Imbert shows the excavation at Lockport, New York.

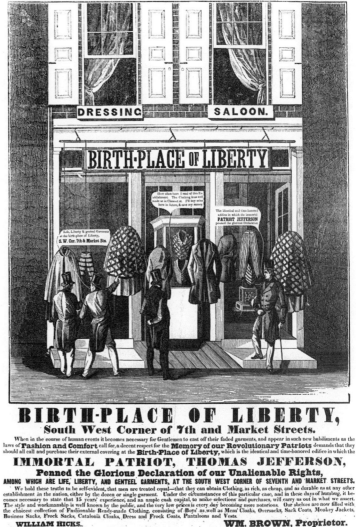

BIRTH-PLACE OF LIBERTY,
South West Corner of 7th and Market Streets.

When in the course of human events it becomes necessary for Gentlemen to cast off their faded garments, and appear in such new habiliments as the laws of **Fashion and Comfort** call for, a decent respect for the **Memory of our Revolutionary Patriots** demands that they should all call and purchase their external covering at the **Birth-Place of Liberty**, which is the identical and time-honored edifice in which the

IMMORTAL PATRIOT, THOMAS JEFFERSON,
Penned the Glorious Declaration of our Unalienable Rights,

AMONG WHICH ARE LIFE, LIBERTY, AND GENTEEL GARMENTS, AT THE SOUTH WEST CORNER OF SEVENTH AND MARKET STREETS.

We hold these truths to be self-evident, that men are treated equal—that they can obtain Clothing, as rich, as cheap, and as durable as at any other establishment in the nation, either by the dozen or single garment. Under the circumstances of this particular case, and in these days of humbug, it becomes necessary to state that 15 years' experience, and an ample cash capital, to make selections and purchases, will carry us out in what we assert. The style and workmanship is well known by the public, and the very low prices is every day becoming more notorious. Our shelves are now filled with the choicest collection of Fashionable Ready-made Clothing, consisting of Boys' as well as Mens' Cloaks, Oversacks, Sack Coats, Monkey Jackets, Business Sacks, Frock Sacks, Catalonia Cloaks, Dress and Frock Coats, Pantaloons and Vests.

WILLIAM HICKS..   WM. BROWN, Proprietor.

An 1830s advertisement for a Philadelphia clothier's shop revises the Declaration of Independence, placing it in the service of consumption.

in many ways. Often they poured public funds directly into these projects. Sometimes they rewarded private investors with direct cash subsidies, special tax exemptions, government backing for privately issued bonds, special banking and lottery franchises, and exclusive corporate charters. Such charters often brought with them lucrative monopoly privileges. A bridgebuilder, for example, might receive exclusive legal rights to use the given river's waterpower for manufacturing purposes.

Expenditures for new and improved roads, bridges, canals, and railroads increased steadily. A truly staggering improvement in internal travel and communication resulted. New York State's Erie Canal produced the most remarkable results. Built at public expense between 1817 and 1825, the canal stretched 364 miles from Buffalo to Albany, linking the Great Lakes and Ohio Valley with the Hudson River, New York City, and the transatlantic trade. Freight rates to the interior fell sharply, giving a great boost to internal commerce.

The era of canals soon melted into the railroad age. A particularly attractive investment, railroads played a key role in opening up the West. Ten thousand miles of railroad track laid in the 1850s helped link recently settled western farmers to the older railroad lines—the New York Central, the Pennsylvania, the Erie, and the Baltimore & Ohio—and the eastern markets. At the same time, eastern investors and their western political allies (such as Illinois senator Stephen A. Douglas) strove to extend this railroad network farther westward, through the unorganized territories and onward to the Pacific Coast.

People and goods now moved at far lower cost: freight rates dropped by about 95 percent between 1820 and 1860. And the speed of travel increased almost as radically. In 1817, the fastest freight shipments from Cincinnati to New York took almost two months. By the early 1850s, a railroad trip between the two took only about a week.

Parallel developments took place in communications. Improvements in printing—particularly the development of a steam press— slashed the price and rapidly multiplied both the number and total circulation of the nation's newspapers after 1830. During the 1840s, the telegraph made it possible for the first time to send information— including commodity prices—instantaneously across vast distances. These changes, too, helped knit local markets together into regional and, ultimately, national ones.

INDIANS IN THE NORTHWEST

This revolution in transportation and communication made possible a vast population increase in the coastal regions and their cities, and an even more dramatic growth in the states and territories of the Great Lakes region (the old Northwest). As in the deep South, however, this expansion of white settlement first required the destruction of a distinct and preexisting Indian society, the seizure of its lands, and the removal of its population.

Leadership of the Indian resistance came from the ranks of the Algonkian-speaking Shawnee tribe. During the seventeenth and eighteenth centuries, the steady pressure of advancing white society had undermined the Shawnees' hunting-farming way of life and drove them into territories already occupied by other tribes. The resulting conflicts further fragmented the Shawnee tribe and scattered individual bands, driving them back and forth across the eastern half of the continent. Desperately trying to resist further encroachments from the East, the Shawnees first supported the French in their losing war with England and her colonies, and then allied with England against the colonists' war for independence.

No sooner had the British signed the Treaty of Paris than American settlers came pouring onto Indian lands in southern Ohio. In two major engagements with U.S. forces in 1790 and 1791, Shawnees and other tribesmen dealt the whites powerful blows, killing over eight hundred troops. But in 1794 at Fallen Timbers, defeat at the hands of well-trained and well-equipped soldiers led by General "Mad Anthony" Wayne (of Revolutionary War fame) turned this tide. In the Treaty of Greenville signed the next year, the Shawnees ceded most of their land east of the Mississippi. What was left was soon invaded by white hunters, trappers, and horsethieves, whose activities further reduced the Shawnees' access to food. "Hear the lamentations of our women and children," tribal leaders pleaded with the U.S. government. "Stop your people from killing our game. At present they kill more than we do. [Just as] they would be very angry if we were to kill a cow or hog of theirs, the little game that remains is very dear to us." In reply, U.S. officials solemnly advised the Shawnees to abandon hunting in favor of agriculture and to cede even more of their lands in return for cash payments. In the meantime, the federal government imposed additional land cessions upon the region's other tribes, often through the medium of particularly pliant "government chiefs."

The conduct of such chiefs drove many young warriors into rebellion. The disintegration of Shawnee society, its growing economic dependence on trade with the whites, and a spreading atmosphere of frustration drove growing numbers of Shawnees to alcohol. Drunkenness and random violence within the community followed, which only deepened the sense of shame and decay. So did the erosion of kinship and family ties and the breakdown of traditional rules of sexual conduct. "The white people have spoiled us," admitted even pro-U.S. Shawnee chief Black Hoof. "They have been our ruin."

This was the chaotic and demoralized setting for a major religious and political awakening that galvanized first the Shawnees and through them other northwestern tribes. The movement's leader and inspiration was a prophet known as Tenskwatawa, or "the Open Door." His name signified that he would show his people the entrance to paradise, "a rich, fertile country, abounding in game, fish, pleasant hunting grounds, and fine cornfields," a place where Indian spirits could follow "the same course of life which characterized them here. They [could] plant, . . . hunt, [or] play at their usual games and in all things [could remain] unchanged." From 1805 through 1808, this movement attracted the fervent support of growing numbers of Shawnees and other hard-pressed tribespeople, principally in Michigan, Illinois, Wisconsin, and Ohio.

The creed that attracted them all was a stern one, as are most religions that strive to regenerate a crisis-stricken population. It demanded of its followers a renewed pride in their identity and past, great self-discipline, and a firm rejection of alien and corrosive forms of behavior.

A former alcoholic, Tenskwatawa demanded temperance from himself and his followers, denouncing whiskey as "poison and accursed." Outbreaks of violence among tribespeople must cease, and warriors must cease "running after women; if a man is single let him take a wife." New fires must be kindled in the lodges, but without the use of the flint or steel acquired from whites. Hunting must be done with bow and arrow, metal goods should be replaced with those fashioned of wood or stone, and the whites' kind of clothing must give way once again to animal skins, leather, and loincloths. Indians must not domesticate animals as the whites did; the meat from such animals was unclean. Rather must they hunt their game in the wild. Nor were they "on any account to eat bread. It is the food of the whites." Instead they must raise only corns, beans, and other traditional crops.

Tenskwatawa also scorned the accumulation of "wealth and ornaments" as a white disease. Indians who succumbed to it would "crumble into dust." Only those who had shared what they had with others would after death "find their wigwam furnished with everything they had on earth." As for the debts into which whites had drawn the Indians, "no more than half" of them must be repaid "because [the Americans] have cheated you."

As this last injunction showed, a movement that began as a spiritual revival was turning its attention to more political matters. In 1808, Tenskwatawa declared his intention to draw a clear "boundary line between Indians and white people" and to forge the political unity among the western tribes that would allow them to defend that boundary, so that "if a white man put his foot over it . . . the warriors could easily put him back."

As the movement toward Indian unity became more and more political and military in emphasis, leadership began to shift from the religious leader Tenskwatawa to his warrior brother, Tecumseh. "The only way to check and stop this evil," Tecumseh declared, "is for all the red men to unite in claiming a common and equal right in the land, as it was at first, and should be yet; for it never was divided, but belongs to all, for the use of each." Unfortunately for Tecumseh, his brother, and the northwestern Indians as a whole, these plans required more advanced military technology and greater political centralization than was compatible with the tribal social structure and traditions that they strove to defend.

Military reverses were not long in coming. In November 1811, some one thousand U.S. troops led by territorial governor William Henry Harrison advanced on Shawnee headquarters at Prophetstown in present-day Indiana. Between six and seven hundred Shawnee warriors battered but failed to break up the whites' encampment on the nearby Tippecanoe River. This military failure badly damaged Tenskwatawa's reputation and weakened his attempt to unify the northwestern Indians.

Tecumseh and Tenskwatawa once more supported British forces against those of the United States in the War of 1812. But high hopes for this alliance collapsed late in October 1813, when the Americans routed a combined force of British and Indians at the battle of the Thames River in Canada. Among the Indian casualties of that defeat was Tecumseh himself.

This was the end of armed resistance to white settlement in the Northwest. By the 1830s, many Shawnees had been removed to settlements in present-day Kansas, and most Indian lands in Ohio, southern Indiana, Illinois, and Michigan had been ceded to the U.S. This made possible the rapid white settlement of this region. The U.S. as a whole more than tripled its population from 1810 to 1860. But the population of Indiana, Illinois, Michigan, Missouri, and Ohio grew twentyfold. In 1810, western states had only a fourth as many residents as those in the Northeast; by 1860, the two regions were about equal.

CROPS AND COMMERCE

Indians were not the only ones to see their way of life radically transformed by the growth of transportation, commerce, and white settlement. These processes also challenged the patterns of economic life, personal relations, and social values of many white farm families. Not least important, the isolation of many of these families faded as the market became more and more important in their lives. That enlarged the range of choices open to family members, which helps explain why so many of the grandchildren and great-grandchildren of Yankee soldiers in the Continental Army left their farms and parents behind them—either to cultivate the lands of western New York, northern Pennsylvania, and the Ohio Valley or to work for wages in New England and the Middle Atlantic states.

At the beginning of the nineteenth century, northern farmers took pride in their status as landowning producers. In particular, they celebrated their freedom from extreme want and social subservience, a freedom they identified with the family farm and economic self-sufficiency. (They shared these attitudes with the slaveless small farmers of the antebellum South.) Rural inequality, to be sure, was widespread, and tenancy blighted parts of New York and other free states as well. Landless farm laborers could be found everywhere. But in the early nineteenth century, the typical northern farm was modest in size and operated by the family that owned it. Temporary work as a laborer usually served as a stepping-stone to acquiring one's own farm. A trip through New York and New England in 1821 convinced the Yankee clergyman Timothy Dwight that "No man here begins life with the expectation of being a mere laborer. All intend to possess, and almost all actually possess, a comfortable degree of prosperity and independence."

"Independence" was the watchword of the small-farm population. Crystallized in the revolutionary era, the ideal signified in economic terms the capacity (among farmers, the ownership of enough good land) to support oneself and one's family. Socially, this gave one the right to look others squarely in the eye as an equal. "Every man," boasted the *New England Farmer*, "is a free, independent landlord, thinks himself, while pursuing a virtuous course, as good as his neighbor, and asks none but his Maker leave to live and thrive." Politically, it implied the right and competence (of the male family head) to vote and exercise the full rights of republican citizenship. Economically, socially, and politically, the small proprietors of town and country cherished their independence as the only alternative to its dreaded opposite—dependence, the condition identified in varying degrees with slaves, indentured servants, rural tenants, propertyless laborers, and women and children generally. A farmer voiced the fears of many in 1831, pleading, "We are willing to work, our wives are willing to work—but spare us, if it be permitted, spare us the humiliation of performing the servile offices, and living in the kitchens of our more fortunate neighbors."

In the eyes of some of these farmers, maintaining and exercising this independence required the aggressive accumulation of wealth. But for most, it meant cultivating enough fertile land to feed one's family decently, to acquire necessary

". . . I HAVE EVERYTHING I COULD WISH"

America's extraordinary material abundance was a recurring theme in letters recent European immigrants wrote home in the early nineteenth century. In the following letter, written in August 1818 from Germantown, Pennsylvania, Alice Barlow describes in detail the bounty of available food and drink. Letters such as this helped lure other Northern Europeans to migrate to America in the decades that followed.

Dear Mother:

I write to say we are all in good health, and hope this will find you so. . . . Tell my brother John I think he would do very well here; my husband can go out and catch a bucket of fish in a few minutes; and John brings as many apples as he can carry, when he comes from school; also cherries, grapes, and peaches. we get as much bread as we can all eat in a day for seven pence; altho' it is now called dear [expensive]. Dear mother, I wish you were all as well off as we now are: there is no want of meat and drink here. We have a gallon of spirits every week; and I have a bottle of porter per day myself, in short I have everything I could wish. . . . Tell little Adam, if he was here, he would get puddings and pies every day. Tell my old friends I shall be looking for them next spring; and also tell my brother John and sister Ann, if they were here, they would know nothing of poverty. I live like an Indian Queen. . . .

Your affectionate daughter,
Alice Barlow

items not made at home, and eventually to buy enough land for grown sons to establish their own homesteads.

Realizing this rural ideal required the labor of all family members. Husbands and sons, by and large, worked the fields. Virtually all the other tasks, including the all-important manufacture of household goods, fell to wives and daughters. A contemporary farm journal reported that women's work amounted to fully half of all farm labor:

> Women . . . picked their own wools, carded their own rolls, spun their own yarn, drove their own looms, made and mended their own chairs, braided their own baskets, wove their own carpets, quilts, and coverlets, picked their own geese, milked their own cows, fed their own calves. . . .

The independent farmer plows the path to prosperity for the Republic on this seal of the Philadelphia Society for Promoting Agriculture.

The writer could have added many other tasks, including delivering babies, nursing the sick, and caring for the elderly. Rural women did not share equally in political and economic opportunity with their husbands, sons, and brothers. But the comparative self-sufficiency that the men celebrated rested heavily on the diverse skills and exertions of their wives, daughters, and sisters.

The individual family's self-sufficiency was not absolute, by any means. Farmers lived in small communities, often bound together by close ties of kinship, religion, and ethnicity. The heart of such a community would be a small village, with little more than a church, a general store, and a few artisans such as carpenters and blacksmiths, who might ply their trades only part-time. An unusual village had a proper schoolhouse, a doctor, or a lawyer. These craftsmen, merchants, and professionals supplied the local residents with the few but essential goods and services unavailable in the home. Farm families aided one another, by lending tools or lending a hand when a particular task (barn-raising, harvesting) required extra help. Payment for any of these goods and services might be in cash, homemade goods, or labor. The independent farmer was thus firmly woven into a dense network of family and neighborly ties that simultaneously encouraged independence and mutual reliance.

Beyond family and community support, rural independence rested on crucial if limited ties to the outside market. Minimal comfort, much less modest prosperity, required contact with traders. Basic items such as salt, sugar, molasses, coffee, tea, tobacco, gunpowder, guns, knives, and axes could not be produced at home. To pay for them, farm families had to produce either a larger crop or more domestic manufactures (such as yarn, thread, or cloth), which could then be bartered directly or sold for cash to buy such goods.

Yet another need pushed farmers into the marketplace. A son expected a farm of his own on coming of age, but dividing a father's homestead among his sons eventually produced small and uneconomical holdings. Fathers therefore needed cash to set sons up on new land—about six hundred dollars for a new farm in the 1830s. Once again, independence and commerce seemed to complement rather than oppose one another. "Our sons," said the ardently pro-commerce *New England Farmer* in 1835, "from the very cradle, breathe the air of independence—and we teach them to owe no man. It is to gratify this love of independence that they rake the ocean and the earth for money."

The transportation revolution also played a critical role in the process. It ended the relative isolation that led to the ideal and reality of near self-sufficiency. It brought mass-produced household goods to

"The Residence of David Twining, 1787." Edward Hicks, a Quaker painter of coaches and signs, completed this painting in the late 1840s. Hicks's idealized representation of a "well-ordered" eighteenth-century farm was based on memories of his childhood in Bucks County, Pennsylvania.

farm families. Declining freight costs made internal trade more profitable for merchants and made "store-bought" items of decent quality available to rural families at declining prices. Some of these goods came from eastern workshops and factories. "The time spent in a factory," explained a Massachusetts observer, "will produce at least ten times as much as it will in household manufactures."

The fortress of self-sufficiency surrendered to the lure of declining prices for manufactured goods. Year after year, more items were available at lower prices. A coffee mill selling for $5 in 1813 sold for only $2 in 1836 and $1.25 in 1855. Between 1809 and 1836, the price of soap and candles fell by about a third. Glassware prices dropped 60 percent between 1810 and 1860, while the cost of cotton mattresses plummeted 86 percent. The same happened to the price of such items as buttons, pins, hooks-and-eyes, and calico cloth. By the 1840s and 1850s, the list of goods that farmers bought already seemed endless. It ranged from stoves and furniture to rugs and kitchenware, from churns and corn shellers to harnesses and carriages. "Formerly," noted a Pennsylvanian in 1836, "no man thought of going to a tailor for a sheet. Now everybody goes to one even for a handkerchief."

Household manufacture for home use thus died out as early as 1820 in parts of New England, and in most other places by the Civil War. It happened soonest in the regions best served by new transportation networks: between 1820 and 1860 the the household manufacture of woolens virtually died out along the Erie Canal.

Rural residents welcomed low-priced, high-quality manufactures. But the need for cash to buy all these goods caused farm families to devote more of their time to producing marketable goods—whatever crops would command the highest price in expanding urban markets. Farmers therefore soon found themselves buying even more of their basic food staples. The New York State Agricultural Society's president wrote in 1851:

> At an early period "production for consumption" was the
> leading purpose; now no farmer would find it profitable "to
> do everything within himself." He now sells for money, and
> it is in his interest to pay for every article that he cannot
> produce cheaper than he can buy.

None of this happened smoothly or simply. As white farmers moved westward, their frontier communities would depend for a while—usually about a decade—on the kind of precommercial, self-sufficient economy that had already disappeared in the East. But when transportation improvements and population caught up with those communities, they repeated the eastern experience. By the 1850s, commercial agriculture had become dominant in the free states. Rural survival—not to mention prosperity—came to depend upon favorable market conditions.

Production for the market prompted significant social changes in the rural community. Sellers had to fight to maintain their market position, and competition began to replace cooperation, pitting farmer against farmer. The *New England Farmer* warned:

> The cultivator who does not keep pace with his neighbors as regards agricultural improvements and information will soon find himself the poorer in consequence of the prosperity that surrounds him. . . . He will be like a stunted oak in the forest, which is deprived of light and air, by its "towering neighbors."

And farmers were also competing with others far away. Improved transportation brought produce from the virgin lands of the West into competition with crops grown on rocky and nearly exhausted New England soils. Commerce through the Erie Canal alone virtually ended grain production in much of the East, and it brought heavy pressure to bear on hog and cattle production there. Between 1840 and 1860, western competition made possible by the railroads effectively wiped out wool-growing in New England.

Merchant middlemen, who connected the inland farmer and the urban consumer, added to the difficulties of marginal farmers. In or-

"Starting for Lowell." An illustration from T. S. Arthur's reform tract *Illustrated Temperance Tales* (1850) showing a young woman leaving her farm family to work in a cotton mill. This picture is accurate in showing that New England farm families often had to rely on income from factory labor. But reformers blamed economic hardship on personal weaknesses—in the case of Arthur's story, the father's alcoholism.

der to increase their profits, they could force down the prices they paid for agricultural goods, and resell those goods at higher prices. Farm families caught between rising costs and dwindling income, and no longer producing their own food and clothing, faced ruin. They had difficulty getting credit from banks, which still specialized in short-term loans that fit mercantile needs, not farm needs. A common complaint appeared in an 1838 *New England Farmer* letter:

> Individuals who are capitalists think in general they can find more profitable investments for their money than to lend it to farmers, who have no other resources than their own labor and enterprise. Bank loans are in general too short and capricious to be safe or convenient for farmers. . . . Banks are only for merchants and manufacturers; and for . . . gamblers and speculators who live upon the hard earnings of labor.

Even when they could be gotten, loans often merely postponed and then deepened the crisis. Unless they could be used to increase productivity and total output, the debt they imposed on the farmer became just another burden. In 1832, one farmer described the impact on traditional community ties: "This business of mortgage has already dispossessed a large portion of the best farmers in New England, and it constantly increases." He feared that "the independent yeomanry of our country" would soon "give place to wretched tenantry," and that "a very few rich men . . . will own the whole soil." A Vermont farmer echoed his sentiments. Successful commercial farmers, he worried, "are increasing their real estate by buying the small farms of their neighbors. [In] this way will be produced a wealthy aristocracy, and a poor, dependent peasantry. Let the farmers of Vermont beware."

Commercialization did fragment the old rural community.

". . . THE TRUTH ABOUT THIS COUNTRY"

For some European immigrants, American society in the 1830s proved a profound disappointment. In this 1834 letter to his mother back home, David Davies, a Welsh immigrant in the coal town of Carbondale, Pennsylvania, suggests how unhappy his prospects had become in America, less than a year after his arrival.

▌IS SOME comfort to me that hundreds of my fellow countrymen are as unfortunate as I am or else I do not know what would become of me. I cannot blame anyone but myself because nothing would do but that I should come to America. It is coal work here and that very stagnant at present and the outlook is poor that any improvement will take place for a long time. Also the news that we get from newspapers and letters makes things worse and, consequently, the more dissatisfied with our situation. . . . This makes everyone here want to return home. I wish that I could persuade Welsh people to believe the truth about this country.

There is no acre to be had under ten shillings, and that covered by trees and wilderness. If a young man lived for fifty years he could not gather all the stones from off it even if he worked every day. If you spent a year here seeing nothing but poor cottages in the woods with the chimneys smoking so that Welsh people could not breathe in them and the jolly Welsh women here losing their rosy cheeks and smiling eyes—what would your feelings be? You would sigh for the lovely land that you had left.

CORRECT LIKENESSES,
TAKEN WITH ELEGANCE AND DESPATCH BY
RUFUS PORTER.

Prices as follows—
Common Profile's cut double, - - $.0 20
Side views painted in full colours, - - 00
Front views, - - - - - 3 00
Miniatures painted on Ivory, - - 8 00
Those who request it will be waited on, at their respective places of residence.

A handbill of about 1820. Itinerant portrait artists offered rural people reasonably priced portraits, using simplified techniques to render enough of a "correct likeness" to satisfy a client. Portraitists and other traveling tradesmen served as scouts for capital, introducing attractive goods and services to the countryside.

Some farmers flourished as commercial producers. They added to their property, hired less fortunate neighbors as farm laborers and domestic servants, and became fervent supporters of further measures designed to increase commerce. Other families supplemented meager farm earnings through outwork, selling large quantities of household manufactures to merchants. Some women worked on shoes, wove straw hats, and sewed shirts for merchant capitalists, who paid them by the piece. Still others made their way into the country's first factories. And many men, with or without their families, headed west, hoping to regain their status as independent yeomen there. "Thousands of illustrious families," an early labor newspaper complained in 1834, "are compelled to take the situation of tenants, or are scattered into factories, and into the kitchens of the rich—or, more happily for them, driven in exile to the remoter West."

Indeed, fully one-third of all those born in Connecticut and New Hampshire, for example, had by 1860 left their home states in search of a second chance, mostly out West. Four of every ten Vermonters did the same. Gold, discovered in California in 1848, was a powerful magnet. The center of northern agriculture moved west too: During 1840, only ten thousand bushels of grain and flour left Chicago for the East. Twenty years later, over fifty million bushels followed that route. Much of this increased yield went to feed the people of New England and the Middle Atlantic states. Some went south, too. And large markets also appeared in famine-stricken Ireland in the 1840s, and elsewhere in Europe during the Crimean War of 1853–55.

Located at key points along the now-bustling East-West trade routes, cities like Buffalo, Pittsburgh, and Chicago boomed. So did construction and youthful western manufacturing, especially mining (lead, copper, iron) and smelting, lumbering, farm equipment, food processing (milling, meatpacking, distilling, and brewing), and production of consumer goods for local markets.

In this way, the West's primary economic ties shifted. Until now, the South had represented the most important market for western corn, hogs, bacon, pork, wheat, and flour. Between 1843 and the Civil War, however, the expanded railroad network, the increased industrialization and urbanization of the East, and the South's growing self-sufficiency in foodstuffs transformed the Northeast into the western farmers' chief customer.

PATHS TO WAGE LABOR

Though some industry began now to arise in the West, three-quarters of the nation's manufacturing employment in 1850 remained concentrated in New England and the Middle Atlantic states. Indeed, the growing western market stimulated the Northeast's decisive transformation into a primarily industrial region specializing in light consumer goods. Speedier travel and lower freight costs multiplied the numbers of people manufacturers could reach with their wares. Commercialized agriculture made it possible to feed the cities, boosted rural demand for those manufactures—and forced many marginal farmers and their families into new fields of labor.

Anyone could see that trade between the burgeoning West and the coastal cities was booming. Very little merchandise had moved westward from the seaport towns in 1810. But by 1835, the value of merchandise flowing westward along the Erie Canal approached $10 million. By 1853, the figure was approaching an incredible $100 million.

The surge in commerce and industry also swelled the number and size of the cities. In 1790, the entire country claimed only twenty-four towns or cities with populations greater than 2,500, and none greater than 50,000. Fewer than one northeasterner in ten lived in a town. But by 1860, there were nearly 400 towns and cities, and more than a third of all northeasterners lived in them. Much of the region's manufacturing took place in small cities and towns. Meanwhile, New York City (with more than a million residents by 1860) and Philadelphia (with over half a million) became the dominant manufacturing cities in the nation.

Urban growth and the development of industry brought with them a third momentous change. More and more people were now making their living in ways that challenged the values of the revolutionary generation. The absolute size of the nation's farm population grew steadily through 1910. But the number of people working outside of agriculture grew considerably faster. Almost seven in every ten working residents of the North had tilled the soil in the days when Thomas Jefferson sang the praises of the independent American farmer. By 1860, the figure was only four in every ten.

More ominously, this shift accompanied a startling growth in the size of the "dependent" population. While indentured servitude all but vanished in the early nineteenth century, those dependent for their survival upon wage labor moved from the fringes of northern society to its center. In 1800, according to one rough estimate, those who worked primarily for wages accounted for only 12 percent of the country's total working population. By the Civil War, however, such people represented 40 percent of the working population, and the great majority of these wage-earners lived and worked in the "free-labor" North.

The rise of industry took varying forms, and so did the rise of its workforce. Old skilled crafts producing consumer goods like clothing and hats, boots and shoes, leather, furniture, barrels, soap and candles, and books and newspapers expanded their output and workforce and altered the work process to meet the rising demand. Thread, yarn, and most textile production, meanwhile, moved from home to factory. And new inventions and methods launched some new industries and caused drastic growth and reorganization in others. Among the affected industries were railroads (locomotives and track), steam engines, textile machinery, sewing machines, as well as ironmaking, coalmining, milling and meatpacking, glassmaking, and a long list of specialized metal products, including machine tools, stoves, firearms, clocks, axes, springs, bolts, and wires. The construction and functioning of new transportation routes and methods and of towns and cities, finally, required the exertions of unprecedented numbers of unskilled laborers.

These various industries involved different types of labor, different forms of economic organization, and people of different social (and sometimes national) backgrounds. Here, we examine four types of industrial wage labor: unskilled labor, skilled craft work, wage labor in the home (outwork), and finally factory production of textiles. But beneath these real and important distinctions, a single, unifying process was at work. Slowly but no less certainly, the nature of work and of the relations among those engaged in it was changing. Far more than just a list of inventions and inventors, of growing output and accumulating profits, this industrial revolution would fundamentally redefine the meaning of life and labor in the United States as a whole.

The Unskilled Laborer

Canals, roads, and railroads furnished employment to thousands of men, especially unskilled laborers. So, too, did the unparalleled growth of towns and cities. Expanding urban populations needed more streets, houses, shops, and factories. Teamsters, carters, porters, warehousemen, dockworkers, sailors, and boatmen loaded, transported, unloaded, and stored the commodities that created rising mercantile fortunes.

Though considered unskilled, much of this labor demanded extremely heavy exertion; human muscle then performed many tasks later done by power-driven machinery. In the 1830s, the Irish actor Tyrone Power observed hundreds of his fellow countrymen struggling to cut a canal through a pestilential Louisiana swamp. He watched them "wading amongst stumps of trees, mid-deep in black mud . . . wheeling, digging, hewing, or bearing burdens it made one's shoulders ache to look upon." Living conditions were just as miserable. The Irish laborers lived in crude log huts "laid down in the very swamp, on a foundation of newly-felled trees, having the water lying stagnant between the floor-logs." A decade later, the shacks of the railroad builders in upstate New York repelled the English novelist Charles Dickens:

The best were poor protection from the weather; the worst let in the wind and rain through the wide breaches in the roofs of sodden grass, and in the walls of mud; some had nearly fallen down and were imperfectly propped up by stakes and poles; all were ruinous and filthy. . . . Hideously ugly old women and very buxom young ones, pigs, dogs, men, children, babies, pots, kettles, dunghills, vile refuse, rank straw and standing water, all wallowing together in an inseparable heap, composed the furniture of every dark and dirty hut.

The physical exertion demanded of canal laborers in Concord, Massachusetts, "working from dark till dark," wrote Ralph Waldo Emerson, "reminds one of negro-driving."

Between 1820 and 1860, the real wages of unskilled day laborers rose about 12 percent per decade. A number of factors qualified the improvement this increase implies. First, most unskilled jobs lasted only a few weeks, sometimes only a day or two. Competition from a growing pool of unemployed made finding work still more difficult. Streams of immigrants from rural America and from Europe fed the pool. So the average day laborer worked only about two hundred days a year. Second, the real wages of the unskilled in 1820 were low in-

"Dumping Ground at the Foot of Beach Street." An 1866 engraving shows people scavenging on garbage barges, searching for coal, rags, and other discarded items that might be used or sold to junk dealers. The picture, according to a *Harper's Weekly* editor, showed how some people in New York "live upon the refuse of respectable folk."

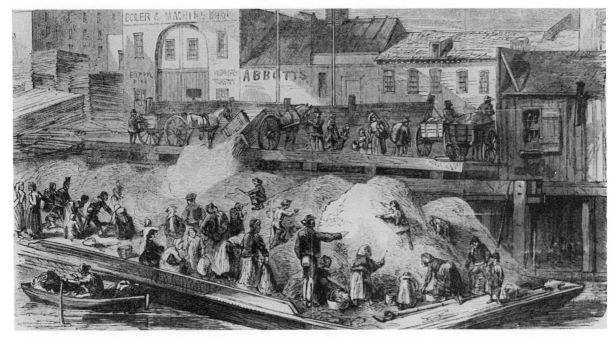

Go West, Young Man! An Illinois
Central Railroad advertisement,
probably directed to immigrants,
posted in New York City in 1853.

deed. In the short run, therefore, increases that occurred failed to pull the incomes of many much above bare subsistence.

Irregular employment and low wages put a premium on increasing the family income. Wives and children entered the commercial economy to help fill minimal everyday needs. Many women labored as outworkers or took in borders. Small children sought jobs in factories, as errand runners, and in casual labor of all kinds. In towns and cities, daughters hired out as live-in domestic servants. In fact, more than half of all female wage-earners in the late antebellum years were domestics. Money wages for domestics averaged just over a dollar a week as late as 1850, though personal expenses were minimized by living with one's employer.

Extreme poverty could bring crime in its wake. In January 1850, John McFealing was arrested for stealing wood from the docks in Newburyport, Massachusetts. He had been unable to find work, and a court investigation described his family: "The children were all scantily supplied with clothing, and not one had a shoe to the feet. There was not a stick of firewood nor scarcely a morsel of food in the house."

Families like the McFealings lived in increasingly crowded and decaying neighborhoods. Boston's North End was one such place. Slightly more than ten thousand of its seventeen thousand residents in 1855 were of Irish birth, mostly unskilled laborers and their families. The area no longer housed the prosperous merchants and master artisans whose substantial homes had by now been subdivided. So had the North End warehouses. Shoddy frame dwellings rose on empty land. The North End's 3,441 families crowded into about one thousand three-story dwellings. "Houses, once fashionable," noted a contemporary, have "become neglected, dreary tenement houses into which the low-paid and poverty-smitten . . . crowd by the dozens." Cholera and other infectious diseases thrived in such neighborhoods, and, according to the Boston physician and pioneer public health worker Josiah Curtis, mortality rates there equaled "anything we have been able to discover in European cities." This was a shocking observation in a society that prided itself precisely on avoiding the social ills of the Old World.

The Artisan

The lives of skilled craftsmen were also disrupted by the growing market. In the young republic, the urban artisan—and especially the master craftsman—had ranked high as an ideal citizen. Thomas Jefferson, who considered the independent yeoman farmers the chief pillars of the new republic, praised artisans in the strongest terms known to him by dubbing them "the yeomanry of the city." The self-employed artisan was respected as a property owner, possessing his own tools, materials, and small shop, as well as the added "property" of the knowledge and skill required to work his trade. Neither aristocratically rich nor degradingly poor, independent artisans won acclaim as "the sinews and muscles of our country," the "very axis of our society." A typical speech at a July Fourth meeting of New York City craftsmen early in the nineteenth century proclaimed:

> You cannot be inflated by distinction; you do not float like the ephemeral bubbles of pride and fashion, on the surface of society; nor are you of that uninformed class too low to be agitated with the current of events, and who, like dull weeds, sleep secure at the bottom of the stream.

Like artisans in an earlier Europe, those in American seaboard towns in the 1790s mostly worked in small teams—a master, a journeyman or two, and a young apprentice—at skilled labor. Tailors, shoemakers, barrelmakers, tanners, blacksmiths, printers, hatters, cabinetmakers, carriagemakers, and many others worked this way, filling orders from a small and well-to-do local market. The master-journeyman-apprentice relationship in these traditional handicrafts was not egalitarian, and in many overcrowded trades it barely paid. Still, many journeymen and apprentices could look forward to opening their own small shops once they learned the necessary skills and saved the capital. John Fanning Watson later recalled the Philadelphia of those days:

> No masters were seen exempted from personal labor in any branch of business—living on the profits derived from many journeymen. . . . Then almost every apprentice, when of age, ran his equal chance for his share of business in his neighborhood, by setting himself up for himself, and, with an apprentice or two, getting into a cheap location, and by dint of application and good work, recommending himself to his neighborhood. . . . Thus every shoemaker or tailor was a man for himself.

That older world—idealized by Watson, to be sure—collapsed during his lifetime as market forces redefined the skilled artisan's power and place.

The changes in the cities paralleled what was occurring in the country. Improvements in transportation destroyed local pockets of craft independence, and they increased competition between craftsmen. Enlarged markets caused a shift from the custom-made production of a few items to larger-scale production on a ready-made basis.

Boston, New York, Newark, and Philadelphia shoemakers, for example, soon competed not only with one another but also with shoes shipped in from Lynn, Massachusetts, the nation's rising center of shoe production. The *Voice of Industry* complained in 1847:

> In proportion as railroads and canals are constructed, . . . mammoth establishments in tanning, shoemaking, saddlery, blacksmithing, and every department of work and skill, send their productions and fabrics to distinct parts of the country . . . constantly killing out their rivals.

Once again, quite a few artisans—especially masters, but some journeymen as well—found ways to prosper in these new conditions. Evidence on antebellum income remains very incomplete, but it does suggest that in the trades least transformed in this period (such as skilled construction work), real wages rose somewhat between 1820 and 1850. But other artisans less favorably situated were often forced to choose between migration to more promising areas and staying put to face decline, debt, and eventual dispossession, losing their shops and perhaps even their tools to more successful neighbors.

Deprived of any means of independent support, such artisans became employees. They worked on materials supplied to them by merchants and produced goods for their employers in exchange for wages. An 1845 New York *Tribune* report depicted life among some of the worst-off craftworkers in this new economic setting. The reporter visited more than fifty

---

"COOKIES AND CAKES . . . ONE CENT APIECE"

In the early nineteenth century, traditional work patterns still limited the pace and intensity of labor in many industries. Below, a ship carpenter recalls the frequent breaks for food and drink that punctuated a typical day in a New York shipyard. Employers increasingly regarded such practices as intolerable obstacles to efficiency and profit.

IN OUR YARD, at half-past eight a.m., Aunt Arlie McVane, a clever kind-hearted woman but awfully uncouth . . . would make her welcome appearance in the yard with her two great baskets, stowed and checked off with crullers, doughnuts, ginger-bread, turnovers, pieces, and a variety of sweet cookies and cakes; and from the time Aunt Arlie's baskets came in sight until every man and boy, bosses and all, in the yard, had been supplied, always at one cent a piece for any article on the cargo, the pie, cake, and cookie trade was a brisk one. Aunt Arlie would usually make the rounds of the yard and supply all the hands in about an hour, bringing the forenoon up to half-past nine, and giving us from ten to fifteen minutes' "breathing spell" during lunch; no one ever hurried during "cake-time."

After this was over we would fall to [work] again, until interrupted by Johnnie Gogean, the English candyman, who came in always at half-past ten, with his great board, the size of a medium extension dining table, slung before him, covered with all sorts of "stick," and several of sticky candy, in one-cent lots. Bosses, boys, and men—all hands, everybody—invested one to three cents in Johnnie's sweet wares, and another ten to fifteen minutes is spent in consuming it. Johnnie usually sailed out with a bare board until eleven o'clock, at which time there was a general sailing out of the yard and into convenient grog-ships after whiskey. . . .

In the afternoon, about half-past three, we had a cake-lunch, supplied by Uncle Jack Gridder, an old, crippled, superannuated ship carpenter. No one else was ever allowed to come in competition with our caterers. Let a foreign candyboard or cake basket make their appearance inside the gates of the yard, and they would get shipped out of that directly.

At about five o'clock p.m., always Johnnie used to put in his second appearance; and then, having expended money in another stick or two of candy, and ten minutes in its consumption, we were ready to drive away again until sundown; then home to supper.

cellars in the city inhabited by shoemakers and their families. Typically, he recounted,

> The floor is made of rough plank laid loosely down, and the ceiling is not quite so high as a tall man. The walls are dark and damp, and a wide desolate fireplace yawns in the center to the right of the entrance. There is no outlet back, and of course no yard privileges of any kind.

Light reached the interior only through a small window high in one wall just above the street outside. All the family's activities took place within the one-room abode:

> In one corner is a squalid bed, and the room elsewhere is occupied by the workbench, a cradle made from a drygoods box, two or three broken and scattered chairs, a stewpan, and a kettle. . . . Here they work, here they cook, they eat, they sleep, they pray.

Similar conditions prevailed among many tailors, hatters, and others employed in production for a big market. In the building trades, workers had less difficulty in good times, but irregular employment plagued them, too. Again, some masters became contractors, employing wageworkers who never rose above journeyman status.

To take maximum advantage of an expanded market and their

Shoemakers in a "ten-footer" shop. A master cordwainer and his journeymen make shoes in a workshop attached to the master's home. By the time this engraving was published in 1880, the shoemaker's "ten-footer" was only a memory.

"Job Visited by a Master Tailor from Broadway." An illustration from the 1841 novel *The Career of Puffer Hopkins* caricatures the growing distinction between masters and journeymen. The master tailor's prosperous outfit, stance, and fancy business address (New York's Broadway) sharply contrast with the journeyman's wretched appearance and workshop-home.

power over growing numbers of workers, employers soon learned to convert expensive skilled work into simpler and cheaper tasks. This transformation often occurred well before the introduction of significant labor-saving machinery. Such specialized tasks could be performed either in centralized workshops under an employer's eye or at home on contract to a merchant. Those unwilling to accept the new system might quickly find themselves without work. "Capitalists," the *New York State Mechanic* indignantly objected in 1842, "have taken to bossing all the mechanical trades, while the practical mechanic has become a journeyman, subject to be discharged at every pretended 'miff' of his purse-proud employer." Simplified tasks, in turn, made it possible to replace skilled journeymen with semiskilled workers, including women and children. In the 1840s and 1850s, thousands upon thousands of immigrant artisans joined the ranks of these semiskilled native workers. These new groups of workers made it even easier for employers to depress the wages and working conditions of all.

While journeymen and apprentices were forced to become wage workers, master craftsmen faced two quite different choices. In the name of loyalty to tradition and to their journeymen and apprentices, they might resist the demands of commerce and merchant-capitalist pressure—a road that usually led to ruin. Or they might go with the winds of change, responding to merchant pressure by pressuring their own employees. Some masters eventually exchanged their worn leather aprons for the more elegant attire of the merchant elite; others elbowed the old merchants aside to become themselves the principal organizers of industrial production.

The transformation of shoe production in Lynn, Massachusetts, illustrates the changes throughout the Northeast. Until about 1760, this small farming and fishing town near Boston boasted only a handful of shoemakers, who custom-made shoes for local clients. A master shoemaker labored with at most a journeyman or two and a couple of youthful apprentices. The division of labor was as yet minimal. Each shoemaker usually cut his own leather, sewed the pieces together, and joined soles and uppers in his own home or small shop (called a "ten-footer" because of its modest size).

But around the turn of the nineteenth century, change came about in response to growing demand for cheaper, more roughly made shoes—many for southern slaves. The number of shoe shops increased, and the division of labor increased. Large masters ceased working alongside their journeymen, moving instead into larger central shops. There they concentrated simply on cutting the leather, leaving the other tasks to journeymen. Gradually, however, even the job of cutting was delegated to workers called clickers. Masters now became bosses (supervising the labor of others) and merchants (selling finished shoes).

Journeymen bitterly resented some masters' changing attitude toward them. One complained:

> They seem to think it is a disgrace to labor; that the laborer is not as good as other people. These little stuck-up, self-conceited individuals who have a little second-hand credit. . . . You must do as they wish . . . or you are off their books; they have no more employment for you.

Even as he wrote, however, shoe production was being subdivided even further. Women, often the wives and daughters of journeymen, increasingly assumed the less skilled work of binding—stitching together the uppers and linings of the shoes. Now working apart from the old masters in the old ten-footers, the journeymen found themselves performing only two tasks, lasting (fitting the uppers over a foot-shaped wooden last) and bottoming (attaching them to the soles).

A large influx into Lynn of part-time rural craftsmen now being uprooted from the soil also contributed to the journeymen's problems. Displaced by the transportation revolution and the commercialization of agriculture, these migrants competed for work with the Lynn-born journeymen, making it easier for employers to hold down pay rates and lengthen the hours of work.

As elsewhere, therefore—and decades before any significant mechanization of production took place—the deepening division of labor

As master artisans' control over their journeymen and apprentices dwindled, their former charges were freer to choose how to spend time away from the workshop. Some, like these two "Killers," joined proliferating urban gangs. This cover illustration is from an 1850 novel that was based on the violent activities of a notorious Philadelphia gang of journeymen, laborers, and apprentices.

and reduction of skill levels brought a decline in most journeymen's prospects. Some might still become masters, but this was now the exception rather than the rule. Apprenticeship declined as well. The developing new system, journeymen said, created distinctions between them and their masters that were "antirepublican in character" and seemed like "those existing between the aristocracy and the laboring classes in Europe." Though real wages rose somewhat between 1830 and 1860, the intensity of work increased as well. Describing the situation in the mid-1840s, shoe worker William Frazier observed simply, "Where we have to sit on our seats from twelve to sixteen hours per day, to earn one dollar, it must be apparent to all that we are in a sad condition." In 1850, the Lynn Board of Health found a shoemaker's life expectancy to be almost twenty years shorter than that of a Massachusetts farmer.

As the Lynn shoe bosses prospered, the wage-labor network that sustained them expanded. Lynn shoes made their way through all parts of the country, and bosses scoured the New England countryside for new workers. Families in economic difficulty, of course, were by now easy to find. Thousands of Massachusetts farmers and fishermen were soon supplementing their incomes by lasting and bottoming shoes at home. Possibly fifteen thousand Massachusetts women took up shoe-binding as outwork, usually part-time, for wages between a third and a half of what male shoemakers earned in the central shops. Reliance on outwork grew; by the 1850s, three out of every five shoes sold by Lynn manufacturers had actually been made outside the city. Rural Yankee labor based in the home remained essential to the region's shoe industry until new machinery and methods drew thousands of outworkers into large factories between 1855 and 1875.

". . . ROUGH WORK IS PERFORMED HERE BY MACHINERY"

Large cabinetmaking (furniture) firms—especially in the Midwest—began to mechanize production earlier than did most other craft-based industries. In 1851, Cincinnati booster Charles Cist proudly described the big new Mitchell and Rammelsberg factory as follows. Note that while machines were used to do the "rough work," skilled craftsmen remained central to the work process.

THIS, WHICH IS one of the heaviest of our furniture establishments, does not, as is generally the case with others, confine its operations to two or three staple articles, but comprehends in its [products] almost every description of cabinet ware and chairs.... The main building ... is six stories high, and filled with workmen and material to its utmost capacity.... In the manufacture of furniture, the rough work is performed here by machinery, with great celerity and exactness—the finishing being, as in other shops, executed by competent and skillful workmen. This concern employs, directly and indirectly, two hundred and fifty persons, and manufactures to the value of two hundred and twenty thousand dollars annually.

The various articles made are cut into lengths and shapes ... by the agency of a series of circular saws. Every process here, from the ripping out and cross-cutting of rough boards, to the finest slitting, progresses with inconceivable rapidity; the saws performing at the rate of from two thousand five hundred to three thousand revolutions in a minute; a speed which renders the teeth of the saw absolutely invisible to the eye.

As many as two hundred pieces of furniture, and the various parts in the same series, prepared and adjusted to fit, as fast as they progress, at a time, are taken from story to story, until on the upper floors they receive their final dressing and finish for the market.... This is but one of the many cabinet ware establishments in Cincinnati, which supply the South, West, and Southwest with materials for housekeeping of all sorts on an extensive scale.

The Outworker

From the 1820s on, more and more work was "put out"; no fewer than eighteen thousand Massachusetts women, for example, braided straw hats at home for wages in the 1830s. In 1831, businessman and philanthropist Mathew Carey estimated that, in the country's four largest cities, twelve or thirteen thousand women worked at home, making paper boxes, hoopskirts, shirts and collars, artificial flowers, ladies' cloaks, and the like. In fact, when outworkers are included, women in 1840 made up almost half of all manufacturing workers in the nation, and about two-thirds of those in New England.

The New York men's-clothing industry demonstrates how the outwork system fit into the overall transformation of work underway in many industries. Until the early 1800s, production followed the traditional pattern. Skilled male tailors catered to a limited upper-class demand for custom-made garments such as breeches, vests, coats, and capes. Working outside the artisanal structure, seamstresses and female dressmakers confined themselves largely to shirts, dresses, children's clothing, and mending.

But in the 1820s, the industry experienced a huge expansion. The protective tariff of 1816, together with cheap cloth produced by New England workers, allowed northern merchants to capture the market in clothing for southern slaves from English suppliers. Gradually, the southern trade expanded to include plantation owners, and the completion of the Erie Canal opened large upstate New York and western markets, too. In the 1840s, an observer noted, "everywhere throughout the country, New York–made clothing is popular over all others." Profits were handsome: in the early 1830s, ready-made clothing sold for five times what it cost to produce.

This profit rested squarely on low overhead costs and low wages. The outwork system allowed manufacturers to replace skilled tailors—working in a master's shop and accustomed to artisanal conditions and pay—with less-skilled women working in isolation in their homes. The 1860 census identified sixteen thousand New York City women clothing workers. Unable or unwilling to abandon their homes and family responsibilities, these women nevertheless needed work. They included the wives and daughters of poor day laborers, declining craftsmen, and men seeking work in the West. But as a rule, these female clothing workers headed their own households. Many of them had been abandoned or widowed, and many had children to support.

In clothing, outwork operated much as it did with shoes. Big merchants, contractors, and large manufacturing firms like Brooks Brothers dominated the industry. By 1860, Brooks Brothers employed only seventy workers in its shops but hired between two and three thousand outworkers. Contractors of much smaller size worked either independently or as subcontractors for the larger firms. Thousands of women labored for the big companies, contractors, and subcontractors. Supplying their own work space, fuel, light, needles, and thread, they received orders and cloth from a merchant or tailor and returned the completed work to him.

Again, employers' profits depended less on productive efficiency than on intensive labor for low wages. Fed by a swelling stream of poor women and families, especially immigrants, competition for outwork increased over time. This kept piece rates pitifully low and continually falling. Such low rates forced outworkers to labor even longer hours. Wagework in the home, furthermore, isolated individuals from each other, making it difficult for the outworkers to band together to defend their common interests.

The invention of the sewing machine in 1846 did not work to their advantage. The machine did reduce the labor required to make each garment, but employers reaped the benefits. They dropped piece rates so low that women often worked fifteen to eighteen hours a day on the new machines just to sustain themselves. Furthermore, their social subordination as women, their isolation from one another, and their poverty made these women easy victims of other abuses such as the arbitrary withholding of wages and sexual harassment.

In 1845 the New York *Daily Tribune* described housing conditions among these workers. Most rented "a single room, perhaps two small

"Hooking a Victim." A lithograph printed around 1850 depicts three prostitutes soliciting on a gas-lit city street. Some women chose prostitution as an alternative to (or to supplement) low-wage domestic or sewing work. Reformers (and artists) sentimentalized and demonized prostitutes, viewing them either as betrayed innocents, victimized by poverty or deceitful seducers, or as "abandoned women" craving sex and liquor.

rooms, in the upper story of some poor, ill-constructed, unventilated house in a filthy street. . . . In these rooms all the processes of cooking, eating, sleeping, washing, and living are indiscriminately performed." These women, the *Tribune* reported, spent "every cent" of their wages on necessities but still often lacked cash to "buy any other food than a scanty supply of potatoes and Indian meal and molasses for the family." The winter cold brought freezing temperatures to their garrets. "They are destitute of the means not only of adding comfortable clothing to their wretched wardrobes," the account concluded, "but of procuring an ounce of fuel." It did not surprise sensitive contemporaries that thousands of such poor women turned to occasional prostitution in search of needed cash.

The Factory Worker

Machines came to the textile industry long before they did to the production of shoes or men's clothing. The companies that introduced mechanization usually paired wealthy New England merchants with individuals experienced in production itself. In 1790, the English immigrant Samuel Slater succeeded in mechanizing the spinning of cotton yarn for the first time in the United States. An old clothier's shop in Pawtucket, Rhode Island, housed his machines, and the Blackstone River supplied the necessary power. Slater had acquired both technical and managerial experience while working as an overseer for one of England's largest cotton manufacturers. The capital for the enterprise came from the wealthy Brown family, a Rhode Island mercantile clan that made its first fortune in the colonial trade in rum and slaves from the West Indies, and later helped transform Providence into one of New England's chief commercial and manufacturing centers.

Encouraged by Slater's early accomplishments, the firm of Almy, Brown, and Slater set out in 1793 to erect the country's first textile factory, a modest, two-and-a-half-story spinning mill located upstream from the original clothier's shop. The factory depended largely upon children to run its spinners, especially during its first years. Adults, often the parents of the children employees, were paid to weave the yarn into fabric in their own homes.

The success of the Slater mill encouraged emulation, and by 1815 southern New England boasted a number of yarn-spinning factories on the Rhode Island model. By 1845 the region was covered with them, particularly in the Blackstone Valley and the valleys of eastern Connecticut. But during the century's second decade, another textile-factory system arose, this one originating in Waltham, Massachusetts. Initiated by a mechanic named Paul Moody, it was financed, owned, and controlled by Francis Cabot Lowell and a growing circle of merchants eventually known as the Boston Associates. In the 1820s, they established a second site in a village later renamed Lowell.

The Waltham system differed from the Rhode Island system in important ways. From the outset, it operated on a larger scale and involved a far greater financial investment. The first Waltham factory, more than ten times as large as the average Rhode Island mill, required an initial outlay of $400,000. A second difference explained the great increase in scale. The system mechanized the entire process of textile production, incorporating power looms as well as power-driven spinning frames. The proprietors, finally, were all absentee owners. While Slater managed his Rhode Island mill, hired agents oversaw the day-to-day operations of the Lowell mills.

There was an additional difference. Unlike the usually rural Rhode Island factories, which found their workforces among rural families, especially children, the urban Lowell mills at first hired mostly young, unmarried Yankee women from the countryside. And because this drew them away from their families' homes, the company constructed special boarding houses for them in Lowell.

The promise of wages attracted these women to Lowell. Most of the first group were firstborn daughters of farm families. The expansion of commerce and transportation seems to have both pushed them out of their parents' homes and attracted them to places like Lowell. Although not drawn from the very poorest farm families, the mill women had nonetheless experienced hard times at home. At the very least, the departure of a daughter meant that a hard-pressed farm family would have one less mouth to feed.

The women also hoped that a stint at the mill would give them

---

"NO. 5 & 7 LOOMS STOPPED—NO WEAVERS . . ."

Finding and disciplining an adequate supply of competent weavers plagued early textile-mill managers. N. B. Gordon managed a small woolen mill in rural Massachusetts. The daily entries in his 1829 diary reveal recurring problems of absenteeism, unpredictable natural conditions, and poor production standards.

January

5: One weaver sick, four looms stopped. Water wheel froze up this morning. Took until 8 o'clock to start it.

6: One weaver still sick. Four looms stopped. Water failed some about 4 o'clock.

8: Last night and yesterday warm, which gave plenty of water this day for all hands. One weaver sick. Four looms stopped.

13: 6 weavers—2 looms stopped. One weaver sick. Sally and Mary Ann Leonard out ¾ of the day by permission.

14: Looms all in operation.

16: Fine warm day. Almira Lowell absent this day and also to be tomorrow, to bury her grandmother. P.M. went to Mr. Carver's to get harness made.

March

23: No. 4 weaver absent ½ day. No. 5 and 6—¼ day each. Extreme cold. Lovell's children did not get in until ½ past 7 a.m. on account of water on the road.

24: Mr. Thayer's party last night broke up 3 o'clock. Morning hands in consequence come in late, and one, No. 6 weaver, not until noon. H. Kingman commenced repairing the old looms.

April

18: No. 6 loom stopped, no weaver. No. 5 weaver quit.

19: Went to Norton after weavers.

21: No. 5 & 7 looms stopped—no weavers. New spinning badly tended.

TIME TABLE OF THE LOWELL MILLS,

Arranged to make the working time throughout the year average 11 hours per day.

TO TAKE EFFECT SEPTEMBER 21st., 1853.

The Standard time being that of the meridian of Lowell, as shown by the Regulator Clock of AMOS SANBORN, Post Office Corner, Central Street.

From March 20th to September 19th, inclusive.

COMMENCE WORK, at 6.30 A. M. LEAVE OFF WORK, at 6.30 P. M., except on Saturday Evenings.
BREAKFAST at 6 A. M. DINNER, at 12 M. Commence Work, after dinner, 12.45 P. M.

From September 20th to March 19th, inclusive.

COMMENCE WORK at 7.00 A. M. LEAVE OFF WORK, at 7.00 P. M., except on Saturday Evenings.
BREAKFAST at 6.30 A. M. DINNER, at 12.30 P.M. Commence Work, after dinner, 1.15 P. M.

BELLS.

From March 20th to September 19th, inclusive.

Morning Bells.	Dinner Bells.	Evening Bells.
First bell,..........4.30 A. M.	Ring out,...........12.00 M.	Ring out,...........6.30 P. M.
Second, 5.30 A. M.; Third, 6.20.	Ring in,...........12.35 P. M.	Except on Saturday Evenings.

From September 20th to March 19th, inclusive.

Morning Bells.	Dinner Bells.	Evening Bells.
First bell,..........5.00 A. M.	Ring out,...........12.30 P. M.	Ring out at...........7.00 P. M.
Second, 6.00 A. M.; Third, 6.50.	Ring in,...........1.05 P. M.	Except on Saturday Evenings.

SATURDAY EVENING BELLS.

During APRIL, MAY, JUNE, JULY, and AUGUST, Ring Out, at 6.00 P. M.
The remaining Saturday Evenings in the year, ring out as follows:

SEPTEMBER.	NOVEMBER.	JANUARY.
First Saturday, ring out 6.00 P. M.	Third Saturday ring out 4.00 P. M.	Third Saturday, ring out 4.25 P. M.
Second " " 5.45 "	Fourth " " 3.55 "	Fourth " " 4.35 "
Third " " 5.30 "		
Fourth " " 5.20 "	DECEMBER.	FEBRUARY.
OCTOBER.	First Saturday, ring out 3.50 P. M.	First Saturday, ring out 4.45 P. M.
First Saturday, ring out 5.05 P. M.	Second " " 3.55 "	Second " " 4.55 "
Second " " 4.55 "	Third " " 3.55 "	Third " " 5.00 "
Third " " 4.45 "	Fourth " " 4.00 "	Fourth " " 5.10 "
Fourth " " 4.35 "	Fifth " " 4.00 "	
Fifth " " 4.25 "		MARCH.
NOVEMBER.	JANUARY.	First Saturday, ring out 5.25 P. M.
		Second " " 5.30 "
First Saturday, ring out 4.15 P. M.	First Saturday, ring out 4.10 P. M.	Third " " 5.35 "
Second ". " 4.05 "	Second " " 4.15 "	Fourth " " 5.45 "

YARD GATES will be opened at the first stroke of the bells for entering or leaving the Mills.

• *SPEED GATES commence hoisting three minutes before commencing work.*

Bells, bells, bells: the mill worker's day in 1853, as dictated by the managers of the Lowell Mills.

some of the economic and cultural opportunities—not least important, a dowry—that straitened agricultural life denied them. Mary Paul of Barnard, Vermont, for example, worked in her early teens as a domestic servant and then boarded with nearby relatives. Seeking her father's consent to work in Lowell, she wrote him, "I think it would be better for me than to stay out here. . . . I am in need of clothes which I cannot get about here and for that reason I want to go to Lowell or some other place." Sally Rice of Somerset, Vermont, had hired out as a farmworker in New York State, but found farm life too exhausting and isolating. She wrote to her parents that she wanted to find work in a Connecticut textile mill: "I am most 19 years old. I must of course have something of my own before many more years have passed over my head. And where is that something coming from if I go home and earn nothing?"

Work in the Lowell mills was never easy and grew harder as time passed. In the early years, the average employee worked twelve hours a day, six days a week. Holidays were few and short: July Fourth, Thanksgiving, and the first day of spring. But the relative scarcity of labor at first and the need to lure women into the mills and keep them there for four or five years dictated tolerable working and housing conditions. The healthy state of the industry and the expansion of the market allowed the company to maintain relatively attractive conditions without suffering financially. From 1814 to 1825, the Boston Manufacturing Company returned a dividend of 20 percent each year.

But the situation changed in the mid-1830s. Increasing competition from new firms brought down prices, especially following the great economic crisis of 1839–43, discussed below. The Boston Associates protected their profits by reducing costs—especially the cost of labor. They combined three methods: speed-up, stretch-out, and the premium system (piece rates). Speed-up meant increasing the rate at which a machine operated. Stretch-out meant increasing the number of machines a worker tended. Between 1840 and 1854, the workload of the average Lowell spinner and weaver more than doubled. Had piece rates remained stable, this extra work would have meant extra income for the workers, too. Instead, the company systematically lowered piece rates, so that weekly wages remained virtually frozen. Meanwhile, housing conditions deteriorated as construction of boarding houses lagged behind the growth of the labor force. Overcrowding resulted; soon most Lowell workers sought housing wherever they could find (and afford) it.

"...A NEW KIND OF MACHINERY"

To the New England farm girls and women who worked in the nation's first textile mills, factory work was a new and sometimes fearful experience. Wrestling with powerful and complicated machinery could be frightening and dangerous. In A New England Girlhood, *Lucy Larcom recounts one such experience in the Lowell mills.*

My return to mill-work involved making acquaintance with a new kind of machinery. The spinning-room was the only one I had hitherto known anything about. Now my sister Emilie found a place for me in the dressing-room, beside her. It was more airy, and fewer girls were in the room, for the dressing-frame itself was a large, clumsy affair, that occupied a great deal of space. Mine seemed as unmanageable to me as an overgrown spoilt child. It had to be watched in a dozen directions every minute, and even then it was always getting itself and me into trouble. I felt as if the half-live creature, with its great, groaning joints and whizzing fan, was aware of my incapacity to manage it, and had a fiendish spite against me. I contracted an unconquerable dislike to it; indeed, I never liked, and never could learn to like, any kind of machinery. And this machine finally conquered me. It was humiliating, but I had to acknowledge that there were some things I could not do, and I retired from the field, vanquished.

"Bell Time." A cross-section of the Lawrence, Massachusetts, workforce as presented to the readers of *Harper's Weekly*. Winslow Homer sketched women, men, and children as they emerged from the city's textile factories at the end of a workday in 1868.

As working and living conditions declined, Irish immigrants (including older women, children, and men) steadily entered the labor force. In 1836, less than 4 percent of the workers in a typical Lowell factory were foreign-born. But that proportion rose to nearly 40 percent by 1850 and 60 percent by 1860. The change reflected two simultaneous trends: the decreasing willingness among the native-born farm women to go to work in ever less attractive mills, and the arrival in the United States of millions of poor Irish peasants fleeing catastrophic famine.

At first the factory bosses treated their foreign-born workers even worse than they did the native-born, forcing the Irish to bear the brunt of speed-up, stretch-out, and declining piece rates, and denying them equal access to higher-paying jobs. This temporarily took some of the pressure off the Yankee women and created deep divisions within the workforce. So

"A SLAVE AT MORN, A SLAVE AT EVE . . ."

This poem about textile work, written in 1833 by Thomas Mann, a teacher, poet, and social critic from Providence, Rhode Island, condemns the personal and political effects of America's growing factory system.

Picture of a Factory Village

For Liberty our Fathers fought,
Which with their blood, they dearly bought,
The Fact'ry system sets at naught.
A slave at morn, a slave at eve,
It doth my inmost feelings grieve;
The blood runs chilly from my heart,
To see fair Liberty depart;
And leave the wretches in their chains,
To feed a vampyre from their veins.
Great Britain's curse is now our own;
Enough to damn a King and a Throne.

did the company policy of segregating native-born and immigrant housing facilities. But as the factory system spread and available labor became more plentiful, these differences in treatment shrank. By 1860, the heavy work and low wages initially reserved for immigrants were the standard for all textile operatives.

The future seemed to belong to the factory, and not only in the field of textiles. "Machinery has taken almost entire possession of the manufacture of cloth," lamented the exiled English democrat Thomas Devyr, then living in the United States.

> It is making steady—we might say rapid—advances upon all branches of iron manufacturing; the newly invented machine saws, working in curves as well as straight lines, the planing and grooving machines, and the tenon and mortise machine, clearly admonish us that its empire is destined to extend itself over all our manufactures of wood.

Indeed, Devyr added, most of the traditional handicrafts, too, had already "foretasted the overwhelming competition of this occult power."

DEPRESSION, RECOVERY, EXPANSION

A major financial panic paralyzed the economy in 1837, and two years later a full-scale, protracted depression set in. Banks failed, transportation and commerce slumped, construction all but ceased, goods went unsold. Untold numbers of businesses had to close their doors. In New York City, an estimated fifty thousand—more than a third of the total labor force—found themselves thrown out of work. One day, a notice appeared offering rural employment for twenty laborers at the low wage of $4 per month plus board; five hundred desperate men responded. The story was the same elsewhere. Thousands were left jobless in Lynn, and those still employed saw their wages halved. A Philadelphia citizens' committee warned that the poor in that city were "dying of want." A similar committee in Boston tried to push the unemployed out of the city.

Full recovery came slowly. By the mid-1840s, however, the pace of business was brisker than ever. Slumps would recur in 1854–55 and in 1857, but overall, the last two decades before the Civil War saw towns and cities, commerce and industry, expand at an unprecedented rate. It had taken half a century (1790 to 1840) for urban residents to increase from 8 percent to 18 percent of the Northeast's total population. Now that percentage doubled again in just twenty years. Industry grew even more rapidly. During this same two decades, the value of the nation's manufacturing and mining output increased

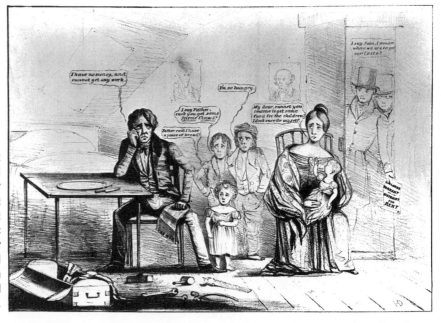

"I have no money, and cannot get any work." An unemployed mechanic and his destitute family face starvation and eviction during the 1837 depression. This Whig lithograph cartoon places the blame on the Democratic Party (represented by the wrinkled portraits of Andrew Jackson and Martin Van Buren tacked on the garret wall).

more than four and a half times. Much more than in earlier decades, the introduction of power-driven machines (such as the sewing machine) sharply boosted the productivity of human labor.

Immigrants made up a big share of the urban population and of the expanding class of industrial wage-earners whose efforts sustained this economic development. During these key twenty years, more than four million human beings uprooted themselves from their native lands (mostly from Ireland, Germany, and Great Britain, fewer from Canada and Scandinavia) and emigrated to the United States. For the America of that day, this was a human tidal wave—equaling nearly a third of the free population of the U.S. in 1840. Only about one in every eight of the newcomers settled in the South, and then principally in the border states and in cities. More went to western farms. Most, however, went to the booming cities of both the North and West, and there they put their distinctive stamp on whole neighborhoods. By the Civil War, at least one out of every three residents of most major cities—including Boston, Lowell, New York, Brooklyn, Rochester, Buffalo, Newark, Pittsburgh, Detroit, Cleveland, Cincinnati, Chicago, St. Louis, Milwaukee, and San Francisco—had been born abroad.

This immigrant wave included a few well-to-do merchants, manufacturers, and professionals, but the overwhelming majority made their living with their hands. Out of every ten immigrants reporting their occupations to American customs officials between 1840 and 1860, roughly two were skilled workers, three had been farmers, and four unskilled laborers. The agricultural and industrial revolutions in Europe—often accompanied by social conflict and government repression—wrenched them out of their communities and drove them abroad in search of sanctuary, though in many places the immigrants found work in occupations that bore the heaviest burdens imposed by American industrialization.

The Irish emigration grew out of just such a complex of factors: economic crunch, class and religious clashes, natural disaster, and resistance to British colonialism. To strengthen its hold over its Irish colony, England had worked for centuries to concentrate land, wealth, religious privilege, and political power in the hands of Ireland's pro-English Protestant minority at the expense of the Catholic majority. In pursuit of increased revenue, meanwhile, the largely Protestant landlord class steadily squeezed the already impoverished Catholic tenants and landless laborers.

Simultaneously, England moved to transform the Emerald Isle into a secure market for British manufactures. Ireland was stripped of its limited tariff protection, crushing much of the country's traditional small industry (especially textiles) under the weight of British competition. Unemployed workers joined landless peasants in search of new ways to survive.

This relentless pressure triggered fierce resistance. In the early nineteenth century, diverse movements raised the centuries-old Irish struggle to new heights of popular mobilization and organization. The same pressures that produced resistance also drove more and more of the dispossessed out of their country. By the 1830s, thousands were leaving every year, most bound for North America. But this emigrant stream became a raging flood in the following decade. In 1845, a blight devastated Ireland's potato crop, and it returned the next few years. The potato blight was not peculiar to Ireland; in fact, it began in North America. But only in Ireland was the rural population already so poor as to be wholly dependent on this single plant. The result was calamitous.

Profiteering, landlord-tenant relations, and colonialism aggravated the disaster. In the midst of the potato famine, corn, cattle, and dairy products continued to be produced in Ireland. But rather than give these foodstuffs to the starving, landlords sold them abroad for profit. "God sent the blight," went an Irish saying, "but the English landlords sent the famine!" When the blight prevented tenants from paying rent, landlords evicted them in droves, often to clear the way for larger commercial farms. The relief law helped the landlords consolidate the land: to qualify for famine relief, a family had to surrender all land in excess of a quarter-acre.

This catastrophe brought death and misery on a staggering scale. The nation lost a third of its population during the 1845–55 famine—

"Ejectment of Irish Tenantry." A wood-engraving from an 1848 edition of the *Illustrated London News* depicts an eviction in Ireland, a common occurrence during the potato famine.

more than a million died from starvation or disease. "One business alone survives!" bitterly observed nationalist leader Thomas Francis Meagher. "That fortunate business, . . . that favored, privileged, and patronized business is the Irish coffin-maker's." At least another million and three-quarters fled their native land—eight in ten bound for the United States, most of the rest for Canada.

Two-thirds of the U.S.-bound Irish settled in New York, Pennsylvania, and New Jersey, overwhelmingly in towns and cities. Most of the rest went to Massachusetts, Connecticut, Ohio, and Illinois. A few managed to buy farms. Others (including those who had gained skills and experience working in England) found employment here as craftsmen, miners, and construction workers.

But the vast majority arrived virtually penniless and without any industrial training. Ireland's stunted agriculture had denied them anything but the most primitive farming experience. The only work in the New World open to the men among them, therefore, was unskilled, temporary, and often heavy. After the mid-1840s, Irish immigrants dominated day labor in most coastal towns and cities. A visiting Irish journalist remarked in 1860, "There are several sorts of power working at the fabric of this Republic: water-power, steam-power, horse-power, Irish-power. The last works hardest of all."

Young Irish women working as domestic servants did more than their share of heavy work. In the last three antebellum decades, prosperous urban families hired them in swiftly rising numbers. While the wealthier employers might divide the household's tasks among the cook, a maid, and a butler, most employed only one all-round maid. It was her responsibility to cook, clean, prepare and serve meals, care for the children, and mend the family's clothing. And then, as one contemporary recalled,

> wood and coal were to be brought from the cellar to all the fires . . . in all sitting rooms. All water required for the kitchen, or bedrooms, or for baths, was drawn from the nearest street pump, and all refuse water and slops were carried out to the street and emptied into the gutter.

Small wonder that these young women commonly worked sixteen hours a day and more.

As for unskilled male day laborers, even though their real daily wages rose over time, as already noted, sporadic employment often meant low annual incomes and wretched living conditions. An 1849 report of the Boston Committee of Internal Health pointed with alarm at "the very wretched, dirty, and unhealthy conditions of a great number of the dwellinghouses occupied by the Irish population," where "each room, from garret to cellar, is filled with a family

". . . THE PESTILENT AIR OF THE STEERAGE"

Herman Melville, the author of Moby Dick, was a cabin-boy on a packet ship sailing between New York and Liverpool, England, in the 1830s. In his novel *Redburn,* Melville describes the conditions of work and life on board the sailing ship *Highlander.* The following selection describes the horrifying conditions experienced by Irish immigrants traveling belowdecks in steerage. Hundreds of thousands of Irish immigrants died on board ship while traveling from Ireland to the United States in the 1840s and 1850s.

DURING THE FREQUENT *hard blows* we experienced, the hatchways on the steerage were, at intervals, hermetically closed; sealing down in their noisome den, those scores of human beings. [It] was beyond question, this noisome confinement in so close, unventilated, and crowded a den: joined to the deprivation of sufficient food, from which many were suffering; which, helped by their personal uncleanliness, brought on a malignant fever. . . .

The cases [soon] increased: the utmost alarm spread through the ship. . . . Many of the panic-stricken emigrants would fain now [to be] domiciled on deck; but being so scantily clothed, the wretched weather—wet, cold, and tempestuous—drove the best part of them again below. Yet any other human beings, perhaps, would rather have faced the most outrageous storm, than continued to breathe the pestilent air of the steerage. . . .

The sight that greeted us, upon entering [steerage], was wretched indeed. It was like entering a crowded jail. From the rows of rude bunks, hundreds of

consisting of several persons, and sometimes with two or more families." Such conditions, the report concluded, allowed "no cleanliness, privacy, or proper ventilation, and little comfort."

But despite these hardships, many found much to cherish in their new land. From Philadelphia, Patrick Dunny wrote his family and friends in the old country to praise America's more democratic atmosphere, using phrases that echo immigrant letters from decades earlier:

> People that cuts a great dash at home, when they come here they think it strange for the humble class of people to get as much respect as themselves. For when they come here it won't do to say I had such-and-such and was such-and-such back at home. But strangers here they must gain respect by their conduct and not by their tongue. . . . I know people here from the town of Newbridge that would not speak to me if they met me on the public road [in Ireland], and here I can laugh in their face when I see them.

meager, begrimed faces were turned upon us; while seated upon the chests were scores of unshaven men, smoking tea-leaves, and creating a suffocating vapor. But this vapor was better than the native air of the place, which from almost unbelievable causes, was fetid in the extreme. In every corner, the females were huddled together, weeping and lamenting; children were asking bread from their mothers, who had none to give. . . .

About four o'clock that morning, the first four died. They were all men; and the scenes which ensued were frantic in the extreme. . . . By their own countrymen, they were torn from the clasp of their wives, rolled in their own bedding, with ballast-stones, and with hurried rites, were dropped into the ocean.

At this time, ten more men had caught the disease. . . .

On land, a pestilence is fearful enough; but there, many can flee from an infected city; whereas, in a ship, you are locked and bolted in the very hospital itself. Nor is there any possibility of escape from it; and in so small and crowded a place, no precaution can effectually guard against contagion. . . .

However this narrative of the circumstances attending the fever among the emigrants on the *Highlander* may appear . . . the only account you obtain of such events, is generally contained in a newspaper paragraph, under the shipping-head. *There* is the obituary of the destitute dead, who die on the sea. They die, like the billows that break on the shore, and no more are heard or seen. . . . What a world of life and death, what a world of humanity and its woes, lies shrunk into a three-worded sentence!

You see no plague-ship driving through a stormy sea; you hear no groans of despair; you see no corpses thrown over the bulwarks; you mark not the wringing hands and torn hair of widows and orphans:—all is a blank. . . .

In some ways Germany's emigration resembled Ireland's. There, too, industrial and agricultural changes undermined the position of farmers and craftsmen, particularly in the Southwest, the center of the emigration of these decades. Peasants and artisans chafed at the tax burdens, social restrictions, and political repression imposed by the old nobility, its armies, its bureaucracies, and its state churches. Far from improving the situation, the endeavors of merchants and industrialists often deepened their economic insecurity. Their new economic order, complained one petition from master craftsmen, forced independent producers "into the abyss of the proletariat." In Germany, too, economic, political, and religious grievances wove themselves tightly together.

But the German experience

"The Irish Harvest." "In many districts of Ireland," says the caption accompanying this 1852 illustration in a Boston weekly, "there are scenes like this which give unmistakable evidence of prosperity, notwithstanding the reports that are constantly reaching us of want and misery in that unfortunate land." Although the British press depicted the ravages of the Irish potato famine, American publications seemed reluctant to unsettle their readers with disturbing images.

differed from the Irish in several important respects. For one thing, skilled craftsmen made up a larger proportion of those leaving Germany. For another, Germany's national crisis produced full-scale revolution in 1848–49. Imbued with values similar to those of Thomas Paine, German craftsmen provided the radical democratic movements and the revolution with much of their driving force and popular following. Hostile alike to medieval survivals and modern wage labor, some of these people sought a new "organization of labor . . . recognizing the equal rights of all producers." To that end, they demanded narrower differences in personal wealth, an end to political and economic burdens on the land and those who worked it, and a range of other measures aimed at improving lower-class life. These included limits on the length of the working day, free universal education, producers' and consumers' cooperatives, and a guaranteed right to employment.

By 1860, a third of all German immigrants lived in the three mid-Atlantic states favored by the Irish, but few settled in New England. More ventured farther west, into Ohio, Indiana, Illinois, Missouri, Michigan, Iowa, and Wisconsin. Germans were more likely than Irish to become farmers, and less likely to become unskilled laborers, factory workers, or domestic servants.

Most importantly, large numbers of German immigrants entered the older urban skilled crafts, especially those producing consumer goods. More than their craft skills won them these jobs. The expansion of the North's light industry brought with it a painful degradation in pay and work conditions for many skilled crafts. Having fewer alternatives than the native-born, immigrants could more easily be induced to accept such objectionable work. Though proud to be "without any strong predilections in favor of foreigners of any kind," the Chicago *Daily Tribune* was nonetheless delighted to find that "our German population" was "fitted to do the cheap and ingenious labor of the country." The low wages particularly cheered the *Tribune* editor, who enthused, "The German will live as cheaply and work infinitely more intelligently than the negro."

Similar forces also stimulated migration to America from England, Scotland, Wales, Canada, Norway, and Sweden. The British government actively encouraged the expansion and mechanization of industry at the expense of both farmers and traditional urban crafts. Again, the results included mass protest movements (most notably trade-unionism and the radical-democratic Chartists) and large-scale migration across the Atlantic. Once in the United States, these immigrants spread out across the free states. About a fourth become farmers. Coming from the most advanced industrial nation of the world, many British workers brought with them more skills and greater experience with modern machinery than any other national group. They were also more at home with the language and customs in the United States. These two factors helped them move quickly into some of the most desirable jobs, especially in construction, in the manufacture of machines and tools, and in the production of textiles, coal, iron, cutlery, glass, and paper.

More than a hundred thousand people migrated from Canada to the United States between 1840 and the Civil War. They included refugees of the unsuccessful nationalist revolts of 1837–38 as well as victims of British trade policies in the lumber, shipbuilding, and provisioning industries of the Maritime Provinces. Especially numerous were French-Canadian farmers in flight from land speculation. Some sought farms in Illinois, Michigan, and Wisconsin. Others obtained wage labor in New England or northern New York State, commonly in textile mills and brickyards or as lumberjacks and farmhands.

From Europe's northern tier, nearly forty thousand Swedes and Norwegians made their way to the United States during the last two antebellum decades. Like other Europeans in this period, Scandinavia's small farmers, tenants, and laborers were plagued by agrarian crisis, semifeudal class relations, and political inequality. Johan Reierson, a leading liberal writer, warned that those of "the producing and working class" who remained in their homeland faced a future of "slavish dependence." Few were surprised when the social groups Reierson described became breeding grounds for religious dissent, protest movements, and emigrant fever.

A Norwegian named Marcus Thrane lent his name to part of this broad popular protest. Inspired by the continental revolutions of 1848, Thrane led a mass movement in his own country of impoverished tenants and laborers. Claiming to number more than twenty thousand by mid-1850—a large figure in a country of less than a million and a half inhabitants—the Thraneites demanded the sale of all state lands to tenants and laborers, special workers' banks, government leniency toward debtors, universal manhood suffrage, a broader and more democratic school curriculum, and an end to corporate-monopolistic trade privileges.

Suppressed by the government in 1851, many of the movement's rank and file joined the emigration already underway. In the United States, most Scandinavians settled in the Northwest, starting in Illinois and Wisconsin, then spreading into northern Iowa, the Minnesota Territory, and Kansas. About half became farmers, a proportion three times as big as the Irish and twice that of the Germans and British. Others gravitated toward agriculture-related industries like lumbering, furniture-making, and the manufacture of farm implements. Many women became domestic servants.

But like other immigrant groups, they brought to their new home a determination to win the independence and freedom denied them in the Old World. Warned by skeptics there that migration would just mean becoming "a foreign slave abroad," a popular Norwegian emigrant's song replied: "America is free. Work is not slavery. . . . In the free land of the West every man is a free-born citizen." This devotion among immigrant working people to the promise of a free-labor society played an important role in U.S. politics during these decades.

IMMIGRANTS AND THE SOCIAL STRUCTURE

Many of these newcomers received a mixed reception in the antebellum United States. A potent blend of social, political, and cultural forces shaped the attitudes of native-born Americans toward the immigrants. One key factor was the way industrial change and expansion combined with the massive European influx to transform the country's labor force.

Few new immigrants were able to refuse work at short pay and long hours. This fact helped ease one of the problems cited by Albert Gallatin—the scarcity of labor, and (at least compared with Europe) its high price. Industrial growth could therefore proceed in America without having to force huge numbers of farmers here into the wage-earning labor force. Furthermore, the commercial and manufacturing expansion that this new source of cheap labor assisted also created a significant number of more desirable positions in towns and cities. A booming economy required more supervisors, merchants, clerks, and other white-collar workers, as well as small employers and highly skilled operatives (especially in the modern metal trades and other newer industries). This enabled a great many native-born working people—who enjoyed important economic, linguistic, and cultural advantages over newer immigrants—to leave unskilled or declining occupations for more attractive ones, or to leave depressed regions for flourishing ones. The resulting improvement in social status and living standards impressed not only those who experienced it but also others, who expected to follow their example.

Some observers concluded from all this that immigration and the congregation of newcomers in low-paid occupations benefited the native-born population as a whole. Massachusetts educator and politician Edward Everett argued that the Irish should be welcomed to America because "their inferiority as a race compels them to go to the bottom" of the occupational scale "and the consequence is that we are all, all of us, the higher lifted because they are here." The Irish, he continued, "do the manual labor. They do it most cheaply, and so they leave those whom they find" in those jobs "free to do other and more agreeable walks of duty." In this way the native-born "are simply pushed up, into foremen of factories, superintendents of farms, railway agents, machinists, inventors, teachers, artists, etc."

Everett greatly exaggerated the changes he observed and certainly misunderstood their causes. But the general tendency he tried to describe was real. Natives and newcomers—and among the newcomers, different nationalities—were increasingly becoming identified with different kinds of jobs, conditions, and incomes. This affected the way each group was viewed. The mental equation between "Irish Catholic" and "unskilled poor," for example, became an unquestioned commonplace. Many of the prospering native-born soon convinced

"Mother Abbess Strangling an Infant." Nativist tracts claimed to reveal loathsome rituals practiced by Catholic clergy. Lurid tales about priests preying on convent nuns and the secret murder of the illegitimate infants fanned nativist sentiments—and enriched authors who exploited their readers' predilections for stories about forbidden sex and violence.

themselves that it was Irishness or Catholicism—and not their own
free-labor economy—that created poverty in America. The Lawrence,
Massachusetts, *Courier*, for example, simply refused to believe that
four hundred native-born laborers lived among their Irish coworkers
in the city's shanty district. An army of anti-immigrant writers, edu-
cators, ministers, and politicians hammered the "nativist" message
home, ascribing most of the nation's ills to the newcomers' rejection
of "American" work-habits, culture, and religion. Irish and German
fondness for liquor and beer deeply offended pious nativists, who
linked temperance to republican morality in general. Treating the
Sabbath as a day of boisterous public celebration likewise infuriated
proper evangelicals. More than a few native workers accepted this nativist viewpoint.

On the other hand, the ethnic transformation of the nation's labor
force was far from immediate or total. While many natives did find
more desirable positions in these years, many others found themselves displaced by lower-paid immigrants. Still others stayed on at
their old jobs, sharing with new foreign-born coworkers the burdens

Cartoonist David Claypoole
Johnston's condemnation of the
nativist rioters who burned down
the Ursuline Convent in
Charlestown, Massachusetts, on
August 11, 1834.

of the industrial revolution. But even sharing hardship by no means guaranteed mutual sympathy, friendship, or support. It was not hard to convince some of the native-born unemployed that immigrants had stolen their jobs. Others stuck in declining occupations found it equally easy to blame that decline on the immigrants. Employers frequently encouraged these nativist attitudes, partly out of genuine conviction, partly to deflect workers' anger away from themselves, partly to undermine their employees' capacity to organize across ethnic lines. During the 1840s and 1850s, bloody brawls repeatedly pitted groups of workers of different origins against one another.

The transformation that enormously enlarged production and began radically to alter class and social relations in the North between 1790 and 1860 gratified many Americans. We need only recollect Daniel Webster's enthusiasm in 1847.

But not all Americans shared Webster's views. The changes he so ardently approved deeply concerned others who had seen them. In May 1865, a committee of the Massachusetts state legislature heard testimony from workers that astonished it. The committee marveled at the "development of machinery for the saving of labor" and at the "progress of invention." But it concluded that

> in the midst of progress and prosperity unrivaled, MAN the producer of all these—the first great cause of all—was the least of all. . . . Instead of the manly and sturdy independence which once distinguished the mechanic and the workingman, we have cringing servility and supineness. Instead of honest pride in the dignity of labor, we have the consciousness of inferiority. . . . Instead of labor being the patent of nobility, it is the badge of servitude.

These citizens of Webster's state feared the consequences of the changes the senator had earlier celebrated. "The first duty of the state," the committee reminded the legislature, "is to protect itself. . . . The state is composed of MEN, and the interest, progress, and the advancement of man is the foundation upon which the state rests."

These Massachusetts legislators differed from Webster in assessing the transformation of society since the American Revolution. More was involved than the far-reaching alterations introduced into the world of work. Those changes were matched by equally dramatic changes in family life, religion, popular culture, and especially politics. Americans debated these changes just as vigorously as they debated the impact of the industrial revolution on the relationship between liberty and equality.

SUNSHINE

AND

THE OLD BREWERY.

FIVE POINTS MISSION
BY THE LADIES HOME MISS SOC

SHADOW

IN

NEW YORK.

7 CHANGING PATTERNS OF SOCIAL LIFE

Popular mid-nineteenth-century publications presented the East's industrializing cities— New York, Philadelphia, and Baltimore—as fractured societies. According to articles, novels, and city guides, each was really *two* cities—one orderly, prosperous, and bathed in "sunlight," the other menacing, poor and steeped in "darkness" (or "gaslight"). In this frontispiece from the 1868 *Sunshine and Shadow in New York,* the symbolic extremes of day and night are represented by a Fifth Avenue mansion and the Old Brewery, an infamous "thieves' den."

THE DEMOCRATIC spirit of the young American nation combined with economic change to affect many other aspects of society as well. "The transition from mother-daughter power [in the home] to water and steam power" in the mill and factory, as one farmer noted in the 1850s, resulted in "a complete revolution in social life and domestic manners." Involved in this revolution were changes in family life, the roles assigned to family members, and more generally the ways in which men and women, boys and girls, thought of themselves and each other.

None of these changes, of course, began abruptly at the turn of the nineteenth century. Many of them began long before and reached full maturity only decades after the Civil War. And as with economic change, these social transformations came at different speeds in different parts of the country and among different groups of people. But during the decades between the achievement of independence and Lincoln's election, the alteration of old family and gender patterns touched all regions and social classes.

In social life, just as in economic, these years witnessed a process of differentiation and division. The strong bonds that had once joined family members to one another, while linking home life to production and work to leisure, now began to dissolve. More and more economic activity took place outside the home. With this shift came a sharper distinction between men's and women's responsibilities as well as new concepts of femininity, masculinity, childhood, and proper public behavior.

Most influential in shaping these concepts were members of prosperous urban families, who judged by their own experiences. Struggling against the current, other Americans evolved a variety of strategies to ensure survival for themselves and their families. In many cases, these strategies required wage labor for women and children, postponed marriages, and strained relations between parents and children, husbands and wives. Judged morally deficient by well-to-do critics, many now found themselves beset by reformers, lawmakers, and ministers determined to improve their characters, correct their behavior, and save their souls.

The same forces that increasingly separated home and production also introduced a firmer division between work and leisure. For the free farm and town population of the colonial era, relaxation and amusement had been integrated into working days and family lives. Stepped-up commerce, urban growth, and wage labor changed this. Faster work rhythms and tightened work discipline forced people to seek their pleasure elsewhere. Slowly but plainly, leisure became a separate and distinct part of life. At the same time, the growth of commerce began to change the nature of leisure activities themselves. More and more they became commodities—something to pay for and observe rather than simply join in free of charge. At the same time, the increasingly distinct manner in which rich and poor relaxed and entertained themselves reinforced a growing sense of alarm that society was polarizing dangerously. That fear, in turn, nurtured a new religious revival.

The evangelical Protestantism that now swept across the United States drew strength from many sources—from democratic thought and economic development, as well as from the important changes under way in the nation's family life and cultural activities. This powerful religious movement expressed—while trying to resolve—some of the most explosive tensions developing within the society. It sought to reach across the chasms that seemed more and more to separate one group from another. The broad sweep of the movement and the power of its message did indeed blunt some of these conflicts. Others, however, defied religious resolution. Even there, however, evangelicalism's impact proved strong, deeply affecting the language and methods with which such conflicts were expressed and fought out.

THE MIDDLE-CLASS IDEAL

For the eighteenth-century white population, life revolved around the household and the family. Most work was performed in the home and absorbed the efforts of all family members. As one New Englander later recalled, farm life in that period had "harnessed all together into the productive process, young and old, male and female, from the boy that rode the plow horse to the grandmother knitting under her spectacles." The various family members performed different if often overlapping tasks. But the combined efforts of all were crucial to the success of this family economy.

On a farm, the men and older boys worked in the fields, growing food or cash crops. Assisted by the children, the women maintained the household, prepared food, and made utensils to use in their own homes, to sell to merchants, or to barter with neighbors for other items.

In the artisan household, the father did his skilled work, perhaps assisted by sons or other boys apprenticed to him. His wife cooked, cleaned, wove, sewed, and cared for the children, the ill, and the elderly; she might also help her husband in his trade or wait on his customers. Any apprentices and journeymen boarded in the master's home, and his wife cooked and cleaned for them as well as her family.

But while their work was essential, women of all classes occupied social positions clearly and firmly below men. Compared with their husbands, brothers, and even their sons, they had more restricted personal opportunities and much more limited legal rights, and their participation in public life was strictly curtailed. In general, a wife was viewed merely as an extension of her husband and family. Her primary responsibility was to fulfill their needs and assist her husband in his work.

In the seven decades after the Revolution the growing importance of the market combined with the spread of democratic beliefs and the accompanying decline of deference to introduce significant changes into these households.

Although farm women, especially on the frontier, continued to make many things for their families' own use well into the nineteenth century, goods bought from others became increasingly common, as we have seen. The experience of a prospering Philadelphia

The frontispiece and title page of a popular 1869 guide to the "Formation and Maintenance of Economical, Healthful, Beautiful, and Christian Homes." Intended to instruct young women on their proper role in the middle-class home, this book was continually expanded and reprinted after its first publication in 1841. Its lessons about Domestic Science ranged from the correct way to raise children to the appropriate type of picture to hang in the parlor.

family illustrates this change. Before 1780, this family had never spent more than ten dollars a year for clothing and household supplies. In that year, the first daughter brought to her marriage a dowry that included a supply of her mother's best wool and flax to make dresses, coats, stockings, and shifts. She also bought some cotton for sheets. Two years later, the second daughter married. She was evidently no longer expected to make all her own clothes and instead bought a calico gown and a petticoat to round out her dowry. She also purchased a set of stoneware teacups, a half-dozen pewter teaspoons, and a teakettle—items her father and mother had never owned. The third and last daughter's dowry included a store-bought silk gown,

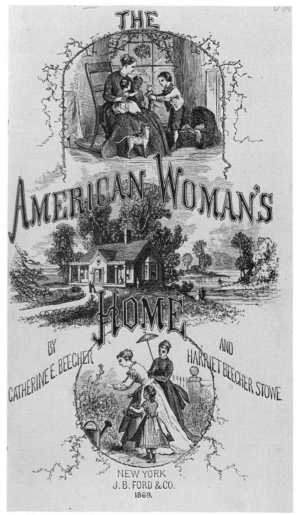

THE AMERICAN WOMAN'S HOME

BY CATHERINE E. BEECHER AND HARRIET BEECHER STOWE

NEW YORK
J. B. FORD & CO.
1869.

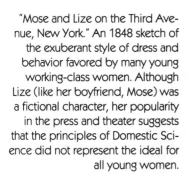

"Mose and Lize on the Third Avenue, New York." An 1848 sketch of the exuberant style of dress and behavior favored by many young working-class women. Although Lize (like her boyfriend, Mose) was a fictional character, her popularity in the press and theater suggests that the principles of Domestic Science did not represent the ideal for all young women.

additional silk for a cloak, a looking glass, china, a tea service, and other finery. This family could afford steadily to replace goods produced in the home with those produced by others.

As the years passed, technological advances also made their presence felt. In the 1830s, iceboxes made it possible to keep fresh foods longer, expanding the diet and reducing the number of trips to market. Around the same time, iron cookstoves began to appear. Their owners no longer had to bend before dangerously open fireplaces or wrestle with the heavy utensils used in them. Many cities now began installing public water systems. For subscribers to this water system who could afford indoor pumps, housework became easier. And for those women who could afford to hire them, probably the greatest household conveniences of all were domestic servants, whose ranks, since 1800, had grown twice as fast as the number of white families.

Even more fundamentally, commercial and industrial development served to dissolve the link between the home life of many families and the ways they earned their livings. This process has been most closely studied among those who benefited most from development—the families of well-to-do merchants, manufacturing employers, master craftsmen, professionals. Among members of this growing group, which came to be called the middle class, historians have uncovered significant changes in the nature and structure of family life, the assignment of responsibilities, the way those responsibilities were carried out, and the ways that men, women, and children thought about themselves and one another.

In these families, fathers increasingly conducted their business in

"The Amazonian Convention." The proceedings of a women's-rights meeting are disrupted by hecklers in an 1859 cartoon published in *Harper's Weekly.*

offices, shops, workshops, and factories separate from their homes. Their involvement in this "public sphere" diverted their energies and attention from household matters. Their wives remained in the home, now freed (and excluded) from most income-producing activities. In the shops of rising master craftsmen, the efforts of wage-earning employees replaced the efforts of family members. In shoemaking, for example, the responsibility for stitching the uppers shifted from the master's wife to people like Sarah Trask, a poor laborer's daughter employed as a shoe outworker in Beverly, Massachusetts. For the master's wife and other women in similar circumstances, therefore, family and home life became a special sphere, one strictly separated from the public sphere of business and politics. They now contributed to the economic health of their families primarily by shrewdly planning their purchases. This growing separation between the genders also gave rise to (and was made more tolerable by) strong friendships among the women who experienced it.

The same economic changes that drew men out of their homes also affected the nature, tempo, and feel of work itself, stripping away its earlier associations with individual freedom and independence, personal creativity, alternating bouts of labor and recreation. The pace quickened, time pressures came more and more to dominate labor, and the relatively cooperative atmosphere of the old artisan workshop gave way to employer-employee tensions.

As the business world became less convivial, writers idealized the home as a unique refuge from the driving economic pressures and personal frictions of the man's working life. And, they added, it was the woman's responsibility to keep it that way. Sarah Josepha Hale, editor of one of the most popular magazines of the 1830s, *Godey's Lady's Book*, instructed her middle-class female readers, "Our men are sufficiently money-making; let us keep our women and children free from the contagion as long as possible."

This bracketing of women, children, and the protected household reflects another of the changes under way. Much more than previously, during the first decades of the century society acknowledged the mother's primacy in the task of childrearing. At the same time, the nature of this task evolved, reflecting not only the increased maternal role but also the development of democratic-republican ideals and recognition of the rapid economic changes reorganizing society. "Republican mothers" increasingly sought to instill habits and standards of behavior, associated with Ben Franklin's *Poor Richard's Almanac*, deemed essential to republican government and personal prosperity. These included the importance of hard work, perseverance, and diligence; frugality, saving, and accumulation; and personal reserve, self-discipline, restraint of the emotions, and steady and temperate habits.

Childrearing now also came to rely less on intimidation and physical punishment and more on affection and patient instruction. Instead of simply recognizing and bending before authority, the child was now expected to understand and internalize the parents' values in order to govern him or herself. Machinist Morton Poole encouraged his sister to strengthen in her son "the liberties which are essential to the formation of a free and independent spirit." In doing so, he continued, she should rely upon "superior understanding" instead of fear and physical punishment, since "a child that is afraid of its parents can never feel that confidence which is necessary to the receiving of information in conversations with its parents."

As Poole's letter suggests, the transmission of information—and in larger quantities than ever—moved to the center of middle-class childrearing in the young republic. The mother's role in the early stages of this process required increased female access to educational facilities. Only a better-educated mother could begin the training of future adults able to confront the novel and swiftly changing society of the antebellum North. Particularly by the 1840s and 1850s, after all, a young man's success generally depended upon skills and methods different from those his father had needed a generation earlier. As artisans divided into employers and wage-earners, for example, sons of master craftsmen tended either to leave the industry completely or to act more as merchants and supervisors than as practicing artisans. Preparing for such roles led them into public high schools rather than apprenticeships.

As parents accorded more importance to the individuality and independence of their offspring, they also began relaxing their grip on their children's marital futures. More room was now left for the wishes of the individuals most directly involved. Of course, people (especially the wealthy) still tended to marry other members of their own social class. But within these limits, personal feelings and choice gained in importance.

Shielded from the harsh public sphere, and as the recognized center of youthful instruction, the mother-supervised home became equated with proper Christian values. Indeed, middle-class women now assumed greater responsibility for overseeing the morals not only of their own households but also, by extension, of the society as a whole: while men saw to the nation's material needs, women would see to its spiritual ones.

But this role did not imply challenging the husband's ultimate power over a wife and her household, much less bringing women directly into political life. To remain morally pure and personally comforting to her family, a woman was to remain under the formal rule of her man. She performed her special domestic role at the pleasure of her husband and could improve the society's moral temper by participating in church affairs and by setting a personal example for other family members. Wives, Sarah Josepha Hale advised, must remain "pure, pious, domestic, and submissive." And the wives of respectable artisans were expected to follow the same precepts. A book addressed to "the American mechanic" in 1840 explained that the proper mate was "patient, resolute, loves her home." Her place, it added, "is eminently at the fireside."

Some women, however, did breach the barrier between the

". . . A DEPENDENT AND ABJECT LIFE"

The resolutions passed at the first women's-rights convention, at Seneca Falls in 1848, parts of which are presented below, demanded that women be given their full political and civil rights as citizens of the United States.

THE HISTORY OF mankind is a history of repeated injuries and usurpations on the part of man toward woman, having in direct object the establishment of a absolute tyranny over her. To prove this, let facts be submitted to a candid world:

He has never permitted her to exercise her inalienable right to the elective franchise.

He has compelled her to submit to laws, in the formation of which she had no voice.

He has made her, if married, in the eye of the law, civilly dead.

He has taken from her all right in property, even to the wages she earns.

. . . In the covenant of marriage, she is compelled to promise obedience to her husband, he becoming, to all intents and purposes, her master—the law giving him power to deprive her of her liberty, and to administer chastisement.

He has monopolized nearly all the profitable employments, and from those she is permitted to follow, she receives but a scanty remuneration. He closes against her all the avenues to wealth and distinction which he considers most honorable to himself. As a teacher of theology, medicine, or law, she is not known.

He has created a false public sentiment by giving to the world a different code of morals for men and women, by which moral delinquencies which exclude women from society, are not only tolerated, but deemed of little account in man.

He has endeavored, in every way that he could, to destroy her confidence in her own powers, to lessen her self-respect, and to make her willing to lead a dependent and abject life.

"Bloomer-ism and Bloomer-fus'em." A cartoon from an 1853 comic almanac takes a swipe at Bloomers, loose-fitting trousers that were advocated by Amelia Jenks Bloomer and other women reformers as a relief from the inhibiting, uncomfortable, but standard corsets, petticoats, and crinoline gowns. Accosted by a police officer for wearing a dress in public, a hapless husband replies: "Oh, it's all owing to my wife, who is a Bloomer, and wears my breeches, and having walked out with my only pair, I could do nothing but put on her petticoats."

domestic and public spheres. Among them were working women, whose families had never accepted the new cult of female domesticity. Others, though, crossed that barrier by following the twisting logic of the domestic ideology itself. Accepting the role of society's moral guardians, they had enrolled in movements for social reform ranging from providing charity to the poor, to opposing alcohol, to pressing for the abolition of slavery. Once involved in such eminently political activity, however, some female activists—unlike most other female reformers—began revising their views about their own political status. "Those who urged women to become missionaries and form tract societies," wrote Lydia Maria Child at the start of the 1840s, "have changed the household utensil to a living, energetic being," and such a changed woman had no desire to "turn into a broom again."

Demands for greater social and economic rights for American women had been raised before this. But only now did an organized movement arise led by women and dedicated to winning for women the full rights of American citizenship—first and foremost, the right to vote. "The investigation of the rights of the slave," wrote Quaker abolitionist Angelina Grimké, "has led me to a better understanding of my own." And indeed, the most prominent leaders of the women's-rights movement of this period—Elizabeth Cady Stanton, Susan B. Anthony, and Lucy Stone—had all been active abolitionists. In July 1848 the village of Seneca Falls, New York, hosted the country's first national women's-rights convention. Attended by some two hundred people, the convention issued a manifesto modeled on the Declaration of Independence, but amplifying it, declaring that "all men and women are created equal." Another convention three years later boldly announced, "We deny the right of any portion of the species to decide for another portion . . . what is and what is not their 'proper sphere'; the proper sphere for all human beings is the largest and highest to which they are able to attain."

PLEBEIAN REALITIES

Women's diaries, letters, and memoirs have made it possible to reconstruct and comprehend the changes in urban middle-class existence during the early industrial revolution. The careful study of family life among less prosperous and literary Americans began more recently and faces greater difficulties. But though the results remain fragmentary, some tentative generalizations can be made.

Relationships within the families of northern wage-earners changed in important ways between the Revolution and the Civil War. Some changes paralleled those occurring among their better-off fellow citizens, but others pointed in a very different direction.

Especially powerful, judging from the behavior of both women and men, was the belief that married women ought not to engage in wage labor. For the family of a self-employed male farmer or artisan, pride in being independent was seriously undermined when the father and husband had to go to work for someone else. But if even those wages were inadequate, and other family members also had to go to work— that would be an even greater humiliation. Opposition to female wage labor also drew strength from fears that the competition of women workers would further undermine the economic position of male breadwinners.

But these sentiments collided with other harsh realities. The poorer the family was, first of all, the less able were youths and women to remain outside the world of commerce. The same processes that turned an economically independent father into a wage-earner often also pushed other family members into the labor market to supplement his inadequate income. Working for wages imposed a second burden upon women of the laboring poor, for whom housework remained difficult; they needed to rely upon kin, neighbors, and coworkers for help. Nonetheless, though wage labor was hard, the personal and economic alternatives appeared to offer even less opportunity for independence, self-improvement, and self-respect. Thus, even those who started working mainly to help sustain their families found that the experience itself could reshape their concepts of family obligation. Some of them came to question, challenge, or even reject both traditional and current notions of their proper role.

On the northwestern frontier, family life among subsistence farmers retained much of its eighteenth-century character even after the Civil War. But further east, prospering commercial farm families identified more strongly with the vision of proper family life championed by middle-class citydwellers.

Still a third pattern appeared among rural northeastern families adversely affected by commercial development. The parents found it ever more difficult to provide for their children. Young men therefore tended increasingly to move away, usually westward, in search of land and opportunity. Though less mobile than their brothers, growing numbers of farm girls did join the paid labor force.

For some, assisting their families financially meant living apart from them, in order to work a few years in domestic service or in the Northeast's multiplying mills and factories. Most stayed in touch with parents, siblings, and more distant relatives by mail. In many cases their new life actually strengthened some family bonds, since they commonly obtained their jobs, housing, and crucial help in adapting to the mill towns through local networks of sisters, cousins, and friends who had arrived before them.

But family ties were nonetheless tested and strained by a stint in

Reformers blamed poverty on the moral failure of working-class households. Giving up on adults, many "missionaries" focused on the children of the poor. This emblem of the Philadelphia House of Refuge suggests the reformers' belief in their capacity to convert children into model citizens.

the mills. New conditions and experiences confronted young women with contradictory demands and temptations. They started work as loyal daughters helping to hold their families together, but many soon found themselves thinking and behaving in very untraditional ways. Living away from home and supporting themselves tended to strengthen their sense of independence. It also led them to reconsider their obligations to parents. "I have earned enough to school me a while," wrote Massachusetts mill worker Lucy Ann, "and have I not a right to do so? Or must I go home, like a dutiful girl, place the money in my father's hands, and then there goes all my hard earnings." In fact, few daughters of farm families—whether mill hands or outworkers—seem to have followed the common European practice of automatically turning wages over to their fathers. Few fathers even made the demand.

Exposure to stimulating new settings and commodities made it harder to contemplate a return to the traditional life of rural women. And the savings accumulated on the job helped a young woman assert her desire for greater personal freedom later on as well. They enabled her to continue supporting herself even after her stint at wagework had ended.

Self-support and savings may also help explain the distinctive marriage decisions that many mill women ultimately made. On average, mill hands married later than women who remained on the farms. While farm women generally married slightly older men, mill girls found mates closer to themselves in age. Mill women also proved less prone to marry farmers. One New England writer observed sadly that farmers' daughters who worked outside agriculture came to "contemn the calling of their fathers, and will nine times out of ten marry a mechanic in preference to a farmer. They know that marrying a farmer is serious business. They remember their worn-out mothers." All this suggests that distance from family and economic independence gave mill women greater freedom of choice and a bigger group of men to select from. And perhaps they felt freer to make such choices, knowing that their own wages formed part or all of their wedding dowries.

But most young farm women who earned wages did so without leaving their parents' homes, through outwork. Indeed, the system's principal attraction probably was that it allowed women to contribute to their family's finances without leaving the home. They could therefore continue to do the essential unpaid household tasks. At the same time, women outworkers received emotional support and practical aid from local relatives and friends, and especially from other females. In some cases, sharing the experiences and problems of common employment in the putting-out system reinforced ties like these.

Relations with males and feelings about marriage appear to have been complex. For most farm women, a successful marriage was the only real route to lasting economic security, and the alternative of a lonely and destitute "spinsterhood" was a frightening one. On the other hand, the risks, burdens, inequalities, and heartaches of marriage were also very real. Historians still have much to learn about marital relations among the rural poor, but the diary kept by Massachusetts outworker Sarah Trask during the 1840s and 1850s illuminates at least one aspect. Her entries reveal deep concern about male drunkenness and male domination of the household in general. A bride "must go just where her husband says," Trask worried, adding that "marriage to me seem a great responsibility . . . and almost all the care come upon the wife." At the same time, her diary registers the wrenching impact on women when their men died or went off to seek their fortunes in the West.

Similar conflicts beset families of the urban laboring poor. As in the colonial era, these people included widows and orphans and those abandoned by male breadwinners. They also included dependents of adult males tramping for work in the West. More numerous, however, were the victims of economic change: farm families uprooted either from the nearby countryside or from Europe, and the longtime city-dwellers upon whom fortune had not smiled. Among such adult males could be found craftsmen, day laborers, peddlers, porters, and factory workers. By the end of the period, immigrants—particularly the Irish—held disproportionately large numbers of the city's most poorly paid jobs. Their family lives and roles bore the distinctive marks of this poverty and of their own attempts to cope with it.

From an early age until marriage, most Irish-American women worked for wages. Their incomes went to support themselves as well as other family members in the United States and in Ireland. Although some took mill or factory work, the largest number went into domestic service; from the 1830s on, they replaced native-born farm women in the kitchens of the middle class. The chief benefit of such work was its security and dependability. Demand exceeded supply, room and board were included, and employment was neither seasonal nor particularly sensitive to fluctuations in the economy. In this respect, the job was better than most of those available to unskilled males.

Irish-American women like these apparently carried Sarah Trask's doubts about marriage a step further, postponing matrimony—or avoiding it altogether—more consistently than any other group of free females in the country. It is not hard to understand why. Marrying and bearing the children of a propertyless immigrant laborer involved great hardship. Furthermore, a domestic servant had to live with the employer, but that was impossible for a wife and mother, so marriage would end such employment—and would cut off funds crucial not only to the woman herself but also to her parents and siblings, in this country and in Ireland. At least as painful, the outside pressures on poor families often caused terrible conflicts within them. The wives of day laborers and ruined craftsmen commonly bore the burdens of their spouses' frustrations, drunkenness, and physical abuse. They also lived with the possibility of abandonment or of being widowed by an industrial accident.

The death or flight of husbands made female household heads commonplace. To support themselves and their children, many women in this position took in lodgers, providing them with shelter, housekeeping service, and meals in exchange for cash. Others joined the ranks of urban outworkers. Some of the poorest married women resorted to the same measures to supplement their husband's inadequate earnings. As with rural outworkers, labor performed for cash had to be combined with household tasks.

Poor wives took just as much pride in their homemaking skills as well-to-do ones. And for the urban poor, successful housekeeping took real skill, along with active cooperation of family members and neighbors. The technological improvements that could ease housework were at first available only to the upper classes; they got indoor plumbing, but the poor hauled pails of water upstairs several times daily from a public pump at the streetcorner or a pipe beside the backyard outhouses. Iron cookstoves and iceboxes were similarly rare among American families before the Civil War.

In the meantime, the bad effects of overcrowding, makeshift housing, disease, and filth—byproducts of urban growth and early industrialization—could be kept under control only with the help of others. Such assistance might mean the difference between survival and starvation during periods of unemployment or illness. At its best, this kind of interdependence created warm and tight-knit relations among the individuals involved. But with resources and living space limited, and other sources

"AND AIN'T I A WOMAN?"

A wide chasm separated the middle-class ideal of domesticity from the arduous labor of many poor working women. Sojourner Truth, born a slave called Isabella in New York State in 1798 and freed in 1827, addressed the issue at a women's-rights convention in 1851. Truth directed her impromptu speech at a group of ministers in the hall who referred to women as delicate and frail creatures who should confine themselves to the home. She contrasted the rhetoric of "separate spheres" with the hard realities of her own life. Although never enslaved, poor immigrant Irishwomen would have understood Truth's point very well.

THAT MAN OVER there says that women need to be helped into carriages and lifted over ditches, and have the best place everywhere. Nobody ever helps me into carriages, or over mud-puddles, or gives me any best place! And ain't I a woman? Look at my arm! I have ploughed, and planted, and gathered into barns, and no man could head [outdo] me! And ain't I a woman? I could work as well and eat as much as a man—when I could get it—and bear the lash as well! And ain't I a woman? I have borne thirteen children, and seen them most all sold off to slavery, and when I cried out with a mother's grief none but Jesus heard me! And ain't I a woman?

If the first woman God ever made was strong enough to turn the world upside down all alone, these women together ought to be able to turn it back, and get it right side up again! And now they are asking to do it, the men better let them!

"Let the Public Look at These Plague-Spots." An illustration from an 1860 edition of the *New York Illustrated News* shows a reporter and artist working on a story about the Glennan family, residents of a shanty district near the city's East River called Dutch Hill. Although newspapers and magazines may have failed to recognize the causes of urban poverty, by midcentury editors consistently dispatched reporters to cover the "dark background of our civilization."

of personal tension plentiful, interdependence could also create friction, hard feelings, and the angry "broom fights" notorious among tenement women.

Clearly, this kind of domestic life did not fit the new middle-class ideals of fatherhood, motherhood, and a cozy and insulated household. Outside observers viewed that divergence with mounting alarm. No aspect of the subject attracted more attention than the condition and behavior of lower-class children and youth.

This issue had caused concern even before the heavy immigrant influx. In the first decades after the Revolution, worries had focused on the rising spirit of self-assertion among craft apprentices. They contradicted their masters, expressed objectionable views, refused to perform certain tasks, and even walked out before their apprenticeships were done.

Why did the apprentices rebel? Conservatives pointed to a general breakdown of social order and individual responsibility that they associated with the decline of strict hierarchy and deference and the development of a more fluid society. One demanded, "Are not husbands and wives, parents and children, masters and servants culpable, very culpable for neglecting the duties of their respective stations?" Others, less alarmed, saw this youthful independence as an echo of the new nation's more democratic spirit: the children "seem to be taught in the cradle that there is freedom of mind," commented one optimistic writer, "and 'tis well they think so."

Whether with censure or praise, most agreed that the strict subordination of apprentices to their masters was on the wane. Underlying this fact were the debasement of urban crafts and the disintegration of the patriarchal artisan household. Apprentices and journeymen evolved from masters-in-training into wage laborers. As workshops grew and cash wages replaced payment in kind, masters no longer housed and fed their assistants and coworkers in their homes. And as the division of labor and mechanization reduced skill levels, and new opportunities opened up elsewhere in the economy, a young man's pride in his apprenticeship shrank. All in all, the decline in the master's authority is not surprising.

From the late 1830s onward, worries about urban youth shifted to another "deplorable and growing evil," this one cited by New York City's chief of police—"the constantly increasing number of vagrant, idle, and vicious children . . . who infest our public thoroughfares." Who were these children and where had they come from? To most middle-class journalists and reformers, the answer was simple: children roamed the streets because their parents were morally bankrupt. An 1856 client report of the New York City Children's Aid Society said, "In such a woman there is little confidence to be put." Indulging "some cursed vice," the agent assumed, had reduced her to poverty in the first place, and "if her children be not separated from her, she will drag them down, too."

A more penetrating explanation points instead to the major social changes of the era. Rural American and immigrant families flowed to the cities, filling them with poor children—just

". . . VAGRANT, IDLE, AND VICIOUS CHILDREN"

In this 1850 letter, New York chief of police George W. Matsell deplored the growth of "juvenile vagrancy" and placed the responsibility on the youngsters' parents.

I deem it my duty to call the attention of your Honor to a deplorable and growing evil which [exists] amid this community, and which is spread over the principal business parts of the city. It is an evil and a reproach to our municipality for which the laws and ordinances afford no adequate remedy.

I allude to the constantly increasing numbers of vagrant, idle, and vicious children of both sexes, who infest our public thoroughfares, hotels, docks, &c. Children who are growing up in ignorance and profligacy, only destined to a life of misery, shame, and crime, and ultimately to a felon's doom. Their numbers are almost incredible, and to those whose business and habits do not permit them a searching scrutiny, the degrading and disgusting practices of these almost infants in the schools of vice, prostitution, and rowdyism, would certainly be beyond belief. The offspring of always careless, generally intemperate, and oftentimes immoral and dishonest parents, they never see the inside of a school-room, and so far as our excellent system of public education (which may be truly said to be the foundation stone of our free institutions) [is concerned], it is to them an entire nullity. Left, in many instances, to roam day and night wherever their inclination leads them, a large proportion of these juvenile vagrants are in the daily practice of pilfering wherever opportunity offers, and begging where they cannot steal. . . . Astounding as it may seem, there are many hundreds of parents in this City who absolutely drive their offspring forth to practices of theft and semi-bestiality, that they themselves may live lazily on the means thus secured,—selling the very bodiies and souls of those in whom their own blood circulates, for the means of dissipation and debauchery.

as most apprenticeships were disappearing, removing one older way of feeding, clothing, housing, instructing, and controlling at least some young males. Hard-pressed parents needed their children's help in holding the family together. The children might do household chores, run errands, look after younger sisters and brothers, buy provisions or borrow them from neighbors—or even beg and scavenge for food, wood, and coal, or for items that could be sold to junk dealers. Boys as young as eight or nine often earned money by peddling hot corn, sweet potatoes, string, pins, or newspapers.

From any point of view, this kind of existence left much to be desired. Scavenging easily shaded off into petty theft, and prostitution attracted many young women denied other sources of income. It was all too common for parents to exploit, abuse, neglect, and even abandon children. In the eyes of the upholders of domestic ideology, these and other ills all sprang from the failure of working-class parents to adopt middle-class norms of morality and family life. Most objectionable was the fact that the children spent so much time on the streets, away from the supervision of their parents.

Of course the parents themselves saw matters differently. Most of them knew and regretted the uglier aspects of their children's lives, but knew also that those lives were deformed by the pressures that bore down on the whole family. It was simply impossible for them to live by middle-class standards. Moreover, impoverished parents were proud of their children's attempts to help the embattled family survive. In their eyes, such youthful endeavors displayed respect for such cherished values as personal responsibility, family loyalty, and economic independence. Furthermore, they believed, lessons learned on the street would prepare their children for adulthood.

SOUTHERN FAMILIES

As in the North, economic change and social status deeply influenced family life in the antebellum South. There, however, chattel slavery remained the hub of economic growth. A family's prosperity, prospects, and legal and social status depended largely on the place it occupied within the particular social structure of slave society.

In the southern hill country, where slave labor and commerce generally played their most limited role, family life and relations between the sexes had changed the least since the eighteenth century. Dominated by small family farms producing mostly for their own use, this upland region shared much with farming areas of the North. The patriarchal family and ties of kinship remained by far the most powerful and important focus of economic and cultural life. Working closely together, the family members produced the overwhelming bulk of the upland region's crops and manufactures. Fathers and teenage sons cleared the land, plowed the fields, and planted and cultivated the crops, while wives and daughters looked after the house, garden, and smaller livestock. One resident of the Tennessee hill country recalled that his father "did all kinds of farm work [while] my mother cooked, sewed, spun thread, wove cloth, and clothed the family of eleven children with the fruits of her labor." Here, too, despite the importance of their contribution to family survival, the wife and young children were strictly subordinated to the will of the husband and father.

Planter society also celebrated strongly patriarchal families. The sexual division of labor here was more sharply defined than in the uplands; in some respects, in fact, it resembled that among the more prosperous families of the urban North. But the economy's basis in slave labor left its peculiar mark on family roles and burdened domestic life with its own contradictions. The father supervised the plantation's production of the staple crop and the financial transactions directly linked to it, including the purchase and sale of slaves. His wife was assigned the domestic sphere and denied access to most aspects of public life. "The proper place for a woman is at home," declared the *Southern Quarterly Review.* "One of her highest privileges [is] to be politically merged in the existence of her husband."

On a plantation, the domestic sphere could be huge, and the mistress supervised much of the work that sustained the plantation from day to day—not only in her family's living quarters (the Big House) but also in the separate kitchen, dairy, smokehouse, and storehouse. She also supervised a broad range of essential tasks: raising, preserving, and cooking food, providing medical care, and producing, buying, and repairing clothing. Related finances—managing the household budget, negotiating with local merchants—also fell within her sphere. If the husband was deceased or temporarily absent, she usually administered the plantation, alone or with the aid of the overseer, and thereby held the family together.

But the parallel to the life of prosperous northern women was not complete. For one thing, urbanization and industrial growth were sharply limited in the South. Everything revolved around the plantation rather than the town or city, so the father was at home, able to control the household and family life, which reduced the domestic power and status of his wife. At the same time, rural isolation limited friendships among women largely to the immediate family. At the same time, the society's dependence on slaves rather than free workers strengthened traditional beliefs in the validity of hierarchy in general, and specifically in the strict subordination of the members of one (supposedly inferior) social group to those of another (supposedly superior). Planters viewed their children, their wives, their poor neighbors, their white employees, and their slaves as being to one degree or another inferior to themselves in social standing, independence, and personal rights. That outlook also made planters responsible for the behavior and welfare of their various "charges"; slavery was seen in family terms, with the master's power over his slaves merely an extension of the father's power over his wife and children. "Do you say that the slave is held to *involuntary service?*" one spokesman asked rhetorically, before offering this justification: "So is the wife. Her relation to her husband, in the immense majority of cases, is made for her and not by her." This linking of slavery with white family relations did not stop the forcible breakup of slave families or prevent planters from enslaving or selling those of their children whom they conceived with female slaves. It did, however, reinforce the patriarch's supremacy within his own home and emphasize still more than in the North the wife's subordinate position.

There were other contradictions as well. On the one hand, the mistress's power over household slaves dwarfed that exercised by northern wives over domestic servants. At the same time, other aspects of the slave system steadily weakened the mistress's position. The planter's sexual access to female slaves strained his ties to his wife and undermined her self-respect and moral authority on the plantation. Though encouraged, like northern women, to turn their attentions to religion, southern mistresses discovered fewer opportunities there for social initiative and self-expression. Northern women's involvement in religious antislavery agitation during and after the 1830s triggered a backlash in the South that curbed both organizations for religious reform and the educational opportunities offered to white women.

Prevailing attitudes even denied the mistress most public credit for contributing to the plantation's upkeep. Chattel slavery discredited hard work, associating those who performed it with the slave's lowly status. Unlike northern businessmen, therefore, planters generally prided themselves on being men of leisure and culture, freed from labor and financial concerns. The popular image of the plantation mistress reflected those values. She must be the very embodiment of leisurely grace, gentility, and refinement. "Maidenly delicacy," affirmed the president of one southern university in 1810, was the very foundation of society. These strictures placed at least one plantation visitor in an awkward position. Strolling the grounds, he came upon the mistress, disheveled and toiling over a salting barrel. Rather than greet her—and thereby accost her in a role deemed unseemly for a southern lady—he could only pretend not to see her and walk on. More important than the minor embarrassment of two individuals, the incident highlights the extremes to which planters went to exile both the image and reality of labor from the Big House.

*

"I Will Come Back." Having purchased his freedom, an Alabama ex-slave named Peter Still bids farewell to his enslaved wife, Vina. Still's self-purchased manumission in 1850—an opportunity few masters offered their slaves—had no effect on his wife, who was owned by a different individual.

Labor belonged in the slave quarters. There, the generalized oppression and brutality of life in bondage lent special value to family ties. Market forces and geographical mobility strained the ties to the utmost. Unlike whites, they could not choose to take advantage of commercial opportunities by moving, but economic pressures could and did lead their masters to move them or to sell them, often separating them from friends and loved ones. By the same token, owners sharply curtailed slaves' ability to form voluntary associations of any kind or to decide how to allocate their labors. Nor could slaves look to state or local governments for social services or other types of assistance.

Thus, with the partial exception of religion, family and kin were the only shield slaves had against the system's physical and psychological pressures, the only reliable source of help, respect, intimacy and warmth. Not least important, the slave family served to nurture a developing African-American culture and transmit it from one generation to another. Cultural prohibitions against marrying a blood cousin encouraged marriage patterns that tied different families together. These ties provided important networks of mutual help and channels of communication among the slave population as a whole.

So it was that slaves strove desperately, against enormous odds, to establish, maintain, and protect their family and kinship bonds. They went through regular marriage rituals in order to stabilize and formalize their relations. Even though slave divorce was permitted, most of these marriages lasted until the death of one partner, unless forcibly broken up by a master. Most slave children grew up knowing both their father and their mother.

Because of the obstacles placed in their way, however, slaves naturally evolved some practices and attitudes unlike those of free people. Where husbands and wives lived on different plantations, for example, responsibilities otherwise kept within the immediate family fell to other kin or community members. Unwed mothers were not stigmatized in the slave community, although they were expected eventually to marry. Slave parents gave their children first and last names that would remind them of their ancestry and kin. Thus it was that J. C. Cohoon's slave Huldah and Lewis Orton named their first son Lewis. And by adopting and keeping the last name of their original owner, even after being sold to another, slaves made it easier to identify and therefore locate family members separated from them by sale. Slaves constantly requested—or demanded—the right to visit spouses and other relatives forced to live apart from them. When Union armies finally put an end to their slave status, millions of African-Americans began the long and difficult task of reuniting their scattered families.

There was some division of labor within the slave family, particularly on large plantations. Men and women alike were required to

Rough rural "sports" as interpreted in the 1841 issue of the *Crockett Almanac*, named after the Tennessee backwoodsman made famous by his self-serving tall tales. Inexpensive comic almanacs combined illustrated jokes on topical subjects with astrological and weather predictions. Opposite, *Harper's Weekly* cartoonist Thomas Nast's version of rough urban "sports"—a riot in New York on St. Patrick's Day, 1867. Nast's portrayal of the Irish, baring their teeth along with other weaponry, was typical—nineteenth-century cartoonists gave each immigrant working-class group the physical traits supposedly characteristic of its "race" and place in the social hierarchy.

labor in the fields, but gang labor was normally organized along sex-segregated lines. Men were generally expected to perform the heaviest fieldwork, like plowing, and fathers supplemented their food by fishing, hunting, and trapping during off-work hours. "My old daddy partly raised his children on game," remembered Louisa Adams of North Carolina in later years. "He caught rabbits, coons, and possums. He would work all day and hunt at night." Women cooked, sewed, knitted, cleaned, and raised the children.

Nevertheless, these gender distinctions remained far less sharp than among whites. Only when their arduous, dawn-to-dark field work was done were women able to undertake their domestic labors. As a result, many mothers had little time to spend with their children. Above all, slavery denied blacks a great many rights and responsibilities that characterized white family life. Their power, authority, and dignity were undermined all along the line, in large matters and small ones. Although slaves tried to make adjustments, the separation of family members by farm boundaries, sale, or migration obviously interfered with stable family life. The regular whipping of slaves—children as well as adults—before the eyes of husbands and

fathers, wives and mothers, starkly demonstrated where real power lay. So did the rape of slave women by owners and overseers, a violation that slaves could challenge only at the risk of death.

BARBECUES, BARN-RAISINGS, AND BEES

For the free rural population of colonial North America, most leisure activities grew out of daily work and community life. Trips to the village or to the occasional fair brought farm people together. So did church, weddings and funerals, and cooperative tasks like harvesting and barn-raising. When neighbors pitched in to raise the frame for a house or barn, they celebrated the task's completion with feasting, singing, and dancing. Public holidays featured barbecues, group singing, praying, parades, lengthy orations, and dramatic readings of historical documents. Amateur theatricals and debates were widely enjoyed, and dancing was extremely popular, even after funerals. The fact that dances were usually held outdoors on the bare

ST. PATRICK'S DAY 1867.

RUM   BRUTAL ATTACK ON THE POLICE. "THE DAY WE CELEBRATE." IRISH RIOT.   Th. Nast.   BLOOD

earth or on the rough wooden floor of a barn influenced the kind of dance steps used—genteel steps were impossible. "When young folks danced in those days," recalled one early Texas settler, "they danced; they didn't glide around; they 'shuffled' and 'double-shuffled,' 'wired' and 'cut the pigeon's wing,' making the splinters fly."

Women gathered at sewing, quilting, and husking bees, for after-church dinners, and to prepare for weddings and baptisms. These occasions offered them a chance to share thoughts and experiences, exchange letters, books, and news, and generally strengthen their personal ties to one another and to the community as a whole. Males got together and compared their physical prowess in logrolling and railsplitting contests, cockfighting and other blood sports, animal hunts—and even, according to the boasts of a few, periodic forays against American Indians. Gambling and heavy drinking accompanied most of these pastimes. Whatever organization was required for most of these activities arose spontaneously.

The forms of entertainment familiar to rural colonial North America survived well into the nineteenth century (and even beyond)—primarily where small communities and traditional work patterns held out longest against the powerful forces of commerce and industry. The lives of yeoman farmers, herders, and hunters of the southern upcountry, for example, as well as southern rivermen and roustabouts, continued to show cycles of intense physical labor alternating with strenuous leisure. Among all of them, similarly, older types of leisure activity remained popular long after they had disappeared—often under the pressure of severe moral disapproval—elsewhere. Decades later, Mark Twain tried to capture something of this

". . . INDIAN REDS AND SILVER GRAYS"

In Sketches of Old Warrenton, North Carolina, Lizzie W. Montgomery *recalled the sport of cockfighting in antebellum North Carolina, suggesting its wide appeal among rural Americans. Such leisure activity alleviated the monotony of everyday life.*

THE PEOPLE OF the present generation can form no idea of the interest excited among the people over chicken fighting, called in sportsman parlance, "cocking mains." These mains were usually fought between chickens owned by gentlemen of different counties, but often between rival strains of birds belonging to people of the same county.

Advertisements of an approaching main as to time and place was made in the local newspaper and by posters at the tavern, cross-roads, and other public places where people were likely to congregate. The place chosen for the main was generally near the county town, and during the time of sport, lasting sometimes a whole week, the hotels and public places, the barrooms and gambling dens, were open night and day, crowded with patrons. On such occasions the town would have the appearance of circus day. Much money was staked on the issue of the contest between the cocks. The strains or stocks of chickens were as important matters among chicken fanciers as were those of race horses to their owners. Even the children and boys knew the peculiarities, the strengths, the weaknesses of the several strains of the fighting chickens, and could talk glibly and intelligently of Stonefence, Indian Reds, Silver Grays, Washington's Grays, Red Eagles, the Blue Hen's Chickens, etc., etc.

Visitors from the adjoining counties of North Carolina and Virginia attended the mains and professional gamblers were sometimes present. The young bloods would drink and gamble and get fleeced.

For many years no serious protest was made against cockfighting, and even after public sentiment had been aroused against the crime, and laws passed against it, it was many years in many communities before the law could be or was enforced.

world in his description of the men who had worked the antebellum Mississippi riverboats:

> Rude, uneducated, brave, suffering terrific hardships with sailorlike stoicism; heavy drinkers, coarse frolickers in moral sties like the Natchez-under-the-Hill of that day; heavy fighters, reckless fellows, every one; elephantinely jolly, foul-witted, profane; prodigal of their money, bankrupt at the end of their trip, fond of barbaric finery; prodigious braggarts; yet in the main, honest, trustworthy, faithful to promises and duty, and often picaresquely magnanimous.

COMMERCIAL AMUSEMENTS

The world Twain so vividly described was radically transformed during his lifetime. As society grew in size and complexity, people in towns and cities formed a broad spectrum of private voluntary societies, church organizations, and fraternal orders. Alongside militias, volunteer fire companies, and mutual-insurance societies there sprang up other groups to bring form and regularity to leisure activities like team sports, singing, hunting, and reading. Some of the most durable and best known were the societies founded in midcen-

"The Soaplocks, or Bowery Boys." An 1847 watercolor depicts the young men who habituated New York's working-class entertainment area, the Bowery. They sport the fashionable long sideburns that gave them their nickname. Around them, posters advertise some of the Bowery attractions the "B'hoys" attended after their workday ended.

Young Democracy at the Theater. As this 1852 lithograph indicates, it was often hard to tell where the performance really was in popular urban theaters. The raucous audience includes an aggressively critical German immigrant (in the center wearing a hat) and an artisan fire "laddie" preoccupied with a hasty meal (on the left).

tury by German immigrants striving to preserve their own distinctive cultural and political traditions in an unfamiliar setting.

The early nineteenth century also saw the development of a third major form of popular leisure. As commercial work separated from home and family life, social life also became its own distinct sphere, increasingly organized and more and more set off from both work and family time. First and most distinctly among urban dwellers, increasingly commercial forms of spectator entertainment became popular. Urbanization had begun to distance people from the natural rural settings of many popular forms of entertainment (barns, lakes, rivers, open fields, forests). The new work discipline likewise restricted older, spontaneous forms of popular entertainment. At the same time, people were exposed to new ideas, new commodities, new fashions, and new forms of entertainment, at prices for the first time within the reach of large numbers. Commercial theater had been the expensive entertainment of the wealthy; now others looking for a little fun might also buy a ticket to the theater or circus, or to P. T. Barnum's American Museum, which offered a glimpse of dwarves, wax figures, jugglers, snake-charmers, bearded ladies, and fortune-tellers. Over time, other diversions appeared: in the 1840s, the race-track; in the 1850s, baseball parks and music halls. The cultural market grew continuously, as did the profits to be gleaned. When Swedish singer Jenny Lind toured the United States in the 1850s, her ninety-five concerts packed halls nationwide and grossed more than $700,000, an enormous sum in that day.

"Winter Evening Amusements—Parlor Theatricals." By the mid-nineteenth century, few urban theaters still catered to mixed-class audiences. Some middle- and upper-class patrons preserved a more genteel atmosphere for their entertainments by holding performances in private homes.

Like many other amusements, theater flourished even more freely in the South than in the North. Evangelical Protestantism, which despised many of these activities as sinfully frivolous, was slower to win favor among the planter elite than among northern businessmen. In the 1840s, a typical European actor's American tour began in Boston, New York, and Philadelphia, but it then went southward toward Baltimore, Washington, Alexandria, Charleston, Savannah, Columbus, Mobile, and New Orleans, and upriver to Natchez and St. Louis. Nor were theater performances restricted to the major cities. More than fifty traveling stock companies brought comedy and drama to all parts of the country. In smaller towns, performances would be held in barns, warehouses, taverns, and dining rooms.

The evolution of the theater most clearly reveals the main forces shaping popular leisure and culture as a whole in this period. The growing size of the theaters themselves reflected the growth of their audience. In the 1820s, New York's Park Theater held twenty-five hundred. Built in the next decade, the Bowery Theater seated three thousand, and in the 1840s the Broadway Theater held four thousand. Within the halls, members of different social classes sat in distinct sections. Artisans and shopkeepers perched on backless benches in the pit (today's orchestra section). Behind and above them were the most expensive sections, box seats occupied by merchants, professionals, and their ladies. Above everything was the gallery (today's balcony), where apprentices, servants, and blacks (if permitted in at all) mingled with prostitutes and other members of the laboring poor.

Reduced prices made this audience diversity possible. In the late 1700s, tickets at New York's Park Theater had cost $2 for the boxes, $1.50 in the pit, and $1 in the gallery. Half a century later, these prices had fallen to 75 cents, 50 cents, and 37½ cents respectively.

The presence, tastes, and, especially, behavior of the boisterous new audience displeased some. During performances, lower-class audience members strolled the aisles, eating and talking freely. Noises from the audience, noted English visitor Frances Trollope in the 1830s, "were perpetual and of the most unpleasant kind."

"NO DAINTY KID-GLOVE BUSINESS . . ."

The audiences that attended urban theaters early in the nineteenth century comprised a cross-section of the city's population. Such mixing of classes at "entertainments" upset many elite observers. From the vantage point of the "pit"—the floor facing the stage—Washington Irving, author of Rip Van Winkle *and* The Legend of Sleepy Hollow, *complained about the rowdy behavior of artisans, journeymen, and apprentices (the "gods" in the upper gallery seats). His observations were printed in the New York* Morning Chronicle *in 1802.*

MY LAST COMMUNICATION mentioned my visit to the theatre; the remarks it contained were chiefly confined to the play and the actors: I shall now extend them to the audience, who, I assure you, furnished no inconsiderable part of the entertainment.

As I entered the house, some time before the curtain rose, I had sufficient leisure to make some observations. I was much amused with the waggery and humor of the gallery, which, by the way, is kept in *excellent* order by the constables who are stationed there. The noise in this part of the house is somewhat similar to that which prevailed in Noah's ark; for we have an imitation of the whistles and yells of every kind of animal.—This, in some measure, compensates for the want of music, (as the gentlemen of our orchestra are very economic of their favors). Somehow or another the anger of the gods seemed to be aroused all of a sudden, and they commenced a discharge of apples, nuts, and ginger-bread, on the heads of the honest folks in the pit, who had no possibility of retreating from this new kind of thunder-bolts. I can't say but I was a little irritated at being saluted aside of my head with a rotten pippin, and was going to shake my cane at them; but was prevented by a decent-looking man behind me, who informed me it was useless to threaten or expostulate. They are only *amusing themselves* a little at our expense, said he, sit down quietly and bend your back to it. My kind neighbor was interrupted by a hard green apple that hit him between the shoulders—he made a wry face, but knowing it was all in joke, bore the blow like a philosopher. I soon saw the wisdom of this determination,—a stray thunder-bolt happened to light on the head of a little sharp-faced Frenchman, dress'd in a white coat and small cock'd hat, who sat two or three benches ahead of me, and seemed to be an

The theaters' dramatic offerings changed as well. Less self-consciously highbrow than previously, theaters mixed large servings of Shakespeare with many other kinds of dramas (including temperance plays like *The Drunkard, or the Fallen Saved* and so-called "equestrian dramas," featuring horses onstage), comedies, musical revues, specialty acts, and blackface minstrel shows that mixed anti-temperance, anticapitalist, and racist themes. Shakespeare owed his enormous popularity among all classes to Americans' great love of melodramas with strong moral themes and larger-then-life heroes who took their fate into their own hands. It also reflected the population's near-worship of the spoken word (as in church sermons, folktales, speeches, and political debates).

Democratic and patriotic themes especially pleased the crowds. Most popular were those plays in which a rough-and-ready American told off (and often enough knocked down) a pompous aristocratic Englishman. Audiences cheered such confrontations enthusiastically, even climbing onto the stage to join the battle. For these people, at least, the early-nineteenth-century theater was still partly a participatory, rather than just a spectator, institution. "When a patriotic fit seized them," Frances Trollope observed, "and Yankee Doodle was called for, every man seemed to think his reputation as a citizen depended on the noise he made." The large Irish immigration that began in the 1830s added to the numbers and fervor on such occasions.

The ability of the early theater to tap deep and powerful feelings among Americans produced some vivid confrontations in this era. During the 1830s and 1840s, for example, the Ameri-

irritable little animal: Monsieur was terribly exasperated; he jumped upon his seat, shook his fist at the gallery, and swore violently in bad English. This was all nuts to his merry persecutors, their attention was wholly turned on him, and he formed their *target* for the rest of the evening.

After the 1850s, mixed-class audiences less often shared the same theaters. Some observers, such as poet Walt Whitman, regretted the change. In this selection from an essay written in the 1880s, he fondly recalled the enthusiasm of the crowds at New York's Bowery Theater. His memories of audience responses to the performances of popular actors such as Edwin Forrest and Junius Brutus Booth contrast sharply with Irving's comments.

RECALLING FROM THAT period the occasion of either Forrest or Booth, any good night at the old Bowery, pack'd from ceiling to pit with its audience mainly of alert, well-dress'd, full-blooded young and middle-aged men, the best average of American-born mechanics—the emotional nature of the whole mass arous'd by the power and magnetism of as mighty mimes as ever trod the stage—the whole crowded auditorium, and what seeth'd in it . . . —bursting forth in one of those long-kept-up tempests of hand-clapping peculiar to the Bowery—no dainty kid-glove business, but electric force and muscle from perhaps 2,000 full-sinew'd men . . . —such sounds and scenes as here [recalled] will surely afford to many old New Yorkers some fruitful recollections.

I can yet remember (for I always scann'd an audience as rigidly as a play) the faces of the leading authors, poets, editors, of those times—Fenimore Cooper, Bryant, Paulding, Irving, Charles King, Watson Webb, N. P. Willis, Hoffman, Halleck, Mumford, Morris, Leggett, L. G. Clarke, R. A. Locke, and others—occasionally peering from the first-tier boxes; and even the great National Eminences, Presidents Adams, Jackson, Van Buren, and Tyler, all made short visits there on their Eastern tours.

. . . The young ship-builders, cartmen, butchers, firemen . . . too, were always to be seen in these audiences, racy of the East River and the Dry Dock. Slang, wit, occasional shirt sleeves, and a picturesque freedom of looks and manners, with a rude good-nature and restless movement, were generally noticeable. Yet there never were audiences that paid a good actor or an interesting play the compliment of more sustain'd attention or quicker rapport. . . .

can actor Edwin Forrest and the Englishman William Charles Mac-ready appealed to different social groups in their competition for pop-ular favor. The elite preferred Macready for his aristocratic bearing, while working people backed the vocally patriotic and democratic Forrest.

In 1849 both actors appeared simultaneously in New York City; anti-Macready posters demanded, "WORKING MEN, SHALL AMERICANS OR ENGLISH RULE IN THIS CITY?" Macready's first night on May 8 turned into pandemonium when hostile audience members hurled everything handy (including their chairs) out of the galleries, shout-ing, "Down with the codfish aristocracy!"

On May 10, an angry crowd of thousands led by young journeymen, both native and foreign-born, gathered outside the Astor Place Opera House, where Macready was again scheduled to perform. Urged by street orators to "burn the damned den of the aristocracy!" members of the crowd hurled paving stones through the windows and tried to break down the doors. Police and the Seventh Regiment responded by shooting directly into the crowd, killing at least twenty-two and wounding more than a hundred forty others. The city was placed under martial law for three days. As one reporter wrote, the riot had revealed "an opposition of classes—the rich and poor, . . . a feeling that there is now in our country, what every good patriot hitherto has considered it his duty to deny—*a high and a low class.*" Social and political change had dramatically forced its way into the world of drama.

Upper-class rage and disgust at lower-class conduct eventually led to a theater system in which different social classes attended different theaters to enjoy different kinds of entertainment at different price scales. Eventually, New York's Park Theater and the Opera House ca-tered to the wealthiest strata, the Bowery Theater entertained the middle layers, and the Chatham Theater drew low-income working people. The same kind of split eventually appeared in other cities and towns as well. In Baltimore, for example, visiting Irish actor Tyrone Power noted that one theater catered to "the sturdy democracy" while another attracted "the aristocracy."

Disorderly public conduct, whether within a theater or on the streets, deeply affronted upper-class urbanites. Their developing no-tions of propriety prized dignity, decorum, and strict self-control above most other virtues. To watch the city's public spaces dominated by such boisterous behavior repelled them and challenged their right to dictate society's moral standards. And precisely because that right remained in doubt, the issue arose time and again. Those enraged by Edwin Forrest's supporters looked with sentiments ranging from disdain to disgust upon some of the rowdier amusements favored by young male workers. Public drunkenness and drinking in taverns and grog shops were staples of lower-class socializing. The saloon itself provided a rare sanctuary from an oppressive workplace and a crowded and often tense household; its inexpensive spirits helped wash away the day's cares, and the company was familiar and congenial. Other diversions that lent excitement to humdrum lives included carousing by and brawling among rival militia companies, volunteer fire brigades, and neighborhood street gangs. Cards, billiards, and bowling also absorbed much time, energy, and cash. In New Orleans in the 1850s, as one newspaper noted, the center of such activities was St. Charles Street:

> Lights glare out of its palaces, dedicated to Bacchus, far into the midnight watches. The banquettes and the saloons are thronged with crowds of the most diverse characters, coming one knows not from whence, and flitting away, at late hours, one knows not whither. There are eating houses and drinking houses, coffee saloons and shooting galleries, billiard rooms and ten-pin alleys, whose din, like that of Babel when language was confounded, astonishes the stranger. . . . St. Charles Street is the theater of a perpetual carnival.

New York's counterpart was the Bowery, with its cheek-by-jowl assortment of groggeries, sideshows, brothels, oyster houses, and gam-

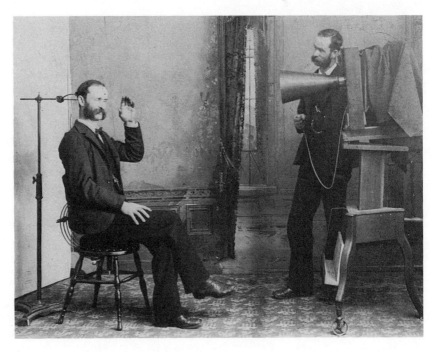

Freeze. Frenchman Louis Daguerre's improvements in photography reached America in the 1840s. Personal portraits were soon the craze, and "daguerreotype" studios sprang up in every city, while traveling daguerreotypists served the countryside. This picture suggests the controlled environment of the early studios. It took so long to properly expose a photographic plate that the subject needed a head brace to hold a pose.

Seeing is not believing: Before-and-after portraits in an 1858 illustrated newsweekly lampoon the widely acclaimed accuracy of photography. The technique for reproducing photographs in print was not perfected until the 1890s, forcing publishers to rely on wood-engravings for inexpensive illustrations.

bling rooms. Betting added a special spice to all sorts of contests between men, just as it did to the violent animal sports that survived into these decades. Professional boxing flourished, drawing big audiences of working people. Especially after the 1830s, Irish immigrants—many of them veterans of bloody "faction fights" in their homeland that set village against village—produced both fighters for the large purses and a growing number of fans. And while respectable society sneered, excited crowds gathered to watch and wager on cockfights, bullfights, dogfights, and bull and bear matches.

On occasion, the level of noise and revelry rose even further. During the thirties, forties, and fifties, Philadelphia mummers, bands of youths (often mockingly made up as women or blacks), marched through the city at Christmastime, assaulted members of despised ethnic or racial groups, and filled the air with fireworks, gunfire, and raucous music. These demonstrations clearly reflected real hostilities between groups of working people—but they also ridiculed, annoyed, and harassed individuals higher up the social ladder, evoking an outraged response. One newspaper in 1833 denounced the "riot, noise and uproar" visited upon "many of our central and most orderly streets." A decade later another paper decried the "riotous spirit raging" there, which had turned Philadelphia into "the theater of disorders which practically nullify civil government." Raucous public celebrations of July Fourth and other holidays—including the weekly Sabbath workbreak—elicited similar expressions of outrage.

Much about these rough-and-tumble amusements was very old indeed. The noisy theater audiences were like those in Shakespeare's day. For centuries, crowds had been protesting actions and attacking individuals they objected to. Newer, at least in North America, was the chasm that now opened between this world and that of the respectable middle class, which gave so much of popular street life its violent and anti-elite character.

No doubt middle-class critics found these incidents particularly galling because they often took place under their noses. The city was only beginning to divide into distinct neighborhoods defined by wealth, and in older cities, this change would be very gradual. As late as 1863, according to one resident, New York's fashionable Washington Square area still encompassed lives of "every variety from luxury to poverty, and almost every branch of industry is represented." So the brawling was inescapable. In any case, Philadelphia's Christmas Eve revelers went out of their way to sharpen the middle class's awareness of them by bringing their season's greetings downtown to the main business and theater district.

Those who missed the street action, whether rich or poor, could read about it in lurid detail in the mass-circulation "penny press" introduced in the 1830s. By 1836, nearly one out of four New York

City residents bought daily papers, a dramatic increase over earlier decades. These newspapers specialized in sensational reports about natural disasters, poverty and degradation, extravagant displays of wealth, and grisly crimes. "These papers are to be found in every street, lane, alley," observed one reporter, and "in every hotel, tavern, and counting house. . . . Almost every porter and drayman, while not engaging in his occupation, may be seen with a paper in his hands."

LEISURE IN THE SLAVE QUARTERS

"Plantation Burial." Funerals were sad occasions in the slave quarters, but they gave African-Americans a chance to confirm their community identity. They were often held at night, so friends and families from neighboring farms could attend.

Of course, the unique conditions in which slave laborers lived affected their leisure and cultural activities and helped make them distinct from those of other groups of American working people. Rural isolation, poverty, and legal restrictions ruled out most of the commercial diversions gaining popularity among whites. At the same time, long working hours and strict discipline left comparatively little time for socializing or other types of amusement beside work songs. Shucking corn—a task that often turned into a kind of com-

petitive team sport complete with spectators, song and dance, food and drink—was an exception to this rule. So was hog-killing. On the other hand, these tasks often involved night work and were performed after regular plantation labor. The celebrations accompanying them were intended as a kind of special incentive or bonus.

On the whole, social gatherings took place on occasional Saturday nights, Sundays, holidays, and rainy days—the few times slaves were not compelled to work. Some masters not only permitted these parties but provided food and drink. Some even attended in person—and thereby altered and sometimes stifled the festive atmosphere. For greater freedom from supervision and control, slaves would sneak out and gather on a weeknight after curfew. Though planters fretted that such midweek revelry weakened the slaves' efforts the next morning, they proved unable to abolish them. At least in part, masters permitted the weekend parties to make the other ones seem unnecessary. That tactic proved only partially successful.

Music at the approved parties came sometimes from a real violin or banjo, more often from instruments handmade from whatever materials were available. "Sometimes," one slave later remembered, "they'd get a piece of tree trunk and hollow it out and stretch a goat's or sheep's skin over it for the drum. . . . They'd take the buffalo horn and scrape it out to make the flute."

The music and dancing were punctuated by storytelling. A favorite type of story was the "trickster" tale, which featured a small but clever hero-animal (Br'er Rabbit is the best-known example) that outwitted stronger but slower-minded villain-animals. These tales originated in Africa and had many shades of meaning. But if whites missed the parallels to daily life under slavery, blacks certainly did not.

To the slaves themselves, the value of these gatherings was obvious. "They are different beings from what they are in the field," explained the escaped slave Solomon Northup. "The temporary relaxation, the brief deliverance from fear and from the lash, produce an entire metamorphosis in their appearance and demeanor." But many owners also understood that the gatherings served as an important safety-valve, releasing powerful pent-

". . . THEY GIVE US THE HUSK"

The secret social gatherings of slaves occasionally vented a hostility to bondage more direct than that expressed in the "trickster" parables. Frederick Douglass remembered a song that gave what he called "not a bad summary of the palpable injustice and fraud of slavery, giving, as it does, to the lazy and the idle the honest comforts which God designed should be given solely to the honest laborer":

We raise the wheat,　　　　And that's the way,
They give us the corn;　　They take us in;
We bake the bread,　　　We skim the pot,
They give us the crust;　They give us the liquor;
We sift the meal,　　　　And say that's good enough for nigger.
They give us the husk;　Your butter and the fat;
We peel the meat,　　　Poor nigger, you can't ever get that!
They give us the skin;　　　　Walk over—

up tensions. "Some will say that this plan will not do to make money," wrote one Alabama slaveholder in 1852, "but I know of no man who realizes more [money] to the hand than I." Frederick Douglass believed that "those holidays were among the most effective means in the hands of the slaveholders of keeping down the spirit of insurrection among the slaves." Without such occasional opportunities, he added, "the rigors of bondage would have become too severe for endurance, and the slave would have been forced to a dangerous desperation."

EVANGELICAL PROTESTANTISM

During the first third of the nineteenth century, a powerful religious upheaval shook the United States. The shock waves produced by this Second Great Awakening reverberated for decades afterward. More Americans than ever before entered active religious life. In western New York State during the 1820s, the powerful emotions aroused at mass prayer meetings hurled converts right off their seats. "If I had had a sword in my hand," reminisced evangelist Charles Grandison Finney, "I could not have cut them off . . . as fast as they fell." Between 1800 and 1860, the most important Protestant denominations affected by this religious revival—Methodists, Baptists, and Presbyterians—saw their combined formal membership multiply more than thirteen times. By the Civil War, Methodists and Baptists alone accounted for about seven in every ten Protestants nationwide, nine in every ten in the South. Just as important as the numbers, the Second Great Awakening transformed the form and content of mainstream American Protestantism in a number of important ways, though many Protestants remained outside the movement.

Evangelicalism was a complex movement growing within—and dividing—many Protestant denominations. The movement included various distinct, even opposing, outlooks, doctrines, and styles, but it is possible to summarize its most important characteristics. Evangelicalism affirmed that anyone could be saved from sin if he or she experienced a profound religious rebirth (or "conversion") and thereafter led an upright Christian life. (This doctrine was called Arminianism, after one of John Calvin's principal religious opponents, the Dutchman Jacobus Arminius.) "I stand as a messenger of God," Albert Barnes told his Pennsylvania congregation in 1829, "with the assurance that all that *will* may be saved." "The will is free," affirmed Finney, "and . . . sin and holiness are voluntary acts of mind."

Instead of accepting existing society, evangelicals believed in changing it by reforming ("perfecting") the individuals who composed it. Christians could accomplish this best through personal ex-

"Evangelist Meeting." A campmeeting in the woods painted by Pennsylvania artist Jeremiah Paul.

ample and by spreading the message of Jesus. "To the universal reformation of the world they stand committed," Finney wrote. Rather than emphasizing the study of lengthy and difficult religious texts, evangelicals simplified Christian doctrine so that common people could more easily interpret and apply it in daily life. Traditional, elaborate, and austere church ceremonies, similarly, made way for services in which the congregation played a much more direct role.

The powerful psychological forces released by evangelical appeals produced many gripping emotional scenes. Less favored in largely Congregationalist New England, this emotional fervor was most visible in the rural South and West, at huge and protracted revival meetings. On such occasions, recalled Kentucky Methodist preacher Peter Cartwright, five to ten thousand people "would collect from forty to fifty miles around" and remain together for days and even weeks on end. For isolated farm families accustomed to a dry and lonely daily routine, these mass gatherings were exciting—even intoxicating—events. Up to thirty ministers of various denominations would cooperate in preaching night and day. In that atmosphere, Cartwright wrote, "I have seen more than a hundred sinners fall

CHANGING PATTERNS OF SOCIAL LIFE

like dead men under one powerful sermon, and I have heard more than five hundred Christians all shouting aloud the high praises of God at once."

The combination of profound repentance and ecstatic joy at these meetings gave rise to many types of unusual behavior. Barton Stone, who in 1801 organized perhaps the largest camp meeting of all, at Cane Ridge, Kentucky, described the intense muscular convulsions known as "the jerks." Some people

> would be affected in one member of the body, and some-
> times the whole system. When the head alone was affected,
> it would be jerked backward and forward, or from side to
> side, so quickly that the features of the face could not be
> distinguished. [They] would often . . . grunt, or bark, . . .
> from the suddenness of the jerk. [But] when the whole sys-
> tem was affected, I have seen the person stand in one place,
> and jerk backward and forward in quick succession, their
> head nearly touching the floor behind and before.

There was no place in this emotional, intensely participatory brand of Protestantism for a highly distinct and powerful church hierarchy. Evangelical ministers came from all walks of life (including farmers and artisans) and often performed their religious functions part-time while continuing to pursue their own occupations. Congregants pre-ferred this arrangement to that of well-paid full-time ministers who "regarded the *fleece* more than the *flock*."

The evangelical movement embraced people from every social class. In a new republic hostile to permanent, inherited class distinc-tions, this proved one of its chief strengths: including different classes within a single religious movement tended to soften the conflicts among them. But the very diversity of the movement's membership guaranteed a diversity in its interpretations. Not all evangelicals understood their doctrines the same way.

In the North, the most fervent supporters of evangelicalism in-cluded the families of the successful master craftsmen, merchants, and farmers who were most quickly adapting to the new, more com-petitive economic order. Such people saw the new religious doctrines as endorsing their own way of life and their evolving outlook. The belief that, with self-discipline and effort, people could influence their afterlives fit their own emphasis on personal initiative, hard work, and hopes for individual advancement in this world. Ministers like Presbyterian Albert Barnes encouraged such sentiments by up-dating the older notion that worldly success reflected spiritual salva-tion. Speaking of the "saved," Barnes declared, "By their fruits they shall be known." For the women of these families, evangelicalism

"The Voting-Place." Evangelical reformers objected to the undisciplined and sometimes violent atmosphere of working-class saloons. But, as indicated in this 1858 engraving of a bar in the Irish "Five Points" section of New York, reformers' concern involved more than the excesses of public drinking. The saloons were the organizing centers for the reformers' rivals, urban political machines like New York's Tammany Hall.

likewise endorsed their seclusion from the business world, their increased authority in the household, and their roles as moral teachers and examples for both the family and society at large. Everywhere, women composed the clear majority of church congregations.

In addition to bolstering their personal values, evangelicalism offered these men and women an effective means to convert others—including their employees—to those values. This was a major concern. Though their personal fortunes were based on commercial and industrial change, businessmen worried about the apparent breakdown of public order that these changes seemed to bring with them. In Rochester, New York, Finney's revivals made a big impact precisely among such entrepreneurs. "I fear the facilities of intercourse in this Country," Congregationalist minister Henry Clark Wright confided to his private journal in 1834, "while increasing the business and moneyed interests of the Nation . . . will by spreading vice and irreligion prove its ruin. Those very things which all regard as improvements will be our destruction."

In the smaller, simpler, deferential world of the past, many social problems were dealt with through informal personal or community

"A German Beer Garden on Sunday Evening." Although German immigrants did not mix politics and liquor, reformers were disconcerted by the atmosphere of their social establishments. Unlike the bars in Irish neighborhoods, the beer gardens catered to whole families. As this 1859 engraving shows, public drinking was only one attraction at a beer garden; but to reformers the presence of women and children suggested immorality.

action. For example: When a few apprentices and journeymen had worked and lived with an individual master, the master had naturally exercised great personal authority. As enterprises grew larger, this relationship became impersonal and strained. Employers withdrew from the work, employees lived separately, and conflicts between the two groups increased. With their personal moral authority eroded, many businessmen hoped the evangelical movement would help bring social life back onto the straight and narrow. The doctrine of free will encouraged such hopes by depicting social conditions (including social ills) not as God-given and fixed but as changeable through pious behavior.

This activist outlook supported the rise of an imposing network of church-linked voluntary organizations pledged to moral reform. Composed largely of women (though usually led or controlled by

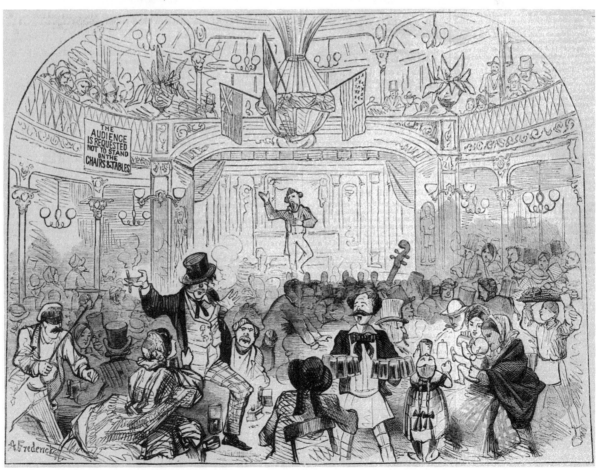

men), this network included societies pledged to fight alcohol and prostitution, enforce a strict puritan Sabbath, encourage public and religious education, and support charitable institutions of all kinds. These groups generally shared the belief that social ills grew out of "the ungoverned appetites, bad habits, and vices" of individuals rather than the workings of society itself. For them, therefore, reform often meant converting the poor to their own ideas about proper family life and personal behavior. Drinking alcoholic beverages, Albert Barnes thus explained, "produces idleness and loss of property," adding that "the man who will not work . . . is the enemy of this country." New York's Children's Aid Society placed poor urban (often Catholic) youngsters with rural Protestant foster-parents—with or without the real parents' approval. The Society's industrial schools and lodging houses taught street girls that "nothing was so honorable as industrious *house-work.*"

The same features that attracted prosperous individuals to evangelicalism also appealed to people of lesser means but high hopes. The promise of personal advancement in the future, if only one lived right and worked hard, spoke to the dreams of many middling shopkeepers, farmers, and craftsmen, especially those less hurt by economic change, such as native-born workers in the building trades. Among this group, evangelical concern with social disorder also struck a sympathetic chord. They worried about the general sense of unrest in the air. They disapproved of the growing ranks of propertyless craft workers and laborers below them, their boisterous and irreverent behavior, and the radical ideas some of them voiced. This disapproval mounted in the 1840s and 1850s as more and more Irish and German immigrants flowed into these low-income occupations. Blaming the poor for their poverty, some native workers found it easiest to point the finger at foreigners with different beliefs, customs, and languages. Conservative evangelicals like these often supported the "nativist" (antiforeign, anti-Catholic) movements of these decades.

Other more radical-minded working people also identified with evangelicalism, but for other reasons. They sought a religion that would help the common people defend and extend their rights. They valued the evangelical demand for personal self-discipline, since a corrupt society offered many lures (alcohol, gambling, prostitution) that trapped common people or distracted them from the defense and exercise of their liberties. To recognize and resist such snares was therefore essential to the cause of working people. The popular form and style of evangelicalism also appealed to them, especially in its rejection of an elitist ministry and of coldly formal church services. For the same reasons, they opposed the power and privileges of the

"FOR TEMPERANCE AND FOR '76!"

At a Fourth of July celebration during Philadelphia's 1835 general strike over the length of the working day, workers sang "The Temperance Strike," a song linking their commitment to free themselves from the evil effects of "demon rum" with their struggle to free themselves from oppressive working conditions. The combination of temperance and social rebellion expressed in this song captured the spirit of self-reform that animated groups like the Washingtonians and irritated the more conservative advocates of coercive laws against liquor and "dissolute behavior" generally.

His chains the tyrant rum, too long
   Has tried to cast around us.
Shall not Mechanics prove too strong,
   When any would confound us?
We shall! we shall! we feel our strength
   And who no sword will draw,
When we for freedom strike at length?
   Hurrah! hurrah! hurrah!

Our Fathers—who may see their like?—
   When trodden down as cattle,
For liberty knew how to strike,
   And win the righteous battle!
And shall their sons be slaves to drink?
   O never! never! Nor
Will Working Men like cowards shrink,
   No, boys!—hurrah! hurrah!

The pledge to Temperance we renew
   For she is Freedom's Daughter—
In generous draughts of mountain dew,
   In cold and limpid water!
Strike hands with us!—for wine like this
   The toper never saw;
E'en Woman's lip such cup may kiss
   Unstained, hurrah! hurrah!

Some strike for wages, some for hours,
   Shall we refuse—O never!
For time and cash we pledge our powers,
   And strike for both for ever!
Then strike who will for "6 to 6,"
   We flinch not in the war;
For Temperance and for '76
   We strike—hurrah! hurrah!

wealthy in church (symbolized by their occupation of choice church pews) and denounced the rich for flaunting their finery there.

Lowell labor leader Sarah Bagley explained the absence of most mill women from church services on these grounds. "Is it strange," she asked in 1846, "that the operatives should stay away from the churches where they see the men filling the 'chief seats' who are taking every means to grind them into the very dust?" Where conservative evangelicals celebrated individualism and private enterprise, their radical counterparts denounced personal greed and the threat it posed to community rights and older Christian values of mutual support and cooperation. God intended, wrote evangelical labor journalist William Young in 1845, that humanity "should be bound together by nature's golden chain ... into one harmonious whole—no slaves—no servants—no masters—no oppressed and no oppressors—but in the language of Christ—'For one is your master, and all ye are brethren.'" "We would thank God most devoutly," wrote Sarah Bagley, "if there could be found a house of worship in Lowell where the Gospel, as preached by ancient disciples, could be heard by every operative."

Less firmly based in the churches than the conservatives, these radical evangelicals were

"Citizens of Maine Emigrating, in Consequence of the Maine Liquor Law." *Fisher's Comic Almanac* comments on the impact of the passage of a state temperance act in 1853.

drawn by their social activism toward a number of religiously in-spired social-reform campaigns, such as those advocating temper-ance, public schools, and the end of slavery. But they approached these issues in a distinctive spirit. If conservative reformers hoped that public schools would help tame the lower classes and create more conscientious and disciplined wives and workers, radicals wanted them to help working people learn and defend their rights as citizens and producers. The same point of view influenced them to form separate reform groups like the Washington Temperance Society and the Sons of Temperance. The result was a tug-of-war between them and the conservatives over the precise nature and goals of re-form as a whole, with one side emphasizing social order and the other popular participation and democratic rights.

ROMAN CATHOLICISM

Roman Catholics made up the country's largest single religious de-nomination. The number of Catholics grew dramatically during the 1840s and 1850s as a result of the huge immigration of Irish, most of them former peasants and laborers. Roman Catholicism contrasted sharply with evangelical Protestant ideals. Its hierarchy was large, ap-pointed from above, and clearly distinguished from parishioners in dress, lifestyle, training, and function. Only members of that hier-archy could perform church ceremonies, which (conducted largely in Latin) remained more elaborate than in any Protestant denomination.

Where evangelicals pursued human perfection, imposing upon themselves the strictest code of behavior, Catholicism adhered to an older and more lenient point of view: human beings were conceived in sin and were incapable of perfection on earth. While the church demanded moral conduct from Catholics, it granted that human frailty would inevitably and repeatedly lead them astray. The way back from sin could be found not in a single conversion, but in regular confession, repentance, and priestly absolution. Deeply respectful of established political and social structures, the Catholic Church was one of the most conservative institutions in the Western world.

In the United States, the imposing solemnity and splendor of their church helped compensate immigrant parishioners for their own poverty. Outside that church, as one sympathetic observer noted, "they have little that is pleasant to the eye or cheering to the sentiment."

But the Irish Catholicism of this era cannot be understood simply by looking at the official structures, ceremonies, and doctrines of the church. In Ireland, the actual religious life of the common people was also heavily influenced by the age-old rhythms, customs, and beliefs of Celtic peasant society. Despite the urgings of parish priests, attendance at Sunday mass generally remained small, and few went to confession or attended communion more than once a year. And while the average Irish villager knew rather little about formal church doctrine, attachment to a number of pre-Christian religious symbols, practices, and even local deities (now transformed into saints) remained strong. Among these were patron saints' festivals (honoring some saints never canonized by the church), the ritual use of bonfires, celebrations of "holy wells," and especially the combination of mourning and revelry that constituted the wake.

This complex religious tradition followed the Irish to the New World. New York's Transfiguration Church (which served the heavily Irish Sixth Ward) was attracting relatively few of that area's mass of unskilled immigrant laborers in 1845. One priest commented that "half of

"CAN THIS BE THE SABBATH . . . ?"

Troubled by evidence of extreme poverty in the nation's industralizing cities, many Protestant reformers set up mission houses in poor, immigrant neighborhoods to minister to the needs of the largely Catholic residents. But a cultural abyss divided reformers from the people they wanted to help. In the House of Industry's 1857 Monthly Record, a shocked Protestant missionary, Louis M. Pease, describes the Sunday activity in the Five Points, a working-class immigrant neighborhood in New York City.

"CAN THIS BE the Sabbath—God's holy day?" I involuntarily exclaimed, as I stood for a moment at the entrance of one of the avenues leading to the Five Points, and beheld the crowd of people pressing up and down Chatham street, while the heavily laden cars passed by, crowded with pleasure-seekers bound for the country, on their weekly holiday excursion. And then, as I walked slowly up Baxter street, to see the rum-shops, the junk-shops, the pawn-shops, the groceries, and the low Jewish clothing-stalls all open, the side-walks lined with apple-stands, and juvenile traffickers in papers and peanuts, while here and there were groups of night-thieves, vagabond boys, and loathsome, shameless girls prematurely ripened into infamous womanhood. Oh! who would suppose that this was the sabbath of the Metropolis of this great and Heaven-blessed country!

our Irish population here is Catholic merely because Catholicity was the religion of the land of their birth" and many "had no clear explicit knowledge of Catholic doctrines." True, most were baptized and married in the church. On the other hand, the wake remained a far more popular ceremony than the official funeral mass. Indeed, more than a few of the immigrants had to be taught how to make the sign of the cross. (The great Irish famine of the 1840s radically altered the shape of Irish society and religion, eventually transforming the latter into its more pious and uniform modern pattern. But the full effect of these changes would be felt in North America only after the Civil War.)

Irish-American loyalty to Catholicism grew out of a number of factors. For one thing, key aspects of evangelical Protestantism were alien to Irish life. Coming from a stable, traditional, overwhelmingly rural and impoverished country, they had little reason to believe that their own will or action could fundamentally alter their fate, and the poverty of most Irish in America reinforced that attitude. In Ireland itself, furthermore, Protestantism was the religion of the hated English conquerors and their Scots-Irish allies. Denied national independence, the Irish majority clung all the more fiercely to their religion. American nativism reinforced that identification among Irish immigrants and, in the words of New York archbishop John Hughes, "tended powerfully to unite Catholics." Finally, in both Ireland and America, the Catholic Church provided a broad array of services—not only spiritual but also social, economic, educational, and charitable—unavailable from any other institution, whether governmental or voluntary.

FREETHINKERS

At the other end of the religious spectrum, another group of nonevangelicals—variously known as freethinkers, rationalists, or religious liberals—stood in the tradition of Thomas Paine and Vermont's Ethan Allen. Staunch democrats, champions of human reason instead of faith, they were deeply suspicious of organized religion and church hierarchies, viewing them as bastions of superstition, privilege, and tyranny. In these respects they resembled radical evangelicals, but their criticism of religion went much further. Some were outright atheists. Others believed in a god, but one who played so small a role in the day-to-day life of human beings as to be almost irrelevant.

In the late eighteenth century, the religious skepticism of the Enlightenment had attracted many members of the colonies' and early republic's upper class. Fears that such ideas might reach the common people and encourage social and political radicalism among them helped discredit this fashion among the elite. Thereafter, free thought found its main support among the less affluent. "Open [religious] infidelity," complained the Rev. Robert Baird in 1844, "has descended to the lower ranks. It now burrows in the narrow streets and lanes and purlieus of our large cities and towns, where it finds its proper aliment—the ignorant and the vicious, to mislead and destroy."

Compared with evangelicals and Catholics, this group was by no means numerous. It derived its importance from the fact that its members—people such as George Henry Evans, Frances Wright, and Robert Dale Owen—often served as labor journalists and as leaders and activists in early trade unions and workingmen's parties. This current found much of its support in the urban crafts, especially those (like shoemaking and tailoring) affected earliest and most deeply by industrial development, the growing division of labor, and declining incomes and working conditions. At the start of the century, many of these artisan rationalists were either native or British-born. Printers, who regarded themselves as the intellectuals of the working classes, also contributed more than their share to the ranks of lower-class freethinkers. By the 1840s and 1850s, as thousands of German immigrants entered the declining handicrafts, the American freethinkers also became increasingly German in leadership and support. Like Newark's radical immigrant journalist Fritz Anneke, they fought an ongoing war against attempts to write evangelical views about alcohol and Sabbath observance into law. In 1853, an angry Anneke wrote,

> This money aristocracy, which has the time and means to take care of its body through the whole week, and which in spite of its hypocritical laws, knows how to serve all worldly desires on the holy Sabbath, strives zealously to deprive the working man of every means of escape from his drudgery.

EVANGELICALS AND SLAVERY

Although it eventually changed the religious face of the North, the Second Great Awakening actually began in the southern United States, specifically in the valleys of Kentucky and Tennessee. In the eighteenth-century South, evangelical Protestantism arose as a religious protest against the planter elite. The movement's converts came primarily from that broad layer of farmers and merchants whose hard work and modest prosperity placed them well above poverty but still below great landed wealth. While some of these people had managed to acquire substantial farms and a handful of slaves, the big planters nevertheless looked down on them, dealt with them in a high-handed manner, and expected to be treated as social superiors, aristocrats. Equally offensive was the big planters' attempt to act like medieval aristocrats, spending extravagantly and flaunting their wealth and possessions.

The dominant Anglican Church—with its formal and somber rituals, autocratic clergy, and firm belief in predestination—fulfilled the spiritual needs of the elite far better than those of the rest of the population. In evangelicalism, these middling folk found a different kind of religion, one able to express their own self-respect and optimism about a better future and to provide a sense of warm mutual support and full membership in the Christian community. The communal self-discipline of their church, furthermore, helped members live an orderly, productive life rather than revel in the pleasures of the flesh—a sin that, they believed, the planter elite shared with those at the very bottom of society.

While southern evangelicals rarely sought legal enforcement of their values, they did wish to change society, if only through the power of personal example and community pressure. This reformist goal at first alarmed many among both rich and poor who clung to the familiar, more stable, deference-based society and religion. For them, an even more objectionable aspect of the new doctrine was its attitude toward slaves and free blacks. During the previous century, the more democratic assumptions contained in evangelical doctrine, especially its belief in the Christian brotherhood of all, regardless of social class, led revivalists to do what southern Protestants had never done before: some Baptist and Methodist preachers launched determined efforts to reach African-Americans, convert them, and draw them into the Christian community. Their success was impressive. By 1800, for example, one out of every five Virginia Methodists was black. More than one congregation in South Carolina and Maryland contained more black members than white.

Some whites followed this train of thought and action still further. If Africans had souls that could be saved like those of white people, they asked, how could one Christian in good conscience enslave another? In the late eighteenth century, especially in the upper South, individual evangelical ministers helped found societies dedicated to ending slavery through gradual emancipation. Anti-evangelical whites responded strongly to these challenges to their traditions. Wealthy ones denounced evangelicals as alien agents of Yankee society and sent evangelical leaders to jail, while the humbler anti-evangelicals expressed disapproval with hard words, sticks, and stones. But the movement's sweeping appeal swamped that resistance, and by the 1790s a clear majority of southern Protestants had entered the evangelical fold.

Black converts to evangelicalism took what they heard from white preachers, added aspects of West African religious belief, and fashioned a novel brand of Christianity that addressed their own special needs, both spiritual and practical. Black and white evangelicalism shared many common texts, symbols, and rituals. But the radically different life conditions imposed by slavery profoundly transformed the inner meaning of those forms.

Three aspects of evangelicalism particularly appealed to African-Americans. The emotional conversion experience, first of all, echoed the deeply emotional religious rituals practiced in West Africa. Secondly, evangelicalism's God intervened actively and continually in human life, thereby bridging the chasm between the mystical and the practical worlds—another parallel to West African religion. This characteristic also fit the African-American experience: usually isolated from urban centers, denied access to education, science, technology and (as much as possible) information in general, and always at the mercy of arbitrary overseers, owners, or other white authorities, slaves easily accepted the idea that human life was dominated by powerful forces beyond control or full comprehension.

The third—and by no means least important—attraction of evangelicalism was the support that it seemed to give to the slaves' longing for dignity, equality, and freedom. The first truly massive wave of black conversions occurred during the second half of the eighteenth century. That was the high point, if only a modest one, of white evangelical antislavery sentiment in the South. Encouraged by that sentiment, most black evangelicals evidently rejected notions (common among most whites) that the Bible justified slavery and that slaves owed loyalty and obedience to their masters. On the contrary, they found condemnation of slavery throughout both the Old and the New Testament. They identified with the suffering of Old Testament prophets and especially with the passion of Jesus, the innocent child of God suffering for the sins of others.

Favorite passages included those from the gospels of Mark and Matthew in which Jesus criticized the rich and powerful and promised deliverance to the poor and downtrodden. Recalling these biblical scenes in emotional group prayer, slaves could openly cry out against oppression and vent their own longing for freedom and justice—without risking summary punishment by their masters. Especially treasured was the Book of Exodus, in which enslaved Israelites threw off their bonds and set out for a promised land while their Egyptian masters suffered dearly for having oppressed them. "We used to have to employ our dark symbols and obscure figures," a former North Carolina slave later recalled, "to cover our real meaning." When the opportunity arose, the same biblical passages provided religious justification for open acts of resistance, major or minor, individual or collective.

As in the story of Exodus, black evangelicals anticipated justice not simply in the next world but—at least eventually—in this one. More specifically, they expected a radical, revolutionary transformation of human society that would prepare the way for the Second Coming of Christ. And when that Judgment Day arrived, they firmly believed, the Lord would reward His long-suffering children and exact heavy payment from their tormentors.

Conversion brought with it still more tangible benefits as well. By accepting Christianity, slaves could claim membership in the same spiritual world as whites. And in that case, were they not God's children, too? If so, didn't they deserve the same rights as any other of His children? White society never answered these questions with a consistent yes, but the Christianization of slaves and free blacks did bring them practical gains. During the early nineteenth century, some independent black congregations were allowed to form, principally in upper South cities. Commonly they were linked to free black denominations in the North, such as the African Methodist Episcopal Church. Although always sponsored and supervised by whites, these churches were the first and only community-wide institutions permitted to the slaves. Their deacons and preachers (commonly free blacks) were some of the only African-Americans whom whites allowed to play any kind of leadership role among slaves. Some black ministers attracted a white following as well.

Finally, in their own brand of evangelical Protestantism, slaves were able to formulate their own common standard of proper behavior. They used it not only to judge their treatment by whites but also—and just as important—to clarify mutual rights and obligations among themselves. In doing so they strengthened their sense of group identity and their ties to one another. At the same time they asserted an increased (if still very restricted) degree of self-regulation and self-rule.

Perhaps ironically, the surge of slave conversions to Christianity played a key role in improving relations between the evangelical churches and the initially hostile slaveholder elite. Beginning in the first quarter of the nineteenth century and culminating between 1820 and 1840, these two groups made peace with one another. Unable to prevent evangelicalism's growth, big planters joined the movement to control it and make it their own. For their part, most church leaders welcomed the new planter approval and sponsorship.

One result of this union was a change in both groups' attitude toward slaves and slavery. Southern evangelicalism shed all ties to or sympathy for emancipationism. Antislavery preachers were either silenced or forced to leave the South. In return, evangelical slaveowners generally dropped their objections to slave religiosity, although most considered separate black churches and black preachers intolerable and set out to suppress both. "Intend to break up negro preaching and negro churches," South Carolina planter James Henry Hammond informed his diary in 1831. "Refused to allow Ben Shubrick to join the Negro Church . . . but promised to have him taken in the church [that] I attended." And: "Ordered night [prayer] meetings on the plantation to be discontinued." Henceforth, planters tried to use religion to bind slaves more tightly to themselves. And these efforts yielded some successes. During his years as a slave, Frederick Douglass was frustrated by the "many good, religious colored people who were under the delusion that God required them to submit to slavery and to wear their chains in meekness and humility." But other blacks defended the independence of their own churches and resisted the preaching of servility.

The experience of one such minister during the 1840s and 1850s— white pastor Robert Ryland of Richmond's First African Baptist Church—may illustrate the point. A defender of slavery, Ryland preached the merits of white supremacy, sermonizing (as one free black recalled) "that God had given all this continent to the white man, and that it was our duty to submit." (To that message one black congregant replied, "I'll be damned! God is not such a fool!") Groups of blacks would linger after regular services at the Richmond church, and other blacks would preach to them. Ryland himself admitted that one of these black preachers "was heard with far more interest than I was." Another witness noticed that at these informal services the "most active were those who had slept during the [Ryland] sermon."

In Baltimore, membership in the African Methodist Episcopal conference more than doubled between 1836 and 1856. In rural districts, where separate black churches were rare, secret "night meetings" often continued despite prohibitions. Twenty years after recording his first decision to suppress independent black religion, planter J. H. Hammond was still wrestling with the problem. His 1851 diary again reports, "Have ordered all church meetings to be broken up except at the Church with a white preacher."

Attempts to force black Christians into the white congregations confronted a second obstacle: white southerners generally disliked sharing their churches and services with blacks. They also worried that prayers, songs, and sermons intended for their own ears (and so filled with references to human freedom and universal brotherhood) would encourage dangerous ideas among slaves. The structure and content of black Christianity therefore remained the object of struggle down through the Civil War and even after. And the marriage between southern evangelicalism and the institution of slavery was soon put to another test as well. In the mid-1840s, northern Methodists and Baptists tried to commit their southern coreligionists to oppose slavery on Christian grounds. When southern congregations resisted, the national denominations split in half.

Among comfortably situated southern white women, evangelical religion played a role similar to that in the North. It celebrated the family household as a comfortable refuge and as the moral cornerstone of society. It also extolled the mother's central position within that household and applauded her abstention from "male" activities. As in the North, women took an active part in church affairs and made up a majority of church members. Evangelicalism's discomfort with rigid social distinctions among its congregants—at least so far as purely religious affairs were concerned—gave women greater spiritual equality and freedom of action that they had previously enjoyed. The conversion experience, in which individual women stood up on their own in church and took the spiritual initiative, loomed large in this pattern. And the churches launched women's educational societies, prayer groups, missionary bodies, and other institutions, further contributing to the development of women's abilities and leading them further into social life.

Nevertheless, the churches' explicit goal for women as well as slaves was to keep this increased religious role within narrow and carefully policed bounds. Evangelical doctrine firmly designated men as society's (and women's) rightful rulers and ultimate authorities. They were, in the words of one southern female writer, "the anointed lords of creation." Far more than in the North, these limits set for women were successfully enforced. No movement for women's rights ever took root in the slave South. Those unable to abide such restrictions—like Angelina and Sarah Grimké, daughters of a South Carolina slaveowner, who protested both slavery and the subordination of women—had to relocate in the North.

For Americans living in the first half of the nineteenth century, little seemed fixed or stable. All around them, on the contrary, the familiar and traditional was undergoing dramatic transformation. Production methods, work rhythms, and class relations were being changed before their eyes. So was one after another aspect of

"SPIRIT, DON'T TALK SO LOUD . . ."

The underground religious life of the slaves proved difficult to uproot, as many a planter discovered. Here a former slave recounts efforts to conduct nighttime "praise meetings" without being caught by the notorious "paddyrollers" (slave patrollers).

BEFORE THE WAR when we'd have a prayer meeting at night, it was almost always held way out in the woods or the bushes somewhere so that the white folk couldn't hear. And when they'd sing a spiritual and spirits began to shout, some of the elders would go amongst the folks and put their hands over their mouths and sometimes put a cloth in their mouths and say: "Spirit, don't talk so loud or the patrol will break us up." (You know they had white patrols that went around at night to see that the niggers didn't cut up no devilment.) And then the meeting would break up, and some would go to one house and some to another, and they would groan awhile, and then go home.

social life. Commercial and industrial development was dissolving the bonds joining work, leisure, household, and family. Meanwhile, the nation found itself increasingly divided into different and often hostile classes, classes that felt themselves different from one another not only in economic terms but also in their family lives and cultural norms.

Altering the form and content of American Protestantism, the Second Great Awakening was a central part of that overall change. It also expressed the hopes and fears of Americans—free and slave, North and South, East and West, in the countryside, towns, and cities—confronted by those changes. Arising in a world in flux, furthermore, evangelicalism itself became a major stimulus to change, including political change. "Religion in America takes no direct part in the government of society," noted French visitor Alexis de Tocqueville at the Awakening's peak, "but nevertheless it must be regarded as the foremost of political institutions of that country." Indeed, Tocqueville added, Americans hold religion "to be indispensable to the maintenance of republican institutions. This opinion is not peculiar to a class of citizen or to a party, but it belongs to the whole nation, and to every rank of society."

During the following decades, Americans of different parties and social ranks found themselves more and more at odds with one another about how republican institutions should function and whose interests they should serve. All sides defended their opinions with religious references, often to the same evangelical creed. In the process, the religion of the Great Awakening became an arena in which Americans struggled with each other about what form the change ought to take.

"The Great Meeting of Foreigners in the Park." An illustration from an 1855 nativist tract, *The Crisis; or, the Enemies of America Unmasked,* depicts a labor demonstration in New York's City Hall Park demanding relief for the unemployed during the 1854–55 panic. This wood-engraving is one of the few images of organized working-class action published before the Civil War.

8 THE FIGHT FOR FREE LABOR IN THE NORTH

THE VICTORY of the American Revolution led to great economic growth, and it transformed political life and thought as well. Belief in democracy, equality, and liberty—at least for adult white males—acquired new strength; these principles became fixed in the minds of common people as rights.

During the infancy of the republic, these two forces—economic development and democratic rights—seemed to form a natural partnership, each sustaining and improving the other. Popular liberty, many believed, made economic expansion possible; by the same token, only economic growth and prosperity could preserve the people's freedom and give it practical meaning, allowing them to improve their standard of living and to rise in social position.

The relationship between prosperity and liberty, though, soon came to seem less simple. True, economic growth meant greater total wealth, which supported a booming population and helped many to improve their situations, if only modestly. But there was a price to pay: economic development led to the dissolution of an existing social structure and traditional way of life. Old and stable ties among people gave way to newer relationships—weaker, looser, and more anonymous. In this changing world, moreover, conditions that spelled economic freedom and opportunity for some meant uncertainty and new forms of economic subservience for others.

In this new situation, new controversies arose from the very principles underlying the American Revolution and republic. Fights erupted over the scope and content of popular rights and freedoms. Workers of all sorts—male journeymen and laborers and female factory operatives and outworkers—resisted the subordinate positions they were being assigned. Old ties—notably those joining journeymen to their masters—began to fray and then snap. Others—binding one wage-earner to others—slowly and unevenly grew stronger.

Working people embraced the Revolution's ideals, which gave them a language that legitimated their demands. But though they used the history of the republican Revolution to justify their struggles, the very novelty of their needs forced them slowly to redefine the tradition to which they appealed. Groups that until then had been excluded from political life, even in the revolutionary period, now began demanding the full rights of American citizens. And indeed, some of the rights they now claimed were new; so were the alliances and organizations they forged to win those rights.

By organizing and mobilizing in defense of their own interests, America's working people also changed the form and content of politics in the early nineteenth century. The nation's main political parties—whether they called themselves Federalists or Antifederalists, Democrats or Whigs—protected the interests of society's elite. But as more and more free white males gained the right to vote, the tone and techniques of political life changed. First the Jacksonian Democrats and then their Whig opponents strove to identify themselves with the hopes and fears of the "common people," the "working man."

Sometimes these attempts involved simple pretense and posturing: by the 1840s, every candidate for public office seemed to be claiming birth in a humble log cabin. But the increasingly politicized working people also won some tangible gains that enhanced their political and economic rights. And when the existing parties declined to make concessions, common people utilized their political experience to organize parties, formulate programs, and run candidates of their own. Thus they helped to shape the social and political contours of the early nineteenth century. Just as important, their actions entered into popular memory and tradition, influencing working people for generations to come.

JOURNEYMEN UNITE

To the urban artisans of the first decades after the Revolution, no day was more symbolic than the Fourth of July. It held a double meaning for these masters, journeymen, and apprentices—at once celebrating their country's liberation from colonial rule and their own personal freedom from social and political domination by others.

In New York's annual celebration, various patriotic contingents paraded behind the banner of the General Society of Mechanics and Tradesmen, with its vivid arm-and-hammer crest and assertive motto, "BY HAMMER AND HAND ALL ARTS DO STAND." Although composed primarily of master craftsmen, the General Society—and bodies like it in Boston, Charleston, Providence, Albany, Portsmouth, and Savannah—sought to represent the common interests of all the artisans. Their charters proclaimed their intention "to promote mutual fellowship, confidence, and good understanding" among all artisans and to foster "a general harmony . . . throughout the whole manufacturing interest of the country." There seemed nothing unusual about masters assuming such a general responsibility. Didn't they play the same role in their own workshops? And wouldn't all journeymen and apprentices one day become masters themselves?

The New York march usually ended at one of the larger churches, where speakers would "swear eternal allegiance to the principles of Republicanism." These principles included the idea that personal independence and community are linked, as well as the notion that democratic self-government is essential—a self-government made possible, in turn, only by the readiness of all citizens to place the good of all above narrowly defined self-interest. But no theme called forth greater eloquence than that of civic equality. In North America's "mighty republic," established through the efforts of mechanics and other working people, all citizens stood on the same ground. None was innately superior to another. "Every man looks with independent equality in the face of his neighbor," proclaimed a typical July Fourth speaker. "Those are exalted whose superior virtues entitle them to confidence; they are revered as legislators, obeyed as magistrates, but still considered as equals."

The orators tailored these broad republican principles to fit the particular shape of life and values in the trades. Members of this artisan audience heard themselves hailed as ideal republicans: apprentice, journeyman, and master worked in harmony according to the general regulations of their trade. Those regulations and the harmony of the workshop benefited all members of the trade—and the society whose needs the skilled artisans served. The master's workshop and his hard-earned skill ensured his economic independence and thus his political dependability. By working with the master and learning from him, the apprentice and journeyman would one day earn independence as well.

Independence, freedom, democracy, equality, craft unity, opportunity—all seemed densely interwoven. And all seemed to depend on the commercial prosperity of the nation. This recurring theme in artisan thought expressed itself, as we have seen, in the mammoth 1788 parade celebrating the new federal Constitution. Songs and flags predicted that the new federal system would usher in a commercial expansion from which all would benefit.

The federal system and the transportation revolution did indeed inaugurate a period of great economic growth in the United States. But contrary to expectation, this prosperity and development led to increased economic inequality among American citizens and sharper conflict between rich and poor, merchant and artisan, master and journeyman.

"Procession of Victuallers." Butchers parade in the streets of Philadelphia in 1821. Their costumes, floats, and banners (including one in the center with the motto, "We Feed the Hungry") display symbols of the butchers' trade.

Faced with the growing wealth and power of the merchants, the master craftsmen organized in self-defense. Before long, however, journeymen were mobilizing on their own to resist the pressures of the masters. In New York, some twenty journeymen tailors struck in response to wage cuts as early as 1768. Such labor conflicts multiplied and deepened after the Revolution. New York cordwainers (shoemakers) downed tools in 1785, three years before the Constitution was written. In 1786, the year of Shays' Rebellion, Philadelphia's journeymen printers went out on strike. During the 1790s, Philadelphia's journeymen cordwainers struck at least three times. "Between employers and employed there are mutual interests," acknowledged New York's journeymen printers—but, they said, the conduct of the masters was undermining this traditional belief. Now "very few" of the journeymen "ever have it in their power to realize a capital sufficient to commence business on their own."

By the turn of the new century, journeymen in some of the most-pressed trades were venturing beyond occasional strikes to more durable organizations. As the pressures upon their working and living conditions became regular, they felt the need to solidify networks of self-defense—there seemed no other way to defend their rights and status as free men. Philadelphia cabinetmakers and chairmakers considered the stakes high, urgently calling for "a plan of union" by which all could obtain "the protection of their mutual independence." Escalating economic conflict was forcing these journeymen to think about themselves in new ways. Notions of the happy harmony of the workshop seemed increasingly outdated, as did the old assumption that the masters could speak for all members of the trade. And as the bonds of trust and loyalty between master and journeyman weakened, new ones appeared linking one journeyman to others, leading to separate and distinct organizations. Members of the journeymen printers' union hesitated to exclude journeymen-turned-masters from their ranks. But in 1817 they, too, concluded

> that the actions of men are influenced almost wholly by their interests, and that it is almost impossible that a Society can be well regulated and useful when its members are actuated by opposite motives and separate interests. This society is a society of *journeymen* printers; and as the interests of the journeymen are *separate* and in some respects *opposite* to those of the employers, we deem it improper that they should have any voice or influence in our deliberations.

The rhythms of the economy often set the tempo for labor conflict. The depression of 1819 closed firms and wiped out jobs, thus largely destroying the unions that had arisen during the previous two decades. The upturn of the 1820s brought greater employment and income. But some employers renewed their offensive against the journeymen, and increased it after a new downturn in 1829. In response, the journeymen rebuilt their own organizations and returned to strikes and other forms of collective self-defense. The resulting confrontations further estranged large employers from journeymen within the trades. At the same time, they cemented bonds of shared interests and mutual support among journeymen within each trade. More and more, however, the new cohesion overflowed occupational categories: journeyman status in general defined the members of the new community, the emerging commonwealth.

Such shifting loyalties sparked mass confrontations between employers and employees, along with a major public debate over economic and political rights and contending notions of social justice. That debate highlighted the increasingly distinct ways in which different groups of citizens now viewed the republican values that had once seemed their common heritage. For a time, in fact, it seemed about to redefine the issues of national politics and redraw the map of party organization.

Capturing some of the journeymen's resentment at new forms of domination by master-employers, the issue of how long the workday should be repeatedly sparked heated conflict. In 1828–29, word circulated that a group of New York employers were about to extend the working day from ten hours to eleven. A mass meeting of angry journeymen and their supporters portrayed that attempt as an antirepublican assault on community standards and popular rights motivated by reckless and unbridled selfishness. The gathering resolved that "ten hours well and faithfully employed is as much as an employer ought to receive, or require, for a day's work." Therefore "those who now undertake to exact an excessive number of hours of toil for a day's work . . . subject themselves to the displeasure of a just community." Such employers become "aggressors upon the rights of their fellow citizens, invaders of their happiness, and justly obnoxious to the indignation of every honest man." A few days later, a crowd five to six thousand strong put teeth in these pronouncements, promising to strike any employer insisting on more than ten hours of labor per day. In the face of this resistance, the employers hastily retreated.

In Philadelphia in 1827, journeymen house carpenters based their stand on their rights and responsibilities as citizens of a democratic republic, winning broad support for their fight to reduce a twelve-hour day to ten. "It is true," one of their pamphlets noted, that "in this favored nation we enjoy the inestimable blessing of 'universal suffrage,' and constituting, as we everywhere do, a very great majority, we have the power to choose our own legislators." The problem was that "this blessing . . . can be of no further benefit to us" unless "we possess sufficient knowledge to make proper use of it." To acquire that knowledge, workers needed more time to read, think, and discuss—and less time chained to the workbench.

Out of this movement arose the country's first citywide federation of craftworkers employed in different trades, the Philadelphia Mechanics' Union of Trade Associations. Asserting that journeymen labored in exchange for a mere subsistence to support "in affluence and luxury the rich who never labour," the Mechanics' Union pledged itself

> to avert, if possible, the desolating evils which must invariably arise from a depreciation of the intrinsic value of human labour; to raise the mechanical and productive classes to the condition of true independence and equality which their practical skill and ingenuity, their immense utility to the nation, and their growing intelligence are beginning imperiously to demand; to promote, equally, the happiness, prosperity, and welfare of the whole community . . . and to assist . . . in establishing a just balance of power, both mental, moral, political, and scientific, between all the various classes and individuals which constitute society at large.

Another turning point had been reached. As the Philadelphia journeymen now saw it, responsibility for upholding republican values had shifted from the shoulders of the masters (or even of the organized trade as a whole) to those of the organized journeymen.

THE WORKINGMEN'S PARTIES OPPOSE MONOPOLY

The Philadelphia Mechanics' Union enjoyed only a brief existence. Before its demise, however, it spawned still another first—the Workingmen's Party of Philadelphia. Similar parties quickly arose in major cities like Boston and New York, and in scores of smaller towns and villages as well. The Albany *Advocate* declared, "Throughout this vast republic, the farmers, mechanics, and workingmen are assembling . . . to impart to its laws and administration those principles of liberty and equality unfolded in the Declaration of our Independence."

The political movement launched with such optimism confronted an immediate challenge—to identify the nature of society's ills and explain how it proposed to cure them. In the ferment of the time, such diagnoses and prescriptions abounded. Certainly the most revolutionary of these flowed from the pen of the self-educated New

"The Verdict of the People." A clerk announces the results of a Missouri election in a painting by George Caleb Bingham. An enthusiastic supporter of the Whig party, states' rights, and slavery, Bingham was praised for his pictures that celebrated the boisterous, "pioneer" roots of America's democracy—even though, by the mid-1850s, when this painting was completed, he had grown disillusioned with politics.

York City machinist Thomas Skidmore. Personal experience, observation, and wide reading had convinced Skidmore that the root of modern inequality was the unequal possession of private property. "As long as property is unequal," Skidmore argued in *The Right of Man to Property*, published in 1829, "then those who possess it *will* live on the labor of others." The only solution was for the dispossessed and other "friends of equal rights" to win control of the government, in order to redistribute property on an equal basis among all adults of all races (Skidmore opposed slavery and supported equal rights for women). To ensure that this new equality survived the passing of generations, inheritance would be abolished. Upon an individual's death, his or her property would revert to society, to be redistributed equally among those then coming of age. Skidmore's plan aimed not to abolish private property but rather—by asserting

society's superior rights over it—to ensure property's equal distribution among all. Such measures, he believed, would eventually produce a nation with "no lenders, no borrowers; no landlords, no tenants; no masters, no journeymen; no Wealth, no Want." Proud, independent self-employment would become general.

Skidmore helped launch and lead the New York Workingmen's movement, and he wrote some of his general ideals into its founding documents. But the Workingmen never adopted Skidmore's radical redistribution plan as their own. Instead they put forward a list of more modest legislative proposals, most of them typical of Workingmen's party platforms around the country. Urging journeymen, small masters, and others of the producing classes to elect "men who, from their own sufferings, know how to feel for ours, and who . . . will be disposed to do all they can to afford a remedy," the city's Workingmen's candidates received some six thousand votes in elections to the state assembly. That was enough to send one man—journeyman carpenter Ebenezer Ford—to the state capital. Six other Workingmen's candidates fell short of Ford's achievement by fewer than fifty votes each. This seemed an auspicious start. But in the election's aftermath, Thomas Skidmore's opponents blamed him and his inflammatory ideas for the Workingmen's failure to attract even more votes. They outmaneuvered him, ejected him from the leadership, and reconstituted their New York Workingmen's Party on a still more moderate political basis.

The rise of independent journeyman unions attested to growing polarization within the workshop—the alienation of propertyless employee from propertied employer, and resulting conflicts over how labor ought to be organized and how its fruits should be distributed. Thomas Skidmore's plan to equalize property was one response to this problem. That was not the solution advanced by most other Workingmen's parties and leaders. To account for deepening inequality in society, they pointed not at questions of labor and property but at political favoritism. Particularly culpable, in their view, was the array of government-conferred monopolies that propped up the system of merchants' capital—the corporate charters regularly granted to private companies engaged in banking, insurance, transportation, communication, and certain fields of manufacturing. Typically bestowed only on the nation's mercantile elite, these charters often guaranteed their owners exclusive legal rights to engage in particular fields of enterprise. Even when Skidmore's influence was at its zenith, for example, the New York Workingmen were denouncing "legislation which has employed all its energy to sustain exclusive privileges" through which the wealthy elite carried out "a rapacious and cruel plunder of the people." In Philadelphia, the *Mechanics' Free Press*, edited by Philadelphia shoemaker and journeymen leader William Heighton, inveighed against "everything which limits individual enterprise, or tends to make the *many* dependent upon the few." He asked,

> Is it equal or just that a few should be empowered by law to monopolise a business to themselves, to the exclusion and disadvantage of the many? Certainly not. All competition may be laudable, when left free to all persons, as it may have a tendency to prove beneficial to the community at large. But charatered monopolies make a few wealthy, to the disadvantage and misery of the mass of the people.

This diagnosis called for a certain kind of prescription. If it was government-endowed privilege and monopoly that caused the nation's social ills, surely true democrats should concentrate on eliminating those privileges. Accordingly, Philadelphia Workingmen's candidates pledged to oppose "all exclusive monopolies." By freeing America from the burdens of "special privilege," they would make it the kind of community long cherished by artisan republicans—one mainly composed of independent, hardworking artisans and farmers enjoying "equal rights" and free of the constant specter of permanent wage labor. These measures were not designed to eliminate the distinction between merchant and artisan, master and journeyman, employer and employee. On the plane of equal rights, it was assumed, relations

"No More Grinding the POOR—But Liberty and the Rights of Man." An engraving printed around 1830 depicts the forces of monopoly attempting to undermine the workingman's vote. While the devil offers an aristocrat the support of his "favourite" newspapers "to grind the WORKIES," a mechanic places his faith in the suffrage.

among these groups would regain the cooperative and friendly character identified with the past.

Though they differed in detail, the proposals of these parties were similar. Priority often went to increasing popular control over the government. Since an enlightened citizenery was needed to make proper use of that government, there must be public school system, paid for with public funds. Such a system would break the elite's monopoly on knowledge, and teach the benefits and workings of republican government to rich and poor children alike. To uproot economic privilege, Workingmen sought to limit or outlaw corporate monopolies, of which chartered banks were deemed the most powerful and insidious. Paper money—then still issued by banks and often worth much less than its face value—which seemed like just another gimmick with which to cheat working people, would also be abolished. So would debtors' prison. Another reform, a mechanics'-lien law, would help craftsmen secure payment for their work. To protect the rights and markets of small producers there would be an end to the use of convict labor to make goods sold on the open market. Public lands in the West would be made available cheaply as homesteads for small farmers—rather than to speculators interested only in reselling for a profit—to give those with little money an alternative to urban or rural wage labor.

Demands like these enjoyed wide popular support, addressing the concerns not only of wage-earners but also of poor small masters and other petty proprietors. In fact, democratic rhetoric, denunciations of monopoly, and calls for greater popular participation in politics became increasingly common during the 1830s and 1840s, not only among the poor or propertyless but in some more affluent circles as well. The economic opportunities of these years had

---

"... THIS MONOPOLY SHOULD BE BROKEN UP"

The Philadelphia Workingmen's Committee assessed the status of public instruction in Pennsylvania in 1830 and issued an eloquent report defending public schooling and arguing for "equal knowledge" as the necessary foundation of "equal liberty." The report was unanimously adopted at a public meeting of "friends of general and equal education."

THE ORIGINAL ELEMENT of despotism is a monopoly of talent, which consigns the multitude to comparative ignorance, and secures the balance of knowledge on the side of the rich and the rulers. If then the healthy existence of a free government be, as the committee believe, rooted in the will of the American people, it follows as a necessary consequence, of a government based upon that will, that this monopoly should be broken up, and that the means of equal knowledge (the only security for equal liberty) should be rendered, by legal provision, the common property of all classes. . . .

It appears, therefore, to the committee that there can be no real liberty without a wide diffusion of real intelligence; that the members of a republic should all be alike instructed in the nature and character of their equal rights and duties, as human beings and as citizens; and that education, instead of being limited, as in our public poor schools, to a simple acquaintance with words and cyphers, should tend, as far as possible, to the production of a just disposition, virtuous habits, and a rational self-governing character.

When the committee contemplate their own condition, and that of the great mass of their fellow laborers, when they look around on the glaring inequality of society, they are constrained to believe that until the means of equal instruction shall be equally secured to all, liberty is but an unmeaning word, and equality an empty shadow, whose substance to be realized must first be planted by an equal education and proper training in the minds, in the habits, in the manners, and in the feelings of the community.

"A Militia Drill Thirty Years Ago." Congress authorized universal militia duty for all males, but inequalities in the system led to calls for reform. The Workingmen's Party in Pennsylvania and New York attacked privately organized elite units whose members' costly uniforms and elaborate ceremonies displayed their wealth and connections. The aristocratic pretensions of "private" units contrasted with the ragtag appearance of "public," neighborhood militias (remembered here in an 1862 lithograph). Public militia service was a financial burden: members lost wages to attend drills and risked fines if they were absent or violated dress codes.

whetted the appetites of men of middling wealth—local merchants, master artisans, investors, farmers, and professionals—who stood outside the charmed circle of the older mercantile elite. These people resented the system of legal monopoly and exclusive privilege for reasons of their own: it restricted their ability to grow wealthy.

At the same time, most states eliminated property qualifications for voting, which signaled a new era in the nation's political life. A new breed of professional politician appeared. These men built their careers and vote-getting organizations on their ability to appeal to the expanding electorate and to dispense growing amounts of government patronage. They returned favors and cemented alliances in part by distributing government jobs among those outside the elite. "The duties of all public officers," President Andrew Jackson declared in his first message to Congress, "are, or at least are capable of being made, so plain and simple that men of intelligence may readily qualify themselves for their performance." Campaign speeches, banners, and brochures, in the meantime, fairly bristled with effusive praise and vows of loyalty to "the working man" and "the producing classes."

In 1832, President Jackson dissolved the second Bank of the United States—a privately owned but federally charatered corporation that, he said, "enjoys an exclusive privilege of banking under the authority of the General Government, a monopoly of its favor and support, and, as a necessary consequence, almost a monopoly of the foreign and domestic exchange." As a large landholder, speculator, and slave-owner, Jackson saw nothing wrong with the coexistence of wealth and poverty: "Distinctions in society will always exist under every government. . . . Equality of talents, of education, or of wealth cannot be produced by human institutions." Indeed, he added, it was the government's responsibility to protect legitimately obtained wealth, since "in the full enjoyment of the gifts of Heaven and the fruits of superior industry, economy, and virtue, every man is equally entitled to protection by law." Problems arose, however, "when the laws undertake to add to these natural and just advantages artificial distinctions, to grant titles, gratuities, and exclusive privileges, to make the rich richer and the potent more powerful."

For the Jacksonian Democrats, as one of their spokesmen put it, "free competition in all departments of social industry" would cure society's main ills. (While some demanded the abolition of chartered corporations, the view that prevailed called simply for making such charters more widely and easily obtainable.) Democrats frequently coupled their antimonopoly stance with support for a number of the specific demands championed by the Workingmen (including the mechanics'-lien law, public education, the end of imprisonment for debt) while opposing nativist, sabbatarian, and temperance legislation. Through these means and others, a party led by wealthy men attracted the votes of many Americans uneasy about economic development and social inequalities.

The Democrats' success induced the opposition Whig Party to follow suit. Even the stately Daniel Webster was shortly trumpeting his father's log-cabin origins. The Whigs employed democratic rhetoric and imagery to attract voters—especially those native-born individuals who were better served by commercial and industrial growth—to their program of protecting tariffs, internal improvements, and moral reform. By ensuring the nation's prosperity, the Whigs promised, this program would simultaneously secure the republican dream—a society offering all Americans the chance to obtain or enhance their personal independence by accumulating wealth and ascending the social ladder. Among the most sincere, persistent, and effective apostles of this creed was the Illinois lawyer and politician Abraham Lincoln.

SOLIDARITY OR CONSPIRACY?

The Workingmen's parties found it difficult to compete in this new political setting. Most of them dissolved during the 1830s, many of their leaders affiliating with the Democrats and a few with the Whigs. But the end of the Workingmen's electoral challenge by no means erased the economic conflicts that had given rise to the challenge. The opposition between masters and journeymen, employers and employees continued to deepen during the 1830s, causing an unprecedented mobilization of labor and a sharpening debate over the principles underlying the American republic.

New York—by now the nation's chief port and soon its leading manufacturing city as well—witnessed much of the unfolding drama. Journeymen carpenters struck in 1833 for higher wages. Recognizing their own stake in the carpenters' cause, organizations of printers, tailors, masons, brushmakers, tobacconists, and ten other trades quickly came to their support; within a month or so the strike was won. This victory—and especially the role played by the expression of solidarity across craft lines—electrified the city's working people. "The noble and energetic efforts" in support of the carpenters, wrote printers' union president John Finch, underscored the general "necessity of combined efforts for the purpose of self-protection." Finch's union promptly issued a leaflet calling on all organized trades to unite in a citywide federation of craft unions.

The call provoked a swift and gratifying response. Journeymen organizations in nine trades attended the first convention of New York's General Trades Union, and three more sent messages of support. In 1834, a GTU parade that included the associations of Newark, New Jersey, as well formed a line of march stretching a mile and a half. The GTU's primary function was to organize support for individual member societies in their efforts to defend their living standards and working conditions. In this connection, it provided support to strikes among bakers, hatters, ropemakers, sailmakers, weavers, leatherworkers, tailors, and others—not only in New York but also in Newark, Poughkeepsie, and even Boston and Philadelphia.

The GTU then moved to strengthen and regularize such far-flung but still informal networks of mutual support and assistance. If this could be accomplished, urged radical printer and former Workingmen's Party leader George Henry Evans, "The rights of each individual would then be sustained by every workingman in the country, whose aggregate wealth and power would be able to resist the most formidable oppression." Meeting in August 1834, the convention that created the National Trades Union (NTU) attracted delegates from Boston, Philadelphia, Brooklyn, Poughkeepsie, and Newark, representing upwards of 25,000 workers.

Never truly national in extent and limited in its day-to-day powers, the NTU aided and gave coherence to a labor upsurge during the next few years that spawned at least sixty new unions and called more than a hundred strikes. The NTU insisted that in a republican society a citizen's conduct and, indeed, the "value of all social institutions" had to be judged by standards of "moral justice" rather than the fickle

"By Hammer and Hand All Arts Do Stand." The artisan's symbol adorns an announcement in New York's General Trades' Union newspaper, *The Union,* calling for a demonstration to support union tailors convicted of conspiracy in 1836.

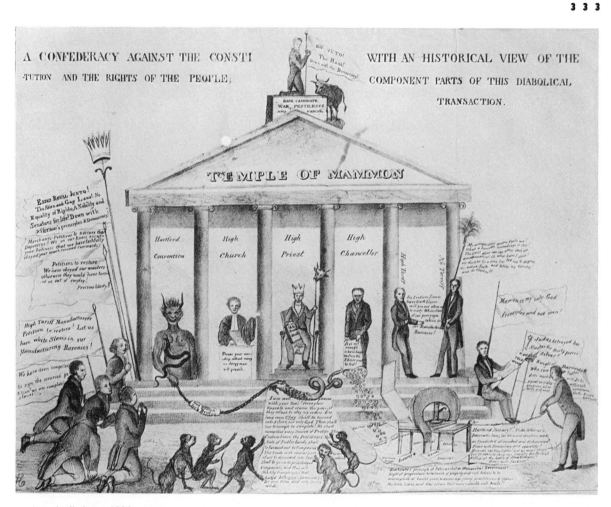

A typically busy 1830s cartoon denounces monopoly and privilege. On the right side of the "Temple of Mammon," a northern manufacturer conspires with a southern planter: "You Southern Barons have black Slaves; will you not allow us to make White Slaves of our poor population in our Manufacturing Baronies?"

judgments of profitability, of supply and demand. From this perspective, the NTU continued, "the social, civil, and intellectual condition of the laboring classes of these United States" had been undermined "by means of the erroneous customs, usages, and laws of society." The result was "the most unequal and unjustifiable distribution of the wealth of society in the hands of a few individuals." That, in turn, imposed upon working people "a humiliating, servile dependency, incompatible with . . . natural equality" and "subversive of the rights of man."

The actions and words of these organized journeymen outraged substantial merchants and employers. They struck back hard in the name of an alternative view of proper republican order, one that identified moral justice with the free play of a free market—a market in which labor constituted a commodity like any other. "The true regulator of prices," held the New York *Journal of Commerce*, "whether of labor, goods, real estate, or anything else, is demand." Certainly, the editor assured, "we wish to see all men, mechanics as well as others, receive an adequate compensation for their labor." But collective organization and activity (in the form of journeymen's unions and work stoppages) in pursuit of that goal was "wicked" and "at war with the order of things which the Creator has established for the general good." Nor could he understand why wage-earners should unite in mutual support when some, at least, would do better through dog-eat-dog competition. In trade unions and strikes, he advised, the best and most skilled workingmen—"whose wages would go up . . . if they would but go on their own merits"—suffered needlessly to aid in "lifting up the unworthy, [even] though they sink themselves."

These two very distinct outlooks—one demanding that economic life conform to republican principles, the other insisting that life in the republic be regulated by the marketplace—clashed head-on in New York in 1836. Over the previous two years, price inflation had proven catastrophic for working people, forcing shoemakers, carpenters, cabinetmakers, farriers (horseshoers), weavers, and others to strike for higher wages. The employers of New York decided to make an example of the journeymen tailors' assiciation, in part because it was one of the strongest unions in the city. In the beginning of 1836, master and merchant tailors refused any longer to honor the pay scale previously negotiated and agreed among themselves not to hire union members. Following practices common among strikers in all trades, the journeymen picketed the shops of the masters and sought to discourage other journeymen from taking their places. A grand jury, however, labeled this conduct "conspiracy," a criminal offense. (A state law passed in 1829 had made illegal any collective action "to commit any act injurious to public morals or to trade and commerce.")

In May, a jury found twenty of the indicted tailors guilty as charged. Judge Ogden Edwards imposed stiff fines and lectured the tailors on the error of their ways, substantially echoing the opinions of the city's employers and pro-employer newspapers. In this "favored land of law and lib-

---

"THE RICH AGAINST THE POOR!"

Shortly after the striking tailors were convicted, a placard appeared in various parts of New York City. Its text was printed within the outline of a coffin, signifying the "coffin of equality." Below are excerpts from that text. The Common Council promptly offered a reward for the apprehension of the anonymous author of this "Coffin Handbill."

THE RICH AGAINST the Poor! Judge Edwards, the tool of the Aristocracy, against the People! Mechanics and Workingmen! A deadly blow has been struck at your Liberty! The prize for which your fathers fought has been robbed from you! The Freemen of the North are now on a level with the Slaves of the South! with no other privileges than laboring that drones may fatten on your lifeblood! Twenty of your brethren have been found guilty for presuming to resist a reduction of their wages! and Judge Edwards has charged an American jury, and agreeably to that charge, they have established the precedent, that workingmen have no right to regulate the price of labor! or, in other words, the Rich are the only judges of the wants of the Poor Man!

erty, the road to advancement is open to all," Edwards explained, "and the journeymen may by their skill and industry and moral worth soon become flourishing master mechanics." Combinations (unions), he added, were by nature alien to American society "and are mainly upheld by foreigners."

The court's attack on the right to organize and strike called forth a storm of protest. A mass rally endorsed by the GTU drew 27,000—more than one in every ten residents of the entire city—to the park across from City Hall. The crowd burned Judge Edwards in effigy, invoked the traditions of 1776, and branded the trial "a concerted plan of the aristocracy to take from them that Liberty which was bequeathed to them as a sacred inheritance by their revolutionary sires." The court proceedings bristled with "principles utterly at variance with the spirit and genius of our Republican government." In defense of "combinations," "conspiracies," and strikes, the protesters recalled an earlier "holy combination"—"that immortal band of Mechanics, who despite the injury inflicted upon 'trade and commerce,' 'conspired, confederated, and agreed' and by overt acts did throw into Boston harbour the Tea that had branded upon it 'Taxation without Representation.'"

WOMEN WORKERS MOBILIZE

As women were drawn into wage labor, they too moved to defend their interests as workers. At times they proved even readier than the men to undertake direct action. In the spring of 1821 the Boston Manufacturing Corporation's Waltham factory without notice cut the wages of all its unmarried male employees. "They are determined," wrote one of their employees in a letter, that "their word shall be law and shall be obeyed." But when "the same trick was played off on the girls, . . . they as one revolted and the work stopped two days in consequence."

This same combativeness sometimes enabled women to lead protests mobilizing workers of both sexes. This was the case in May 1824, when mill owners in Pawtucket, Rhode Island, attempted to relieve pressure on their profits by extending the workday in their shops by one hour and cutting piece rates paid to the young female weavers by one-fourth. In the strike that ensued, women weavers occupied the front ranks, drawing in their wake not only male coworkers but also great numbers of neighbors and other townfolk.

By linking their individual fates more directly and clearly to large social forces and to mutual aid, wage labor both forced and helped working women to intervene more boldly in social and political life. This was dramatically shown in the case of New York City needlewomen. Despite the comparatively isolated nature of the outwork

During the 1840s the *Offering*
published writing by women
working in the Lowell mills.
Contributions to the publication,
which was supported by the city's
textile companies, promoted the
morality and industry of mill
women, carped occasionally about
working conditions, but avoided
any harsh criticism of employers.
On the *Offering* cover, a pure
textile maiden, book in hand,
stands adjacent to a beehive
(representing industriousness).

system in which they worked, sixteen hundred women joined the
New York Tailoresses' Society, founded in 1831, and fought a series
of wage cuts decreed by merchants and contractors. In the process,
they advanced views about their rights as workers, citizens, and
women that raised many an eyebrow.

For women merely to form a labor organization demanded extraordinary bravery; it directly challenged traditional values taught them
by their parents and celebrated by society at large. "It needs no small
share of courage," affirmed Sarah Monroe, a leader of the Tailoresses'
Society, "for us, who have been used to impositions and oppression
from our youth up to the present day, to come before the public in
defense of our own rights." Nearly a full generation before the birth
of the women's-rights movement, Monroe's associate Lavinia Waight
denounced the fact "that females are oppressed in almost every stage
of action to which the circumstances of their existence render them
liable" and, further, "incapacitated from the duties of legislation,
and other matters of equal importance." "My friends," Monroe demanded, "if it is unfashionable for the men to bear oppression in
silence, why should it not also become unfashionable with the
women?" Or, she added, turning the increasingly fashionable notions
of supposed feminine delicacy to her own use, "do they deem us more
able to endure hardships than they themselves?"

When the tailoresses struck in February 1831, they asserted their
sisterhood with females in other trades and places. They hoped their
strike for "a just price for our labor" would "excite the oppressed of
our sex in other places to similar salutary exertions." Two years later,
women shoebinders from Lynn and neighboring towns convened in a
Quaker meetinghouse to form a protective organization of their own.
"Women as well as men," they announced, using the language of both
the Declaration of Independence and the Constitution, "have certain
inalienable rights, among which is the right at all times of 'peaceably
assembling to consult upon the common good.'"

Female textile-mill operatives called strikes in nearby Lowell, Massachusetts, in both 1834 and 1836. They, too, considered themselves
heirs to the nation's democratic-republican rights and traditions. In
February 1834, hundreds walked out of the mills in protest against
wage reductions. As in Pawtucket a decade earlier, the manufacturers
cited declining profits to justify the proposed piece-rate cuts. And just
as in Pawtucket, the Lowell women rejected the argument. "The op-
pressing hand of avarice would enslave us," declared a workers' statement, "and to gain their object, they gravely tell us of the pressure of
the times."

The women were aware that the expansion of the industry had
stimulated competition and pinched the profits of the owners. But
they refused on this account to surrender the small measure of inde-

pendence that existing wages had allowed them. "If any [owners] are in want," they jested, "the Ladies will be compassionate and assist them; but we prefer to have the disposing of our charities in our own hands; and as we are free, we would remain in possession of what kind Providence has bestowed upon us, and remain daughters of freemen still." Unlike the New York tailoresses, who were outworkers, Lowell women worked together and usually lived together in company-owned boardinghouses. This gave them an unusual degree of mutual familiarity and support that now strengthened their organization.

The 1834 Lowell strike eventually involved one-sixth of Lowell's total mill workforce, but this strength was not enough to make the companies back down. Within a week, most mills were again operating near capacity. The companies found it easy to recruit other rural women to tend the machines. This was true both because of the economic pressures on many New England farm families and because tending machines did not call for much skill or experience.

But the spirit of the Lowell women was not broken. When mill owners moved two years later to raise rents in their boardinghouses, they again ran into organized resistance. Women called workplace meetings, marched through the town, and thronged to outdoor rallies. This second walkout proved more successful. Many more joined this strike, for one thing, and organization and tactics improved, halting operations in some departments. The strikes succeeded in limiting or eliminating threatened increases for room and board in much of the town.

This militancy from working women evoked a varied response. Lowell industrialists were deeply insulted by the

". . . THE FEEBLE THREATS OF TORIES IN DISGUISE"

When women textile workers in Lowell, Massachusetts, went out on strike in 1834 in response to a pay reduction, they depicted their plight as a betrayal of the nation's republican ideals. Below are reprinted a petition, a resolution, and a song written by the strikers.

UNION IS POWER. Our present object is to have union and exertion, and we remain in possession of our own unquestionable rights. We circulate this paper, wishing to obtain the names of all who imbibe the spirit of our patriotic ancestors, who preferred privation to bondage and parted with all that renders life desirable—and even life itself—to produce independence for their children. . . .

All who patronize this effort we wish to have discontinue their labor until terms of reconciliation are made.

Resolved. That we will not go back into the mills to work unless our wages are continued as they have been.
Resolved. That none of us will go back unless they receive us all as one.
Resolved. That if any have not money enough to carry them home that they shall be supplied.

Let oppression shrug her shoulders
        And a haughty tyrant frown,
And little upstart Ignorance,
        In mockery look down.
Yet I value not the feeble threats
        Of Tories in disguise,
While the flag of Independence
        O'er our noble nation flies.

jection of their paternalistic stance. The textile companies denounced the meetings and demonstrations as unfeminine; it was nothing but an "amazonian display," sneered one.

And the women got little support from the rest of the labor movement. Most male unionists regarded the employment of women as yet another attack on their own independence, dignity, and traditions; it weakened the family by leading women out of the home and away from their proper roles as daughter, wife, and mother. Male workers prided themselves on being good providers, on earning enough to support their families. The employment of women challenged that source of male pride.

It also seemed to menace male wages by enlarging the labor pool and increasing the competition for jobs, and accelerating the decline of skill standards. In 1819, New York City's journeymen tailors threatened a strike against the employment of women in the "slop" (ready-made) shops. In Philadelphia, the tailors' union of the 1820s organized makers of custom-made fine garments but not those engaged in slop work. This was considered "work of women, and . . . not . . . so dignified a subject of employment as the former, which men alone have the honor to make."

By the 1830s, the erosion of the older artisan system had deflated some of these pretensions and taught a few basic lessons about the need for solidarity among workers regardless of the differences among them. In Philadelphia, printer Thomas Hogan and weaver John Ferral helped organize women textile operatives and paper workers and spoke in their defense. Male shoemakers there had always opposed

The latest model. A mill woman stands in unlikely repose beside a Fale and Jenks spinning frame in this promotional engraving. The benign relationship of the figure to the machine may have served to reassure nineteenth-century observers that factory work would not debase "virtuous womanhood."

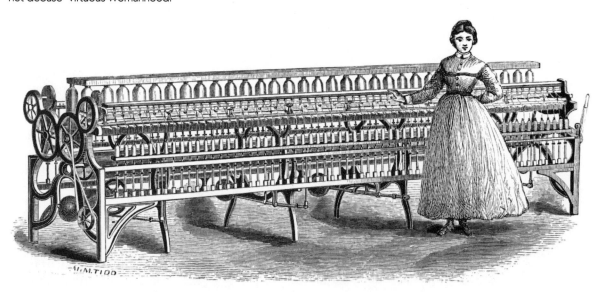

Maine weavers. In a tintype taken around 1860, four young textile workers pose with their shuttles.

the employment of women, but when women shoeworkers went on strike, the male trade union came to their aid, reviling the "heart-less" shoe bosses for trying to "crush a suffering class of females." Resolving to take the women "under our wing to sink or swim with us," the men established a solidarity committee to lead a joint strike. Male cigarmakers in Philadelphia followed a parallel course.

Time and experience were broadening the scope of labor solidarity. Much, however, remained unchanged. Male workers who supported strikes among women often did so in the hope that higher wages for women would discourage employers from hiring them. And the NTU's Committee on Female Labor still held that "the physical organization, the natural responsibilities, and the moral sensibility of women prove conclusively that her labors should be only of a domestic nature." Working women remained unconvinced. The women shoebinders of Lynn named their organization the Society for the *Protection and Promotion* of Female Industry.

UNSKILLED LABOR ORGANIZES

Organization for self-defense was especially difficult for the great mass of unskilled laborers, in part because their numbers grew so quickly during the decades of the transportation revolution. The fact that their work usually required even less training than textile work left them especially vulnerable to job competition from many sources, particularly from migrants leaving farms in America and Europe. Fleeing landlords, poverty, and political oppression, more than fifty thousand Irish reached the United States during the 1820s. A hundred seventy thousand more arrived during the 1830s.

Although this exodus included some better-off families and skilled craftsmen, the vast majority were leaving labor in the fields and—often penniless upon landing in the New World—found no alternative here to unskilled labor. The life of the day laborer was hard indeed. As with the outworking tailoresses, it was not unusual for laborers to have part or all of their wages arbitrarily withheld by employers. Job competition and frequent layoffs due to seasonal and economic changes kept them on the move from site to site, from one town or state to another. This constant movement further weakened attempts to build stable labor organizations. Another barrier was the widespread contempt among artisans for permanent wageworkers, especially unskilled ones. Horror at the prospect of falling into the ranks of wageworkers provided a good deal of the impetus of journeymen artisans' movements. The lowly day laborers at first seemed to be fitting objects of pity or horror, not natural allies against a common foe. This attitude effectively excluded day laborers from most labor organizations, isolated them, and threw them back upon their own resources.

Despite these obstacles, the unskilled did organize and fight, especially those working in canal and railroad construction gangs, on the docks, and aboard ships. Organization often took the form of secret societies, especially among the Irish, who brought with them a long tradition of underground resistance. Protest actions frequently involved threats and physical reprisals against individual employers, strikebreakers, and police. Such "exotic" acts, sniffed the New York *Journal of Commerce*, had "been imported along with the dregs and scum of the old world." No doubt forms of struggle born in Ireland did affect the level of violence used here. Equally important, though, was the truly desperate situation of the laborer, the greater difficulties involved in organizing those without a valuable skill, and the readiness of employers and public authorities to treat those deemed "dregs and scum" with a kind of brutality still usually spared the more respectable craftsmen.

The construction of Maryland's Chesapeake and Ohio Canal was typical (there were similar conflicts on the Pennsylvania Canal, the Baltimore and Ohio Railroad, and elsewhere.) By 1832, many of the Chesapeake and Ohio laborers had been recruited from one place, Ireland's County Cork, and had organized a militant secret society to defend working conditions and wage rates. Those who refused to join the society were driven off the work site.

The company, determined to break up this body, brought in a new levy of Irish laborers—from County Longford. The members of the existing society viewed the new hires as threats to their own security, and fights broke out. In January 1834, pitched battles with hundreds on each side caused many deaths and arrests. President Andrew Jackson, self-proclaimed friend of the working man, sent a detatchment of federal troops to quell the labor trouble.

The society stubbornly clung to life. In May 1838, the canal company failed to pay the wages of its employees, who responded by destroying the work done but not remunerated. Three companies of state militia were sent this time. Now, however, the authorities began to feel the limits imposed on them by America's democratic traditions—and by a civilian militia. The militiamen sympathized with the strikers—so much so (noted Brigadier General O. H. Williams) that some refused to answer the call to arms. And if they were forced to fight, they warned, they would rather "fight for the Irish."

In the cities, protests by the unskilled could be more open and organized.

In New York, two to three hundred dockers and stevedores walked off work in 1828 in response to layoffs and pay cuts. In 1834, there were work stoppages by sailors, ship and construction laborers, riggers, and stevedores. Two years later, against the background of the journeymen tailors' strike in New York and

". . . NEW-FANGLED NOTIONS OF AMERICAN LIBERTY"

As late as the 1830s, European immigrant workers secured passage to the United States by signing contracts of indenture in exchange for transportation. The following report from Washington, D.C., printed in the October 29, 1829, Boston Courier, indicates how quickly such unskilled laborers could learn the language of liberty in their new home.

WE LEARN THAT the laborers who recently arrived in this city from England, and who entered into indentures to serve the Chesapeake and Ohio Canal Company for four months, for the expenses of their passage, were brought up on Thursday last before Judge Cranch, on a writ of *habeas corpus*. These men had positively refused to comply with their engagements upon their arrival in this country on the ground, as we learn, that they could not make themselves slaves, and were under no obligations to serve the company, and therefore [had] been imprisoned. These new-fangled notions of American liberty were, however, wholly subverted by the decision of Judge Cranch, who has remanded them to prison, there to remain until they consent to comply with their solemn engagement, and thus discharge the debt which they have voluntarily contracted.

the subsequent trial, police and militia were used to defeat strikes among construction laborers, stevedores, and riggers, leading to increased collaboration between laborers and craftsmen and even some talk about a general strike.

But cooperation between skilled and unskilled workers developed most quickly in Philadelphia. The early and steady erosion of craft status and pride there had also undermined the journeyman's condescension toward the laborer. During the mid-1830s, Philadelphia's trade union federation supervised the first major relaxation of craft exclusiveness. House carpenters who had previously disdained "half-trained" workers energetically appealed in 1835 to all in their trade to join a united strike for a shorter workday. Shoemakers, cigarmakers, and others did likewise.

In May 1835, the coalheavers on the city docks walked off the job to demand shorter hours, and their march through the city streets triggered the first general strike in the nation's history. Catching sight of the march, shoemakers rushed out of their shops and fell into line shouting, "We are all day laborers!" Members of other trades followed, and throughout the week other working people voted to join the strike. The excitement reached even the outlying textile mills and the homes of outworkers. A stunning, triumphant success, the strike brought shorter hours for many groups of workers, either immediately or in a few months' time. The laborers gained both a wage increase and a city ordinance making ten hours the legal working day on all public projects.

Until now, Philadelphia's new General Trades Union had refused admission to the laborers' union. But in the year after the general strike, joint action between the skilled and unskilled occurred more and more frequently. As a result, the GTU reversed itself and voted to bring the laborers into its ranks—the first time a skilled-workers' federation had reached so dramatically and decisively across the chasm that once separated them from the unskilled. It was a momentous event.

DEPRESSION TAKES ITS TOLL

This unprecedented mobilization of working people was dramatically cut short by economic crisis—financial panic in 1837 and a depression that began in 1839 and continued on into the early 1840s.

In all the main centers of industry and commerce, working men and women abruptly found themselves without work or income of any kind. At least as many managed to remain employed only part-time or at drastically reduced wages.

The labor movement plunged into crisis. With so many jobs lost and so many people desperate for work at any pay, strike threats

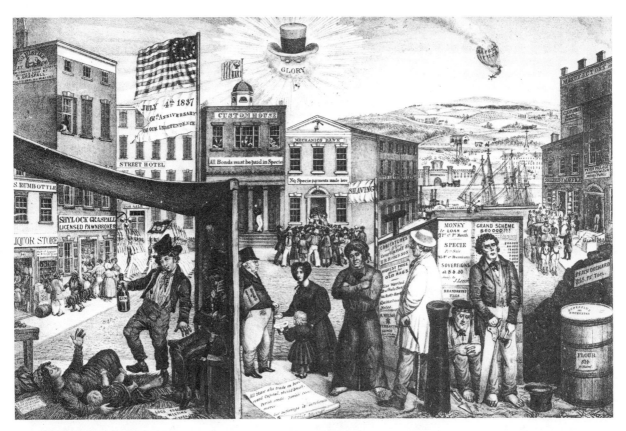

"The Times." The ravages of the depression are cataloged and blamed on the Jackson administration in this 1837 lithograph by a Whig printmaker. In the foreground, a family descends into alcoholism, a mother and child beg for charity, and unemployed workers stand about. In the background, citizens line up outside of a pawnbroker's establishment, while others make a run on a bank. Signs all around announce the devaluation of currency and lack of credit. Above the dismal scene shines Andrew Jackson's well-known beaver hat, spectacles, and clay pipe.

quickly lost their power. With so many of their members out of work, and being helpless to defend the wages and conditions of the rest, unions dissolved.

For employers, that was the depression's silver lining. A hat manufacturer boasted that his employees were now free of "the moral gangrene of Trades Union principles" and worked without "the inconveniences" and "injustice" of "regular combinations and periodical strikes." The New York *Journal of Commerce* instructed its well-to-do readers to seize the moment and henceforth "employ no men who do not forever abjure the unions." The opportunity had now arrived to eradicate labor organizations, the editor noted, and "it should be done thoroughly."

But if hardship helped employers extinguish the new labor organizations, it also fanned the flames of antibusiness sentiment. New York City's flour riot of 1837 made that unmistakably clear. A mass meeting to demand "Bread, Meat, Rent, Fuel!" attracted four to five thousand angry, hungry, shivering people to City Hall Park on the afternoon of February 10. Most of the prepared speeches were rather tame, but members of the crowd mounted soapboxes to vent more passionate feelings. They denounced landlords and their high rents, and merchants holding back food from starving neighbors. One speaker informed his listeners that Mr. Eli Hart, head of Hart and Company, commission merchants, "has now fifty-three thousand barrels of flour in his store," and suggested that the meeting "go and offer him eight dollars a barrel for it"—a price deemed just, but considerably below the going rate. And if Mr. Hart rejected the modest bid? "If he will not take it," the speaker concluded cautiously, "we shall depart in peace."

The crowd did march down to Hart's store, but once there proved less patient than the speaker. Mr. Hart soon arrived with a detachment of police armed with clubs. The protesters grabbed the clubs and broke them into splinters. The mayor himself hurried to the scene, mounted a flight of steps, and called upon those assembled to disperse. Before he could finish speaking, sticks and stones filled the air, forcing him to flee.

At last the crowd grasped one of the building's heavy iron doors, tore it from its hinges, and used it as a battering ram to force open other doors still in place. People now surged into the store, spotted the barrels of flour, and rolled them one after the other out onto the street. There the barrels were opened, their contents either distributed among the crowd or thrown onto the pavement.

The arrival of more police, reinforced by the state militia, momentarily halted the proceedings. Police arrested many and marched them off toward jail. Soon, however, the crowd regrouped and resumed the offensive. One large group set off in pursuit of the police and their prisoners. Eventually overtaken and attacked, the police had their clothes literally torn off their backs; some of their prisoners were freed.

By nine o'clock that night the

". . . THEY WERE DESPERATE MEN AND WOULD HAVE WORK OR FOOD"

Here is a Buffalo, New York, newspaper account of a protest by a thousand Irish day laborers at the Welland Canal in August 1842. The laborers had come to the canal in response to the canal company's handbill promising jobs. When they appeared, however, they found no jobs were to be had. What followed recalls the New York City flour riot five years earlier. Despite the editor's view of the immigrant laborers as "wild"—a common prejudice of the times—a sense of the workers' goals, determination, and concept of justice emerges from the report.

THE LABORERS assembled in immense masses with banners bearing various devices and inscriptions and proceeded to supply their wants with the strong hand. All efforts to arrest their proceedings were unavailing. The Catholic priest resident there informed the authorities that all his efforts to restrain them had proven useless and they were desperate men and would have work or food. The town was completely given up to them, none daring to make any resistance. Several stores and mills were plundered of goods and flour, and an American schooner . . . boarded and plundered of the pork which formed her cargo. We have not heard that any lives were lost, but our informant says it was a terrible thing to see so many hundreds of men frenzied with passion and hunger with no restraint upon the impulses of their wild natures.

The Theater of Artisan Republicanism. After the depression and collapse of the Workingmen's Party, insurgent "shirtless" Democrats in New York City challenged their political party's conservative leadership. Laborers, journeymen, and small master-craftsmen gathered around the charismatic figure of Mike Walsh, an Irish immigrant artisan and newspaper editor, who combined rough street tactics with provocative calls for social reform. Part of Walsh's appeal derived from a calculated public image that owed a lot to styles of performance in working-class theater. In this engraving from a collection of his speeches, Walsh strikes a standard actor's pose.

battle was over and the crowd finally dispersed. The point, however, had been made. The depression had broken up most labor organizations, but it had not reconciled working people to the absolute rule of the marketplace, to the commandment that "the true regulator of prices, whether of labor, goods, real estate, or anything else, is demand." Alternative conceptions of popular rights and community justice retained their strength. People believed they had a right to food at a reasonable price. If market fluctuations would not guarantee that price, citizens had other and more direct measures available. Hurling barrels out of Hart and Company's windows earlier that evening, a crowd member had proclaimed defiantly, "Here goes flour at eight dollars a barrel!"

THE SEARCH FOR SOLUTIONS

"Whoever looks at the world at it is now," Thomas Skidmore had written in 1829, "will see it divided into two distinct classes: proprietors, and nonproprietors; those who own the world, and those who own no part of it. If we take a closer view of these two classes, we shall find that a very great proportion even of the proprietors are only nominally so; they possess so little that in strict regard to truth they ought to be classed among the nonproprietors."

More and more people expressed sentiments like these during the early nineteenth century. The increasing national wealth alone

"Obscene Orgies and Pernicious Teachings." John Humphrey Noyes's utopian community in Oneida, New York, as represented in the *National Police Gazette*. The Oneida community, founded in 1848, extended the idea of communal property to sexual relationships and the bearing of children. Although popular publications like the *Police Gazette* titillated their readers with images of licentiousness, Oneida's "sexual communism" was carefully controlled and, unlike other utopian experiments, lasted over thirty years.

seemed to remedy nothing: growth in commerce, productivity, and total output seemed only to deepen the chasm between rich and poor and further erode values of mutual assistance and community rights. "No one can observe the signs of the times with much care," wrote Bostonian Orestes Brownson during the depression of 1839–43, "without perceiving that a crisis as to the relation of wealth and labor is approaching." Nor would old remedies serve:

> In this coming contest there is a deeper question at issue than is commonly imagined, a question which is but remotely touched in your controversies about United States Banks . . . , chartered banking and free banking, free trade

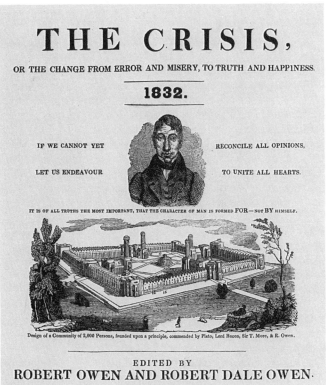

"The Change from Error and Misery, to Truth and Happiness." Robert Owen and the design of his New Harmony utopian community in Indiana appeared on the title page of *The Crisis,* written by Owen and his son in 1833.

and corporations, although these controversies may be paving the way for it to come up.

The real source of the social conflict Brownson anticipated was the whole "system of labor at wages." If America were truly to become a society grounded in equality, he concluded, "there must be no class of our fellow men doomed to toil through life as mere workmen at wages."

Attempts to stem the growth of wage labor took a variety of forms. Some tried to build entire new communities based on collective ownership of property and infused with the spirit of cooperation instead of competition. Viewing North America as a new world still in the making, European emigrants had begun erecting their model utopian societies early in the eighteenth century. A religious movement called the Shakers founded the largest of these; by the 1830s, it claimed more than six thousand members. Cooperative communities like Hopedale and Brook Farm (both in New England) drew upon the doctrines of the more radical evangelicals and took the need to change human society very seriously. Led by Universalist minister Adin Ballou, residents of Hopedale also participated in many other social-reform movements of the day, including the peace movement, temperance, women's rights, and antislavery. Brook Farm, founded in 1841, likewise expressed Christian disenchantment with commercializing and industrializing America. The colony's founder, Unitarian minister George Ripley, decried

the glaring inequalities of conditions, the hollow pretensions

". . . WHO SHALL PRACTICE VIRTUE UNDER CIRCUMSTANCES LIKE THESE?"

Following his arrival in the United States in 1824, Robert Owen, aided by his son, Robert Dale Owen, spread the message of social reform and cooperative socialism across the country. Owen was even invited twice in 1825 to address the House of Representatives on his theories of social organization. Although Robert Owen left America in 1827, his son stayed on to continue the struggle for social reform in America. In 1829, he cofounded and coedited (with Frances Wright) the Free Enquirer, *a weekly newspaper. In an editorial, Robert Dale Owen commented on a report detailing the deplorable status of working women in the city of Philadelphia.*

THE FIRST AND obvious conclusion to be deduced from the Philadelphia report is that several kinds of labor are, in that city, most inadequately rewarded; so inadequately that incessant and skillful industry from females engaged in these branches [of industry] is insufficient to procure them an honest support. . . .

I [wish] I could find terms to express the extreme importance which I attach to this subject. Not as it regards alone the poor, destitute victims to whom the report more immediately refers; but as it involves the interests of all the working and all the commercial classes of our country. . . .

I pray our readers' undivided attention to the facts now presented to them. In Philadelphia, women who are willing to work, and who do work, at tedious, sedentary employments, early and late, day after day, obtain for food and clothing SIXTEEN DOLLARS per annum: that is to say, *if* they be expert, and *if* they be constantly employed. . . . Is there, then, a possibility for women so employed honestly to maintain themselves?

This is not a tempting, it is a constraining to vice. IT IS A CONDEMNING TO PROFLIGACY UNDER PENALTY OF STARVATION. It is very easy to talk of character and of virtue in a drawing room; but who shall practice virtue under circumstances like these?

of pride, the scornful apathy with which many urge the
prostration of man, the burning zeal with which they run
the race of selfish competition with no thought for the ele-
vation of their brethren.

In the 1820s at New Harmony, Indiana, and elsewhere, industrial-
ist Robert Owen sought to apply ideas about social reform developed
in his native England. Some of these ideas fit particularly well in the
new world. Like many Americans, for example, Owen was excited
by the possibilities opened up by the development of industry and
technology. Rising productivity made it possible to produce more
and more goods and services while expending less and less human
labor. A permanent and growing prosperity should thus produce the
leisure time necessary for rest and relaxation, physical and cultural
development.

But for all to reap the harvest of industrial development, Owen
believed, mankind must replace the existing economic system with
one based on human cooperation. In such a society there would be
"no personal inequality, or gradation of rank and station; all will be
equal in their condition." Like many other communitarians, Owen
also sought to restore to women the equal rights so long denied them.
His words and actions exercised a wide appeal across the social spectrum. Participants in Owen's communities included business people,
professionals, farmers, mechanics, and laborers.

A kindred movement, called Associationism, based on the ideas of
French visionary Charles Fourier, gained popularity here during the
1840s and 1850s. Nearly thirty phalanxes (as their communities were
called) arose in those decades, appearing as far west as Michigan,
Iowa, and Wisconsin. And a variety of German cooperative colonies
in Pennsylvania, Ohio, Iowa, and elsewhere attracted groups of immigrant workers, farmers, and professionals.

One of those drawn to these cooperative colonies was Mary Paul,
the Vermont farmer's daughter and textile-mill operative encountered
earlier. In 1853–54, her Lowell stint and a term of domestic service
behind her, Paul entered the North American Phalanx in Redbank,
New Jersey. Her enthusiastic letters home breathe her attraction to
doctrines of sexual and economic equality. At the phalanx, Mary Paul
wrote, she would "not be confined to one kind of work but could do
almost anything," including "*housework* if I choose and that without
degrading myself" like a domestic servant. Equally exciting was the
prospect of receiving "better pay without working as hard as at any
other place." This possibility was directly linked to the issue of wom-
en's rights. "You know," she reminded her father, that in society at
large "men often get more than double the pay for doing the same
work that women do." Such discrimination was forbidden among As-

sociationists. "*All* work there, and all are paid alike. Both men and women have the *same pay* for the *same* work."

Between the American Revolution and the Civil War, more than a hundred experimental communities appeared. But great obstacles beset the communitarian experiments from the start. With limited resources, most found it difficult to match the temptations held out by the competitive world outside. For the same reason, even modest economic setbacks could spell disaster for communities already operating so close to the financial edge.

Critics cited these failures as proof that the whole attempt had been futile. Mary Paul felt differently. "I know," she added, "many will exult in the downfall of this place, but [they] are shortsighted." In just one year at the phalanx, she had "already seen enough to convince me that Association is the true life. And although all the attempts that have ever yet been made towards it have been failures . . . my faith in the principle is as strong as ever, stronger if possible." Associationist doctrines contained flaws, she judged, but they "have enough of truth in them to keep them alive until the world shall be ready for them." Of this point, Mary Paul was certain: "There is a better day coming for the world."

"Nashoba, April 12, 1828." Influenced by Robert Owen and New Harmony, Frances Wright established an interracial utopian community, Nashoba, near Memphis, Tennessee. Its white and black residents (including slaves purchased by Wright) worked and lived together. Believing that racism could be defeated only by the "amalgamation of the races," Wright permitted interracial sexual relationships in the Nashoba community. Even abolitionists condemned the experiment. This is a sketch by Charles-Alexandre Lesueur, a French artist-naturalist who spent ten years at New Harmony.

Cooperative enterprises embodied some of the same values as cooperative communities, but on a smaller scale. In the communities, people tried to organize a completely cooperative way of life on the periphery of American society. Cooperative enterprises challenged the wage-labor system in the midst of that society. Lynn shoemakers as well as Lowell textile operatives organized cooperative workshops. Under the leadership of exiled Chartist B. S. Treanor, Irish tailors in Boston did the same. So did German tailoresses in Cleveland. Indeed, working people established cooperative enterprises in virtually every major town and city of the North and West. Jointly owned by those who performed the labor that sustained them, producer and consumer cooperatives arose in various ways. Sometimes cooperatives were launched as permanent institutions, conceived from the start as durable alternatives to enterprises based on wage labor aimed primarily at profit-making. Sometimes strikers established cooperatives as temporary measures, to help sustain themselves. Striking journeymen printers launched Cincinnati's *Daily Unionist* as well as the German-language New York *Abendzeitung.* And some cooperatives founded as temporary measures outlived their original purpose.

Alongside both cooperative colonies and cooperative enterprises, concern about the evolution of American society spawned a third solution: agitation for land reform. In an overwhelmingly agrarian society, the ideal of economic independence naturally evoked visions of the small, family-owned farm. The calamitous crises of 1837 and 1839 and the trade-union crackup they brought on, the steady expansion of wage labor and tenancy during the subsequent economic revival, and then the acquisition of great chunks of

". . . CRUSHING THE PRODUCERS OF WEALTH TO THE VERY DUST"

In 1845, the Boston Mechanics' and Laborers' Association founded a cooperative society. A committee of that association drafted the statement excerpted below to explain the purpose and methods of cooperation.

IT IS OUR belief that the same causes of evil and suffering are operative in this country, that, in the Old World, are developed to giant magnitude, and are crushing the producers of wealth to the very dust, and that unless a speedy change can be effected in our social condition the time is not far distant when the laborers of the United States will be as dependent, as oppressed, and as wretched as are their brethren in Europe. Here, as there, the soil, motive power, and machinery are monopolized by the idle few; all the sources of wealth, all the instrumentalities of life, and even the right and privilege of industry are taken away from the people. Monopoly has laid its ruthless hands upon labor itself, and forced the sale of the muscles and skill of the toiling many, and under the specious name of "wages" is robbing them of the fruits of their industry. Universal monopoly is the bane of labor not less in America than in Europe. . . .

The remedy lies in a radical change of principle and policy. Our isolated position and interests, and our antisocial habits, must be abandoned. The Money-power must be superseded by the Man-power. Universal Monopoly must give place to Societary ownership, occupancy, and use. . . . The direction and profits of industry must be kept in the hands of the producers. Laborers must own their own shops and factories, work their own stock, sell their own merchandise, and enjoy the fruits of their own toil. Our Lowells must be owned by the artisans who build them, and [by] the operatives who run the machinery and do all the work. And the dividend, instead of being given to the idle parasites of a distant city, should be shared among those who perform the labor. Our Lynns must give the fortunes made by the [shoe] dealer and employer, to those who use the awl and work the material.

Frances Wright wearing the classical republican dress adopted by New Harmony residents. A painting probably by August Hervieu, a French artist who came to the United States in 1827 to teach drawing at the Nashoba colony.

territory from Mexico and American Indians—each of these developments increased popular support for proposals to make farmland available for small cultivators.

The federal government owned huge tracts of unimproved soil in the West. Some of it went to war veterans. Most was given in subsidy to private railroad companies or sold in large tracts on the open market. Both railroad grants and these public sales restricted the access of would-be small farmers to the soil. Boasting much readier access to money, big land companies, banks, and wealthy individual speculators bought up enormous quantities of public land. By 1860, speculators owned over twenty million acres in Illinois and Iowa alone—nearly a quarter of the land in those states—and nearly half of all the privately held land in Minnesota.

Interested in short-term profits rather than agriculture itself, the speculators simply jacked up the price of land and resold it in smaller plots to homesteaders. Railroad companies made similar use of the lands given to them. In each case, the result was the same: heavier financial burdens on the actual farmers. These only added to the difficulties imposed by the rising costs of commercial farming. Unable to buy land on these terms, some would-be homesteaders became farm laborers or tenants of large landowners. Those who did buy their own farms frequently went into debt to do so. Later unable to meet their payments, many of them lost both their homesteads and their life savings.

Reformers protested these government land policies and the speculation and landlordism they encouraged. Demanding that public lands go to the needy, reformers aimed to resist the growth of wage labor and tenancy. And both the leadership and the mass support of the land-reform movement reflected its multinational appeal. The best known and most energetic land reformer in these years was George Henry Evans, a Welsh-born printer and Workingmen's Party leader. Employing the democratic antimonopoly language of the times, Evans and his allies denounced the concentration of land in the hands of a minority, branding it "the king monopoly, the cause of the greatest evils." By stripping people of their basic rights as American citizens and members of the human community, it condemned them to degrading servitude on a mass scale. "If any man has a right on the earth," Evans insisted, "he has a right to land enough to raise a habitation on. If he has *a right to live,* he has a right to land enough for his subsistence. Deprive anyone of these rights, and you place him at the mercy of those who possess them." Without *"free soil,"* he concluded, trade unions and other efforts at self-defense were futile; public land must be made available free of charge, and only to those who would actually settle on and till it.

Demonstrating its broad appeal and strong links to northern antebellum reform thought, land reform attracted individuals associated with a broad spectrum of early-nineteenth-century democratic causes. Among them stood exiled Chartists like Thomas Devyr of Ireland, previously active in the Hudson Valley rent wars; John Cluer of Scotland, a leading New England advocate of a shorter working day; and James T. Pyne of England, a former leader of the New York Workingmen's Party. So did other Workingmen's Party leaders like John Commerford, John Ferral, James Marshall, and John Windt, as well as W. F. Young, editor of the Lowell *Voice of Industry*. They were joined by large numbers of communitarians as well; by the leader of the insurrectionary movement for democratic electoral reform in Rhode Island, Thomas Dorr; by New York City's colorful Irish gang leader and populist Democrat Mike Walsh; and by the Whig lawyer, teacher, and future Republican Party cofounder Alvan Bovay.

Since the beginning of European settlement in the New World, the promise of free land for homesteads had lured millions across the Atlantic. That promise had lost none of its power during the antebellum era, drawing native-born and immigrant working people alike to agitation for land reform. The National Trades Union linked "the interests and independence of the laboring class" to the land question, asserting that "if these public lands were left open to actual settlers" rather than speculators, surplus workers would be "drained off" from the cities into agriculture, relieving urban unemployment and job competition while simultaneously increasing the "demand for the produce of mechanical labor." Lynn's shoe workers warmly endorsed demands for free soil. As one of them, typically anguished by the prospect of permanent wage-labor status, demanded, "Where shall we go but on to the land? Deprive us of this and you reduce us to the condition of the serfs of Europe." And Lowell's labor newspaper, the *Voice of Industry*, prescribed a "simple and certain remedy" for the ills of the factory system: "free soil." Other labor organizations throughout the North and West took up one or another version of this refrain.

Immigrants from Germany—where marginal farmers and craftworkers were being driven steadily out of the countryside—were also enthusiastic about land reform. The best-known German-American land-reform advocate was Hermann Kriege, who in the mid-1840s took up the argument made a decade earlier by the NTU. By easing urban overcrowding, Kriege argued, land reform would eliminate the principal cause of antiforeign sentiment in the U.S. "If once the soil is free," he wrote, "then every honest workingman," regardless of birthplace, would be treated by all Americans as a "blessing to our republic." In 1850, Wilhelm Weitling's national congress of German-

American craftworkers endorsed the same principles; many other independent German land-reform societies also flourished.

At its inception, the land-reform movement in the United States had no direct connection with antislavery sentiment. Indeed, by the end of his life, George Henry Evans—once the champion of Nat Turner and fierce critic of slavery—was explicitly advocating participation in the land-reform movement instead of participation in the abolitionist campaign. Hermann Kriege, the German land reformer, followed suit and died (in 1852) a staunch member of the Democratic Party, the principal national vehicle of the slaveowning aristocracy. In later years, however, the seemingly separate threads of westward expansion, free labor, free land, and the future of slavery would all become tightly interwoven. That process would hasten the coming of the American Civil War.

THE LABOR MOVEMENT AFTER THE DEPRESSION

During the 1840s, the cultural diversity and national conflicts within the new working class for a time weakened its powers of resistance. The depression of 1839 had effectively destroyed most of the labor organizations painfully constructed during earlier decades. The slowness of the economic recovery in the early 1840s left many workers

"A BILLION OF ACRES OF UNSOLD LANDS"

This 1855 poem laments governmental policies allowing huge areas of the public domain to go to railroads and land speculators. A supporter of land reform, the poet Augustine Duganne insists on giving the soil to the landless.

A billion of acres of unsold land
  Are lying in grievous dearth;
And millions of men in the image of God
  Are starving all over the earth!
Oh! tell me, ye sons of America!
  How much men's lives are worth! . . .

To whom do these acres of land belong?
  And why do they thriftless lie?
And why is the widow's lament unheard—
  And stifled the orphan's cry?
And why are the poor-house and jail so full—
  And the gallows-tree built high? . . .

Those millions of acres belong to Man!
  And his claim is—that he needs!

still unemployed. And the continual breakdown of skilled labor into unskilled reduced the bargaining power of still others.

The reduced combativeness of labor in the 1840s could be seen in the factories of Lowell, where the relatively independent young women originally employed steadily gave way to Irish immigrants. Preoccupied with supporting themselves and their dependents here and across the Atlantic, the new employees at first showed little enthusiasm for unions or strikes. This remained true even when mill owners repeatedly slashed pay rates while accelerating their speed-up and stretch-out campaigns. And the Lowell experience was repeated in many other places.

By the later 1840s, however, this employers' heaven was already beginning to dissolve. A brisk business pace now strengthened workers' hands; years of long hours, low wages, and deteriorating conditions hardened their resolve.

Just as important, some immigrants initially impressed with how much better things were in the New World began to see a darker side to American life. "The rich and distinguished stand here higher above the law than in any other country," exclaimed one German-born Pittsburgher. Here in America, he went on, "in the land that boasts of its humanity, that claims to be at the very top of civilization . . . the laboring classes are treated in as shameful a manner as in Europe, with all its ancient prejudices." A group of Boston Irish put it more bluntly, denouncing "the petty domineering of would-be tyrants" who profited from their poverty. Led by exiled Chartist B. S. Treanor, Irish tailors there resolved that a "fundamental change must take place in our social and industrial relations" or labor would be crushed under the "despotic weight of capital."

By about 1850, efforts to improve wages and working conditions and to organize working people had picked up again. The old ten-hour movement, weakened during the 1840s, grew. Groups of immigrant and native-born workers began reaching out for mutual support. Irish craftsmen in eastern cities organized unions of tailors, carpenters,

And his title is sealed by the hand of God—
  Our God! who the raven feeds:
And the starving soul of each famished man
  At the throne of justice pleads! . . .

Who hath ordained that the few should hoard
  Their millions of useless gold?—
And rob the earth of its fruits and flowers,
  While profitless soil they hold?
Who hath ordained that a parchment scroll
  Shall fence round miles of lands,—
    When millions of hands want acres
    And millions of acres want hands.

'Tis a glaring *lie* on the face of day . . .
  This robbery of men's rights!
'Tis a lie, that the word of the Lord disowns—
  'Tis a curse that burns and blights!
And 'twill burn and blight till the people rise,
  And swear, while they break their bands—
    That the hands shall henceforth have acres
    And the acres henceforth have hands!

"A Panic in Wall Street." A "truthful and vivid account" in *Harper's Weekly* of the 1857 financial panic. This wood-engraving portrays the "essential personages of a Wall Street scene," including a penny-pinching "Jewish capitalist" (second from left in foreground), a smiling loan-shark (center), and "the victim of an unexpected failure" (seated right). As in most nineteenth-century illustrations, this wood-engraving served as a diagram of social "types" that appeared in literature and theater, if not in actuality.

shoemakers, cabinetmakers, bakers, masons and stonecutters, blacksmiths, and printers, among others. The great mass of unskilled Irish laborers began to band together in larger numbers; the localized and clannish secret societies of the 1830s increasingly gave way to public, legal organizations. The New York Laborers' Union Benevolent Association, formed in 1843, embraced many different kinds of laborers and by 1850 claimed six thousand members. The association focused mainly on demands for higher wages and an end to competition from convict labor. In Brooklyn and Boston, predominantly Irish longshoremen built organizations of their own with similar aims.

An important development came to Lowell in 1859, when, after almost two decades of quiescence, between three and five hundred female mill operatives walked off their jobs. That was only about 6 percent of the city's total workforce, and the strike was ultimately lost. But what was significant was that for the first time, most of the strikers were Irishwomen, now ready to make claims on their new homeland.

German craftsmen, many of them highly politicized and deeply influenced by the 1848 revolution, mobilized and organized even more quickly. In October 1850, the first national congress of German-American craftworkers convened in Philadelphia. The initiative came from Wilhelm Weitling, a self-taught radical tailor. There, delegates representing more than four thousand working people founded the Allgemeine Arbeiterbund (General Workers' League). When Weitling's organization later declined, others arose to take its place. These maintained close ties with a broad range of cultural and political societies of German-Americans. The motto adopted by several of these groups echoed the popular democratic slogan of 1848: "Welfare, Education, and Freedom for All."

At first, groups of immigrant workers commonly stood aloof from and even opposed to one another. But by collaborating among themselves and repeatedly using one national group to depress the pay and conditions of another, employers gradually taught their employees a hard lesson. To defend themselves effectively, mutual distaste and suspicion would have to be overcome—or at least sufficiently tempered to permit united organization.

This growth during the 1850s of active labor solidarity—across ethnic as well as occupational lines—manifested itself in three major waves of strike action and union-building. The first occurred in 1850, the second in 1853, and the third in 1858–60. Each of these mobilizations, in turn, encouraged the creation of citywide bodies to which large numbers of trade unions and other groups devoted to labor reform affiliated. Explaining its own appearance, Cincinnati's new General Trades Union in 1853 expressed the impulse driving labor unity forward in other cities, too. "All trades," declared the GTU's founding meeting, "have an equal and identical interest" and "if united . . . could better resist the encroachments of capital" in the struggle "of right against might."

It was often the more experienced and worldly German craftworkers who first sought to bridge the gap separating them from native-born and Irish workers. New York's German cabinetmakers resolved to reor-

". . . THE LABORER SHALL ENJOY THE FULL FRUITS OF HIS INDUSTRY"

In 1850, a powerful wave of strikes swept the industrial centers of the country. One result was the creation of local federations of trade unions and other groups pledged to labor reforms. Among them was the United Trade and Laborers' Organization of Allegheny County, which represented many of the Pittsburgh area's organized English-speaking workers. The following excerpt from its Platform of Principles reflects a general outlook and specific demands typical of such organizations at midcentury.

THE FACT THAT a man is born is evidence that he has a right to life and a share of its enjoyments, and any system of society which deprives him of these is false. . . . All material wealth is produced by labor—physical and mental—and the laborer shall enjoy the full fruits of his industry, and any system of society or government which deprives him of these is false. . . . As the Workingmen compose the great mass of the population of the country, they should control its legislation. . . . Prominent among the changes which the people should demand are the following:

First. A general Incorporation Law which will enable workingmen to associate and become their own employers.

Second. The Homestead of the family should be exempt from execution and be made inalienable; but dishonest debtors should not be permitted to escape punishment.

Third. The public lands should be given, in limited quantities, to actual settlers, and under no circumstances should they be permitted to go into the hands of speculators.

Support for such views crossed ethnic lines, as the following response from Pittsburgh's German Workingmen's Congress indicates. Broad agreement on such principles helped unite workers of different nationalities and religions over the course of the 1850s.

In this brother Union of workingmen based on equality, justice, and love of man, we discover that the Great Ruler of the Universe has clearly manifested this important truth, that the earth, and all the elements necessary for the happiness and well-being of the race, belong alike to the whole of mankind; and there can be no just or natural right existing on the part of a select or elect few to monopolize that which of right belongs equally to all for use.

"If I Don't Kill Something Else Soon, *I'll Spile!*" An 1856 drawing comments on Know-Nothing violence in Baltimore. The scene is populated by members of nativist gangs with names like "Blood-Tubs," "Cut-Throats," and "Plug-Uglies."

ganize their union "for the accommodation of all nations." And German blacksmiths and wheelwrights likewise declared, "We all belong to one great family—the Workingmen's family." Some mainly Irish organizations also came to stress the importance of multinational unity. The banner of the New York longshoremen featured the national flags of eight different European nations and the Stars and Stripes together with the word "Unity." Above this display were the words "We know no distinction but that of merit." A violent 1850 New York City tailors' strike for a time united German, Irish, and native workers on an unprecedented scale.

Mounting immigration in the next few years continued to aggravate ethnic frictions within the swiftly expanding working class, but there were also instances of cooperation across ethnic lines. During the economic crises of 1854–55 and 1857, such instances caused a wave of fear in conservative business and political circles in several cities. Trapped between inflated prices and staggering unemployment, large crowds of jobless workers of various nationalities held angry mass meetings. In New York City in January 1855, eight thousand native, Irish, and German workers demanded laws outlawing eviction of tenants unable to pay their rent, providing large-scale employment of the jobless on public works, and giving free land to the landless. Former Workingmen's leader John Commerford drew cheers from the crowd by proposing that the city government employ jobless workers to build low-rent public housing. Upper-class critics, both native- and foreign-born, scorned such calls for government action as "foreign" or "European." But "this has been the policy of the aristocracy at all times," Commerford argued. "They wish to separate the American mechanics from the German, and the German from the Irish; they want to keep you in a divided condition so that you cannot concentrate your action for the benefit of yourselves and fellow workingmen"; furthermore, the same people who oppose government aid to the poor are happy to accept it themselves. "Shall those," he asked, "who have received the millions that have been appropriated to individuals, states, railroads, and the various companies who confederate for the purpose of swelling the army of accumulating plunderers"— shall such people "tell us to [lie] down and wallow in the inferiority of the condition with which they have provided us?"

"LOOK AT THE HORDES OF DUTCH AND IRISH THIEVES AND VAGABONDS . . ."

Nativist—anti-immigrant—appeals to American-born workers and merchants were common throughout the 1840s and 1850s. The following election circular, printed in the New York Daily Plebeian *on April 20, 1844, conveys a sense of how fear of immigrants was manipulated by politicians in search of votes and by businessmen looking to further divide the urban working class.*

LOOK AT THE hordes of Dutch and Irish thieves and vagabonds, roaming about our streets, picking up rags and bones, pilfering sugar and coffee along our wharves and slips, and whatever our native citizens happen to leave in their way. Look at the English and Scotch pick-pockets and burglars, crowding our places of amusement, steam-boat landings, and hotels. Look at the Italian and French mountebanks, roaming the streets of every city in the Union with their dancing monkeys and hand-organs, all as an excuse for the purpose of robbing us of our property the first favorable opportunity. Look at the wandering Jews, crowding our business streets with their shops as receptacles for stolen goods, encouraging thievery and dishonesty among our citizens. Look at the Irish and Dutch grocers and rum-sellers monopolizing the business which properly belongs to our own native and true-born citizens.

". . . WE ARE STRONG AND GETTING STRONGER"

Immigrants responded to nativist attacks in various ways. In this 1847 letter to the New York Champion of American Labor, *one foreign-born worker warned of the effects of nativism on mutual support between American- and foreign-born workers in the United States.*

YOU INTEND TO shut out the foreigners or naturalized citizens of this country from any benefit that will arise from your plans to get better wages. . . . You use the word *American* very often and nothing at all is said about *naturalized citizens,* but if you think to succeed without the aid of foreigners you will find yourself mistaken; for we are strong and are getting stronger every day, and though we feel the effects of competition from these men who are sent here from the poorhouses of Europe, yet if you don't include us to get better wages by shutting off such men, why, you needn't expect our help.

ON THE EVE OF WAR

Though the growing sectional crisis tended to hide their significance, important events now foreshadowed something of the nature, scope, and power of the labor movement of later decades. The labor militancy of the 1850s carried on its crest an important organizational advance. Attempts to build nationwide trade unions had begun in the labor crisis of the 1830s. That impulse became much stronger in the decade before the Civil War, as national unions arose among hat-finishers, cigarmakers, typesetters, plumbers, painters, stonecutters, shoemakers, and iron-molders. Some disappeared almost as fast as they arose, and the cohesion of most proved tenuous, the national body merely advising its local units. But even these steps represented breakthroughs, and laid the groundwork for the larger and more successful efforts at national labor organization that would come in the wake of the Civil War.

The case of the national union of iron-molders—founded largely at the instigation of William H. Sylvis—illustrates the overall development. Sylvis's own life, in fact, tells us much about the labor movement in these decades.

Born in 1828, William Sylvis worked in his father's wagon shop in Armagh, Pennsylvania, for a while. But during the 1840s, he sought training and work as a molder in the iron industry, then mushrooming to meet demands for industrial tools and machinery. At first this expansion meant good wages for the few workers with the skills required. But the lure of higher pay steadily increased the number of would-be molders, eventually allowing foundry owners to reduce wages and stiffen working conditions. Simultaneously, iron production was becoming concentrated in the hands of a small number of larger companies able to afford the new and expensive equipment needed. The cost of opening an independent foundry soared, so when Sylvis tried to open his own foundry, the venture ended in disaster. Sylvis soon found himself trudging Pennsylvania's roads in search of wage work.

In 1852, Sylvis married and the next year settled in Philadelphia. There he attempted to support a growing family on the meager wages of a journeyman molder. During the 1830s and 1840s, journeymen molders had already formed several local unions around the country. But like most unions of the day, these were generally loose, localized, and temporary affairs, typically organized to negotiate a single agreement or to call a single strike, and not enduring afterward.

The Philadelphia molders were among the first workers to move toward a more durable organization. Their 1855 constitution declared, "In the present organization of society, laborers single-handed are powerless . . . but combined there is no power of wrong they may not openly defy." Two years later, when some of Sylvis's coworkers struck over a 12 percent wage cut, Sylvis joined the strike as well as the picket committee.

At length, the Philadelphia molders met defeat; the 1857 depression simply cut the ground from under them. This time, however, defeat failed to destroy the union itself. Soon elected union secretary, Sylvis threw himself into the job of strengthening it and its ties to other molders' associations around the country. The rise of a national market had convinced Sylvis that molders had to organize nationally as well. He therefore played a central role in founding the National Molders' Union in 1859. Largely through Sylvis's efforts, this early national union more than doubled its size during its first year in existence.

Frank Leslie's Illustrated Newspaper covers a strike. Preceded by the local militia, women shoemakers demonstrate in the streets of Lynn, Massachusetts, on March 7, 1860. In contrast to their failure to cover previous labor actions, illustrated newspapers published a number of images of the 1860 strike, as though editors were aware that the shoemakers' protest marked the beginning of a new era of industrial conflict.

The Lynn shoemakers also stepped up their activity as the Civil War approached. Declining wages, repeated layoffs, and the disruptions occasioned by the introduction of the sewing machine finally exploded in 1860 in the largest strike the nation had ever seen. During the next two months, over twenty thousand men and women downed tools—more than a third of all shoe workers in Massachusetts.

The strikers held that their cause was the defense of the individual's dignity and independence against the threat of a dependence that approached slavery. To emphasize that point, they linked their struggle to symbols of national independence, launching the strike on George Washington's birthday. Their "Cordwainer's Song" rallied strikers to defend their rights as free citizens and "sink not to the state of slave." On March 7, eight hundred female strikers marched through the wintry streets of Lynn behind a banner proclaiming, "American ladies will not be slaves: Give us a fair compensation and we labor cheerfully."

The Lynn strikers turned out in huge street demonstrations, fought the use of scab labor, and battled the town marshal when he and his deputies intervened on the side of the bosses. To no avail: bolstered by additional police, the employers won the day. Lack of funds and divisions in the workforce also plagued the strike effort.

"AN EMPTY POCKET'S THE WORST OF CRIMES!"

The Hutchinson family was one of the country's most popular singing groups in the nineteenth century. Their successful stage performances combined entertainment with a social reform message; Hutchinson songs often took up the causes of abolitionism and woman's suffrage. As natives of Lynn, Massachusetts, the Hutchinsons were particularly aware of the plight of the city's shoeworkers. "The Popular Creed," first sung at shoeworkers' meetings, later became a standard song of the labor movement.

Dimes and dollars! Dollars and dimes!
An empty pocket's the worst of crimes!
If a man's down, give him a thrust!
Trample the beggar into the dust!
Presumptuous poverty, quite appalling!
Knock him over! Kick him for falling!
If a man's up, oh, lift him higher!
Your soul's for sale, and he's the buyer!
Dimes and dollars! Dollars and dimes!
An empty pocket's the worst of crimes!

I know a poor but worthy youth,
Whose hopes are built on a maiden's truth;
But the maiden will break her vow with ease,
For a wooer whose charms are these:
A hollow heart and an empty head,
A face well tinged with the brandy's red,
A soul well trained in villainy's school,
And cash, sweet cash!—he knoweth the rule.
Dimes and dollars! Dollars and dimes!
An empty pocket's the worst of crimes!

I know a bold and honest man,
Who strives to live on the Christian plan.
He struggles against fearful odds—
Who will not bow to the people's gods?
Dimes and dollars! Dollars and dimes!
An empty pocket's the worst of crimes!

So get ye wealth, no matter how!
No question's asked of the rich, I trow!
Steal by night, and steal by day
(Doing it all in a legal way!)
Dimes and dollars! Dollars and dimes!
An empty pocket's the worst of crimes!

Despite their defeat, though, the determined mobilization of the Lynn strikers set the terms for the massive labor confrontations of the coming decades. More immediately, the strikers' repeated invocation of the slavery theme carried with it a significance of its own. The implied equation between shoe bosses and slave-masters illuminated the particular concerns—and ambivalences—that northern labor brought to the political conflict then dividing the country. As the Lynn strike began, a newspaper reporter overheard some journeymen debating the relative merits of free-labor and slave-labor society. As published in the New York *Daily Tribune,* part of the exchange went as follows:

> "What is the use," said one of them, who seemed to take an interest in politics, "of our making such a fuss about the slaves of the South? I tell you we are almost as much oppressed as they are. In fact, in one sense we are worse oppressed, for they don't work so many hours in the week as we do; and they get a living: while most of us couldn't live, with our families, if we couldn't get trusted for the necessaries of life, which we never expect to be able to pay for at this rate."
>
> His opponent seemed to hesitate, and a bystander put in, "We are worse treated than the slaves of the South, in every sense, so far as I can see."
>
> "Yes," said the first speaker, "I don't know but we are."
>
> The second party to the controversy now spoke up with some earnestness. "You know, gentlemen, we are not a quarter as bad off as the slaves of the South, though we are, by our —— foolishness, ten times as bad off as we ought to be. They can't vote, nor complain, and we can. And then just think of it; the slaves can't hold mass meetings, nor 'strike,' and we haven't lost that privilege yet, thank the Lord." (LOUD CHEERS)

Escape. The icon, or symbol, that appeared on notices about
fugitive slaves in the classified section of the Mobile, Alabama,
Commercial Register in the 1830s.

9 THE STRUGGLE OVER SLAVE LABOR

AMONG THE sources of conflict in the young North American republic, African-American slavery proved the most profound and explosive. Eventually, indeed, it absorbed or overshadowed all others. Densely interwoven with matters of race, religion, family, property, political and legal philosophy, and partisanship, the crux of the issue was the proper status and rights of labor.

To slaveowners, the centrality of the labor issue was obvious. Their whole way of life depended on the efforts of enslaved black workers. As one South Carolina planter bluntly explained, "Slavery with us is no abstraction but a great and vital fact. Without it our every comfort would be taken from us. Our wives, our children made unhappy—education, the light of knowledge—all, all lost and our people ruined forever." That black labor sustained southern society was of course no mystery to slaves, either. Gazing upon the soil of the South, as one black South Carolina field hand later put it, they saw "land that is rich with the sweat of our face and the blood of our back."

For decades, most white Americans accepted the slave-labor system. Non-slaveholders in the South declined to challenge it, many instead extolling black bondage as the bedrock of southern white liberty. In the free states, larger numbers disapproved of slavery on principle but deemed it a matter of importance primarily to the South. Slaves, however, refused to accept their lot passively. Some turned to collective force, attempting against all odds to rise in revolt against their masters. Others sought their freedom through escape. The rest resisted the burdens and humiliations of slavery the only way they could—by covertly frustrating the owners' plans and setting limits on the owners' effective power.

Directly and indirectly, the beliefs and actions of African-Americans compelled white society to reexamine its values and assumptions. Revolts, escapes, day-to-day resistance, and free-black organizations disturbed the peace and challenged the values of individual whites. Slaveowners responded to these initiatives in ways that menaced and infuriated people outside the system. Planters' belligerence, intended to shore up slavery in the South, seemed increasingly to threaten free labor throughout the country. The Republican Party arose in the 1850s in response to that threat. "The present political contest," a Republican leader in Maine write toward the decade's close, "when resolved into its simplest elements is the ever-enduring and never-ending warfare between free and servile labor." "There is but one issue in this prolonged and bitter contest," proclaimed the pro-Republican Chicago *Press and Tribune*. "It is this, *shall labor be degraded?*"

SLAVES RESIST AND ADAPT

The odds had always been heavily against slave revolts. Whites composed the great majority of the North American population, and their rapid settlement of the countryside deprived potential black insurrectionists of a safe refuge from which to resist recapture.

With freedom unlikely through insurrection, slaves had to find ways to survive in bondage. Some accepted their subordinate place within southern society, an acceptance that was aided by slaveowner-sanctioned churches. But adapting to the reality of slavery did not mean accepting that it was just or permanent. Much less did it guarantee strict obedience to a master's wishes.

On the contrary. Unable to break their bonds, slaves nonetheless strove to assert their humanity and defend their minimal interests.

They evolved an elaborate code of conduct that permitted them to limit their burdens without the masters fully understanding what was afoot. Slaves pretended stupidity, forcing masters and overseers to explain the simplest task time and time again. By destroying tools and injuring livestock (always apparently by accident), they convinced masters of their genuine inability to work too hard or to undertake certain tasks at all. By feigning pregnancy, slave women could temporarily avoid some of the heavier work in the fields. Through theft, all might improve their diet or add to their meager personal possessions. And by slipping away from the farm or plantation and then escaping to the North or to Canada, slaves could not only emancipate themselves but also raise the morale and assertiveness of others still in bondage. Most runaways were eventually caught. But when one made his or her way to freedom, those left behind noted the success. One field hands' song ran,

> Go 'way, Ol' Man,
> Go 'way, Ol' Man
> Where you been all day?
> If you treat me good
> I'll stay till Judgment Day,
> But if you treat me bad,
> I'll sho' to run away.

Unable to recognize their slaves as human beings like themselves, who shared their own desires for personal freedom and material betterment, slaveowners generally interpreted slave behavior as proof of innate inferiority. African-Americans, they argued, were by nature stupid, lazy, and dishonest. "They break and destroy more farming utensils," complained one planter,

> ruin more carts, break more gates, spoil more cattle and horses, and commit more waste than five times their number of white laborers do. They are under instruction relative to labor from their childhood, and still when they are gray-headed they are the same heedless botches; the negro traits predominate over all artificial training.

Another planter exclaimed, "To keep a diary of their conduct would be to record nothing short of a series of violations of the laws of God and man." Those laws, however, looked somewhat different to the slave. "They always tell us it's wrong to lie and steal," recalled former slave Josephine Howard, "but why did the white folks steal my mammy and her mammy? . . . That's the sinfullest stealing there is."

Despite insuperable barriers, slave revolts did break out again and again throughout the history of the "peculiar institution." In these revolts we can see the feelings, values, aspirations, and abilities that slaves normally had to conceal from their masters. For one thing slaves interpreted and used the values, language, and symbols of republicanism and evangelical Protestantism that were regularly invoked by the nation that held them captive. All social groups in white society in these years—merchants, manufacturers, planters, small farmers, and wage-earners—identified with one version or another of the American revolutionary heritage. When conflicts erupted among them, all sides claimed to uphold that tradition. African-Americans —those most flagrantly denied democratic rights—made use of that same democratic and revolutionary heritage, along with religious beliefs of both African and Christian origin, to express their own ideals and demands.

Another common element of the slave revolts was the prominent part played by urban, educated, and skilled slaves, whose experience gave them a broader view than that of the average field hand.

Equally important was the existence of open conflict within the white population. At the least, such divisions promised rebels some essential maneuvering room. But they might even end the slaves' political isolation, leading to alliances that could affect the odds of a rebellion's success.

Masters could rarely predict which of their slaves might lead a conspiracy or join an uprising. The owners chose to believe their slaves were content. They were usually unaware of day-to-day slave resistance—both because it was concealed by the slaves' acting skill and because their own social blindness led them to regard their slaves as childlike, docile, even if shiftless and clumsy, "Sambos." And yet, this image of the contented slave could never fully calm the slaveholders' deepseated fear that, given capable leadership and the right circumstances, these humble, smiling, shuffling people would rise up and cut their master's throats. Virginia congressman John Randolph reported that "the night bell never tolls for fire in Richmond, that the mother does not hug the infant more closely to her bosom. I have been witness to some of the alarms in the capital of Virginia."

One of these alarms shook Virginia's capital in 1800, during Randolph's first term in the House, when slave blacksmith Gabriel Prosser organized an insurrection aiming to seize the city. Prosser apparently believed that strained relations between France and the United States had finally given way to war—which, if true, would have made success more likely. He was better informed about both the American Revolution and the incidence of antislavery sentiment. Thus Prosser and his followers reportedly planned to kill all whites in their path save those they deemed friendly—Quakers, Methodists, and Frenchmen. The insurrectionists would carry out their plans,

Death of Capt. Ferrer, the Captain of the Amistad, July, 1839.

The *Amistad* Rebellion. In July 1839, captive West Africans rebelled and took over the Spanish slaveship *Amistad*. They ordered the owners to sail to Africa but, instead, the *Amistad* was taken on a meandering course, finally waylaid by a U.S. Navy brig. The Africans were charged with the murder of the captain and jailed in New Haven, Connecticut. Abolitionists came to their support; ex-President John Quincy Adams represented them in court. After a long legal battle, the Supreme Court freed the "mutineers" in 1841. The following year they returned to Africa.

furthermore, under a banner proclaiming "Death or Liberty," a slogan that fellow Virginian Patrick Henry would easily have recognized.

A generation later, in 1822, a free black carpenter of Charleston, South Carolina, named Denmark Vesey organized one of the broadest and best-planned insurrectionary conspiracies in southern history. Born a slave, Vesey had managed to purchase his liberty in the year of Gabriel Prosser's revolt. His wide travels as a merchant seaman left him not only literate but multilingual. His confederates included other craftsmen, house servants, and a slave foreman, and together they fashioned an arsenal including hundreds of bayonets, daggers, and pike heads. Had the rising succeeded, Vesey and his lieutenants evidently planned to sail for the self-governing black state of Haiti.

This conspiracy, like Prosser's, was betrayed. The effective impossibility of maintaining absolute secrecy undid most such plots. To suppress the revolt and terrorize other would-be rebels, the white authorities arrested 131 Charleston blacks and hanged 37 that summer.

Testimony at the Vesey trials reveals the influence of both religious and political ideas among the plotters. To encourage his confederates, we learn, Vesey regularly read aloud from the Bible "about how the children of Israel were delivered out of Egyptian bondage." He also attended closely to news bearing on the future of slavery, such as the enduring independence of the self-governing black state born of Haiti's eighteenth-century slave revolt. The South Carolina elite acknowledged Vesey's spiritual kinship to revolutionaries of other nations and ages. "Let it never be forgotten," concluded one white Charlestonian,

> that our NEGROES are truly the *Jacobins* of the country; that they are the *anarchists* and the *domestic enemy*; the *com-*

mon enemy of civilized society, and the barbarians who would, IF THEY COULD, become the DESTROYERS *of our race.*

In the summer of 1831, an insurrection erupted in tidewater Southampton, Virginia, sending a new thrill of fear through the South. Its leader was Nat Turner, a bondsman who in the presence of whites had usually acted the polite, respectful, eager-to-please servant so dear to the hearts of slaveowners. And then, late that August, Turner and a group of confederates killed approximately sixty whites in a desperate, ultimately unsuccessful, bid for freedom.

Nat Turner was a religious leader, a "self-called" Baptist minister whose mission was revealed to him during a vision in the fields. In prison his captors taunted him, "Do you not find yourself mistaken now?" But the armed prophet continued to draw strength from the

"Joseph Cinque." "Our hands are now clean for we have striven to regain the precious heritage we received from our fathers." A portrait of the leader of the *Amistad* rebellion painted by Nathaniel Jocelyn.

symbolism of Christianity. "Was not Christ crucified?" he answered. A letter printed in the Richmond *Whig* a month after Turner's capture placed responsibility for his religious zealotry on the heads of white evangelical preachers and their "ranting cant about equality." It was they who had infected "an imagination like Nat's" with "the possibility of freeing himself and race from bondage; and this by supernatural means."

Prosser, Vesey, Turner, and their supporters influenced the course of national history and have justly captured the imagination of modern historians and novelists. But the most sustained and successful military efforts waged by African-Americans against enslavement have often been overlooked. These efforts occurred in the context of the two so-called Seminole Wars, the first one in 1812, the second in 1835. Until its annexation by the United States in 1819, Florida had provided a haven for lower-South slave runaways (known as "maroons"). Here they found a refuge rare on the continent: a swampy terrain that was difficult to penetrate but rich enough in food to support isolated groups of fugitives. They also found something else, just as important—allies, in the form of the Seminole nation.

True, some Seminoles held African-Americans they had bought as slaves. But slavery among the Seminoles resembled the traditional slavery of Africa more than it did the commercially oriented slavery fashioned by European settlers and their descendants. The Seminoles' slaves lived on small farms with their own families and enjoyed most of the rights and liberties of full members of the tribe. The absence in Seminole Florida of a rigidly racist society—anchored in slave-driven production for profit—enabled black fugitives from the United States to find acceptance as members of Seminole society.

The First Seminole War broke out in 1812 when U.S. marines invaded Florida. Seminoles and black maroons repelled the invaders. American military reports indicated that the fiercest resistance came from the black fugitives, some of whom led in the fighting. The Second Seminole War began in 1835. Partly the result of American efforts to drive all southwestern Indian tribes beyond the Mississippi, the war was also encouraged by slavetraders, slaveowners, and would-be slaveowners hoping to get their hands on the African-Americans living among the Seminoles. The fighting, expected to last only a few months, actually lasted seven years and cost the lives of some sixteen hundred U.S. troops and a financial loss of between $30 and $40 million. According to a contemporary account, "The negroes, from the commencement of the Florida war, have, for their numbers, been the most formidable foe, more bloodthirsty, active, and revengeful than the Indian." The most militant of the Indian leaders, Osceola, counted many Afro-Indians among his supporters. Even more alarming to whites, slaves on nearby American-owned plantations actively collaborated with the insurgent Seminoles and Afro-Indians. Hundreds actually escaped servitude and joined the Seminole ranks. American general Thomas Sidney Jessup wrote in late 1836, "This, you may be assured, is a negro, not an Indian, war."

The war dragged on largely because the whites were bent on reenslaving recent plantation runaways living among the Seminoles. Finally stalemated, General Jessup considered offering milder terms, hoping thereby to separate the Afro-Indians from the full-blooded Seminoles. He would send the blacks to the Indian (Oklahoma) Territory while allowing the Seminoles to remain in southern Florida. "Separating the negroes from the Indians," he wrote in 1838, would "weaken the latter more than they would be weakened by the loss of the same number of their own people." But white military commanders developed other reasons for wanting to exile rather than recapture the black warriors. They felt that, having tasted comparative freedom and proven themselves in battle, reenslaved black warriors would only escape once again into the swamps, where they would prove more dangerous than ever. "Ten resolute negroes," warned one officer, "with a knowledge of the country, are sufficient to desolate the frontier, from one extent to the other." Another added that "If . . . the swamps of Florida . . . become the resort of runaways" the maroons "might impose upon the general government a contest, quadruplicate in time and treasure than that now being waged."

Ultimately the Second Seminole War ended in a U.S. victory, but by no means an unconditional one. The victors had to allow the fugitive slaves among the Seminoles to accompany the Indians westward rather than be returned to their white former owners. The Afro-Seminole resistance speaks eloquently of the courage, determination, and military capacity that existed among blacks in the antebellum South. If the successes scored there proved unique, that was only because other preconditions—above all, a strong and numerous ally—existed nowhere else in the South.

DISSENT AND DEMOCRACY IN THE SOUTH

Not that the white South was free of turmoil. The Workingmen's agitation that gripped New England and the Middle Atlantic states during the late 1820s and 1830s found an echo among southern whites as well. Sympathetic newspapers appeared in Delaware, Maryland, Virginia, South Carolina, and Missouri. Various groups of printers, steamboat hands, and dockworkers supported trade unions, and city-wide federations arose in Baltimore, Washington, D.C., and Savannah. In Wilmington, Delaware, the Association of Working People of New Castle County declared that "the poor have no laws; the laws are made by the rich and of course *for* the rich" and called upon members of the producing classes to "give your votes to no man who is not pledged to support your interests." Northern Workingmen would readily have recognized many of the demands the association raised, including calls for public education, the end of imprisonment for debt, a mechanics'-lien law, the reduction of taxes levied upon "the farmer, mechanic, and working man," freedom from homestead foreclosure, simplification of laws and legal procedures, and the elimination of property requirements for officeholding.

The focus on the legal system and on qualifications for voting and officeholding reflected the belated survival in the South of elitist norms of government. Effectively excluded from political life by post-Independence state constitutions drawn up by planters and their representatives, white southerners of little or no property now demanded equal rights. Some state legislatures responded soon. Elsewhere, as in Georgia, North Carolina, Virginia, and Maryland, the popular movement encountered stiffer opposition. In response, the reformers prepared to circumvent established state governments to achieve their goals. Mass meetings called provocative extralegal assemblies to draft new and more democratic state constitutions. One of these, convened in Georgia in 1831, pointedly reminded the populace that they "have an undoubted right, in their sovereign capacity, to alter or change their form of government, whenever in their opinion it becomes too obnoxious or oppressive to be borne. That crisis . . . has arrived, when the people should assert their rights, and boldly and fearlessly maintain them." The Georgia assembly called for the popular election of delegates to a constituent convention that it called on its own authority.

Confronted with such organized determination, Georgia's legislature relented. So did those of Maryland, Virginia, North Carolina, Mississippi, and Tennessee. During the 1830s, property qualifications for voting and officeholding were abolished in most southern states, and many appointive offices became elective. The Wilmington Association of Working People went even further, proposing that women be granted the vote as well. Women composed a majority of the population, it pointed out. "Wherefore should they be denied the immunities of free men? Does anyone deem that their interference in public affairs would be prejudicial to the general interest?"

But these reforms—those achieved as well as those still pursued—remained limited. Aimed at reducing the economic and political power exercised by the great planters over the lives of white farmers and craftsmen, this popular movement rarely addressed the basic source of the planters' power and of their own weakness—chattel slavery. Competition, actual or potential, from enslaved black artisans and laborers depressed the wages of white workers and the income of white farmers. At least equally important, a social structure, culture, and legal code based on a system of unfree labor frequently restricted the freedom of movement, organization, and protest of white workers.

There were whites in the South who were hostile to the slave regime. Southern antislavery societies—usually dominated by Quakers, Methodists, or Baptists—did exist during the first third of the century, especially in the upper South, where slavery was already beginning to decline. Perhaps some white craftsmen or farmers supported them. We know of instances in which white artisans and tenant farmers encouraged and even helped individual slaves to escape from their masters. Westward migration, in the meantime, drew an unknown number of discontented small property-owners out of the South and into the new states of Tennessee and Kentucky and on into southern Ohio, Indiana, Illinois, and Missouri. Living and holding a few slaves in Kentucky, Abraham Lincoln's father, Thomas, came to repudiate bound labor and joined an antislavery Baptist congregation there before moving on into Indiana and then Illinois.

The vast majority of southern white workers and farmers, however, neither left the slave states nor betrayed any sympathy for the slaves. Many evidently believed the enslavement of blacks bolstered the prosperity and liberties of all whites, slaveowning and slaveless alike. Others felt threatened by the slave system but tried simply to coexist with it while limiting its direct damage to themselves. Thus, white mechanics in the 1830s strove repeatedly to force blacks (slave and free alike) out of their occupations. Some politicians expressed sympathy for such demands, but to write them into law and enforce them would have limited the freedom of the

". . . SO CHEAPENED THE WHITE MAN'S LABOR"

Far from viewing black workers as allies, most southern white workers saw them as competitors to be excluded from their trades. Below is an open letter from a white Georgia artisan complaining in 1838 about black competition and demanding preferential treatment for white workers.

GENTLEMEN:

... I am aware that most of you have [such a] strong antipathy to encouraging the masonry and carpentry trades of your poor white brothers, that your predilections for giving employment in your line of business to ebony workers have either so cheapened the white man's labor, or expatriated hence with but a few solitary exceptions, all the white masons and carpenters of this town.

The white man is the only real, legal, moral, and civil proprietor of this country and state. . . . By white men alone was this continent discovered; by the prowess of white men alone (though not always properly or humanely exercised), were the fierce and active Indians driven occidentally: and if swarms and hordes of infuriated red men pour down from the Northwest, like the wintry blast thereof, the white men alone, aye, those to whom you decline to give money for bread and clothes, for their famishing families ... would bare their breasts to the keen and whizzing shafts of the savage crusaders—defending negroes too in the bargain, for if left to themselves without our aid, the Indians would or can sweep the negroes hence, "as dewdrops are shaken from the lion's mane."

The right, then, gentlemen, you will no doubt candidly admit, of the white man to employment in preference to negroes, who *must* defer to us since they live well enough on plantations, cannot be considered impeachable by contractors. . . . As masters of the polls in a majority, carrying all before them, I am surprised the poor do not elect faithful members to the Legislature, who will make it penal to prefer negro mechanic labor to white men's. . . .

Yours respectfully,
J. J. Flournoy

planters to make use of their property in whatever way they saw fit. No southern legislature was prepared to do that.

Angered by such failures but unwilling to champion emancipation, whites generally blamed their woes upon the helpless black population. Frederick Douglass remembered a white ship's carpenter in Maryland named Thomas Lanman who had murdered two slaves. Regularly boasting of the crime, Lanman added that "when others would do as much as he had done, they would be rid of the d—d niggers." Douglass experienced this attitude more directly in 1836. Hired out by his owner as a caulker in a Baltimore shipyard, Douglass was severely beaten by white workers who resented his presence among them. While such tactics occasionally achieved limited results—Douglass's master pulled him out of the shipyard—they left slavery intact, with the slaveowners astride southern society.

SLAVERY AND SECTIONAL CONFLICT

Many in the revolutionary generation had hoped for a different outcome. Especially after independence, prominent patriot planters like Washington and Jefferson expressed views about slavery that encouraged hopes for the system's eventual, peaceful demise. Human bondage, they then held, was an evil, unpleasant institution left over from the days of British colonialism; while it had unfortunately become too important to the region's economy to be uprooted immediately, it would undoubtedly decline with the passage of years.

This did not appear to be so farfetched. The Revolution certainly strengthened libertarian principles in the country, and proof of freedom's advance abounded. White indentured servitude disappeared in the early nineteenth century. In the northern states, an anemic slave system expired. Surely it could not survive much longer in the South alone. And, as though in promise of things to come, thousands of upper-South slaves did soon win individual manumission. But for the South, this proved a false spring of freedom. Beginning in the 1790s, the cotton boom brought not decline to southern slavery but revival and prosperity. Among southern whites, organized opposition to human bondage declined.

Before long, thus, the North and South found themselves dependent upon sharply differing labor systems. As they diverged in perceived needs as well as social, political, and even religious values, the future of chattel slavery became a source of mounting sectional friction. Jefferson's election and the decline of the Federalist Party (based in the Northeast) seemed to assure slaveowners a sympathetic central government. But how long would that remain true? In 1790, the populations of North and South were about equal, and so was their representation in Congress. But during the next few decades, the North's population grew faster, and the balance of power in Congress began to shift accordingly. By 1820, the slave states found themselves with just 42 percent of the votes in the House of Representatives; only in the Senate was parity maintained.

The long-term implications of these changes became clear in 1819. In that year, the Missouri Territory applied for admission to the Union as a slave state. New York congressman James Tallmadge, Jr., promptly confirmed planter fears that the North would apply its political power to weaken chattel slavery. As a condition for Missouri's statehood, Tallmadge proposed that no additional slaves be admitted within its borders and that all slave children born there following statehood be emancipated at age twenty-five. Although fourteen northern congressmen voted against Tallmadge's proposal, eighty-seven voted in favor, enough for a majority. The Senate, where the slaveowners were stronger, voted to impose no restrictions on slavery in Missouri. But the Senate alone could not admit a state into the Union.

Henry Clay, Speaker of the House, finally engineered a compromise. Missouri would be admitted with no restrictions on slavery. At the same time, the line of Missouri's southern border (at 36 degrees 30 minutes latitude) would be extended westward through the rest of the Louisiana Purchase. Henceforth, no territory north of that line would be admitted to the Union as a slave state. The Missouri Compromise also opened the way for the statehood of Maine, blocked in the Senate until the Missouri issue was resolved.

Many in the North bitterly denounced the 1820 compromise as a slaveholder victory. But planters were unhappy, too: the entire affair confirmed their suspicions about the North's attitude toward their labor system. And the freewheeling debate in Congress had given a public forum to subversive ideas. Free blacks living in the capital had filled the House galleries during the debates and listened intently to antislavery speeches. Who knew how far those words might travel? These fears multiplied when whites learned that slave revolutionary Denmark Vesey had encouraged his comrades of 1822 by reading from an antislavery speech by New York senator Rufus King.

Determined to block the use of federal power against slaveowner interests, South Carolina seized the political initiative. The tariff of 1828, known to southern critics as the "tariff of abominations," provided the pretext. Before the northern and southern economies began sharply to diverge, Carolinians such as John C. Calhoun had supported protectionism. By the early 1830s, however, they despised tariffs on imported manufactures as an arbitrary tax levied by the industrializing North upon the agricultural South. In November 1832, the state's planter leadership met in special convention and declared the tariff "null, void, no law, nor binding upon this state, its officers, or citizens." It would no longer be enforced or collected in the state.

Behind this stance stood sentiments stronger and calculations deeper than those connected simply with the tariff. By nullifying this federal law, South Carolina meant to serve notice that it would allow the federal government to impose upon it *no* law harmful to planter interests. The 1828 tariff was bad, explained low-country planter Robert J. Turnbull. But

> great as is this evil, it is perhaps the least of the evils which attend an abandonment of one iota of the principle in controversy. Our dispute involves questions of the most fearful import to the institutions and tranquillity of South Carolina. I fear to name them. The bare thought of these is enough to rouse us to resistance were there no other motive.

Though sympathetic toward his fellow planters, President Andrew Jackson considered the Carolinians' fears exaggerated and responded angrily to their attack on the federal government—of which he was, after all, chief executive. He promptly reinforced the federal fort in Charleston Harbor and obtained a "force bill" from Congress authorizing the use of the military to implement federal law. Once again, Henry Clay and others managed to fashion a compromise. Congress agreed to reduce tariffs over the next nine years, and in early 1833 South Carolina repealed its nullification act. But to demonstrate its continued belief in the right of states to veto federal law, South Carolina also nullified Jackson's force bill. This defiant gesture kept the states-rights claim alive, but it could not conceal the defeat of the nullification strategy at this stage.

ABOLITION AND REACTION

The fabulous success of King Cotton and the entrenchment of southern slavery led more and more opponents of the "peculiar institution" to abandon hopes for peaceful and gradual change. Imbued with faith in the North's "free-labor" system and inspired by the spirit of the Great Awakening, William Lloyd Garrison and a group of like-minded people embraced the demands for immediate abolition of slavery and full civil equality for blacks. Their journal, the *Liberator*, began publication in Boston on New Year's Day 1831.

This was not abolitionism's birth date. Groups of free blacks in Boston and other northern cities had espoused the same doctrine for decades. Garrison himself credited his "colored friends" with helping

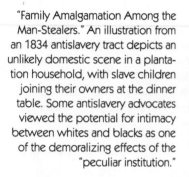

"Family Amalgamation Among the Man-Stealers." An illustration from an 1834 antislavery tract depicts an unlikely domestic scene in a plantation household, with slave children joining their owners at the dinner table. Some antislavery advocates viewed the potential for intimacy between whites and blacks as one of the demoralizing effects of the "peculiar institution."

him abandon the gradualism and colonization schemes characteristic of the earlier white antislavery movement. Five years before the *Liberator* appeared, members of the Massachusetts General Colored Association were already pursuing abolition and the advancement of free blacks. One of these people was David Walker, the freeborn son of a slave father. Walker had left his native North Carolina for Boston as a youth and there earned a living by selling new and used clothing. He soon became a leading figure in that city's growing free-black community and an agent and writer for the New York *Freedom's Journal*, the nation's first newspaper published by African-Americans.

In 1829, Walker published a seventy-six-page *Appeal*. It caused a sensation. Its militant tone and uncompromising message marked a fundamental breach with most earlier antislavery literature. Its very form indicated its departure: it was a call to action by the slaves rather than a plea for mercy from their owners. "Brethren," Walker urged, "arise, arise! Strike for your lives and liberties. Now is the day and the hour." When he did address white readers it was to hurl their principles in their faces, quoting to them "ALL MEN ARE CREATED EQUAL, that they are endowed by their Creator with certain inalienable rights; that among these are life, liberty, and the pursuit of happiness." Walker claimed for slaves the rights proclaimed "in this *Republican Land of Liberty*," adding: "and tell us no more about colonization, for America is as much our country as it is yours." "Remember, Americans," he warned, "that we must and shall be free, and enlightened as you are, will you wait until we shall, under God, obtain our liberty by the crushing arm of power? Will it not be dreadful for you? I speak, Americans, for your own good." During the *Liberator*'s first difficult years of existence, free blacks like Walker constituted a majority of its subscribers and the hard core of its circulation agents.

The abolitionist movement—along with slave revolts and the nullification crisis—led to some important changes in the behavior of slaveowners and their representatives. One of these altered the very manner in which they described chattel slavery. Previously referred to apologetically as a necessary but temporary evil, black bondage was now transformed (in John C. Calhoun's 1837 words) into "a good—a positive good," an institution beneficial alike to planters, slaves, and all other social groups.

Defenders of the new creed developed their arguments along two different lines. Some, like Calhoun himself, held up slave labor as in all respects superior to wage labor. Sharpening social conflicts in the North, this group held, testified to the superiority of outright bondage. "There is and has always been, in an advanced stage of wealth and civilization," Calhoun told the U.S. Senate, "a conflict between labor and capital. The condition of society in the South exempts us from the disorders and dangers resulting from this conflict." This fact demonstrated, he asserted, "how vastly more favorable our condition of society is to that of other sections for free and stable institutions." During the 1850s, George Fitzhugh, a spokesman of Virginia's tidewater planters, carried such reasoning to its logical conclusion. Since slavery was so far superior to other labor systems, he argued, it followed that *all* laboring classes ought to be enslaved. "Free society!" spat one Georgia newspaper. "We sicken at the name. What is it but a conglomeration of greasy mechanics, filthy operatives, small-fisted farmers, and moonstruck theorists . . . hardly fit for association with a southern gentleman's body servant."

"LET NO MAN OF US BUDGE ONE STEP . . ."

In a work that soon came to be known as Walker's Appeal, *Daniel Walker in 1829 demanded the complete and immediate emancipation of slaves in the United States, challenging the prevailing beliefs among most white critics of slavery that emancipation should come gradually and that free blacks should be sent abroad to distant colonies.*

WILL ANY OF us leave our homes and go to Africa? I hope not. Let them commence their attack upon us as they did on our brethren in Ohio, driving and beating us from our country, and my soul for theirs, they will have enough of it. Let no man of us budge one step, and let slaveholders come to beat us from our country. America is more our country, than it is the whites'—we have enriched it with our *blood and tears.* The greatest riches in all America have arisen from our blood and tears:—and will they drive us from our property and homes, which we have earned with our *blood*?

. . . Throw away your fears and prejudices then, and enlighten us and treat us like men, and we will like you more than we do now hate you; and tell us now no more about colonization, for America is as much our country, as it is yours.—Treat us like men, and there is no danger but we will all live in peace and happiness together. For we are not like you, hardhearted, unmerciful, and unforgiving. What a happy country this will be, if the whites will listen.

Although logically consistent, arguments like Calhoun's and Fitzhugh's failed to win wide popular support. Few slaveholders were ready to embrace so frankly antidemocratic a doctrine. Nor could many southern white working people cheer such ominous sentiments. The more popular defense of chattel slavery, therefore, increasingly distinguished between the character and rights of whites and of blacks, justifying slavery only for those of African ancestry.

In 1835, South Carolina's governor, George Duffie, explained to his state's legislature that blacks were "destined by providence" for bondage. They were "in all respects, physical, moral, and political, inferior to millions of the human race" and therefore "unfit for self-government of any kind." During the next twenty-five years, proslavery politicians, professors, physicians, and publicists dutifully elaborated the racist argument, offering a battery of pseudo-scientific "evidence" in its defense. Racist doctrine was scientific nonsense, but it served three important purposes for the slaveowners. First, it justified the bondage of African-Americans by ruling out all arguments based on universal human rights. Second, it undermined the status and claims of free blacks. Third, it accomplished both these objectives without explicitly threatening the rights of poor southern whites, whose support (or at least toleration) the slaveholders required.

"GUARDED FROM WANT, FROM BEGGARY SECURE . . ."

The following poem, entitled "The Hireling and the Slave," argues that slavery not only guaranteed a stable labor force but also benefited blacks by providing them with a secure life. The poem was written in 1856 by southerner William J. Grayson.

Taught by the master's efforts, by his care
Fed, clothed, protected many a patient year,
From trivial numbers now to millions grown,
With all the white man's useful arts their own,
Industrious, docile, skilled in wood and field,
To guide the plow, the sturdy axe to wield,
The Negroes schooled by slavery embrace
The highest portion of the Negro race;
And none the savage native will compare,
Of barbarous Guinea, with its offspring here.

If bound to daily labor while he lives,
His is the daily bread that labor gives;
Guarded from want, from beggary secure,
He never feels what hireling crowds endure,
Nor know, like them, in hopeless want to crave,
For wife and child, the comforts of the slave,
Or the sad thought that, when about to die,
He leaves them to the cold world's charity,
And sees them slowly seek the poor-house door—
The last, vile, hated refuge of the poor. . . .

The master's lighter rule insures
More order than the sternest code secures;
No mobs of factious workmen gather here,
No strikes we dread, no lawless riots fear; . . .

Seditious schemes in bloody tumults end,
Parsons incite, and senators defend,
But not where slaves their easy labors ply,
Safe from the snare, beneath a master's eye;
In useful tasks engaged, employed their time,
Untempted by the demagogue to crime,
Secure they toil, uncursed their peaceful life,
With labor's hungry broils and wasteful strife.
No want to good, no faction to deplore,
The slaves escape the perils of the poor.

THE NEGRO AS HE WAS.

THE NORTHERN LABORER.

THE NEGRO AS HE IS.

THE SOUTHERN LABORER.

The benefits of slavery. Two pages from a proslavery tract published around 1860 present the contrasting fates of unfree and free labor: while fortunate slaves are civilized and, in old age, cared for by benevolent masters, the northern wage worker faces only exhaustion and destitution.

The South could now stand firmly behind its "peculiar institution." By 1858, James Henry Hammond, a governor of South Carolina and later U.S. senator, could recall that in the days of Washington and Jefferson, the South had "believed slavery to be an evil—weakness—disgrace—nay a sin." Fortunately, however, "a few bold spirits took the question up; they compelled the South to investigate it anew and thoroughly, and what is the result? Why, it would be difficult to find a southern man who feels the system to be the slightest burden on his conscience."

"Free Negroes in the North."
Apologists for slavery often
constructed a grotesque picture of
free blacks in the North. According
to this etching published during the
Civil War, without the supervision
of benevolent masters, northern
African-Americans descended into
violence and degradation.

Planters defended their society with more than rhetoric. Beginning in the late 1820s and 1830s and steadily escalating through the Civil War, the master class launched a reign of terror aimed at suppressing all those deemed dangerous to the institution of chattel slavery. Southern free blacks became a special target of this campaign. They were known to aid runaway slaves. The appearance of free-black districts in southern cities gave runaways havens in which they might go undetected by white society. Demands by free blacks for greater civil freedoms stimulated parallel ideas among slaves. Free-black schools and churches could offer slaves assistance and models that planters strove hard to deny them. Indeed, the very status of "free black" offered slaves a goal to which they could aspire. Free black Denmark Vesey's attempted revolt gave shape and substance to all such planter fears. Individual manumission now became more difficult and rarer than ever, and state governments moved to strip free blacks of the few liberties they had previously won.

Repression broadened over time. Convinced that Prosser, Vesey, and Turner had all been inspired by antislavery writings, Virginia and North Carolina declared it illegal to teach slaves to read. State and local governments suppressed opposition to—and even querulous doubts about—chattel slavery. This ban covered books, newspapers, schools, politics, and all other public forums. Meanwhile, Georgia offered a $5,000 reward for the trial and conviction "under the laws of this state" of William Lloyd Garrison. A reward of $1,000 was offered for the delivery of David Walker's corpse, $10,000 if he were captured and returned to the South alive.

Results were achieved either through law or by extralegal mob action. In July 1835, a Charleston crowd broke into the local post office, seized stacks of antislavery literature, and publicly set them afire. State officials endorsed the deed, and Andrew Jackson's postmaster general, Amos Kendall, refused to interfere. Any postmaster refusing to deliver "inflammatory papers," Kendall thought, "would stand justified before the country and all mankind." In his annual message to Congress that year, President Jackson went still further, calling for legislation to prohibit, "under severe penalties, the circulation in the Southern States, through the mail, of incendiary publications intended to instigate the slaves to insurrection."

NORTHERN WORKERS AND THE ANTISLAVERY MOVEMENT

The crushing of slave rebellions, the campaign against southern free blacks, and the crackdown on southern civil liberties all failed to break antislavery resistance. On the contrary, hardnosed planter tactics helped increase northern sympathy for abolitionism. In 1832–33, this growing support made possible the founding of the American Antislavery Society. In the next few years, the AAS spread its literature throughout the country. By 1836 it had printed and distributed more than a million pieces of literature, mostly by mail, some of them in the South.

Ever since the 1790s, antislavery petitions had been sent to Congress from various parts of the country. During the AAS's first few years in this field, the number of petitions reaching Congress soared from a mere twenty-three to more than four hundred thousand. But planters were no more tolerant of antislavery propaganda in Congress than in the mails. As the petitions proliferated, southern congressmen insisted that the House of Representatives reject them without consideration. By May 1836, the House instituted a regular "gag rule" according to which "all petitions, memorials, resolutions, propositions, or papers relating in any way or to any extent whatever to the subject of slavery" shall be tabled and "no further action shall be taken thereon." Similar rules held sway until 1844. But the petitions continued to pour in. Those arriving during 1838 and 1839 alone, according to one estimate, contained more than two million signatures.

Who signed these petitions? We can get some idea by returning to New York City. Between 1829 and 1839, New Yorkers sent thirteen petitions to Congress urging the abolition of slavery in the District of

Columbia. (They picked Washington, D.C., because that was one place where Congress exercised direct and undisputed rule.) About four in every ten known signatories were craftsmen, and three in ten were small shopkeepers. The signatures of three groups of craftsmen appear with marked frequency—shoe- and leatherworkers, printers, and those employed in the garment trades. These were the occupations suffering the most severe attacks as a result of the city's industrialization. Stepped-up conflict in these trades fostered an atmosphere unusually friendly to radical doctrines. The democratic impulse that led these workers to demand equal rights for themselves helped make them opponents of slavery.

Workingmen's Party leader George Henry Evans voiced this outlook. "We are now convinced," he wrote, that "EQUAL RIGHTS can never be enjoyed, even by those who are free, in a nation which contains slaveites enough to hold in bondage two millions of human beings." Evans published the only newspaper in the city (the *Daily Sentinel*) that defended Nat Turner's insurrection. Regretting the bloodshed, Evans blamed it on the slaveowners themselves, noting that the rebels

> no doubt thought that their only hope . . . was to put to death, indiscriminately, the whole race of those who held them in bondage. If such were their impressions, were they not justifiable in doing so? Undoubtedly they were, if freedom is the birthright of man, as the declaration of independence tells us. . . . Those who kept them in slavery and ignorance alone are answerable for their conduct.

But most white workers shared the racist attitudes of the surrounding society. They despised slavery, slaves, and free blacks alike, regarding all three as inherently degraded and dangerous to independent labor and republican order. The proportionally tiny black population of the free states lived on the margin of society, confined to menial and low-paid occupations. Few black males could obtain work above the level of unskilled laborer, coachman, waiter, or barber. Women subsisted as domestic servants, laundresses, and dressmakers. They were excluded economically and treated as pariahs socially. As Frederick Douglass recalled, free blacks of the North were routinely

> denied the privileges and courtesies common to others in the use of the most humble means of conveyance—shut out from the cabins on steamboats, refused admission to respectable hotels, caricatured, scorned, scoffed, mocked, and maltreated by anyone, no matter how black his heart, so he has a white skin.

Bolstered by southern-born migrants, one midwestern state after another went even further, legally excluding free blacks altogether during the antebellum era. Those white working people who considered such treatment just were of course opposed to abolitionism. Newspapers and politicians warned them that emancipation would send a torrent of former slaves northward, there to drive down the wages and respect enjoyed by white labor.

But even workers who opposed slavery withheld active support from the abolitionist movement for some time. Even among those sympathetic to the slaves themselves, few felt strongly enough to commit their time and energy to the cause. Most were preoccupied with more immediate economic goals, seeing little connection between these and the question of slavery in the South.

Abolitionists did little to explain that connection. Led by businessmen, clergy, and others who enthused about the benefits of the North's emerging system of industrial capitalism, the organized abolitionists often expressed contempt for trade unions and workingmen's parties. The grievances of those legally enslaved were obvious to Garrison, but how could those enjoying legal freedom claim to be similarly oppressed? Under the "free-labor system," he believed, the worthy and hardworking were rewarded and only the lazy and undeserving remained poor. On this question, in short, Garrison endorsed the viewpoint of northern employers. "The worst enemies of the people," Garrison judged, were those who told the "poor and vulgar" to view "the opulent as the natural enemies of the laboring classes."

So matters stood until the abolitionists' campaign of pamphlets and letters triggered a series of riots against them, not only in the South but in the North as well. In Cincinnati and Utica, antiabolitionist mobs included many prominent merchants and allied professionals from old and established families. They were men rooted in the declining system of merchants' capital, who felt threatened by abolitionism as by all causes hostile to inequality and special privilege.

Just such a figure organized the 1834 antiabolitionist attacks in New York City. The editor of the New York *Courier and Enquirer*, James Watson Webb, saw himself as the champion of an older and more refined America, the America of gentlemen merchants. Webb even tried to live out his nostalgia, fighting duels, beating impudent "inferiors" on the streets with his walking cane. But for the antiabolitionist and antiblack violence, Webb found skilled workingmen to do his bidding.

George Henry Evans promptly denounced the attacks as assaults on the civil liberties essential in a democratic republic. As for the targets of the violence, Evans observed, "Let the mobites imagine themselves in the situation of the blacks, and if they have any feeling of manhood about them they will cease their senseless opposition to a righteous cause."

SLAVERY AND WESTWARD EXPANSION

Despite other differences, most antebellum northerners agreed on at least one issue—the need to facilitate rapid settlement of the western territories. Speculators, promoters, merchants, and manufacturers enthused over business prospects there. Small proprietors and working people valued the greater economic independence and security that life in the newer West seemed to offer.

A parallel consensus had grown up in the South, likewise buttressed by economic, social, and political considerations. Two human currents flowing into the same underpopulated region need not cause more than minor cultural frictions and readjustments. But in the circumstances at hand, it meant rivalry, conflict, and ultimately full-scale war, because each group carried with it not just different customs and values but the irreconcilably opposed systems of labor, social relations, and politics that characterized the North and South. Postponed for decades by both Democratic and Whig politicians, the decisive confrontation between free-labor and slave-labor societies finally occurred during the contest for the West.

Proslavery forces demanded western expansion for a variety of reasons. For one thing, soil there was considerably more fertile than in the Southeast. Greater fertility meant richer yields and higher profits, a pressing consideration for commercial planters. The southwestward spread of the slave-labor system also aided planters in the upper South, where slavery was declining, by giving them a place to sell their excess slaves at a profit.

Planters needed to expand their system for social and political reasons as well. Within the South, friction dogged relations among different sectors of the white agricultural population. Planters insisted that the slave system benefited all southerners, a claim that won widespread support among other low-country whites as well. But the passage of time was steadily reducing the relative size of the planter class. By 1830, almost two-thirds of all southern white families owned no slaves at all. Three decades later, the slaveless constituted three-quarters of the white population. This development worried planters and poor farmers alike, and threatened to further alienate the upper and lower strata of rural white society. As in the North, such worries directed attention westward. Perhaps, in the rich and open land of the territories, small farmers might find greater economic opportunity. They might even enter the privileged ranks of the slaveowners.

A third factor, and possibly the most important one, stimulated the slaveowners' appetite for new territory—the very rapid growth of a non-slaveholding and increasingly antislavery North. To prevent the free states from using the federal government against the interests of slaveholders, the latter needed to retain equal representation in the Senate, if not in the House of Representatives. That meant admitting one new slave state into the Union for every free one.

All these considerations impelled the geographical extension of slavery: it was a matter of expand or die. "There is not a slaveholder in this House or out of it," one Georgia politician told Congress in the 1850s, "but who knows perfectly well that whenever slavery is confined within certain specified limits, its future existence is doomed." Like-minded congressmen and presidents cast hungry glances at Cuba and other Caribbean and Central American states. Proslavery adventurers mounted invasions of Mexico, Cuba, and Nicaragua. Most importantly, attempts to expand the domain of slavery led to the annexation of Texas and the outbreak of full-scale war with Mexico in 1846.

Americans had already begun to settle in the Mexican province of Coahuila-Texas by the beginning of the century, but systematic colonization began in earnest during the 1820s, organized by Virgina-born Stephen Austin. Most of those rallying to Austin's colony came from the trans-Allegheny South plus Missouri. By the summer of 1832, the number of settlers was nearly six thousand and growing fast. Although Mexico formally outlawed slavery in 1829, about a thousand slaves continued to live in the province. Austin had secured a special provincial law permitting slavery to operate under a different name—"permanent indentured servitude."

Initially cordial, relations with the Mexican government quickly soured due to continuing conflicts over slavery, tariffs, and especially the increasingly open maneuvers of the United States to annex Texas. In 1835, hostilities finally broke out between the Mexican regime and the American colonists. Early the next year, four thousand troops under the Mexican nationalist leader Antonio López de Santa Anna advanced on San Antonio. On the way, they wiped out a small force of American rebels entrenched at the Alamo mission. On April 21, however, a rebel army under Sam Houston decimated Santa Anna's troops on the banks of the San Jacinto River.

The new Republic of Texas was now a fact, and its leaders quickly sought U.S. statehood. Northern hostility to admitting this immense slaveholding republic deferred annexation for nearly a decade. In 1844, however, the Democratic Party platform bracketed support for Texas annexation with the demand—popular among northern farmers—for the annexation of all of Oregon (a region claimed by both England and the United States). Farmers from the Old Northwest had been eyeing Oregon's Willamette Valley for years; by 1843 thousands of wagons were already following the Oregon Trail west from Missouri. Since it was clear that Oregon would soon become a territory, Congress approved the annexation of the Lone Star republic in December 1845.

Not satisfied with Texas, newly elected president James Polk, a Tennessee Democrat, turned his attention to the rest of Mexico early the next year. Additional annexations required war, which his administration promptly provoked. "As war exists," the president then told Congress, "we are called upon by every consideration of duty and patriotism to vindicate with decision the honor, the rights, and the interests of our country." Many Americans agreed. Illinois representative Stephen A. Douglas, fervent champion of westward expansion, helped boost the war spirit in Congress and branded critics "traitors." Most slaveholders eagerly looked forward to carving new slave states out of the additional lands to be won. "Every battle fought in Mexico," cheered the Charleston *Courier* of South Carolina,

> and every dollar spent there, but insures the acquisition of territory which must widen the field of Southern enterprise and power in the future. And the final result will be to readjust the power of the confederacy, so as to give us control over the operation of government in all time to come.

Elsewhere, however, the war was seen as a slaveholders' adventure, which encouraged opposition. A majority in the House of Representatives objected that the war had been "unnecessarily and unconstitutionally begun by the President of the United States." And while a prowar demonstration on May 20, 1846, occupied one part of New York's City Hall Park, George Henry Evans and John Commerford addressed an antiwar rally in another. Having "great reason to believe" that the Mexican War was the work of Texans and their business allies, the meeting urged "the Commander in Chief of the army to withdraw his forces, now on the Rio Grande, to some undisputed land belonging to the United States." And if war proved finally unavoidable, the meeting concluded, then the American sponsors of prowar meetings and messages "ought to be the first to volunteer, and the first to leave for the seat of war." Opposition found strength among northeastern farmers and some businessmen, too. The Massachusetts state legislature denounced the war and its "triple object of extending slavery, of strengthening the 'Slave Power,' and of obtaining control of the Free States" by gaining a slave-state majority in the Senate.

This vocal opposition probably cut the war short, but it could not prevent Mexico's further dismemberment. In March 1848, the Senate approved a peace treaty giving the provinces of California and New Mexico to the United States and moving the Texas-Mexican border southward from the Nueces River to the Rio Grande.

Victory over Mexico transferred almost 1.2 million square miles of land—half Mexico's national territory—and nearly eighty thousand Spanish-speaking people, mostly of mixed Spanish-Indian descent, to

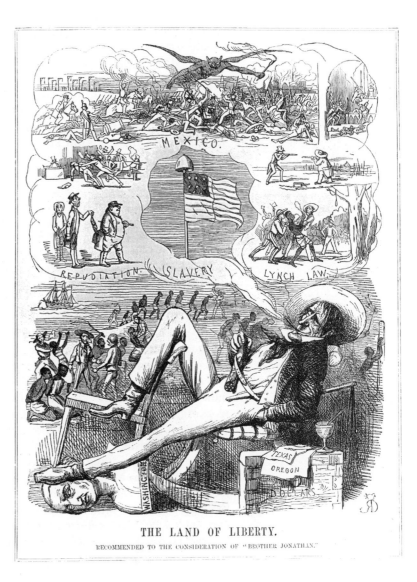

THE LAND OF LIBERTY.
RECOMMENDED TO THE CONSIDERATION OF "BROTHER JONATHAN."

Actions speak louder than words: "The Land of Liberty" is the ironic title of this cartoon published in an 1847 edition of the British satirical weekly *Punch*.

the United States. These people would perform the low-paid labor needed to make agriculture, ranching, mining, and industry in the region profitable. The discovery of gold in California buoyed the entire national economy and added to an already substantial westward population shift. By 1860, furthermore, some thirty-five thousand Chinese had immigrated to California, mostly to work in the mining camps. This vast expansion exhilarated many Americans. Didn't the war demonstrate the country's growing military prowess and finally seal its "manifest destiny" to dominate the continent from sea to sea?

As it turned out, however, it also greatly sharpened the internal conflict in the United States by drastically raising the stakes. The debate over what to do with the new land—specifically, whether to permit slavery there—aroused emotions that ultimately produced civil war.

Congressman David Wilmot, a Pennsylvania Democrat, opened the debate in 1846, when President Polk had barely gotten his war with Mexico under way. At Wilmot's initiative, the House of Representatives voted to prohibit slavery in any territory acquired through that war. Though defeated in the Senate, the Wilmot Proviso by 1849 had nonetheless received the endorsement of all but one northern state legislature.

Wilmot's attempt to block slavery in the West won widespread and fervent support among common people in the free states. Some opposed slavery and even racial discrimination anywhere. This sentiment was strongest in New England, where an 1846 convention of working people protested the fact that "there are at the present time three millions of our brethren and sisters groaning in chains on the Southern plantations." Wishing "not only to be consistent but to secure to all others those rights and privileges for which we are contending ourselves," the convention declared its refusal to do anything "to keep three millions of our brethren and sisters in bondage" and called upon other labor groups "to speak out in thunder tones" along the same lines. (The Richmond, Virginia, *Enquirer*, on the other hand, ridiculed the shoe workers of Lynn, Massachusetts—"a people working all day on brogan shoes for the negroes at the South," but "who go to Abolition prayer meetings at night.")

But Wilmot drew strong support even from the majority not yet committed to nationwide abolition, much less to political or social equality between black and white. Wilmot himself vigorously denied feeling any "morbid sympathy for the slave" and objected to seeing his proposal described "as one designed especially for the benefit of the black race." He preferred dubbing it the "White Man's Proviso." George Henry Evans, once an outspoken enemy of slavery, became convinced that the fight against chattel slavery must be postponed until the war against wage slavery was won.

But if most northerners disdained blacks and, while disliking slavery, also feared the effects of abolition, they also hotly opposed the extension of slavery beyond its present borders. Northern farmers wanted western lands held free for settlement as homesteads, and many urban working people shared the farmers' dream. This was the sentiment that Evans and other land-reformers had so effectively tapped. These would-be western farmers did not want those lands preempted by slave plantations. Other urban workers and small producers hoped eventually to populate the West's towns and cities. They had no desire to dwell among slaves and slaveowners, nor to compete with slave labor, nor to face the multiple indignities, political restrictions, industrial stagnation, and depressed wages and conditions that they believed slavery had imposed upon free white workers in the South. Even those workers and farmers who expected to remain in the East wanted the West kept free for their children and grandchildren.

To all these people, slavery signified the death of everything they cherished or aspired to—personal independence, mutual respect, political equality, the right to enjoy the fruits of their own labor. In criticizing their own employers, therefore, Lynn shoemakers, Lowell mill operatives, and so many other workers equated them with slaveowners. That is also why, when protesting their own condition, they referred to themselves as wage slaves. With so negative a view of slavery, they could hardly relish having the institution gain new vigor by spreading further west. Though only a minority of all northern workers were abolitionists, that was true partly because most others expected slavery to remain restricted to the South until it eventually died out—but that would not happen if slave territory were increased.

This explains why the Wilmot Proviso was so appealing, and why local free-soil clubs sprang up so quickly throughout the Northeast and upper Midwest in 1846. By joining these clubs, workers, farmers, and shopkeepers—native-born and immigrant alike—announced that they would not tolerate chattel slavery in the territories acquired from Mexico.

The nation had reached a turning point. By waging and winning the Mexican War, Polk fused the issues of land reform ("free land") and opposition to the spread of chattel slavery ("free soil"). In the process, he confounded all those who considered them distinct or even counterposed questions.

The dispute over the spread of slavery now took center stage in American politics and stayed there for the next decade and a half, splintering the two main political parties, Whigs and Democrats

This 1848 lithograph cartoon comments on the formation of the Free-Soil Party in 1848. Free-Soil presidential candidate Martin Van Buren, whose political career included alliances with slaveholding interests, is shown entering a "marriage of convenience" with the forces of the antislavery Liberty Party. The racial stereotypes are typical of the visual representation of African-Americans in the antebellum period.

alike. In 1840, abolitionists had formed the Liberty Party and were soon running candidates for office. In 1844, their presidential candidate, James G. Birney, received 62,300 votes, about 3 percent of the free-state total. Four years later, ex-president Martin Van Buren bolted Democratic ranks to become the candidate of the new Free-Soil Party. Though not an abolitionist, Van Buren ran on a platform that coupled opposition to the westward spread of slavery with support for "the *free* grant [of land] to *actual settlers.*" Some leading land-reformers participated in the Free-Soil Party's founding convention, and in some midwestern states the influence of land-reformers in the new party was especially obvious.

Although some wealthy northerners like Gerrit Smith were active abolitionists, most of the economic elite saw matters very differently. In most cases morally opposed to slavery, they opposed the organized antislavery movement with still greater energy. Their reasons were many: A mass campaign against slavery would dangerously polarize

MARRIAGE OF THE FREE SOIL AND LIBERTY PARTIES.

the nation. It would infuriate the slaveowners, whom the northern elite counted on as business and political partners. It would undermine the two major political parties and threaten the federal union itself. Whig leader and financier Philip Hone characteristically denounced Free-Soilers as "Ishmaelites whose hand is against everybody, the firebrands who are ready to tear down the edifice of government to erect altars for the worship of their own idols."

Still, Free-Soil candidate Van Buren received almost 300,000 votes in 1848, nearly one ballot in every seven cast in the free states that year. Especially successful among small farmers, the Free-Soil Party found support among certain industrial workers as well. Lynn shoemakers proved quite receptive, and the party carried that city. Three years later, in 1851, Free-Soilers and Democrats combined forces in Lowell to elect a slate of state legislators pledged to both the ten-hour workday and the containment of slavery. That same year, the new German Sozialistischer Turnerbund, a large athletic, cultural, and political organization, announced that it "in general subscribes to the principles underlying the radical Free-Soil Party and urges all members to support that party in every way possible." German Free-Soilers of New York City vowed "to carry out land-reform measures in the most radical manner" and announced themselves "strictly opposed to Slavery in whatever shape it might be seen."

Free-black spokesmen Samuel Ringold Ward, Henry Highland Garnet, Charles L. Remond, Henry Bibb, and Frederick Douglass all attended the first Free-Soil convention. Many other free blacks likewise supported that party as an opening wedge in the larger fight against slavery everywhere. They did so despite the new party's rejection of abolitionism *per se* and despite the antiblack sentiments expressed by some party leaders. Events themselves, they felt, would force free-soilers to reexamine these prejudices. "It is nothing against the actors in this new movement," wrote Frederick Douglass later,

> that they did not see the end from the beginning—that they did not at first take the high ground that further on in the conflict their successors felt themselves called upon to take. . . . In all this and more it illustrates the experience of reform in all ages, and conforms to the laws of human progress.

THE COMPROMISE OF 1850

The next act of the drama also revolved around the issues raised by the Mexican War. The Gold Rush of 1849, which carried thousands of emigrants into California Territory, raised the question of statehood. In 1850, congressional leaders considering California's appli-

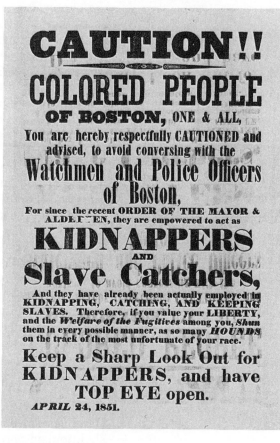

CAUTION!!
COLORED PEOPLE
OF BOSTON, ONE & ALL,
You are hereby respectfully CAUTIONED and advised, to avoid conversing with the
Watchmen and Police Officers of Boston,
For since the recent ORDER OF THE MAYOR & ALDERMEN, they are empowered to act as
KIDNAPPERS
AND
Slave Catchers,
And they have already been actually employed in KIDNAPPING, CATCHING, AND KEEPING SLAVES. Therefore, if you value your LIBERTY, and the *Welfare of the Fugitives* among you, *Shun* them in every possible manner, as so many *HOUNDS* on the track of the most unfortunate of your race.

Keep a Sharp Look Out for KIDNAPPERS, and have TOP EYE open.
APRIL 24, 1851.

The Fugitive-Slave Law. A notice posted by Boston abolitionist Theodore Parker in 1851.

cation attempted to defuse the free-soil issue once and for all. A series of resolutions adopted after lengthy debate rejected the idea of forbidding slavery in the West by federal law. California was admitted to the Union as a free state. New Mexico and Utah became territories without the federal government's prohibiting slavery there. To placate the antislavery population, another bill banned the slave trade (but not slavery itself) in the District of Columbia. To sweeten the pot for the slaveowners, on the other hand, a new Fugitive-Slave Law was enacted, denying jury trials to accused runaway slaves and empowering any marshal pursuing them to force local citizens to join the hunt.

One target of the new law was the "underground railroad," a network of thousands of free blacks and white sympathizers who concealed, guided, housed, clothed, and sheltered runaway slaves in the course of their northward flight. The best-known of these "conductors" was Harriet Tubman, who escaped from slavery in Maryland only in 1849. During the next decade, Tubman returned to the South nineteen times, repeatedly risking recapture and summary punishment, in order to liberate more than three hundred others. In the North, local vigilance committees kept the railroad functioning. Much of its meager funds came from impoverished free blacks. Members of the New York committee were able to pledge only fifty cents a month; those in Philadelphia, even less.

During the last prewar decade, the number of successful escapes increased markedly, especially from the slave states that bordered the free North. Though many slaves escaped through the underground railroad, more made their way with the help of only one or two people. The escapes affected far more than the few thousand directly involved; news traveled through the slaves' "grapevine telegraph," emboldening many others still in bondage. At the same time, recent escapees like Frederick Douglass became the most powerful and effective antislavery spokespeople in the country. The new Fugitive-Slave Law, its proponents hoped, would not only reduce the number of escapes but also drive earlier escapees like Douglass and Tubman back into hiding.

Leaders of both major parties congratulated themselves on the 1850 compromise. They believed they had finally buried the dangerous slavery issue and thereby rescued the Union from conflict and division. "Much . . . may be effected by a conciliatory temper and

Unveiled. After passage of the Fugitive-Slave Law, escaped slave women living in the North sometimes wore veils when they appeared in public to avoid identification by slave-catchers.

discreet measures," declared prominent Whig Philip Hone. "All praise to the defenders of the Union!" Former Democratic presidential candidate Lewis Cass (whose defeat in 1848 owed much to competition from the Free-Soil Party) in 1850 declared confidently, "I do not believe any party could now be built in relation to this question of slavery. I think the question is settled in the public mind." Political and business leaders organized mass meetings in New York, Boston, Philadelphia, Pittsburgh, and Cincinnati, in support of the 1850 compromise.

Many workers and farmers also approved the new agreement in hopes that it would prevent the disruption of the Union. Many, but not all. Mass meetings denounced the compromise for failing to outlaw slavery in the West and for including a fugitive-slave law. In June, the land-reformers of the National Industrial Congress denounced slavery as a "moral, social, and political evil" and decried "the idea that to satisfy the South, and to secure the perpetuation of the Federal Union, the people of the United States must agree that the Slave as well as the Free Area shall be extended." A large anticompromise meeting in Allegheny City, near Pittsburgh, heard land-reformer John Ferral, veteran of the Workingmen's movement of the twenties and thirties, attack the Fugitive-Slave Law in strong terms. Speaking for the free-soil movement's most democratic wing, Ferral proposed a state constitutional amendment enfranchising black males, and the meeting approved his proposal. Antislavery Whigs like John P. Hale, Salmon P. Chase, William

---

"WHAT A DISGRACE TO A CITY CALLING ITSELF FREE . . ."

Harriet Brent Jacobs's Incidents in the Life of a Slave Girl, *published in 1861, was one of the few narratives of slavery written by a woman. Having escaped from her master in 1845, Jacobs—along with other fugitive slaves—found herself once more imperiled when Congress passed the Fugitive-Slave Law. She here describes the impact of the 1850 law on the African-American community of New York City.*

ABOUT THE time that I reentered the Bruce family, an event occurred of disastrous import to the colored people. The slave Hamlin [James Hamlet], the first fugitive that came under the new law, was given up by the bloodhounds of the north to the bloodhounds of the south. It was the beginning of a reign of terror to the colored population. The great city rushed on in its whirl of excitement, taking no note of the "short and simple annals of the poor." But while fashionables were listening to the thrilling voice of Jenny Lind in Metropolitan Hall, the thrilling voices of poor hunted colored people went up, in an agony of supplication, to the Lord, from Zion's church. Many families, who had lived in the city for twenty years, fled from it now. Many a poor washerwoman, who, by hard labor, had made herself a comfortable home, was obliged to sacrifice her furniture, bid a hurried farewell to friends, and seek her fortune among strangers in Canada. Many a wife discovered a secret she had never known before—that her husband was a fugitive, and must leave her to insure his own safety. Worse still, many a husband discovered that his wife had fled from slavery years ago, and as "the child follows the condition of its mother," the children of his love were liable to be seized and carried to slavery. Everywhere, in those humble homes, there was consternation and anguish. But what cared the legislators of the "dominant race" for the blood they were crushing out of trampled hearts?

. . . I was subject to it; and so were hundreds of intelligent and industrious people all around us. I seldom ventured into the streets; and when it was necessary to do an errand for Mrs. Bruce, or any of the family, I went as much as possible through back streets and by-ways. What a disgrace to a city calling itself free, that inhabitants, guiltless of offence, and seeking to perform their duties conscientiously, should be condemned to live in such incessant fear, and have nowhere to turn for protection! This state of things, of course, gave rise to many impromptu vigilance committees. Every colored person, and every friend of their persecuted race, kept their eyes wide open.

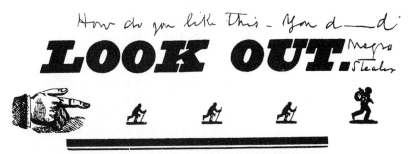

"Negro Dogs." An 1856 advertisement for track dogs.

Seward, George Julian, Thaddeus Stevens, Benjamin Wade, and Charles Sumner rode into Congress on the crest of this popular reaction. Others embarked upon direct action. In Boston, Philadelphia, Syracuse, Chicago, and elsewhere, blacks and their white allies used force to protect fugitives from their hunters, sometimes attacking and even killing the pursuers. It was against this background that *Uncle Tom's Cabin*, Harriet Beecher Stowe's 1852 story about slavery and slave-hunters, appeared as a serial in an abolitionist newspaper. When published as a book, it sold 300,000 copies in one year, electrifying northern readers.

Contrary to the hopes of its sponsors, then, the Fugitive-Slave Law inflamed antislavery feeling in the country. So long as slavery seemed geographically contained and remote, free-state residents could try to ignore it, considering it someone else's worry and someone else's sin. But by welcoming slave-hunters into the free states and requiring even antislavery citizens to aid them, the new law put an end to those illusions. Like the Mexican War a few years earlier, the Fugitive-Slave Law seemed to bear out the abolitionist claim that chattel slavery endangered freedom everywhere, not merely in the South.

As if seeking to confirm that thesis, Democratic senator Stephen A. Douglas of Illinois presented his Kansas-Nebraska Bill to Congress in January 1854, to speed the creation of new states in the land of the Louisiana Purchase. Kansas and Nebraska both fell north of the latitude of Missouri's southern border; by the terms of the Missouri Compromise, therefore, they should have been admitted as free states. To win the support of southern senators, Douglas added a provision explicitly annulling the Missouri Compromise, thus removing all federal barriers to the spread of slavery throughout the entire West. Douglas's doctrine of "popular sovereignty" left the future of slavery in each individual territory or state to be decided locally. The Senate passed the Kansas-Nebraska Act on March 3. On May 22, the House added its assent by a narrow margin, and Democratic president Franklin Pierce signed it into law a week later.

The response was nearly instantaneous. Antislavery congressmen Salmon P. Chase, Charles Sumner, Gerrit Smith, Joshua Giddings, Edward Wade, and Alexander De Witt issued an impassioned and widely circulated manifesto calling the new law "a criminal betrayal of precious rights." In the West, they said, "it has been expected, freedom-loving emigrants from Europe, and energetic and intelligent laborers from our own land, will find homes of comfort and fields of useful enterprise." But Douglas's law would turn this great expanse "into a dreary region of despotism, inhabited by masters and slaves." That alone would exclude free labor, since "freemen, unless pressed by a hard and cruel necessity, will not, and should not, work beside slaves. Labor cannot be respected where any class of laborers is held in abject bondage."

Freedom or Death. Soon after passage of the Fugitive-Slave Law, Margaret Garner fled from her Kentucky master with her four children. Slave patrollers followed her to Ohio. Faced with capture, Garner killed two of her children rather than have them return to slavery. The surviving children were taken from her and, on the return trip to Kentucky, Garner drowned herself in the Ohio River. Her story inspired an acclaimed nineteenth-century painting by Thomas S. Noble (on which this engraving is based) and Toni Morrison's Pulitzer Prize novel, *Beloved*.

"A Bold Stroke for Freedom." On Christmas Eve, 1855, patrollers finally caught up with a group of teenaged slaves who had escaped by wagon from Loudon County, Virginia. But the posse was driven off when Ann Wood, leader of the group, brandished weapons and dared the pursuers to fire. The fugitives continued on to Philadelphia.

Widely reprinted, and translated, this appeal realized its intended effect. A wave of anger that dwarfed opposition to the 1850 compromise swept the North and West. By the time the House passed Douglas's bill, more than three hundred rallies had mobilized tens of thousands of people of all social backgrounds espousing all shades of free-soil sentiment.

At one end of the spectrum stood some of the leading merchants and bankers in major northern cities. Long advocates of compromise and friendly relations with the slaveowners, they now pled with the South to withdraw the bill in order to avoid inflaming the already dangerous antislavery sentiment in the North. Boston merchant and Whig leader Amos Lawrence begged the slaveowners to "pause before they proceed further to disturb the peace which we hoped the Compromise of 1850 would have made perpetual." His counterparts in Newark regretted that the bill threatened to "open anew the whole controversy and conflict between the free and slaveholding states," a polarization "destructive of peace and harmony of the States, dangerous to the interests of the Republic, and causing serious apprehensions for the perpetuity of the Republic."

At the other end of the free-soil spectrum stood those opposed to slavery everywhere. Such people denounced the Kansas-Nebraska Bill not for causing bad sectional feelings but because (as one meeting declared) it "authorizes the further extension of slavery," while "we have, do now, and shall continue to protest most emphatically against both white and black slavery."

Between the compromisers and the antislavery militants, finally, stood many others who insisted that the West be kept free for white settlement alone. A resolution adopted at a free-soil meeting in Pittsburgh in 1854 conveyed this sentiment:

> If the Douglas Nebraska bill should ever go into peaceful operation, which we doubt, it would completely Africanize the heart of the North American continent and divide the Free States of the Atlantic from the Free States of the Pacific by colonies of African boundmen and thereby exclude the free white race of the North from lands purchased by the whole nation from France. . . .

During the next two years, Kansas-Nebraska flames burned even higher as free-soil and proslavery forces alike began pouring into Kansas. Confronted by a free-soil majority, the proslavery forces quickly resorted to armed intimidation and violence. When antislavery forces

Bleeding Kansas. A daguerreotype of a free-state artillery battery, taken in Topeka, Kansas Territory, during the summer of 1856.

In 1859 the Kansas abolitionist Dr. John Doy, called a slave-stealer by his enemies for his forays into Missouri to free slaves, was kidnapped by proslavery partisans and imprisoned in Missouri. This photograph shows Doy surrounded by the friends who subsequently rescued him.

responded, undeclared guerrilla war followed. One of those involved was a man named John Brown.

Standard accounts commonly portray Brown as a solitary, atypical, even bizarre individual. And there is some truth in that portrait. Brown was unusual in many ways—for one thing, he felt things more deeply and acted more decisively than most others. But Brown was also very much the product of his time and place, and both his feelings and actions—if more extreme than those of his neighbors—reveal much about the world that produced him.

In 1800, the year of Gabriel Prosser's attempted slave revolt, John Brown was born into a family of New England stock, deeply attached to the country's revolutionary traditions and stirred by the great religious awakenings of the age. Over the years, he tried his hand at various occupations to support himself and his growing family, seeking and sometimes achieving a modest prosperity. But Brown prized other things above commercial success. "To get a little property together," he once wrote his son, "is really a low mark to be firing at through life." Personal independence, democracy, equal rights, self-discipline, and self-respect—the traditional republican values of the North's small producers—meant more. The quickening commercialization of American life disturbed Brown, seeming to threaten both his world and moral code. And the crisis of 1837, which wiped him out along with so many others, confirmed his worst fears. As the years went by, Brown's views about society and its ills grew clearer. He "thought that society ought to be organized on a less selfish basis," one of his associates would recall,

> for while material interests gained something by the deification of pure selfishness, men and women lost much by it. He said that all great reforms, like the Christian religion, were based on broad, generous, self-sacrificing principles. He condemned the sale of land as chattel and thought that there was an indefinite number of wrongs to right before society would be what it should be.

But of all society's wrongs, none repelled Brown so thoroughly as human bondage. Here was truly the "sum of all villainies," the starkest challenge to all the social and religious beliefs that shaped his outlook on life. Like his father before him, Brown aided fugitive slaves. In 1831, he and his neighbors cheered at the news of Nat Turner's insurrection. "The slaves have risen down in Virginia," cried one community elder, "and are fighting for their freedom as we did for ours. I pray God that they may get it." In 1851, Brown worked with free blacks to bolster resistance to the fugitive-slave law.

In the mid-1850s, five of John Brown's sons moved west to Kansas as free-soil homesteaders. Encountering armed groups of southerners determined to force slavery upon the territory, they called on their father for aid, and he soon joined them. In the often brutal fighting that followed in "Bleeding Kansas," John Brown earned a reputation for ferocity, tenacity, and an uncompromising hostility to slavery and racism generally. Especially obnoxious to Brown, remembered one of his allies, was "that class of persons whose opposition to slavery was founded on expediency," those who were "desirous that Kansas should be consecrated to free white labor only, not to freedom for all and above all." Brown "soon alarmed and disgusted" such people "by asserting the manhood of the Negro race, and expressing his earnest antislavery convictions with a force and vehemence" alien even to many free-soilers.

Despite the partisan interference of a Democratic president and his appointed representatives, free-state forces in Kansas had effectively prevailed by mid-1858. That victory, however, ended neither the broader dispute over slavery nor John Brown's role in it. The battle in Kansas, in fact, only stoked the flames of national conflict and convinced Brown that a final reckoning was near. And if it was only violence that had kept Kansas free, he asked, how could peaceful methods alone secure the same ends throughout the country? His brother Jeremiah reported unhappily that "since the trouble growing out of the settlement of the Kansas Territory, I have observed a marked changed in brother John." He "has abandoned all business, and has become wholly absorbed by the subject of slavery." When Jeremiah urged moderation, John replied

> that he was sorry that I did not sympathize with him [but] that he knew that he was in the line of his duty, and he must pursue it, though it should destroy him and his family. He . . . was satisfied that he was the chosen instrument in the hands of God to war against slavery.

The country would hear from this singleminded man again.

A NEW PARTY ALIGNMENT

For decades, the concerted efforts of politicians North and South had staved off a direct confrontation between the slave-labor and wage-labor systems. Geographical separation of the two systems had of course made compromise easier. Now the Kansas-Nebraska Act— and, even more dramatically, "Bleeding Kansas"—turned geography

William Walker's "filibusters" relax after the battle of Granada. Supported by fifty-eight mercenaries, the Tennessee-born William Walker "invaded" Nicaragua in May 1855. Within six months he succeeded in exploiting civil unrest in the country and declared himself president. Walker's government, which opened the country to slavery, was recognized by the United States in 1856. But a year later, he was overthrown by forces financed by former sponsor Cornelius Vanderbilt.

itself into the focus of conflict. In 1855, Congressman Abraham Lincoln wrote a Kentucky friend:

> You spoke [in 1819] of "the peaceful extinction of slavery" and used other expressions to indicate your belief that the thing was, at some time, to have an end. Since then we have had thirty-six years of experience, and this experience has demonstrated, I think, that there is no peaceful extinction of slavery in prospect for us. . . . Our political problem now is "Can we, as a nation, continue together *permanently—forever—*half slave and half free?"

During the 1850s, that question broke the country's two old political parties wide open and added a new one, the Republican Party, pledged to barring slavery from the western territories. The Whig disintegration began early. The conduct of Whig president Zachary Taylor during the 1850 compromise failed to satisfy ardently proslavery voters, dooming the party's future prospects in the South. The Whig remnant, meanwhile, now found itself deeply divided between procompromise ("Cotton Whig") and anticompromise ("Conscience Whig") factions. Some Whigs made an attempt to eclipse the antislavery movement by whipping up nativist sentiment and mobilizing it behind the new American Party (the "Know-Nothing" Party); the movement made quick gains but then collapsed even more suddenly. The slavery question had simply become unavoidable: in mid-1855, the Know-Nothing Party itself split into proslavery and antislavery wings.

Democrats, meanwhile, suffered a series of splits and defections beginning in 1848 with the founding of the Free-Soil Party of 1848. In 1854 and 1855, massive numbers of midwestern free-soil Democrats bolted the party to support a series of *ad hoc* anti-Nebraska electoral slates. The formation of a national Republican Party in 1856 cut deeply into northern Democratic support, and two years later the Democrats suffered another major blow when Stephen Douglas objected to Buchanan's policy in "Bleeding Kansas," threatening to divide the party into northern and southern wings.

The Republican Party coalesced out of the large but amorphous anti-Nebraska movement of 1854. The Republican platform of 1856 denounced slavery as immoral, insisted on halting the further westward expansion of slavery, and rejected the politics of nativism. Party leaders included some prosperous northern businessmen, such as Thaddeus Stevens of Pennsylvania and Zachariah Chandler of Michigan. Prominent among them were rising manufacturers, often from relatively humble backgrounds, who had been competing against the established mercantile elite for many years. But many of the North's largest merchants and some manufacturers with important southern ties threw their political support to the Know-Nothings or northern Democrats. Leading Republicans were more commonly middle-class men (especially lawyers, professional politicians, editors and journalists) who accepted the values of the North's free-labor industrial system and were ready to fight for it—more so than much of the elite itself.

The new party attracted supporters from many backgrounds. Politically, they included antislavery Whigs, Democrats, former Free-Soilers, and Know-Nothings. One of its earliest organizers, Alvan Bovay, was a veteran land-reformer and former associate of George Henry Evans. Labor leader and land-reformer John Commerford became a Republican spokesman in New York.

The great bulk of those rallying to the new party's banner during the 1850s were small farmers, small shopkeepers, and skilled urban working people, most of them native-born. In the wake of their defeated strike in 1860, the shoe workers of Lynn split their tickets. They refused to vote for Republican candidates for local office because the shoe bosses controlled the local Republican organization. But they gave stunning majorities to Republicans at the state level and to the slate of Republican electors committed to Abraham Lincoln for president. Free blacks supported the Republicans, as they had the Free-Soilers, as the best way to advance the larger fight to uproot slavery everywhere and eventually to secure full democratic rights for all African-Americans.

The response of other nationalities was mixed. Republican strength among immigrant farmers and workers from Britain and Scandinavia grew steadily during the 1850s. Germans were divided: Some of the wealthiest German-American businessmen, like so many of their native-born colleagues, clung to the Democratic Party for fear of angering southern customers, losing southern markets, and in general encouraging social and political conflict in the country. Conservative German religious leaders (notably Catholic and Old Lutheran) and their loyal parishioners similarly resisted the Republican appeal. But German-born small proprietors, liberal and radical-democratic intellectuals, and craftworkers seemed to offer one of the firmest potential pillars of the Republican organization. Frederick Douglass was describing this group and its spokesmen when he praised "the many noble and high-minded men, most of whom, swept over by the tide of the revolution of 1849, have become our active allies against oppression and prejudice." Such immigrants might have voted their antislavery principles more easily and in larger numbers, German Republicans argued, had it not been for the obvious power of sabbatarianism and nativism in many state-level Republican organizations.

Some Irish-Americans moved toward the Republicans in 1856, but their own profound grievances against the "free-labor system," suspicion of nativist elements among the Republicans, fear of splitting their beloved American republic, loyalty to a Democratic Party that had accepted them when others would not, and fears of job competition from an expected flood of low-wage ex-slaves—all these factors combined to keep the vast majority of this group in the Democratic column in 1860.

In 1856, despite all the difficulties facing it, the Republican Party and its presidential candidate, John C. Frémont, rolled up impressive gains in the North, proving the new party was there to stay. Victory went to Democrat James Buchanan, and nativist candidate Millard Fillmore garnered about 20 percent of the popular vote nationally. But Frémont (with no party organization in the slave South) carried eleven out of the sixteen free states and 45 percent of all ballots cast in the North. The tremendous increase registered over Van Buren's Free-Soil vote only eight years earlier reflected the drastic transformation that the Kansas-Nebraska question had wrought in popular thinking. The Republican campaign slogan—"Free soil, free labor, free men"— summarized the goals and ideals that drove millions into its ranks, almost overnight.

Frémont's dramatic gains, in turn, accelerated the already rapid drive toward national conflict. Observing the deepening isolation of their northern political allies, southern planters began to see the majority in the free states as hopelessly hostile to slavery. To them it seemed only a matter of time before Republicans gained control of the national government and used its power to undermine slavery everywhere—first in the West, then in the old South. These specific fears grew out of other, more general worries about southern society and its internal frictions and conflicts. Most immediately, what impact would a Republican national government have upon the slave population?

Throughout the South, blacks were once again paying close attention to national politics, pondering the significance of this new division of the white population, hoping for liberation through a Republican victory. Nor was the slave attitude passive. The 1856 election brought with it stories of slave insurrection plans in at least six southern states. "The recent Presidential canvass has had a deleterious effect on the slave population," reported a Nashville, Tennessee, editor in alarm. "The negroes manifested an unusual interest in the result and attended the political meetings of the whites in large numbers. This is dangerous." A Memphis colleague agreed: "If this eternal agitation of the slavery question does not cease we may expect servile insurrections in dead earnest." In the meantime, individual Republican leaders (such as the Blair family in Maryland and Missouri) and writers (such as Cassius Clay in Kentucky and Hinton Helper of the Carolina hill country) began courting "the non-slaveholding whites of the South." Helper's book *The Impending Crisis of the South* aided Republicans among southern-born residents of the Midwest. Its immediate impact in the South seemed minor, but planters feared its long-term effect and severely punished those caught circulating it. Increasingly numerous German-born craftsmen in Richmond, Baltimore, St. Louis, San Antonio, and New Orleans likewise seemed dangerous sources of potential pro-Republican sentiment.

Even before it achieved national supremacy, then, Republicanism threatened slaveowners on their own soil. So it was with growing seriousness that southern politicians threatened to safeguard their human property and social power by pulling their states out of the federal union and beyond the reach of the Republicans.

TOWARD A SHOWDOWN

During the late 1850s, the nation continued to lurch away from compromise and toward a final showdown. Demands from proslavery firebrands for more and more guarantees for the slave-labor system, already mounting by the end of the 1840s, proliferated further. Some demanded the resumption of the Atlantic slave trade. More called for an automatic southern veto over all federal legislation affecting southern interests. Souring on immigration, southern politicians tried to limit the rights of the foreign-born. Southern congressmen also blocked homestead legislation. A law turning western land over to independent small farmers, exclaimed the Charleston *Mercury*, would be "the most dangerous abolition bill which has ever been directly passed by Congress."

In 1857, a Supreme Court filled with southerners and their sympathizers rejected the claim of the Missouri slave Dred Scott that he had become free when his master took him out of the South and into a free state (Illinois) and a free territory (Wisconsin). Chief Justice Roger B. Taney, a Jackson appointee, pronounced unconstitutional all laws restricting the free movement of property, including human property. Indeed, he asserted further, Scott had no right to bring suit at all, because since the founding of the American republic no black person in the United States had enjoyed any "rights which the white man was bound to respect." Followed to its logical conclusion, replied horrified northerners, this opinion could lead to legalizing slave ownership not only in all the territories but in the free states as well.

This was the charged atmosphere in which John Brown and some two dozen associates—black and white, slave and free—launched their October 1859 raid on the federal arsenal at Harpers Ferry, Virginia. Their plans called for seizing the arms stored there, liberating the slaves of the immediate vicinity, and then retreating into Virginia's Allegheny Mountains. There they hoped to fortify a base from which to encourage, assist, and defend additional escapes and insurrections. The constitution that Brown drafted for this projected haven bore the unmistakable imprint of utopian-cooperative ideals. "All captured or confiscated property, and all property [that is] the product of the labor of those belonging to this organization and their families, shall be held as the property of the whole, equally, without distinction," it declared.

Brown's plan was probably hopeless from the start, pitting a handful of poorly armed people against virtually the entire white population of Virginia—and the South—plus the armed forces of the United States government. A detachment of U.S. Marines under Colonel Robert E. Lee and Lieutenant J. E. B. Stuart soon surrounded the insurgents, subjected them to withering fire, and finally captured most of the survivors. Brown himself, mortally wounded, was promptly tried, convicted, and sentenced to death.

"Men cannot imprison, or chain, or hang the soul," Brown wrote in one of his last letters. "I go joyfully in behalf of millions that 'have

"The Arraignment." A *Harper's Weekly* artist sketched John Brown and his co-conspirators as they were charged with treason and murder in a Charlestown, Virginia, courtroom.

no rights' that this great and glorious, this Christian republic, 'is bound to respect.'" Brown rejected Taney's version of the republic's traditions. The Dred Scott decision, he held, marked "a strange change in morals, political as well as Christian, since 1776."

Brown had some prophetic words for the South's political leadership as well:

> You may dispose of me very easily, I am nearly disposed of now. But this question is still to be settled—this Negro question, I mean; the end of that is not yet. You had better—all you people at the South—prepare yourselves for a settlement of this question.

Though unsuccessful, the Harpers Ferry raid reverberated through the country. Southern leaders pointed to it as the final proof of the North's violent intentions. Republican moderates like Abraham Lincoln hastily condemned Brown's deed. Ominously for the South, though, others rejected Brown's tactics but saluted his values and goals. White abolitionists, southern slaves, and free blacks nationwide grieved at Brown's execution and proclaimed him a martyr in the American revolutionary pantheon. Churchbells throughout the North pealed in mourning when Brown died. When Baltimore police in 1859 broke into the caulkers' ball, an annual free-black affair, they found the hall draped in banners bearing John Brown's likeness and a bust of him inscribed, "The martyr—God bless him."

In 1860, therefore, matters came to a head. The Democratic Party—the last major national bastion of the compromise forces—could not agree on a single platform and candidate. The slavery issue had simply be-

---

"YOU HAVE BEEN BRAVE ENOUGH TO REACH OUT YOUR HANDS . . ."

In the days before his execution, John Brown received many letters of support from free blacks throughout the North. A black woman in Kendalville, Indiana, wrote Brown offering her thanks and speculating on the steps America would have to take to erase the "national sin" of slavery.

Kendalville, Indiana, Nov. 25

Dear Friend:

Although the hands of Slavery throw a barrier between you and me, and it may not be my privilege to see you in your prison-house, Virginia has no bolts or bars [that can stop me from sending you] my sympathy. In the name of the young girl sold from the warm clasp of a mother's arms to the clutches of a libertine or a profligate, in the name of the slave mother, her heart rocked to and fro by the agony of her mournful separations, I thank you, that you have been brave enough to reach out your hands to the crushed and blighted of my race. You have rocked the bloody Bastille; and I hope that from your sad fate great good may arise to the cause of freedom. . . . I would prefer to see Slavery go down peaceably by men breaking off their sins by righteousness and their inequities by showing justice and mercy to the poor; but we cannot tell what the future may bring forth. God writes national judgments upon national sins; and what may be slumbering in the storehouse of divine justice we do not know. We may earnestly hope that your fate will not be a vain lesson, that it will intensify our hatred of Slavery and love of freedom, and that your martyr grave will be a sacred altar upon which men will record their vows of undying hatred to that system which tramples on man and bids defiance to God. . . .

F.E.W.

come too explosive. Democrats divided their party and their electoral strength into two halves, one in the North and one in the South. A weak echo of the old Whig and Know-Nothing forces dubbed itself the Constitutional Unionist Party and made a futile last attempt to delay action on the slavery issue still longer.

The North and West went heavily Republican, giving that party 54 percent of their total popular vote, with Douglas's northern Democrats picking up most of the rest. Only New Jersey resisted Abraham Lincoln's triumphal sweep of the free states. In the South, the small urban vote generally went to the Constitutional Unionists, while the rural majority went heavily to Breckinridge and his fire-eating southern Democrats. Lincoln's majority in the North and West proved sufficient to elect him president. That election, in turn, opened one of the most important and dramatic chapters in the nation's history. It signaled, as one observer noted, "the beginning of the Second American Revolution."

The Republican victory in 1860 grew organically out of the social, economic, cultural, and political development of the United States during the preceding half-century. By preserving slave labor in half the country, the first American Revolution stopped far short of the Declaration of Independence's stated goal—a society based on the principle that "all men are created equal." For a number of decades, national leaders worked long, hard, and successfully to hold together

An 1860 anti-Lincoln cartoon portrays the presidential candidate trying to conceal the antislavery essence of the Republican platform.

"THE NIGGER" IN THE WOODPILE.

a nation divided into two different societies based on two distinct labor systems.

At last, the growth, development, and expansion of the country as a whole and of the two societies within it brought the compromise era to an end. For each society, as it matured, developed needs, interests, and values that the other found increasingly dangerous and ultimately unacceptable. Slaveowners and their supporters became more and more committed to chattel slavery and everything it required, viewing it as the essential prop to their own independence, while the North's vaunted "free society" became an object of fear and loathing to them. And while northerners hotly disagreed among themselves about the meaning of "free labor," most came to view an expanding slavery as the most direct challenge—and threat—to the American republic and their own rights, freedoms, and aspirations within it. The ongoing resistance by slaves, free blacks, and white sympathizers (including revolts and rumors therof, abolitionist agitation, and a rising tide of slave escapes) and the response it evoked from the slaveholders kept the issue alive and illuminated the stakes involved.

The dispute over the future of the West expressed the growing sectional clash, destroyed the old two-party system, and gave life to Republicanism. "Bleeding Kansas" and Harpers Ferry revealed how sharp the conflict had become and anticipated the way it would at last be resolved.

Even in death, John Brown symbolized the speed with which the nation drove toward that resolution. In late 1859, Brown died a traitor's death, brought to the gallows by U.S. troops led by Colonel Robert E. Lee. Two short years later, U.S. troops marched into battle against Confederate general Lee. On their lips was a fighting song called "John Brown's Body." His truth, they sang, went marching on.

Matthew Dripps, The United States and Territories, 1876

PART THREE

WAR, RECONSTRUCTION, AND LABOR

1860 – 1877

THE DRAMATIC events that unfold in this part constitute America's second revolution. Like the first revolution, the second was the bloody culmination of decades of conflict over what kind of society America should be. The North's ultimate victory in the Civil War settled finally the issue of slavery, changing the status of four million enslaved African-Americans and assuring the nation's future development under industrial capitalism. The second revolution also resulted in a fundamental expansion of constitutional guarantees of citizenship and political equality, just as the colonists' victory in the first revolution and the new citizens' persistent demands had resulted in the Bill of Rights. And, like the American Revolution, the Civil War and its aftermath demonstrate that the behavior and beliefs of working people—black and white—were essential in determining the outcome of these momentous events.

None of this could be imagined when war finally broke out in April 1861. The South seceded from the Union to maintain the system of racial slavery upon which the region's very identity was based. Northern whites went to war, for the most part, not to free the slaves, but only to limit slavery's expansion westward and to prevent the South's departure from the Union. But the North's war aims changed in the face of unexpected military defeats and the unanticipated actions of slaves. African-Americans escaped from slavery in huge numbers. Many of them, along with northern free blacks, demanded the right to fight for the Union, and ultimately, nearly 200,000 African-Americans served in the Union Army, helping turn the tide in the war's final two years.

A broad coalition—farmers, workers (including recent immigrants), businessmen, and politicians—emerged to support the Republican party's policy of total war against the South. Like the similar coalition of colonists that sustained America's war for independence, this second wartime coalition formed the core of support for what would become Republican policies towards the South after the war.

The Confederacy's defeat raised as many questions as it answered. Slavery was now destroyed, but what kind of labor system would replace it? African-Americans were now free, but what would they do with their new freedom? How would their former masters react? Who would lead the South now? The period called Reconstruction was the attempt to answer these questions.

The freedpeople knew exactly how they wanted the questions answered. To them, emancipation meant the right to speak and act as free people, to reunite their families, and to end their automatic deference towards whites. And freed men and women acted decisively to guarantee these freedoms; their claims of individual rights quickly grew into collective demands for education, the ownership of land, and finally full political participation.

Southern whites had a very different notion of what Reconstruction should mean. Former slaveowners wanted a rapid return to stability and a continuation of their rule. Small farmers and workers did not want to face economic or political competition from millions of former slaves. Few whites could abide the freedpeople's demands for political and social equality.

Although most northern whites also abhorred the idea of racial equality, few wanted the South to return to its prewar ways. Most industrialists were committed to rebuilding the ravaged South as quickly as possible on free-labor principles, transforming slaves into wage laborers. Working people, though they did not want to compete with African-Americans for jobs, were unwilling to accept the slaveowners' continued domination over the freedpeople. Republican Party politicians, intent on blunting the political power of the Dem-

ocrats and the former slaveholders, needed the votes of the newly en-
franchised freedpeople to build their party in the south.

As we will see, these diverse objectives resulted in sharp conflict
and a growing sense of crisis. No group won all of its demands—least
of all the freedpeople. They did win important victories, especially
citizenship and the right to vote. But freedpeople's quest for land of
their own remained unfulfilled.

Nonetheless, these gains and the increasingly radical policies of
the Republican Party engendered intense opposition among southern
whites. Opposition soon turned ominous. The rise of the brutal Ku
Klux Klan after 1867 halted the freedpeople's progress. Within a decade, the southern elite had reestablished its control, thanks to the
moderate Republicans who came to dominate the northern party
after 1870. Reconstruction ended tragically for freedpeople, who saw
their traditional antagonists returned to economic and political
power.

Meanwhile, the North was also being transformed. Developments
that began in the midst of the war accelerated after 1865. Within a
few years, a transcontinental railroad system linked the North to the
far West. Industrial manufacturing multiplied. The staggering increase in national wealth that followed was made possible by unprecedented numbers of immigrants, millions of whom came from
northern and eastern Europe and China to fill the growing ranks of
America's postwar industrial working class.

The wartime political coalition that had linked farmers, workers,
and businessmen in the North broke apart in the face of these
changes. The severe industrial depression that began in 1873 forced
Americans to realize that their nation, too, was suffering the wrenching dislocations and class divisions already evident in Europe: increasingly, great wealth and opulence coexisted with grinding poverty
and human misery. This widening gulf helped revive the labor movement.

The celebration of the nation's centennial in 1876 only served to
obscure this gulf. The following year America experienced its first
nationwide industrial rebellion as hundreds of thousands of railroad
strikers and their supporters brought the nation to a standstill. The
end of Reconstruction and the nationwide railroad strike in 1877
mark the end of an era. Decades of conflict about the status of slavery
had ended; now a new drama pitting capital against labor was about
to begin.

SEQUEL TO
"KINGDOM COMING."

BABYLON

IS FALLEN!

SONG AND CHORUS.

WORDS AND MUSIC BY

HENRY C. WORK.

CHICAGO:

PUBLISHED BY ROOT & CADY, 95 CLARK STREET.

10 THE CIVIL WAR: AMERICA'S SECOND REVOLUTION

Illustrated sheet-music cover, 1863.

LINCOLN'S election forced the hand of the slaveholders. Although the new president had promised not to interfere with slavery where it already existed, he had pledged himself to stop its further expansion. But, as we have seen, southern leaders believed that slavery needed to expand in order to survive. This belief, along with their fears that the Republican victory would lead inevitably to slave rebellion, caused the southern slaveholding class to embark on the path of secession. By seceding from the United States, southerners proclaimed that they were unwilling to become a permanent minority in the nation, a status that would inevitably undermine the institution of slavery and the society upon which it was based.

When northerners went to war to keep the South in the Union, they also sought to maintain rather than transform a society. Like southerners, most northerners had somewhat idealized notions of the society they were fighting to preserve. These deeply felt beliefs, rooted in the traditions of the Revolution, included the ideal of opportunity, opportunity for freeborn workers and farmers to attain a degree of economic independence, to end life a little higher on the social scale than they had started. Northerners believed that this free-labor ideal was profoundly threatened by slavery's continuing spread through the western territories. Like southerners, they went to war to defend, rather than change, the world they knew.

But, unexpected by both sides, the Civil War became a total war, a brutal ordeal in which over six hundred thousand Americans, white and black, gave their lives. And as it became a total war, it also became a revolution. The slaveholders had gone to war to preserve both slavery and their dominance over southern society. But the war's end found slavery dead and the loyalty of non-slaveholders to the old ruling class considerably weakened. Northerners had fought to protect their free-labor society. But the very course of the war dramatically accelerated the pace of economic change, transforming American society in the midst of war and in its aftermath.

Most revolutionary of all was the Civil War's effect on the status of the nation's four million African-Americans. Despite the intentions of the vast majority of whites in both South and North, the war ended with the total abolition of slavery. How did such an unforeseen change happen? Military and diplomatic considerations played a large role in shaping the famous legal documents—the Emancipation Proclamation and the Thirteenth Amendment to the Constitution—that registered the legal abolition of slavery. But the actual uprooting of the institution on plantations throughout the southern and border states was a highly uneven process, occurring in strikingly different ways over the course of the war's four years. Central to this process were the actions of the slaves themselves, hundreds of thousands of whom fled slavery and offered their labor and their lives to put an end to America's "peculiar institution."

THE SOUTH SECEDES

In November 1860, American voters elected Abraham Lincoln as their sixteenth president. Within three months, and as a direct response to Lincoln's election, slaveholders had led seven states of the lower South out of the Union and had formed an independent nation, the Confederate States of America. They did so because they believed that secession was the only way to protect the institution of slavery. Secession set off a crisis that rocked America, prompting some northerners to seek a compromise between the secessionists and the victorious Republicans. But the slaveholders demanded far more than most Republicans could accept. Compromise efforts failed, and in April 1861 the nation plunged into war.

South Carolina led the secession movement, declaring its independence on December 20, 1860, just over a month after Lincoln's election. In the early weeks of 1861, Mississippi, Florida, Alabama, Georgia, Louisiana, and Texas, the states most dependent on slavery, proclaimed their independence from the Union. On February 9, a month before Lincoln had even taken office, representatives from these seven states met in Montgomery, Alabama, to establish the Confederacy. They adopted a provisional constitution and elected a Mississippi slaveowner and former U.S. senator, Jefferson Davis, as their president.

Large slaveholders like Davis led the secession movement because they believed that Lincoln's victory placed the future of slavery in doubt. On the surface, such fears seemed unfounded. "Do the people of the South really entertain fears that a Republican administration would, *directly* or *indirectly*, interfere with their slaves, or with them, about their slaves?" Lincoln asked a southern acquaintance, Alexander H. Stephens, shortly after his election. "If they do, I wish to assure you . . . that there is no cause for such fears." But the Republicans, true to their free-soil principles, did plan to keep slavery from expanding. Lincoln summed up the issue to Stephens (who later became vice-president of the Confederacy): "You think slavery is *right* and ought to be extended; while we think it is *wrong* and ought to be restricted. That I suppose is the rub."

But even attempts to limit slavery's expansion badly frightened southern slaveholders. As we have seen, southern planters believed that their peculiar institution needed to grow in order to survive. "Expansion seems to be the law and destiny and necessity of our institutions," argued a slaveholder at Alabama's secession convention. "To remain healthful and prosperous within . . . it seems essential that we should grow without." For men like this, Lincoln's election marked the beginning of the end of slavery. Independence seemed the only way out.

Slaveholders had more immediate reasons for supporting secession. Many feared that a Republican government in Washington would inevitably lead to a massive uprising of slaves. John Brown's raid on Harpers Ferry had greatly intensified the South's ongoing fears of slave insurrection. After the raid, a southern newspaper warned that the region was "slumbering over a volcano, whose smoldering fires may, at any quiet starry midnight, blacken the social sky with the smoke of desolation and death." Some believed that the South was being infiltrated by abolitionists who were "tampering with our slaves, and furnishing them with arms and poisons to accomplish their hellish designs." In the wake of Brown's raid, "vigilance committees" of slaveholders and their supporters sprang up all over the South; one such committee in Mississippi lynched twenty-three suspected slave rebels in a single three-week period.

The Republicans' victory, coming in the midst of this hysteria, sparked new fears. The victory of those they called "black Republicans," argued some slaveholders, would encourage the spread of "subversive" ideas throughout the South. Eventually these ideas would come to "infect" the slave quarters, inciting slaves to revolt. "Now that the black radical Republicans have the power I suppose they will [John] Brown us all," punned one South Carolinian.

Many slaveholders feared that slavery could not withstand the open debate on its future that Republicans seemed determined to conduct. Slaveholders were particularly concerned about the sentiments of those whites (a full three-quarters of the southern white population) who did not own slaves. "I mistrust our own people more than I fear all of the efforts of the Abolitionists," a politician in South Carolina had admitted in 1859. Men like this feared that the victorious Republicans would exploit social and economic inequalities among southern whites to build their political party in the region. "They will have an Abolition party in the South, of Southern men," warned a southern newspaper after Lincoln's election. "The contest for slavery will no longer be one between the North and the South. It will be in the South between people of the South." Only complete southern independence, many planters believed, could effectively isolate southern yeomen from their potential Republican allies in the North and thus protect the institution of slavery.

These fears kept secessionists from putting their plans to a popular test. Of the seven states that seceded in early 1861, only Texas allowed voters to speak directly on the question. A delegate to South Carolina's secession convention summed up a widely held view when he noted that "the common people" did not understand the issues involved. "But who ever waited for the common people when a great movement was to be made?" he asked. "We must make the move and force them to follow."

Many of the South's common people did indeed follow the Confederacy, and not because they were forced. Though some urban workers and some small farmers in the mountains remained loyal to the Union and opposed secession, most southern yeomen initially supported the Confederacy. As we have seen, many yeomen in the lower South had started farming cotton in the 1850s, growing dependent on planters for help with marketing and labor. These close economic ties—as well as ties of kinship—led them naturally to support secession.

"The First Flag of Independence Raised in the South, by the Citizens of Savannah, Ga. November 8, 1860." According to this lithograph, the earliest symbol of secession was the "Don't Tread on Me" snake—an image familiar to many Americans, having appeared on numerous flags and banners during the American Revolution.

Though they also planted some cotton, yeomen in the up-country were more likely to cling to economic self-sufficiency and their traditional way of life. For them, it was fear that the growth of northern capitalism threatened their self-sufficiency that made them turn to slaveholders to protect their economic and cultural independence. This alliance was cemented by the planters' successful appeal to white racial unity in the face of the exaggerated fear that the Republicans would free the slaves and introduce racial equality in the South. Slaveholders and yeomen alike could agree with the southern leader who said of secession, "These are desperate means, but then we must recollect that we live in desperate times."

Times were desperate in the North as well. Southern secession wreaked havoc on the northern economy, which now faced a financial panic and the prospect of a replay of the depression of 1857. The cities of the Northeast and the towns along the Ohio River were hit hardest.

Stock-market prices plummeted, banks shut their doors, factories laid off workers, and unsold goods piled up on docks.

Many northern businessmen thought they could not afford to accept southern independence: merchants and textile manufacturers worried about the permanent loss of the southern cotton crop, and bankers feared that southerners would not repay their loans. With these economic considerations added to their political concerns about national unity, many businessmen called for compromise, for peace at almost any price.

Many northern working people, fearing that the economic strains of southern independence would lead to mass unemployment, joined in the call for compromise. On February 22, a group of trade-unionists from eight northern and border states met in Philadelphia. They denounced the secessionist "traitors," but also called for efforts to resolve the issue peacefully. "Our Government never can be sustained by bloodshed," they proclaimed, opposing "any measures that will evoke civil war." Working-class support for compromise stemmed not only from economic considerations, but also from a deep loyalty to the world's only political democracy, what the Philadelphia trade-unionists called "the best form of government ever instituted by man."

But the price of peace would be high. In the most elaborate of various compromise schemes, Kentucky's Senator John J. Crittenden proposed that the North accept a return to the principles of the 1820 Missouri Compromise. In all western territory now held by the United States, slavery would be prohibited north of 36° 30' and permanently protected south of it, including land "hereafter acquired"— an open invitation to the acquisition of more southern territory for slavery. Crittenden also proposed constitutional amendments that would prohibit Congress from abolishing slavery in the District of Columbia, forbid federal interference with the internal slave trade, and provide compensation for any slaveholder prevented from recovering escaped slaves in the North.

Measures like this were naturally opposed by northern free blacks and abolitionists. Frederick Douglass spoke for them when he said, "If the Union can only be maintained by new concessions to the slaveholders, if it can only be stuck together and held together by a new drain on the negro's blood, then . . . let the Union perish."

But the Republican leadership also opposed formulas that allowed for the expansion of slavery. "Free soil," after all, was a guiding principle of the party. With Lincoln secretly advising Republican congressmen to "entertain no proposition for a compromise in regard to the extension of slavery," Congress defeated the Crittenden measures.

In so doing, Congress expressed the political commitments of the Republican rank-and-file: the workers, farmers, and small businessmen who had elected Lincoln president. Flooding Congress with letters, ordinary citizens demanded that their party leaders remain true to free-soil principles and reject compromise. "Artful politicians—rich merchants and speculators, whose god is money—will counsel peace, regardless of principle," wrote one citizen to his Republican congressman. "See that you yield not to their solicitations."

Chicago became a storm center of the fight against compromise. Led by the substantial population of German-American artisans and laborers, the city's Republican societies angrily denounced Chicago businessmen who were "doing everything they possibly can . . . to support the compromisers." Trumpeting the city's commitment to antislavery principles, one newspaper proudly announced that, in Chicago at least, "Cotton has not usurped the function of Conscience."

By March, when Lincoln was sworn in as president, the voice of the Republican rank-and-file had been heard. Although Lincoln's new secretary of state, William Seward, continued to favor compromise, in the face of such rank-and-file and congressional determination, he had little room to maneuver. As the Democratic New York *Herald*

"The March of the Seventh Regiment down Broadway." Newspaper artist Thomas Nast sketched the tumultuous send-off of New York's national guard regiment on April 19, 1861. Eight years later Nast completed this oil painting of the scene.

put it, there was "a power behind him, in the Republican camp, stronger than his own."

These were the circumstances Lincoln faced as he took control of the national government. Not yet prepared to force the South back into the Union through military means, the new president nevertheless needed to make a demonstration of strength to satisfy his militant free-soil supporters. Attention focused on Fort Sumter in Charleston Harbor, where a small Union garrison was running low on food and medical supplies. Lincoln dispatched reinforcements to Fort Sumter, but fearing moves that would appear to make the North the aggressor, promised they would go into action only if the Confederates blocked a peaceful effort to send in supplies. On April 8 a Union supply ship set sail for Charleston Harbor.

The new Confederate government now faced a dilemma. It could attack the Union vessel and bear the responsibility for firing the first shot of the war. Or it could allow the supplies to be delivered, thus permitting what it had labeled a foreign power to maintain a fort in one of its major harbors. Jefferson Davis and his advisors chose an aggressive course, demanding the unconditional surrender of the Fort Sumter garrison. The commanding officer refused and on April 12 Confederate guns opened fire. Two days later Fort Sumter surrendered. The Civil War had begun.

FOR UNION—OR AGAINST SLAVERY?

The two sections now faced very different tasks. The South did not have to "win" a war in order to maintain its independence. It had only to defend its own territory and force the North to halt military action. The North, on the other hand, to accomplish its goal of maintaining the Union, had to bring the South to its knees. In military terms, this meant invading the South and isolating it from potential allies abroad. Most northern policy-makers believed that they could accomplish these ends without challenging the institution of slavery. They never intended to involve slaves in the war.

But from the first shot, slaves saw it differently. Knowing that their future depended on the outcome of the Civil War, slaves looked for chances to join the conflict. As we will see, the actions of slaves, both individually and collectively, had a profound impact not only on the course of the war, but also on the aims for which it would be fought: The North went to war in April 1861 to preserve the Union and to stop the expansion of slavery. By January 1863, because of the aggressive and largely unanticipated actions of African-Americans, the North was fighting not merely to stop the expansion of slavery, but to abolish it entirely.

In the wake of Fort Sumter, northerners across the social spectrum lined up behind Lincoln's war policy. Manufacturers and merchants, intent upon maintaining economic links with the cotton South, had been the loudest advocates of compromise. Now they rushed to support Lincoln, hoping that force would succeed in keeping the South in the Union where compromise had earlier failed.

The outbreak of fighting galvanized northern workers, including those who had endorsed compromise. Their concern for national unity was now expressed as firm support for the Union war effort. William Sylvis—who had been a leader in the Philadelphia workers' endorsement of the Crittenden compromise—now raised an army company among his fellow iron-molders. Small unions across the country collapsed as their members rushed to recruiting stations. Foreign-born workers seemed particularly patriotic. Germans organized ten regiments in New York State alone, while New York City's Irish formed the soon-to-be-famous Sixty-Ninth Regiment and the Irish Brigade. For foreign-born workers, to fight for the Union was to prove to the world the soundness of political democracy and to defend it for all working people.

Midwestern farmers and farm laborers, the backbone of the free-soil movement, enlisted in large numbers, making up nearly half the Union Army.

"Contrabands" in Virginia, May, 1862.

Equally enthusiastic were the 225,000 African-Americans now living in the free states. At the sound of the alarm bell, recalled one northern black, "Negro waiter, cook, barber, bootblack, groom, porter, and laborer stood ready at the enlisting office." And a recruiting meeting of Cleveland blacks proclaimed, "Today, as in the times of '76, we are ready to go forth and do battle in the common cause of our country." Their country, however, was not yet ready for them. Secretary of War Simon Cameron quickly announced that he had no intention of calling up black soldiers; local authorities drove his point home by prohibiting African-American recruitment meetings as "disorderly gatherings." "In Boston, Providence, New York, Philadelphia, Cleveland, and Columbus, black men have offered their services and been rejected," reported a leading African-American newspaper in May 1861.

Northern optimism contributed in part to this hasty rejection. Although four slave states that had previously rejected secession—Virginia, North Carolina, Arkansas, and Tennessee—joined the Confederacy after Fort Sumter, northern leaders remained confident that the South would be subdued easily. "Jeff Davis and Co. will be swinging from the battlements at Washington at least by the 4th of July," predicted newspaperman Horace Greeley. "This much-ado-about-nothing will end in a month," echoed a Philadelphia newspaper. The North did possess important advantages—more than twice the population of the South, a growing industrial base, and a better transportation network, all of which had tremendous military value. Given these advantages, there seemed little need to call on the assistance offered by northern free blacks. Added to these factors was the fear that whites would not enlist if blacks were allowed to serve in the Union Army.

But there was a deeper reason. Lincoln and his advisers were wary lest the war for the Union become a war against slavery. Despite the quick secession of the upper South, four crucial border slave states (Missouri,

". . . WILL YOU ALLOW US THE POOR PRIVERLIGE OF FIGHTING"

A letter to Secretary of War Simon Cameron from two Cleveland black citizens seeking to join the Union Army suggests the eagerness of free blacks in the North to fight against the Confederacy.

Cleveland, O., 15 Nov. 1861.

Sir:
The following particulars, hereafter mentioned, have been laid before the Hon. S. P. Chase, Sec of the Treas, and his reply to us is that "we apply to you direct."

Theirfore, we would humbly and respectfully State, that, we are Colard men (legal voters) all voted for the presant administration. The question now is will you allow us the poor priverlige of fighting—and if need be dieing—to suport those in office who are our own choise. We belive that a reigement of colard men can be raised in this State, who we are sure, would make as patriotic and good Soldiers as any other.

What we ask of you is that you give us the proper athroity to rais such a reigement, and it *can* and SHALL be done.

We could give you a Thousand names as ether signers or as refferance if required. . . .

W. T. Boyd,
J. T. Alston
P.S. we waite your reply.

SOME COLORS WON'T STAND.

An 1862 cartoon from the northern satirical weekly, *Vanity Fair*, depicts the Confederacy's president trying to gain diplomatic recognition from a skeptical Great Britain. "I hardly think it will wash, Mr. Davis," Britannia comments in the cartoon's caption, "We hear so much about your colors running."

Kentucky, Maryland, and Delaware) remained in the Union. Any threat to slavery might well drive these states into the Confederacy's waiting arms, and enlisting black soldiers would show that slavery's future in the Union was not entirely secure.

These concerns accounted for Lincoln's reaction to the exceedingly tense situation in Missouri. In August 1861, General John C. Frémont, the famous explorer and former Republican presidential candidate who now commanded Union military forces in the West, proclaimed martial law in Missouri and issued an order that freed the slaves of all Confederate sympathizers in the state. Black and white abolitionists hailed Frémont's action as a brilliant military move and a bold step for freedom. But furious Unionist slaveholders in Missouri and the other border states called on Lincoln to reverse Frémont's order. Noting that Frémont's move would "alarm our Southern Union friends" and "perhaps ruin our rather fair prospects for Kentucky," the president hastily followed their advice.

Yet slaves and their supporters believed that the war had indeed opened a door to freedom. As the war began, a northern black newspaper spoke for most African-Americans, slave and free, when it concluded that "out of this strife will come freedom, though the methods are not yet clearly apparent." In order to be ready to act, slaves carefully followed the course of the war, learning about battles and Union troop movements on the "grapevine telegraph." Though northern intentions remained unclear, most slaves realized that if Union troops came, they would undermine the authority of slaveholders and make freedom a distinct possibility. Even in the deep South, far from the early battles, far from the Union Army, slaves were heartened by events. At the outset of the fighting, a white Alabama farmer wrote to Jefferson Davis that slaves in his region "very hiley hope that they will soon be free." Concealing their hopes from the slaveholders (as they had long concealed their real feelings), the slaves awaited their chances.

They first appeared in tidewater Virginia. The Confederate commander there triggered events by impressing nearly all the male slaves in the area to build fortifications. Local slaveholders, objecting to this infringement of what they regarded as their property rights, began "refugeeing" slave men, sending them out of the area. Another reason for this policy was the slaveholders' growing inability to maintain discipline on plantations as the war unfolded. The slaves, of course, resisted both impressment and removal, which would mean separation from their loved ones. Instead they took another course: escape.

On the night of May 23, 1861, three Virginia slaves escaped and paddled up the river to the Union outpost at Fortress Monroe, requesting sanctuary from its commanding general, Benjamin Butler. Butler was a Democratic politician from Massachusetts, and no abolitionist. Yet realizing that the Confederacy would use slaves against the Union, he decided to give the runaways military protection, refusing the pleas of their owner that they be returned. The slaves, Butler proclaimed, were "contraband" of war, property that rebel slaveowners had forfeited by their very act of rebellion.

News of Butler's decision spread like wildfire among the slaves in the region. Two days later eight runaway slaves arrived at what they called "Freedom Fort." The next day they were joined by another fifty-nine African-American men and women. And Lincoln endorsed Butler's contraband policy in rebel Virginia as a legitimate tactic of war. The North now possessed a formula that allowed it to strike at the institution of slavery, the linchpin of the southern economy—without proclaiming general abolition and thus alienating the loyal border states.

The Union forces needed every weapon they could muster. Despite the North's material superiority, in the first two years of the Civil War the South seemed to have all the advantages. First, southerners were fighting on their own ground. This gave them both a knowledge of the terrain and a distinct psychological edge, often expressed as arrogance about their military superiority. A wartime southern textbook proposed these problems for southern children to solve:

1. A Confederate soldier captured 8 Yankees each day on 9 successive days. How many did he capture in all?
2. If one Confederate soldier can kill 90 Yankees, how many Yankees can 10 Confederate soldiers kill?
3. If one Confederate soldier can whip 7 Yankees, how many soldiers can whip 49 Yankees?

Second, although the South had only 40 percent as many people as the North, the availability of slaves freed a much larger proportion of whites for military service. Finally, the martial tradition of the slave-holding class now took on a crucial military significance. Southerners had dominated the nation's military academies and officers' corps. Many of these southerners now fought for the Confederacy, leaving the North with few effective military leaders.

These advantages were apparent at Bull Run, in northern Virginia, in the first major battle of the Civil War. On July 21, 1861, twenty-two thousand southerners, led by General Thomas "Stonewall" Jackson, pushed back an attack by thirty thousand Union troops. Although only six hundred men lost their lives, the battle of Bull Run gave Americans their first taste of the carnage that lay ahead. Northern civilians, who had traveled to the battle site to picnic and witness an afternoon of martial jousting, ended up fleeing for their lives to escape Confederate artillery.

The defeat at Bull Run gave the North a tremendous shock.

"... TO DEPRIVE THEIR MASTERS OF THEIR SERVICES"

On May 27, 1861, four days after he decided personally to allow escaped slaves to stay at Fortress Monroe, General Benjamin F. Butler once again wrote the general-in-chief of the army. Butler commented on the use of slave labor in support of the Rebel cause, concluding that it was a problem "of very serious magnitude." Male slaves were laboring on the construction of Confederate fortifications; at the same time planters were sending slave women and children south, away from the front. Butler's letter considers the military, political, and humanitarian aspects of this situation and asks for some guidance from federal officials.

AS A MATTER of property to the insurgents [sheltering the escaped slaves] will be of very great moment, the number that I now have amounting as I am informed to what in good times would be of the value of sixty thousand dollars. Twelve of these negroes I am informed have escaped from the erection of the batteries on Sewall's Point which this morning fired upon my expedition as it passed by out of range. As a means of offense therefore in the enemy's hands these negroes when able-bodied are of the last importance. Without them the [Confederate] batteries could not have been erected at least for many weeks. As a military question it would seem to be a measure of necessity to deprive their masters of their services. How can this be done? As a political question and a question of humanity can I receive the services of a Father and a Mother and not take in the children? Of the humanitarian aspect I have no doubt. Of the political one I have no right to judge. I therefore submit all this to your better judgment. . . .

"The Stampede from Bull Run—From a Sketch by Our Special Artist." Northern illustrated newspapers dispatched "special artists" to cover the war. These artists' sketches, engraved on wood blocks and published in *Harper's Weekly, Frank Leslie's Illustrated Newspaper,* and other periodicals, were the North's major source of war imagery. A few short-lived southern illustrated papers appeared, but it was the *Illustrated London News* that most actively portrayed the Confederate point of view. Its "special artist" Frank Vizetelly sketched this rout of Union forces on July 21, 1861.

In its wake, Congress began to move against slavery, attempting to make Butler's contraband policy more systematic. On August 6, 1861, Congress passed its first confiscation act, proclaiming that any slave-owner whose slaves were used by the Confederate Army would thereafter lose all claim to those slaves. Although far from a clearcut declaration of freedom, the act provided slaves and abolitionists with a basis for further action.

Slaves now moved quickly. In every region touched by the war, African-American men, women, and children fled to Union camps. They requested protection, offering in return their labor and their knowledge of the local terrain and Confederate troop movements. But masters often followed runaway slaves into the camps and demanded that their property be returned. Although none were returned from Fortress Monroe, some commanders (following the letter of the confiscation act) returned slaves who had not served the Confederacy, or simply prevented them from entering their camps in the first place.

But the persistence of the slaves and their determination to gain freedom gradually led many Union officers and ordinary soldiers to help
shield escapees from slavecatchers intent on returning them to servitude. In November 1861, Secretary of War Cameron, who had earlier opposed black enlistment, now publicly supported the radical
idea of arming slaves to fight for the Union, labeling as "madness"
the policy of leaving the enemy "in peaceful and secure possession of
slave property."

Lincoln, again acting to calm angry loyal slaveholders, forced Cameron to backtrack, and in January 1862 removed him from his position. But antislavery sentiment was growing in Congress, inside the
Union Army, and in the North as a whole. At the forefront of the
antislavery group in Congress was a handful of abolitionists who
sought to use the war to strike down the "peculiar institution." These
so-called Radical Republicans never represented more than a minority of the Congress. But they were able to help shape its legislation by
constantly emphasizing the military benefits to be gained by striking
at the institution of slavery. "You will observe that I propose no crusade for abolition," wrote the Radical Massachusetts senator Charles
Sumner in November 1861. Emancipation "is to be presented strictly
as a measure of military necessity."

The military argument for emancipation took on greater force as
the war dragged on through 1861 and 1862. The Union's navy began
a blockade of southern ports that grew ever more effective. In April
1862 the navy captured the major southern port city of New Orleans.
Even more significant, Union troops commanded by Ulysses S. Grant
won in the same month a battle at Shiloh in western Tennessee. Shiloh was a grisly bloodbath, a new kind of battle in which soldiers
pushed forward yard by yard under heavy fire. When it was over nearly
four thousand men lay dead, more than sixteen thousand wounded.
Grant's troops were too exhausted to follow up their victory. But the
Confederacy had lost a battle it could not afford to lose. Now the vast
western regions of the Confederacy, the very heart of the slave South,
lay open to invasion.

Union advances deep into the cotton belt during 1862 gave Union
soldiers a chance to observe slavery at first hand. Many—although
certainly not all—were repulsed by what they saw. After visiting several captured plantations near New Orleans and discovering a number
of instruments used to torture slaves, a Union soldier concluded that
he had seen "enough of the horror of slavery to make one an Abolitionist forever." A Union officer wrote from Louisiana, "Since I am
here, I have learned what the horrors of slavery was. . . . Never hereafter will I either speak or vote in favor of slavery." Such changes in
attitude made some Union soldiers more sympathetic to the plight of
runaway slaves who sought protection behind Union lines.

But changing individual attitudes were less important in determining the status of runaway slaves than a growing sense that the Union could gain a distinct advantage by employing African-American labor in support of the war effort. The willingness of slaves to act as Union spies, reporting on Confederate troop movements in these regions, also disposed some Union officers to give them freedom. "The Negroes are our only friends," wrote a Union officer in northern Alabama. "I shall very soon have watchful guards among the slaves on the plantations bordering the river from Bridgeport to Florence, and all who communicate to me valuable information I have promised the protection of my Government."

Military reversals encouraged antislavery sentiment as well. In the summer of 1862, Confederate troops led by Stonewall Jackson won a series of stunning victories in Virginia's Shenandoah Valley, setting off panic in the North. The panic increased when Union general George B. McClellan, known for his proslavery views and his vacillating approach to military strategy, ordered retreat following the crucial Seven Days' campaign at Richmond, Virginia, in June and July. The Confederate Army in Virginia, commanded by Robert E. Lee, now prepared to invade the North itself.

As the war turned against the North, the North turned against slavery. In July 1862, Congress passed its second confiscation bill, which declared that the slaves of anyone who supported the Confederacy should be "forever free of their servitude, and not again held as slaves." This act encouraged more slaves to do what many had been doing since the war started: desert their masters for freedom behind Union lines. Acceding to pleas from free blacks, slaves, and some Union officers, the congressmen who passed this bill also authorized the president to employ African-Americans in the military. The militia act, passed the same day, allowed "persons of African descent" to be employed in "any military or naval service for which they may be found competent."

"... THE NEW LIFE OF FREEDOM"

The following description, from the war diary of Union general George Gordon, suggests the growing flood of slave contrabands that poured into Union Army camps in northern Virginia from the earliest days of the war.

THE EFFECT OF messages to the colored people to come within our lines began to be more and more apparent in the numbers of men, women, and children, with all sorts of baggage that continued to crowd upon us. The men found work in the quartermaster's department at eight dollars a month and one ration, while the women were employed on wages in washing and in cooking. . . .

Quickly following upon the heels of this [group], came another exodus of negroes, singly and in families, white, black, and blue, with all their children and with their household goods, in all sorts of trunks, parcels, and boxes. I was on my way to the front . . . when I encountered this motley crowd, shouting with joy at their deliverance. No manifestations of regret did they utter, no solicitude did they express; but with a perfect trust, mothers and children laid down their weary loads, and waited to begin the new life of freedom. . . . The next day they went down to Fortress Monroe, and thence wherever they pleased.

By the end of the summer, the numbers of black men (and to some extent, women) employed by the Union Army began growing rapidly. African-Americans built fortifications and roads, chopped wood, carried supplies, guarded ever-lengthening supply lines, and (on naval vessels) shoveled coal. They also worked in more skilled jobs, piloting boats and driving teams. The work was often hard and heavy, and though pay was promised, blacks often received their wages late—or not at all. Though they protested this treatment, they also believed that their labor played a central role in a military struggle for freedom.

For men who had left families in slavery when they escaped to Union lines, their joy in reaching freedom was mixed with the pain of separation. John Boston, a Maryland slave, ran to freedom early in the war and found employment as a servant to a Union officer. A letter to his still-enslaved wife in 1862 illustrated the mixed emotions of many runaway slaves: "This day I can Adress you thank god as a free man. . . . As the lord led the Children of Israel to the land of Canon So he led me to a land Whare freedom Will rain in spite of earth and hell." But Boston's triumph was clouded by concern about seeing his family again: "I trust the time Will Come When We Shall meet again," he wrote. "And if We don't meet on earth We Will meet in heven Whare Jesas ranes."

Even when whole families escaped together, there were problems. Union officers, while seeing the labor of black men as crucial, wanted little to do with women, children, and the elderly. Though some women were employed as laundresses and cooks, their numbers were small compared with those of male laborers. Yet African-American men often made it clear that they would not work unless their families had food and shelter. To stem the general disorganization of large numbers of women and children congregating near military camps, commanders began to establish "contraband camps" in the fall of 1862.

The growing numbers of contrabands and their willingness to labor for the Union cause helped change the attitudes of ordinary white soldiers toward the idea of emancipation. Writing home early in 1863, a Minnesota sergeant explained:

> I have never been in favor of the abolition of slavery until
> . . . this war has detirmend me in the conviction that it is
> a greater sin than our Government is able to stand—and
> now I go in for a war of emancipation and I am ready and
> willing to do my share of the work.

The president's own views on emancipation reflected a similar shift. Like Congress and the public, Lincoln was influenced by the turn in the North's military fortunes. But he was also affected by a crucial diplomatic objective: the need to prevent international recognition of southern independence.

The Confederacy desperately needed such recognition. In the long run, international support would undermine the Union cause and might help persuade the North to accept southern independence. Of more immediate concern, the agricultural South looked abroad for the manufactured products needed in a modern war. Attention focused mainly on Britain, the leading market for southern cotton and a potentially important supplier of goods. Many British political leaders sympathized with the Confederacy. Their sympathy increased as the Union blockade of southern ports grew more effective, for it had a disastrous effect on the British economy. In the Lancashire textile region, which depended entirely on the South for its raw cotton, thousands of workers lost their jobs, turning some of them into supporters of the Confederacy as well.

Nevertheless, working people throughout England had long maintained a hatred of both slavery and the southern slaveholding aristocracy. The democratic sentiments that underlay this hatred could not be fully mobilized until the North officially took a strong antislavery position. A firm Union commitment to the complete emancipation of the slaves might turn the tide, giving the North an edge in the battle for public opinion and preventing Britain's recognition of the Confederacy.

In response to these diplomatic considerations, the deteriorating military situation, and the unrelenting pressure of slave "contrabands," Lincoln decided in the summer of 1862 to issue a proclamation emancipating all slaves. He withheld its announcement, waiting for a Union victory that would make the proclamation a sign of strength rather than one of weakness. The opportunity came in the fall of 1862, when Lee led his army north into Maryland. On September 17, in the bloodiest battle yet (even bloodier days would soon follow), Union troops brought Lee's advance to a standstill at Antietam. Nearly five thousand men lost their lives on that day; another three thousand would die later of wounds.

Antietam was the victory Lincoln required. Five days later, he announced his preliminary Emancipation Proclamation to the assembled cabinet. On January 1, 1863, the final edict was issued. It proclaimed that slaves in areas still in rebellion were "forever free" and invited them to enlist in the Union Army. Nonetheless, the proclamation seemed a conservative document. Its provisions exempted 450,000 slaves in the loyal border states as well as 275,000 slaves in Union-occupied Tennessee and tens of thousands more in Louisiana and Virginia. It also justified the abolition of southern slavery on military rather than moral grounds.

Despite the limitations of the Emancipation Proclamation, its announcement set off wild cheering among white and black abolitionists in Boston and celebration and prayer among fugitive slaves in Washington, D.C. There was even jubilation among the slaves in loyal border states who were exempted from the proclamation's provisions. African-Americans, slave and free alike, understood, in ways that white Americans only partially did, that the aims of the war had been dramatically changed. The Emancipation Proclamation augured a total transformation of southern society, rather than the mere reintegration of the slave states when the Union proved victorious. Although Lincoln had admonished Congress in 1861 that the war not turn into "a violent and remorseless revolutionary struggle," by 1863 that is precisely what it had become.

SOLDIERS' LIVES

If the northern victory at Antietam gave Lincoln the victory he needed to issue the Emancipation Proclamation and begin the active enlistment of black soldiers, it did not mark an overall change in the North's fortunes on the battlefield. In the following months the war continued to go poorly for the Union. Against a superior Union force, Confederate troops won an important victory in December 1862 at Fredericksburg, Virginia, inflicting twelve thousand Union casualties, while suffering only five thousand of their own. In the same month, Confederate cavalry cut Union supply lines in the West, preventing a much larger Union force from seizing the strategic river town of Vicksburg, Mississippi. By early 1863 the war reached a stalemate. Then in May, Lee's army defeated a Union force twice its size at Chancellorsville, Virginia, setting the stage for a Confederate thrust north into Pennsylvania. These victories reflected not only the South's advantage in fighting on its own terrain and its officers' greater talents, but also the generally disorganized nature of the northern war effort.

Despite having more than twice as many soldiers, northern officers seemed unable to press their clear advantages in the war's first two years. Early battles, while intense, were separated by long periods of inactivity. Tradition dictated that both armies take the winter months off, building semipermanent winter camps to await the spring thaw. One estimate suggests that in its first two years of operation, the Union's Army of the Potomac spent a total of only one month in actual battle.

The war's casual pace fulfilled the expectations of both northern and southern soldiers. Most were too young to remember, much less to have experienced, any organized war (America's last war, with Mexico, was fully two decades earlier). Popular notions of battle were

"Cavalry Charge at Fairfax Court House, May 31, 1861." Early in the war, artists often drew highly romantic and very inaccurate pictures. Such feats as firing from the saddle were viewed with great amusement by soldiers in the field, who enjoyed seeing illustrations of their exploits almost as much as they criticized their inaccuracies.

largely derived from articles and pictures in popular magazines. Most young men expected war to be conducted in an orderly, even chivalrous fashion. They were in for a rude shock. A young private wrote home that his idea of combat had been that the soldiers "would all be in line, all standing in a nice level field fighting, a number of ladies taking care of the wounded, etc., etc., but it isn't so."

One reason it wasn't had to do with the extraordinary range of the muzzle-loading rifles used by both sides, which quickly turned early battlefields into scenes of sheer chaos and carnage. Although an individual soldier could fire only a few times a minute, the Enfield and Springfield rifles were murderously effective at great distances, thanks in large measure to the fact that their barrels were spirally grooved ("rifled") to spin the bullets and extend their range. In the early battles, soldiers marched in tight formation toward an enemy that began killing and wounding them from a quarter of a mile away.

The first Civil War battles thus put a premium on the individual courage of ordinary soldiers, valuing their willingness to move forward relentlessly under withering fire. In the face of such efficient killing, fixed infantry formations soon gave way to the realities of self-defense and protection. By 1863 the nature of battle had changed considerably, relying on heavy fortifications, elaborate trenches, and distant heavy mortar and artillery fire—more like World War I than the American Revolution or even the Mexican War.

But battles alone, while obviously important, were not enough to determine the ultimate success of either side. More mundane factors—sanitation, consistent supplies of materials and food, and sufficient medical care—proved equally important as the war wore on. As we will see, the North's stronger industrial base gave it an ability to solve such logistical problems after 1863, an ability that the largely agricultural Confederacy clearly lacked.

Overall, the Civil War proved to be an exhausting, trying experience for the ordinary infantrymen who bore the brunt of the fighting. One Vermont soldier wrote after a major battle that he was "so completely worn out that I can't tell how many days there has been in the last two weeks. . . . I went without sleeping or eating." The hardships and discomforts experienced on both sides extended far beyond actual fighting. Many solders went into battle in ragged uniforms, even

"Maryland and Pennsylvania Farmers Visiting the Battle-field of Antietam." As the war progressed and artist-reporters experienced battle firsthand, their illustrations often became more realistic. F. H. Schell sketched the carnage after the battle of Antietam and the morbid curiosity of the local inhabitants.

without shoes. A Georgia major reported after Manassas that he "carried into the fight over one hundred men who were barefoot, many of whom left bloody foot-prints among the thorns and briars through which they rushed."

Supplies of rations on both sides were sporadic at best; food was often adulterated, and even that was in short supply. Staples of the Union Army diet were bread (actually, an unleavened biscuit called hardtack), meat, beans, and coffee, the latter drunk in enormous quantities. Confederate troops got even less, subsisting on cornmeal and fatty meat. Vegetables and fruit were scarce on both sides, making scurvy common. Confederate rations were so short that after some battles, officers sent details to gather food from the haversacks of Union dead. "I came nearer to starving than I ever did before," noted a rebel soldier in Virginia. In fact, as the war progressed, the Confederate government actually reduced rations to its soldiers; Union soldiers' diet, on the other hand, improved because of the greater scope and efficiency of the North's supply system.

Disease proved a greater adversary than enemy soldiers. "There is more dies by sickness than gets killed," complained a recruit from New York in 1861. His assessment was chillingly accurate. For every soldier who died as a result of battle, three died of disease. Caused or made worse by contaminated water, bad food, and exposure, diseases such as measles, dysentery, typhoid, and malaria became major killers. One soldier stationed in Louisiana described an outbreak of malaria:

> Two-thirds of the regiment are buried or in hospital. It is woeful to see how nearly destitute of comforts and of at-

"A Harvest of Death, Gettysburg, July 1863." Photographers also covered the war, following the Union Army in wagons that served as traveling darkrooms. Their equipment was bulky and the exposures had to be long, so they could not take action photographs during battle. But photography was graphic; this picture taken on the morning of July 4th showed the northern public that dying in battle lacked the gallantry often represented in paintings and prints.

tendance the sick are. They cannot be kept in their wretched bunks, but stagger about, jabbering and muttering insanities, till they lie down and die in their ragged, dirty uniforms.

African-American troops fared worst of all. The death rate for black Union soldiers from disease was nearly three times greater than for northern white soldiers, reflecting their generally poorer health upon entry into Union service and the heavy physical labor to which they largely were assigned.

Medical assistance was often primitive. One commentator described military hospitals in the war's early years as "dirty dens of butchery and horror." After the battle of Shiloh, General Grant's medical director told of "thousands of human beings . . . wounded and lacerated in every conceivable manner, on the ground, under a pelting rain, without shelter, without bedding, without straw to lie upon, and with but little food. . . . The agonies of the wounded were beyond all description." Army doctors on both sides provided little relief. "I believe the Doctors kills more than they cure," wrote an Alabama private in 1862; "Doctors haint Got half Sence." Little wonder that ordinary soldiers often resisted being sent to hospitals, despite serious wounds or illness.

The morale of ordinary soldiers, Rebel and Yankee alike, reflected their performance on the battlefield and the relative comfort of camp life. As food, sanitation, and medical care deteriorated on both sides in the war's initial year and the horrors of battle sank in, a shockingly large number of soldiers de-

---

"I HAVE NEVER CONCEIVED OF SUCH TRIALS . . ."

Severe shortages of food, clothing, and medical care plagued soldiers in both the Union and Confederate armies throughout the war. Below are two letters from soldiers to their families, lamenting the travails of army life.

CONFEDERATE SOLDIER AFTER THE LONG MARCH FROM YORKTOWN TO RICHMOND, SEPTEMBER 1862

I have never conceived of such trials as we have passed through. We were for days together without a morsel of food, excepting occasionally a meal of parched corn. . . . The army was kept on the march day and night, and the roads were in some places waist deep in mud. . . . Many of the men became exhausted and some were actually stuck in the mud and had to be pulled out. . . . The men on the march ran through the gardens . . . devouring every particle of vegetables like the army worm, leaving nothing at all standing. Whenever a cow or hog were found it was shot down and soon despatched.

WOUNDED UNION SOLDIER, BATON ROUGE, JUNE 1863

I never wish to see another such time as the [day I was wounded]. The surgeons used a large Cotton Press for the butchering room and when I was carried into the building and looked about I could not help comparing the surgeons to fiends. It was dark and the building lighted partially with candles; all around on the ground lay the wounded men; some of them were shrieking, some cursing and swearing, and some praying; in the middle of the room was some ten or twelve tables just large enough to lay a man on; these were used as dissecting tables and they were covered with blood. Near and around the tables stood the surgeons with blood all over them and by the sides of the tables was a heap of feet, legs, and arms. On one of these tables I was laid, and being known as a colonel, the Chief Surgeon of the Department was called and he felt of my mouth and then wanted to give me chloroform: this I refused to take and he took a pair of scissors and cut out the pieces of bone in my mouth: then gave me a drink of whiskey and had me laid away.

serted. At Antietam, Confederate general Lee estimated that one-third to one-half of his soldiers were "straggling"—that is, absent without leave. Early the next year, Union general Hooker reported that one in four soldiers under his command similarly were absent. Morale problems in the Union Army were compounded by the fact that the North kept losing battles to seemingly inferior Confederate forces; many Union soldiers were openly critical of their leaders by 1863. A Massachusetts private concluded that "there is very little zeal or patriotism in the army now; the men have seen so much more of defeat than of victory and so much bloody slaughter that all patriotism is played out."

As we will see, a string of Union victories, beginning at Gettysburg, Pennsylvania, and Vicksburg, Mississippi, in July 1863, helped improve Yankee morale and instill in the northern population a will to see the war through to victory. At the same time, Confederate morale—both in the army and on the homefront—sank into despair. What turned the tide for the Union was not simply improved army leadership and better tactics. The North's pronounced economic advantage over the South finally came into play, improving the supply of armaments, food, and clothing to Union troops.

WAR TRANSFORMS THE NORTH

Despite military setbacks in 1861 and 1862, the Union grew stronger as the war progressed. Northern factories steadily turned out the weapons, ammunition, blankets, clothing, shoes, and other products so essential to victorious armies. Its shipyards built the fleets that blockaded southern ports. Since the early 1800s, the North had been the center of American industrial development. By 1860, manufacturing establishments in the North outnumbered those in the South six to one; there were 1.3 million industrial workers in the North, compared to 110,000 in the South. The emerging system of industrial capitalism—a system based predominantly on railroads, factories, cities, and wage labor—could be put to military use. The war did not cause these developments; as we have seen in previous chapters, they began much earlier in the nineteenth century. But the war did dramatically speed the pace of change. The war also gave birth to the modern American state, dominated by a national government far more powerful than anything the nation had known previously.

Ironically, the original economic effects of the war had been little short of disastrous. New England textile production declined precipitously as the flow of raw southern cotton dried up. Shoe factories, relying heavily on the South for their market, fell silent. The large seaboard cities of the Northeast, whose very lifeblood was trade, suffered greatly.

Women filling cartridges at the U. S. Arsenal at Watertown, Massachusetts.

By 1863, however, the economic picture had changed dramatically. Coalmining and iron production boomed in Pennsylvania. New England woolen manufacture took up the slack left by the decline of cotton. Merchants dealing in war orders made handsome profits and industrialists ran their factories at a frenzied pace.

The economic boom of 1863–64 was inextricably linked to a vast expansion of the federal government's power. Direct orders from the War Office for blankets, firearms, and other goods did much to spark the manufacturing upturn. The government also stimulated economic activity by granting large contracts to northern railroads to carry troops and supplies and by making loans and land grants that would finance the railroads' dramatic postwar expansion. Congress also instituted a steep tariff on imported manufactured goods, giving American manufacturers protection from competition and encouraging industrial development. Such policies had long been demanded by northern industrialists; with southern Democrats removed from the halls of Congress, Republican congressmen now rushed to meet these demands.

Perhaps the federal government's most significant long-term contribution to the economy was the creation of a national currency and a national banking system. Before the Civil War, private banks (chartered by the states) issued their own banknotes, which were used in most economic transactions; the federal government paid all of its expenses in gold or silver. Various wartime acts of Congress revolutionized this system, giving the federal government the power to create currency, to issue federal charters to banks, and to create a national debt (which totaled $2 billion by war's end). These developments had important long-term consequences, helping to shape the full flowering of industrial capitalism after the war. But they also had profound short-term effects as well. In order to finance the war, the government used its new power to flood the nation with $400 million in treasury bills, commonly called "greenbacks." The federal budget mushroomed from $63 million in 1860 to nearly $1.3 billion in 1865; the federal bureaucracy had grown to be the nation's largest single employer by war's end. These federal actions provided a tremendous stimulus to industry and were greeted, on the whole, with enthusiasm by northern manufacturers.

In the minds of industrialists, the need for a new supply of workers was second only to the need for currency and banking reform. As over half a million workers left their jobs for the Union Army and the pace of production accelerated, a major labor shortage emerged. Employers dealt with the problem in a variety of ways, all of which turned out to have important consequences for northern society as a whole.

Mechanization offered the most thoroughgoing way of solving the problem, though machines were more widely introduced in agriculture than in industry. Reapers and mowers had been developed and used in the decade prior to the war. The shortage of agricultural labor now greatly hastened their adoption by midwestern farmers. "The severe manual toil of mowing, raking, pitching, and cradling is now performed by machinery," noted the *Scientific American* in 1863. "Man simply oversees the operations and conducts them with intelligence." The war similarly quickened the trend towards mechanization in the manufacture of clothing and shoes.

Immigration was another way to remedy the labor shortage. Here industrialists led the way, forming organizations like the Boston Foreign Emigrant Aid Society and the American Emigrant Company to encourage migration from the European countryside to American factories, mines, and mills. They were extremely successful. Immigration had fallen off sharply in the first two years of the war, with only about 90,000 immigrants arriving in 1861 and again in 1862—less than half the level of the preceding five years. But by 1863 the number of immigrants had reached the pre-1860 level again. The figure climbed to nearly 200,000 in 1864 and to over 300,000 in 1865. Irish, Germans, and British dominated this increased flow of immigrants into the country.

The entry of women into new sectors of the work force also helped ease the labor shortage. Women took over much of the work on northern farms.

Take your gun and go, John,
Take your gun and go,
For Ruth can drive the oxen,
And I can use the hoe,

went the words to a popular verse called "The Volunteer's Wife." A missionary traveling through Iowa in 1863 reported that he "met more women driving teams on the road and saw more at work in the fields than men."

But the labor of women was not confined to the farm. Already major participants in the industrial work force before the war, women were now hired in ever larger numbers in the factories and armories churning out northern war orders. Most important to the war effort were the thousands of "sewing women," who worked under government contract in their own homes (often in crowded tenements) to make the uniforms worn by Union soldiers. Some of the newer industrial jobs women held were temporary; when the war ended so did their employment. But in other areas, such as the nursing profession, women made permanent inroads. Despite strong initial opposition, women struggled successfully to obtain work in northern hospitals. By the end of the war, they had almost entirely replaced men in taking care of the sick. Opportunities for women also opened up in teaching and in government clerical work. Finally, during the Civil War, women began their entry into retail sales and food processing, areas that would have large concentrations of women workers in later years.

The Civil War, then, created new opportunities for some. But all in all, northern working

"... AND THEN I MUST WORK FOR MYSELF"

The following letter, written by a sewing woman in November 1863 to the New York Sun, *reveals the kinds of jobs and the low wages available to northern working women during the war.*

WHEN THIS REBELLION broke out, my brothers joined the Army, and then I must work for myself and help support my mother and my little sister. I would read the advertisements in the paper and go answer them. . . .

A well-known hat manufactory on Broadway wanted five hundred hands. I applied for work. The proprietor . . . promised me 62 cents per dozen. I knew I could not make a dozen per day; but what was I to do? I wanted work, and must get it, or starve. My mother and myself worked from early morning until late at night, but could not make more than $2.50 each per week. . . . Are we nothing but living machines, to be driven at will for the accommodation of a set of heartless, yes, I may say souless people . . .? They ought to read the commandment, "Thou shall not kill." But they are murderers that die on feather beds. . . .

Men join the army and leave us with our employers to battle with. I trust that we will have kind friends to aid us; it is a good work. If we were paid better it would save many young girls from worse than poverty. Let us act as one, and I feel sure that with the blessings of God, and assistance of our fellow beings, we will succeed.

E.S.P., A Working Girl

people suffered tremendously during the war years. Their main problem was inflation. As greenbacks flooded the economy and as consumer goods fell into short supply, prices climbed rapidly—about 20 percent faster than wages. Skilled workers, whose labor was in high demand, might be able to keep up. But unskilled workers were hit hard by inflation, particularly the sewing women, who had almost no bargaining power and who were often exploited by unscrupulous contractors. "We are unable to sustain life for the prices offered by contractors, who fatten on their contracts by grinding immense profits out of the labor of their operatives," wrote a group of Cincinnati seamstresses to President Lincoln in 1864.

Northern workers tried to improve their plight in a variety of ways. From 1863 through 1865, there were dozens of strikes as workers in a number of trades began to form unions to demand higher wages. Many workers also looked to Lincoln and the federal government for help. The Republicans, after all, had pledged themselves to protecting the rights of free labor.

But government proved to be a better friend of business than of labor. Employers successfully lobbied a number of state legislatures to pass laws prohibiting strikes. They also persuaded the increasingly powerful federal government to help block workers' efforts to organize. When workers at the Parrott arms factory in Cold Spring, New York, struck for higher wages in 1864, the government sent in two companies of troops, declared martial law, and arrested the strike leaders. The army similarly intervened in labor disputes in St. Louis and in the Pennsylvania coalfields. All three strikes were crushed.

These experiences led many workers to criticize the federal government and its ruling Republican Party. Even more upsetting were the huge profits that industrialists garnered as production boomed. Profits in the woolen industry nearly tripled, railroad stocks climbed to unheard-of prices, and government contractors made huge gains—sometimes by supplying inferior goods

". . . IF WAGES ARE NOT PERMITTED TO KEEP PACE"

The problem of wartime inflation and tainted food is described in the following account taken from a July 1863 issue of Fincher's Trades Review, *an important labor newspaper of the period.*

TWO YEARS AGO, the man who received $1.50 per day, could satisfy his wants with that sum just as well, if not better, than he can now with $3.00 per day. Nearly every article of consumption has doubled, and if wages are not permitted to keep pace with the cost of necessaries, the producer is daily robbed of one-half his earnings. . . . Rents will soon range from 15 to 20 percent higher; and many articles heretofore used by the families of workingmen are now wholly beyond their means.

It will be found, also, that workingmen are subjected to other ills by the fictitious value placed upon the necessaries of life. Flour has become classified into several brands, which plainly indicate impurity in one or more of them, and means something more than the mere color of the wheat; hence, the purchaser of second or third quality is apt to eat his share of worms and other insects, or nauseate his stomach with musty, sour bread. . . . The vegetable and chemical trash mixed up with a small portion of [coffee] is enough to weaken the digestive organs of an ostrich. Tea undergoes the same fraudulent process, and our lady readers cannot be too careful in the selection of the article. These adulterations, in many cases, must result in shattered health, if not premature death. . . .

THE IRREPRESSIBLE CONFLICT.

In this cartoon from *Vanity Fair,* an Irish longshoreman tells a black worker seeking employment on New York's waterfront: "Well, ye may be a man and a brother, sure enough; but it's little hospitality ye'll get out of yer relations on this dock, me ould buck!" The sharp competition for unskilled jobs contributed to the New York draft riot.

at vastly inflated prices. To working people suffering the ravages of inflation, such extraordinary profits seemed, to say the least, unfair.

This situation raised the hopes of opposition Democrats in their continuing effort to bring the war to an end. The Civil War had deeply divided the Democratic Party in the North. Although some party leaders supported Lincoln and the war effort, many (called Copperheads after the poisonous snake) rallied behind Ohio politician Clement L. Vallandigham in opposing the war. These antiwar Democrats sought desperately to build working-class support for their position.

They enjoyed considerable success, particularly in the large eastern cities, where inflation was running rampant and where immigrant workers had long supported Democratic political machines. Racism was the strongest weapon in the party's arsenal. As the Civil War increasingly became a war against slavery, many antiblack white workers gave their support to the peace wing of the Democratic Party.

The clear injustice of the Republicans' draft law added fuel to this fire. The Conscription Act of March 1863 provided that draftees would be selected by an impartial lottery. But it also allowed an individual to pay a $300 fee to the government in place of serving or to pay a substitute to take his place. Many unskilled workers were lucky to earn $300 in an entire year. They deeply resented both the draft law's profound inequality and the recent expansion of the North's war aims to include emancipation of the slaves.

The resentment of the urban poor reached the boiling point in July 1863, when the new draft law went into effect. Riots against the law broke out in the cities across the North. In New York, where war-induced inflation had caused tremendous suffering, implementation of the draft triggered three days of the worst rioting Americans had ever seen. Violence and looting quickly spread through the entire city. Rioters, many of them poor and unskilled Irish immigrants, attacked and killed Protestant missionaries, Republican draft officials, and wealthy businessmen. Homes in the city's wealthy neighborhoods were looted. Bitterness caused by years of hardship and discrimination suddenly exploded in a massive urban rebellion.

Tragically, but not surprisingly, New York City's small free-black population became the rioters' main target. Immigrant workers, determined not to be drafted to fight for the freedom of a people they despised, turned on black New Yorkers in rage. One observer reported that he saw "a black man hanged . . . for no offense but his Negritude." Rioters lynched at least a dozen African-Americans and looted

"Buying a Substitute in the North during the War." From *Sketches from the Civil War in North America,* a collection of etchings by Baltimore "Copperhead" artist A. J. Volck. A German immigrant dentist, Volck depicted the Union Army as composed of immigrant and native-born deviants and criminals. He was moved less by the inequities of the northern draft law than by his sympathy for the South.

The New York Draft Riots: Lynching
of a black man on Clarkson Street.

and burned the city's Colored Orphan Asylum. Leading trade-unionists joined middle-class leaders in condemning the riots, but to no avail. The violence ended only when Union troops were rushed back from the front to put down the riot by force. The troops included New York's own Irish Brigade, whose members, in the process of securing the city's working class wards, had to fire on their countrymen. When it finally ended, over one hundred New Yorkers lay dead.

Thus as it unfolded, the war encouraged both a quickening of economic change and a heightening of social tensions in the North. These tensions gave Democratic leaders much room for maneuver, because they could link the long-standing racism of the northern white population with workers' growing resentment at the wartime inequities now evident in the North. The Democrats' explicit challenge proved short-lived, however; July 1863 also marked the beginning of the Union's military turnaround.

That month, the Union won two decisive victories.

In the eastern theater, Union forces turned back a major Confederate drive, defeating Lee's army at Gettysburg, Pennsylvania, on July 4. The battle was a disaster for the South: four thousand of its men lay dead; another twenty-four thousand were recorded as wounded or missing.

In the West, troops under Grant's command, using an audacious mobile strategy, followed by a direct siege, finally succeeded in capturing the Confederate city of Vicksburg, Mississippi. Thirty thousand Confederate soldiers surrendered after Vicksburg's fall. In the long run, this victory was even more important than Gettysburg, for it gave the Union Army control of the richest plantation region in the South. With the northern victory at Vicksburg the curtain went up on the most important act of the Civil War: the destruction, root and branch, of American slavery.

AFRICAN-AMERICANS IN THE WAR

After the Union capture of Vicksburg in July 1863, African-American slaves intervened decisively in the Civil War in two interrelated ways. First, as the war moved South, slaves in greater and greater numbers deserted their owners to join the Union's advancing forces. Slave labor was crucial to the South's economy and military effort, and this

massive transfer of labor from the Confederacy to the Union had a tremendous impact on the course of the war. Second, ex-slaves overcame initial white objections to their use as front-line soldiers, serving with distinction in the Union Army and contributing directly to key northern victories. As they fought for Union victory, African-Americans helped assure that nothing short of universal emancipation would be the outcome of the war.

Grant's capture of Vicksburg gave northern forces control of the Mississippi Valley, the heart of the new South. In November 1863, General George H. Thomas followed with a major victory in the battle of Chattanooga, opening up much of the South's remaining territory to Union invasion. As 1864 began, Union forces were twice those of the Confederacy, and the southern armies were suffering from low morale and dwindling supplies, especially of food. The North's war of attrition had begun to pay dividends.

The changing Union fortunes helped turn the tide of northern pub-

Private Pryor makes the news. In 1864 T. B. Bishop photographed escaped slave Hubbard Pryor before and after he enlisted in the Forty-Fourth U. S. Colored Infantry. By the time the photographs were transferred to wood-block, appearing in the July 2 edition of *Harper's Weekly* as "The Escaped Slave" and "The Escaped Slave in the Union Army," the "after" Private Pryor had changed. He had become the kind of romantic soldier of which the *Weekly*'s editor thought his readers would approve.

lic opinion. As the memory of the draft riots of 1863 faded, white northerners' support for Lincoln, and indirectly for abolition, began to grow. Wartime experiences doubtless changed the attitudes of many, who saw the "peculiar institution" and the suffering it inflicted on African-Americans firsthand. By the end of the war, such experiences had been translated, at least in a limited way, into changes in racial attitudes and even in the law. Ohio, California, and Illinois repealed statutes barring blacks from testifying in court and serving on juries. In May 1865, Massachusetts passed the first comprehensive public-accommodations law in American history. Earlier, San Francisco, Cincinnati, Cleveland, and even New York City (despite the virulent racism witnessed in the 1863 draft riot) had desegregated their streetcars. The logic of a war against the enslavement of southern blacks now was extended, at least partially, to encompass rights for free blacks in the North.

These developments boded ill for the Democratic Party. In 1864, the party nominated George B. McClellan, the one-time Union commander, as their candidate for president. McClellan ran on a peace platform, and while he managed to attract many working people who had traditionally supported the Democrats and who now bore the heaviest burden of the war, his efforts failed in the end. Coming on the heels of Union general Sherman's capture of Atlanta, the election gave Lincoln a stunning victory and a clear mandate to continue the war to its conclusion.

The rapid Union advances after 1864 enhanced slaves' opportunities for seizing their freedom. Despite the desperate efforts of slaveowners to remove them from areas of combat, whenever the Union Army moved through plantation regions, thousands of slaves put down their tools, gathered up their belongings, and headed for the Union lines. The climax of this movement occurred during Sherman's march through Georgia. Nearly eighteen thousand slaves—men, women, and children—left their plantations to join the victorious Union Army in its march to the sea.

The approach of Union troops also affected slaves who did not flee. "He won't look at me now," said one white woman of her mother's butler as the northern army approached. "He looks over my head, he scents freedom in the air." Slaves suddenly became less willing to work and refused to take punishment they had accepted in the past. And they also began to talk openly of the advancing Union Army. As she prepared Sunday dinner for her master, a cook in eastern Virginia greeted each blast of nearby Union cannons with "Ride on, Massa Jesus." Slaves frequently interpreted events in religious terms. But freedom was to be realized on earth, not in heaven, and it was not to be long in coming. "Now they gradually threw off the mask," a slave later remembered of this moment, "and were not afraid to let it be known that the 'freedom' in their songs meant freedom of the body in this world."

As more and more ex-slaves came under Union protection, major problems arose. Frequently short on rations, clothing, and medical supplies, Union officers were not sure what to do with the growing numbers of men and women. Some even turned away contrabands, who then risked capture by Confederate forces and even re-enslavement. But by the end of the war, nearly a million ex-slaves, about one-fourth of the African-Americans in the South, were under some kind of federal custody. As we have seen, the government established a number of military-run "contraband camps," where ex-slaves were put to work for wages as government laborers. But many of these camps were sadly overcrowded, disease-ridden, and poorly administered, and they created tremendous dissatisfaction among the ex-slaves.

Most objectionable was the fact that the government sometimes broke its promise to pay wages. This was a serious failure, for southern blacks believed that the end of slavery would mean an end to unpaid labor. The wife of a black Union soldier expressed this belief when she wrote to her husband, "Do the best you can and do not fret too much for me, for it won't be long before I will be free and then all we make will be ours." Contrabands understood full well the role that their labor was playing in the Union war effort; they expected the government to recognize that contribution with appropriate compensation.

After 1863, slaves aided the northern war effort directly, as the Union finally began to recruit African-Americans into the military. The response was overwhelming. By the end of the war, nearly 200,000 African-

SLAVES FLEE TO FREEDOM

The following account of South Carolina slaves flocking to meet a regiment of black Union troops is drawn from the testimony of Harriet Tubman, famous for her success in helping hundreds of escaped slaves before the war. Tubman had joined forces with the First South Carolina Volunteers, made up largely of escaped slaves, in raiding plantations and leading slaves to freedom.

"I NEVER SAW such a sight," said Harriet; "we laughed, and laughed, and laughed. Here you'd see a women with a pail on her head, rice smoking in it just as if she'd taken it from the fire, young one hanging on behind, one hand hanging around her forehead to hold on, another hand digging into the rice pot, eating with all its might; holding on to her dress two or three more; down her back a bag with a pig in it. One woman brought two pigs, a white one and a black one; we took them all aboard; named the white pig Beauregard, and the black pig Jeff Davis [two prominent Confederate officials]. Sometimes the women would come with twins hanging around their necks; appears like I never seen so many twins in my life; bags on their shoulders, baskets on their heads, and young ones tagging behind, all loaded; pigs squealing, chickens screaming, young ones squalling." And so they came pouring down to the gunboats. When they stood on the shore, and the small boats put out to take them off, they all wanted to get in at once. After the boats were crowded, they would hold on to them so that they could not leave the shore. The oarsmen would beat them on their hands, but they would not let go; they were afraid the gunboats would go off and leave them, and all wanted to make sure [that they were on] one of these arks of refuge. At length Col. Montgomery shouted from the upper deck, above the clamor of appealing tones, "Harriet, you'll have to give them a song." Then Harriet lifted up her voice and sang:

Of all the whole creation in the east or the west,
The glorious Yankee nation is the greatest and the best.
Come along! Come along! don't be alarmed,
Uncle Sam is rich enough to give you all a farm.

Americans (one out of five black adult males in the entire country) had served in either the Union army or navy, constituting a full one-tenth of the total number of men in uniform. More important was the fact that nearly 80 percent of black soldiers had been recruited in the slave states. By fighting for the Union, these men struck a blow for their own and their people's freedom. George W. Hatton, a black sergeant with Company C, First Regiment, U.S. Colored Troops, captured the sense of momentous change when he observed in 1864 that "though the Government declared that it did not want Negroes in this conflict, I look around me and see hundreds of colored men armed and ready to defend the Government at any moment; and such are my feelings, that I can only say, the fetters have fallen—our bondage is over."

The first black Union regiment had been organized in 1862, but only with the Emancipation Proclamation did Lincoln give his support to the active recruitment of African-American soldiers. White opposition to black enlistment, which had been so strong in the early months of the war, began to dissipate as Union manpower needs grew. Now even outright racists could support black recruitment. "When this war is over and we have summed up the entire loss of life it has imposed on the country," wrote Iowa's governor, Samuel Kirkwood, "I shall not have any regrets if it is found that a part of the dead are *niggers* and that *all* are not white men."

Recruitment policies sometimes reflected this racism. In Louisiana and Mississippi, for example, army squads swept through plantation slave quarters, impressing all able-bodied men into the military. "The Soldiers have taken my husband away . . . and it is against his will," protested one black woman in a letter to the government. African-Americans throughout the South condemned these policies, which tore families apart and undermined any real exer-

"Assault of the Second Louisiana (Colored) Regiment on the Confederate Works at Port Hudson, May 27, 1863." The bravery of black soldiers is extolled in the pages of *Frank Leslie's Illustrated Newspaper.*

MEN OF COLOR
To Arms! To Arms!
NOW OR NEVER
THREE YEARS' SERVICE!
BATTLES OF LIBERTY AND THE UNION
FAIL NOW, & OUR RACE IS DOOMED
SILENCE THE TONGUE OF CALUMNY
VALOR AND HEROISM
PORT HUDSON AND MILLIKEN'S BEND,
ARE FREEMEN LESS BRAVE THAN SLAVES
OUR LAST OPPORTUNITY HAS COME
MEN OF COLOR, BROTHERS AND FATHERS!
WE APPEAL TO YOU!
STRIKE NOW!

A recruiting poster directed to free African-Americans in Pennsylvania, 1863.

cise of freedom. A handwritten manifesto distributed among New Orleans blacks in 1863 pointed to the similarities between "a rebel master and a Union master. . . . One wants us to make Cotton and Sugar . . . the Union master wants us to fight the battles under white officers."

But in the border states, the situation was very different. Because they remained in the Union, four border slave states (Delaware, Kentucky, Maryland, and Missouri) had been exempted from the Emancipation Proclamation. Slaves in these states who enlisted in the Union Army were granted their freedom, nonetheless. Slaveholders in these loyal states did everything in their power to prevent their slaves from joining the army, including assault, the harsh treatment of family members left behind, and even murder. Despite these actions, the proportion of military-age slave men joining the army in these four states was staggering, ranging from 25 to 60 percent. By enlisting in the Union Army, slaves gave the "peculiar institution" in the border states a blow from which it could never recover.

African-American soldiers quickly distinguished themselves in battle. In May 1863, Louisiana black regiments fought with great gallantry and almost reckless disregard for their own lives in the assault on Port Hudson, downriver from Vicksburg. Two weeks later, exslaves helped fight off a Confederate attack at Milliken's Bend in the same region. "The bravery of the blacks in the battle of Milliken's Bend completely revolutionized the sentiment of the army with regard to the employment of negro troops," wrote the assistant secretary of war. "I heard prominent officers who formerly in private had sneered at the idea of the negroes fighting express themselves after that as heartily in favor of it." The valor of African-American troops at Port Hudson and Milliken's Bend helped assure Grant's success in taking Vicksburg the following month.

African-American soldiers had to be courageous, for they faced not only death on the battlefield, but torture and death if they were captured. The Confederate government had threatened that any blacks taken prisoner would be treated as slaves in rebellion and be subject to execution. Although this did not become a general Confederate policy because Lincoln threatened northern retaliation, at Fort Pillow, Tennessee, in April 1864, Confederate troops cold-bloodedly murdered black Union soldiers who had surrendered. By the end of the war, 37,000 black soldiers had given their lives for freedom and the Union.

To some extent, the courage of African-American soldiers helped undermine the ingrained racism of white northerners who served with them. Rank-and-file white soldiers, for example, gave three cheers to a Tennessee black regiment after one hard-fought battle. "One year ago the regiment was unknown, and it was considered . . .

very doubtful whether Negroes would make good soldiers," a white commander noted. "Today the regiment is known throughout the army and is honored."

Nevertheless, racism followed African-Americans into the army. They were segregated in camps, given the most menial jobs, and treated as inferiors by white recruits and officers. "We are treated in a Different manner to what other Regiments is," a black recruit wrote to Abraham Lincoln. "Instead of the musket It is the spade and the Whelbarrow and the Axe."

Particularly galling was the early Union policy of paying black soldiers considerably less than whites. This inequality outraged African-American troops. Many now realized that their fight was not only against southern slavery, but against northern discrimination as well. Black soldiers who openly struggled against this discrimination, like Third South Carolina Volunteers' sergeant William Walker, paid dearly for their courage. Walker, who refused to take orders until given equal pay, was charged with mutiny and executed by firing squad in February 1864. But the protests continued. "The patient Trusting Descendants of Afric's Clime, have dyed the ground with blood, in defense of the Union, and Democracy," an African-American army corporal wrote to Lincoln. "We have done a Soldier's Duty. Why can't we have a Soldier's pay?"

In June 1864 the War Department finally equalized wages among black and white recruits. But the struggle itself had begun to transform African-American soldiers. They now understood that the battle for equality would go on after the war was over and that it would be fought in the North as well as the South. Not surprisingly, black army veterans would lead many of the future struggles for African-American rights.

Many setbacks lay ahead for the ex-slaves. But their participation in the struggle for freedom left a deep mark on the African-American soldiers and on the southern black commu-

---

". . . I HOPE TO FALL WITH MY FACE TO THE FOE"

The heroism of black troops at Port Hudson and Milliken's Bend was only the first of a string of such examples of African-American bravery under fire. On July 18, 1863, the Massachusetts Fifty-Fourth, a regiment made up of free northern blacks and escaped slaves, unsuccessfully attacked Fort Wagner, the Confederate stronghold guarding the entrance to South Carolina's strategically vital Charleston Harbor. After the battle, Frederick Douglass's son Lewis, a sergeant in the Fifty-Fourth, wrote the following letter to his future wife.

My Dear Amelia:
I have been in two fights, and am unhurt. I am about to go in another, I believe to-night. Our men fought well on both occasions. The last was desperate— we charged that terrible battery on Morris Island known as Fort Wagoner, and were repulsed with a loss of [many] killed and wounded. I escaped unhurt from amidst that perfect hail of shot and shell. It was terrible.... Should I fall in the next fight killed or wounded I hope to fall with my face to the foe....

My regiment has established its reputation as a fighting regiment—not a man flinched, though it was a trying time. Men fell all around me. A shell would explode and clear a space of twenty feet, our men would close up again, but it was no use we had to retreat, which was a very hazardous undertaking. How I got out of that fight alive I cannot tell, but I am here. My dear girl, I hope again to see you. I must bid you farewell should I be killed. Remember, if I die, I die in a good cause. I wish we had a hundred thousand colored troops—we would put an end to this war.

nity as a whole. "Suppose you had kept your freedom without enlisting in this army," said a black corporal. "Your children might have grown up free and been well cultivated so as to be equal to any business, but it would have been always flung in their faces—'Your father never fought for his own freedom'—and what could they answer? Never can say that to this African Race anymore."

WAR TRANSFORMS THE SOUTH

While the destruction of slavery was the most dramatic result of the Civil War, it was by no means the only one. In the South as in the North, conflict between the various social classes intensified. The Confederate government's growing power and its encouragement of industrialization contributed a great deal to this conflict, which tore the social fabric of the Confederacy. But there was a more important and immediate cause: by 1864 the South was visibly losing the war. Military defeat ushered in social change.

Widespread popular dissatisfaction actually began when the Confederate Congress introduced a draft in April 1862. This, the first conscription act in American history, came a full year before the Union passed its own draft law. Concerned with the weariness of troops in the field and by Grant's successes in the West, Jefferson Davis concluded that the Confederacy's ability to prosecute the war required conscription.

But other southerners maintained that the very idea of a national (that is, a Confederate) draft undermined southern traditions of states' rights. Georgia's governor, Joseph E. Brown, for example, attempted to block implementation of the act, arguing that it conflicted with the same states'-rights principles that had been used to justify secession in the first place. "No act of the Government of the United States prior to the secession," Brown proclaimed, "struck a blow at constitutional liberty so [fatal] as has been stricken by this conscription act." Many ordinary southerners agreed. "I volunteered for six months and I am perfectly willing to serve my time out, and come home and stay awhile and go again," wrote a Georgia soldier to his family, "but I don't want to be forced to go."

Inequalities in the execution of the law incited opposition as well. As in the North, those with money did not have to fight: a draftee was allowed to hire a substitute to serve in his place. As if this were not enough, another law passed in October 1862 exempted any white man owning twenty or more slaves from service in the army. The growing unruliness of plantation slaves in the absence of overseers or owners explains, at least partially, this special exemption. Practically, though, it meant that the large slaveowners, the very ones who had led the South into war, had exempted themselves from dying in it.

The point was not lost on the non-slaveholding whites who fought and died for the Confederacy. Opposition to the draft grew rapidly, especially among small farmers in the mountains. "All they want is to get you pumpt up and go to fight for their infernal negroes," said one farmer from Alabama, "and after you do there fighting you may kiss there hine parts for all they care." Throughout the South, non-slaveholders used an increasingly popular phrase to describe the Civil War. It was, they said, "a rich man's war and a poor man's fight."

Impressment, introduced by the Confederacy in 1863, also caused discontent. It allowed the Confederate Army to take food, animals, or other property from farmers, paying for these goods at prices fixed far below market value. A group of farmers from Floyd County, Georgia, told of "armed men traversing our 'neighborhoods' taking, in many instances, the last animal fit for beef, and insulting all who dare to claim their right to food." "These seizures are not impressment," the farmers complained; they "are robbery." Along with a more stringent tax bill introduced the same year, impressment placed a heavy burden on the small, food-producing farm families that had the least to gain from a Confederate victory, further penalizing them for their unenthusiastic support for the southern cause.

By taking farm products destined for the market and rerouting them to the army, impressment also intensified a food shortage in the southern cities, which by 1863 had reached crisis proportions. A number of factors led to the food shortage. Although overwhelmingly agricultural, the South had from its earliest days built its economy for the most part on cotton, tobacco, and other distinctly nonedible staples. Grain and livestock were produced in South Carolina, central Virginia, and middle Tennessee, but by 1863 the latter two areas had fallen under Union control. The absence of a good railroad or canal system in the South, coupled with the Union blockade of coastal shipping, hindered distribution of what food there was.

As a result, the specter of starvation came to haunt the cities of the South. Even the people of Richmond, the capital of the Confederacy, were no strangers to hunger. Until March 1863, Richmond's urban poor blamed their plight on the high prices charged by shippers, storekeepers, and others who profited from the food shortage. Then, when government agents began

". . . AND THE REBS BURNT THE LAST BALE"

Jesse Wade, a Georgia up-country farmer, describes Confederate impressment policies and how they led many poor southerners to oppose the southern cause.

THE REBEL ARMY treated us a heap worse than Sherman did. . . . I had four bales of cotton, and the Rebs burnt the last bale. I had hogs, and a mule, and a horse, and they took [them] all. They didn't [even] leave my wife [a] bedquilt. [After] they took what they wanted, they put her out of the house and set fire to it. [None of] my boys fought against the Union; they were conscripted [into the Confederate army] with me, [but] one night we went out on guard [duty] together . . . and [we] just put for the Yankees. All the men that had a little property went in for the war, but the poor people were against it.

"Sowing and Reaping." A northern view of southern white womanhood and secession after the 1863 Charleston bread riot. The first illustration shows southern women "hounding their men on to Rebellion," while the second portrays them later "feeling the effects of Rebellion and creating Bread Riots."

using impressment to take scarce food from city markets to feed the army, the poor found a new target for their anger.

On April 2 a group of women, mostly the wives of Richmond iron-workers, marched to the governor's mansion, demanding that he provide food. When asked by a curious passerby if the march was some sort of celebration, a young woman in the growing throng answered affirmatively. "We celebrate our right to live," she said solemnly. "We are starving. As soon as enough of us get together we are going to the bakeries, and each of us will take a loaf of bread. This is little enough for the government to give us after it has taken all our men." The protest turned into a major riot, ending only when Jefferson Davis personally threatened to have troops open fire on the women. That spring there were also food riots in Atlanta, Macon, and several other cities in Georgia and North Carolina. In Mobile, Alabama, crowds of rioters carried signs reading, "Bread or blood."

That urban food riots could occur at all in the South points to an important and unforeseen consequence of the Civil War. The population of southern cities had grown dramatically. Although southerners had gone to war to protect an essentially rural society, the war was beginning to transform that society. New Orleans had been the only really large southern city prior to the war. Now Atlanta mushroomed, and Richmond's population more than doubled. Smaller cities also grew tremendously. Mobile's population, for example, climbed from twenty-nine thousand people in 1860 to forty-one thousand five years later.

The creation of a large governmental and military bureaucracy triggered Richmond's rapid growth. But the main factor behind the growth of cities was industrialization. Despite its traditional hostility to graceless Yankee capitalists, the South was beginning to industrialize. By 1863, for example, more than ten thousand people in Selma, Alabama, worked in war industries—industries that had not existed three years earlier.

Military necessity provided the spur to industrialization. No longer able to buy industrial goods from the North and handicapped by the Union blockade in its trade with Europe, the South had to either industrialize or die. Thus, the thirty thousand troops that defended Vicksburg in 1863 depended almost exclusively on clothing and equipment manufactured in Mississippi. Factories in Natchez, Columbus, Jackson, and other towns turned out ten thousand garments and eight thousand pairs of shoes a week. According to a local newspaper, these factories, like others that made tents and blankets, had "sprung up almost like magic." At the base of the South's new industries were the huge Tredegar ironworks in Richmond, which employed over twenty-five hundred men by January 1863.

In the end, the South's industrial revolution proved abortive. The victorious Union Army destroyed factories and machinery all across the region as the war drew to a close. More importantly, even at its height, southern industrialization was a creation of government rather than of an independent class of industrial capitalists. The South in 1865 was not even a pale reflection of industrializing New England.

And yet, as in the North, industrialization did trigger wider social change. It led, for instance, to a dramatic change in established gender roles, as large numbers of women took jobs in the new factories. Change had also come to the countryside, where women had to take on full responsibility for farm management; as one soldier wrote to his wife on a Georgia farm, "You must be a man and woman both while the war lasts." But factory work undermined traditional ideas of women's roles most drastically. Women flocked to the mills to make not only clothing but also powder, cartridges, and other armaments. When a roomful of explosives blew up in a Richmond factory in March 1863, most of the sixty-nine workers killed were women.

Industrialization also led to a vast expansion of the region's small urban working class and to the breakup of the old social order in the cities of the South. Led by skilled craftsmen in the war industries, workers formed unions, went on strike, and tried to put political pressure on the Confederate government. Although the movement was weaker and more isolated in the South than in the North, its very existence showed how fast the South was changing in the midst of war.

Of all the problems facing urban working people, inflation was the most difficult. Food shortages forced food prices up, while the blockade and the military focus of southern industry led to rapid inflation in manufactured consumer goods. Finally, the government issued more and more treasury notes to finance the war. In January 1864 it took twenty-seven Confederate dollars to buy what one dollar had bought in April 1861—an inflation rate of 2,600 percent in less than three years!

Southern urban workers could not keep up with this kind of inflation. When Virginia legislators introduced a bill in the fall of 1863 to control food prices, a large crowd of Richmond workers expressed not only their support for price controls, but also their sense of the emerging lines of class conflict in southern society. "From the fact that he consumes all and produces nothing," they proclaimed, "we know that without [our] labor and production the man with money could not exist."

Nevertheless, the urban working class remained a relatively insignificant political force. The small farmers and their families were the ones who constituted the backbone of the Confederacy and who bore the war's heaviest burdens. On the whole, rural southerners remained loyal to the Confederacy and its leaders. Yet eventually, taxation, impressment, inflation, and the inequities of the draft began to take their toll. To these grievances were added the devastation of war: since most of the war was fought in the upper South rather than in the cotton-growing regions of the lower South, small non-slaveholding farmers saw their crops, their animals, and sometimes their very farms destroyed. As the outcome of the

". . . WE WERE FORCED TO DO WITHOUT"

In this account, an Alabama woman recalls how wartime shortages forced farm households either to substitute homemade goods for store-bought ones or to do without.

WITHIN A FEW months after the war began our supply of cloth began to give out. We lived far from the cities and large towns, and the country stores never kept large stocks on hand. All cloth that was suitable for the use of the soldiers was used up at once and more could not be purchased except by sending quite a long distance and by paying very high prices. So very soon our people had to return to the old way of making cloth at home on homemade hand looms. This was slow work, and it was the most tedious of all our home duties, and it kept nearly all of the women and girls busy. . . .

During the war we were forced to do without many things that we formerly had bought from stores. For some of these things nothing could be substituted, but for many of them others were used which we pretended served the purpose almost as well as the originals. We had to pretend about many things in those days.

war became clear by 1864, small farmers began to drift toward the cause of peace.

"A rich man's war and a poor man's fight" had seemed a cynical phrase in 1862. By 1864 it had become the rallying cry of the peace movement. The Washington Constitutional Union, a secret peace society with a large following among farmers in Georgia, Alabama, and Tennessee, elected several of its members to the Confederate Congress. The Heroes of America, another secret organization with strength in North Carolina, provided Union forces with information on southern troop movements and encouraged desertion from the Confederate Army. By war's end, more Confederate soldiers had deserted than remained in uniform. In some isolated mountainous regions of the South, draft evaders and deserters formed guerrilla groups that killed draft officials and actively impeded the war effort.

Here then was another unintended consequence of the Civil War. When they led the South out of the Union in 1861, slaveholders had been motivated in part by a desire to ensure the loyalty of yeoman farmers. But the war seemed to have the opposite effect—far from preserving social harmony between slaveholders and white farmers, or slaveholders and white workers, it undermined that harmony. Although dissent interfered with the war effort only in a limited way, it did prepare the way for a much more massive disaffection of southern farmers and workers in the years following the war.

THE WAR'S END

By mid-1864, the northern policy of total warfare had begun to pay off. Robert E. Lee's Virginia army, badly weakened by death and desertion, was pushed back toward Richmond by a superior Union force, led by General Grant. Invading northern troops in Georgia, under the command of General William Tecumseh Sherman, finally forced Hood's army to retreat to Atlanta, one of the most important cities in the South, in late August. Early the following month, Sherman's army swept into Atlanta, cutting the South in half. A sense of impending doom spread across the Confederacy.

Now, while African-American soldiers helped protect Sherman's army by defeating Hood's forces in the battle of Nashville, Sherman began his famous three-hundred-mile march across Georgia, from Atlanta to the sea. His troops cut a path fifty to sixty miles wide, destroying crops, livestock, and houses before reaching Savannah in late December. Sherman's army, which was entirely white, paid little heed to the thousands of slaves uprooted in the process, many of whom tried to attach themselves to the Union forces. The troops turned many away, and a number of slave contrabands were subsequently captured by marauding Confederate forces and re-enslaved.

"'Marching On!'—The Fifty-Fifth Massachusetts Colored Regiment Singing John Brown's March in the Streets of Charleston, February 21, 1865."

Sherman's callous actions caused a scandal in Washington; the re-enslavement of contrabands posed a significant political and moral issue for the federal government.

In January 1865, Lincoln dispatched Secretary of War Edwin Stanton to Georgia to investigate the charges. In an extraordinary meeting held in Savannah, Stanton and Sherman met with twenty black ministers to hear their complaints about mistreatment of contrabands and to inquire what, in their opinion, African-Americans wanted, now that slavery was ending. The ministers spoke movingly of the war lifting "the yoke of bondage"; freed slaves now "could reap the fruit of our own labor" and, by being given land, could "take care of ourselves, and assist the Government in maintaining our freedom." Four days later, Sherman responded to the ministers' demands by issuing his famous Field Order Number 15, setting aside more than 400,000 acres of captured Confederate land to be divided into small plots for the freed slaves. Perhaps as significant as Sherman's order was the fact that a major official of the national government had traveled to Georgia to ask ordinary African-Americans what they wanted. The Civil War had truly revolutionary consequences.

Those consequences were far-reaching. As defeat loomed at the end of 1864, Confederate leaders themselves began to talk of emancipating the slaves. At almost the same moment as Stanton and Sherman were meeting with the black Savannah ministers, Jefferson Davis called for the general recruitment of slaves into the Confederate Army, with their payment to include freedom for themselves and their families. The Confederate Congress ultimately passed such a law in early 1865, but it came too late to allow African-Americans to actually enlist. The passage of the law demonstrated a startling fact nonetheless: southern planters who had seceded from the Union to protect the institution of slavery were now openly adopting policies that would inevitably destroy it. The Civil War had indeed turned southern society upside down.

The war now entered its final months. In February, Sherman led his troops north from Georgia. They marched through South Carolina and North Carolina, wreaking havoc, destroying the remnants of the plantation system in the South. Meanwhile in Virginia, Grant's

"A JUBILEE OF FREEDOM"

The meaning of freedom for enslaved African-Americans can be glimpsed in the following report from Charleston, South Carolina, published in the New York Daily Tribune *on April 4, 1865—just a few days before Lee's surrender. Charleston boasted one of the largest and most important African-American communities in the antebellum South. Two months after the Confederate Army fled, the city's black men and women organized a parade to celebrate their emancipation. The parade numbered thousands of marchers and included dramatic tableaux, banners, and songs. Like their white working-class counterparts who held similar events in the decades before the war, African-Americans used such public celebrations to symbolize their deeply held beliefs and feelings.*

It was a jubilee of freedom, a hosannah to their deliverers. First came the marshals and their aides, followed by a band of music; then the Twenty-First [U.S. Colored] Regiment; then the clergymen of the different churches, carrying open Bibles; then an open car drawn by four white horses. In this car there were fifteen colored ladies dressed in white—to represent the fifteen recent slave states. A long procession of women followed the car. Then the children—1,800 in line, at least. They sang:

John Brown's body lies a mould'ring in the grave,
We go marching on!

This verse, however, was not nearly so popular as one which rapidly sup-

troops finally overwhelmed Lee's besieged army in Richmond. In one of the war's most dramatic moments, seasoned African-American troops under Grant's command led the final assault on Richmond; black soldiers were among the first Union troops to enter the capital of the Confederacy. They marched in carrying the Stars and Stripes and singing the anthem to John Brown, much to the amazement of Richmond's citizenry, black and white. Finally, in April 1865, with fewer than thirty thousand soldiers remaining under his command, Lee surrendered. In an agreement signed at a courthouse in Appomattox, Virginia, the Civil War came to an end.

The actual legal abolition of slavery had come from Washington a few months earlier. In 1864 the Republican Party had endorsed a constitutional amendment that would end slavery in America forever. On January 31, 1865, Congress finally passed the Thirteenth Amendment to the Constitution, prohibiting slavery and involuntary servitude in any lands within the jurisdiction of the United States.

Lincoln's assassination a week after Appomattox seemed to mark the end of an era. Conflict between two social systems—one based on slavery, the other on free labor—had plagued the nation since the American Revolution. More than six hundred thousand Americans had died to make a second revolution, resolving once and for all the issue of slavery. In the process, nearly four million Americans who had once been slaves were freed. All Americans now had to confront difficult new questions in the spring of 1865.

planted all the others, until along the mile or more of children, marching two abreast, no other sound could be heard than

We'll hang Jeff Davis on a sour apple tree!
As we go marching on!

After the children came the various trades. The fisherman, with a banner bearing an emblematical device and the words, "The Fishermen welcome you, [U.S. Army] General [Rufus] Saxton." . . . The carpenters carried their planes, the masons their trowels, the teamsters their whips, the coopers their adzes. The bakers' crackers hung around their necks; the paper-carriers [had] a banner, and each a copy of the Charleston Courier; the wheelwrights a large wheel; and the fire companies, ten in number, their foremen with their trumpets.

A large cart, drawn by two dilapidated horses, followed the trades. On this cart was an auctioneer's block and a black man with a bell represented a Negro trader. This man had himself been sold several times, and two women and a child who sat on the block had also been knocked down at auction in Charleston.

As the cart moved along, the mock-auctioneer rang his bell and cried out: "How much am I offered for this good cook? She is an excellent cook, gentlemen. . . . Who bids?"

"Two hundred's bid! Two-fifty. Three hundred."

"Who bids? Who bids?"

Women burst into tears as they saw this tableau and, forgetting that it was a mimic scene, shouted wildly:

"Give me back my children! Give me back my children!"

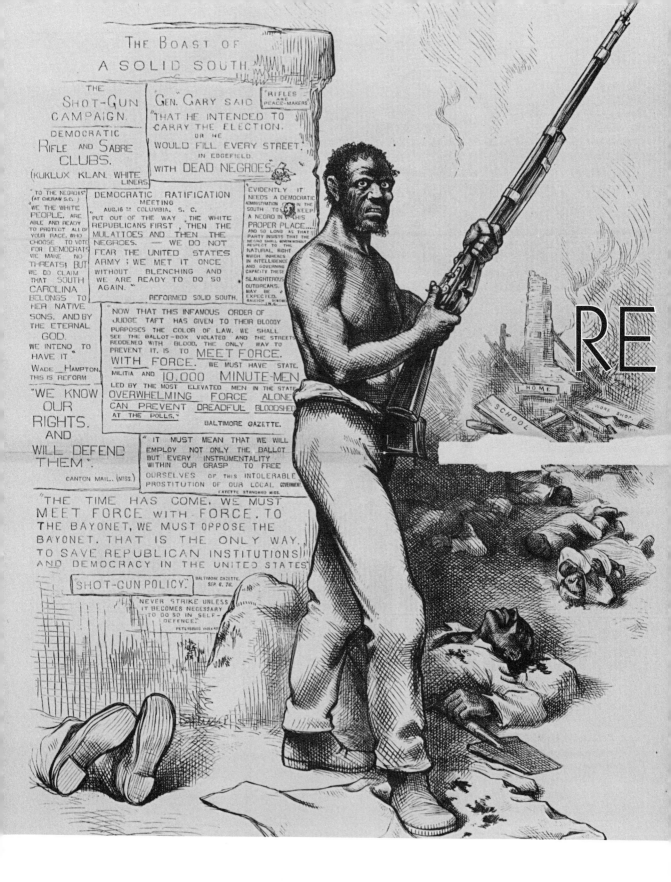

EMANCIPATION AND CONSTRUCTION

11

"He Wants a Change, Too."
A cartoon by Thomas Nast
in *Harper's Weekly*, 1876.

THE UNION victory in April 1865 settled two major debates, but everything else was in doubt. The Union was preserved; slavery was dead and African-Americans could now be free. But who would hold economic and political power in the postwar South? How would the land be worked? How would labor be organized? Above all, what would freedom mean for the ex-slaves?

Answers to these questions would emerge only after a decade and a half of intense political and social struggle, a struggle that contemporaries hopefully called Reconstruction. There were four main sets of actors in this drama: the old planters, who fought to maintain their wealth, their power, and their control over the labor of the former slaves; the freedpeople, who sought land, education, and freedom from the planters' domination; the northern Republicans, who sought to put their party on a solid basis nationally and to expand

4 6 5

the free-labor system in the South; and, to a lesser degree, the white yeomen farmers, who struggled—sometimes, as in North Carolina and Georgia, in alliance with African-Americans and Republicans—to maintain their beleaguered political and economic independence.

The role of the northern Republicans in this drama tells us something very important about Reconstruction. It was truly a national experience, involving not only the transformation of the South, but also a profound change in the very character of American society and politics. In this sense Reconstruction, though played out largely in the South, had vast national implications, very much like the civil-rights movement in our own era.

Yet, Reconstruction, like the civil-rights movement, was also an intensely local, even personal experience. Individual blacks, from the first moments of their newly won freedom, repeatedly asserted their rights to reunite their families, to found their own churches where they could worship as they chose, to own land on which they could labor as free men and women, to educate themselves and their children, and finally to exercise the full rights of American citizenship. African-Americans' unceasing efforts to secure such rights, individually and collectively, made them central players in the Reconstruction drama. In less than a decade, they helped transform themselves legally and politically from chattel property, possessing no rights that white Americans were bound to respect, to full, voting citizens of the United States. Although such status would prove short-lived, the actions of African-Americans helped make Reconstruction a truly revolutionary era that, like the Revolution a century earlier, resulted in a fundamental expansion of political rights for ever larger numbers of America's citizens.

REHEARSALS FOR RECONSTRUCTION

Reconstruction began not in 1865, but in the midst of the Civil War itself. By the end of 1862 the Union Army had captured and occupied the string of islands off the coast of South Carolina as well as much of southern Louisiana, including the city of New Orleans. In both of these regions slavery rapidly disintegrated, profoundly changing the lives of black slaves and white plantation owners. As a result, sharp conflicts emerged between ex-slaves, planters, and federal authorities. The nature of these conflicts made the Civil War experience of these two regions what one historian has called a "rehearsal for Reconstruction," revealing the agendas of both whites and blacks for the post-slavery era.

On November 8, 1861, Union troops captured the South Carolina Sea Islands and began an occupation that would last the rest of the war. The islands' wealthy cotton planters fled to the mainland when the Union Army arrived. But, despite their threats and pleading, the ten thousand slaves on the islands refused to go with them, hiding in swamps and cotton fields to avoid being carried back to slavery. Sea Island slaves had long enjoyed a relative measure of autonomy and control over their labor in the cotton fields. For these black men and women, the coming of the Union Army offered the possibility of ending "massa's hollerin'" and "missus' scoldin'."

In a scene repeated throughout the islands, planter John Chaplin ordered a slave, Moses Mitchell, to row him to Charleston. "You ain't gonna row no boat to Charleston," Mitchell's wife called out to him. "You go out that back door and keep a-going." Hearing the Union guns, Mitchell's son asked his mother where the thunder was coming from. "Son," she explained, "that ain't no thunder, that Yankees come to give you Freedom."

But what kind of freedom would the Yankees bring? As we have seen, official northern war aims in 1862 did not include the abolition of slavery, although some northern whites were committed to such a policy. In the spring of 1862 just such a group of antislavery northerners sought to establish "a productive colony" on the islands that "would serve as a womb for the emancipation at large." They hoped to demonstrate that black people were "reasoning beings" with a "capacity for self-government." The northern reformers established schools and churches designed to prepare the freedpeople for full American citizenship. Some of them also dreamed of a time when the islands would be divided into small farms, worked by ex-slaves who owned their own land.

Other northern arrivals to the Sea Islands had different aims. Economist and manufacturer Edward Atkinson, for example, was as much committed to cotton production as he was to demonstrating black equality; in fact, he saw the two as inextricably linked. Atkinson envisioned not an economy based on an independent land-owning yeomanry (something he feared would spell the doom of cotton), but rather one in which black workers would be employed on cotton plantations for decent wages. For Atkinson, as for most southern employers when the war ended, the key question was "Will the people of African descent work for a living?"

In March 1863, one year after the northerners arrived on the islands, the federal government began to sell the lands deserted by the old planters. Pooling their resources, a group of Sea Island blacks managed to buy two thousand acres. Over the next few years, they demonstrated that they were indeed willing to work for a living—but only so long as they were working for themselves. African-Americans throughout the islands, according to one northern observer, "had all set their minds on owning for themselves and swore they'd never work for a white man." In their desire for land and independence, Sea Island blacks revealed themselves to be little different in their aspirations than most nineteenth-century white Americans.

And like most small farmers, landowning African-Americans also showed that they preferred growing corn and other foodstuffs for their own consumption rather than cotton for the market. Cotton was a powerful symbol of their long years in slavery. During the Union bombardment of 1861, many Sea Island blacks had destroyed cotton gins as the most immediate emblems of their oppression. For them, freedom meant "no more driver, no more cotton."

Unfortunately for the freedpeople, the largest tracts of Sea Islands land were purchased not by ex-slaves, but by northern investors. Eight thousand acres of the best land went to a combine represented by Edward Philbrick, an engineer from Boston. Like Atkinson, Philbrick firmly believed that cotton production was indispensable to national prosperity. But, as a longtime abolitionist, he also maintained that cotton could be produced cheaper by wage labor than by slave labor. He heralded the experiment on the Sea Islands as a way of showing that the abandonment of slavery did not mean the abandonment of cotton production.

Conflict continually plagued Philbrick's efforts to produce cheap cotton. The freedpeople who ended up working for him had not abandoned their desire to own their own land. On one farm, the hands told Philbrick bluntly that "the plantation belonged to them by right, that they were born and brought up on the land, that their masters had run away and left them in possession of the land, and no white man, except their old master, had a right to take the land from them." On other farms, freed slaves denied altogether the legitimacy of their former masters' claims to the land.

But if they could not work their own land, the former slaves on Philbrick's plantation made sure that they would be paid well for their labor; they forced him to raise their daily wages. Other northern planters who came to the Sea Islands faced similar demands. Island agricultural workers successfully fought for "task" payment, a system under which they would receive pay for each task performed, rather than a daily wage. Most freedpeople in the region had worked on a task system during slavery, and they greatly preferred it to the gang system, in which they were heavily supervised and did not control their own labor time.

The northern planters in the Sea Islands bitterly resisted the continuation of the task system. "If he goes to the house for an axe he's to be paid extra for it," a northern planter complained about one of his workers. "It's well enough to pay a man for all he does, but who can carry on a farm in such a way as that?" According to northerner William Waters, the task system put the employers "in a very awkward position, as the negroes decide how many tasks they will work, putting you entirely at their mercy." But in the face of such determination, employers had to give in, and the freedpeople on the islands came as close as possible in these years of wartime Reconstruction to functioning as their own bosses. "You have no idea how independent these negroes are," Waters wrote to his son, a complaint that whites would make repeatedly across the South after 1865.

A second rehearsal for Reconstruction also took shape in the midst of the Civil War, one that provided a far more complete picture than the Sea Islands of what was to come. In April 1862, the Union Navy captured New Orleans, the largest city in the South and the nation's leading cotton port. General Benjamin Butler's troops soon began shaping a new order throughout the rich sugar lands of southern Louisiana. African-Americans in Louisiana, as in the Sea Islands, emerged from slavery with a definite agenda for freedom. But the continuing presence of the old slaveholders (who, unlike their Sea Island counterparts, had not fled), combined with President Lincoln's decision to seek their political allegiance, made Louisiana's freed slaves much less successful in achieving their aims.

Ex-slaves in southern Louisiana sought land, economic independence, and, above all, protection for their families. The family had stood at the very center of African-American life under slavery, and when the war came, freedpeople throughout Louisiana used the presence of Union troops to attempt to strengthen and sustain their families. Early in the war, slaves managed to escape together as families to the Union lines or to reconstitute their families after escaping individually. In the later years of occupation, freedpeople turned to military chaplains and northern missionaries to sanctify their marriages in white law. Black men serving in the military also tried to persuade their officers to liberate members of their families still held in slavery.

". . . IT'S SLAVERY OVER AGAIN"

In this speech, delivered in the summer of 1865 to the freedpeople of the South Carolina Sea Islands, Martin R. Delany, a longtime black abolitionist, a Union Army officer, and now a federal official, condemns those northerners who purchased cotton plantations in the area and exhorts resident African-Americans to resist wage labor. Delany's words were recorded by Alexander Whyte, Jr., a white Union Army officer who thought Delany's views too radical.

I CAME TO talk to you in plain words so as you can understand how to throw open the gates of oppression and let the captive free—In this state there are [hundreds of thousands] of able, intelligent, honorable negroes, *not an inferior race*, mind you, who are ready to protect their liberty. The matter is in your own hands. . . . I want to tell you one thing: Do you know that if it was not for the black man this war never would have been brought to a close with success to the Union, and the liberty of your race . . . ? I want you to understand that. Do you know it? Do you know it? Do you know it? (Cries of "Yes! Yes! Yes!") They can't get along without you. [Yet,] yankees from the North . . . come down here to drive you as much as ever. It's slavery over again: northern, universal U.S. slavery. But they must keep their clamps off. . . . They don't pay you enough. I see too many of you are dressed in rags and shoeless. These yankees talk smooth to you, oh, yes! Their tongue rolls just like a drum. (Laughter.) But it's slavery over again as much as ever it was.

Almost as important as the family was education. Northern reform groups such as the American Missionary Association built schools in occupied Louisiana, but it was African-Americans themselves who fought hardest for education. Their enforced illiteracy under slavery had been a serious handicap, and now they were determined to learn at least the rudiments. Blacks throughout the state simply refused to work on plantations, even to support the Union war effort, unless schools were set up. Though extremely hesitant at first, General Nathaniel Banks (who had replaced General Butler late in 1862) was forced to accede to their demands. By the end of the war, the freedpeople of Louisiana had gained over 120 new federal schools, serving nearly thirteen thousand black students.

But developments in Louisiana were not all so positive. Although the state's planters soon discovered that they could not protect the institution of slavery itself, they sought federal support for a contract-labor system that would allow them to keep control of their former slaves. In February 1863, General Banks gave in to their demands. Under the new labor arrangement, planters would provide workers with food and clothing and either one-twentieth part of the annual crop or a fixed monthly wage. In return, the Union Army would induce the freedmen "to return to the plantations where they belong" and require them "to work diligently and faithfully for one year, to maintain respectful deportment to their employers and perfect subordination to their duties."

Most Louisiana planters applauded the agreement, for they assumed that coercion was essential to keep order and discipline among their workers. But African-American laborers were not prepared to give up the benefits of freedom so quickly. Many simply refused to work under the new system. Others went on strike against their employers, demanding higher wages and passes to leave their plantations whenever they liked.

Though he recognized that the planters needed to be held in check—he issued an order in January 1864 that expressly prohibited them from using flogging or other cruel punishments against their workers—Banks nonetheless held to his labor system and increasingly relied on federal troops to maintain discipline on plantations. He was backed up in Washington, for his position on black labor reflected President Lincoln's basic war strategy. Lincoln believed that the key to winning the war, bringing the Confederate states back into the Union, and making emancipation secure lay in winning the loyalty of white southerners. To that end he was more than willing to let planters control black labor. Lincoln saw Louisiana as a testing ground for his strategy; he even exempted southern Louisiana from the Emancipation Proclamation (although he pressed the new state government there to abolish slavery itself).

Louisiana, however, presented another possible approach to Recon-

"The First Schoolhouse Built for the Instruction of Freedmen." Black soldiers from the Port Hudson, Louisiana, "Corps d'Afrique" pose with textbooks in front of their school.

struction. Rather than courting the planters, Lincoln could have encouraged antiplanter sentiment by turning to the city of New Orleans. The largest and richest city of the South, it resembled Boston or Philadelphia more than it did other southern cities. Ninety percent of its free families owned no slaves, for example, and nearly 40 percent of its population were immigrants—mostly the Germans and Irish who dominated its large working class. Also, thousands of northern-born people lived in New Orleans. Although not necessarily sympathetic to the freedpeople, many of the city's white residents distrusted the planter class and even felt loyalty toward the Union.

New Orleans was also the center of the most powerful free-black community in the deep South. Ten thousand of the city's African-Americans had been free prior to the Civil War. These urban free blacks did not always share the interests of Louisiana's rural blacks, and some supported Banks's harsh labor programs. But they were ready to fight for their own objectives: by the end of 1863, free blacks in New Orleans had organized a powerful movement to secure the vote for all black Louisianans "born free before the rebellion." They argued that their support for the Union war effort gave them a claim to full American citizenship.

Both white and black Unionists came together in the Free State General Committee, which was organized in 1863 to press for complete abolition in Louisiana. "A large majority are as radical as we ever were," wrote a northern Republican working with the group. "A col-

Edisto Island, South Carolina, 1862.
Freedpeople plant sweet potatoes.

ored delegation of intelligent free men were admitted, which was more than would have been done in Ohio." But because the full Free State Committee balked at their demand for the vote, the African-Americans of New Orleans decided early in 1864 to take their case to Washington. They brought Lincoln a petition that called for abolition and for granting the vote to the state's blacks, especially those who had served in the Union Army.

Some of Louisiana's urban white Unionists supported the petition. On the advice of Banks, however, Lincoln rejected the demands of New Orleans's free blacks and continued to place his hopes in the moderate planters. In December 1863, the president had announced the terms of his Proclamation of Amnesty and Reconstruction, which included his famous "ten-percent plan." The plan allowed any Confederate state to seek readmission to the Union if ten percent of its voters took an oath of loyalty to the Union. Lincoln did suggest to Louisiana's 1864 constitutional convention that it consider granting the franchise to particularly "intelligent" blacks and to black soldiers. In 1865, in the last speech of his life, Lincoln publicly endorsed limited black suffrage for the first time, but still refused to make it a condition for a state's readmission. The war's end and Lincoln's assassination in the spring of 1865 thus left the political status of African-Americans entirely undecided.

The wartime experiences of southern Louisiana and the Sea Islands demonstrated that the demise of slavery would bring with it an intense struggle between whites and blacks over the meaning and extent of freedom for the newly freed slaves. These two rehearsals for Reconstruction foreshadowed larger political and economic struggles that would emerge after the war.

EMANCIPATION AND THE MEANING OF FREEDOM

Emancipation came in different ways at different times across the South. Hundreds of thousands of African-Americans fled slavery over the course of four years of war; others had to wait until the spring of 1865 and the Union army's arrival to break "slavery's chain." Southerners, black and white, now faced a world turned upside down by war and emancipation.

On plantations and in towns and cities across the South, ex-slaves discovered diverse ways to give expression to their new freedom. The meaning of freedom for a newly emancipated slave could be as specific and personal as the decision to take a new name, to reject a name imposed by a former master. Or it could mean the ability to dress as one pleased, to wear colorful clothes or a hat. Or it could take

Wedding. A chaplain marries an African-American couple in the offices of the Vicksburg Freedmen's Bureau.

the form of refusing to be deferential to one's former owner. A South Carolina planter was "utterly disgusted" by what he saw as "excessively insolent" behavior by ex-slaves in Charleston soon after the end of the war:

> It is impossible to describe the condition of the city—It is so unlike anything we could imagine—Negroes shoving white persons off the walk—Negro women drest in the most outré style, all with veils and parasols, for which they have an especial fancy.

In Richmond, Virginia, freedpeople held meetings without securing white permission. They also walked in Capitol Square, an area previously restricted to whites, refusing to give up the sidewalks when whites approached. In these and in countless other ways, large and small, freed slaves demonstrated that the end of slavery meant the end of petty control by whites over their lives.

Freedom also meant the ability for thousands of freed slaves to travel, to move around unrestricted. This allowed countless thousands of former slaves to search far and near for loved ones who had been sold away or who had been displaced during the war's upheavals. Some searches covered hundreds of miles and several states. A northern correspondent reported meeting a middle-aged ex-slave—"plodding along, staff in hand, and apparently very footsore and tired"— who had walked six hundred miles in search of his wife and children. As one government official noted, for many ex-slaves "the work of emancipation was incomplete until the families which had been dispersed by slavery were reunited." Even successful searches could have unhappy endings. One ex-slave, after finding his former wife, decided that a meeting would be too painful:

> I want to see you and I don't want to see you. I love you just as well as I did the last day I saw you, and it will not do for you and I to meet. I am married, and my wife have two children, and if you and I meets it would make a very dissatisfied family.

Freedom also made it possible for ex-slaves to formalize long-standing family relationships. Slaves who had been unable to marry before the war because of separation or their master's objections, as well as those who had been allowed to "marry" only informally, sought out northern missionaries and Union officers to officially register and solemnize their unions. Many children who had lost their parents during the war were now legally adopted by relatives or friends.

LESSON XV.

cook	wash	pig	too
crows	dawn	dig	two
food	bound	hoe	scrub
wake	clean	plow	bake
home	know	noise	eyes
cheer	knives	knéel	school

What letter is silent in hoe? in clean? Say just, not *jist*
catch, not *cotch*; sit, not *set*; father, not *fåder*.

THE FREEDMAN'S HOME.

SEE this home! How neat, how warm,
how full of cheer, it looks! It seems as
if the sun shone in there all the day long.
But it takes more than the light of the sun
to make a home bright all the time. Do
you know what it is? It is love.

Reading, writing, and role-models: The textbooks prepared by northern reformers for freed men and women contained more than practical lessons. Besides instructions on spelling, reading, and pronunciation, this page from *The Freedman's Second Reader* presents a "model" black household that exhibits the gentility of the northern middle-class ideal of the family.

Freedom took on collective and institutional reality as well. The year following the war saw a tremendous upsurge in African-American demands for education. The belief in education, a fundamental nineteenth-century American value linked to the ideal of an educated citizenry in a democracy, ran particularly deep in a people who had been prohibited from learning to read or write under slavery (over 90 percent of adult blacks in the South were illiterate in 1860). "If I never does do nothing more while I live," a freedman in Mississippi vowed, "I shall give my children a chance to go to school, for I considers education the next best thing to liberty." Pragmatism and ideals were often mixed. Elderly ex-slaves wanted to be able to read "the word of God" for themselves. Others wanted to read and to do sums so they could protect themselves in the world of free labor and signed contracts. A Louisiana freedman decided that "leaving learning to your children was better than leaving them a fortune; because if you left them even five hundred dollars, some man having more education than they had would come along and cheat them out of it." Some plantation workers even made schools an absolute condition before signing labor contracts.

Whatever their motivations, freed slaves succeeded in building and maintaining schools and in hiring black teachers all across the South in 1865 and 1866. Often they were forced to rely on their own scarce resources; other times they got help from northern missionary groups and the federal government. Freedpeople converted some places that symbolized the oppression of slavery—such as the old slave markets in New Orleans and Savannah—into schoolhouses. Within a few weeks of Sherman's occupation of Savannah in December 1864, a large number of black residents, led by a group of ministers, formed the Savannah Education Association. By February 1865 the association had raised nearly $1,000 from the African-American community and had hired fifteen black teachers, who began their work with six hundred pupils.

Freed slaves also quickly established churches independent of white control. Religion had been a fundamental institution in slave days. But while slaves had often conducted their own clandestine religious services, most had worshipped in biracial churches under their owners or white preachers—who had used the New Testament to urge blacks to accept their enslavement and to obey their masters.

Freedpeople now took control over their religious lives. They challenged white domination of biracial congregations and even replaced white preachers with blacks, as did the black members of the Front Street Methodist Church in Wilmington, North Carolina, early in 1865. When these efforts failed, as they frequently did, many African-Americans abandoned white-dominated churches entirely to found their own institutions.

Black congregants often pooled meager resources to build new church buildings as permanent symbols of their desire to practice their religion as they chose. The African Methodist Episcopal (AME) Church was the most famous of these independent churches, but many black congregations were entirely independent of or only loosely affiliated with other, largely white denominations. "The Ebony preacher who promises perfect independence from White control and directions carries the colored heart at once," observed an officer of the American Missionary Association. Baptist churches attracted the largest number of freedpeople after the war, largely because the church's decentralized, democratic structure allowed for popular ministers, enthusiastic worship services, and local control of church affairs.

The independent black church rapidly became the moral and cultural center of African-American community life, the first institution fully controlled by black men. Preachers, along with schoolteachers and ex-soldiers, emerged as community leaders, and churches often held political meetings. Religion and politics mixed easily in the first years after the war; Florida AME minister Charles Pearce thought that he could not fulfill his duties as a minister if he did not "look out for the political interests of his people."

On September 29, 1865, 115 black men, most of them ex-slaves, held a Convention of Freedmen at the AME church in Raleigh, North Carolina, electing a black preacher from the North as their chairman. Dozens of such conventions, meetings, and rallies were held across the South in 1865 and 1866. They raised demands for full civil equality and called for universal manhood suffrage, which, in the words of one delegate, was "an essential and inseparable element of self-government." The freedmen's conventions were the first steps taken by ex-slaves toward the independent political activity that would characterize Reconstruction.

But these steps made by freed slaves toward defining their own freedom and creating institutions to defend and extend it were not unopposed. The definition of African-American freedom was a point of constant conflict between black and white southerners. The realities of daily life after the Civil War, and the power that white southerners still held, set boundaries on black freedom.

Henry Watson's plantation in Alabama typified this struggle. In June 1865, Watson's ex-slaves, who had chosen to remain on the plantation after emancipation, quit work. According to Watson's brother-in-law, who was helping to manage the place, they "rebelled" against the authority of the overseer, and "set up claims to the plantation and all on it." Watson's former slaves remained "idle and doing nothing"; he responded in January 1866 by proposing a harsh labor contract that included rules requiring workers to obey "all orders from the manager . . . under all circumstances" and forbidding them to leave the plantation "without written permission from the manager." But the freedpeople rejected this contract in "a loud voice and most defiant manner." They were not prepared to submit to the absolute authority Watson sought to impose. In disgust, Watson rented the plantation to his overseer, who leased individual plots to the freed slave families.

That was not the only way Watson's workers demonstrated their interpretation of freedom. "The women," Watson complained in 1865, "say that they never mean to do any more outdoor work, that white men support their wives, and they mean that their husbands shall support them." All over the South, black married women sought to move out of field labor and to concentrate on household duties. And on the Watson plantation, they stuck to this objective. "The female laborers are almost invariably idle," wrote Watson months later; they "do not go to the field but desire to play the lady and be supported by their husbands 'like the white folks do.'" Even though women's household labor was hard—it included not only cooking, cleaning, and child-rearing, but also tending a garden and chickens, preserving food, and making clothes—Watson could not understand the unwillingness of black married women to labor in the fields except as a desire to be "idle."

Such actions enraged most whites long accustomed to African-American subservience. During the first year of freedom, countless incidents of violence were directed against freed slaves. When in the course of a dispute an Arkansas ex-slave

"WE ARE AMERICANS BY BIRTH . . ."

The following selection from The Address of the Colored State Convention to the People of the State of South Carolina *on November 24, 1865, shows how freedpeople justified their demands for equality in the language of the Declaration of Independence and the Constitution.*

WE HAVE assembled . . . to confer together and to deliberate upon our intellectual, moral, industrial, civil, and political condition as affected by the great changes which have taken place in this State and throughout the whole country. . . .

Heretofore we have had no avenues opened to us or our children—we have had no firesides that we could call our own; none of those incentives to work for the development of our minds and the aggrandizement of our race in common with other people. The measures which have been adopted for the development of the white men's children have been denied to us and ours. The laws which have made white men great, have degraded us, because we were colored, and because we were reduced to chattel slavery. But now that we are free men, now that we have been lifted up by the providence of God to manhood, we have resolved to come forward, and, like MEN, speak and act for ourselves. . . . In making this appeal to you, we adopt the language of the immortal Declaration of Independence, that "all men are created equal," and that "life, liberty, and the pursuit of happiness" are the right of all; . . . that the Constitution of the United States was formed to establish justice, to promote the general welfare, and secure the blessings of liberty to all the people of the country; that resistance to tyrants is obedience to God—[these] are American principles and maxims; and together they form the constructive elements of the American Government.

We think we fully comprehend and duly appreciate the principles and measures which compose this platform; and all that we desire or ask for is to be placed in [such] a position that we could conscientiously and legitimately defend, with you, those principles against the surges of despotism to the last drop of our blood. . . . We are Americans by birth, and we assure you that we are Americans in feeling; and, in spite of all wrongs which we have long and silently endured in this country, we would still exclaim with a full heart, "O, America! with all thy faults we love thee still."

told her former white mistress, "I am as free as you, madam," the white woman struck her. Later that day, learning that a "negro had sauced his wife," the planter horsewhipped the black woman and "clubbed his whip and struck her severely over the head."

Assertions of independence could be treated even more harshly. A North Carolina black man packed up his clothes and told his former owner's wife that he was leaving because his family was given food inferior to that of other plantation workers. A quarrel followed; later in the day, the former owner shot the freedman. He later justified this murder by noting that in "contradicting" his wife, the freedman's "language and manner became insolent."

Freedpeople's desire for land also met tremendously violent opposition from whites. The quest for land was almost universal among the ex-slaves. Like other nineteenth-century Americans, they longed for economic independence and believed that without it, freedom was incomplete. "Every colored man will be a slave, and feel himself a slave," a black soldier argued, "until he can raise his own bale of cotton and put his own mark upon it and say this is mine."

Freedpeople argued that they were entitled to land in return for their years of unpaid labor, which had created the wealth of the cotton South and the industrialized North. "Our wives, our children, our husbands, have been sold over and over again to purchase the lands we now locates upon; for that reason we have a divine right to the land," argued freedman Baley Wyat in a speech in Yorktown, Virginia, protesting the eviction of blacks from land they had been assigned by the Union Army during the war. "And then didn't we clear the land, and raise the crops of corn, of cotton, of tobacco, of rice, of sugar, of everything? And then didn't them large cities in the North grow up on the cotton and the sugar and the rice that we made? . . . I say they has grown rich, and my people is poor."

Freedpeople put forward other justifications for being allowed to keep land confiscated by the Union Army. Without land, they argued, they would remain in a fundamentally subservient position when confronted with the economic power of their former owners. "Give us our own land and we take care ourselves," declared one freed slave. "But without land, the old massas can hire us or starve us, as they please." This same understanding had moved the black Savannah ministers who prompted General Sherman's Field Order Number 15 early in 1865, which allowed twenty thousand African-American families to farm hundreds of thousands of acres of confiscated plantation land on the Georgia and South Carolina coast.

Many southern blacks firmly believed that the federal government, particularly through the Freedmen's Bureau, would now help them achieve economic self-sufficiency by distributing land among the freedpeople. Established by the Republican-dominated Congress just

Traveling: African-Americans exercised their new freedom in many ways; one of them was traveling where and when they chose. This engraving is from Edward King's *The Great South*, one of many postwar surveys of southern life. Northerners were curious to learn about the region that they had defeated in war.

before the end of the war, the Bureau of Freedmen, Refugees, and Abandoned Lands was created to assist the freed slaves throughout the South by issuing supplies, providing medical aid, establishing schools, dividing confiscated plantation lands, and supervising contracts between the freedmen and their employers. The bureau was headed by General Oliver O. Howard, and many of its nine hundred officials and agents were army officers. Committed to ideals of self-sufficiency, they did much to aid blacks with education and medical care.

But in many areas of the South, the Freedmen's Bureau also adopted extremely coercive labor policies. In the spring of 1865, the bureau issued stringent orders that restricted blacks' freedom of movement and required them to sign one-year labor contracts with large landowners. If freedmen refused to sign these contracts, which were based on the Louisiana model worked out during the war by General Banks and eventually expanded throughout the whole Mississippi Valley, the bureau withheld relief rations. "Freedom means work," declared General Howard in 1865, and his policies ensured that African-Americans would continue to work the lands of their former masters.

But the Freedmen's Bureau did not always support the planters' interests. Blacks throughout the South turned to the bureau to protest brutality, harsh working conditions, and the hostility and inattention of local courts and police, forcing the bureau to hear complaints and take action against employers. Although such requests often went unanswered, most bureau agents were at least committed to guiding the South toward northern patterns of free labor relations, what one Tennessee agent called "the noblest principle on earth." While they supported coercive contracts as a way of getting the South on its feet in the short run, bureau agents also believed that in the long run a contract had to be, as a leading northern Republican put it, "a free transaction in which neither coercion nor protection is necessary." Howard and others hoped that eventually the market alone would determine wages and working conditions in the South.

Despite the bureau's policies and limitations, many freed slaves continued to believe that the federal government, having abolished slavery, would now confiscate the slaveowners' land and distribute it among the freedpeople. "This was no slight error, no trifling idea," reported an observer in Mississippi, "but a fixed and earnest conviction as strong as any belief a man can ever have." A black laborer in Georgia was so certain that the confiscation would occur that he offered to sell, in advance, to his former master, a share of the plantation he expected to receive "after the division." Freedpeople even decided on the actual date that the government would announce the new policy: January 1, 1866, the third anniversary of the Emancipation Proclamation and the starting date for new labor contracts. Meetings of freed slaves were held across the South to discuss the forthcoming land distribution. There was much agitation in plantation areas among blacks and whites alike as the date approached. Many freedpeople refused to sign new contracts as a way of putting additional pressure on the planters. Whites were especially concerned about what the government would do and how the freed slaves would react if they were denied access to land. There were even fears of a "Christmas rebellion" by freed slaves. New Year's Day 1866 passed, however, without either the expected division or the rebellion.

Plantation owners vehemently opposed any form of black land-ownership, whether government-sponsored or individually realized. By the summer of 1865, they had convinced Andrew Johnson—who became president when Lincoln was assassinated in April 1865—to take back even the limited land grants made under Sherman's field order. When General Howard personally delivered the news to freedpeople in the South Carolina Sea Islands, asking them to "forgive" their former masters and return the land to them, his request was met with open resentment and outrage. One Sea Islander told Howard:

> You ask us to forgive the landowners of our island. *You* only lost your right arm in war and might forgive them. The man who tied me to a tree and gave me thirty-nine lashes and who stripped and flogged my mother and my sister and who will not let me stay in his empty hut except I will do his planting and be satisfied with his price and who combines with others to keep away land from me knowing I would not have anything to do with him if I had land of my own—that man, I cannot well forgive.

Planters and freedpeople alike understood that black landownership would destroy the whites' basic control over black labor and lead to the total collapse of the plantation economy. "The negroes will become possessed of a small freehold, will raise their corn, squashes, pigs, and chickens, and will work no more in the cotton, rice, and sugar fields," said one Alabama newspaper; "their labor will become unavailable for those products which the world especially needs." If even a few independent black farmers succeeded, concluded one Mississippi planter, "all the others will be dissatisfied with their wages no matter how good they may be and thus our whole labor system is bound to be upset."

The labor system of the South had been based for a century and a half on slavery, a severe form of regimentation, and maintaining a similar system of regimentation became the only conceivable and most important objective of the planters. A South Carolina planter spoke for most of his fellows when he claimed that freedpeople were "not controlled by the same motives as white men, and unless you have power to compel them, they'll only work when they can't beg or steal enough to keep from starving." "Three-fourths of the [white] people assume that the negro will not labor except on compulsion," wrote one northern observer, concluding correctly that planters "have no sort of conception of free labor. They do not comprehend any law for controlling laborers, save the law of force."

In order to secure "the law of force," planters looked to their state governments, which rapidly came back under their control by the end of 1865. The struggle over the meaning and extent of freedom for African-Americans now shifted to the arena of politics.

LEGISLATING RECONSTRUCTION

In the first months after the war, former Confederate supporters resumed control over state governments throughout the South. These men, hostile to the ideals and intentions of Republican politicians and their constituents, were able to reassert their political dominance as a result of the lenient pardoning policies of President Andrew Johnson.

Johnson, a southerner, had been a senator from Tennessee before the Civil War. But he had been no friend of the slaveholders, a group he referred to as "an odious and dangerous aristocracy." Originally a tailor by trade and entirely self-taught, Johnson had long resented the power that slaveholders held in his region, identifying personally and politically with the region's white yeoman farmers. When his state seceded from the Union, he remained in his seat in the Senate, the only senator from a seceding state to do so. This act led Lincoln to put him on his ticket as vice-president in 1864.

But Johnson's hostility to the planters did not make him a supporter of African-Americans' objectives. One senator believed that at heart he was "as decided a hater of the negro . . . as the rebels from whom he had separated." The president further believed that the slaves had participated with their masters in the oppression and exploitation of small farmers across the South. Calculating that he could win broad political support in the South, Johnson made no effort to initiate a sweeping reconstruction; in May 1865 he offered total amnesty to white southerners who would swear basic loyalty to the Union. Members of the social and political elite, who were excluded from this automatic amnesty, were allowed to petition the president for a pardon. Johnson also had to appoint interim governors for the southern states, and in many instances he chose southern conservatives, men who had opposed secession but were hostile to the gains secured by African-Americans since 1863. William Marvin, appointed governor of Florida, told the state's blacks not to "delude themselves" into believing that emancipation implied civil equality or the vote. Freedpeople, Marvin insisted, should return to the plantations, labor diligently, and "call your old Master—'Master.'"

For full readmission to the Union, Johnson demanded a number of concessions from the southern states. State constitutional conventions, representing southern whites who had received amnesty, would have to amend their constitutions to ratify the Thirteenth Amendment, which abolished slavery; repudiate Confederate debts; and nullify the ordinances of secession. Once they had complied, southern states were free to organize elections and reestablish governments.

This process proceeded rapidly in nearly all of the southern states in the fall of 1865, although several of the new legislatures were slow to accept the abolition of slavery. Meanwhile southern planters and Confederate officials flooded Johnson's desk with requests for pardons, most of which were granted. Believing that secession had been the work of evil individuals rather than the logical outcome of a struggle between two social systems, Johnson held that the request for a pardon represented a true repentance of sin. He also believed that only the planters possessed the experience, prestige, and power to "control" the volatile black population, and that they were therefore

A racist Democratic broadside during the 1866 election campaign.

the best basis for the South's reconstruction. For Johnson, Reconstruction was now complete.

Many northerners, however, were shocked by the outcome of the 1865 elections. Ex-Confederate officials were elected in large numbers. Representatives elected to fill vacated southern seats in Congress, for example, included the vice-president of the Confederacy, four Confederate generals, five Confederate colonels, six Confederate cabinet officers, and fifty-eight Confederate congressmen. Although the newly elected state governments in the South were dominated by more moderate elements, mainly former Whigs, Unionists, and "reluctant" secessionists, these men shared with the ex-Confederates a determination to rebuild the South's plantation society. In Louisiana, former Confederate officers wore their uniforms in the legislature.

Not surprisingly, the new state governments immediately began to pass legislation in the interests of the planter class. And the central demand of the planters was the creation of what a New Orleans newspaper called "a new labor system, prescribed and enforced by the state." Southern legislators responded with the passage of the so-called Black Codes. Essentially a series of rigid labor-control laws, the Black Codes attempted to ensure planters an immobile and dependent black labor supply lacking economic alternatives.

The laws differed somewhat from state to state, but most had the same basic provisions. If a freedman was found without "lawful employment," he could be arrested, jailed, and fined. If he could not pay the fine, he could be hired out to an employer, who would pay the fine and deduct it from the worker's wages. In practice, any freedman who refused to work at a prevailing wage could be arrested as a vagrant. Other provisions prevented African-Americans from entering any employment except agricultural labor or domestic work, allowed black children to be apprenticed to white employers for indefinite periods of time without the consent of their parents, and severely punished even petty theft. The overall effect of the Black Codes was thus to set the status of newly emancipated African-Americans in the South as landless agricultural laborers, with no bargaining power and restricted mobility. The state government now replaced the master, who had exercised such summary power under slavery. "Mississippi has abolished slavery," commented a group of blacks protesting that state's code. "Does she mean it or is it [only] a policy for the present?" A Republican leader in Louisiana put it more directly when he suggested that the Black Codes were intended "for getting things back as near to slavery as possible."

Although the Black Codes were never effectively enforced, largely because of a labor shortage throughout the South in 1865 and 1866 and opposition from Freedmen's Bureau agents, their passage did have one result: many members of Congress and their constituents became enraged that such laws could be passed in the first place.

In 1865, the Republicans held a three-to-one majority in Congress. Representative Thaddeus Stevens of Pennsylvania and Senator Charles Sumner of Massachusetts led a minority of congressmen called the Radical Republicans, whose political roots lay in the antislavery movement of the 1840s and 1850s. These legislators had long opposed the expansion of slavery and had supported federal action to abolish it entirely during the Civil War. Now in 1865 they sought a vast increase in federal power to obtain new rights for the freedpeople and to revolutionize social conditions in the South. They were the most bitter critics of Johnson's lenient approach to Reconstruction.

A far greater number, however, considered themselves "moderate" Republicans. Led by Senators William Pitt Fessenden of Maine and Lyman Trumbull of Illinois, these men generally opposed African-American enfranchisement and sought to maintain good relations with President Johnson. The moderates hoped for a rapid reunification of the nation and a return to good business relations between North and South.

But, like the Radicals, the moderates were profoundly disturbed by the results of what they called Andrew Johnson's "experiment"—the return of many ex-Confederate leaders to positions of influence and the near-slave status to which the freedpeople had been subjected by the Black Codes. In December 1865, when Congress finally reconvened, Radicals and moderates joined in refusing to seat the newly elected southern representatives, citing the constitutional provision that "each House shall be the Judge of the Election, Returns, and Qualifications of its own Members."

This act inaugurated a confrontation with President Johnson and resulted in what can only be described as a sweeping political revolution. Within four years, voting rights and civil rights were established for African-Americans, and democratic political institutions had been created in the South. This

---

". . . WE ARE WILLING TO TAKE OUR MUSKETS"

The following letter, addressed to a U.S. Army commander from the black citizens of Yazoo City, Mississippi, complains about various aspects of the state's Black Codes.

Yazoo City, January 20, 1867

Dear Sir

By Request I Send you the Proceeding of this Place. The Law in regard to the freedman is that they all have to have a written contract. Judge Jones, mayor of this place, is enforcing the Law. He says they have no right to rent a house nor land nor reside in town without a white man to stand for them. He makes all men pay Two Dollars for Licenses and he will not give a License without a written contract. Both women and men have to submit or go to Jail.

His Deputy is taking the people all the time. Men that are traveling are stopped and put in jail or Forced to contract. If this is the Law of the United States we will submit, but if it is not we are willing to take our muskets and serve three years Longer to have more liberty. We the undersigned Look to you for Protection and hope you will give it. You can write to any white man of this place and he can testify to the same.

Yours Respectfully,
[signed by twelve men]

transformation did not go as far as freedpeople and their allies in Congress had hoped. But it did set the stage, as we shall see, for the next act in the Reconstruction drama, the participation of blacks and poor whites in reconstructed southern state governments.

At the end of 1865, the Radicals established a joint committee of Congress to investigate the situation in the South. In the next few months army officers, white southern Unionists, Freedmen's Bureau officials, newspaper reporters, and a handful of freedpeople gave testimony before the joint Congressional committee. Their evidence presented a clear picture of conditions in the South, a picture of growing anti-Union sentiment, violence, and systematic oppression of the freedpeople. Joseph Stiles, a white Virginian loyal to the Union, informed the committee that the attitudes of white southerners were "changing for the worse" as a result of President Johnson's leniency:

> It seems to me that the rapid promotion of rebels, the old politicians, to places of trust and honor, has had a great tendency to render treason popular instead of odious. . . . I think that the disloyal feeling of the people is more intense now than it was immediately after the surrender of Lee's army.

Richard Hill, one of the few black witnesses called to testify, informed the joint Committee that if the recently elected southern representatives were allowed to sit in Congress, "the condition of the freedmen would be very little better than that of slaves." Such evidence led many congressmen to conclude that a constitutional amendment was necessary to guarantee the rights of the freedpeople—who were, after all, the only large group of loyal southerners.

In the meantime, Republican congressmen rallied behind two bills designed to protect freedpeople immediately. The first extended the life of the Freedmen's Bureau and expanded its powers. The second, the Civil Rights Bill, conferred U.S. citizenship on the freedpeople, granted them "full and equal benefit of all laws," and gave federal courts the power to defend their rights against interference from individual state governments. In one sweeping act, Congress nullified the Supreme Court's 1857 Dred Scott decision (which had denied basic citizenship to African-Americans), undermined the Black Codes, and expanded the powers of the federal courts. Both bills marked a dramatic break from the deeply rooted American tradition of states' rights. But the situation in the South was so serious that congressional backers hoped President Johnson would agree to their approach.

But instead, Johnson was outraged. He was now fully committed to his own approach to Reconstruction and condemned his most effective congressional critics, Sumner and Stevens, as "disunionists" and traitors. Johnson vetoed both the bills as unconstitutional infringements of states' rights, arguing that the bills' "distinction of race and color" is "made to operate in favor of the colored and against the white race."

The Democratic Party was encouraged by Johnson's vetoes. Weakened by the Civil War, Democrats now attempted to use race-baiting as the basis for their return to power. One southern Democratic editor applauded the president for opposing the "compounding of our race with niggers, gipsies, and baboons." If Congress declared African-Americans citizens, asked another Democrat, "how long will it be . . . before it will say the negro shall vote, sit in the jury box, and intermarry with your families?"

But for moderate Republicans, Johnson's vetoes were the last straw. "Those who formerly defended [the president] are now readiest in his condemnation," said one moderate Republican leader. On April 6, Congress overrode Johnson's veto of the Civil Rights Bill, the first time in U.S. history that a major piece of legislation was passed over

"The Massacre at New Orleans." Thomas Nast's view of Andrew Johnson's role in the July 1866 riot.

the president's objection. (Three months later, Congress also overrode Johnson's veto of the bill to extend the Freedmen's Bureau.) Congress was prepared now to go even further. Between April and July, the joint committee in Congress, dominated by the moderates, prepared a constitutional amendment to get around Johnson's use of the veto and to guarantee civil rights to southern blacks.

The Radicals in Congress sought a more sweeping approach. Stevens and Sumner envisioned not just civil rights for African-Americans but a total transformation of southern society. Sumner wanted to give blacks full voting rights, an action that he believed would provide the Republican Party with its only hope for future political power in the South. Stevens went even further, arguing that if the vote was to have any meaning it needed to be backed up with economic power. Stevens called for confiscating the land of the planters and distributing it among the ex-slaves. "The whole fabric of southern society must be changed," he proclaimed, "and never can it be done if this opportunity is lost." At this stage, however, the best that the Radicals could hope for was the Fourteenth Amendment, and they reluctantly gave it their support.

The main provision of the Fourteenth Amendment, which passed both houses of Congress in June 1866, granted full citizenship to African-Americans and prohibited states from denying them "equal protection of the laws." This alone was a sweeping transformation of the constitutional balance of power. Hitherto, states had been seen as the guardians of the rights of their citizens against the power of the federal government. Now the roles were reversed.

On voting rights the Fourteenth Amendment was less clear. States were not required to grant black men suffrage, but if they chose not to do so, their representation in Congress would be reduced in direct proportion. To have allowed the southern states to count the new black citizens for purposes of determining congressional representation without also allowing them to vote would have given the South an enormous political advantage, significantly greater even than the infamous three-fifths compromise originally enshrined in the Constitution. But most Republicans were not yet prepared to take the obvious next step of guaranteeing voting rights to black men. Though displeased with the weakness of the Fourteenth Amendment on this issue, Radicals had little alternative but to support it.

One group of Americans took a different position. As we have seen earlier, the movement for women's rights had long been intertwined with the abolitionist movement. Now, as the members of Congress worked to pass the Fourteenth Amendment, women's-rights activists called on them to place women and men on an equal footing. When Congress refused to consider pressuring states to grant voting rights to women, Elizabeth Cady Stanton and Susan B. Anthony, leaders of the women's-rights and abolitionist movements, broke with the abolitionists and began searching for other allies in their drive for the vote. This would lead the increasingly independent women's movement into a complicated relationship with the labor movement, as we will see.

But the big question at the moment was how Johnson would respond to the congressional actions. His decision was not long in coming. The president strongly condemned Congress's refusal to seat the southern representatives, and urged the southern legislatures to reject the new amendment. Encouraged by Johnson's position, all but one southern state (ironically Tennessee, Johnson's home state) refused to ratify the Fourteenth Amendment. Now attention turned to the North. The congressional elections in fall 1866 became a referendum on the Fourteenth Amendment and on the merits of Johnson's approach to Reconstruction.

Johnson campaigned against Republican congressmen throughout the North, but to no avail. Northern voters might not have been prepared to accept African-American equality or the confiscation of southern plantations. But they were outraged by the Confederates' return to political power in the South and by the creation of a southern labor system that bore a striking resemblance to slavery. The Union had won the war, but now appeared to be losing the peace. As one northern newspaper noted, the former Confederates seemed to have "simply changed their base from the battlefield to the ballot box."

"Selling a Freedman to Pay His Fine." "Special artist" James E. Taylor toured the South for *Frank Leslie's Illustrated Newspaper* after the Civil War, when the notorious Black Codes were being enforced. He sketched this scene in front of the county courthouse in Monticello, Florida, during the winter of 1866–67.

Moreover, on the eve of the campaign came reports of increasing antiblack violence throughout the South. In Memphis in May and in New Orleans in July, local authorities stood by or actively participated as whites slaughtered blacks in orgies of racist violence. The Memphis riot took the lives of forty-six African-Americans; the one in New Orleans left thirty-four blacks dead along with three of their white supporters. The riots revealed what one northern newspaper called "the demoniac spirit of the southern whites toward the freedmen." Coming just before the fall election, such naked brutality helped turn northern public opinion away from President Johnson's policy of leniency and toward the Radical Republican program.

In these circumstances it was not surprising that the November elections gave Republicans a stunning victory. They held their three-to-one majority in Congress and retained power in every northern state as well as in West Virginia, Missouri, and Tennessee. And among Republicans, the Radicals were the biggest winners.

The Republican mandate, along with continuing southern resistance to the Fourteenth Amendment, encouraged the Radicals in Congress to present an even more sweeping plan for Reconstruction early in 1867. Arguing that the existing southern state governments would never ratify the Fourteenth Amendment, they convinced Congress to enact a bill that temporarily reduced the southern states to the status of territories under military rule. This alone, they believed, would have important positive benefits in the short run. But in the long run, the Radicals proposed three crucial changes for the South. First, they argued for the disfranchisement of ex-Confederates, giving blacks and loyal whites a chance to organize state governments without any interference from the conservative southern Democrats. Secondly, they argued for the confiscation and redistri-

---

"NO MATTER WHAT HIS RACE OR COLOR. . . . AN EQUAL RIGHT TO JUSTICE"

In this speech made before the House of Representatives on January 3, 1867, Radical leader Thaddeus Stevens argued powerfully for Congress to take the initiative to impose suffrage for black men and to disfranchise all former Confederates.

WE HAVE BROKEN the material shackles of four million slaves. We have unchained them from the stake so as to allow them locomotion, provided they do not walk in paths which are trod by white men. We have allowed the unwonted privilege of attending church, if they can do so without offending the sight of their former masters. We have even given them that highest and most agreeable evidence of liberty . . . , the "right of work." But in what have we enlarged their liberty of thought? In what have we taught them the science and granted them the privilege of self-government? We have imposed upon them the privilege of fighting our battles, of dying in defense of freedom, and of bearing their equal portion of taxes; but where have we given them the privilege of ever participating in the formation of the laws for the government of their native land? . . . Think not I would slander my native land; I would reform it. Twenty years ago I denounced it as a despotism. Then, twenty million white men enchained four million black men. I pronounce it no nearer a true Republic now when twenty-five million of a privileged class exclude five million from all participation in the rights of government. . . .

But it will be said, as it has been said, "This is negro equality!" What is negro equality . . . ? It means, as understood by honest Republicans, just this much, and no more: every man, no matter what his race or color . . . has an equal right to justice, honesty, and fair play with every other man; and the law should secure him those rights. . . .

bution of land, giving blacks an economic basis for political independence. Thirdly, they advocated massive federal assistance for southern schools, allowing blacks to gain the literacy and skills necessary to protect their own rights.

Moderate Republicans still held the decisive power in Congress, however, and were not prepared to accept these demands. But, in an effort to undercut the Radicals' much more sweeping program, moderates finally embraced the principle of black voting rights. The Reconstruction Act of March 1867, the centerpiece of what became known as congressional or "Radical" Reconstruction, passed over President Johnson's veto. The Reconstruction Act divided the former confederate states into five military districts. In each of these states there would be new constitutional conventions in which blacks would participate, backed up by protection from federal troops. These conventions were mandated to draft new constitutions, which had to include provisions for African-American suffrage. Newly elected state legislatures were also required to ratify the Fourteenth Amendment as a condition for their readmission to the Union.

The guarantee of black voting rights that was at the center of the Reconstruction Act seemed to many Americans to represent the final stage of a sweeping political revolution. In February 1867, a journalist writing in the *Nation* magazine summed up how the Civil War had revolutionized northern politics:

> Six years ago, the North would have rejoiced to accept any mild restrictions upon the spread of slavery as a final settlement. Four years ago, it would have accepted peace upon the basis of gradual emancipation. Two years ago, it would have been content with emancipation and equal civil rights for the colored people without extension of the suffrage. One year ago, a slight extension of the suffrage would have satisfied it.

Clearly, a great deal had changed in the nation. At the end of the war, only a handful of Radical Republicans had in fact supported black suffrage. Two years later Congress had overridden a presidential veto to enshrine African-American suffrage in federal law. The next act in the Reconstruction drama now opened in the South, where black and white southerners would have to deal with the consequences of these sweeping federal actions.

RADICAL RECONSTRUCTION IN THE SOUTH

Passage of the Reconstruction Act in March 1867 caused two related developments in the South: the political and economic power of the planter class was significantly undercut and political activity among

Electioneering in the South.
Harper's Weekly, 1868.

freedpeople flourished. Strikes, rallies, and protests by freedpeople broke out in cities all over the South during 1867—including Charleston, Savannah, Richmond, Mobile, and New Orleans, and small towns like Meridian, Mississippi, and Tuskegee and Livingston, Alabama—demanding political and economic rights. In South Carolina, hundreds of freedpeople refused to pay taxes to the existing planter-dominated state government. The onset of Radical Reconstruction thus inaugurated a massive and unprecedented movement of freedpeople into the political arena.

The first organized expression of this movement was the dramatic growth of the Union League (or Loyal League) among freedpeople, local chapters of which sprang up across the South in the spring and summer of 1867. The Union League began during the war as a national organization that encouraged the Union cause. With the passage of the Reconstruction Act, the Union League dispatched white and black organizers all over the South to found local chapters. They functioned locally as political clubs, initially providing a civics education for new members, encouraging support for the Republican Party and its candidates, and informing members of the party's political successes across the South. But local chapters soon broadened the league's educational mission to include more aggressive economic and political activities. The Union League helped build schools and churches, organized militia companies to defend communities from white violence, and called strikes and boycotts for better wages and fairer labor contracts. A number of local chapters were even organized on an interracial basis. One such racially mixed league meeting in North Carolina in the summer of 1867 discussed plans for a Fourth of July celebration and debated questions, such as disfranchisement, debtor relief, and public education, that League members expected to be raised in the forthcoming state constitutional convention.

In the fall of 1867, southerners, black and white, began electing delegates to these constitutional conventions. The participation of freedpeople in the elections was truly astonishing: between 70 and 90 percent of eligible black males voted in every state in the South, and a total of 265 African-Americans were elected as delegates. Not surprisingly, Union Leaguers played a major role in the conventions. Of the hundred delegates elected to Alabama's November constitutional convention, as many as half were league members.

These conventions were of tremendous symbolic and practical importance. For the first time in American history, blacks and whites met together to prepare constitutions under which they would be governed. The constitutions they produced were among the most progressive in the nation. They established public schools for both races, created social-welfare agencies, reformed the criminal law, and drew up codes that more equitably distributed the burden of taxation. Most important of all, the constitutions guaranteed black civil and political rights, completing what one Texas newspaper called "the equal-rights revolution." Universal manhood suffrage was approved (although in some states, ex-Confederates were briefly barred from voting).

The intensity of black political participation demonstrated in these elections represented a dramatic turning point in southern politics. After 1867 the southern Republican Party won elections and dominated all of the new state governments. African-Americans were prominent in many of these governments. Although they represented an actual majority only in South Carolina's legislature, blacks held six hundred legislative seats in southern states. Furthermore, between 1868 and 1876, southern states elected fourteen black representatives to the U.S. Congress, two black U.S. senators, and six black lieutenant governors. Perhaps as important, literally thousands of African-Americans served local southern governments as supervisors, voter registrars, aldermen, mayors, magistrates, sheriffs and deputies, members of local school boards, and justices of the peace.

The southern Republican Party, unlike its northern counterpart, was, in the words of one black Republican leader, "emphatically the poor man's party." As we shall see, the party ultimately came to include some poor white southerners as well as poor black ones. But nearly 80 percent of southern Republican voters were black. Though frequently illiterate, African-Americans across the South welcomed their chance to participate actively in politics. "We are not prepared for this suffrage," admitted one ex-slave at the South Carolina constitutional convention in 1868. "But we can learn. Give a man tools and let him commence to use them, and in time he will learn a trade. So it is with voting."

Because of its central role in their emancipation and enfranchisement, freedpeople demonstrated a near fanatical loyalty to the Republican Party after 1867, a loyalty that would last six decades. The Republican Party thus joined the church and the school as a central institution in the lives of the freedpeople. George Houston, an Alabama Union League organizer and Sumter County voter registrar, proudly asserted that "I am a Republican, and I will die one. I say the Republican Party freed me, and I will die on top of it." The intensity of Houston's commitment to the Republican Party found its echo in cities, towns, and rural areas all over the South in the late 1860s and after.

In St. Mary's Parish, Louisiana, for example, African-Americans had organized Radical or Republican clubs on every third or fourth plantation by the late 1860s. "We organized those clubs with the intention of teaching the people what they were to vote for and what the constitution meant," recalled one black activist. "We had those meetings weekly all the time, and we had men of the most influence and intelligence among our people to speak to them, and to tell them what the constitution meant." Planters resented this new activism. A Texas planter complained that once a week during the summer of 1867 "the negroes from the entire county" left work and traveled to nearby Waco for political rallies.

Unlike their rank-and-file supporters, black elected officials were often educated, politically sophisticated, and likely to have been free before the Civil War (in either the South or the North). Of the black men elected to state or federal office in this period, about four-fifths were literate and over one-quarter had been free before the war. Henry M. Turner, for example, was born in South Carolina and served during the war as a minister in the AME Church and as an army chaplain. He settled in Georgia after the war and was elected to the state legislature in 1867.

At the local level, however, indigenous political leaders often emerged from the ranks of the freedmen. James Alston, for example, was a slave-born shoemaker and musician in Macon County, Alabama; he headed the Union League chapter in Tuskegee, became the county registrar of voters, and later represented Macon County in the state legislature. Such small-town artisans possessed the skill and independence to represent the growing African-American population in southern towns and villages as well as their rural constituents. Moreover, their work experience, which involved a good deal of contact with whites, helped them link the black community with potential white allies in local Union League and Republican Party organizations.

White allies were essential. Only in South Carolina and Mississippi were blacks in the majority. If the Republican Party was going to survive in the South, it would need to develop a coalition that included some white support. In the early years of Radical Reconstruction, the party received that support from several quarters.

Most visible among the white Republicans were those whom conservative white southerners labeled "carpetbaggers." The term, which is still used to denote greedy outsiders, described white northerners who came to the South (with their belongings packed in carpetbags) to make money through politics. Such a characterization was generally inaccurate. Some of the so-called carpetbaggers were themselves black and anything but greedy. Martin Delany, for example, had risen to the rank of major in the Union Army and then served in the Freedmen's Bureau before settling down in Charleston. Many

The Alabama state legislature, 1867.

white carpetbaggers were similarly sincere in their commitment to ensuring black rights and to transforming the South into a virtuous republican society. A number of them were former Union Army officers or Freedmen's Bureau agents who had come to the South before the advent of Radical Reconstruction. The Massachusetts-born governor of Mississippi, Adelbert Ames, for example, first came to the state as a U.S. Army officer and then as a military governor—not as a political adventurer. Some northerners who had originally come South to make money in cotton did eventually turn to politics, but even these men usually shared a firm belief in the ideals of Radical Reconstruction. Northerner Albert T. Morgan, the sheriff of Yazoo County, Mississippi, for example, moved into politics after the failure of his cotton crop in 1867. But along with other northerners, Morgan tried to use his political office to secure for "the freedpeople the right to life, liberty, and the pursuit of happiness."

Even more important to Republican successes in the South were the so-called scalawags. Given this label by southern conservatives who saw them as traitors, scalawags were native white southerners who supported the Republican Party for a wide variety of reasons. Some were ex-Whigs, wealthy planters who nevertheless saw the South's future as one built on industrialization, urbanization, and the construction of a wage-labor system similar to that of the North. Specifically they sought governmental support for railroads and industry and the establishment of a stable banking and currency system. Because southern Democrats, representing the old elite, could not support these programs, the ex-Whigs turned to the Republicans and pragmatically accepted black voting rights.

But far more of the scalawags were poor yeoman farmers. In the mountainous areas that reached from West Virginia down into Georgia, Alabama, and Mississippi, they had long resented the large planters who held the best land, owned huge numbers of slaves, and dominated political affairs. The mountains had been strongholds of Unionist sentiment, where the Civil War had been denounced as "a rich man's war, a poor man's fight." Wartime Unionism provided a vital link to postwar Republicanism.

But economic changes in the postwar South added a new ingredient to the yeomen's support for the Republicans. Before the war, yeomen had lived largely outside the market economy, producing most of their own food and necessities of life. But after the war, many of them were drawn in to cotton planting—within a decade, 40 percent of all cotton in the South was grown by whites. Catastrophic crop failures in 1866 and 1867 hit these up-country families hard, and many fell deep into debt. Hoping to obtain relief from new state governments, large numbers of up-country white farmers began flocking to the Union League as early as 1866. And the passage of

White Supremacy Forever! Anti–Union League handbill, 1867.

the new state constitutions containing provisions for homesteading and debtor relief led these men, like their black counterparts, to become strong supporters of the southern Republican Party.

Most of the Republican Party's southern adherents, then, were poor people, black and white, with a strong hostility to the planter aristocracy. In Georgia, the Republican Party called on "poor men" to vote for the party of "relief, homesteads, and schools"; their nominee for governor proclaimed himself the "workingman's candidate." The "bottom rail," black and white, responded to such platforms across the South, voting overwhelmingly in 1867 and 1868 to reconstruct their state governments and to allow them to develop laws designed to benefit all citizens.

During their period in power—from two years in Tennessee to eight in South Carolina—southern Republican governments managed to construct the beginnings of a social-welfare state for their citizens. Building on the tremendous commitment of the freedpeople to education and continuing the work begun by the Freedmen's Bureau, reconstructed state governments in the South created a public school system where none had existed before. These schools remained segregated by race, and were better in the cities than in the countryside, but there was real progress nonetheless. Texas had fifteen hundred public schools by 1872. By 1876, the crest of Reconstruction-era educational reform, about half of all southern children—white and black—were enrolled in school. And not only children went to school: a northern correspondent reported in 1873 that in Vicksburg, Mississippi, "female negro servants make it a condition before accepting a situation, that they should have permission to attend the night-schools."

Although school integration made little progress in these years, several Radical governments did pass laws eliminating racial discrimination in other public accommodations, notably streetcars, restaurants, and hotels. In 1871, Texas barred segregation in public transportation. Arkansas, Mississippi, Louisiana, and Florida made it illegal for railroads, hotels, and theaters to deny "full and equal rights" to any citizen. South Carolina, with a black majority in the Republican-controlled legislature, passed a series of tough laws after 1869 requiring equal treatment in all public accommodations and in any business chartered or licensed by municipal, state, or federal authority. Although much of this legislation proved ineffective and unenforceable, it did indicate that Radical Republican governments were committed to ending legal segregation.

Laws helping both black and white landless agricultural laborers were another achievement of Radical rule. "We favor laws to foster and elevate labor," proclaimed the Republicans of Georgia. "We denounce all attempts of capital to control labor by legislation." Radical Republicans repealed the notorious Black Codes and passed lien laws that gave farmworkers (both black and white) a first claim on crops if their employers went bankrupt. "Under the laws of most of the Southern states, ample protection is afforded to tenants and very little to landlords," complained one planter in 1872. South Carolina went beyond protection, creating a state Land Commission with the power to buy land, and resell it to landless laborers on long-term credit. By 1876, despite initial corruption and mismanagement, fourteen thou-

"Colored Rule in a Reconstructed (?) State." Although Thomas Nast was an ardent supporter of equal rights, he often resorted to racial and ethnic stereotypes in his *Harper's Weekly* cartoons. Incensed by the lack of decorum displayed by some African-American legislators, Nast drew the figure of "Columbia," symbol of the nation, chiding: "You are aping the lowest whites. If you disgrace your race in this way you had better take back seats."

sand African-American families (about one-seventh of the state's black population) had acquired homesteads, as had a handful of white families. But other southern Republican governments rejected land distribution; most chose instead to increase the property-tax rate paid by large landowners, shifting some of the burden from the poor to those best able to pay for states' growing social-welfare programs.

Having local Republican officials, black and white, who sympathized with the plight of the landless farmers proved especially beneficial to the rural poor. Locally elected magistrates and justices of the peace, many of them black, adjudicated contract disputes between planters and their laborers—and usually decided in favor of the laborers. In Georgia's coastal McIntosh County, for example, Tunis Campbell, a freeborn African-American from the North, served as both state senator and justice of the peace for the county. Campbell integrated trial juries and undermined the power of local planters to enforce stringent work rules against their laborers. By 1870, men like

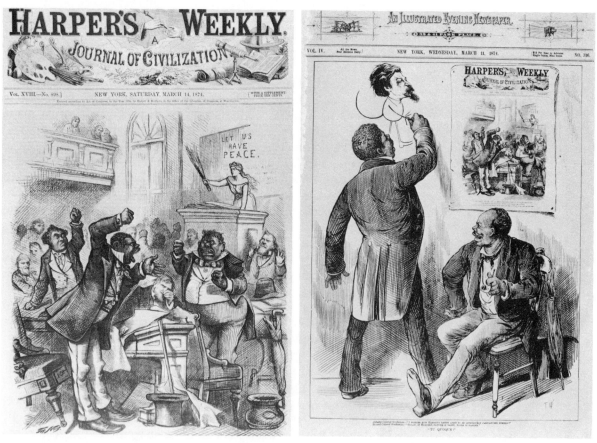

Campbell succeeded in transforming local law enforcement in the South. Planters frequently complained about "the negro magistrate, or majesty, as they call him," who sided with laborers because he depended upon their votes for his "offices and emoluments." Freedpeople, on the other hand, viewed local officials such as Campbell as "the champion of their rights and the bearer of their burdens."

Poor laborers thus gained a significant bargaining edge in their economic relations with the planters. This became particularly clear in the late 1860s, when the economy improved and black agricultural workers could demand and often receive higher wages. With the repeal of the Black Codes, which prevented the "enticement" of workers to other jobs, "the power to control [black labor] is gone," lamented one southern newspaper. Planters' power had been eroded further by the rise of local Union Leagues. Freedpeople were thus enabled to negotiate a new kind of compromise with planters on to how the land would be worked and who would reap its bounty.

The compromise emerged in the late 1860s. Rather than working in gangs for wages, individual black families worked small plots independently, renting land from the planter for cash or, more commonly, for a fixed share of the year's crop. By 1870, this "sharecropping" had become the dominant form of black agricultural labor, especially in the vast cotton lands. Sharecropping was a far cry from the freedpeople's objective of owning their own land, and later in the century, as we will see, it became connected to a credit system that drastically reduced the economic freedom of sharecroppers, both black and white. But in the short run, sharecropping did free black workers from the highly regimented gang-labor system, allowing them a good deal of control and autonomy over their work, their time, and their family work arrangements. Many landowners were therefore unhappy with the system. Sharecropping "is the wrong policy," one planter complained. "It makes the laborer too independent; he becomes a partner, and has a right to be consulted." As if to prove this very point, an Alabama sharecropper informed his former master that he (the sharecropper) was now "part owner of the crop, and as I have all the rights that you or any man has, I shall not suffer them abridged."

These very real economic and legal gains did not occur without cost, however. The southern Republican Party, which made all of this possible, experienced constant tensions within its ranks. A fragile coalition of wealthy ex-Whigs, northern politicians, rural ex-slaves, free urban blacks, and poor white yeomen, the party could not take a single position without alienating at least part of its constituency.

Although made up overwhelmingly of poor people, the Republican Party had leaders who were generally in favor of economic expansion, and thus of business. They wanted to use state governments to pro-

"I Wonder How Harper's Artist Likes to Be Offensively Caricatured Himself?" Nast gets a taste of his own medicine in this answering cartoon on the cover of the New York *Daily Graphic*. Such consciousness in the press about offensive imagery would not last long. By the 1880s, with the end of a national commitment to black equality, racist stereotypes characterized virtually all published cartoons and illustrations.

mote transportation and industry. These economic policies, when combined with large increases in state spending on schools and social programs for a free population that had nearly doubled in size, led to tremendous increases in taxes. But because the abolition of slavery also meant the elimination of the taxes on slaves, the tax burden fell increasingly not only on the wealthy planters but also on poor whites who owned little property. This fact contributed powerfully to the gradual defection, from 1867 on, of many poor whites from the Republican Party.

Revelations of political corruption among Republican officials also contributed to the growing disaffection of white voters. Although government patronage and individual bribery were as common after the Civil War in the North as in the South, southern Republicans could ill afford the hint of scandal added to growing doubts among whites about their radical egalitarian political program. The taint of corruption clung to southern Republican politicians after 1867, compromising the possibilities of achieving the Radical program.

The Republican Party thus began to lose political power and influence among its white constituents in several southern states. By 1869, Tennessee and Virginia had become the first states to return to conservative Democratic control. The process that conservatives called "redemption" had begun.

RETREAT FROM RECONSTRUCTION

Beginning in 1867, southern Democrats employed a combination of violence, economic intimidation, and fraud to regain political control and thus "redeem" the South. But this could not have happened without a sharp movement of both northern public opinion and the northern Republican Party away from the original goals of Radical Reconstruction. The first sign of retreat was Congress's failure to implement a federal law to confiscate planters' lands and distribute them among the freedpeople.

Throughout 1867, Radicals Charles Sumner and Thaddeus Stevens put forward a number of confiscation schemes, appealing to beliefs in independence and widespread landownership that were rooted in American political thought from the beginning. "No people will ever be republican in spirit and practice where a few own immense manors and the masses are landless," Stevens proclaimed. "Small independent landholders are the support and guardians of republican liberty."

But northern businessmen and their allies among the moderate Republicans effectively blocked these efforts. Part of their opposition stemmed from equally deep beliefs that government had no business redistributing property. "No man in America has any right to anything which he has not honestly earned, or which the lawful owner has not thought proper to give him," argued an editorial in the pro-business *Nation* magazine in 1867. But even more important than these views were fears among northern businessmen that confiscation would mean an end to plantation production of cotton and the "retreat" of freedmen into self-sufficient rather than market agriculture. Since raw cotton remained the nation's single largest export, reduced production would mean serious loss of foreign revenue. The wartime concerns of northern cotton planters such as Atkinson and Philbrick continued to haunt northern businessmen, leading them to oppose meaningful land reform.

The 1867 elections in the North gave another sign that outside the South the commitment to the political and civil rights of African-Americans was nearing its limits. Republicans were defeated in a number of northern states, forcing party leaders to reconsider even moderate plans to continue to assist southern blacks. Representatives to New York's 1867 constitutional convention refused to approve the extension of the franchise to the state's African-American citizens. Some Republicans believed that the racism of the northern population was the cause of these defeats. "The Negro question lies at the bottom of our reverses," argued Republican editor Horace Greeley. "Thousands have turned against us because we propose to enfranchise the Blacks." Furthermore, many northerners had simply been worn out by the long political battles. While the Black Codes and Confederate rule had led northerners to support the Republicans overwhelmingly in 1866, the removal of these overt signs of southern intransigence now tended to weaken that support.

A third sign that northern enthusiasm for Reconstruction was waning was the failure of the drive to impeach Andrew Johnson. Angered by Johnson's subversion of their Reconstruction program through deliberately ineffective enforcement and his removal of Edwin Stanton, Lincoln's secretary of war, from the cabinet, Radical Republicans managed in 1868 to persuade the House of Representatives to vote a bill of impeachment against the president. In the subsequent trial before the Senate, however, moderate Republicans cast the deciding votes and Johnson was narrowly acquitted.

The key to the moderates' defense of Johnson lay not in substantive support for his policies, but rather in a conservative belief in the sanctity of the presidency as an institution crucial to the maintenance of social order. "Whether Andrew Johnson should be removed from office, justly or unjustly, [is] comparatively of little consequence," wrote one moderate Republican senator, "but whether our government should be Mexicanized and an example set which would surely, in the end, utterly overthrow our institutions, [is] a matter of great consequence."

The final sign of northern retreat was the nomination and election of Ulysses S. Grant as president in 1868. A popular Union Army general, Grant himself had never advocated sweeping reform in the South. His ascendency coincided with the emergence of a new group of moderate leaders in the Republican Party. These men, the "Stalwarts," had none of the idealism of the Radical Republicans. Their sole objective was to maintain the power of the Republican Party, and under them, the great principles of Radical Reconstruction were replaced by simple political careerism.

These developments indicated that northern politicians were now prepared to leave the fate of the South, economically if not yet politically, in the hands of "the best men"—the former slaveowners, whom many northerners had viewed only a few years earlier as traitors. The northern Republicans even decided now to remove large numbers of federal troops from the South, troops originally dispatched in 1867 to protect freedpeople's rights and to minimize electoral violence.

Large planters thus would be left to "redeem" the South as they saw fit. They initially justified their actions with overt appeals to racism. As one planter put it, "God intended the niggers to be slaves." But the racism of their rhetoric cloaked another motivation: planters wanted a government-enforced labor system that would help them reassert control over agricultural labor. "The first thing to be done is to secure Home Government for Home Affairs," said one leading southern Democrat. "We must get control of our own labor."

As southern whites began to return to the Democratic Party, the presence of black voters stood as the major obstacle to full redemption and the return of conservative rule. Because African-Americans had never received their own land, they depended on planters for employment, even under the evolving system of sharecropping. Large planters tried to use their economic power over labor to influence the freedpeople's political activities. In Alabama, for example, a landlord required two black laborers to sign the following contract before he would hire them: "That said Laborers shall not attach themselves, belong to, or in any way perform any of the obligations required of what is known as the 'Loyal League Society,' or attend elections or political meetings without the consent of the employer." A Mississippi Democrat advised landlords

to use the great and all-powerful weapon that is in our control; we should not falter in the pledge to ourselves and our neighbors to discharge from our employ and our friendship forever, every laborer who persists in the diabolical war that has been waged against the white man and his interests ever since the negro has been a voter.

On the whole though, this economic pressure was not very successful. One planter complained bitterly that the Civil War and the Radical program had totally destroyed "the natural influence of capital on labor, of employer on employee." The result was that "negroes who will trust their white employers in all their personal affairs . . . are entirely beyond advice on all political issues." Because blacks could not be dissuaded from their loyalty to the Republican Party, planters looked to more violent methods of intimidation to get results.

The Ku Klux Klan provided their most important, and effective, weapon. Founded by Confederate veterans in Tennessee in 1866, the Klan began to grow rapidly after the advent of Radical Reconstruction. Though many of its rank-and-file members were poor men, attracted by the organization's banner of white supremacy, its leaders were mainly prominent planters and their sons. A white minister who traveled through Alabama in 1867 reported that "the leading men of the state" had created the Klan:

> They had lost their property, and worst of all, their slaves were made their equals and perhaps their superiors, to rule over them. They said there was an organization, already very extensive, that would rid them of this terrible calamity. . . . On my arrival at Huntsville, I learned of the organization of the Ku Klux Klan. It seemed to answer precisely the design expressed by these men.

By 1868 the Klan had a wide following across the South. Klan nightriders terrorized individual freedmen who deserted their employers or complained about low wages. Black Civil War veterans were targeted. So were freedpeople who had succeeded in breaking out of the plantation system and renting or buying land on their own. The latter were in particular danger because, having gotten a piece of land and a cabin, they were physically isolated. According to one Georgia freedman, "whenever a colored man acquires property and becomes in a measure independent, they take it from him."

The Ku Klux Klan played an important political role as well: it was in essence the paramilitary arm of the southern Democratic Party. The Klan systematically employed violence beginning in the spring of 1868 against freedpeople's organizations, especially the Union League and local Republican parties. Hooded Klansmen broke up meetings, threatened and lynched Radical and Union League leaders,

Klansman. A captured member of the Ku Klux Klan poses for a photographer in Holly Springs, Mississippi, after turning state's evidence in the 1871 prosecution of Klan members.

and succeeded in driving many black voters away from the polls all across the South. Estimates suggest that fully one in ten black delegates to the 1867–68 state constitutional conventions and one in five Union League leaders became victims of Klan terrorism during Reconstruction.

Klan violence against Radical politicians continued unabated after 1868. Abram Colby, a member of the Georgia legislature, testified that in October 1869 Klansmen

> took me to the woods and whipped me three hours or more and left me for dead. They said to me, "Do you think you will ever vote another damned radical ticket?" . . . I said, "If there was an election tomorrow, I would vote the radical ticket." They set in and whipped me a thousand licks more, with sticks and straps that had buckles on the ends of them.
>
> Q—What is the character of those men who were engaged in whipping you?
>
> A—Some are first-class men in our town. One is a lawyer, one a doctor, and some are farmers.

The targets of Klan violence were rarely chosen at random. James Alston, an early Union League organizer and by 1870 a Republican member of the Alabama legislature, reported that he was shot by the Klan because of his political activities. Alston had been one of five African-American Radicals from his area who had gone to Washington for Grant's inauguration in 1869. When asked about the fate of the other four, he replied, "I am the only man that is living. Everyone [else] is killed that went there to the inauguration of Grant." Such targeted violence by the KKK profoundly affected Reconstruction politics. Even though freedpeople, particularly those organized into Union Leagues in towns and cities, fought back valiantly, the Klan succeeded in destroying Republican organizations and demoralizing entire communities of freedpeople across the South.

In the face of such incredible violence and despite its general movement away from support of Reconstruction, the Republican-controlled Congress finally acted. In 1869 Congress approved the Fifteenth Amendment to the Constitution (which was ratified by the necessary number of states in 1870). Representing the essence of political compromise, the amendment declared that the right of U.S. citizens to vote could not "be denied or abridged" by any state "on account of race, color, or previous condition of servitude." This wording allowed numerous "nonracial" means of limiting the suffrage: southern states would later introduce poll (voting) taxes and literacy tests to restrict black voting. Moreover, the amendment said nothing about the right to hold elective office. Nevertheless, the Fifteenth Amendment demonstrated that moderate Republicans were not yet willing to stand by and allow their party to be terrorized and destroyed in the South by Klan violence.

Reports of increasing Klan attacks on freedpeople throughout the South forced the Republican majority to act. A series of grisly events in the small railroad town of Meridian, Mississippi, in March 1871 had shocked the nation and galvanized the Republicans. Three African-American leaders, who had organized local freedpeople to resist Klan "nightriders," had been arrested by the Meridian authorities. They were charged with delivering "incendiary speeches" and put on trial on March 6. In the midst of the first day's proceedings,

"Dedicated to the Men of the South Who Suffered Exile, Imprisonment and Death for the Daring Service They Rendered Our Country as Citizens of the Invisible Empire." By the turn of the century, popular novels like Thomas Dixon's *The Traitor* transformed the bloody record of the Ku Klux Klan (now softened by the euphemism "Invisible Empire") into tales of gallantry, sacrifice, and latter-day knighthood.

shots rang out in the courtroom—probably fired by a white spectator—killing two of the defendants and the Republican judge. In the
rioting that followed, thirty freedpeople were brutally murdered,
many of them members of the town's Union League chapter.

A joint congressional committee was appointed to hear testimony
in Washington and across the South (including in Meridian) from victims of racist violence. Several witnesses estimated that thousands of
freedpeople and their white allies had been killed and beaten by the
Klan in the previous four years.

Aghast at tales of such carnage, and fearing the possible demise of
the Republican Party in the South, Congress passed a series of enforcement acts, which imposed harsh penalties on those who used
organized terrorism for political purposes. In April the Ku Klux Klan
Act became law; for the first time, certain individual crimes against
citizens' rights were offenses
punishable under federal law.
Later in the year, President
Grant declared martial law in
parts of South Carolina and dispatched U.S. Army troops to the
Carolinas. Hundreds of Klansmen were indicted and tried by
the U.S. attorney general in
South Carolina, North Carolina,
and Mississippi. The federal government had broken the Klan's
back, at least temporarily. The
election of 1872, which saw
Grant reelected, was in fact the
most peaceful in the entire Reconstruction period.

But 1872 was the end, rather
than the beginning, of the federal presence in the South. Although the Ku Klux Klan Act
and the enforcement acts were
indeed strong federal laws, their
mere existence could not end
political violence—only contin-
uous, vigorous enforcement of
those laws could do that. Other
groups like the KKK rapidly
arose in the South after 1872,
using violence to achieve Democratic victories. Their success

"KILL HIM, GOD DAMN HIM . . ."

*The testimony offered by freedpeople at the 1871 congressional hearings on
the Ku Klux Klan detailed a horrifying litany of brutal violence and intimidation.
In her testimony before the committee in the courthouse in Demopolis,
Alabama, Betsey Westbrook recounts the murder of her husband, Robin
Westbrook.*

THEY CAME UP behind the house. One of them had his face smutted and
another had a knit cap on his face. They first shot about seven [shotgun] barrels
through the window. One of them said, "Get a rail and bust the door down."
They broke down the outside door.... One of them said, "Raise a light." ...
Then they saw where we stood and one of them says, "You are that damned
son of a bitch Westbrook." The man had a gun and struck him on the head.
Then my husband took the dog-iron and struck three or four of them. They got
him jammed up in the corner and one man went around behind him and put
two loads of a double-barreled gun in his shoulders. Another man says, "Kill
him, God damn him," and took a pistol and shot him down. He didn't live
more than half an hour.

My boy was in there while they were killing my husband and he says,
"Mammy, what must I do?" I says, "Jump outdoors and run." He went to the
door and a white man took him by the arm and says, "God damn you, I will fix
you too," but he snatched himself loose and got away.

Q—Did you know any of these men?

A—Yes, sir. I certainly knowed three.

Q—What were they mad at your husband about?

A—He just would hold up his head and say he was a strong Radical [Repub-
   lican]. He would hang on to that.

illustrates a crucial point: the Democrats assumed that neither Congress nor the president would act decisively to prevent political violence and fraud. And indeed, after the 1872 election, Republicans in the North continued their steady retreat from the defense of African-American rights in the South. This retreat, as much as the actions of southern racists, contributed to the ending of Reconstruction.

The retreat was made easier by the nearly total collapse of Radical Republican leadership in the Congress after 1870. Thaddeus Stevens died in 1868, embittered and apprehensive about the future. "The death of Stevens is an emancipation for the Republican Party," rejoiced a leading Stalwart. In the following two years, many of the most prominent Radicals lost their seats in Congress. Although Charles Sumner kept his Senate seat, he was stripped of power by the new party leaders.

With the eclipse of the Radicals and the vast expansion of the national economy, the Republican Party became ever more attuned to the interests of business. Interested in investment possibilities in the South, businessmen and their political allies became increasingly weary of Reconstruction. By 1870 most of the leading business newspapers had turned against the Radicals' southern policy, arguing that it had paralyzed southern business and discouraged investment. In May 1870 a group of what the *Nation* called "businessmen of the highest character" from New York and Boston examined conditions in the South "with reference to investments" and found them very discouraging. Particularly upsetting were the debtor-relief provisions adopted by many of the southern state governments. "No one will invest or emigrate, so long as . . . laws are made to prevent the collection of debts," noted one northern businessman.

This growing dissatisfaction with Reconstruction was a key factor in the revolt within the Republican Party in 1872. A group calling themselves Liberal Republicans held a convention and nominated the prominent editor Horace Greeley to run against Grant for the presidency. Deeply disturbed by accounts of corruption in the Grant administration, the Liberals called for the establishment of a professional civil service. Although many Liberals had once been Radicals, they seemed to have little trust in political democracy and placed their greatest faith in members of the upper classes, whom they called "the best men."

The Liberals opposed continued federal intervention in the South, believing that planters, the "best men" of the South, should be allowed to rule paternalistically over black laborers and white yeomen alike. They saw this as the surest way to end the turmoil of Reconstruction. Although Grant won the 1872 election convincingly, in part because of his decision to dispatch army troops to the South to prevent election violence, the Liberal revolt signaled the growing dis-

"A Prospective Scene in the 'City of Oaks,' 4th of March, 1869." A September, 1868, edition of the Tuscaloosa *Independent Monitor* proposes the treatment its local Republican opponents should receive on inauguration day if the Republicans lose the upcoming presidential election. The editor of the Democratic newspaper was the Grand Cyclops of the Ku Klux Klan in Tuscaloosa.

satisfaction with Reconstruction that would soon dominate the Republican Party.

The Panic of 1873 launched a severe nationwide depression that dealt the final blow to Reconstruction. Across the South, the depression drove many black renters back into the ranks of sharecroppers or laborers and sharply reduced black workers' wage levels. White planters increased their economic control and reasserted their political power through the Democratic Party.

The depression also prompted northern businessmen to abandon the last remnants of Reconstruction. "There is a pretty general impression [among businessmen] in the country that the financial crisis of 1873 was owing in great part to the paralysis of the South," noted one northern observer. "What the South now needs is capital to develop her resources, but this she cannot obtain till confidence in her state governments can be restored, and this will never be done by federal bayonets," wrote a New York businessman in 1875. "We have tried this long enough. Now let the South alone."

Leaving the South alone meant accepting white rule and a resurgent Democratic Party. In Mississippi, the Democrats retook power in 1875 and devised the "Mississippi Plan," which became a model for redemption in what was left of the reconstructed South: South Carolina, Louisiana, and Florida.

The Democrats' first step was to drive whites who continued to be loyal to the Republicans into the Democratic Party. This was accomplished through economic pressure, social ostracism, and threats of physical violence. Democrats simply made it "too damned hot for [us] to stay out," explained one white Republican who gave in to the pressure. "No white man can live in the South in the future and act with any other than the Democratic Party unless he is willing and prepared to live a life of social isolation and remain in political oblivion."

The second step was to use a combination of economic and physical coercion to keep blacks from voting. One Democratic newspaper pledged to "carry the election peacefully if we can, forcibly if we must." Landlords informed blacks that they could expect no further work if they voted Republican. Democrats also organized rifle clubs and attacked Republican picnics and rallies. Such violence proved to be the Democrats' most effective tool.

Vicksburg, Mississippi, was the scene of the worst violence. In December 1874, responding to continuing harassment of Republicans, Vicksburg's black sheriff called on local blacks to help maintain the peace. But African-Americans were outnumbered and outgunned. White terrorists attacked a group of armed black deputies, killing thirty-five. With black voters intimidated, the Democrats won the county elections that same month, encouraging further violence throughout the state. "The same tactics that saved Vicksburg will save the State, and no other will," trumpeted a Democratic newspaper several months later.

Black people throughout Mississippi protested the rising tide of violence and called on Republican governor Adelbert Ames to give them protection. "I beg you most fulley to send the United [States] soldiers here," wrote one citizen of Yazoo to the governor. "They have hung six more men since the killing of Mr. Fawn; they won't let the Republicans have no ticket." But the violence continued. It was directed primarily at local Republican leaders such as Richard Gray in Noxubee County. According to a fellow black Republican, Gray was "shot down walking on the pavements . . . because he was nominated for treasurer, and furthermore, because he made a speech and said he never did expect to vote a Democrat ticket, and also advised the colored citizens to do the same."

In response to this terrorism, Governor Ames organized a state militia. Black men all around the state volunteered to serve in it, but Ames hesitated to arm them, perhaps fearing that this step would only result in greater violence. Democratic violence continued; by election day, Republican supporters were thoroughly intimidated. Many stayed away from the polls and the Democratic Party carried the state by thirty thousand votes. Mississippi had been "redeemed."

Only federal intervention could have prevented what occurred in states such as Mississippi and Alabama. But President Grant's administration, which had acted forcefully against the Klan in Mississippi and elsewhere in the South in 1871, turned down Ames's re-

---

". . . THE BLOOD AND TREASURE OF THE PEOPLE SPENT IN VAIN"

This February 1875 petition to the U.S. Congress from Alabama's black Republican legislators laments the deteriorating political conditions in the state in the aftermath of "redemption" and the resurgence of the Democratic Party.

THE DEMOCRATIC PARTY of Alabama has made, and is now making, a deliberate and persistent attempt, as shown by their leaders in the present general assembly, to change the penal code and criminal laws of Alabama so as to place the liberty and legal rights of the poor man, and especially of the poor colored man, who is generally a Republican in politics, in the power and control of the dominant race, who are, with few exceptions, the landholders, and Democratic in politics. . . .

We need not remind you how such a policy is at variance with all the results intended to be wrought out by the war for the preservation of the Union. That was a conflict of ideas as well as of armies. The issue was free-labor institutions and principles against slave-labor institutions and principles. It was a conflict between these two types of civilization. And yet, while the slave-labor system did not triumph at Appomattox, they are thus seen to be practically triumphant in Alabama. After the war came reconstruction, by which the free-labor type of civilization was believed to have been firmly established throughout the entire South. . . . But no sooner does the Democratic Party accede to power in Alabama than its leaders propose to forget not only all that has been done and promised, but to undo, as fast as possible, that which was wrought out by the war, and all that has since been promised in connection therewith. It would practically reverse the verdict wrought out at the point of the bayonet, reverse the policy of Reconstruction, and strike out of existence not only our free-State constitutions, but the laws made in pursuance thereof, thus violating the fundamental conditions of the readmission of Alabama into the Union. If this is allowed to be done, it is not difficult to perceive that the war for the Union was a grand mistake, and the blood and treasure of the people spent in vain.

Strawman. An unrepentant southern rebel discovers the true nature of the federal government's commitment to defend African-American rights. "Come on, boys!" he shouts in this 1874 cartoon, "Old Grant's bluster about our killing Republicans is only a military scarecrow, after all."

quest in 1875 for federal troops to be used against the Mississippi Democrats. The North no longer seemed outraged by political violence directed against freedpeople.

Northern working-class voters, like northern businessmen, clearly had tired of Reconstruction. Preoccupied by the depression, and still unconvinced by arguments for equal rights for African-Americans, working people turned away from the radicalism of the mid-1860s. Capitalizing on this weariness, Democrats scored important northern victories in the elections of 1874 and took control of the House of Representatives, ensuring that southern blacks would receive no further protection from Congress. And Democrats now looked hopefully toward the presidential election of 1876.

The Democrats chose New York's reform governor Samuel J. Tilden as their candidate for president, while Republicans nominated Rutherford B. Hayes, the governor of Ohio. Although initial returns gave Tilden the election, disputes about the votes from three southern states still in Republican hands (Louisiana, South Carolina, and Florida) threw his victory into question.

A specially appointed electoral commission composed of ten congressmen and five Supreme Court justices ruled 8–7 in February that the disputed votes in the three states belonged to Hayes. But there was no guarantee that the Democratic majority in the House of Representatives would accept this decision, and many felt the nation faced another civil war. Leading Republicans now moved to the fore, working out a secret understanding with southern Democrats in Congress to assure the latter's acquiescence in Hayes's inauguration.

In exchange for this Democratic support, the Republicans promised to give southern Democrats a fair share of federal appointments and to provide federal assistance for southern railroad development. The Republicans also promised to remove the federal troops remaining in the South. In April 1877, President Hayes pulled out the few remaining federal troops from the capitals of Louisiana and South Carolina, allowing Democrats to return to power. Neither the southern Republican Party nor the freedpeople who were its most ardent supporters could rely any longer on federal protection against violence and intimidation. The curtain finally rang down on the long drama of Reconstruction.

THE END OF RECONSTRUCTION

Within two decades, southern Democrats solidified their iron rule of the region through a series of measures that disfranchised large numbers of voters, especially African-Americans. South Carolina established a literacy requirement for voting and Georgia instituted a poll tax. Other states passed voter-registration laws that discriminated against poor and black citizens. The Fourteenth and Fifteenth Amendments were effectively nullified by such actions across the South. Along with outright fraud and continuing violence, these techniques served ultimately to destroy the Republican Party (and other opposition parties) in the South.

The process took a long time to run its course, however. Republicans maintained some strength in the South, polling as much as 40 percent of the vote through the 1880s and 1890s. Local Union League chapters survived into the early 1890s. African-Americans continued to vote and even hold office until their complete disfranchisement around the turn of the century.

In the area of labor legislation, however, the results of redemption were much quicker to appear. As the Democrats took control of the southern states through the 1870s, they reinstated some of the provisions of the Black Codes. Laborers in several states now faced criminal penalties for violating labor contracts. Justices of the peace had been important in upholding laborers' claims in disputes during Reconstruction; now new ones were appointed by conservative legislatures rather than elected by local residents. Landownership by poor whites and blacks almost disappeared, and the initial advantages of sharecropping were overwhelmed by growing indebtedness and the resurgent power of the planter class.

Even more ominously, a convict-lease system was established in many states that allowed planters to use unpaid convict labor on their lands—which gave the planters a huge economic advantage and threatened all free laborers. Convicts, 90 percent of whom were black, were poorly clothed and fed and often abused by guards. Also, a series of laws were introduced to restrict mobility among landless laborers. These developments harked back not only to the vagrancy laws of the Black Codes, but to slavery itself.

Freedpeople had few options in the face of growing repression. Most settled in and tried as best they could to live their lives within the constraints of the New South. As in slave times, the church, the family, and the larger community provided African-Americans with cultural and social resources for survival.

But many could not tolerate staying in the South. Beginning in the mid-1870s colonization schemes, which proposed migration to Africa or to midwestern states such as Kansas, became popular among freedpeople. Henry Adams, a Union Army veteran from Louisiana and a colonization organizer, claimed to have signed up sixty thousand from all parts of the South. "This is a horrible part of the country," he wrote. "It is impossible for us to live with these slaveholders of the South and enjoy the right as they enjoy it." Although not many made the journey to Africa, tens of thousands of southern blacks, taking the biblically inspired name Exodusters, did migrate to Kansas. Few succeeded in establishing themselves on Kansas farmland, however; most Exodusters had to settle for menial jobs in the state's towns. But few returned to the "redeemed" South.

Life was indeed oppressive in the South after Reconstruction ended, but the fact that thousands of freedpeople were able to emigrate at all indicates that they had at least succeeded in

". . . LAND WHERE WE CAN HAVE A HOME"

This letter to the National Emigrant Aid Society from a group of North Carolina freedpeople lists their reasons for wanting to migrate to Kansas.

August 1, 1879

We the people of the 2nd Congressional District, North Carolina, have a Strong Desire to Emigrate to Kanses Land Where we can Have a Home. Reason and why:

1. We have not our rights in law.
2. The old former masters do not allow us anything for our labor. . . .
3. We have not our Right in the Election. We are defrauded by our former masters.
4. We have not no [right] to make an honest and humble living.
5. There is no use for the Colored to go to law after their Rights; not one out of 50 gets his Rights.
6. The Ku [Klux] Reigns. . . .
7. We Want to Get to a land Where we can Vote and it not be a Crime to the Colored Voters. . . .
8. Wages is very low [here]

Nearly all of the laborers have families to take care of and many other things we could mention, but by the help of God we intend to make our start to Kansas land. We had Rather Suffer and be free, than to suffer [the] infamous degrades that are Brought upon us [here] . . .

Rev. S. Heath
Moses Heath
Lenoir Co., N.C.

All Colored People
THAT WANT TO
GO TO KANSAS,
On September 5th, 1877,
Can do so for $5.00

IMMIGRATION.

WHEREAS, We, the colored people of Lexington, Ky., knowing that there is an abundance of choice lands now belonging to the Government, have assembled ourselves together for the purpose of locating on said lands. Therefore,

BE IT RESOLVED, That we do now organize ourselves into a Colony, as follows:— Any person wishing to become a member of this Colony can do so by paying the sum of one dollar ($1.00), and this money is to be paid by the first of September, 1877, in installments of twenty-five cents at a time, or otherwise as may be desired.

RESOLVED, That this Colony has agreed to consolidate itself with the Nicodemus Towns, Solomon Valley, Graham County, Kansas, and can only do so by entering the vacant lands now in their midst, which costs $5.00.

RESOLVED, That this Colony shall consist of seven officers—President, Vice-President, Secretary, Treasurer, and three Trustees. President—M. M. Bell; Vice-President—Isaac Talbott; Secretary—W. J. Niles; Treasurer—Daniel Clarke; Trustees—Jerry Lee, William Jones, and Abner Webster.

RESOLVED, That this Colony shall have from one to two hundred militia, more or less, as the case may require, to keep peace and order, and any member failing to pay in his dues, as aforesaid, or failing to comply with the above rules in any particular, will not be recognized or protected by the Colony.

Exodusters, 1877: A handbill urging African-Americans to leave Kentucky and join a new settlement in Kansas.

preventing the reinstitution of slavery. Moreover, many of the gains secured during the Civil War and Reconstruction could not be erased by redemption. African-Americans came out of this era having won control over their family and religious lives; having secured, however briefly, national legal guarantees of equal rights, including suffrage; and, perhaps most important, having created a legacy of successful collective action that their heirs would draw upon in future struggles for civil rights. Nonetheless, by 1877 the free-labor society that black Americans and their Radical Republican allies had tried so hard to create during Reconstruction had become but a distant ideal.

Frederick Douglass—the nation's preeminent African-American leader, whose career spanned the Abolitionist crusade, the drama of war and emancipation, and, finally, the tragedy of the postwar era— summed up the political and moral lessons of Reconstruction:

You say you have emancipated us. You have; and I thank you for it. But what is your emancipation?

When the Israelites were emancipated they were told to go and borrow of their neighbors—borrow their coin, borrow their jewels, load themselves down with the means of subsistence; after, they should go free in the land which the Lord God gave them. When the Russian serfs had their chains broken and given their liberty, the government of Russia—aye, the despotic government of Russia—gave to those poor emancipated serfs a few acres of land on which they could live and earn their bread.

But when you turned us loose, you gave us no acres. You turned us loose to the sky, to the storm, to the whirlwind, and, worst of all, you turned us loose to the wrath of our infuriated masters.

12 INDUSTRIAL LABOR AFTER THE WAR

Railroad-riot extra:
The Pittsburgh
railyards aflame.
From
*Frank Leslie's
Illustrated
Newspaper,*
August 4, 1877.

IN 1876 America celebrated the hundredth anniversary of its independence. At a gala Centennial Exposition in Philadelphia, Americans marveled at the wonderful new inventions of the industrial age: Thomas Alva Edison's "multiplex" telegraph, which could transmit several messages on one line, Christopher Schole's typewriter, and Alexander Graham Bell's telephone. At the center of the exposition stood the huge eight-thousand-horsepower Corliss steam engine, a fitting symbol of the nation's spectacular industrial growth.

But beneath the optimistic symbolism of the centennial lay a more disturbing reality. In 1876 America was in the fourth year of the worst economic depression it had ever experienced. The nation was overrun with unemployed workers, thousands of whom tramped through the countryside looking for work.

The depression also brought a wave of bitter industrial conflicts. The climax came a year after the centennial, when railroad strikes erupted in dozens of towns and cities across the country, resulting in the loss of over a hundred lives and the destruction of millions of dollars' worth of property. Federal troops were called in to suppress the strikes, and to prevent what many businessmen and press commentators feared was an imminent revolution.

How had the nation, buoyed by the decisive northern victory in the Civil War and the political and economic possibilities it inaugurated, once again reached the point of open warfare? How had the optimism of the 1876 celebration of the nation's unity and independence degenerated so quickly into the brutal conflict of the 1877 railroad strike? The answers to these questions lay in the extraordinary economic and geographical expansion of the nation that followed the war and the challenge that expansion posed to political and philosophical ideals of independence and equality long cherished by most Americans.

RAILROADS AND THE WEST

The rapid opening of the West was the most important economic development in the years just after the Civil War. When the war began, American settlement extended from the Atlantic seaboard to the tier of states west of the Mississippi River and from the eastern slope of the Sierra Nevada mountain range to the Pacific Coast. The vast expanse of land between these areas was occupied primarily by American Indians. This situation changed rapidly after the war. Hastened by railroad construction, the discovery of mineral resources, and the final defeat of Indian resistance, the vast lands west of the Mississippi River were largely settled in the twenty-five years between 1865 and 1890.

The railroad turned the dream of western settlement into a reality. Between 1867 and 1873, railroad companies laid 35,000 miles of railroad track in the United States—as much as was built in the three decades before the Civil War. The crowning achievement was a line that spanned the continent, linking the Atlantic and Pacific coasts. In 1862 Congress had chartered the Union Pacific and Central Pacific corporations to construct a line between Omaha, Nebraska, and Sacramento, California. Seven years later the line was completed. A golden spike—hammered into place with great ceremony at Promontory Point, Utah, in 1869—marked the climax of the transportation revolution that had begun early in the nineteenth century.

The largest government subsidies in American history financed this railroad boom. Government support for internal improvements was not in itself new. Canals and turnpikes had been heavily subsi-

Vignettes showing some of the tribulations railroad passengers faced as they encountered the new and rapid form of transportation.

dized by state and local governments in the antebellum period, and in the 1850s Congress had realized that a transcontinental line would require major assistance. But the sheer scale of government aid after the Civil War far surpassed anything earlier: between 1862 and 1872, Congress gave away more than 100 million acres of public land to railroad companies and provided them with over $64 million in loans and tax breaks.

The Republican congressmen who voted for these huge grants and loans argued that railroads were needed to open up the western lands to independent farmers. They linked their assistance to the railroads with what appeared to be a pathbreaking land bill, the Homestead Act of 1862. The act allowed any adult citizen or permanent immigrant to claim 160 acres of public land for a $10 fee; final title to the land would be granted after five years of residence. Such a law had long been a demand of the urban labor movement, and its supporters heralded it as the salvation of the laboring man. "Should it become a law," wrote the Radical Republican George Julian before it was passed, "the poor white laborers . . . would flock to the territories, where labor would be respectable, [and] our democratic theory of equality would be put in practice."

A vast expansion of farming in the West in fact followed closely on the heels of the railroads. In the ten years after the transcontinental line was completed, Kansas attracted 347,000 new settlers, with similarly dramatic increases in the other Plains states. All in all, more land was put under cultivation in the thirty years between 1870 and 1900 than in the previous two hundred and fifty years of American history.

Only about a tenth of the new farms in these years were acquired under the Homestead Act, however. Despite the claims of its supporters, the act did not go nearly far enough in encouraging settlement of the Great Plains by urban workers. The land was free, but a city laborer, making perhaps $250 a year, could not even pay the entry fees to file a claim, let alone raise the substantial funds necessary to buy farm equipment and move to the West. More importantly, large mining and lumber companies quickly took advantage of a provision of the law that allowed a homesteader to obtain full title to his land by paying $1.25 or $2.50 an acre for it. Large companies paid individuals to stake claims, and quickly acquired huge tracts of land at prices well below their actual value. Later amendments to the act (particularly the Desert Land Act of 1877) made the acquisition of western land by large companies even easier. George Julian's vision of a West settled by poor urban laborers seemed to be undercut by the actual workings of the Homestead Act.

The rapid expansion of the mining frontier in these years also undermined the hopes of workers. By the mid-1850s the California gold rush had come to an end and little opportunity remained for the independent prospectors who had panned for gold in the state since 1849. Major discoveries of silver and gold in Colorado and Nevada in 1858 and 1859 drew these independent miners to the Rockies and eastern Sierras, where boom towns like Virginia City sprang up in mountainous canyons almost overnight. The 1860s and early 1870s witnessed further discoveries in Montana, Idaho, Wyoming, and the Black Hills of Dakota.

But mining here was very different from that in California. The mines of Colorado and Nevada (often three thousand feet deep or more) required much more capital and technology than had been necessary in California. As a result, the individual prospectors who discovered veins of precious metals like Nevada's spectacular Comstock Lode were rapidly displaced by large mining companies. Eastern and European investors provided the capital to buy heavy machinery, and the companies employed large numbers of wage-earning miners in impersonal (and often unsafe) settings. The industrialization of hard-rock mining, the emergence of powerful mining syndicates, and the movement of independent prospectors into the ranks of wage-earning employees stood in stark contrast to the dream of a free and open West.

The cattle industry also grew rapidly in this period. A tough breed of cattle called longhorns, introduced by the Spanish, had long roamed wild on the plains of southern Texas. After the Civil War, enterprising men realized that they could buy cattle for as little as $3 or $4 a head in Texas and sell them in northern markets for $25 to $50 a head. It was then a matter of driving the cattle across the plains to the new railhead cattle towns such as Sedalia, Missouri, or Abilene, Kansas. The famous "long drives" of the 1860s brought tremendous profits to a number of Texans, turned Abilene and Sedalia into thriving boom towns, and gave the cowboy a permanent place in American mythology.

But this period of the cattle industry was short. The high profits brought a flood of capital from England, Scotland, and the East that turned cattle-raising into a large-scale business. And as cattlemen began raising stock closer to the railroad lines in Kansas and Missouri, the romance of the long drives came to an end. The cowboy's more demanding tasks were eliminated and he became simply a cowhand—a wageworker on horseback—who lived on a ranch and sorted the cattle to be shipped to market.

The rapid settlement of the Plains and Far West, greatly speeded by the building of the railroads, led to violent conflict between the settlers and the American Indians of the region. Miners quickly dispersed and destroyed the peaceful tribes inhabiting the mountains of California, Utah, and Nevada. The conflict on the Great Plains was more protracted. In treaties signed in the 1830s, the United States government had solemnly pledged much of the Great Plains region to American Indians. The non-Indian settlement of the West led the government to break these treaties and to declare a new policy in 1867. Indians would thereafter be concentrated on two reservations in Dakota Territory and in Oklahoma Territory.

Although a number of tribal leaders were persuaded to accept the new terms, a good many other Indians resisted the drastic reduction of their lands and (what was even worse) the destruction of their nomadic culture by the boundaries of the reservation system. Between 1869 and 1876, these "nontreaty" Indians carried out guerrilla warfare against white settlers and United States troops throughout the

West. The warfare reached its climax in 1876, when the powerful Sioux nation moved into open rebellion in response to the movement of miners into the Black Hills of the Dakota reservation. Led by Chiefs Sitting Bull and Crazy Horse, the Sioux won a major victory when they annihilated the troops of General George A. Custer at the Little Big Horn River in southern Montana. But the victory was short-lived. A shortage of supplies and overpowering odds led to the defeat of the Sioux by the fall of 1877.

Even more important than government policy and military action was the destruction of the buffalo between 1867 and 1883. The bison that roamed the West in giant herds provided both food and shelter for the Plains Indians (the skins were used for tents and robes), essential for their nomadic life. In the late 1860s "sportsmen" killed many of the buffalo on the northern plains, as did railroad crews in search of meat; they were joined by professional hunters after a Pennsylvania tannery discovered in 1871 that buffalo hides could be used for commercial leather. Using powerful, long-range rifles, and shooting from railroad cars or from horseback, these hunters rapidly slaughtered millions of the beasts: once numbering over 13 million, buffalo had all but disappeared from the Great Plains by the mid-1880s. With the buffalo gone, American Indians had little choice but to move to the new federal reservations. Though cultural resistance to the reservation system would continue, culminating in the rapid spread of the Ghost Dance religion among the Sioux in 1890–91, by the late 1870s direct physical resistance by American Indians had come to an end.

Now a vast network of railroad lines crisscrossed the Plains where Indians had once hunted the buffalo. But the railroads did more than settle the West with white farmers, ranchers, and

---

"THIS WAS TO BE OUR LAND FOREVER . . ."

Iron Teeth, a Cheyenne woman, provided a vivid account of the conflicts that arose in the 1870s between federal troops and the Indian tribes they were trying to relocate.

SOLDIERS BUILT FORTS in our Powder River country when I was about thirty-two years old. The Sioux and the Cheyennes settled at the White River agency, in our favorite Black Hills country. This was to be our land forever, so we were pleased. But white people found gold on our lands [in 1874]. They crowded in, so we had to move out. My husband was angry about it, but he said the only thing we could do was go to other lands offered to us. We did this.

Many Cheyennes and Sioux would not stay on the new reservations, but went back to the old hunting grounds in Montana. Soldiers went there to fight them. In the middle of the summer [1876] we heard that all of the soldiers [led by General George A. Custer] had been killed at the Little Bighorn River. My husband said we should go and join our people there. We went, and all of our people spent the remainder of the summer there, hunting, not bothering any white people nor wanting to see any of them. When the leaves fell, the Cheyenne camp was located on a small creek far up the Powder River.

Soldiers came [on November 29, 1876] and fought us there. Crows, Pawnees, Shoshones, some Arapahoes, and other Indians were with them. They killed our men, women, and children, whichever ones might be hit by their bullets. We who could do so ran away. My husband and my two sons helped in fighting off the soldiers and enemy Indians. My husband was walking, leading his horse, and stopping at times to shoot. Suddenly, I saw him fall. I started to go back to him, but my sons made me go on, with my three daughters. The last time I ever saw [my husband], he was lying there dead in the snow. From the hilltops we Cheyennes saw our lodges and everything in them burning.

Ride the Train and Shoot a Buffalo! One of the short-lived attractions of western railroad travel was the opportunity to join a buffalo hunt—often without having to leave the comfort of your railroad carriage. In this 1870 promotional photograph, the official taxidermist displays his wares outside of the Kansas Pacific Railroad's general offices.

miners. They also began to transform the very fabric of American economic life. Through its large subsidies to the railroads, the federal government helped to create extremely powerful corporations, which became America's first big businesses. The Pennsylvania Railroad, then the nation's largest single business enterprise, employed over 20,000 workers by the early 1870s. And the railroads' tremendous need for capital led them to adopt and popularize a variety of modern managerial methods, including the limited-liability corporation. The number of railroad stockholders expanded, and large boards of directors—usually including several powerful bankers—replaced the old-fashioned individual entrepreneurs who had both owned and managed their own concerns. This new separation of ownership and control gave the railroad corporation a permanence and impersonality unknown in antebellum times.

The railroads were also the first businesses to face the problem of economic competition in all its severity. This was the result of two interrelated factors. First, the railroads had extremely high fixed expenses, which they had to meet even if they were not operating. These expenses included not only the maintenance of equipment and tracks but also the regular payment of interest on the bonds used to finance their construction. These constant costs encouraged railroads to continue operations even during bad times, when rates could fall to very low levels.

Second, railroads had a strong incentive to utilize as much of their capacity as possible. Since it was nearly as expensive to haul empty cars to a point where they were needed as it was to haul the same cars loaded with freight, railroads were willing to offer extremely low rates to shippers of goods. In areas where two or more lines competed for the same traffic, the result was a series of disastrous rate wars.

The combination of high fixed costs and an incentive to utilize maximum capacity left the railroad industry in a state of chaos. In some areas of the nation, some railroads went bankrupt while others emerged as monopolies. In other areas, railroads formed "pools" that tried to end cutthroat competition by setting rates and dividing up traffic. From the standpoint of railroad managers, such practices seemed essential to survival. But the railroad pools undermined the "free competition" constantly lauded as the key to American prosperity and virtue.

"The American Frankenstein." Inspired by Mary Shelley's novel about a man-made monster who turned upon its creator, this cartoon depicts the railroad trampling the rights of the American people. "Agriculture, commerce, and manufacture are all in my power," the monster roars in the cartoon's caption. "My interest is the higher law of American politics."

Railroads also created a small group of extremely wealthy entrepreneurs who became known as the Robber Barons: Cornelius Vanderbilt, Jay Gould, Jim Fisk, and Collis P. Huntington all built immense personal fortunes through railroad promotion and consolidation. When Vanderbilt died in 1877, he left his son William a fortune of $100 million, a figure unheard of in earlier times. By way of comparison, a decent annual wage in 1877 for ten to twelve hours of labor, six days a week, was $350.

These railroad men rapidly translated their economic might into political power. They hired armies of lobbyists whose activities in Washington and in state capitals gained the corporations even more subsidies and land grants and protected them from regulation and taxation. "The galleries and lobbies of every legislature," observed a Republican leader, "are thronged with men seeking . . . an advantage" for one corporation or another. Railroad promoters, managers, and financiers began to form the basis of a powerful new political elite.

The pattern of development in the 1860s and 1870s made many Americans doubt the future of their nation. A civil war fought to destroy the power of one ruling class (the southern slaveholders) seemed to be producing another—even more powerful—oligarchy. And this oligarchy was emerging in part as a result of the rapid and uncontrolled development of the West, the very region where the dream of a free and open republic should have been fulfilled.

INDUSTRY AND WORKERS

The pace and intensity of industrialization accelerated dramatically after the Civil War. Cities grew rapidly. New immigrants flooded into them. As a result, the number of workers in manufacturing and construction leapt from two million in 1860 to over four million in 1880. In 1860 there were about as many self-employed people as wage-earners. Twenty years later, far more people relied on wages. The ideal of economic independence and self-sufficiency became less and less possible for most Americans to attain.

The most dynamic industries were those involved in processing the natural resources of the rapidly developing West. Meat production, for example, was transformed. Before the 1870s, cattle were driven on hoof to towns and cities throughout the nation, where local butchers slaughtered them and prepared the beef. The refrigerated railroad car in the early 1870s transformed this system. Gustavus Swift, a New Englander who came to Chicago in 1875, realized that cattle could be slaughtered and packed in huge packing houses there, and then be shipped ready for market to cities throughout the nation. In 1878 Swift started what soon became one of America's largest companies; things would never be the same for the local butcher.

"Pork Packing in Cincinnati." An 1873 promotional lithograph diagrams, bloodlessly, assembly-line meatpacking, from slaughter to preserving.

Oil-refining was another large new industry. In 1859, Edwin Drake drilled America's first oil well in Pennsylvania. The lucrative business of refining the oil grew up in Pittsburgh, Philadelphia, and Cleveland, attracting many businessmen and leading to a period of intense competition similar to that which plagued the railroads. John D. Rockefeller, whose Standard Oil Company dominated the Cleveland petroleum business by 1871, saw this competition as the main problem facing the industry. Rather than supporting price-fixing pools, which he referred to as "ropes of sand," Rockefeller brought pressure on other oil refiners to sell out to him. By the late 1870s Standard Oil was a virtual monopoly, controlling about nine-tenths of the nation's oil-refining capacity.

But such large-scale processing industries were just the tip of the iceberg. A wide variety of both old and new industries grew tremendously in the decades after the Civil War, many of them spurred on by all the railroad construction. Railroads needed enormous amounts of stone, iron, and lumber, and thus directly stimulated those industries.

What with the railroads' demand for rails, locomotives, and bridges, the output of pig iron tripled, from under a million tons in 1865 to almost three million tons in 1873. At the same time, the size of iron-producing firms increased dramatically. In 1862, for example, the Cambria ironworks in Pennsylvania was a small and inefficient firm. Seven years later the company owned 40,000 acres of land, four blast furnaces, and forty-two puddling furnaces, and it employed 6,000 workers. This trend toward concentration continued through the next decade. Between 1869 and 1879 both the number of workers and the amount of capital investment in iron nearly doubled, while the number of firms remained about constant.

The growing iron industry needed more and more coal. As a result, coal production leapt from under 17 million tons in 1861 to nearly 72 million tons in 1880. In some regions, such as Allegheny County, Pennsylvania, which produced as much soft coal as the rest of the nation combined in 1869, individual mining companies remained relatively small. The sixty-six mines in this region averaged less than 100 miners each. In newer areas of coal production, such as northern Illinois, however, large companies quickly emerged. By 1873 the Chicago, Wilmington, and Vermillion Coal Company employed 900 men in the new town of Braidwood—half the miners in the area. Many of these newer, larger mines and coalfields were in fact developed and owned by railroads, guaranteeing adequate supplies—and control over an industry essential to railroads' survival.

Railroads provided more than a demand for specific products such as coal and iron. They also created the rapid, reliable shipping needed for a truly national market. This in turn encouraged manufacturers to produce in larger quantities and to experiment with low-cost mass-production methods. Small producers who had once dominated local markets now faced competition from products made in distant factories and hauled—by the railroads—to every area of the United States. "Of the nearly three millions of people employed in the mechanical industries of this country, at least four-fifths are working under the factory system," the pioneer statistician Carroll D. Wright estimated in 1880. In the production of carriages, wagons, furniture, and other wood products, the factory rapidly replaced the home and the small shop as the center of work.

Large numbers of sewing women continued to labor under the old outwork system, producing clothing in the tenements of New York and Boston. Feathers, paper flowers, and buttons were also made by women outworkers, and many male tailors worked at home. But the vast expansion of the market brought about important changes in outwork. In clothing, for example, it encouraged contractors, who provided women with raw materials and paid them for their finished product, to seek out ways of increasing output. Between 1860 and

A group of immigrants pose beside a Central Pacific train stopped at Mill City, Nevada, en route to California in 1880.

1880 they began to introduce the newly invented sewing machine to meet the higher demand. Now sewing women working in their own homes, who already had to foot the bill for heat and light, had to either buy or rent sewing machines. And contractors lowered the prices paid to women for their piecework, to take advantage of the greater speed at which they worked. The effect of these changes on sewing women's income was disastrous. "I have worked from dawn to sundown, not stopping to get one mouthful of food, for twenty-five cents," reported one woman tailor in 1868.

Yet it was the factory, not the outwork system, that represented the wave of the future. The history of shoemaking in Lynn, Massachusetts, was typical. By 1855 the once-proud craft of shoemaking had already been subdivided into less skilled tasks. This increasingly complex division of labor had been accompanied by the growth of outwork—Lynn, the largest shoe producer in the United States, sent work out to women throughout New England. But as the national market expanded along with transportation and population, the outwork system looked less and less efficient to manufacturers. They had to transport raw materials and finished products back and forth as far as 150 miles; the resulting delays kept Lynn manufacturers from competing as effectively as they might in this new national market.

Their problems were resolved with the invention of the McKay stitcher (an adaptation of the sewing machine) in 1862. The stitcher allowed manufacturers to end outwork, employ more male workers, and centralize production in large factories in Lynn itself. The factory represented a turning point in the history of the shoe industry, because it allowed for the first time the direct supervision of workers by employers and their foremen. Now discipline became tighter and work was performed more steadily. "The men and boys are working as if for life," observed a visitor to a Lynn factory.

Factory cities like Lynn were extremely dynamic in this period. Between 1850 and 1873, for example, Paterson, New Jersey, grew from a market town of 11,000 people to a sprawling city of over 33,000, with many of its residents laboring in the new locomotive, iron, machinery, and textile industries. In the late 1860s industry grew faster in cities like Lynn and Paterson than in large cities like New York and Boston.

But the growth of the large cities was also impressive. By 1880 more than 4 million Americans were living in cities larger than 250,000; forty years earlier, only one city had been that large. No longer was urban growth confined to the eastern seaboard. Chicago, which had 30,000 people in 1850, had become, a mere forty years later, the sixth-largest city in the world, with a population of over a million. Linked by the spreading railroad network, cities like St. Louis, Cleveland, and San Francisco also grew tremendously. The modern American city emerged in the first decade after the Civil War: urban services, including professional fire and police protection, rudimentary sanitation and health facilities, and public transportation (in the form of streetcars) were instituted in these years.

And large cities, with their expanding services and job opportunities, attracted the most immigrants. In 1880 nearly 90 percent of Chicagoans were immigrants or their children; in Milwaukee, Detroit, New York, Cleveland, San Francisco, and St. Louis the proportion was almost as high. The massive influx of Europeans had powered the first spurt of industrial growth around 1850, for they, along with New England farm women, had constituted the first American wage-earning class. The years of economic depression and war from 1857 to 1865 greatly slowed the pace of immigration. But after the Civil War, immigration picked up again—and this time on an even more massive scale: about 5 million people entered the United States between 1815 and 1860, but more than double that figure came between 1860 and 1890.

As before, most immigrants came from northern and western Europe, where agricultural crisis prompted them to leave home. The combined effects of the railroads and cargo steamers brought large areas of the world (particularly Russia, India, and the United States) into competition with the traditional wheat-producing regions of Sweden, England, and eastern Germany. As wheat prices fell, tens of thousands of farm people in these countries emigrated to the New World rather than face continued hardship at home. When the Austro-Hungarian Empire officially granted the right to emigrate in 1867, Bohemians and Moravians (from what is today Czechoslovakia) joined their ranks.

Not all the immigrants of this period were from the countryside. Britain and Germany, in particular, contributed a large number of immigrants from urban and industrial backgrounds. Coal-miners from Durham, Scotland, and Wales and iron puddlers from England's Black Country brought crucial skills to the most dynamic sectors of the American economy. German immigrants became both laborers and artisans in more traditional handicrafts, such as baking, brewing, and upholstering, and made up the majority of craftsmen in St. Louis, Chicago, and a number of other large cities.

Most immigrants ended up working in the least-skilled sectors of the workforce. They hauled goods on the docks and in warehouses, built roads and streetcar lines, and labored at building sites. Most importantly, it was overwhelmingly immigrants who built America's railroad network—especially the Irish, in the East, and the Chinese, who worked on the Central Pacific's line from California through the Sierras to Utah.

Chinese immigration to the

"PESTILENCE IN THE CIGAR"

This 1874 article from the New York Sun describes the sort of conditions faced by immigrants in New York City. Employers had established tenement "factories" to undermine the control of skilled workers—in this case unionized cigar rollers and finishers—by eliminating centralized craft workshops, thus forcing workers to labor at home. By 1874, seven thousand Bohemian men, women, and children worked and lived in tenement factories, bunching, stripping, and casing cigars.

THE BOHEMIAN QUARTER of New York is on the east side.... The [forty] cigarmakers' tenement [factories] are mostly within those limits.... These houses are usually twenty-five feet by fifty, and so the lighted rooms are as a rule ten by ten feet in area. The dark room ... is barely six feet square at the utmost.... In these houses, when full, as they usually are, will be found at least 100 workers.

Entering the narrow hall, ... the olfactories are at once startled by a pungent odor, so strong in some instances as to make a sensitive person sneeze "on sight," or rather "on smell." This is, of course, from the tobacco.... It was said that in cold weather the odor was so overpowering and pungent, doors and windows being closed, that persons unaccustomed thereto were compelled to shut their eyes in pain. Yet about four thousand people eat, cook, and sleep, as well as work, in these places. Young children fall asleep from the narcotic effects of the pervading odor. Women suffer greatly from it, especially in diseases peculiar to the sex. It is also a prolific source of eye diseases.

A number of principal cigar manufacturers have taken to hiring these tenements and subletting them to their employees, who are therefore compelled to live in the same place and atmosphere as that in which they work.

The occupation of tenements for this purpose began about three years ago, but until this year there were not over half a dozen so occupied. The system is growing rapidly. With employers merely governed by avarice, this is no wonder, when the profits are considered.

On Stampede Pass, after the blizzard. Chinese workers constructing a tunnel on the Northern Pacific Railway clear a switchback (a zig-zag, uphill road) in the Cascade Mountains of Washington in the 1880s.

Pacific Coast began in the 1850s, when famine in China triggered an exodus to gold-rush California; by 1860 nearly one Californian in ten was Chinese. When the Central Pacific began to build its end of the transcontinental line in the 1860s, however, it recruited laborers directly from China. Its agents paid an individual's outfitting and passage in return for a $75 promissory note, the debt to be repaid within seven months of beginning work on the railroad. Eventually, over ten thousand Chinese laborers found their way to the grading camps and construction crews of the Central Pacific.

Here they found the most brutal conditions of work known in America. In the winter of 1866, heavy snows covered the Chinese encampments in the Sierra Nevada mountains. The laborers had to dig chimneys and air shafts through the snow and live by lantern light. Yet, under orders from Charles Crocker, who directed labor for the Central Pacific, construction continued. On Christmas Day, 1866, a local newspaper reported that "a gang of Chinamen employed by the railroad were covered up by a snow slide and four or five died before they could be exhumed." Even when not facing such dangers, the Chinese labored for ten grueling hours a day at roughly two-thirds the wages paid to whites. The experience of the Chinese in America was harsher than that of any other immigrant group—partly because they were "contract laborers," recruited on a basis much like the indentured servitude of the colonial period.

A labor law, passed by Congress in 1864 as part of the Republican Party's program of economic development, permitted employers to recruit contract laborers abroad, though they rarely did it in these years. Nonetheless, the contract-labor law was now opposed by many working people, who felt that it symbolized the undermining of the free-labor society that had abolished slavery by force of arms. And contract labor was not the only challenge to the values of a free-labor society. The dramatic increase in wage labor and the enormous expansion of wealth—direct results of the spectacular growth of industry following the Civil War—also raised fundamental questions about the survival of traditional American ideals and values.

Business leaders and their intellectual supporters tried to create a rationale for these vast new changes in American economic and social life. They did it by combining two concepts: "laissez-faire" in economics and "Social Darwinism" in social and political relations. The theory of laissez-faire (roughly, "leave it alone" in French), rested on a belief that economic growth could result only from the free and unregulated development of the market, governed entirely by laws of supply and demand. The theory maintained that any attempt by government or unions to interfere with industry would have a disastrous effect on prosperity. Social Darwinism, the application of British scientist Charles Darwin's ideas about animal evolution to social relations, argued for a similar hands-off approach to problems. Sociologists and economists like Herbert Spencer and William Graham Sumner took Darwin's concept of "the survival of the fittest" and used it to explain the economic success of the few capitalists ("the strong") and the increasing impoverishment of many workers ("the weak") in the new industrial age. They argued that this process resulted in society's continuing improvement; to deny this basic "law" was to violate nature. Sumner, for example, used Darwinian concepts to justify the existence of the wealthy:

> Millionaires are a product of natural selection. . . . It is because they are thus selected that wealth—both their own and that entrusted to them—aggregates under their hands. . . . They may fairly be regarded as the naturally se-

lected agents of society for certain work. They get high wages and live in luxury, but the bargain is a good one for society.

Not all Americans could agree with such formulations, however. Even the generally conservative New York *Times* expressed concern in 1869 when it noted that little workshops were "far less common than they were before the war," and that "the small manufacturers thus swallowed up have become workmen [for] wages in the greater establishments." This descent of the once proud and independent mechanic to the level of a dependent wage-earner had profound implications. According to the *Times*, it was producing "a system of slavery as absolute if not as degrading as that which lately prevailed [in] the South." In the South, of course, wealthy white planters had been the masters and African-Americans had been the slaves. But now in the North, the *Times* noted, "manufacturing capitalists threaten to become the masters, and it is the white laborers who are to be slaves." More than any other single fact, this development lay behind the rapid growth of the American labor movement in the years after the Civil War.

WORKERS' STRUGGLES

The years from 1866 to 1873 marked a new stage in the development of the American labor movement. Although the actual number of workers in labor organizations would rise to higher levels later, a greater proportion of industrial workers joined trade unions during these years than in any other period in the nineteenth century. By 1872 there were thirty national trade unions in the United States and hundreds of local ones. Together these organizations embraced over 300,000 workers.

Trade unions emerged out of a series of intense struggles with employers over wages, hours, and working conditions. The struggle to limit the length of the workday to eight hours was especially important and triggered union organization in a number of trades. Workers' ideological traditions also helped to spark the labor upsurge, as they had the movement that had existed before the Civil War. Native-born workers, white and black, drew on the egalitarian ideals and the republican traditions of the American Revolution in building their individual unions and the labor movement as a whole. And German, Irish, and British immigrants carried with them new, often radical, political ideas about collective action and distinctive forms of struggle and organization, including socialism and anarchism. The melding of these two traditions shaped the politics and ideology of the postwar American labor movement.

"Serenading a 'Blackleg' on his Return from Work." Jonathon Lowe of *Frank Leslie's Illustrated Newspaper* sketched coalminers and their families harassing a scab during a strike in the Cherry Valley region of Ohio in 1874.

The National Molders' Union had been founded in 1859 and had grown in strength during the war, becoming one of the most important of the new unions. The power of the molders lay in their possession of valuable skills in an industry that was expanding rapidly. But they were also deeply committed to the egalitarian legacy of the American Revolution. "We assume to belong to the order of men who know their rights, and knowing, dare maintain them," proclaimed a molder in Troy, New York. This defiant egalitarianism underlined the efforts of iron-molders as they built one of the strongest unions America had ever seen. Their president, William H. Sylvis, was a tireless worker for the union cause and one of the most able men in the labor movement. As we will see, he would later help found and lead the first national organization of American workers.

Molders in the rapidly growing city of Chicago stood in the forefront of the organization; at the giant McCormick reaper works they had organized a local during the inflation-ridden Civil War. Through a series of successful strikes between 1862 and 1864, the McCormick molders managed to maintain their real wages and obtain wage increases for the unskilled workers in the plant as well. The molders' local continued to gain ground after the war ended, and by 1867 stood at the head of local efforts to shorten the working day to eight hours.

Manufacturers across the nation were unified in their opposition to the eight-hour day. "As long as the present order of things exists, there will be poor men and women who will be obliged to work," noted one employer who wanted to maintain a ten-hour workday, "and the majority of them will not do any more than necessity compels them to do." Concerned with its effect on their profits, manufacturers vowed to fight the eight-hour day with a vengeance.

Illinois presented a major test of the employers' resolve. The Republican-controlled Illinois legislature had passed a law declaring eight hours to be "the legal workday in the State," and the governor had signed it in March 1867. Employers were required to conform to the new legislation beginning May 1. Chicago workers, elated with the seeming victory, took to the streets on the day the law went into effect, in a spectacular parade that featured six thousand marchers, floats, and exuberant brass bands.

The workers' celebration, however, was to prove short-lived. Chicago employers simply refused to obey the new law. The employers' resistance had been encouraged by the failure of state legislators to incorporate a penalty for noncompliance into the new law. Chicago workers once again took to the streets, but this time in a massive city-wide work stoppage, demanding that the new law be enforced. The iron-molders led the way, followed by German and native-born machinists; Irish workers

"EIGHT HOURS AND NO SURRENDER!"

The following description of Chicago's May 1, 1867, parade, taken from the next day's Boston Daily Evening Voice, *conveys not only a sense of the workers' elation at winning passage of a state law mandating the eight-hour workday, but also a feeling of how momentous the victory seemed. The parade is reminiscent of similar parades of workers in support of the U.S. Constitution eighty years earlier.*

MAGNIFICENT DEMONSTRATION BY CHICAGO'S WORKERS!
MOTTOES AND SLOGANS ON THE BANNERS.
THE MASS MEETINGS.

The Eight-Hour Bill became law yesterday, and to celebrate, the workers of the city turned out by thousand with bands, banners, and the badges of their trades. The demonstration was grandiose and impressive.

The procession . . . , extending for more than a mile, made a deep impression on the thousands of onlookers who had gathered in the streets. . . . They covered the stairs, the windows, and even the roofs of the houses where the procession passed by. An almost countless number of banners, flags, slogans, etc. were carried by the marchers. Following are some of the mottos:

"In God We Trust."
"Eight Hours and No Surrender!"
"To the Advantage of the Next Generation."
"Illinois on the Side of Reform."
"The Workers' Millennium. . . ."

The day laborers were represented by a four-horse wagon, on which rode several day laborers with their various tools.

The Molders' Union participated with an eight-horse wagon on which were displayed all the materials, tools, and machinery needed for molding. . . .

Next was a delivery wagon with a coffin bearing the inscription "Death and Burial to the Ten-Hour System. . . ."

Then another delivery wagon appeared, again with a coffin on which were inscribed the words "Death and Burial of the Chicago *Times*"; above the coffin hanging from a gallows was a dummy with a veiled head. . . .

shut down nearly all of the packinghouses and rolling mills in Chicago's Bridgeport neighborhood. On May 6, a crowd of strikers estimated at 5,000, many of them armed, marched through the city's industrial areas, closing factories and battling police.

But the strike never became general and was badly weakened by hostility from the same politicians who had passed the law. Calling for liberation of Chicago from "the riot element," Illinois Republicans united behind the mayor when he called out the Dearborn Light Artillery to suppress the strikers on May 7. Republican hostility to the demands of Chicago workers occurred at the same moment when the national party had taken the bold step of passing the Reconstruction Act, guaranteeing the right to vote for recently freed slaves by creating military governments across the South. The guarantee of rights in the Republicans' free-labor ideology apparently did not extend to support of the eight-hour day. Chicago workers bitterly denounced Republican politicians for deserting their cause, but little could be done. By the middle of June most workers, including the molders, had gone back to work on a ten-hour basis.

Even this defeat, though, did not set back the city's iron-molders too far. The union began to grow again after 1869. Although molders lost a strike at one large Chicago foundry in 1872, almost all of the McCormick molders were enrolled in the union by the next year.

Coalminers also built powerful unions in this period, particularly in the hard-coal region of eastern Pennsylvania. Conditions in the region were very harsh, "little better than semi-slavery" according to one mining clerk. Miners were paid only for the coal they extracted; they worked long hours under extremely hazardous conditions. Mining accidents took the lives of over six hundred workers in a seven-year period in the region. On top of this, miners were frequently cheated out of their rightful earnings—both when

"MONEY MONOPOLIES"

In a speech given to the September 1868 Labor Reform Party Convention, one of several alternative labor parties that sprang up in this period, Iron Molders' president William Sylvis railed against the power of "Money monopolies" and implored workers to use their vote to regain their rights and restore the virtue of the American republic.

MEN TALK TO me of our independence and boast of our constitutional government, and all that it guarantees to us; but with these spread-eagle gentlemen I do not agree. These things will do very well for Fourth-of-July orations, but not for everyday life. Workingmen do not live in imagination, but upon cold, practical facts; and the facts are, that the workingmen of this nation are oppressed more than the same class in any other country. It is true, we have no king—no political king—but here we have monopolies, banking monopolies, railroad monopolies, land monopolies, and bond monopolies, that supply the place of kings, dukes, lords, etc., and their rule is getting to be more intolerable than is found anywhere else. If we have no political king, we have money kings, and they are the worst kings in the world. We, by our labor, have been putting into motion millions of little streams of wealth, and a false financial and money system has been directing them into the pockets of a few individuals, while we remain poor and powerless. No, not powerless, for we have yet one way of escape. The ballot-box is still open. We in this State have yet no law allowing the Legislature to do our voting for us. If we will use the ballot effectively, we will soon be freed from the golden rule that now crushes the vitality out of the industry of the whole nation. This we are now trying to do. This is the object of the Labor Reform Party; and we are ready to make common cause with any other party or people who will adopt our principles and get on our platform.

company "weighmen" short-weighted the coal they had dug and when they had to pay exorbitant prices at company-owned stores.

By the end of the 1860s, miners had organized an effective trade union, the Workingmen's Benevolent Association (WBA), under the leadership of John Siney. Born in Ireland, Siney had been raised in the textile region of Lancashire, England, where he had imbibed the spirit of trade-unionism. In 1867, he led a successful strike of four hundred miners against a wage cut, and in the following year he organized the WBA. By 1869 the organization had a membership of over thirty thousand.

Part of the WBA's strength lay in the highly competitive structure of the mining industry, which prevented employers from uniting against their men. But more important was the WBA's policy of unionizing workers throughout an entire industry. Rather than organizing each category of worker in separate "craft" unions, the WBA merged skilled miners and unskilled surface workers into the same union; it also brought together Irish Catholics, the native-born, and British Protestants in one organization. The WBA thus presented employers with a united front they could not afford to ignore.

The achievements of the WBA reflected Siney's experience with the British trade-union movement. In 1870, after a bitter six-month strike, the WBA forced Pennsylvania mining operators to accept the principle of a "sliding scale." This principle, by which wages would rise or fall according to the market price of coal, had long been an established practice of British coal unions. The WBA also successfully lobbied the Pennsylvania legislature for a mining-inspection law similar to the one in England. The law helped win better and safer working conditions for Pennsylvania miners.

Soft-coal miners in northern Illinois, many of them Scottish immigrants who carried with them a strong trade-union tradition, also organized in this period. In 1873, the Miners' National Association was formed, with Siney as its president, to organize all American mineworkers in one great industrial union.

Although their unions were new, miners and iron-molders could build upon traditions of organization and struggle with deep roots in the early nineteenth century. This was also true for the shoemakers, who built the powerful Knights of St. Crispin (named after the patron saint of shoemakers) after the Civil War. The focus of their protest was the new factory system. The onetime artisans who entered the large new factories, like those in Lynn, Massachusetts, had been accustomed to making their own day-to-day decisions about production and setting their own work pace. Now they found themselves working under a new order wholly under the control of the manufacturer, subjected to a work pace determined by machines. In combatting this new regime, shoemakers could build on a long tradition of artisanal

"The Eight-Hour Movement." Workers demonstrate for the eight-hour day along New York's Bowery in June, 1872. The production of cigars (much in evidence in this engraving) was one of the city's major industries, undergoing rapid change in the 1870s as production moved from craftwork in small shops to manufacture in factories and tenement houses.

struggle and belief in "equal rights" that had culminated, as we have seen, in the great shoemakers' strike of 1860.

The shoe-factory workers organized the Knights of St. Crispin in 1867. Through a series of successful strikes, the organization grew rapidly and by 1870 had a membership of nearly fifty thousand—making it the largest labor union in the nation. Women shoe workers also organized in this period, forming the Daughters of St. Crispin to fight what they called "the unjust encroachments upon our rights." And defying the wave of anti-Asian feeling sweeping the nation, the Crispins organized a local of Chinese workers who had been brought to North Adams, Massachusetts, to break a shoemakers' strike in 1870. One of the first organizations of factory workers, the Crispins practiced solidarity as well as preaching it.

Organization of particular racial and new-immigrant groups into separate unions was common in the postwar period. Concentration in particular industries or workplaces as well as language and cultural differences proved difficult obstacles for unions to overcome, assuming they were willing to make the effort in the first place. But, as we will see, while the chance to be in labor organizations with their fellow countrymen initially attracted some foreign-born workers to unions, it was not at all clear whether or how the postwar labor leaders would build bridges from these ethnic organizations to the larger labor movement.

The organization of German immigrants—who established separate craft unions, trades councils, and political organizations in this period—followed this pattern. As the major port city, New York was a particularly important center of German-American activity. Under the leadership of Adolph Douai and Friedrich Sorge, German tailors, cigarmakers, and twenty-one other unions founded the New York Arbeiter-Union, a German trades council, in 1868. But many German workers believed that organizing trade unions was simply the first step in a much broader social transformation. They ultimately sought the abolition of private ownership of production and its replacement by a socialist system in which workers themselves would hold political power and run the nation's industries in a democratic fashion. These beliefs led Douai and Sorge to establish a section of the International Workingmen's Association (IWA) in New York in 1868.

Founded by the German revolutionary Karl Marx in London in 1864, the IWA held that "the final object" of the labor movement was "the abolition of all class rule."

By 1872, there were twenty sections of the IWA in New York City. German-American socialists played a leading role in the great eight-hour-day strikes of that year. Nearly a hundred thousand workers went out in the spring of 1872, seeking the enforcement of an eight-hour-day law passed in 1867. As in Illinois five years earlier, New York employers resisted the strikes, pointing to the role of the German-American workers as a sign that the strikes were motivated by "a spirit of communism ... entirely foreign to the disposition of our industrial population." American employers, like their European counter-

". . . THIS DEMON OF PRIVATE RICHES"

In his January 6, 1877, editorial in the Labor Standard, *a New York City newspaper, Joseph McDonnell, an Irish immigrant and IWA member, likened the capitalist system to a savage killer who slowly destroys his victims.*

THERE IS NO lion, no tiger, no anaconda so cruel as capital is. . . . [Animals] kill because they act in self-defense from starvation. . . . They kill and that is the end of it. But the capitalistic system kills by inches; it takes hold of the poor child and works him slowly to death within one or two dozen years; it takes hold of poor defenseless women and leaves them no choice but either to go speedily down by prostitution and self-contempt, or by excruciating work for a starving family; it takes hold of the proud, but poor [Negro] freeman, and gradually, almost insensibly reduces him to voluntary slavery, or to the worship of Mammon—the sole God of nowadays. It kills mind, morals, and body, it kills intelligence, reason, virtue, and health. . . . It destroys freedom and humanity wherever it sets its foot. And the worst feature about it is that the poor victims rarely perceive what is the cause of all this; or when they are aware of it, are already too far gone to help themselves. No republic, no constitutional liberty in all the world's history was proof [against] this demon of private riches; and our own proud democratic republic is already by it reduced to the mere semblance of its former self. The cathedral, the pulpit, the stage, the press, and the school are its salaried servants . . . and the state and respectable society applaud it.

parts in the same period, had been terrified by the collective spirit and militant action demonstrated in 1871 during the Paris Commune (thus "communists"), when workers took over and ran the city in the midst of war between France and Germany. "Anticommunism" on the part of American business and governmental leaders would grow dramatically throughout the 1870s. Yet, despite such opposition, the eight-hour strikes were partially successful, and organized socialism continued to grow in these years.

Many native-born workers shared the German immigrants' distrust of industrial capitalism and the wage system, if not their more militant ideology. Some turned to cooperation as an alternative to capitalist competition. To circumvent the monopoly power of the railroads, cooperative distribution and purchase of agricultural products had been developed in the late 1860s by small farmers organized into local chapters of the Grange, or Patrons of Husbandry. Worker-run cooperative stores, mimicking the Granger co-ops, appeared all over the nation in the early 1870s, particularly in textile and mining towns. Cooperatively owned factories also sprang up between 1868 and 1873, mostly iron foundries and shoe companies. Members of the middle class hailed cooperation as an alternative to strikes and as a way of turning workers into procapitalist businessmen. But, though they usually failed from lack of funds and business experience, working-class cooperatives reflected a deep dissatisfaction with the unfettered individualism celebrated by industrial capitalism. Cooperation, argued one advocate, would make workers "independent of the capitalist employer," end "ceaseless degradation," and establish a new civilization in which "reason directed by moral principle" would prevail and universal brotherhood would flourish.

THE NATIONAL LABOR UNION

The resurgence of working-class militancy after the war was capped by the formation of a new federation of labor organizations, covering workers in diverse crafts and industrial occupations, the National Labor Union (NLU). Founded in Baltimore in 1866 and led by iron-molder William Sylvis until his early death in 1869, the NLU focused national attention on the demands of American workers. Larger and broader than its forerunner of the 1830s, the National Trades Union, the NLU marked a new stage in working-class organization, the emergence of a nationwide institution that linked wage workers together in a broad community of interest. The NLU's vision of this community was limited in crucial respects: reflecting the racism of most white workers, it condemned the Chinese, and it only gave lip service to the rights of African-American and women workers. Nevertheless, the organization represented the strongest statement to date of American workers' egalitarian and collective traditions.

The NLU focused attention on the central demand of workers in the period after the Civil War: the "all-absorbing subject of Eight Hours." The NLU's attempt to obtain a national eight-hour-day law for all American workers, however, ran up against intense opposition, not only from employers, but from leading ideologues of the Republican Party as well. Liberal Republicans like E. L. Godkin, who had used the free-labor ideology to oppose slavery and support Reconstruction in the South, might have called for shortening the hours in the workday. But their deep commitment to laissez-faire and the rights of private property prevented them from doing so. Godkin and other Republican intellectuals attacked the eight-hour day as if it challenged the very basis of civilization itself.

Ira Steward, a self-educated Boston machinist and a leader in the eight-hour movement, met this opposition head on. Steward maintained that the whole system of wage labor—and not reforms such as the eight-hour day—undermined freedom and civilization. He believed that the employer's profit was based on the exploitation of the worker and, as a veteran of the antislavery movement in Massachusetts, drew a comparison between northern industrial capitalism and southern slavery to make his point. Just as the motive for "making a man a slave was to get his labor, or its results, for nothing," Steward argued, so "the motive for employing wage-labor is to secure some of its results for nothing; and, in point of fact, larger fortunes are made out of the profits of wage-labor, than out of the products of slavery."

The eight-hour day, according to Steward, would totally transform this system. As hours were shortened and wages rose, profits would decline. In the end, this would lead to the gradual elimination of the capitalist "as we understand him." As the anachronistic wage system passed from the scene, replaced by one based on cooperation, the full dreams of an independent citizenry would be realized. The result would be "a republicanization of labor, as well as a republicanization of government." With this statement, Steward had taken a long step toward adapting the antislavery and republican traditions of thought to the new industrial age.

Steward's reliance on this republican tradition gave his analysis tremendous popularity among working people who had only recently helped win a war against the southern planters. Workers quickly took up Steward's argument, stressing the comparison between southern slavery and northern "wage slavery." Only an eight-hour day would allow the worker to feel "full of life and enjoyment," asserted a Massachusetts bootmaker, because "the man is no longer a slave, but a man." "Eight hours a day, a legal day's work for Freemen," proclaimed the masthead of Philadelphia's *Fincher's Trades Review,* the most important labor newspaper of the 1860s. Workers even referred to eight hours as a "jubilee," the word used by southern blacks to describe their newly won freedom; in the same vein, workers also adapted the Civil War song "John Brown's Body" to serve the eight-hour movement. When a Philadelphia labor newspaper defended the eight-hour day by declaring that "property is a tyrant and the people are its slaves," it carried the argument to its logical extreme.

Drawing this parallel, however, did not necessarily put northern white workers squarely on the side of black workers. While most of the political and economic struggles of Reconstruction centered around agricultural labor in the South, African-American workers in the region's cities and towns were also embarking on new paths of struggle in the late 1860s and early 1870s. The introduction of Radical Reconstruction in 1867 helped trigger the militant upsurge. Dockworkers in port towns led the way: in New Orleans, Charleston, Mobile, and Savannah, black longshoremen engaged in militant and often successful strikes for higher wages and elimination of discriminatory laws and employment policies. Black longshoremen in Pensacola, Florida, organized a Workingmen's Association by 1868 and through a series of strikes in the early 1870s managed to maintain their jobs against competition from emigrating Canadian dockworkers. The wave of labor militancy was not limited to the docks: African-American sawmill workers in Jacksonville, Florida, for example, organized a Labor League in the early 1870s to fight for a minimum wage of $1.50 a day. And black wage laborers in small towns and cities in Alabama linked up with others on plantations to organize the Alabama Labor Union in 1870. Though blacks were also sometimes hired as strikebreakers, African-American workers were often militant in their struggle for unions.

Some leaders of the NLU, particularly the iron-molder William Sylvis and the ship-carpenter Richard Trevellick, argued for the need for white workers to support these struggles. At its first congress in 1866, the NLU had called on its constitutent unions

> to help inculcate the grand, ennobling idea that the interests of labor are one; that there should be no distinction of race or nationality; no classification of Jew or Gentile, Christian or Infidel; that there is but one dividing line— that which separates mankind into two great classes, the class that labors and the class that lives by others' labors.

To put the point more concretely, NLU leaders noted that "if these general principles be correct, we must seek the cooperation of the African race in America."

Many of the trade unions affiliated with the NLU, however, had policies that excluded blacks from membership, and in 1867 the organization came to a grinding halt on the question of pushing these unions to organize African-American workers. Sylvis took a pragmatic line, arguing that "if the workingmen of the white race do not conciliate the blacks, the black vote will be cast against them." But a committee assigned to study the question reported that "we find the subject involved in so much mystery, we believe that it is inexpedient to take action on the subject in this National Labor Congress." Unwilling to interfere with the exclusionist practices of the craft unions, the NLU began backing off from the entire issue, leaving black workers to fend for themselves.

In the face of this white working-class hostility or indifference, African-American workers set about creating their own labor institutions. Calling the exclusion of blacks from trade unions "an insult to God and injury to us, and disgrace to humanity," a national convention of African-Americans meeting in Washington in 1869 created the Colored National Labor Union (CNLU). Led by the onetime Baltimore caulker Isaac Meyers, the new organization attracted the backing of prominent figures in the black community such as Frederick Douglass.

In some ways the CNLU was more conservative on questions of class than its white counterpart. "There is not a natural antagonism between capital and labor," declared Myers in his address to the organization's 1871 convention. "Their relationship and interest are mutual." Such beliefs were the result, at least in part, of actual experience. In 1865, Myers and other black craftsmen had been driven from the Baltimore shipyards by a strike of white workers opposed to the employment of African-Americans. White merchants in Baltimore helped the black workers establish a cooperative shipyard of their own, thus providing the basis for Myers's personal belief in the "mutuality" of labor and capital. In his convention address, Myers denounced strikes as the work of "brainless leaders" and called on black laborers to be honest, industrious, and frugal enough to become capitalists themselves. Yet Myers also realized that even industrious workers were often exploited by employers and must be guaranteed the right to organize labor unions. The Colored National Labor Union remained firmly committed to support for the Republican Party, and cooperation between the CNLU and the NLU—which wanted to form a separate political party of labor—broke down partly over this issue. Yet, in the long run, the discrimination practiced by the white unions had a far greater effect than political differences in hindering working-class solidarity across racial lines.

White workers were even less sympathetic toward Chinese workers. Almost every important labor leader opposed Chinese immigra-

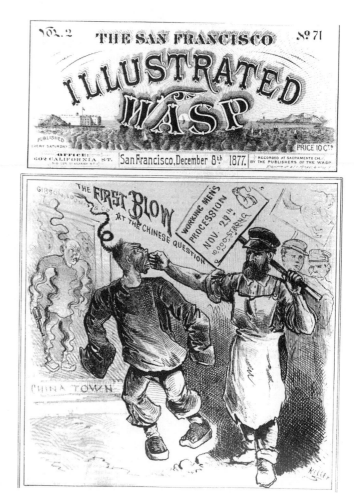

Working-class racism is expressed
in no uncertain terms on the cover
of the *San Francisco Illustrated
Wasp*, 1877.

tion; the labor movement was one of the strongest forces lobbying for
a law to exclude Chinese. The primary argument was that "docile"
Chinese labor would be used by employers to lower the standard of
living of U.S. workers and take their jobs away.

The docility of the Chinese was largely mythical. In the spring of
1867, for example, Chinese railroad workers in the Sierras had gone
on strike. Demanding higher wages and an eight-hour day, between
three thousand and five thousand laborers put down their tools. The
Central Pacific Railroad offered to raise their wages from $31 to $35 a
month, but the strikers held firm, insisting on $45 a month and a
two-hour reduction in the working day. The Central Pacific management condemned the strike as a "conspiracy" and considered the possibility of transporting ten thousand southern blacks to replace the

Chinese. But Charles Crocker, who managed labor for the Central Pacific, developed a more powerful strategy to combat the strike: he cut off the workers' food supply, starving them into submission. "I stopped the provisions on them, stopped the butchers from butchering, and used [other] such coercive measures," Crocker bragged. The strike was broken within a week.

Despite such examples, white workers continued to argue for the exclusion of the Chinese on the grounds that they competed with whites for jobs. In fact such competition was largely illusory, since Chinese immigrants gravitated to the lowest-paying jobs at the bottom of the employment ladder, especially laundry work and unskilled labor, previously abandoned by whites. This fact mattered little, however, for underlying white workers' hostility to the Chinese was a deep belief in white racial supremacy. Labor newspaper editor John Swinton, an otherwise progressive and humane working-class leader, probably spoke for many workers when he argued that "the Mongolian blood is depraved and debased blood. The Mongolian type of humanity is an inferior type—inferior in organic structure, in vital force or physical energy, and in the constitutional conditions of development." Such racial-classification schemes were pervasive in the postwar period, when even educated middle-class Americans used pseudo-scientific theories (Social Darwinism being only the most obvious example) to justify their belief in the inevitability of their social and political dominance. But there were other grounds for bias; other labor leaders insisted that they opposed the Chinese because the corporations hired them as indentured, not free, labor. Richard Trevellick, for example, tried to avoid accusations of racism by saying he opposed "the importation but not the free immigration of the Chinese," and Sylvis's silence on the question indicates that he was not happy with the anti-Chinese sentiment that was extremely widespread among the white workers and their leaders.

So was opposition to working women's struggle for equality. Wage-earning women—nearly one-quarter of the total nonfarm labor force in 1870—turned to a variety of tactics to defend and improve their conditions and wages in this period. In 1869, for example, sewing women in Boston petitioned the Massachusetts legislature to provide them

". . . AS MUCH RIGHT HERE AS YOU OR I"

Although most laborers and leaders resorted to racist arguments to justify the exclusion of the Chinese, a few, mostly in the radical and socialist wing of the movement, were more sympathetic. Here is a letter from B. E. Jewett in the May 1878 Detroit Socialist:

THE CHINAMAN COMING here of his own accord, and at his own expense of accumulated earnings, has as much right here as you or I or any German, Russ, Switzer, Frank, Turk, Pole, Irish, or Ethiopian in the land; and true Socialism demands that as air, land, and water are eternally free to the whole race who wish to live, they shall NOT be debarred their privilege. For if they are ignorant, vile, or needy, it is our duty as first occupants in this land to instruct in intellectual and moral duties and give them the means of performing them as, if we were in their land, it would be their duty to do unto us.

with public housing. Although the legislature ignored the request, the petition broke new ground in demanding state intervention to remedy oppressive working conditions.

Working women in many occupations turned to trade-unionism to improve their working conditions and wages. Female cigarmakers, umbrella-sewers, and textile and laundry workers all formed short-lived local unions in these years. But they received little support from white male workers. There were thirty national unions in the early 1870s, but only two—the cigarmakers and the printers—admitted women into their ranks. Most organized working men believed that the presence of women in the paid labor force was either a temporary phenomenon or part of a strategy of employers to lower wages. Clinging to the myth that "all men support all women," they kept women out of their unions in an effort to keep them out of their trades.

This opposition came to a head in 1869, when the NLU expelled the feminist leader Susan B. Anthony. The conflict was complex, and stemmed in part from Anthony's efforts to train female workers to take the jobs of striking New York printers.

But many male workers opposed Anthony because her vision of total female equality—including women's right to vote—threatened traditional male domination. She and other leaders of the women's movement, including Elizabeth Cady Stanton and Lydia Maria Child, argued that women had a right to all that men sought—"a chance to earn an honest living . . . sufficient to enable them to invest in building societies, and have houses and homes of their own, and make them just as independent as anybody in the country." This was simply too much for many of the members of the NLU. "The lady goes in for taking women away from the washtub, and in the name of heaven who is going there if they don't?" asked one printer in arguing for Anthony's expulsion.

"HOW MUCH BETTER TO HAVE THESE GIRLS INDEPENDENT . . ."

In a speech delivered on April 29, 1869, at a convention of Boston working women, a Miss Phelps described the plight of wage-earning women employed in unskilled and low-paying jobs.

THERE ARE BEFORE me now women whom I know to be working at the present time for less than twenty-five cents a day. Some of the work they do at these rates from the charitable institutions of the city. These institutions give out work to the women with the professed object of helping them, at which they can scarcely earn enough to keep them from starving; work at which two persons, with their utmost exertions, cannot earn more than forty-five cents a day. These things, I repeat, should be known to the public. They do not know how the daughters of their soldiers fare. I do. They have a little aid, to be sure, from the state, but it is only a little, and they have today to live in miserable garrets without fire; and during the cold winters with scanty food and insufficient clothing, they go out daily to labor along these beautiful streets. Do not you think that they feel the difference between their condition and that of rich, well-dressed ladies who pass them? If they did not, they would be less than human. But they work on bravely and uncomplainingly, venturing all things for the hope of the life that is to come. . . . Last winter many of them did not get work enough at even ten cents a garment to live upon, and were obliged to ask charity. They get it doled out to them, but at what a loss of self-respect, of independence! How much better to have these girls independent, earning their own living, enjoying their own homes, than that they should be compelled to go to station houses for soup! That is what many of them had to do last winter. The people have wondered how these girls live. Can you imagine how you should live upon twenty cents a day? Rent is one or two dollars at the lowest, and there is your clothes and your food. Count it up. Where does it come from?

"The Fifteenth Amendment Illustrated." A cartoon in the 1870 edition of *Die Vehme* (*The Star Chamber*), a short-lived St. Louis satirical weekly, supports woman's suffrage at the expense of African-Americans, Chinese, and illiterate immigrants.

"I believe in woman doing her work and men marrying them, and supporting them."

The experience of the young labor movement after the Civil War, then, was decidedly mixed. On the one hand, the many struggles waged across the land encouraged a sense of class awareness. The struggle for eight-hour-day laws focused this awareness of class and marked the labor movement's decisive break with the outlook of the Republican Party, while still deepening the broader antislavery tradition. On the other hand, class awareness and the demand for "equal rights" were sharply limited by the labor movement's discriminatory policies and actions against women and black workers and by its deep hostility to Chinese laborers. The post–Civil War labor movement's broad and encompassing vision of egalitarianism and commitment to mutuality and collective action was ultimately undermined by such racism and sexism. As a result, the labor movement remained limited, and in the end it proved unable to respond effectively to the challenge of the economic depression that began in 1873.

DEPRESSION AND CONFLICT

The depression of 1873 brought the economic boom to an abrupt halt. The depression was triggered on September 18 by the collapse of Jay Cooke and Company, one of the country's great investment houses. In a matter of days panic led to runs on a number of banks across the

"Panic, as a Health Officer, Sweeping the Garbage out of Wall Street." Despite the ghastly appearance of the figure portraying financial panic, this New York *Daily Graphic* cover cartoon of September 29, 1873, subscribes to the belief that such financial "busts" cleanse the economy.

country, and the New York Stock Exchange shut down for over a week—the first time it had ever closed. The financial failures were followed by five years of serious deflation and the longest and severest industrial depression of the century.

Construction of railroads and buildings ground to a halt in 1873–74, and tens of thousands of businesses, large and small, went bankrupt. By 1876, half the nation's railroads had defaulted on their bonds and half the iron furnaces were silent. Prices of capital and consumer goods spiraled downward as surviving businesses engaged in cutthroat competition to keep customers.

The nation had experienced economic downturns and even depressions before: 1837 and 1857 were the most severe. But the depression that began in 1873 was different in both kind and degree. To begin with, it lasted fully sixty-five months, making it the longest period of uninterrupted economic contraction in American history.

Even more disturbing was the depression's human cost. The nation's wholehearted embrace of capitalist development after the Civil War had made many more Americans wholly dependent on industrialization for their basic survival. By 1874 fully a million workers were without work. In some cities, unemployment approached 25 percent of the workforce; New York counted some 100,000 unemployed workers in the winter of 1873–74. "The sufferings of the working classes are daily increasing," wrote one Philadelphia worker the following summer. "Famine has broken into the home of many of us, and is at the door of all." A New York labor paper reported that "thousands of homeless men and women are to be seen nightly sleeping on the seats in our public parks, or walking the streets," and predicted that "the suffering next winter will be tremendous."

Workers who lived in small towns could—and did—tend little garden plots or hunt as a way to survive the hard times. Workers in large cities were forced to go "on the tramp" to try to find work. The American countryside was suddenly flooded with men wandering from town to town in search of jobs—often using the very network of railroads that earlier had linked the nation in a single prosperous market. It was at this moment that the popular image of the rail-riding "tramp" was born.

In this context, the struggle

for public relief and jobs became far more pressing than that for the eight-hour day. Mass meetings of workers in cities across the nation demanded jobs. New York labor leaders in the winter of 1873 demanded to know what would be done "to relieve the necessities of the 10,000 homeless and hungry men and women of our city whose urgent appeals have apparently been disregarded by our public servants." Rejecting what they called "the grudgingly given and debased bread of charity," they called on officials to create jobs financed by the sale of government bonds. Their request was denied, and subsequent meetings of the unemployed in New York were brutally suppressed by the police.

Socialists took a leading role in the movements of the unemployed that sprang up in Chicago, St. Louis, and several other large cities. As a result, socialism moved out of its relative isolation in German neighborhoods and began to build a larger following among native-born workers. When rival political factions in the movement put aside their differences and formed the Workingmen's Party of the United States in 1876, the socialist movement took a major step toward organizing all, not just immigrant, workers.

But the demand for jobs rarely brought results. Business leaders and editors were not even inclined to provide the "debased bread of charity," let alone embark on major jobs programs. The *Nation* magazine summed up this attitude best when its editor, E. L. Godkin, wrote in its Christmas 1875 issue that "free soup must be prohibited, and all classes must learn that soup of any kind, beef or turtle, can be

"The Red Flag in New York—Riotous Communist Workingmen Driven from Tompkins Square by the Mounted Police, Tuesday, January 13th, 1874." Demonstrations by workers and their allies demanding relief and job programs often were met with official violence—and were treated with hostility by the nation's press.

had only by being paid for." In Chicago, the Relief and Aid Society, which had been set up after the fire that devastated the city in 1871, refused to distribute the $600,000 in its coffers to unemployed workers. Its superintendent maintained that any of the unemployed men "loafing around the streets" could find work "if they were not too lazy to look for it."

Businessmen and their supporters tended to use Social Darwinist theories to explain what was happening. They viewed the depression as a necessary, if painful, process that would weed out inefficient businesses and allow only the strongest and most creative capitalists (and, by extension, workers) to survive. Any action taken by the government to interfere with this "natural" process would violate laissez-faire ideals and thus damage the entire social fabric. The future progress and prosperity of the nation would thus be compromised.

"A Tramp's Morning Ablutions." An early morning scene in New York's Madison Square during the summer of 1877. To the annoyance of more affluent urban residents, city parks all over the United States served as homes for many of the country's unemployed.

Annoyance gave way to fright as thousands of unemployed men wandered the country in search of work. The "tramp menace," many argued, required a repressive response—and advertisements like this exploited the pervasive fear.

Business and government leaders were inclined to blame the suffering of working people on "the ignorance, indolence, and immorality" of the poor, and attacked public-works schemes as a form of imported "communism." "The dangerous classes," symbolized above all by the tramp, became the target of their attack—not the economic system that had created the tramp in the first place.

The depression nearly destroyed the young labor movement. There were nearly thirty national trade unions in 1873 and only eight or nine at the end of the decade; the number of members dropped from 300,000 to about 50,000 (in New York City, it fell from 45,000 to 5,000). And wage gains won since the Civil War were lost: New York building tradesmen, for example, had earned $2.50 to $3.00 for an eight-hour day in 1872; three years later, they were working a ten-hour day for $1.50 to $2.00.

But as craft unions declined, activism among some groups of industrial workers increased. Between November 1873 and July 1874, a wave of railroad strikes swept the nation. Engineers, brakemen, and machinists on eighteen railroads walked off their jobs—mainly in response to wage cuts. Although not represented by trade unions, the railroad workers effectively disrupted railroad traffic through a variety of actions: removing coupling pins from freight cars, tearing up sections of track, and cutting telegraph lines. Railroad companies convinced a number of state governors to send in militias, and nearly all of the strikes were eventually defeated. Nevertheless, the strikes indicated the determination of rank-and-file workers to resist attacks on their living standards.

The most dramatic industrial conflict of the mid-1870s was the Long Strike in eastern Pennsylvania. Many of the early miners in the region had been Irish Catholic immigrants. In the early 1860s, they attempted to redress their grievances by employing the violent and secret methods long practiced among poor Irish tenant farmers. Between 1860 and 1867 there were sixty-three unsolved murders in the region, many of them attributed by the employers and the press to a secret and shadowy organization known as the "Molly Maguires." A number of the victims were foremen notorious for "short-weighting" or for other offenses against mineworkers. Although the role of the Molly Maguires in these 1860s attacks was never definitely established, sharp conflict continued to plague the eastern Pennsylvania coalfields.

By 1868 the Workingmen's Benevolent Association (WBA) had emerged as a powerful union representing the regions's miners, who were engaged in conflicts with many mining operators. In the early 1870s, however, the mining industry was in the midst of a major transformation. Franklin Gowen, president of the Reading Railroad, began to eliminate the cutthroat competition that plagued the industry by buying out many smaller mining concerns. By 1874, Gowen was the largest coal operator in eastern Pennsylvania and was ready to take on the WBA, providing leadership for all the operators. He first stockpiled his coal and then, in the winter of 1874–75, shut down his mines. The bitter ensuing struggle lasted for five months. Gowen later bragged that he had spent $4 million to save his company from "the arbitrary control of an irresponsible trades union."

The shutdown caused tremendous hardships for the mineworkers. "Hundreds of families rose in the morning to breakfast on a crust of bread and a glass of water," reported one observer. "Day after day, men, women, and children went to the adjoining woods to dig roots and pick up herbs to keep body and soul together." The strike was also marked by tremendous violence. "Coal and iron police" hired by Gowen shot indiscriminately into crowds of workers, while WBA members attacked strikebreakers with clubs and stones. Although they possessed great courage and determination, the miners finally had to concede defeat. They returned to work in nonunion mines with a 20 percent wage cut.

Now Gowen pressed his victory to a final conclusion. In 1873 the coal operator had hired the Pinkerton National Detective Agency to infiltrate the miners' organizations. Pinkerton was a private company that had achieved some fame for protecting railroad property at a time when local police forces were notoriously weak. The agency now entered a new phase of its history as a leading antilabor force.

James McParlan—a Pinkerton operative—lived among the Irish miners of eastern Pennsylvania for several years. In 1876 he came forward as a leading witness in a series of sensational murder trials. McParlan testified that these murders were the result of a conspiracy by the Molly Maguires, the same secret society that had stood ac-

The Molly Maguires. An illustration from *The Mollie Maguires and the Detectives,* Allan Pinkerton's self-serving account of his detective agency's infiltration of the secret society of Irish miners. Pinkerton's work in the service of the Reading Railroad typified the widespread use of private police by railroads and other businesses to suppress unions.

cused a decade earlier of the murders of dozens of mine foremen. McParlan claimed that the "Mollies" dominated the WBA and other Irish organizations in the region. Despite questions about the validity of McParlan's testimony, twenty miners were found guilty and sentenced to death. Equally important, because of widespread press coverage, the Molly Maguire trials helped link trade-unionism and terrorism in the public mind. As a result, unionism in Pennsylvania mining was totally destroyed and would not reemerge until the end of the century.

Employers used many means to break the wave of strikes that marked the 1870s depression. When miners in Ohio's Hocking Valley went on strike in 1874, for example, employers imported African-American workers from southern and border cities to take their place. "We'll flood the whole area with blacks before we are done with this thing," one mine operator told a reporter. The ploy was possible largely because of the failure of Radical Reconstruction—freed blacks in the South were never able to buy enough land to be economically independent, so it was only logical that they accept the offer of industrial jobs in the North. And—equally important—the unwillingness of unions to admit black workers gave African-Americans little reason to refuse to take white workers' jobs in the first place.

Industrial conflict was intense during the 1870s depression: employers adopted harsh strategies to destroy unions, and unionism declined. As a result, workers turned increasingly toward political activity. "Hundreds of the ablest men in the [labor] movement have lost hope in . . . the organizations known as trade unions," noted the

Iron Molders' Journal in 1875. "Hence we find them no longer urging the organization of labor into trade and labor unions, but urging organization for political purposes."

The relationship of workers to politics had grown increasingly complicated. Many working-class immigrants, especially the Irish, retained a strong loyalty to the Democratic Party. As we have seen, big-city Democratic political machines provided numerous services to urban immigrants, and the party was far more tolerant than the Republicans toward the Catholic Church, the saloon, and other cultural and social institutions within the immigrant community. At the same time, the Democratic Party continued to emphasize hostility toward blacks, which heightened its appeal to white workers with deeply ingrained racist beliefs.

On the other hand, many workers (especially Protestants) supported free labor, temperance, and economic development—all tenets of the Republican Party. In particular, some labor leaders identified strongly with the Republican Party in the late 1860s and extended its antislavery and free-labor ideology to a critique of the entire wage system. But the Republicans didn't accept this critique; they opposed eight-hour-day laws, as we have seen, contributing to a breakdown of the labor-Republican alliance. Working-class dissatisfaction with the Republicans increased dramatically during the depression of the 1870s.

After 1872 the Republicans retreated from free-labor ideals and Radical Reconstruction, and the Democratic Party gained in the 1874 congressional elections, leading to a national political stalemate. The Republican and Democratic parties, which had been diametrically opposed a mere decade earlier, now seemed indistinguishable. Moreover, politicians in both parties enjoyed the fruits of the post–Civil War spoils system: businessmen used outright bribery to guarantee the support of politicians, Republican and Democratic alike.

Workers were growing dissatisfied with both parties, and some activists now looked for other, independent roads to political influence. The main vehicle was the Greenback Party, organized on a national level by farmers in 1875. The new party stood for governmental action to expand the currency with paper "greenbacks" that were not tied to the nation's gold reserves—a reform intended to inflate prices, thus benefiting debtors and providing capital needed for economic growth. Key labor figures, such as Richard Trevellick, A. C. Cameron, and John Siney, endorsed the new party, and it won some working-class support in the presidential election of 1876.

Ira Steward, who had worked so hard for third-party support for the eight-hour day, vehemently protested this new departure. He believed that the eight-hour day would lead to a gradual elimination of capitalists altogether, but that an expanded currency would have no such sweeping consequences. Nonetheless, many labor leaders rallied to the Greenback cause, marking their final rejection of the Republican Party, which after 1872 grew more and more committed to the ideology of laissez-faire.

But the Greenback Party offered no real threat to Republican dominance. As the Republican Party moved away from its radical free-labor program in the South, it increasingly emphasized other aspects of its agenda, particularly economic development. It continued to draw some working-class support through high protective tariffs—which, it was hoped, would ensure high levels of employment in domestic industry. But more and more the party looked to businessmen as its most important social base. The inauguration of Republican Rutherford B. Hayes following the tense electoral dispute of 1876—aided by the active intervention of railroad owners such as the Pennsylvania Railroad's Tom Scott—gave party leaders confidence that they were following the correct course.

Businessmen were equally confident by 1877. Though the country had not yet emerged from the depression, the major problem of cutthroat competition was gradually being eliminated by the emergence of large monopolies in a number of basic industries. And unionism was clearly in retreat. The public hanging of ten accused Molly Maguires in June 1877 seemed to close the book on a defeated post–Civil War labor movement.

Within a month, however, it would be clear that this confidence was profoundly misplaced. The railroad strike of July 1877 shook the foundations of business complacency with the force of a mighty explosion.

THE GREAT UPRISING OF 1877

The railroad strike of July 1877 represented a turning point in American history. In two short weeks, the strike spread through fourteen states from coast to coast. It left over a hundred people dead and millions of dollars' worth of property destroyed. The uprising of 1877 was the first truly national strike in American history and the first one in which the federal government placed its full power (in the form of the army) on the side of business, a development that would be repeated. Though the strike failed in the short run, it marked the birth of a working-class movement far broader and more powerful than anything seen before. In a deeper sense, the strike registered the fact that class relations had become a central issue of national life and that the United States would not be able to avoid the class-based conflict that had plagued Europe since the birth of industrial capitalism.

The Great Uprising of 1877 was brought on by the hard times of the depression. Railroad workers had suffered one wage reduction after another since 1873: brakemen, for example, now earned a mere $1.75 for an extremely hazardous twelve-hour day. In Massachusetts forty-two railroad workers died each year in accidents, and brakemen commonly lost a finger or a hand on the job. After the railroad strikes of 1873–74 were defeated, union members were blacklisted, and unions were nearly nonexistent.

Against this background, executives from four of the largest railroads met in March 1877 to formalize a pooling arrangement. We have seen how pools had been used to end destructive competition. But the presidents of the four railroads—the Pennsylvania, the New York Central, the Erie, and the Baltimore and Ohio—added a new dimension by adopting a plan to cut wages. A wage cut was hardly necessary at this point—the railroads had already cut costs substantially, and several actually paid stock dividends at the same time as they announced their wage cuts. But cutting wages was an accepted practice when unemployment was high and workers' power to resist was limited. John Garrett, president of the Baltimore and Ohio, explained the railroads' actions: "The great principle upon which we joined to act was to earn more and to spend less."

The railroad workers, however, had been pushed beyond the limits of endurance. When the B&O implemented its 10 percent wage cut on July 16, workers in Martinsburg, West Virginia, staged a spontaneous strike, vowing to shut down the railroad yards until wages were restored. This proved to be the spark that ignited the Great Uprising. On July 19, President Hayes ordered federal troops into West Virginia to protect the B&O and the nation from the "insurrection."

But the use of federal troops in a domestic labor dispute created a wave of popular anger that spread the strike. In Baltimore, the Maryland state militia fired on huge crowds of workers, leaving eleven dead and forty wounded. Work stoppages rapidly spread north and west along the railroad lines to Pennsylvania, where the strike reached its most dramatic climax.

Pittsburgh was dominated by the Pennsylvania Railroad, the largest corporation in America. Residents of the city had been particularly hard hit by the depression of the 1870s and blamed the railroad for much of their misery. When railroad workers in Pittsburgh went on strike on July 19 under the banner of the recently revived Trainmen's Union, they were immediately supported by the city's iron workers. "We're in the same boat," said one iron-roller at a strike meeting held that evening. "I won't call employers despots, I won't call them tyrants, but the term 'capitalists' is sort of synonymous and will do as well." The railroad workers had the sympathy of much of Pittsburgh's population—including the city's militia companies, largely composed of workers—so railroad officials looked for outside help. On July 20, the adjutant general of Pennsylvania ordered the Philadelphia militia to Pittsburgh. As Tom Scott, president of the Pennsylvania Railroad, put it from his Philadelphia headquarters, "My troops will see that the trains pass."

The Philadelphia troops reached Pittsburgh the next day. A crowd of strikers and sympathizers greeted them with hoots and hisses; suddenly the troops began thrusting their bayonets at members of the crowd. Several rocks were thrown at the troops, who answered with a volley from their rifles. Panic followed. "Women and children rushed frantically about, some seeking safety, others calling for friends and relatives," wrote a newspaper reporter at the scene. "Strong men halted with fear, and trembling with excitement, rushed madly to and

July 22, 1877. The interior of the Pennsylvania Railroad's upper roundhouse after the battle between the Philadelphia militia and Pittsburgh strikers. From a series of 44 stereographs by S. V. Albee sold commercially as "The Railroad War." Stereographs were cards with "double photographs" that, when viewed through a "stereoscope," looked three-dimensional. By the 1870s stereoscope-viewing was one of the most popular forms of home entertainment.

fro, trampling upon the killed and wounded." When the gunfire finally ended, twenty people, including a woman and three small children, lay dead.

As news of the killing spread, a vast crowd, including thousands of workers from the mills, mines, and factories in the surrounding area, gathered at the railroad yards. By dawn they had set fire to dozens of freight cars and burned the Philadelphia militiamen out of the railroad roundhouse into which they had retreated. As the Philadelphians fled for their lives, new shooting erupted, killing twenty more Pittsburgh residents and five militiamen. Working people from all over the Pittsburgh region, most of them unemployed, then systematically burned and looted Pennsylvania Railroad property. Striking Pittsburgh workers and other residents quickly formed citizens' patrols to restore calm to the city's streets and prevent further looting. With the arrival of federal troops, the citizens' patrols were disarmed and the local strike ended.

In the next few days the strike spread across the Midwest. Workers took over entire towns, shutting down work until employers met their demands. The same railroad and telegraph lines that unified the nation and laid the groundwork for the full emergence of industrial capitalism also linked and unified the workers' protest. The strike spread as far as Galveston, Texas, and San Francisco. Without any central organization (most national unions, as we have seen, were defunct), the conflict gave rise to local committees that provided unity and direction to the strike.

Nonetheless, the strike was not the same everywhere. In Terre Haute, Indiana, for example, workers struck in the last week of July. Yet the specific features of the town, especially its lack of heavy industry, its close contact between workers and employers, and its native-born homogeneity, gave the strike a particular cast. Workers constantly reiterated their "full faith" in the "honor and integrity" of the local railroad president. Although they were genuinely angered by the railroads and the growing role of monopoly in national life, Terre Haute strikers' awareness of

". . . THE GRAND ARMY OF STARVATION"

At a rally called on July 23, Albert Parsons, a printer and a leader of the Workingmen's Party, addressed ten thousand striking Chicago workers and their supporters. Parsons's speech evoked widely held republican ideals; his opening image of a "grand army of starvation" recalls the victorious Union Army in the Civil War—the Grand Army of the Republic.

WE ARE ASSEMBLED as the grand army of starvation. Fellow workers, let us recollect that in this great Republic that has been handed down to us by our forefathers from 1776, that while we have the Republic we still have hope. A mighty spirit is animating the hearts of the American people today. When I say the American people I mean the backbone of the country—the men who till the soil, guide the machine, who weave the material and cover the backs of civilized men. . . . [We] have demanded of those in possession of the means of production . . . that they be not allowed to turn us upon the earth as vagrants and tramps. . . . We have come together this evening, if it is possible, to find the means by which the great gloom that now hangs over our Republic can be lifted and once more the rays of happiness can be shed on the face of this broad land.

WARNING
TO THE PEOPLE
BY THE MAYOR

I again warn all idlers
and curious people, especially all women and children,
to keep off the public streets
as the authorities in case of
necessity will not be responsible for the consequences.

MONROE HEATH,
MAYOR.

Chicago's mayor absolves himself
of responsibility, July 1877.

themselves as members of a distinct social class remained fleeting.

In Chicago, on the other hand, the strike quickly became a city-wide general strike that touched off open class warfare. Roving groups of strikers, led by brass bands playing the "Marseillaise"—the revolutionary anthem of the European working-class movement—swept through industrial areas of Chicago calling workers out of shops and factories, regardless of occupation. Although unemployment was not as severe in Chicago as in Pittsburgh, working people had suffered many wage reductions and had been driven to the breaking point by the depression. Socialists in the newly formed Workingmen's Party of the United States exercised leadership in Chicago and urged the city's workers to take disciplined action.

But city officials responded with extraordinary force. Police were ordered by the mayor to fire their pistols into crowds of strikers. The first such confrontation was at the giant McCormick reaper works, where two strikers were shot dead. As police broke up meetings and charged through working-class neighborhoods, men and women fought back with grim determination. Chicago's businessmen rallied to the cause of "law and order," with bankers, lawyers, and merchants organizing squads of special police to combat what they called "stray strikers and tramps." The strike in Chicago was notable for the unity maintained between German, Bohemian, and Irish workers and for the participation of women. "The women are a great deal worse than the men," proclaimed one journalist unsympathetic to the strikers, claiming that nearly one-fifth of the crowds were made up of women. The strike in Chicago came to an end only with the appearance of troops and artillery on the streets of the city.

Socialists were also active in the St. Louis strike. Here thousands of workers participated in a largely peaceful general strike. They shut down virtually all of the city's industries while government officials fled the city. Black workers in St. Louis took an active role in the strike, shutting down canneries and docks. When an African-American steamboat worker, addressing a crowd of white workers, asked, "Will you stand to us regardless of color?" the crowd responded, "We will! We will! We will!"

Such racial unity did not characterize all local strikes, though. The racism that had been institutionalized in the labor movement of the late 1860s and early 1870s now took a more ominous direction. In the far West, white hostility toward Chinese immigrants put its imprint on the strike as well. In San Francisco a crowd that met to discuss strike action ended up rampaging through the city's Chinese neighborhoods, killing several residents and burning buildings.

But the strike was directed mainly against the railroads and the unchecked corporate power they typified. Working people in 1877 were seeking not to overthrow capitalism as a whole, but to set limits on the unbridled economic power of corporate leaders and to assert workers' right to an equitable share of the economic bounty they helped produce. As a worker on the Wabash railroad told his foreman at the height of the strike, "We are striking not for a few cents, but for principles, and the spirit of liberty, equality, and fraternity so actuates us, that we will stay on the strike till the last one of our brothers on the other roads receive their rightful pay." This sense of social justice and demand for dignity ran like an electric current through the strike. A Pittsburgh militiaman reported that all of the strikers he talked to felt "that they were justified in resorting to any means to break down the power of the corporations."

Businessmen and their supporters took a different point of view. For them the railroad strike represented a revolutionary attempt to interfere with established property rights. They would not tolerate, as one letter writer to a newspaper put it, "this style of men, without a dollar, giving permission to capitalists to use their property under certain conditions." Many spokesmen for "respectable society" blamed the strikes entirely on tramps, the foreign-born, and "communists," and called for constructing armories in major cities, and reorganizing and rearming state militias.

Though the strikers were defeated in the short run, the railroad strike of 1877 marked the beginning of a revival of the labor movement. In 1878, the Greenback Party (renamed the Greenback-Labor Party) polled an impressive number of working-class votes, and in the 1880s the labor movement would grow again, now on a far more massive scale than in the 1860s. The railroad strike, by polarizing social classes and forcing all Americans to choose sides between capital and labor, helped revive the flagging labor movement. One labor leader, looking back to 1877, wrote, "Pittsburgh, with its sea of fire caused by burning freight cars, roundhouses, and depots, was the calcium light which illumined the skies of our social and industrial life."

"Waiting for the Reduction of the Army." As this 1878 cartoon from the New York *Daily Graphic* indicates, in the aftermath of the "Great Uprising," Indians, trade unionists, immigrants, and tramps were increasingly grouped together in the press as symbols of disorder and opposition to the nation's progress.

CONCLUSION

A NEW PHASE IN AMERICAN HISTORY

IN THE two centuries following European colonization, Americans grew more and more divided over which labor system—slave or free—should define the nation's identity and provide the basis for its economic development. Capitalism's emergence in the North early in the nineteenth century and the resulting growth of wage labor posed fundamental challenge to the South, which had erected a social order based on the geographic expansion of large plantations and slave labor. A series of political compromises succeeded after 1820 in blunting, but not resolving, the growing conflicts between the two systems. By 1860, most southern whites—rich and poor alike—embraced an ideology that depended on the enslavement of African-Americans to define both individual and regional identities. Most northerners believed in a very different order of things. Their ideal society was one dominated by free-labor values, including economic self-sufficiency and individual independence and mobility. Most northerners could thus avoid the extremes of ostentatious wealth and degraded dependency that characterized the South, though many wage laborers were in fact bound economically to conditions that were far from ideal.

These two fundamentally different ways of life irrevocably came to blows in the Civil War. The total defeat of the slave system after four years of bitter conflict seemed to confirm the essential truth of the free-labor ideal. The northern victory and the period of Radical Reconstruction that followed offered the hope of revolutionizing the South, creating a free-labor society on the ruins of slavery. Workers in the North sought to restructure their own society as well, giving expanded meaning to the concept of free labor. "So must our dinner tables be reconstructed," demanded a group of Boston workers in 1865, "our dress, manners, education, morals, dwellings, and the whole Social System."

The linking of the East and West by the transcontinental railroad only four years after the war seemed to open up the limitless continent for the benefit of all citizens. Even eastern wage laborers could now aspire to own a western homestead. Economic independence, the ability to escape "hireling" status, seemed within the grasp of all.

But the course of America's economic and political development between 1865 and 1877 undermined these expectations. By 1877, in the South, the old planters had returned to political power and a new system of agricultural labor had emerged. While it was an improvement over slavery, this system of agricultural production bore little resemblance to the free-labor ideal. Developments in the West and North were equally disturbing. Free western land never became as widely available as many had hoped, and huge areas were controlled by railroad, mining, and ranching enterprises that employed thousands of wage workers. Meanwhile, in the East and Midwest, a period of extremely rapid industrialization created a permanent wage-earning class that constituted a majority of the population. A decade after the Civil War, the promise of individual advancement and economic independence embodied in the nation's free-labor ideology had faded.

As a result of these profound changes and unrealized expectations, American workers organized a new and powerful labor movement between 1865 and 1873. Hundreds of thousands of shoemakers, coal-miners, iron-molders, and other workers—skilled and unskilled, native and foreign-born—joined local and national labor organizations. They succeeded in winning better wages and sometimes even formal contracts and recognition of their unions. Although the labor movement of the period was marred by racism directed against African-American and Chinese immigrant workers and did not fully embrace the organization of women workers, it nonetheless expressed a qualified egalitarian outlook that drew together many strands from the free-labor ideology and the republican heritage that emerged from the Revolution and Reconstruction eras. The labor movement spoke of equality and independence, mutuality and social obligation, and collective political action to correct injustice. At the same time, and often in response to the challenge posed by the emerging labor movement, business leaders and their spokesmen put forward a strikingly different viewpoint centered on notions of acquisitive individualism, the iron law of supply and demand in the marketplace, and the philosophies of laissez-faire and Social Darwinism.

The struggle between these opposing worldviews was greatly accelerated by the terrible depression of the 1870s, which produced misery and class conflict on a scale never seen before in the United States. The massive railroad strikes of 1877 dramatically revealed deep class divisions, marking the beginning of a new phase of American history. A new question—"the question of labor and capital, work and wages," in the words of a South Carolina newspaper—now stood at the center of the nation's political and social life. Growing conflict between labor and capital for control of America's political and economic institutions and its cultural and intellectual ideals would shape the nation's future in the decades to come.

SOURCES

These references indicate some of our intellectual debts to colleagues in the profession and point readers toward some of the most important work in U.S. history published during the last three decades and earlier.

Chapter 1: Europe Colonizes the Americas

Adorno, Rolena, "Paradigms Lost: A Peruvian Indian Surveys Spanish Colonial Society," *Studies in the Anthropology of Visual Communication*, 5 (1979), pp. 78–96.

Aston, T. H., and C. H. E. Philpin, eds., *The Brenner Debate: Agrarian Class Structure and Economic Development in Pre-Industrial Europe* (1985).

Axtell, James, *The European and the Indian: Essays in the Ethnohistory of Colonial North America* (1981).

Baud, Michel, *A History of Capitalism, 1500–1980* (1983).

Braudel, Fernand, *Capitalism and Material Life, 1400–1800* (1973).

Brenner, Robert, "Agrarian Class Structure and Economic Development in Pre-Industrial Europe," *Past and Present*, 70 (1976), pp. 30–75.

Cipolla, Carlo M., *The Fontana Economic History of Europe: Vol. 1: The Middle Ages* (1972); *Vol. 2: The Sixteenth and Seventeenth Centuries* (1974).

———, *Before the Industrial Revolutions: European Society and Economy, 1000–1700* (1976).

Coleman, D. C., *The Economy of England, 1450–1750* (1977).

Cronon, William, *Changes in the Land: Indians, Colonists, and the Ecology of New England* (1984).

Crosby, Alfred W., Jr., *The Columbia Exchange: Biological and Cultural Consequences of 1492* (1972).

Davidson, Basil, *The African Slave Trade: Precolonial History, 1450–1850* (1961).

———, *A History of West Africa to the Nineteenth Century* (1966).

———, *Africa in History* (1974).

Davis, Ralph, *The Rise of the Atlantic Economies* (1973).

Driver, Harold E., *Indians of North America* (1969).

Elliott, J. H., *The Old World and the New, 1492–1650* (1972).

Frank, Andre Gunder, *World Accumulation, 1492–1789* (1978).

Franklin, John Hope, *From Slavery to Freedom: A History of Negro Americans* (1967).

Fredrickson, George M., *White Supremacy: A Comparative Study in American and South African History* (1981).

Genovese, Eugene D., *The World the Slaveholders Made: Two Essays in Interpretation* (1969).

Harrison, J. F. C., *The Common People of Great Britain: A History from the Norman Conquest to the Present* (1985).

Hill, John Edward Christopher, *The Century of Revolution, 1603–1714* (1961).

——, *Reformation to Industrial Revolution: A Social and Economic History of Britain, 1530–1780* (1968).

——, *The World Turned Upside Down: Radical Ideas During the English Revolution* (1972).

——, "A Bourgeois Revolution?" in J. G. A. Pocock, ed., *Three British Revolutions: 1641, 1688, 1776* (1980).

Hilton, R. H., *The Decline of Serfdom in Medieval England* (1969).

——, *The English Peasantry in the Later Middle Ages* (1975).

Hobsbawm, Eric, "The General Crisis of the European Economy in the Seventeenth Century, II," in Trevor Aston, ed., *Crisis in Europe, 1560–1660* (1965).

Honour, Hugh, *The European Vision of America* (1975).

——, *The New Golden Land: European Images of America from the Discoveries to the Present Time* (1975).

Huggins, Nathan I., *Black Odyssey: The Afro-American Ordeal in Slavery* (1979).

——, Martin Kilson, and Daniel M. Fox, *Key Issues in the Afro-American Experience*, 2 vols. (1971).

Jennings, Francis, *The Invasion of America: Indians, Colonialism, and the Cant of Conquest* (1975).

Katz, Friedrich, *The Ancient American Civilizations* (1972).

Leon-Portilla, Miguel, ed., *The Broken Spears: The Aztec Account of the Conquest of Mexico* (1962).

Lerner, Robert E., *The Age of Adversity: The Fourteenth Century* (1968).

MacCormack, Sabine, "*Pachacuti*: Miracles, Punishments, and Last Judgement: Visionary Past and Prophetic Future in Early Colonial Peru," *American Historical Review*, 93 (1988), pp. 960–1006.

Mintz, Sidney, and Richard Price, *An Anthropological Approach to the Afro-American Past: A Caribbean Perspective* (1976).

Morgan, Edward, *American Freedom, American Slavery: The Ordeal of Colonial Virginia* (1975).

Nash, Gary, ed., *Red, White, and Black: The Peoples of Early America* (1982).

Parry, J. H., *Exploration in the Age of the Renaissance* (1966).

——, *The Spanish Seaborne Empire* (1966).

Quinn, David Beers, *The Elizabethans and the Irish* (1966).

Rodney, Walter, *How Europe Underdeveloped Africa* (1974).

Sacks, Karen, *Sisters and Wives: The Past and Future of Sexual Equality* (1979).

Salisbury, Neal, *Manitou and Providence: Indians, Europeans, and the Making of New England, 1500–1643* (1982).

Sauer, Carl O., *Sixteenth Century North America: The Land and the People as Seen by Europeans* (1971).

Tawney, R. H., *The Agrarian Problem in the Sixteenth Century* (1961).

Vega, Garcilaso de la, *The Incas: The Royal Commentaries of the Inca, Garcilaso de la Vega, 1539–1616* (1961).

Wallerstein, Immanuel, *The Modern World System: Capitalist Agriculture and the Origins of the European World Economy in the Sixteenth Century* (1976).

——, *The Modern World System II: Mercantilism and the Consolidation of the European World Economy, 1600–1750* (1980).

Walzer, Michael, *The Revolution of the Saints: A Study in the Origins of Radical Politics* (1974).

Williams, William Appleman, *The Contours of American History* (1966).

Wolf, Eric R., *Europe and the People Without History* (1982).

Wrightson, Keith, *English Society, 1580–1680* (1982).

Chapter 2: Slavery and the Growth of the Colonies

Bailyn, Bernard, "Politics and Social Structure in Virginia," in James Morton Smith, ed., *Seventeenth-Century America: Essays in Colonial History* (1959).

Berlin, Ira, "Time, Space, and the Evolution of Afro-American Society on British Mainland North America," *American Historical Review*, 85 (1980), pp. 44–78.

Breen, T. H., "A Changing Labor Force and Race Relations in Virginia, 1660–1710," *Journal of Social History*, 7 (1973–74), pp. 3–25.

———, ed., *Shaping Southern Society: The Colonial Experience* (1976).

———, *Puritans and Adventurers: Change and Persistence in Early America* (1980).

———, and Stephen Innes, *"Myne Owne Ground": Race and Freedom on Virginia's Eastern Shore, 1640–1676* (1980).

Carr, Lois Green, and Loren S. Walsh, "The Planter's Wife: The Experience of White Women in Seventeenth-Century Maryland," *William and Mary Quarterly*, 34 (1977), pp. 542–71.

Carter, Edward C., II, John C. Van Horne, and Charles E. Brownell, eds., *Latrobe's View of America, 1795–1820: Selections from the Watercolors and Sketches* (1985).

Craven, Wesley Frank, *White, Red, and Black: The Seventeenth-Century Virginian* (1971).

Davis, Harold E., *The Fledgling Province: Social and Cultural Life in Colonial Georgia, 1733–1776* (1976).

De Pauw, Linda Grant, and Conover Hunt, *Remember the Ladies: Women in America, 1750–1815* (1976).

Diamond, Sigmund, "From Organization to Society: Virginia in the Seventeenth Century," in Stanley N. Katz, ed., *Colonial America: Essays in Politics and Social Development* (1976).

Dunn, Richard S., *Sugar and Slaves: The Rise of the Planter Class in the English West Indies, 1624–1713* (1972).

Galenson, David, *White Servitude in Colonial America: An Economic Analysis* (1981).

Gutman, Herbert, *The Black Family in Slavery and Freedom, 1750–1925* (1976).

Hofstadter, Richard, *America at 1750: A Social Portrait* (1973).

Honour, Hugh, *The European Vision of America* (1975).

———, *The New Golden Land: European Images of America from the Discoveries to the Present Time* (1975).

Isaac, Rhys, *The Transformation of Virginia 1740–1790* (1982).

Jordan, Winthrop D., *White Over Black: American Attitudes Toward the Negro, 1550–1812* (1968).

Kay, Marvin L. Michael, "The North Carolina Regulation, 1766–1776: A Class Conflict," in Alfred F. Young, ed., *The American Revolution: Explorations in the History of American Radicalism* (1976).

Klein, Rachel N., "Ordering the Backcountry: The South Carolina Regulation," *William and Mary Quarterly*, 38 (1981), pp. 661–80.

Kulikoff, Allan, "The Origins of Afro-American Society in Tidewater Maryland and Virginia 1700 to 1790," *William and Mary Quarterly*, 35 (1978), pp. 226–59.

———, *Tobacco and Slaves: The Development of Southern Cultures in the Chesapeake, 1680–1800* (1986).

Littlefield, Daniel C., *Rice and Slaves: Ethnicity and the Slave Trade in Colonial South Carolina* (1981).

Main, Gloria, *Tobacco Colony: Life in Early Maryland, 1650–1720* (1982).

Matthews, Donald, *Religion in the Old South* (1977).

Menard, Russell, "From Servant to Freeholder: Status Mobility and Property Accumulation in Seventeenth-Century Maryland," *William and Mary Quarterly*, 30 (1973), pp. 37–64.

———, "The Maryland Slave Population, 1658–1730: A Demographic Profile of Blacks in Four Counties," *William and Mary Quarterly*, 32 (1975), pp. 29–54.

Mintz, Sidney, and Richard Price, *An Anthropological Approach to the Afro-American Past: A Caribbean Perspective* (1976).

Morgan, Edmund, *American Slavery, American Freedom: The Ordeal of Colonial Virginia* (1975).

Morgan, Phillip D., "Work and Culture: The Task System and the World of Lowcountry Blacks, 1700–1880," *William and Mary Quarterly*, 39 (1982), pp. 564–99.

———, "Black Life in Eighteenth-Century Charleston," *Perspectives in American History*, 1 (1984), pp. 187–232.

Morris, Richard B., *Government and Labor in Early America* (1946).

Rawick, George, *From Sundown to Sunup: The Making of the Black Community* (1972).

Rutman, Darrett B., and Anita H. Rutman, *A Place in Time: Middlesex County, Virginia, 1650–1750* (1984).

Smith, Abbott Emerson, *Colonists in Bondage: White Servitude and Convict Labor in America, 1607–1776* (1947).

Tate, Thad W., and David L. Ammerman, eds., *The Chesapeake in the Seventeenth-Century: Essays on Anglo-American Society and Politics* (1979).

Washburn, Wilcomb E., *The Governor and the Rebel: A History of Bacon's Rebellion in Virginia* (1957).

Wood, Peter H., *Black Majority: Negroes in Colonial South Carolina from 1670 Through the Stono Rebellion* (1974).

Woodmason, Charles, *The Carolina Backcountry on the Eve of the Revolution*, edited by Richard J. Hooker (1953).

Chapter 3: Free Labor and the Growth of the Northern Colonies

Allen, David Grayson, *In English Ways: The Movement of Societies and the Transferral of Local Law and Custom to Massachusetts Bay in the Seventeenth Century* (1981).

Anderson, Fred, *A People's Army: Massachusetts Soldiers and Society in the Seven Years' War* (1984).

Axtell, James, *The European and the Indian: Essays in the Ethnohistory of Colonial North America* (1981).

——, *The Invasion Within: The Contest of Cultures in Colonial North America* (1985).

Bailyn, Bernard, *The New England Merchants in the Seventeenth Century* (1955).

——, *The Peopling of British North America: An Introduction* (1986).

Berlin, Ira, "Time, Space, and the Evolution of Afro-American Society on British Mainland North America," *American Historical Review*, 85 (1980), pp. 44–78.

Bonomi, Patricia U., *A Factious People: Politics and Society in Colonial New York* (1971).

Boyer, Paul, and Stephen Nissenbaum, *Salem Possessed: The Social Origins of Witchcraft* (1974).

Breen, T. H., *Puritans and Adventurers: Change and Persistence in Early America* (1980).

Bushman, Richard L., *From Puritan to Yankee: Character and the Social Order in Connecticut, 1690–1765* (1967).

——, *King and People in Provincial Massachusetts* (1985).

Clark, Christopher, "The Household Economy, Market Exchange and the Rise of Capitalism in the Connecticut Valley, 1800–1860," *Journal of Social History*, 13 (1979), pp. 169–89.

Countryman, Edward, "'Out of the Bounds of Law': Northern Land Rioters in the Eighteenth Century," in Alfred Young, ed., *The American Revolution: Explorations in the History of American Radicalism* (1976).

Craven, Wesley Frank, *The Colonies in Transition 1660–1713* (1968).

Cronon, William, *Changes in the Land: Indians, Colonists, and the Ecology of New England* (1983).

Davis, T. J., *Rumor of Revolt: The "Great Negro Plot" in Colonial New York* (1985).

Demos, John, *A Little Commonwealth: Family Life in Plymouth Colony* (1970).

——, *Entertaining Satan: Witchcraft in the Culture of Colonial New England* (1982).

Dunn, Mary Maples, *William Penn, Politics, and Conscience* (1967).

Galenson, David W., "British Servants and the Colonial Indentured System in the Eighteenth Century," *Journal of Southern History*, 44 (1978), pp. 41–66.

Greene, Jack P., and J. R. Pole, eds., *Colonial British America: Essays in the New History of the Early Modern Era* (1983).

Greven, Philip J., Jr., *Four Generations: Population, Land, and Family in Colonial Andover, Massachusetts* (1970).

——, "Family Structure in Seventeenth-Century Andover, Massachusetts," in Stanley Katz, ed., *Colonial America: Essays in Politics and Social Development* (1976).

Gura, Philip F., *A Glimpse of Sion's Glory: Puritan Radicalism in New England, 1620–1660* (1984).

Henretta, James A., "Economic Development and Social Structure in Colonial Boston," *William and Mary Quarterly*, 22 (1965), pp. 75–92.

——, "Families and Farms: *Mentalité* in Pre-Industrial America," *William and Mary Quarterly*, 35 (1978), pp. 3–32.

——, and Gregory H. Nobles, *Evolution and Revolution: American Society, 1600–1820* (1987).

Heyrman, Christine Leigh, *Commerce and Culture: The Maritime Communities of Colonial Massachusetts* (1984).

Innes, Stephen C., *Labor in a New Land: Economy and Society in Seventeenth-Century Springfield* (1983).

Jedrey, Christopher, *The World of John Cleaveland* (1979).

Jennings, Francis, *The Invasion of America: Indians, Colonialism, and the Cant of Conquest* (1975).

——, *The Ambiguous Iroquois Empire: The Covenant Chain Confederation of Indian Tribes with English Colonies from its Beginnings to the Lancaster Treaty of 1774* (1984).

———, *Empire of Fortune: Crowns, Colonies & Tribes in the Seven Years War in America* (1988).

Kammen, Michael, *Colonial New York: A History* (1975).

Koehler, Lyle, *A Search for Power: The "Weaker Sex" in Seventeenth-Century New England* (1980).

Lemon, James T., *The Best Poor Man's Country: A Geographical Study of Early Southeastern Pennsylvania* (1972).

Lockridge, Kenneth, "Land, Population and the Evolution of New England Society, 1630–1790," *Past and Present*, 39 (1968), pp. 62–80.

———, *A New England Town, The First Hundred Years: Dedham, Massachusetts, 1636–1736* (1970).

Maier, Pauline, "Popular Uprisings and Civil Authority in Eighteenth-Century America," *William and Mary Quarterly*, 27 (1970), pp. 3–35.

Mark, Irving, *Agrarian Conflicts in Colonial New York 1711–1775* (1940).

McManus, Edgar J., *A History of Negro Slavery in New York* (1966).

Merrill, Michael, "Cash is Good to Eat: Self-Sufficiency and Exchange in the Rural Economy of the United States," *Radical History Review*, 4 (1977), pp. 41–71.

Morgan, Edmund S., *The Puritan Dilemma: The Story of John Winthrop* (1958).

Morris, Richard B., *Government and Labor in Early America* (1946).

Museum of Graphic Art, *American Printmaking: The First 150 Years* (1969).

Nash, Gary B., *The Urban Crucible: Social Change, Political Consciousness, and the Origins of the American Revolution* (1979).

———, *Race, Class, and Politics: Essays on American Colonial and Revolutionary Society* (1986).

Nobles, Gregory H., *Divisions Throughout the Whole: Politics and Society in Hampshire County, Massachusetts, 1740–1775* (1983).

Norton, Mary Beth, *Liberty's Daughters: The Revolutionary Experience of American Women, 1750–1800* (1980).

Parker, Barbara Neville, and Anne Bolling Wheeler, *John Singleton Copley: American Portraits* (1938).

Randel, William Peirce, *The American Revolution: Mirror of a People* (1973).

Rediker, Marcus, *Between the Devil and the Deep Blue Sea: Merchant Seamen, Pirates, and the Anglo-American Maritime World, 1700–1750* (1987).

———, "Good Hands, Stout Heart, and Fast Feet: The History and Culture of Working People in Early America," in Geoff Eley and William Hunt, eds., *Reviving the English Revolution: Reflections and Elaborations on the Work of Christopher Hill* (1988).

Reidy, Joseph P., "'Negro Election Day' and Black Community Life in New England, 1750–1860," *Marxist Perspectives*, 3 (1978), pp. 102–17.

Rothman, David J., *The Discovery of the Asylum: Social Order and Disorder in the New Republic* (1971).

Rutman, Darrett B., *Winthrop's Boston: Portrait of a Puritan Town, 1630–1649* (1965).

Salinger, Sharon V., *"To Serve Well and Faithfully": Labor and Indentured Servants in Pennsylvania, 1682–1800* (1987).

Salisbury, Neal, *Manitou and Providence: Indians, Europeans, and the Making of New England, 1500–1643* (1982).

Slotkin, Richard, *Regeneration Through Violence: The Mythology of the American Frontier, 1600–1860* (1973).

Smith, Abbott Emerson, *Colonists in Bondage: White Servitude and Convict Labor in America, 1607–1776* (1947).

Snyder, Martin P., *City of Independence: Views of Philadelphia Before 1800* (1975).

Thompson, E. P., "The Moral Economy of the English Crowd in the Eighteenth Century," *Past and Present*, 50 (1971), pp. 76–136.

Tracy, Patricia, *Jonathan Edwards, Pastor: Religion and Society in Eighteenth-Century Northampton* (1979).

Ulrich, Laurel Thatcher, *Good Wives: Image and Reality in the Lives of Women in Northern New England, 1650–1750* (1980).

Young, Alfred F., "English Plebeian Culture and Eighteenth-Century American Radicalism," in Margaret Jacob and James Jacob, eds., *The Origins of Anglo-American Radicalism* (1984).

———, "George Robert Twelves Hewes (1742–1840): A Boston Shoemaker and the Memory of the American Revolution," *William and Mary Quarterly*, 38 (1981), pp. 561–623.

Zuckerman, Michael, *Peaceable Kingdoms: New England Towns in the Eighteenth Century* (1970).

Chapter 4: "The Greatness of This Revolution"

Adams, Willi Paul, *The First American Constitutions: Republican Ideology and the Making of the State Constitutions in the Revolutionary Era* (1980).

Appleby, Joyce, "Republicanism and Ideology," *American Quarterly*, 37 (1985), pp. 461–73.

Bailyn, Bernard, *The Ideological Origins of the American Revolution* (1967).

Beard, Charles A., *An Economic Interpretation of the Constitution of the United States* (1913).

Berlin, Ira, *Slaves Without Masters: The Free Negro in the Antebellum South* (1974).

——, "The Revolution in Black Life," in Alfred F. Young, ed., *The American Revolution: Explorations in the History of American Radicalism* (1976).

——, and Ronald Hoffman, eds., *Slavery and Freedom in the Age of the American Revolution* (1983).

Berthoff, Rowland W., and John M. Murrin, "Feudalism, Communalism, and the Yeoman Freeholder: The American Revolution Considered as a Social Accident," in Stephen G. Kurtz and James H. Hutson, eds., *Essays on the American Revolution* (1983).

Brigham, Clarence S., *Paul Revere's Engravings* (1969).

Brown, Richard D., *Revolutionary Politics in Massachusetts: The Boston Committee of Correspondence and the Towns, 1772–1774* (1970).

Brown, Richard Maxwell, "Back Country Rebellions and the Homestead Ethic in America, 1740–1799," in Richard Maxwell Brown and Don E. Fehrenbacher, eds., *Tradition, Conflict, and Modernization: Perspectives on the American Revolution* (1977).

Buel, Joy Day, and Richard Buel, Jr., *The Way of Duty: A Woman and Her Family in Revolutionary America* (1984).

Bushman, Richard L., "Massachusetts Farmers and the Revolution," in Richard Jellison, ed., *Society, Freedom, and Conscience: The American Revolution in Virginia, Massachusetts, and New York* (1976).

Countryman, Edward, *A People in Revolution: The American Revolution and Political Society in New York, 1760–1790* (1981).

——, *The American Revolution* (1985).

Cresswell, Donald H., comp., *The American Revolution in Drawings and Prints: A Checklist of 1765–1790 Graphics in the Library of Congress* (1975).

Cummings, William P., and Hugh F. Rankin, *The Fate of a Nation: The American Revolution Through Contemporary Eyes* (1975).

Davis, David Brion, *The Problem of Slavery in the Age of Revolution, 1770–1823* (1975).

Debo, Angie, *A History of the Indians of the United States* (1970).

Egnal, Marc, and Joseph Ernst, "An Economic Interpretation of the American Revolution," *William and Mary Quarterly*, 29 (1972), pp. 3–32.

Ernst, Joseph Albert, *Money and Politics in America: A Study in the Currency Act of 1764 and the Political Economy of the Revolution* (1973).

Ferguson, James E., *The American Revolution: A General History, 1763–1790* (1974).

Foner, Eric, *Tom Paine and Revolutionary America* (1976).

Foner, Philip S., *Blacks in the American Revolution* (1975).

Graymont, Barbara, *The Iroquois and the American Revolution* (1972).

Gross, Robert A., *The Minutemen and Their World* (1976).

Hill, Draper, ed., *The Satirical Etchings of James Gillry* (1976).

Hobsbawm, Eric, *The Age of Revolution: Europe, 1789–1848* (1977).

Hoerder, Dirk, "Socio-Political Structures and Values, 1750s–1780s," in Erich Angermann et al., eds., *New Wine in Old Skins: A Comparative View of Socio-Political Structures and Values Affecting the American Revolution* (1976).

Hoffman, Ronald, *A Spirit of Dissension: Economics, Politics, and the Revolution in Maryland* (1973).

——, and Peter J. Albert, eds., *Sovereign States in an Age of Uncertainty* (1982).

——, et al., eds., *An Uncivil War: The Southern Backcountry During the American Revolution* (1985).

Honour, Hugh, *The European Vision of America* (1975).

Isaac, Rhys, *The Transformation of Virginia, 1740–1790* (1982).

Kaplan, Sidney, *The Black Presence in the Era of the American Revolution, 1770–1800* (1973).

Kerber, Linda K., *Women of the Republic: Intellect and Ideology in Revolutionary America* (1980).

Labaree, Benjamin W., *The Boston Tea Party* (1964).

Lemisch, Jesse, "Jack Tar in the Streets: Merchant Seamen in the Politics of Revolutionary America," *William and Mary Quarterly*, 25 (1968), pp. 371–407.

Lockridge, Kenneth A., "Social Change and the Meaning of the American Revolution," *Journal of Social History*, 6 (1972–73), pp. 397–439.

Lynd, Staughton, and Alfred F. Young, "After Carl Becker: The Mechanics and New York Politics, 1774–1801," *Labor History*, 5 (1964), pp. 215–76.

Maier, Pauline, *From Resistance to Revolution: Colonial Radicals and the Development of American Opposition to Britain, 1765–1776* (1972).

———, *The Old Revolutionaries: Political Lives in the Age of Samuel Adams* (1980).

Main, Jackson Turner, *The Anti-Federalists: Critics of the Constitution, 1781–1788* (1961).

Martin, James Kirby, and Mark E. Lender, *A Respectable Army: The Military Origins of the Republic, 1763–1789* (1982).

Marston, Jerrilyn Greene, *King and Congress: The Transfer of Political Legitimacy, 1774–1776* (1987).

Middlekauff, Robert, *The Glorious Cause: The American Revolution, 1763–1789* (1982).

Millis, Walter, *Arms and Men: A Study of American Military History* (1956).

Morgan, Edmund S., and Helen M. Morgan, *The Stamp Act Crisis: Prologue to Revolution* (1953).

Museum of Graphic Art, *American Printmaking: The First 150 Years* (1969).

Nadelhaft, Jerome J., *The Disorders of War: The Revolution in South Carolina* (1981).

Nash, Gary, *The Urban Crucible: Social Change, Political Consciousness, and the Origins of the American Revolution* (1979).

———, *Forging Freedom: The Formation of Philadelphia's Black Community, 1720–1840* (1988).

Nobles, Gregory H., *Divisions Throughout the Whole: Politics and Society in Hampshire County, Massachusetts, 1740–1775* (1983).

Norton, Mary Beth, *The British-Americans: The Loyalist Exiles in England, 1774–1789* (1972).

———, *Liberty's Daughters: The Revolutionary Experience of American Women, 1750–1800* (1980).

O'Donnell, James H., *Southern Indians and the American Revolution* (1973).

Olton, Charles S., *Artisans for Independence: Philadelphia Mechanics and the American Revolution* (1975).

Palmer, R. R., *The Age of the Democratic Revolution: A Political History of Europe and America, 1760–1800*, 2 vols. (1959; 1964).

Rose, Willie Lee Nichols, *Slavery and Freedom* (1982).

Rosswurm, Steven, *Arms, Country, and Class: The Philadelphia Militia and the "Lower Sort" During the American Revolution* (1987).

Royster, Charles, *A Revolutionary People at War: The Continental Army and the American Character, 1775–1783* (1979).

Ryerson, Richard Alan, *The Revolution Is Now Begun: The Radical Committees of Philadelphia, 1765–1776* (1978).

Shy, John, *A People Numerous and Armed: Reflections on the Military Struggle for American Independence* (1976).

Steffen, Charles G., *The Mechanics of Baltimore: Workers and Politics in the Age of Revolution, 1763–1812* (1984).

Szatmary, David, *Shays' Rebellion: The Making of an Agrarian Insurrection* (1980).

Wallace, Anthony F. C., *The Death and Rebirth of the Seneca* (1970).

Wilentz, Sean, *Chants Democratic: New York City and the Rise of the American Working Class, 1788–1860* (1984).

Wood, Gordon S., "Rhetoric and Reality in the American Revolution," *William and Mary Quarterly*, 23 (1966), pp. 3–32.

———, *The Creation of the American Republic, 1776–1787* (1969).

Young, Alfred, *The Democratic Republicans of New York: The Origins, 1763–1797* (1967).

———, ed., *The American Revolution: Explorations in the History of American Radicalism* (1976).

———, "George Robert Twelves Hewes (1742–1840): A Boston Shoemaker and the Memory of the American Revolution," *William and Mary Quarterly*, 38 (1981), pp. 561–623.

Chapter 5: The Growth of the Slave South

Allman, John M., II, "Yeomen Regions in the Antebellum Deep South: Settlement and Economy in

Northern Alabama, 1815–1860," Ph.D. dissertation, University of Maryland (1979).

Berlin, Ira, *Slaves Without Masters: The Free Negro in the Antebellum South* (1974).

——, and Herbert G. Gutman, "Natives and Immigrants, Free Men and Slaves: Urban Workingmen in the Antebellum American South," *American Historical Review*, December 1983, pp. 1175–1200.

——, and Ronald Hoffman, eds., *Slavery and Freedom in the Age of the American Revolution* (1983).

Bonner, James C., "Profile of a Late Antebellum Community," *American Historical Review*, 49 (1944), pp. 663–80.

Bruchey, Stuart, ed., *Cotton and the Growth of the American Economy, 1790–1860* (1967).

Crowe, Eyre, *With Thackeray in America* (1893).

Curry, Leonard P., *The Free Black in Urban America, 1800–1850* (1981).

David, Paul A., Herbert Gutman, Richard Sutch, Peter Temin, and Gavin Wright, *Reckoning with Slavery: A Critical Study in the Quantitative History of American Negro Slavery* (1976).

Davis, Allen F., and Mark H. Haller, eds., *The Peoples of Philadelphia: A History of Ethnic Groups and Lower-Class Life, 1790–1840* (1973).

Davis, David Brion, *The Problem of Slavery in the Age of Revolution, 1770–1823* (1975).

Douglass, Frederick, *The Life and Times of Frederick Douglass* (1969).

Eaton, Clement, *The Growth of Southern Civilization, 1790–1860* (1961).

Edmunds, R. David, "American Expansion in the 19th Century: A Second Look," paper delivered at the Newberry/Smithsonian Conference on the Impact of Indian History on the Teaching of American History, Washington, D.C. (1985).

Faust, Drew Gilpin, "Culture, Conflict, and Community: The Meaning of Power on an Ante-Bellum Plantation," *Journal of Social History*, Fall 1980, pp. 83–98.

Fields, Barbara Jeanne, *Slavery and Freedom on the Middle Ground: Maryland During the Nineteenth Century* (1985).

Fogel, Robert W., and Stanley L. Engerman, *Time on the Cross: The Economics of American Negro Slavery* (1974).

Foust, James D., "The Yeoman Farmer and Westward Expansion of U.S. Cotton Production," Ph.D. dissertation, University of North Carolina at Chapel Hill (1968).

Fox-Genovese, Elizabeth, and Eugene D. Genovese, *Fruits of Merchant Capital: Slavery and Bourgeois Property in the Rise and Expansion of Capitalism* (1983).

Gallman, Robert, "Self-Sufficiency in the Cotton Economy of the Antebellum South," *Agricultural History*, January 1970, pp. 5–23.

Genovese, Eugene D., *The Political Economy of Slavery: Studies in the Economy and Society of the Slave South* (1965).

——, *The World the Slaveholders Made: Two Essays in Interpretation* (1969).

——, *Roll, Jordan, Roll: The World the Slaves Made* (1974).

Goldfield, David R., *Cotton Fields and Skyscrapers: Southern City and Region, 1607–1980* (1982).

Gray, Lewis Cecil, *History of Agriculture in the Southern United States to 1860* (1958).

Gutman, Herbert G., *Slavery and the Numbers Game: A Critique of 'Time on the Cross'* (1975).

——, *The Black Family in Slavery and Freedom, 1750–1925* (1976).

Hahn, Steven, *The Roots of Southern Populism: Yeoman Farmers and the Transformation of the Georgia Upcountry, 1850–1890* (1983).

Hilliard, Sam Bowers, *Atlas of Antebellum Southern Agriculture* (1984).

Hutchinson, W. K., and S. Williamson, "The Self-Sufficiency of the Antebellum South: Estimates of the Food Supply," *Journal of Economic History*, September 1971, pp. 591–612.

Johnson, Guion Griffis, *Ante-Bellum North Carolina* (1937).

Jones, Jacqueline, *Labor of Love, Labor of Sorrow: Black Women, Work, and the Family from Slavery to the Present* (1985).

Joyner, Charles, *Down by the Riverside: A South Carolina Slave Community* (1984).

McPherson, James M., *Ordeal by Fire: The Civil War and Reconstruction* (1982).

Miller, Elinor, and Eugene D. Genovese, eds., *Plantation, Town, and Country* (1974).

Morgan, Philip D., "The Task System and the World of Lowcountry Blacks, 1700–1800," *William and Mary Quarterly*, 39 (1982), pp. 563–99.

——, "The Ownership of Property by Slaves in the

Mid-Nineteenth-Century Low Country," *Journal of Southern History*, 49 (1983), pp. 399–420.

North, Douglass C., *The Economic Growth of the United States, 1790–1860* (1966).

Oakes, James, *The Ruling Race: A History of American Slaveholders* (1982).

Osofsky, Gilbert, ed., *Puttin' on Ole Massa: The Slave Narratives of Henry Bibb, William Wells Brown, and Solomon Northup* (1969).

Otto, John S., "Slaveholding General Farmers in a 'Cotton County,'" *Agricultural History*, April 1981, pp. 167–78.

Owsley, Frank L., "The Pattern of Migration and Settlement on the Southern Frontier," *Journal of Southern History*, May 1945, pp. 147–76.

Rose, Willie Lee, ed., *A Documentary History of Slavery in North America* (1976).

———, *Slavery and Freedom* (1981).

Rothstein, Morton, "The Antebellum South as a Duel Economy: A Tentative Hypothesis," *Agricultural History*, October 1967, pp. 373–82.

Stampp, Kenneth M., *The Peculiar Institution: Slavery in the Ante-Bellum South* (1956).

Starobin, Robert S., *Industrial Slavery in the Old South* (1970).

Sullivan, John, "Jackson Caricatured: Two Historical Errors," *Tennessee Historical Quarterly*, 31 (1972), pp. 39–44.

Sydnor, Charles, *The Development of Southern Sectionalism* (1968).

Thornton, J. Mills, *Politics and Power in a Slave Society: Alabama, 1800–1860* (1978).

Tushnet, Mark V., *The American Law of Slavery* (1981).

Usner, Daniel H., Jr., "American Indians on the Cotton Frontier: Changing Economic Relations with Citizens and Slaves in the Mississippi Territory," *Journal of American History*, September 1985, pp. 297–317.

Wade, Richard C., *Slavery in the Cities: The South, 1820–1860* (1964).

White, Richard, *The Roots of Dependency: Subsistence, Environment, and Social Change Among the Choctaws, Pawnees, and Navajos* (1983).

Wish, Harvey, ed., *Ante-Bellum: Writings of George Fitzhugh and Hinton Rowan Helper on Slavery* (1960).

Woodman, Harold, "The Decline of Cotton Factorage After the Civil War," *American Historical Review*, July 1966, pp. 1219–36.

Wright, Gavin, *The Political Economy of the Cotton South: Households, Markets, and Wealth in the Nineteenth Century* (1978).

Wright, J. Leitch, Jr., *The Only Land They Knew: The Tragic Story of the American Indians in the Old South* (1981).

Young, Mary, "Indian Removal and Land Allotment: The Civilized Tribes and Jacksonian Justice," *American Historical Review*, 64 (1958), pp. 31–45.

———, "The Cherokee Nation: Mirror of the Republic," *American Quarterly*, 33 (1981), pp. 502–24.

Chapter 6: The Free-Labor North, 1790–1860

American Philosophical Society, *A Rising People: The Founding of the United States, 1765–1789* (1976).

Appleby, Joyce, "Commercial Farming and the 'Agrarian Myth' in the Early Republic," *Journal of American History*, 68 (1982), pp. 833–49.

Berthoff, Roland W., *British Immigrants in Industrial America, 1790–1950* (1953).

Bidwell, Percy W., and John I. Falconer, *History of Agriculture in the Northern United States, 1620–1860* (1941).

Billington, Ray Allen, *The Protestant Crusade, 1800–1860: A Study of the Origins of American Nativism* (1964).

Blegen, Theodore C., *Norwegian Migration to America: 1825–1860* (1931).

Blewett, Mary H., "Shared But Different: The Experience of Women in the Nineteenth Century Work Force of the New England Shoe Industry," *Essays from the Lowell Industrial History Conference on Industrial History* (1981).

Brady, Dorothy, "Relative Prices in the 19th Century," *Journal of Economic History*, 24 (1964), pp. 172–85.

Bruchey, Stuart, *The Roots of American Economic Growth, 1607–1861* (1968).

Clark, Christopher, "Household Economy, Market Exchange and the Rise of Capitalism in the Connecticut Valley, 1880–1860," *Journal of Social History*, 13 (1979), pp. 169–89.

Clark, Victor S., *A History of Manufactures in the United States, Vol. I: 1607–1860* (1929).

Cochran, Thomas C., *Frontiers of Change: Early Industrialism in America* (1981).

Conzen, Kathleen N., *Immigrant Milwaukee, 1836–1860: Accommodation and Community in a Frontier City* (1976).

Cole, Donald B., *Immigrant City: Lawrence, Massachussetts, 1845–1921* (1963).

Commons, John R., et al., *A History of Labour in the United States, Vol. 1* (1918).

Danhof, Clarence, *Change in Agriculture: The Northern United States, 1820–1870* (1969).

Davis, Lance, et al., *American Economic Growth: An Economist's History of the United States* (1972).

Dawley, Alan, *Class and Community: The Industrial Revolution in Lynn* (1976).

Diner, Hasia R., *Erin's Daughters in America: Irish Immigrant Women in the Nineteenth Century* (1983).

Dublin, Thomas, *Women and Work: The Transformation of Work and Community in Lowell, Massachusetts, 1826–1860* (1979).

Dudden, Fay E., *Serving Women: Household Service in Nineteenth-Century America* (1983).

Edmunds, R. David, *The Shawnee Project* (1983).

Ehrlich, Richard L., ed., *Immigrants in Industrial America, 1850–1920* (1977).

Engerman, Stanley L., "Up or Out: Social and Geographic Mobility in the United States," *Journal of Interdisciplinary History*, 5 (1975), pp. 469–89.

Faler, Paul G., *Mechanics and Manufacturers in the Early Industrial Revolution: Lynn, Massachusetts, 1780–1860* (1981).

Faulkner, Harold U., *American Economic History* (1960).

Feldblum, Mary Alice, "The Formation of the First Factory Labor Force in the New England Cotton Textile Industry, 1800–1848," Ph.D. dissertation, New School for Social Research (1977).

Foner, Philip S., *History of the Labor Movement in the United States, Vol. I* (1947).

Gates, Paul W., *The Farmer's Age: Agriculture, 1815–1860* (1960).

Gombrich, E. H., *Art and Illusion: A Study in the Psychology of Pictorial Representation* (1969).

Gross, Robert A., "Culture and Cultivation: Agriculture and Society in Thoreau's Concord," *Journal of American History*, 69 (1982), pp. 42–61.

Gutman, Herbert G., *Work, Culture, and Society in Industrializing America* (1976).

Hacker, Andrew, *The Triumph of American Capitalism: The Development of Forces in American History to the Beginning of the Twentieth Century* (1965).

Hahn, Steven, and Jonathan Prude, eds., *The Countryside in the Age of Capitalist Transformation: Essays in the Social History of Rural America* (1985).

Handlin, Oscar, *Boston's Immigrants, 1790–1880: A Study in Acculturation* (1959).

Hansen, Marcus Lee, *The Atlantic Migration, 1607–1860* (1961).

Henretta, James A., *The Evolution of American Society, 1700–1815: An Interdisciplinary Analysis* (1973).

————, "Families and Farms: *Mentalité* in Pre-Industrial America," *William and Mary Quarterly*, 35 (1978), pp. 3–32.

Hounshell, David A., *From the American System to Mass Production, 1800–1932: The Development of Manufacturing Technology in the United States* (1984).

Hutchinson, E. P., *Immigrants and Their Children* (1956).

Jaffee, David, "An Artisan-Entrepreneur's Portrait of the Industrializing North, 1790–1860," *Essays from the Lowell Conference on Industrial History*, (1985).

Jensen, Joan M., "Cloth, Butter, and Boarders: Women's Household Production for the Market," *Reviews in Radical Political Economy*, 12 (1980), pp. 14–24.

Johnson, Malcolm, *David Claypool Johnston: American Graphic Humorist, 1798–1865* (1970).

Johnson, Paul, "The Modernization of Mayo Greenleaf Patch: Land, Family, and Marginality in New England, 1766–1818," *New England Quarterly*, 55 (1982), pp. 488–516.

Jones, Maldwyn Allen, *American Immigration* (1960).

Kessler-Harris, Alice, *Out to Work: A History of Wage-Earning Women in the United States* (1982).

Kulik, Gary, "Pawtucket Village and the Strike of 1824: The Origins of Class Conflict in Rhode Island," *Radical History Review*, 17 (1978), pp. 5–37.

Laurie, Bruce, *Working People of Philadelphia, 1800–1850* (1980).

McGrane, Reginald C., *The Panic of 1837* (1924).

McVay, Georgianne, "Yankee Fanatics Unmasked: Cartoons on the Burning of a Convent," *Records of* the American Catholic Historical Society of Phila-delphia, 83 (1972), pp. 159–68.

Merrill, Michael, "Cash Is Good to Eat: Self-Sufficiency and Exchange in the Rural Economy of the United States," *Radical History Review*, Winter 1977, pp. 42–71.

Miller, Kerby A., *Emigrants and Exiles: Ireland and the Irish Exodus to North America* (1985).

Montgomery, David, "The Working Classes of the Pre-Industrial American City, 1780–1830," *Labor History*, 9 (1968), pp. 3–22.

———, "The Shuttle and the Cross: Weavers and Artisans in the Kensington Riots of 1844," *Journal of Social History*, 5 (1972), pp. 411–46.

National Bureau of Economic Research, "Output, Employment, and Productivity in the United States After 1800," *Studies in Income and Wealth*, 30 (1966).

Nettels, Curtis P., *The Emergence of a National Economy, 1775–1815* (1962).

Nevins, Allan, ed., *The Diary of Philip Hone, 1828–1851* (1927).

North, Douglass C., *Growth and Welfare in the American Past* (1966).

———, and Robert Paul Thomas, eds., *The Growth of the American Economy to 1860* (1968).

Parker, William N., ed., *Trends in the American Economy in the Nineteenth Century* (1960).

Pessen, Edward, *Riches, Class, and Power Before the Civil War* (1973).

Pred, Allan, "Manufacturing in the Mercantile City, 1800–1840," *Annals of the Society of American Geographers*, 56 (1966), pp. 307–25.

Prude, Jonathan, *The Coming of Industrial Order: Town and Factory Life in Rural Massachusetts, 1810–1860* (1983).

Rock, Howard, *Artisans of the New Republic: The Tradesmen of New York City in the Age of Jefferson* (1979).

Rosenblum, Gerald, *Immigrant Workers: Their Impact on American Labor Radicalism* (1973).

Ross, Steven J., *Workers on the Edge: Work, Leisure, and Politics in Industrializing Cincinnati, 1788–1890* (1985).

Shammas, Carole, "How Self-Sufficient Was Early America?" *Journal of Interdisciplinary History*, 13 (1982), pp. 247–72.

Smith, Billy G., "The Material Lives of Laboring Phil-adelphians, 1750 to 1800," *William and Mary Quarterly*, 38 (1981), pp. 163–202.

Stansell, Christine, *City of Women: Sex and Class in New York, 1789–1860* (1986).

Taylor, George Rogers, *The Transportation Revolution* (1951).

Temin, Peter, *Jacksonian Economy* (1969).

Thernstrom, Stephen, *Poverty and Progress: Social Mobility in a Nineteenth-Century City* (1964).

Tryon, Rolla M., *Household Manufactures in the United States, 1640–1860* (1917).

Walker, Mack, *Germany and the Emigration, 1816–1885* (1964).

Ware, Norman, *The Industrial Worker, 1840–1860* (1924).

Wilentz, Sean, *Chants Democratic: New York City and the Rise of the American Working Class, 1788–1850* (1984).

Williamson, Harold F., ed., *The Growth of the American Economy* (1944).

Williamson, Jeffrey, "American Prices and Urban Inequality Since 1820," *Journal of Economic History*, 36 (1976), pp. 303–33.

Chapter 7: Changing Patterns of Social Life

Ahlstrom, Sidney, *A Religious History of the American People* (1972).

Barney, William L., "Patterns of Crisis: Alabama White Families and Social Change, 1850–70," *Sociology and Social Research*, 63 (1979), pp. 524–43.

Blewett, Mary H., "I Am Doomed to Disappointment: The Diaries of a Beverly, Massachusetts, Shoebinder, Sarah E. Trask, 1849–51," *Historical Collections of the Essex Institute*, 17 (1981), pp. 192–210.

Boyer, Paul, *Urban Masses and Moral Order in America, 1820–1920* (1978).

Brown, Joshua, "The 'Dead-Rabbit'-Bowery Boy Riot: An Analysis of the Antebellum New York Gang," MA thesis, Columbia University (1976).

Buckley, Peter George, "To the Opera House: Culture and Society in New York City, 1820–1860," Ph.D. dissertation, City University of New York (1984).

Clinton, Catherine, *The Plantation Mistress: Woman's World in the Old South* (1982).

Cott, Nancy, *The Bonds of Womanhood: "Women's Sphere" in New England, 1780–1835* (1977).

Curtis, L. Perry, *Apes and Angels: The Irishmen in Victorian Caricature* (1971).

Darroch, A. Gordon, "Migrants in the Nineteenth Century: Fugitives or Families in Motion," *Journal of Family History*, 6 (1981), pp. 257–77.

Davis, Susan G., "All-me-knack"; or, a Working Paper on Popular Culture," unpublished paper (1980).

———, "'Making Night Hideous': Christmas Revelry and the Public Order in 19th-Century Philadelphia," *American Quarterly*, 34 (1982), pp. 185–99.

———, "The Popular Uses of Public Space in Philadelphia, 1800–1850," unpublished paper presented at the American Studies Association Biennial Meeting (1983).

Dodd, Jill Siegel, "The Working Classes and the Temperance Movement in Antebellum Boston," *Labor History*, 19 (1978), pp. 510–32.

Dolan, Jay P., *The Immigrant Church: New York's German and Irish Catholics, 1815–1865* (1975).

Douglas, Ann, *The Feminization of American Culture* (1977).

Dublin, Thomas, ed., *Farm to Factory: Women's Letters, 1830–60* (1981).

DuBois, Ellen Carol, *Feminism and Suffrage: The Emergence of an Independent Women's Movement in America* (1978).

Dulles, Foster Rhea, *A History of Recreation: America Learns to Play* (1965).

Faust, Drew Gilpin, "Culture, Conflict and Community: The Meaning of Power on an Ante-Bellum Plantation," *Journal of Social History*, 14 (1980), pp. 83–97.

Gordon, Linda, *Women's Body, Women's Rights: A Social History of Birth Control in America* (1980).

Gorn, Elliot, "'Gouge and Bite, Pull Hair and Scratch': The Social Significance of Fighting in the Southern Backcountry," *American Historical Review*, 90 (1985), pp. 18–43.

Grimsted, David, *Melodrama Unveiled: American Theater and Culture, 1800–1850* (1968).

Groneman, Carol, "Working-Class Immigrant Women in Mid-Nineteenth-Century New York: The Irish Woman's Experience," *Journal of Urban History*, 4 (1978), pp. 255–73.

Hahn, Steven, *The Roots of Southern Populism: Yeoman Farmers and the Transformation of the Georgia Upcountry, 1850–1890* (1983).

Haltunen, Karen, *Confidence Men and Painted Women: A Study of Middle-Class Culture in America, 1830–1870* (1982).

Hogan, William Ransom, "Amusements in the Republic of Texas," *Journal of Southern History*, 3 (1937), pp. 397–421.

Jentz, John Barkley, "Artisans, Evangelicals, and the City: A Social History of Abolition and Labor Reform in Jacksonian New York," Ph.D. dissertation, City University of New York (1977).

Johnson, Paul, *A Shopkeeper's Millennium: Society and Revivals in Rochester, New York, 1815–1837* (1978).

Keller, Morton, *The Art and Politics of Thomas Nast* (1968).

Larkin, Emmet, "The Devotional Revolution in Ireland, 1850–1875," *American Historical Review*, 77 (1972), pp. 625–52.

Laurie, Bruce, *Working People of Philadelphia, 1800–1850* (1980).

Lazerow, Jama, "A Good Time Coming: Religion and the Emergence of Labor Activism in Antebellum New York," Ph.D. dissertation, Brandeis University (1982).

Lebsock, Suzanne, *The Free Women of St. Petersburg: Status and Culture in a Southern Town, 1784–1860* (1984).

Lees, Lynn H., and John Modell, "The Irish Countrymen Urbanized: A Comparative Perspective on the Famine Migration," *Journal of Urban History*, 3 (1977), pp. 391–408.

Lerner, Gerda, "The Lady and the Mill Girl: Changes in the Status of Women in the Age of Jackson, 1800–1840," *Midcontinent American Studies Journal*, 10 (1969), pp. 5–14.

Levine, Lawrence W., "William Shakespeare and the American People: A Study in Cultural Transformation," *American Historical Review*, 89 (1984).

———, *Highbrow/Lowbrow: The Emergence of Cultural Hierarchy in America* (1988).

Levine, Susan, "Women and the Family in the Antebellum North," unpublished research paper (1983).

MacFarragher, John, *Women and Men on the Overland Trail* (1979).

Matthaei, Julie A., *An Economic History of Women in America: Women's Work, the Sexual Division of Labor, and the Development of Capitalism* (1982).

Matthews, Donald, *Religion in the Old South* (1977).

McLoughlin, William G., "Pietism and the American Character," *American Quarterly*, 17 (1965), pp. 163–86.

———, *Revivals, Awakenings, and Reform* (1978).

Miller, David W., "Irish Catholicism and the Great Famine," *Journal of Social History*, 9 (1975), pp. 81–98.

Nadel, Stanley, "Kleindeutschland: New York City's Germans, 1845–1880," Ph.D. dissertation, Columbia University (1981).

Norton, Mary Beth, *Liberty's Daughters: The Revolutionary Experience of American Women, 1750–1800* (1980).

———, "The Evolution of White Women's Experience in Early America," *American Historical Review*, 89 (1984), pp. 593–619.

O'Brien, John T., "Factory, Church, and Community: Blacks in Antebellum Richmond," *Journal of Southern History*, 44 (1978), pp. 509–36.

Post, Albert, *Popular Freethought in America, 1825–1850* (1943).

Raboteau, Albert J., *Slave Religion: The 'Invisible Institution' in the Antebellum South* (1978).

Rorabaugh, W. J., *The Alcoholic Republic: An American Tradition* (1979).

Rose, Willie Lee, *Slavery and Freedom* (1982).

Ryan, Mary P., *Womanhood in America: From Colonial Times to the Present* (1979).

———, *Cradle of the Middle Class: The Family in Oneida County, New York, 1790–1865* (1981).

Saxton, Alexander, "Blackface Minstrelsy and Jacksonian Ideology," *American Quarterly*, 27 (1975), pp. 3–28.

Schiller, Dan, *Objectivity and the News: The Public and the Rise of Commercial Journalism* (1981).

Scott, Anne Firor, *The Southern Lady: From Pedestal to Politics, 1830–1930* (1970).

Smith, Timothy, *Revivalism and Social Reform: American Protestantism on the Eve of the Civil War* (1980).

Smith-Rosenberg, Carroll, *Disorderly Conduct: Visions of Gender in Victorian America* (1985).

Stansell, Christine, "Women, Children, and the Uses of the Streets: Class and Gender Conflicts in New York City, 1850–60," *Feminist Studies*, 8 (1982), pp. 309–36.

Strasser, Susan, *Never Done: A History of American Housework* (1982).

Taft, Robert, *Photography and the American Scene: A Social History, 1839–1889* (1938).

Wade, Richard C., *The Urban Frontier: Pioneer Life in Early Pittsburgh, Cincinnati, Lexington, Louisville, and St. Louis* (1959).

Walters, Ronald C., *American Reformers, 1815–1860* (1978).

Warner, Sam Bass, Jr., *The Private City: Philadelphia in Three Periods of Growth* (1968).

———, *The Urban Wilderness: A History of the American City* (1972).

Wyatt-Brown, Bertram, "The Anti-Mission Movement in the Jacksonian South: A Study in the Regional Folk Culture," *Journal of Southern History*, 32 (1975), pp. 501–29.

———, *Southern Honor: Ethics and Behavior in the Old South* (1982).

Chapter 8: The Fight for Free Labor in the North

Arky, Louis H., "The Mechanics' Union of Trade Associations and the Formation of the Philadelphia Workingmen's Movement," *Pennsylvania Magazine of History and Biography*, 76 (1952), pp. 142–76.

Blau, Joseph L., ed., *Social Theories of Jacksonian Democracy: Representative Writings of the Period 1825–1850* (1954).

Blewett, Mary H., "Shared But Different: The Experience of Women in the Nineteenth Century Work Force of the New England Shoe Industry," *Essays from the Lowell Industrial History Conference on Industrial History* (1981).

———, "Work, Gender, and the Artisan Tradition in New England Shoemaking, 1780–1860," *Journal of Social History*, 17 (1983), pp. 249–70.

Curry, Leonard P., *The Free Black in Urban America, 1800–1850: The Shadow of a Dream* (1981).

Darling, Arthur B., "The Workingmen's Party in Massachusetts, 1833–34," *American Historical Review*, 29 (1923), pp. 81–86.

Davis, Susan G., *Parades and Power: Street Theatre in Nineteenth-Century Philadelphia* (1986).

D'Emilio, John, and Estelle B. Freedman, *Intimate Matters: A History of Sexuality in America* (1988).

Dorfman, Joseph, "The Jacksonian Wage-Earner Thesis," *American Historical Review*, 54 (1947), pp. 296–306.

Dublin, Thomas, *Women at Work: The Transformation of Work and Community in Lowell, Massachusetts, 1826–1860* (1979).

Ernst, Robert, *Immigrant Life in New York City: 1825–1863* (1949).

——, "The One and Only Mike Walsh," *New-York Historical Society Quarterly*, 36 (1952), pp. 43–65.

Green, Fletcher M., "Democracy in the Old South," *Journal of Southern History*, 12 (1946), pp. 3–23.

Hammond, Bray, *Banks and Politics in America* (1957).

Harrison, J. F. C., *Quest for the New Moral World: Robert Owen and the Owenites in Britain and America* (1969).

Hofstadter, Richard, *The American Political Tradition and the Men Who Made It* (1948).

Horton, James Oliver, and Lois E. Horton, *Black Bostonians: Family Life and Community Struggle in the Antebellum North* (1979).

Hugins, Walter, *Jacksonian Democracy and the Working Class: A Study of the New York Workingmen's Movement, 1829–1837* (1960).

Hurley, Jean, "The Irish Immigrant in the Early Labor Movement, 1820–1862," MA thesis, Columbia University (1959).

Huston, James L., "Facing an Angry Labor: The American Public Interprets the Shoemakers' Strike of 1860," *Civil War History*, 28 (1982), pp. 197–212.

Litwack, Leon F., *North of Slavery: The Negro in the Free States, 1790–1860* (1961).

Marshall, Lynn L., "The Strange Stillbirth of the Whig Party," *American Historical Review*, 72 (1966–67), p. 445–68.

Morris, Richard B., "Andrew Jackson, Strikebreaker," *American Historical Review*, 55 (1949), pp. 54–68.

Nadworny, Milton J., "New Jersey Workingmen and the Jacksonians," *Proceedings of the New Jersey Historical Society*, 67 (1949), pp. 185–98.

Neufeld, Maurice F., "Realms of Thought and Organized Labor in the Age of Jackson," *Labor History*, 10 (1969), pp. 5–43.

Pessen, Edward, *Most Uncommon Jacksonians: The Radical Leaders of the Early Labor Movement* (1967).

Rezneck, Samuel, "The Social History of an American Depression," *American Historical Review*, 40 (1935), pp. 662–87.

Schiller, Dan, *Objectivity and the News: The Public and the Rise of Commercial Journalism* (1981).

Shalhope, Robert E., "Republicanism and Early American Historiography," *William and Mary Quarterly*, 39 (1982), pp. 334–56.

Sullivan, William A., "Did Labor Support Andrew Jackson?" *Political Science Quarterly*, 62 (1947), pp. 569–80.

——, "Philadelphia Labor During the Jackson Era," *Pennsylvania History*, 15 (1948), pp. 305–20.

——, "The Industrial Revolution and the Factory Operative in Pennsylvania," *Pennsylvania Magazine of History and Biography*, 78 (1954), pp. 476–94.

Tyler, Alice Felt, *Freedom's Ferment: Phases of American Social History from the Colonial Period to the Outbreak of the Civil War* (1944).

Welsh, Peter C., "Henry R. Robinson: Printmaker to the Whig Party," *New York History*, 53 (1972), pp. 25–54.

Wilentz, Sean, "On Class and Politics in Jacksonian America," *Reviews in American History*, 10 (1982), pp. 45–63.

——, *Chants Democratic: New York City and the Rise of the American Working Class, 1788–1850* (1984).

Wittke, Carl, *The Utopian Communist: A Biography of Wilhelm Weitling, Nineteenth-Century Reformer* (1950).

Young, Alfred F., " 'By Hammer and Hand All Arts Do Stand': Mechanics and the Shaping of the American Nation, 1760–1820," unpublished paper (1983).

Chapter 9: The Struggle Over Slave Labor

Aptheker, Herbert, *American Negro Slavery Revolts* (1943).

Bauer, Raymond A., and Alice H. Bauer, "Day-to-Day Resistance to Slavery," *Journal of Negro History*, 27 (1942), pp. 388–419.

Berwanger, Eugene H., *The Frontier Against Slavery: Western Anti-Negro Prejudices and the Slavery Extension Controversy* (1967).

Brock, W. R., *Conflict and Transformation: The U.S., 1844–1877* (1973).

Brown, Richard H., "The Missouri Crisis, Slavery, and the Politics of Jacksonianism," *South Atlantic Quarterly*, 65 (1966), pp. 55–72.

Cole, Arthur C., *The Irrepressible Conflict: 1850–1865* (1934).

Crandall, Andrew W., *The Early History of the Republican Party, 1854–1856* (1930).

Danhof, Clarence H., "Farm-Making Costs and the

'Safety Valve': 1850–60," *Journal of Political Economy*, 49 (1941), pp. 317–59.

Duberman, Martin, *The Antislavery Vanguard: New Essays on the Abolitionists* (1965).

DuBois, W. E. B., *John Brown* (1919).

Eaton, Clement, "Class Differences in the Old South," *Virginia Quarterly Review*, 33 (1957), pp. 357–70.

Finnie, Gordon E., "The Antislavery Movement in the Upper South Before 1840," *Journal of Southern History*, 35 (1969), pp. 319–42.

Foner, Eric, *Free Soil, Free Labor, Free Men: The Ideology of the Republican Party Before the Civil War* (1970).

———, *Politics and Ideology in the Age of the Civil War* (1980).

Foner, Philip S., *Business and Slavery: The New York Merchants and the Irrepressible Conflict* (1941).

Fredrickson, George M., *The Black Image in the White Mind: The Debate on Afro-American Character and Destiny, 1817–1914* (1971).

Freehling, William W., *Prelude to Civil War: The Nullification Controversy in South Carolina, 1816–1836* (1965).

Genovese, Eugene D., *From Rebellion to Revolution: Afro-American Slave Revolts in the Making of the Modern World* (1979).

Harding, Vincent, *There Is a River: The Black Struggle for Freedom in America* (1981).

Holzer, Harold, Gabor S. Boritt, and Mark E. Neely, Jr., *The Lincoln Image: Abraham Lincoln and the Popular Print* (1984).

Johnson, Reinhard O., "The Liberty Party in Massachusetts, 1840–1848: Antislavery Third Party Politics in the Bay State," *Civil War History*, 28 (1982), pp. 237–65.

Lebowitz, Michael, "The Jacksonians: Paradox Lost?" in Barton J. Bernstein, ed., *Towards a New Past* (1968).

Lofton, Williston, "Abolition and Labor," *Journal of Negro History*, 33 (1948), pp. 249–83.

Magdol, Edward, *The Antislavery Rank and File: A Social Profile of the Abolitionist Constituency* (1986).

Mark, Irving, and Eugene L. Schwaab, *The Faith of Our Fathers: An Anthology Expressing the Aspirations of the American Common Man, 1790–1860* (1952).

Morris, R. B., "Labor Controls in Maryland in the Nineteenth Century," *Journal of Southern History*, 14 (1948), pp. 385–400.

Mullin, Gerald W., *Flight and Rebellion: Slave Resistance in Eighteenth-Century Virginia* (1972).

Nye, Russell B., *Fettered Freedom: Civil Liberties and the Slavery Controversy* (1949).

Oates, Stephen B., *The Fires of Jubilee: Nat Turner's Fierce Rebellion* (1975).

———, *To Purge This Land with Blood: A Biography of John Brown* (1984).

O'Connor, Thomas H., *Lords of the Loom: The Cotton Whigs and the Coming of the Civil War* (1968).

Osofsky, Gilbert, "Abolitionism, Irish Immigrants, and the Dilemmas of Romantic Nationalism," *American Historical Review*, 80 (1985), pp. 889–912.

Perry, Lewis, and Michael Fellman, eds., *Antislavery Reconsidered: New Perspectives on the Abolitionists* (1979).

Porter, Kenneth Wiggins, "Florida Slaves and Free Negroes in the Seminole War, 1835–1842," *Journal of Negro History*, 28 (1943), pp. 390–421.

Potter, David M., *The Impending Crisis: 1848–1861* (1976).

Quarles, Benjamin, *Black Abolitionists* (1969).

Rayback, Joseph G., "The American Workingman and the Antislavery Crusade," *Journal of Economic History*, 3 (1943), pp. 152–63.

Richards, Leonard L., *"Gentlemen of Property and Standing": Anti-Abolition Mobs in Jacksonian America* (1970).

Sewell, Richard H., *Ballots for Freedom: Antislavery Politics in the United States, 1837–1860* (1976).

Stampp, Kenneth, *And the War Came: The North and the Secession Crisis, 1860–61* (1954).

———, *The Imperiled Union: Essays on the Background of the Civil War* (1980).

Stewart, James B., *Holy Warriors: The Abolitionists and American Slavery* (1976).

Sydnor, Charles S., *The Development of Southern Sectionalism, 1819–1848* (1948).

Tise, Larry E., *Pro-Slavery a History of the Defense of Slavery in America, 1701–1840* (1987).

Walters, Ronald G., *The Antislavery Appeal: American Abolitionism After 1830* (1978).

Wish, Harvey, "The Slave Insurrection Panic of 1856," *Journal of Southern History*, 5 (1939), pp. 206–22.

———, ed., *Antebellum: Three Classic Works on Slavery in the Old South* (1960).

Woodward, C. Vann, *American Counterpoint: Slavery and Racism in the North-South Dialogue* (1964).

Zahler, Helene S., *Eastern Workingmen and National Land Policy, 1829–1862* (1941).

Chapter 10: The Civil War

Andreano, Ralph, ed., *The Economic Impact of the American Civil War* (1967).

Baker, Jean H., *Affairs of Party: The Political Culture of Northern Democrats in the Mid-Nineteenth Century* (1983).

Barney, William L., *The Secessionist Impulse: Alabama and Mississippi in 1860* (1974).

Berlin, Ira, et al., eds., *Freedom: A Documentary History of Emancipation, 1861–67, Series II: The Black Military Experience* (1982).

Bernstein, Iver C., "The New York City Draft Riots of 1863 and Class Relations on the Eve of Industrial Capitalism," Ph.D. dissertation, Yale University (1985).

Brewer, James H., *The Confederate Negro: Virginia's Craftsmen and Military Laborers, 1861–1865* (1969).

Brock, William R., *Conflict and Transformation: The United States, 1844–1877* (1973).

Channing, Stephen A., *Crisis of Fear: Secession in South Carolina, 1852–1860* (1970).

Cook, Adrian, *The Armies of the Streets: The New York City Draft Riots of 1863* (1974).

Cornish, Dudley Taylor, *The Sable Arm: Negro Troops in the Union Army, 1861–1865* (1966).

Current, Richard N., *The Lincoln Nobody Knows* (1958).

Curry, Leonard P., *Blueprint for Modern America: Non-Military Legislation of the First Civil War Congress* (1968).

Degler, Carl N., *The Other South: Southern Dissenters in the Nineteenth Century* (1974).

Donald, David, *Why the North Won the Civil War* (1960).

———, *Lincoln Reconsidered: Essays on the Civil War Era* (1966).

DuBois, W. E. B., *Black Reconstruction in America, 1860–1880* (1935).

Durden, Robert, *The Gray and the Black: The Confederate Debate on Emancipation* (1972).

Ellison, Mary, *Support for Secession: Lancashire and the American Civil War* (1972).

Engerman, Stanley L., "The Economic Impact of the Civil War," *Explorations in Entrepreneurial History*, 3 (1966), pp. 176–99.

Escott, Paul D., *After Secession: Jefferson Davis and the Failure of Confederate Nationalism* (1978).

Fields, Barbara J., *Slavery and Freedom on the Middle Ground: Maryland During the Nineteenth Century* (1985).

Fite, Emerson, *Social and Economic Conditions in the North During the Civil War* (1910).

Fleming, Walter, *Civil War and Reconstruction in Alabama* (1905).

Foner, Eric, *Free Soil, Free Labor, Free Men: The Ideology of the Republican Party Before the Civil War* (1970).

———, *Politics and Ideology in the Age of the Civil War* (1980).

———, *Nothing But Freedom: Emancipation and Its Legacy* (1983).

Foner, Philip S., *Business and Slavery: The New York Merchants and the Irrepressible Conflict* (1941).

Franklin, John Hope, *The Emancipation Proclamation* (1963).

Gates, Paul W., *Agriculture and the Civil War* (1965).

Genovese, Eugene D., *Roll, Jordan, Roll: The World the Slaves Made* (1974).

Gutman, Herbert G., *The Black Family in Slavery and Freedom, 1750–1925* (1976).

Hahn, Steven, *The Roots of Southern Populism: Yeoman Farmers and the Transformation of the Georgia Upcountry, 1850–1890* (1983).

Harrison, Royden, *Before the Socialists: Studies in Labor and Politics, 1861–1881* (1965).

Hoole, W. Stanley, *Vizetelly Covers the Confederacy* (1957).

Johnson, Michael P., *Toward a Patriarchal Republic: The Secession of Georgia* (1977).

Kessler-Harris, Alice, *Out to Work: A History of Wage-Earning Women in the United States* (1982).

Luraghi, Raimondo, *The Rise and Fall of the Plantation South* (1978).

Massey, Mary E., *Bonnet Brigades* (1966).

McCrary, Peyton; Clark Miller; and Dale Baum, "Class and Party in the Secession Crisis: Voting Behavior in the Deep South," *Journal of Interdisciplinary History*, 8 (1978), pp. 429–57.

McPherson, James M., *The Negro's Civil Rights War: How Negroes Felt and Acted During the War for the Union* (1965).

——, *Ordeal by Fire: The Civil War and Reconstruction* (1982).

——, *Battle Cry of Freedom* (1988).

Mohr, Clarence L., "Southern Blacks in the Civil War: A Century of Historiography," *Journal of Negro History*, 69 (1974), pp. 177–95.

Montgomery, David, *Beyond Equality: Labor and the Radical Republicans, 1862–1872* (1967).

Moore, Barrington, *Social Origins of Dictatorship and Democracy: Lord and Peasant in the Making of the Modern World* (1966).

Neely, Mark E., Jr.; Harold Holzer; and Gabor S. Boritt, *The Confederate Image: Prints of the Lost Cause* (1987).

Paine, Albert Bigelow, *Th. Nast: His Period and His Pictures* (1904).

Parish, Peter, *The American Civil War* (1975).

Potter, David M., *Lincoln and His Party in the Secession Crisis* (1942).

——, *The Impending Crisis: 1848–1861* (1976).

Quarles, Benjamin, *The Negro in the Civil War* (1953).

Rose, Willie Lee, *Rehearsal for Reconstruction: The Port Royal Experiment* (1964).

Scheiber, Harry N., "Economic Change in the Civil War Era: An Analysis of Recent Studies," *Civil War History*, 11 (1965), pp. 396–411.

Sellers, Charles, ed., *The Southerner as American* (1960).

Silbey, Joel H., *A Respectable Minority: The Democratic Party in the Civil War Era, 1860–1868* (1977).

Smith, George, and Charles Judah, eds., *Life in the North During the Civil War* (1966).

Stampp, Kenneth M., *And the War Came: The North and the Secession Crisis, 1860–1861* (1950).

——, *The Imperiled Union: Essays on the Background of the Civil War* (1980).

Taft, Robert, *Photography and the American Scene: A Social History, 1839–1889* (1938).

Thomas, Emory M., *The Confederacy as a Revolutionary Experience* (1971).

——, *The Confederate Nation: 1861–1865* (1979).

Thompson, W. Fletcher, Jr., *The Image of War: The Pictorial Reporting of the American Civil War* (1959).

Thornton, J. Mills, III, *Politics and Power in a Slave Society: Alabama, 1800–1860* (1978).

Trefousse, Hans L., *The Radical Republicans: Lincoln's Vanguard for Radical Justice* (1969).

Van Doren Stern, Philip, *They Were There: The Civil War in Action as Seen by Its Combat Artists* (1959).

Wiley, Bell Irvin, *The Life of Johnny Reb: The Common Soldier of the Confederacy* (1943).

——, *The Life of Billy Yank: The Common Soldier of the Union* (1952).

Chapter 11: Emancipation and Reconstruction

Benedict, Michael Les, *The Impeachment and Trial of Andrew Johnson* (1973).

——, *A Compromise of Principle: Congressional Republicans and Reconstruction, 1863–1869* (1974).

——, "Southern Democrats in the Crisis of 1876–1877: A Reconsideration of *Reunion and Rebellion*," *Journal of Southern History*, 46 (1980), pp. 489–524.

Berlin, Ira, et al., eds., *Freedom: A Documentary History of Emancipation, 1861–1867, Series I, Volume I: The Destruction of Slavery* (1985).

——, et al., eds. "The Terrain of Freedom: The Struggle over the Meaning of Free Labor in the U.S. South," *History Workshop Journal*, 22 (1986), pp. 109–30.

Brock, William R., *An American Crisis: Congress and Reconstruction, 1865–1867* (1963).

——, *Conflict and Transformation: The United States, 1844–1877* (1973).

Carter, Dan T., *When the War Was Over: The Failure of Self-Reconstruction in the South, 1865–1867* (1985).

DuBois, W. E. B., *Black Reconstruction in America, 1860–1880* (1935).

Fitzgerald, Michael, "The Union League Movement in Alabama and Mississippi," Ph.D. dissertation, UCLA (1986).

Foner, Eric, *Politics and Ideology in the Age of the Civil War* (1980).

——, *Nothing But Freedom: Emancipation and Its Legacy* (1983).

——, *Reconstruction: America's Unfinished Revolution, 1863–1877* (1988).

Franklin, John Hope, *Reconstruction: After the Civil War* (1961).

Gerteis, Louis S., *From Contraband to Freedman: Federal Policy Towards Southern Blacks* (1973).

Gillette, William, *Retreat from Reconstruction, 1869–1879* (1979).

Gutman, Herbert G., *The Black Family in Slavery and Freedom, 1750–1925* (1976).

Hahn, Steven, *The Roots of Southern Populism: Yeomen Farmers and the Transformation of the Georgia Upcountry* (1983).

Holt, Thomas, *Black Over White: Negro Political Leadership in South Carolina During Reconstruction* (1977).

Hyman, Harold M., ed., *New Frontiers of the American Reconstruction* (1966).

Jones, Jacqueline, *Labor of Love, Labor of Sorrow: Black Women, Work, and the Family from Slavery to the Present* (1985).

Keller, Morton, *The Art and Politics of Thomas Nast* (1968).

Kolchin, Peter, *First Freedom: The Responses of Alabama's Blacks to Emancipation and Reconstruction* (1972).

Kousser, J. Morgan, *The Shaping of Southern Politics: Suffrage Restriction and the Establishment of the One-Party South, 1880–1910* (1974).

Leslie, James W., "Ferd Havis: Jefferson County's Black Republican Leader," *Arkansas Historical Quarterly*, 37 (1978), pp. 240–51.

Litwack, Leon F., *Been in the Storm So Long: The Aftermath of Slavery* (1979).

Marzio, Peter C., *The Democratic Art: Pictures for a 19th Century America* (1980).

McCrary, Peyton, *Abraham Lincoln and Reconstruction: The Louisiana Experiment* (1978).

McFeely, William S., *Yankee Stepfather: General O. O. Howard and the Freedmen* (1968).

——, *Grant: A Biography* (1981).

McKitrick, Eric L., *Andrew Johnson and Reconstruction* (1960).

McPherson, James M., *Ordeal by Fire: The Civil War and Reconstruction* (1982).

——, and J. Morgan Kousser, eds., *Region, Race, and Reconstruction: Essays in Honor of C. Vann Woodward* (1982).

Montgomery, David, *Beyond Equality: Labor and the Radical Republicans, 1862–1872* (1967).

Morris, Robert C., *Reading, 'Riting, and Reconstruction: The Education of Freedmen in the South, 1861–1870* (1981).

Nathans, Elizabeth Studley, *Losing the Peace: Geor-gia Republicans and Reconstruction, 1865–1871* (1968).

O'Brien, John T., "Reconstruction in Richmond," *Virginia Magazine of History and Biography*, 89 (1981), pp. 259–81.

Painter, Nell Irvin, *Exodusters: Black Migration to Kansas After Reconstruction* (1971).

Perman, Michael, *Reunion Without Compromise: The South and Reconstruction, 1865–1868* (1973).

——, *The Road to Redemption: Southern Politics, 1869–1879* (1984).

Powell, Lawrence N., *New Masters: Northern Planters During the Civil War and Reconstruction* (1980).

Ransom, Roger L., and Richard Sutch, *One Kind of Freedom: The Economic Consequences of Emancipation* (1977).

Ripley, C. Peter, *Slaves and Freedmen in Civil War Louisiana* (1976).

Roark, James, *Masters Without Slaves: Southern Planters in the Civil War and Reconstruction* (1977).

Robinson, Armstead L., "Beyond the Realm of Social Consensus: New Meanings of Reconstruction for American History," *Journal of American History*, 68 (1981), pp. 276–97.

Rose, Willie Lee, *Rehearsal for Reconstruction: The Port Royal Experiment* (1964).

Shugg, Roger W., *Origins of Class Struggle in Louisiana: A Social History of White Farmers and Laborers During Slavery and After, 1840–1875* (1939).

Sproat, John G., *The Best Men: Liberal Reformers in the Gilded Age, 1865–1877* (1968).

Stampp, Kenneth M., *The Era of Reconstruction* (1965).

——, and Leon F. Litwack, *Reconstruction: An Anthology of Revisionist Writings* (1969).

Sterling, Dorothy, ed., *We Are Your Sisters: Black Women in the Nineteenth Century* (1984).

Trelease, Allen W., *White Terror: The Ku Klux Klan Conspiracy and Southern Reconstruction* (1971).

Tunnell, Ted, *Crucible of Reconstruction: War, Radicalism, and Race in Louisiana, 1862–1877* (1984).

Wayne, Michael, *The Reshaping of Plantation Society: The Natchez District, 1860–1880* (1983).

Wharton, Vernon L., *The Negro in Mississippi, 1865–1890* (1947).

Wiener, Jonathan M., *Social Origins of the New South: Alabama, 1860–1885* (1978).

———, "Class Structure and Economic Development in the American South, 1865–1955," *American Historical Review*, 84 (1979), pp. 970–1006.

Williamson, Joel, *After Slavery: The Negro in South Carolina During Reconstruction, 1861–1877* (1965).

Woodman, Harold D., "Sequel to Slavery," *Journal of Southern History*, 43 (1977), pp. 523–54.

———, "Post-Civil War Southern Agriculture and the Law," *Agricultural History*, 53 (1979), pp. 319–37.

Woodward, C. Vann, *Reunion and Reaction: The Compromise of 1877 and the End of Reconstruction* (1951).

Chapter 12: Industrial Labor After the War

Andrist, Ralph K., *The Long Death: The Last Days of the Plains Indians* (1964).

Barth, Gunther, *Bitter Strength: A History of the Chinese in the United States, 1850–1870* (1964).

Billington, Ray A., and Martin Ridge, *Westward Expansion: A History of the American Frontier* (1982).

Broehl, Wayne G., Jr., *The Molly Maguires* (1974).

Bruce, Robert V., *1877: Year of Violence* (1959).

Chandler, Alfred D., *The Visible Hand: The Managerial Revolution in American Business* (1977).

Cochran, Thomas C., and William Miller, *The Age of Enterprise: A Social History of Industrial America* (1942).

Commons, John R., and associates, eds., *History of Labor in the United States, Vol. I* (1918).

———, *A Documentary History of American Industrial Society* (1958).

Dawley, Alan, *Class and Community: The Industrial Revolution in Lynn* (1976).

Debouzy, Marianne, "Workers' Self-Organization and Resistance in the 1877 Strikes," in Dirk Hoerder, ed., *American Labor and Immigration History* (1983).

Degler, Carl N., *The Age of Economic Revolution, 1876–1900* (1973).

Diamond, Sigmund, ed., *The Nation Transformed: The Creation of an Industrial Society* (1963).

Dubofsky, Melvyn, *Industrialism and the American Worker, 1865–1920* (1985).

Dubois, Ellen Carol, *Feminism and Suffrage: The Emergence of an Independent Women's Movement in America, 1848–1869* (1978).

Fine, Sidney, *Laissez Faire and the General-Welfare State: A Study of Conflict in American Thought, 1865–1901* (1956).

Foner, Eric, *Politics and Ideology in the Age of the Civil War* (1980).

Foner, Philip S., *History of the Labor Movement in the United States, Vol. I* (1947).

———, *Organized Labor and the Black Worker, 1619–1973* (1974).

———, *The Great Labor Uprising of 1877* (1977).

Gordon, David M.; Richard Edwards; and Michael Reich, *Segmented Work, Divided Workers: The Historical Transformation of Labor in the United States* (1982).

Greenberg, Brian, *Worker and Community: Response to Industrialization in a Nineteenth-Century American City, Albany, New York, 1850–1884* (1985).

Grob, Gerald N., *Workers and Utopia: A Study of Ideological Conflict in the American Labor Movement, 1865–1900* (1961).

———, "The Workers' War for Economic Opportunity," in Government Printing Office, *200 Years of American Worklife* (1977).

Gutman, Herbert G., "Reconstruction in Ohio: Negroes in the Hocking Valley Coal Mines in 1873 and 1874," *Labor History*, 3 (1962), pp. 243–64.

———, *Work, Culture, and Society in Industrializing America* (1976).

———, *Power and Culture: Essays on the American Working Class* (1987).

Hacker, Louis, *The Triumph of American Capitalism: The Development of Forces in American History to the End of the Nineteenth Century* (1940).

Harris, William H., *The Harder We Run: Black Workers Since the Civil War* (1982).

Harvey, Katherine A., *The Best-Dressed Miners: Life and Labor in the Maryland Coal Region, 1835–1910* (1969).

Hobsbawm, E. J., *The Age of Capital, 1848–1875* (1975).

Jones, Maldwyn Allen, *American Immigration* (1975).

Kessler-Harris, Alice, *Out to Work: A History of Wage-Earning Women in the United States* (1982).

Kirkland, Edward C., *Industry Comes of Age: Business, Labor, and Public Policy, 1860–1897* (1961).

Lens, Sidney, *The Labor Wars: From the Molly Maguires to the Sitdowns* (1973).

Licht, Walter, *Working for the Railroad: The Organization of Work in the Nineteenth Century* (1983).

Lingenfelter, Richard E., *The Hardrock Miners: A History of the Mining Labor Movement in the American West, 1863–1893* (1974).

McNeill, George E., ed., *The Labor Movement: The Problem of Today* (1887).

Miller, Stuart C., *The Unwelcome Immigrant: American Images of the Chinese, 1785–1882* (1969).

Montgomery, David, *Beyond Equality: Labor and the Radical Republicans, 1862–1872* (1967).

———, "Labor in the Industrial Era," in Richard B. Morris, ed., *A History of the American Worker* (1983).

———, *The Fall of the House of Labor: The Workplace, the State, and American Labor Activism, 1865–1925* (1987).

Nee, Victor G., and Brett de Barry Nee, *Longtime Californ': A Documentary Study of an American Chinatown* (1972).

Nevins, Allan, *The Emergence of Modern America, 1865–1878* (1927).

Ozanne, Robert, *A Century of Labor Management Relations at McCormick and International Harvester* (1967).

Paul, Rodman W., *Mining Frontiers of the Far West, 1848–1880* (1963).

Porter, Glenn, *The Rise of Big Business, 1860–1910* (1973).

Roediger, David, " 'Not only the Ruling Classes to Overcome, but also the so-called Mob': Class, Skill, and Community in the St. Louis General Strike of 1877," *Journal of Social History*, 19 (1985), 213–39.

———, "Ira Steward and the Anti-Slavery Origins of American Eight-Hour Theory," *Labor History*, 27 (1986), pp. 410–26.

Ross, Stephen J., *Workers on the Edge: Work, Leisure, and Politics in Industrializing Cincinnati, 1878–1890* (1985).

Rudolph, Frederick, "Chinamen in Yankeetown: Anti-Unionism in Massachusetts in 1870," *American Historical Review*, 53 (1947), pp. 1–29.

Salvatore, Nick, "Railroad Workers and the Great Strike of 1877: The Views from a Small Midwest City," *Labor History*, 21 (1980), pp. 522–45.

Saxton, Alexander, *The Indispensable Enemy: Labor and the Anti-Chinese Movement in California* (1971).

Slotkin, Richard, *The Fatal Environment: The Myth of the Frontier in the Age of Industrialization, 1800–1890* (1985).

Sproat, John G., *The Best Men: Liberal Reformers in the Gilded Age, 1865–1877* (1968).

Takaki, Ronald T., *Iron Cages: Race and Culture in Nineteenth-Century America* (1979).

Trachtenberg, Alan, *The Incorporation of America: Culture and Society in the Gilded Age* (1982).

Utley, Robert M., *The Indian Frontier of the American West, 1846–1890* (1984).

Walkowitz, Daniel J., *Worker City, Company Town: Iron and Cotton-Worker Protest in Troy and Cohoes, New York, 1855–1884* (1978).

Ware, Norman, *The Labor Movement in the United States, 1860–1895* (1929).

West, Richard Samuel, *Satire on Stone: The Political Cartoons of Joseph Keppler* (1988).

CREDITS

vard University. **47:** Anonymous (after an engraving by Simon van de Passe), after 1616, oil on canvas, 30¼ × 25¼ inches—National Portrait Gallery, Smithsonian Institution. **49:** John Carter Brown Library, Brown University. **51:** Anonymous, *The Fortunate Transport. Rob Theif: or the Lady of ye Gold Watch Polly Haycock*, engraving, 1760–80, 11¼ × 15¾ inches—Colonial Williamsburg. **55:** Edwards, *List of Maps . . .* (1794)—Rare Books and Manuscripts Division, New York Public Library, Astor, Lenox, and Tilden Foundations. **58:** American Antiquarian Society. **59:** Joshua Frye and Peter Jefferson, "A Map of the Most Inhabited Part of Virginia . . ." (1775)—Maryland Historical Society. **61:** B. Martyn, *Reasons for Establishing the Colony of Georgia* (1733)—Rare Books and Manuscripts Division, New York Public Library, Astor, Lenox, and Tilden Foundations. **64:** Thomas Coram, oils on paper, after 1775—Gibbes Art Gallery/Carolina Art Association, Charleston. **68:** Anonymous, watercolor, c. 1800—Abby Aldrich Rockefeller Folk Art Center, Williamsburg, Virginia. **70:** Benjamin Henry Latrobe, *An overseer doing his duty. Sketched from life near Fredericsburg, March 13, 1798*, pencil, pen and ink, watercolor, 7 × 10¼ inches—Maryland Historical Society. **71:** George Roupell, *Peter Manigault and His Friends*, c. 1760, black ink and wash, 10³⁄₁₆ × 13³⁄₁₆ inches—Henry Francis duPont Winterthur Museum. **72:** Benjamin Henry Latrobe, *Nondescripts attracted by a neighbouring barbecue, near the Oaks, Virginia*, 1796, pencil, pen and ink, wash, 6¹⁵⁄₁₆ × 10¹⁵⁄₁₆ inches—Maryland Historical Society. **76:** Benjamin Henry Latrobe, *Bunn, the black smith, at a Campmeeting near Georgetown*, August 6, 1809, pencil, pen and ink, 8 × 12¾ inches—Maryland Historical Society.

Chapter 3: Free Labor and the Growth of the Northern Colonies

Documents: 88: ". . . The Indians in old times . . .": James Axtell, ed., *The Indian Peoples of Eastern America* (1981). **102:** ". . . Stones and brickbats": Charles Henry Lincoln, ed., *Correspondence of William Shirley* (1912). **104:** ". . . Plough deep, while sluggards sleep": Richard Saunders, ed., *Poor Richard: The Almanacks for the Years 1733–1758* (1964). **105:** "Forty shillings reward": (a) *New York Weekly Journal*, August 29, 1737; (b) *New York Mercury*, March 19, 1761. **119:** ". . . We are debarred Englishmen's liberty": Fred Anderson, ed., *A People's Army: Massachusetts Soldiers and Society in the Seven Years' War* (1984). **124:** ". . . Always oppressed by the rich": *New York University Law Quarterly Review*, 19 (1942).

Illustrations: 78: *The Book of Trades, or Library of the Useful Arts* (1807)—American Social History Project. **81:** John Foster, *Mr. Richard Mather*, woodcut, 6⅛ × 4⅞ inches, 1670—American Antiquarian Society. **87:** John Underhill, *Newes from America: or a New Discoverie of New England* (1638)—Rare Books and Manuscripts Division, New York Public Library, Astor, Lenox, and Tilden Foundations. **90:** Mary Rowlandson, *A Narrative of the Captivity, Sufferings and Removes of Mrs. Mary Rowlandson* (1773)—Rare Books and Manuscripts Division, New York Public Library, Astor, Lenox, and Tilden Foundations. **94:** *Father Abraham's 1760 Almanac* (1759)—American Antiquarian Society. **96:** *New England Primer* (1767)—Rare Books and Manuscripts Division, New York Public Library, Astor, Lenox, and Tilden Foundations. **98:** William Birch, *Preparation for War to defend Commerce*, line engraving, 11½ × 13⅝ inches, 1800—Free Library of Philadelphia. **100:** John Singleton Copley, *Joseph Sherburne*, oil on canvas, 1767–70, 50 × 40 inches—Metropolitan Museum of Art. **101:** John Singleton Copley, *James Tilley*, oil on copper, 1757, 13¾ × 10¼ inches—M. Knoedler and Company,

New York. **103:** John Singleton Copley, *Paul Revere*, 1768–70, oil on canvas, 35 × 28½ inches—Gift of Joseph W., William B., and Edward H. R. Revere, Museum of Fine Arts, Boston. **106:** Historical Society of Pennsylvania. **107:** James Hulett, *A View of the House of Employment, Almshouse, Pennsylvania Hospital, & part of the City of Philadelphia*, line engraving, c. 1767, 13½ × 18⅝ inches—Library Company of Philadelphia. **110:** Anonymous, *At the Loom*, oil on canvas, c. 1795—American Folk Art Gallery, Downtown Gallery Papers, Archives of American Art, Smithsonian Institution. **111:** *Hutchin's Improved: being an Almanack for 1761* (1760)—American Antiquarian Society. **112:** Edmund Vincent Gillon, Jr., *Early New England Gravestone Rubbings* (1966). **114:** John Ashton, *Chap-books of the Eighteenth Century* (1882)—Prints and Photographs Division, Library of Congress. **121:** (James Smithers) Morgan Edwards, *Materials towards a History of the American Baptists*, I (1770)—Library Company of Philadelphia. **123:** Henry Dawkins, *The Paxton Expedition, Inscribed to the Author of the Farce, by HD*, line engraving, 1764, 13¹¹⁄₁₆ × 7⁵⁄₁₆—Library Company of Philadelphia.

Chapter 4: "The Greatness of This Revolution"

Documents: 137: "In praise of liberty": *Boston Gazette*, August 19, 1765. **139:** "Let every man do his duty . . .": James Hawkes, *A Retrospect of the Boston Tea Party* (1834). **144:** "Remember the ladies . . .": L. H. Butterfield and Marc Friedlaender, eds., *Adams Family Correspondence*, Vol. 1 (1963). **154:** ". . . I took my stand:" John Dann, *The Revolution Remembered* (1980). **158:** ". . . Common sense and a plain understanding": Eric Foner, *Tom Paine and Revolutionary America* (1976). **161:** ". . . We cannot live without bread": Eric Foner, *Tom Paine and Revolutionary America* (1976). **164:** ". . . Inalienable right to freedom": Herbert Aptheker, *A Documentary History of the Negro People in the United States*, Vol. 1 (1951). **172:** "This federal ship will our commerce revive": *New York Packet*, August 5, 1788. **173:** ". . . Moneyed men, that talk so finely": *Massachusetts Gazette*, January 25, 1788.

Illustrations: 126: Benjamin Franklin, *Pennsylvania Gazette*, May 9, 1754—Rare Books and Manuscripts Division, New York Public Library, Astor, Lenox, and Tilden Foundations. **131:** *The Colonies Reduced. Design'd and Engrav'd for the Political Register*, 2⅜ × 3⅞ inches, 1767—Prints and Photographs Division, Library of Congress. **136:** *The Pennsylvania Journal and Weekly Advertiser*, October 24, 1765—Prints and Photographs Division, Library of Congress. **138:** Daniel-Nicholas Chodowiecki, *Historisch-genealogischer Calender, oder Jahrbuch der merkwürdigsten neuen Welt* (1784)—Prints and Photographs Division, Library of Congress. **142:** Paul Revere, *The Bloody Massacre perpetrated in King Street Boston on March 5th. 1770 . . .*, etching (hand-colored), 1770, 7¾ × 8¾ inches—Prints and Photographs Division, Library of Congress. **143:** American Social History Project. **145:** Philip Dawe(?), *A Society of Patriotic Ladies, at Edenton in North Carolina*, mezzotint, 1775, 13¾ × 10 inches—Prints and Photographs Division, Library of Congress. **147:** *London Magazine*, April 1774—Rare Books and Manuscripts Division, New York Public Library, Astor, Lenox, and Tilden Foundations. **149:** Philip Dawe(?), mezzotint, 1774, 14 × 9½ inches—Prints and Photographs Division, Library of Congress. **151:** *The Congress or Necessary Politicians*, etching, 1775?, 8 × 6½ inches—Prints and Photographs Division, Library of Congress. **152:** Amos Doolittle, *The Battle of Lexington, April 19th, 1775*, line engraving (hand-colored), 1775, 13 × 17½ inches—Print Collection, Miriam and Ira Wallach Division of Art, Prints, and Photographs, New York Public Library, Astor, Lenox, and Tilden Foundations. **153:** British

Museum. **154:** Concord Museum, Concord, Massachusetts. **155 (top):** Massachusetts Historical Society. **155 (bottom):** Benjamin West, *Colonel Guy Johnson*, 1776, oil on canvas, 79¾ × 54½ inches—National Gallery of Art, Washington, D.C. **163:** *Bickerstaff's Boston Almanack for 1787* (c. 1787)—National Portrait Gallery, Smithsonian Institution. **167:** New-York Historical Society. **170 (left):** *The Lady's Magazine and Repository of Entertaining Knowledge*, (December 1, 1792)—Library Company of Philadelphia. **170 (right):** *Keep Within Compass*, c. 1785–1805, sepia engraving, 9⁵⁄₁₆ × 7⅛ inches—Henry Francis duPont Winterthur Museum. **176:** Frederick Kemmelmeyer, *General Washington, Reviewing the Western Army at Fort Cumberland the 18th of October, 1794*, c. 1794, oil on paper backed with linen, 18⅛ × 23⅛ inches—Henry Francis duPont Winterthur Museum. **177:** James Gillray, engraving, 1791, 13¹³⁄₁₆ × 9¾ inches—American Philosophical Society Library.

Part Two: Free Labor and Slavery, 1790–1860

178: *A New Map of the United States of America* (1857)—Map Division, New York Public Library, Astor, Lenox, and Tilden Foundations.

Chapter 5: The Growth of the Slave South

Documents: 188: "... Beyond the great river": House Document 102, 22nd Cong., 1st Sess. (1832). **199:** "My master has sold Albert to a trader ...": Ulrich B. Phillips, ed., *Life and Labor in the Old South* (1929). **206–7:** "The bargain was agreed upon ...": Solomon Northup, *Twelve Years a Slave* (1853). **208:** "The colored man has no redress ...": John W. Blassingame, ed., *Slave Testimony* (1977). **212:** "We weren't allowed to sit down": Dorothy Sterling, ed., *We Are Your Sisters: Black Women in the Nineteenth Century* (1984). **216:** "... He had been too free with the niggers": Frederick Law Olmsted, *A Journey in the Seaboard Slave States* (1856).

Illustrations: 182: Prints and Photographs Division, Library of Congress. **186:** Thomas Clarkson, *The History of the Rise, Progress, and Accomplishment of the African Slave-Trade by the British Parliament* (1808)—American Social History Project. **187:** David Claypoole Johnston, 1828, engraving with stipple, 6⅛ × 4⅜ inches—American Antiquarian Society. **189:** George Catlin, *Seminolee*, 1838, pencil drawing—New-York Historical Society. **191:** Lewis Miller, *Virginia Sketchbook*—Abby Aldrich Rockefeller Folk Art Center, Williamsburg, Virginia. **192:** Prints and Photographs Division, Library of Congress. **193:** (August Hervieu) Frances Trollope, *Domestic Manners of the Americans* (1832)—Rare Books and Manuscripts Division, New York Public Library, Astor, Lenox, and Tilden Foundations. **194:** C. E. H. Bonwill, *Frank Leslie's Illustrated Newspaper*, February 6, 1864—General Research Division, New York Public Library, Astor, Lenox, and Tilden Foundations. **196:** Currier & Ives, 1872, lithograph, 9 × 12½ inches—Prints and Photographs Division, Library of Congress. **197:** Prints and Photographs Division, Library of Congress. **198:** John Winston Coleman, *Slavery Times in Kentucky* (1940). **200:** Eyre Crowe, 1862, oil on canvas, 13 × 21 inches—Kennedy Galleries, Inc., New York. **201:** Mary O'H. Williamson Collection, Prints and Photographs Department, Moorland-Spingarn Research Center, Howard University. **203:** New-York Historical Society. **205 (top):** *Harper's Weekly*—American Social History Project. **205 (bottom):** *Illustrated London News*, December 5, 1863—American Social History Project. **209:** Prints and Photographs Division, Library of Congress. **211:** George Bourne, *Slavery Illustrated in Its*

Effects upon Women (1837)—Prints and Photographs Division, Library of Congress. **218:** "A Winter in the South," *Harper's New Monthly Magazine* (September 1857)—American Social History Project.

Chapter 6: The Free-Labor North, 1790–1860

Documents: 232: "... I have everything I could wish": Edith Abbott, ed., *Historical Aspects of the Immigration Problem* (1926). **237:** "The truth about this country": Alan Conway, ed., *The Welsh in America* (1961). **244:** "Cookies and cakes ... one cent apiece": Herbert G. Gutman, *Work, Culture, and Society in Industrializing America* (1976). **248:** "... Rough work is performed here by machinery": Charles Cist, *Sketches and Statistics of Cincinnati in 1851* (1851). **252:** "No. 5 & 7 looms stopped—no weavers ...": Gary Kulik, Roger Parks, and Theodore Z. Penn, eds., *The New England Mill Village, 1790–1860* (1982). **254:** "... A new kind of machinery": Lucy Larcom, *A New England Girlhood* (1889). **255:** "A slave at morn, a slave at eve ...": Gary Kulik, Roger Parks, and Theodore Z. Penn, eds., *The New England Mill Village, 1790–1860* (1982). **260–61:** "... The pestilent air of the steerage": Herman Melville, *Redburn* (1849).

Illustrations: 220: Manchester Historic Association. **225:** George Inness, oil on canvas, 1855, 33⅞ × 50¼ inches—Gift of Mrs. Huttleston Rogers, National Gallery of Art, Washington, D.C. **226:** Cadwallader Colden, *Memoir on the Celebration of the Completion of the New York Canals* (1825)—Metropolitan Museum of Art. **227:** New-York Historical Society. **233:** "The Plan of a Farm Yard," *Columbian Magazine*, October 1786—American Philosophical Society Library. **234:** Edward Hicks, 1845–48—Abby Aldrich Rockefeller Folk Art Center, Williamsburg, Virginia. **236:** Timothy Shay Arthur, "The Factory Girl," *Illustrated Temperance Tales* (1850)—American Antiquarian Society. **238:** American Antiquarian Society. **241:** Stanley Fox, *Harper's Weekly*, September 29, 1866—American Social History Project. **242:** American Museum of Immigration, National Park Service, U.S. Department of the Interior. **245:** (M. Newhall) David N. Johnson, *Sketches of Lynn, or the Changes of Fifty Years* (1880)—U.S. History, Local History, and Genealogy Division, New York Public Library, Astor, Lenox, and Tilden Foundations. **246:** Cornelius Mathews, *The Career of Puffer Hopkins* (1841)—American Social History Project. **247:** George Lippard, *The Killers. A Narrative of Real Life in Philadelphia ...* (1850)—Library Company of Philadelphia. **250:** Serrell and Perkins, *New York by Gas-light. Hooking a Victim*, c. 1850, lithograph—Museum of the City of New York. **253:** Museum of American Textile History, North Andover, Mass. **255:** Winslow Homer, *Harper's Weekly*, July 25, 1868—American Social History Project. **257:** Henry R. Robinson, *The Effects of Loco-Foco Pledges*, 1838, lithograph—New-York Historical Society. **259:** *Illustrated London News*, December 16, 1848—American Social History Project. **262:** *Gleason's Pictorial and Drawing-room Companion*, December 11, 1852—American Social History Project. **265:** William Hogan, *Synopsis of Popery as It Was and as It Is* (1854)—General Research Division, New York Public Library, Astor, Lenox, and Tilden Foundations. **266:** *Scraps* (1835)—Boston Athenaeum.

Chapter 7: Changing Patterns of Social Life

Documents: 276: "... A dependent and abject life": Philip S. Foner, ed., *We, the Other People* (1976). **281:** "And ain't I a woman?": Philip S. Foner, *History of Black Americans* (1983). **283:** "... Vagrant, idle, and vicious children": George W. Matsell, Appendix, New York City *Board of Aldermen Documents* (1850). **290:** "... Indian reds and silver grays": Lizzie W. Montgomery, *Sketches of Old Warrenton, North Carolina* (1924). **294–95:** "No dainty kid-glove business ...": (a) Bruce I. Granger and Martha Hartzog, eds., *Letters of Jonathan Oldstyle* (1977); (b) Justin Kaplan, ed., *Walt Whitman: Poetry and Prose* (1982). **300:** "... They give us the husk": Frederick Douglass, *The Life and Times of Frederick Douglass* (1892). **307:** "For temperance and for '76!": Bruce Laurie, *Working People of Philadelphia, 1800–1850* (1980). **309:** "Can this be the sabbath ... ?": *Five Points Monthly Record*, May 1857. **316:** "Spirit don't talk so loud ...": Lawrence W. Levine, *Black Culture and Black Consciousness: Afro-American Folk Thought from Slavery to Freedom* (1977).

Illustrations: 268: Matthew Hale Smith, *Sunshine and Shadow in New York* (1868)—American Social History Project. **272:** Catherine E. Beecher and Harriet Beecher Stowe, *The American Woman's Home or, Principles of Domestic Science* ... (1869)—General Research Division, New York Public Library, Astor, Lenox, and Tilden Foundations. **273:** James Baillie, 1848, lithograph—New-York Historical Society. **274:** J. M'Nevin, *Harper's Weekly*, June 11, 1859—General Research Division, New York Public Library, Astor, Lenox, and Tilden Foundations. **277:** *Fisher's Comic Almanac* (1853)—Historical Society of Pennsylvania. **279:** C. G. Childs, Philadelphia House of Refuge—Print Collection, Miriam and Ira Wallach Division of Art, Prints, and Photographs, New York Public Library, Astor, Lenox, and Tilden Foundations. **282:** *New York Illustrated News*, February 11, 1860—General Research Division, New York Public Library, Astor, Lenox, and Tilden Foundations. **287:** Kate E. R. Pickard, *The Kidnapped and the Ransomed, Being the Personal Recollection of Peter Still and His Wife "Vina," after Forty Years of Slavery* (1856)—General Research Division, New York Public Library, Astor, Lenox, and Tilden Foundations. **288:** *Crockett Almanac* (1841)—Prints and Photographs Division, Library of Congress. **289:** *Harper's Weekly*, April 6, 1867—American Social History Project. **291:** Nicolino Calyo, c. 1847, watercolor on paper, 10⅞/16 × 14⅞ inches—New-York Historical Society. **292:** *The Old Soldier* (1852)—American Antiquarian Society. **293:** *Frank Leslie's Illustrated Newspaper*, January 27, 1867—General Research Division, New York Public Library, Astor, Lenox, and Tilden Foundations. **297:** A. H. Wheeler, 1893—Prints and Photographs Division, Library of Congress. **298:** *Frank Leslie's Illustrated Newspaper*, February 13, 1858—General Research Division, New York Public Library, Astor, Lenox, and Tilden Foundations. **299:** John Antrobus, 1860, oil on canvas, 53 × 81½ inches—Historic New Orleans Collection. **302:** Jeremiah Paul, n.d., oil on board, 19 × 28 inches—Spanierman Gallery, New York. **304:** *Harper's Weekly*, November 13, 1858—American Social History Project. **305:** *Harper's Weekly*, October 15, 1859—American Social History Project. **308:** *Fisher's Comic Almanac* (1853)—Historical Society of Pennsylvania.

Chapter 8: The Fight for Free Labor in the North

Documents: 329: "... This monopoly should be broken up": *Working Men's Advocate*, March 6, 1830. **334:** "The rich against the poor!": *New York Courier and Enquirer*, June 8, 1836. **337:** "... The feeble threats of Tories in disguise": *The Man*, February 22, 1834. **341:** "... New-fangled notions of American liberty": *Boston Courier*, October 29, 1829. **344:** "... They were desperate men and would have work or food": *Buffalo Commercial Advertiser*, August 27, 1842. **348:** "... Who shall practice virtue under circumstances like these?": Philadelphia *Free Enquirer*, May 6, 1829. **351:** "... Crushing the producers of wealth to the very dust": *The Awl*, Jan-

uary 18, 1845. **354–55:** "A billion of acres of unsold lands": Augustine Duganne, *Poetical Works* (1855). **357:** "... A right to life": *New York Tribune*, May 14 and July 31, 1850. **359 (top):** "Look at the hordes of Dutch and Irish thieves and vagabonds ...": New York *Daily Plebian*, April 20, 1844. **359 (bottom):** "... We are strong and getting stronger": *Champion of American Labor*, April 17, 1847. **362:** "An empty pocket's the worst of crimes!": *The Awl*, 1844.

Illustrations: 318: (Cunnington) J. Wayne Laurens, *The Crisis, or the Enemies of America Unmasked* (Philadelphia, 1855)—American Social History Project. **322:** Joseph Yeager (after John Lewis Krimmel), 1821, aquatint and etching with watercolor, 14⅜ inches × 23¾ inches—Gift of the Estate of Charles M. B. Cadwalader, Philadelphia Museum of Art. **326:** George Caleb Bingham, 1854–55, oil on canvas, 46 × 65 inches—Boatmen's National Bank of St. Louis. **328:** Kilroe Collection, Butler Library, Columbia University. **330:** David Claypoole Johnston, 1862, lithograph, 10⅞ × 16 inches—American Antiquarian Society. **332:** *The Union*, June 14, 1836—Rare Books and Manuscripts Division, New York Public Library, Astor, Lenox, and Tilden Foundations. **333:** Anonymous, 1833, lithograph—Library Company of Philadelphia. **336:** *Lowell Offering*, December 1845—Museum of American Textile History, North Andover, Mass. **338:** James Geldard, *Hand-book on Cotton Manufacture* ... (New York, 1867)—Rare Books and Manuscripts Division, New York Public Library, Astor, Lenox, and Tilden Foundations. **339:** Museum of American Textile History, North Andover, Mass. **343:** Henry R. Robinson (after a drawing by Edward W. Clay), 1837, lithograph, 19 × 12 inches—J. Clarence Davies Collection, Museum of the City of New York. **345:** (S. H. Gimber) Michael Walsh, *Sketches of the Speeches and Writings of Mike Walsh ... Compiled by a Committee of the Spartan Association* (1843)—New-York Historical Society. **346:** Edward Van Every, *Sins of America, as "Exposed" by the Police Gazette* (1931). **347:** Robert Owen and Robert Dale Owen, *The Crisis, or the Change from Error and Misery, to Truth and Happiness* (1833)—Rare Books and Manuscripts Division, New York Public Library, Astor, Lenox, and Tilden Foundations. **350:** Charles-Alexandre Lesueur, April 19, 1828, pencil drawing—No. 43122, Musée d'Histoire Naturelle du Havre. **352:** Prints and Photographs Division, Library of Congress. **356:** Thwaites, *Harper's Weekly*, October 10, 1857—American Social History Project. **358:** Maryland Historical Society. **361:** *Frank Leslie's Illustrated Newspaper*, March 17, 1860—New-York Historical Society.

Chapter 9: The Struggle Over Slave Labor

Documents: 374: "... So cheapened the white man's labor": Athens (Georgia) *Southern Banner*, January 13, 1838. **379:** "Let no man of us budge one step ...": Daniel Walker, *Walker's Appeal* (1829). **380:** "Guarded from want, from beggary secure ...": Eric McKitrick, ed., *Slavery Defended: The Views of the Old South* (1963). **396:** "What a disgrace to a city calling itself free ...": Harriet Brent Jacobs, *Incidents in the Life of a Slave Girl* (1861). **409:** "You have been brave enough to reach out your hands ...": Carter G. Woodson, ed., *The Mind of the Negro as Reflected in Letters Written During the Crisis, 1800–1860* (1926).

Illustrations: 364: Richard Brough, *Commercial Register*, June 16, 1832—Prints and Photographs Division, Library of Congress. **369:** John W. Barber, *A History of the Amistad Captives* (1840)—Prints and Photographs Division, Library of Congress. **370:** New Haven Colony Historical Society. **378:** George Bourne, *Pictures of Slavery in the United States of America* (1834)—Prints and Photographs Division, Library of Congress. **381:** From the private collections of Larry E. Tise, Harrisburg, Pennsylvania. **382:** V. Blada (A. J. Volck), *Sketches from the Civil War in North America, 1861, '62, '63* (1863)—Print Collection, Miriam and Ira Wallach Division of Art, Prints, and Photographs, New York Public Library, Astor, Lenox, and Tilden Foundations. **389:** *Punch* (1847)—General Research Division, New York Public Library, Astor, Lenox, and Tilden Foundations. **392:** National Museum of American History, Smithsonian Institution. **394:** Boston Public Library. **395:** William Still, *The Underground Rail Road* (1872)—American Social History Project. **397:** Abraham Chapman, comp., *Steal Away: Stories of the Runaway Slaves* (1971). **398:** *Harper's Weekly*, May 18, 1867—American Social History Project. **399:** William Still, *The Underground Rail Road* (1872)—General Research Division, New York Public Library, Astor, Lenox, and Tilden Foundations. **400, 401:** Kansas State Historical Society. **403:** J. W. Orr, *Frank Leslie's Illustrated Newspaper*, May 3, 1856—General Research Division, New York Public Library, Astor, Lenox, and Tilden Foundations. **408:** Porte Crayon, *Harper's Weekly*, November 12, 1859—American Social History Project. **410:** Currier & Ives, 1860, lithograph, 12 × 11⅞ inches—Museum of the City of New York.

Part Three: War, Reconstruction, and Labor, 1860–1877

412: Matthew Dripps, *Topographical Map of the United States and Territories, based on official surveys of the United States Government* . . . (1876), 37 × 21 inches—Map Division, New York Public Library, Astor, Lenox, and Tilden Foundations.

Chapter 10: The Civil War

Documents: 426: ". . . Will you allow us the poor priverlige of fighting": Herbert Aptheker, *A Documentary History of the Negro People in the United States*, Vol. 1 (1951). **429:** ". . . To deprive their masters of their services": Ira Berlin et al., eds., *Freedom: A Documentary History of Emancipation, 1861–1867, Series 1, Volume 1: The Destruction of Slavery* (1985). **432:** ". . . The new life of freedom": George Henry Gordon, *A War Diary of Events in the War of the Great Rebellion, 1863–1865* (1882). **439:** "I have never conceived of such trials . . .": (a) Bell I. Wiley, *The Life of Johnny Reb: The Common Soldier of the Confederacy* (1943); (b) Bell I. Wiley, *The Life of Billy Yank: The Common Soldier of the Union* (1952). **443:** ". . . And then I must work for myself": New York *Sun*, November 17, 1863. **444:** ". . . If wages are not permitted to keep pace": *Fincher's Trades Review*, July 1863. **451:** Slaves flee to freedom: Joan Jensen, ed., *With These Hands: Women Working the Land* (1981). **454:** ". . . I hope to fall with my face to the foe": Carter G. Woodson, ed., *The Mind of the Negro as Reflected in Letters Written during the Crisis, 1800–1860* (1926). **456:** ". . . And the Rebs burnt the last bale": J. T. Trowbridge, *The South: A Tour of Its Battlefields and Ruined Cities* (1866). **459:** ". . . We were forced to do without": "Dale County and Its People During the Civil War: Reminiscences of Mary Love Edwards Fleming," *Alabama Historical Quarterly*, 19 (1957). **462–63:** "A jubilee of freedom": New York *Tribune*, April 4, 1865.

Illustrations: 416: Lilly Library, Indiana University. **421:** R. H. Howell (after Henry Cleenewercke), 1861, lithograph with tintstone, 13 × 14 inches—Boston Athenaeum. **423:** Wayne David Geist. **425:** James Gibson—United States Army Military History Institute. **427:** *Vanity Fair*, July 12, 1862—General Research Division, New York Public Library, Astor, Lenox, and Tilden Foundations. **430:** *Illustrated London News*, August 17, 1861—American Social History Project. **436:** *Harper's Weekly*, June 15, 1861—American Social History Project. **437:** *Frank Leslie's Illustrated*

Newspaper, October 18, 1862—General Research Division, New York Public Library, Astor, Lenox, and Tilden Foundations. **438:** (T. H. O'Sullivan) Alexander Gardner, *Gardner's Photographic Sketch Book of the War*, Vol. 1 (1866)—Prints and Photographs Division, Library of Congress. **441:** Winslow Homer, *Harper's Weekly*, July 20, 1861—American Social History Project. **445:** *Vanity Fair*, August 2, 1862—General Research Division, New York Public Library, Astor, Lenox, and Tilden Foundations. **446:** V. Blada (A. J. Volck), *Sketches from the Civil War in North America, 1861, '62, '63* (1863)—Print Collection, Miriam and Ira Wallach Division of Art, Prints, and Photographs, New York Public Library, Astor, Lenox, and Tilden Foundations. **447:** *Illustrated London News*, August 8, 1863—American Social History Project. **448–49:** Freedmen and Southern Society Project, University of Maryland; *Harper's Weekly*, July 2, 1864—American Social History Project. **452:** F. H. Schell, *Frank Leslie's Illustrated Newspaper*, June 27, 1863—American Social History Project. **453:** Library Company of Philadelphia. **457:** *Frank Leslie's Illustrated Newspaper*, May 23, 1863—General Research Division, New York Public Library, Astor, Lenox, and Tilden Foundations. **461:** *Harper's Weekly*, March 18, 1865—American Social History Project.

Chapter 11: Emancipation and Reconstruction

Documents: 469: ". . . It's slavery all over again": Herbert G. Gutman Archive, American Social History Project. **477:** "We are Americans by birth . . .": Philip S. Foner and George E. Walker, eds., *Proceedings of the Black State Conventions, 1840–1865* (1979). **484:** ". . . We are willing to take our muskets": Ira Berlin, Joseph P. Reidy, and Leslie S. Rowland, eds., *Freedom: A Documentary History of Emancipation, 1861–1867, Series II: The Black Military Experience* (1982). **489:** "No matter what his race or color . . . an equal right to justice": *Congressional Globe*, 39th Cong., 2nd Sess. (1867). **506:** "Kill him, god damn him . . .": House of Representatives Report 22, 42nd Cong., 2nd Sess. (1871). **509:** ". . . The blood and treasure of the people spent in vain": Senate Miscellaneous Document 107, 43rd Cong., 2nd Sess. (1876). **512:** ". . . Land where we can have a home": Senate Report 693, 46th Cong., 2nd Sess. (1880).

Illustrations: 464: *Harper's Weekly*, October 28, 1876—General Research Division, New York Public Library, Astor, Lenox, and Tilden Foundations. **471:** Chicago Historical Society. **472:** H. P. Moore, 1862—New-York Historical Society. **473:** *Harper's Weekly*, June 30, 1866—General Research Division, New York Public Library, Astor, Lenox, and Tilden Foundations. **475:** American Tract Society, *The Freedman's Second Reader* (1865)—AMS Press, New York (used with permission). **479:** (J. Wells Champney) Edward King, *The Great South* . . . (1875)—American Social History Project. **482:** Prints and Photographs Division, Library of Congress. **486:** Thomas Nast, 1867, oil on canvas, 7 feet 10¾ inches × 11 feet 6½ inches—Prints and Photographs Division, Library of Congress. **488:** *Frank Leslie's Illustrated Newspaper*, January 19, 1867—General Research Division, New York Public Library, Astor, Lenox, and Tilden Foundations. **491:** W. L. Sheppard, *Harper's Weekly*, July 25, 1868—American Social History Project. **494:** Alabama Department of Archives and History. **496:** Prints and Photographs Division, Library of Congress. **498:** *Harper's Weekly*, March 14, 1874—American Social History Project; New York *Daily Graphic*, March 11, 1874—American Social History Project. **503:** Herb Peck, Jr., Collection. **505:** (L. D. Williams) Thomas Dixon, Jr., *The Traitor: A Story of the Fall of the Invisible Empire* (1907)—American Social History Project. **508:** Tuscaloosa *Independent Monitor*, September 1, 1868—Alabama Department of Archives and History. **510:** *Harper's Weekly*, September 26, 1874—American Social History Project. **513:** Kansas State Historical Society.

Chapter 12: Industrial Labor After the War

Documents: 520: "This was to be our land forever . . .": Joan Jensen, ed., *With These Hands: Women Working the Land* (1981). **528:** "Pestilence in the Cigar": New York *Sun*, September 26, 1874. **533:** "Eight Hours and No Surrender!": Boston *Daily Evening Voice*, May 1, 1867. **534:** "Money Monopolies": James C. Sylvis, *The Life, Speeches, Labors, and Essays of William H. Sylvis* (1872). **537:** ". . . This demon of private riches": *Labor Standard*, January 6, 1877. **543:** ". . . As much right here as you or I": *Detroit Socialist*, May 4, 1878. **544:** "How much better to have these girls independent . . .": Herbert G. Gutman Archive, American Social History Project. **546:** ". . . A 'tramp and vagabond'": *National Labor Tribune*, September 7, 1875. **556:** ". . . The grand army of Starvation": Chicago *Inter-Ocean*, July 25, 1877.

Illustrations: 514: *Frank Leslie's Illustrated Newspaper*, August 4, 1877—American Social History Project. **517:** Thomas Worth, *Harper's Weekly*, September 20, 1873—American Social History Project. **521:** Richard Benecke, *Kansas & Pacific Railroad Album*—DeGolyer Library, Southern Methodist University. **522:** Frank Bellew, New York *Daily Graphic*, April 14, 1874—American Social History Project. **524:** H. F. Farny, 1873, chromolithograph, 26¼ × 37½ inches—Prints and Photographs Division, Library of Congress. **526:** American Association of Railroads. **529:** Special Collections Division, University of Washington Libraries. **532:** *Frank Leslie's Illustrated Newspaper*, September 5, 1874—American Social History Project. **536:** Matt Morgan, *Frank Leslie's Illustrated Newspaper*, June 29, 1872—American Social History Project. **542:** *San Francisco Illustrated Wasp*, December 8, 1877—California Section, California State Library. **545:** Joseph Keppler, *Die Vehme*, April 2, 1870—General Research Division, New York Public Library, Astor, Lenox, and Tilden Foundations. **546:** Frank Bellew, New York *Daily Graphic*, September 29, 1873—American Social History Project. **547:** Matt Morgan, *Frank Leslie's Illustrated Newspaper*, January 31, 1874—American Social History Project. **548:** *Frank Leslie's Illustrated Newspaper*, July 21, 1877—American Social History Project. **549:** *Frank Leslie's Illustrated Newspaper*, April 7, 1877—American Social History Project. **551:** Allan Pinkerton, *The Mollie Maguires and the Detectives* (1877)—American Social History Project. **555:** S. V. Albee, "The Railroad War"—Paul Dickson Collection. **557:** Chicago Historical Society. **558:** Ph. G. Cusachs, New York *Daily Graphic*, June 14, 1878—American Social History Project.

CONTRIBUTORS

STEPHEN BRIER cofounded the American Social History Project and has been its director since 1981. He also served as the producer of the ASHP's *Who Built America?* video series. Brier has written a number of articles on nineteenth-century coalminers.

JOSHUA BROWN, who selected the illustrations and wrote the captions, has been the ASHP's art director since 1981. He also served in that capacity and as scriptwriter for the Project's video series. Brown's artwork and articles on social and cultural history have appeared in a number of scholarly and popular journals.

DAVID BRUNDAGE, an assistant professor of community studies at the University of California, Santa Cruz, was an ASHP staff writer from 1983 through 1985. He has written on working-class life and culture in nineteenth-century Denver.

EDWARD COUNTRYMAN, contributing author, is a professor of comparative American studies at the University of Warwick, England, and author of numerous books and articles on the revolutionary era, including *The American Revolution* (1985).

DOROTHY FENNELL, currently the director of the Program in Industrial and Labor Relations, Cornell University Extension, was an ASHP staff writer from 1983 through 1985. She has written on Pennsylvania's post-Revolution Whiskey Rebellion.

ERIC FONER, consulting editor, is DeWitt Clinton Professor of History at Columbia University and is the author of books on colonial and nineteenth-century America, including *Reconstruction: America's Unfinished Revolution* (1988).

HERBERT G. GUTMAN was Distinguished Professor of History at the Graduate Center of the City University of New York. He cofounded the ASHP and supervised its work until his death in 1985. His books include *Work, Culture, and Society in Industrializing America* (1976), *The Black Family in Slavery and Freedom* (1976), and *Power and Culture: Essays on the American Working Class* (1987).

BRUCE LEVINE, an assistant professor of history at the University of Cincinnati, was the ASHP's director of research and writing from 1981 through 1986. He has written extensively on the role of German-American radicals in the nineteenth-century labor movement.

MARCUS REDIKER, contributing author, is an associate professor of history at Georgetown University and is the author of *Between the Devil and the Deep Blue Sea: Merchant Seamen, Pirates, and the Anglo-American Maritime World, 1700–1750* (1987).

ALFRED YOUNG, consulting editor, is professor of history at Northern Illinois University and is the author of numerous articles and collections on the revolutionary era, including "George Robert Twelves Hewes: A Boston Shoemaker and the Memory of the American Revolution" (1981).

INDEX

Page numbers in *italics* refer to illustrations on sidebar documents.

Abilene, Kans., cattle industry in, 519
abolitionism, abolitionists, 377–411
  African-Americans as, 164–65
  Evangelicalists and, 312, 314–15,
    374
  feminists and, 277, 286, 487–88
  labor movement and, 326, 384,
    390–91, 393, 422–23
  land reformists and, 354, 391
  in revolutionary era, 164
  utopian communities and, 348, *350*
  violence and, 384, *400*, 401
Adams, Abigail, 129, 144
Adams, Henry, 512
Adams, John, 128, 149, 157, 222
  American Revolution and, 133, 139,
    149
  political beliefs, 159–60, 176
  women and, 144
Adams, John Quincy, 183, *369*
Adams, Louisa, 288
Adams, Samuel, 116, 117, 139–40,
  157, 172
Address of the Colored State
  Convention to the People of the
  State of South Carolina, 477
advertising, *227*
Africa:
  diversity of, 19
  rise of slavery in, 18–19
Africa, West, 19–27
  early map of, *19*
  kingdoms of, 21
  precolonial societies of, 8, 19–22
  slave trade and, 19–27
  trade goods of, 22–23
  women in 20, 21
African-American culture, 65–70,
  299–301, 512
  American Revolution and, 165
  beginnings, 27, 65–68
  festivals, 106–7

  kinship ties, 68, 287
  language, 67
  names in, 70, 473
  in northern colonies, 106–7
African-Americans:
  American Revolution and, *155*, 165
  Civil War and, 418, 424, 426–35,
    439, 448–55, 460–61, 462–63
  conventions, 476
  cotton and, 468
  elected officials, 492–93, 498–99
  families, 183, 184, 198–99, 207–8,
    287–89, 396, 433, 466, 467, 469,
    474
  Ku Klux Klan violence against,
    503–6
  labor movement and, 538, 540–41,
    551, 560
  land ownership, 466, 467, 478–81
    487, 489–90, 511
  lynchings, 420, 446, *447*
  Reconstruction and, 466–513
  religion, 198, *205*, 287, 311–17, 368,
    369, 466, 475–76
  Republican Party and, 492–93
  see also free blacks; slavery; slaves
African Methodist Episcopal Church,
  314, 315, 476
African Union Society, 165
Age of Revolution, 177
agriculture:
  American Indian, 10–11, 13
  in Europe, 16
  mechanization of, 442
  in northern colonies, 80, *94*, 96–97,
    120
  in northern states, 231–38, 442, 443
  in pre-colonial Africa, 21
  in southern colonies, 8, 18, 37, 54,
    60–65, 71, 135, 165
  in southern states, 184–87, 189–95,
    201–19, 456

  in West, 518
  see also specific crops
Alabama:
  Civil War and, 460
  ex-slaves of, 476–77, 502
  railroads, 214
  secession, 419
  slavery, 184, 204
Alamance, Battle of, 76
Alamo, 387
Albany *Advocate,* 325
Albee, S. V., *555*
alcohol, 290, 296–97, 306
  American Indians and, 86, 88, 229,
    230
  immigrants and, 266, *304, 305*
  see also saloons
Allegheny County, Pa., 525
Allen, Ethan, 123, 159, 310
Allgemeine Arbeiterbund, 356–57
Allson, Robert, 199
almshouses, *107*
Almy, Brown, and Slater, 251
Alston, J. T., 426
Alston, James, 493, 504
American Antislavery Society, 383
American Emigrant Company, 442
American Indians, *see* Indians,
  American
American Missionary Association, 470
American Museum, 292
American Party, *see* Know-Nothing
  Party
American Revolution, 129–77, 437
  class division in, 143–45, 148–51,
    158–63, 166–69
  coalitions in, 128, 136, 146, 148,
    156–57, 160, 175
  economic problems after, 160–63,
    171, 185
  fighting in, 151–56, *152, 153*
  leaders of, 128–29

American Revolution (*continued*)
  legacy of, 128–29, 165, 175–77, 375, 466, 531, 532
  loyalists and, 150–51, 166
  pamphleteers of, 96, 136, 144
  prelude to, 129–35, 136–45, 146–51
  rise of new government from, 156–65
  state constitutions after, 159–63
  women and, 144–45, 154, 160–61, 170, 174–75
American Woman's Home (Beecher and Stowe), 272
Ames, Adelbert, 495, 509
Amish people, 83
Amistad Rebellion, 369, 370
Amoskeag Manufacturing Company, 220
Andros, Edmund, 88
Anglican Church (Church of England), 29, 32, 70, 312
Anneke, Fritz, 311
Anthony, Susan B., 277, 487–88, 544
Antietam, Md., battle of, 434, 435, 437, 440
Appomattox, Va., 463
Arkansas:
  agriculture, 190, 195
  Reconstruction, 497
  secession, 426
  settling, 190, 195
  slavery, 184, 477–78
Arminianism, 301
Arminius, Jacobus, 301
armories, 441, 443
art:
  itinerant portraiture, 238
  in northern colonies, 99
  in pre-colonial Africa, 21
Arthur, T. S., 236
Articles of Confederation, 168, 169
artisans, 242–48, 321–35
  American Revolution and, 128, 136, 141–45, 151–52
  decline of, 274–75, 338
  families of, 271
  from Germany, 262, 356, 357–58, 405, 407, 423, 528
  industrial revolution and, 243–48
  journeyman-master relationship, 242–48, 305, 321–25
  labor politics of, 321–35
  occupations, 243
  in shipping industry, 224–25
  in village communities, 233
Ashanti people, 25
Associationism, 349–50
Association of Working People of New Castle County, 372–73

Astor Street Opera House riot, 296
Athens, Ga., 213
Atkinson, Edward, 467, 468, 501
Atlanta, Ga., Civil War and, 450, 456, 458, 460
Attucks, Crispus, 141
Austin, Stephen, 387
Aztecs, 8
  gold and, 10, 11, 15
  social structure of, 10

Bacon, Nathaniel, 57–58
Bacon, Sir Francis, 35, 36
Bacon's Rebellion, 54, 57–58, 60, 77
Bagley, Sarah, 307
Baird, Rev. Robert, 311
Ball, Charles, 211
Ballou, Adin, 348
Baltimore, George Calvert, Lord, 46, 84
Baltimore, Md., 358
  free blacks in, 204, 409
  religion in, 315
  slaves in, 216, 217
  theater in, 296
Baltimore and Ohio Railroad, 228, 341, 554
Bank of the United States, 330–31
banks, 329
  failures, 256, 422
  farmers and, 237
  national system, 441–42
  in South, 214
Banks, Nathaniel, 470, 472, 479
Baptist Church, 85, 121, 301, 312, 316, 374
Barbot, Jean, 26
Barlow, Alice, 232
Barlowe, Arthur, 40
Barnes, Albert, 301, 303, 306
Barnum, P. T., 292
Barrow, Bennett, 199–200
Beecher, Catherine E., 272
Belcher, Andrew, 108–9
Belknap, Ruth, 112
Bell, Alexander Graham, 515
Beloved (Morrison), 398
Benin, 20, 21, 22, 23
Berkeley, John, Lord, 82
Berkeley, William, 53, 56–58
Bibb, Henry, 393
Bible, 313, 369
"Billion of Acres of Unsold Lands" (Duganne), 354–55
Bill of Rights, U.S., 173–75
Bingham, George Caleb, 326
Birney, James G., 392
Bishop, T. B., 449

Black Codes, 483–84, 485, 497, 499, 501, 511, 512
Black Hills of Dakota, 518, 520
Black Hoof, 229
blacks, *see* African-Americans; free blacks; slaves
Blackstone Valley, 251
Blair, Rev. James, 66
Blair family, 406
Bloomer, Amelia Jenks, 277
Bloomers, 277
"Bold Stroke for Freedom," 399
Booth, Junius Brutus, 295
Boston, John, 433
Boston, Mass., 80, 81, 106, 109, 525
  abolitionists of, 377–78, 435
  economy of, 104, 118, 139, 142
  growth of, 97–98
  insurrection in, 162–63
  labor movements in, 325, 351, 355, 356
  North End of, 242
  politics of, 116, 137
  poverty in, 242, 256
Boston Associates, 252, 254
Boston Committee of Internal Health, 260
Boston *Courier*, 341
Boston *Daily Evening Voice*, 533
Boston Foreign Emigrant Aid Society, 442
Boston *Gazette*, 137, 141
Boston Manufacturing Company, 254, 335
Boston Massacre, 133, 141–42, 142, 143
Boston Mechanics' and Laborers' Association, 351
Boston Tea Party, 134, 137, 138, 139
Boston Weekly News-Letter, 69
Bovay, Alvan, 353, 405
bow and arrow, 10, 230
Bowdoin, James, 163
Bowers, James L., 217
Bowery Theater, 293, 295, 296
boxing, 298
Boyd, W. T., 426
Braddock, Edward, 118
Bradstreet, Anne, 111
Brant, Joseph, 155
Brazil, 25
  sugar plantations of, 8, 18
bread, 108
Breckinridge, John Cabell, 410
Br'er Rabbit, 300
bridges, 226, 227
British East India Company, 133, 135
Broadway Theater, 293
Brook Farm, 348

Brooks Brothers, 249–50
Brown, Hagar, 199
Brown, Jeremiah, 403
Brown, John, 401–3, *408*, 411
    Harpers Ferry raid, 407–9, 419, 420
Brown, Joseph E., 455
Brown family (Rhode Island), 251
Brownson, Orestes, 347–48
Buchanan, James, 402, 404, 406
buffalo, 520, *521*
Buffalo, N.Y., 238, 344
Bull Run, Va., battle of, 429–30, *431*
Bureau of Freedmen, Refugees, and
    Abandoned Lands, 478–79, *482*,
    485, 487, 497
Burke, Emily, 207, 213
Burn, Mary Hay, 129
butchers, *322*
Bute, John Stuart, Lord, 137–38
Butler, Benjamin F., 428, 429, 430, 469,
    470
Byrd, William, II, 164
Byzantium, 17

cabinetmakers, 323, 357–58
Cabot, John, 81
cacao, 18
Caldwell, James, 141
Calhoun, John C., 376, 379, 380
California, 529
    annexation, 389
    gold in, 238, 390, 393
    race laws, 450
    statehood, 393–94
Calvin, John, 301
Calvinism, 121
Cambria ironworks, 525
Cameron, A. C., 552
Cameron, Simon, 426, 431
Campbell, Tunis, 498–99
Canada:
    immigration from, 257, 263, 540
    as slave refuge, 367
canals, 226, 227–28, 240–41, 340–41,
    456, 516–17
Cane Ridge, Ky., 303
Cannon, James, 158
Career of Puffer Hopkins, 246
Carey, Mathew, 249
Caribbean, *see* West Indies
Carolina, 60–63
    division of, 63
    exports, 71
    slavery, 60–62
    see also North Carolina; South
        Carolina
carpenters, 324, 332, 342
Carpenters' Company, 109
carpetbaggers, 494–95

Carr, Patrick, 141
Carter, John, *193*
Carteret, Sir George, 82
Cass, Lewis, 396
Catholic Church, 308–10, 405, 552
    in England, 29, 35, 104
    growth of, 308, 309–10
    in Ireland, 258, 309, 310
    Protestant views of, *265*, 266, 308–9
Catlin, George, *189*
cattle industry, 54, 56, 62, 236, 519,
    523
Census, U.S., 185, 213, 249
Centennial Exposition, 515
Central Pacific Railroad, 516, 528–30,
    542–43
Chancellorsville, Va., battle of, 435
Chandler, Zachariah, 404
Chaplin, John, 467
Chappel, Alonzo, *143*
Charles I, king of England, 33, 54, 81,
    84, 85, 140
Charles II, king of England, 55, 56, 58,
    82
Charleston, S.C., 62, 369, 383, *457*,
    461, 462–63, 491
Charleston *Courier*, 388
Charleston *Mercury*, 407
Charleston *Standard*, 217–18
Chartists, 263
Chase, Salmon P., 397, 398
Chatham Theater, 296
Chattanooga, Tenn., battle of, 449
Cherokee Indians, 175, 187, 188, 189
Chesapeake and Ohio Canal, 341
Chicago, Ill., 238
    abolitionism and, 423
    1873 depression and, 549
    Great Uprising and, 557
    growth, 238, 527
    iron-industry strike in, 532–34
Chicago, Wilmington, and Vermillion
    Coal Company, 525
Chicago *Daily Tribune*, 263
Chicago *Press and Tribune*, 366
Chickasaw Indians, 187, 188, 189
Child, Lydia Maria, 277, 544
childbirth, 110–11, *112*
children:
    change in raising of, 275–76
    as slaves, 207, 288, 376, 483
    in South, 285
    urban vagrancy, 283
    work, 242, 246, 251, 252
Children's Aid Society, 283, 306
China:
    immigrants from, 390, 528–30, 536,
        538, 541–43, 557, 560
    trade with, 225, 226

Choctaw Indians, 187, 188, 189
Church of England (Anglican Church),
    29, 33, 70, 312
cigarmakers, 528, *536*, 537
Cincinnati, Ohio, 357, 385, 450
Cincinnati *Daily Unionist*, 351
Cinque, Joseph, *370*
Circuit Court Act (1769), 75
circuses, 292
cities:
    gangs in, *247*
    growth, 238, 239, 527
    immigration and, 264–65, 527
    neighborhoods as class divisions of,
        298
    occupations in, 240
    poverty, 241, 256
    services, 527
    slaves in, 83, 106, 109, 204, 213, 214,
        215–16
    see also specific cities
Civil Rights Bill (1866), 485–87
Civil War, 417–63, 523, 559
    advantages of North in, 426, 437,
        440
    advantages of South in, 429
    African-Americans and, 418, 424,
        426–35, 439, 448–55, 460–61,
        462–63
    battles, 429–30, *431*, 432, 434, 435,
        436, 437, 438, 439, 440, 447–49,
        460, 462–63
    beginnings, 356, 409–11, 424
    casualties, 418, 429, 431, 434, 435,
        438, 447–48, 453, 463
    desertions, 439–40, 460
    draft, 445–47, 459
    economy and, 440–45, 458–59
    end, 462–63
    food riots, 456–57
    goals of North and South, 424, 435
    legacy, 418, 440, 447, 455, 463
    lives of soldiers in, 435–40
    turning point, 447–49
    weapons, 436, 437
Clay, Cassius, 407
Clay, Henry, 376, 377
Cleveland, Ohio, 351, 426, 450, 524,
    527
clothing industry, 249–51, 384, 442,
    443, 444, 458, 525–26
Cluer, John, 353
coal industry, 215, 237, 441, 444, 525
    labor movement and, 534–35,
        549–50
cockfighting, 290, 298
Cogbill, Richard, 201
Cohoon, John Cowper, Jr., 183, 184,
    196, 197, 199, 287

Colby, Abram, 504
Cold Spring, N.Y., 444
Colorado, 518
Colored National Labor Union, 541
Colored Orphan Asylum, 447
Columbus, Christopher, 7, 8, 9, 14, 17
Columbus, Miss., 458
commerce, expansion of, 223, 226, 228
Commerford, John, 353, 359, 388, 405
Committees of Correspondence, 150
Commons, John, 151
Common Sense (Paine), 136–37, 144, 158–59, 160, 177
communications, 228
Compromise of 1850, 393–403
Comstock Lode, 519
Confederate Army, 456, 460, 462
Confederate Congress, 455, 460, 462
Confederate States of America, 417–24, 501
  antiwar movement in, 460
  compromise sought by, 422–23
  flag, *421*
  founding, 418–19
  Great Britain and, *427*, 434
  popular support, 420
  taxes, 456, 459
Congo, Kingdom of, 21, *23*
Congregationalism, 302, 304
Congress, U.S., 169, 375
  abolitionism and, 383, 393–94, 396–97, 422–23, 431, 432
  American Indians and, 188
  Ku Klux Klan and, 506
  North-South balance of, 375–76, 387
  powers, 168
  Reconstruction and, 483–90
  slave importation banned by, 186, 200, 203, 206
  tariffs set by, 441
Connecticut, 116, 120, 238
  textile industry of, 251, 254
Conscription Act (1863), 445–46
Constitution, U.S., 165, 166–75, 184, 336, 477
  Bill of Rights and, 173–75
  commerce and, 171, 174
  drafting, 166
  Fifteenth Amendment, 504–5, 511
  Fourteenth Amendment, 487–89, 490, 511
  ratification, 171–74
  slavery and, 171, 174, 175, 186
  Thirteenth Amendment, 418, 463, 482
Constitutional Convention, 148
Constitutional Unionist Party, 410
construction, growth of cities and, 523

consumer goods:
  in rural North, 235, 271–73
  urban, 239–40
Continental Association, 148, 161
Continental Congresses, 148, 153, 157, 166
contrabands, *425*, 428, 429–35, 450–51, 460–61
contract labor system, 470, 479, 530
Convention of Freedmen, 476
convicts:
  forced migration of, 50
  labor of, 356, 512
cookstoves, iron, 273, 281
Cooke, Elisha, Jr., 116, 117
cooperative agriculture, 538
cooperative enterprises, 351
cooperative factories, 538
Copley, John Singleton, 99, *100, 101, 103, 104, 113*
Copperhead Democrats, 445, *446*
corn, 90, 195, 201, 299–300, 468
Cornwallis, Charles, Lord, 154
Cortez, Hernando, 10, 156–16
Coster, Robert, 34
cotton, 184–219, *192, 195, 196, 209,* 440–41, 456, 468, 495, 501
  Civil War and, 434
  commission merchants of, 191–92
  economic effects, 185
  economics, 186, 191–96, 214, 420–21, 422
  growth of industry, 184–87, 189–95, 222
  slavery and, 183–86, 189–90, 204–205, *209*, 211–19, 375
  varieties, 186
cowboys, 519
craftsmen, *see* artisans
Crazy Horse, 520
Creek Indians, 187, 188, 189
crime:
  by city gangs, *247*
  poverty and, 242
Crimean War, 238
Crittenden, John J., 422, 425
Crocker, Charles, 529, 543
Cromwell, Oliver, 32, 33, 83–84, 85, 148
Cuba, 387
Culpepper, Lord, 53
Currency Act (1764), 130, 135
Currier and Ives, *196*
Curtis, Josiah, 242
Cushing, William, 163, 165
Custer, George A., 520

Daguerre, Louis, *297*
daguerreotypes, *297*
Dakota Territory, 518, 519
dances, 289–90
Darwin, Charles, 530
Daughters of Liberty, 144–45
Daughters of St. Crispin, 536
Davenport, James, 120, 121
Davies, David, 237
Davis, Jefferson:
  Civil War and, 424, 428, 455, 456, 462
  as Confederate president, 418, *427*
Dearborn Light Artillery, 534
debtor's prison, 329, 373
Declaration of Independence, 156–57, 165, 277, 336, 410, 477
"Declaration of the People" (Bacon), 57
Declaratory Act (1766), 132, 134, 143
DeLancey, Oliver, 118
DeLancey family, 99, 117, 148
Delany, Martin R., 469, 494
Delaware:
  Civil War and, *427*, 453
  government, 159
  slavery in, 215
Delaware, Lackawana, and Western Railroad, *225*
Delaware Indians, 12
Democratic Party, *257*, 320, 331, *345*, 354, 387
  abolitionism and, 386, 391–92, 393, 395–96, 404–5, 406, 409–10
  after Civil War, *482*, 486, 489
  Civil War and, 441, 445, *446*, 450
  immigrants and, 552
  Ku Klux Klan and, 503, 506–7
  "redemption" of South by, 500, 502, 508–9
  Republican Party compared with, 552
Denys, Nicholas, 88
depressions:
  of 1839–43, 256, 342–45, 347, 354, 546
  of 1857, 361, 421, 546
  of 1861, 421–22
  of 1873, 508, 510, 515–16, 545
Desert Land Act (1877), 518
Detroit, Mich., 527
Detroit Socialist, 543
Devyr, Thomas, 256, 353
De Witt, Alexander, 398
Dickens, Charles, 240–41
Dickinson, John, 96, 149
Diggers, 33, 34–35
"Digger's Song" (Winstanley and Coster), 34–35

diseases:
  brought to New World, 8, 13–14, 18, 37, 85, 86
  during Civil War, 438–39
  encountered in New World, 62, 80
  in Europe, 17
  poverty and, 242, *282*
divorce:
  in American Indian societies, 13
  of slaves, 287
Dixon, Thomas, *505*
dockworkers, 340, 341, 342, 372, 528, 540
Domestic Manners of the Americans (Trollope), *193*
Donne, John, 35
"Don't Tread on Me" snake, *126*, *421*
Doolittle, Amos, *152*
Dorr, Thomas, 353
Douai, Adolph, 537
Douglas, Stephen A., 228, 388, 397–98, 410
Douglass, Frederick, 207, 216, 271, 300, 301, 315, 375, 384, 393, 395, 405, 422, 513, 541
Douglass, Lewis, 454
dowries, family life and, 272–73
Doy, John, *401*
draft laws, 445–46, 455–56, 459
Drake, Edwin, 524
Drake, May, 198
Dred Scott decision, 407, 409, 485
"Drunkard, or the Fallen Saved," 295
Duffie, George, 380
Duganne, Augustine, 354–55
"Dumping Ground at the Foot of Beach Street," *241*
Dunmore, John Murray, Lord, 164
Dunny, Patrick, 261
Dwight, Timothy, 232

Eastern Abenaki Indians, 14
Edison, Thomas A., 515
education, 329, 373
  in Civil War South, 429
  ex-slaves and, 470, *471*, 475, 490, 492, 497
Edwards, Jonathan, 120–21
Edwards, Ogden, 334–35
effigies, hanging and burning of, 137, 138, 335
electioneering, *491*
elections:
  of 1844, 392
  of 1848, 393, 396, 406
  of 1856, 406
  of 1860, 409–10, 417, 418–19
  of 1865, 481–83

of 1866, *482*, 488–89
of 1867, 492–93, 501
of 1868, 502
of 1872, 506, 507
of 1874, 510
of 1876, 510–11, 553
emancipation, 418, 473–81
  education and, 475, 490, 492, 497
  land reform and, 466, 467, 478–81
  personal expressions of, 473–74
  violence toward ex-slaves after, 477–78, 479, *486*, 489
  women and, 477
  see also Reconstruction
Emancipation Proclamation, 418, 434–35, 452, 453, 470, 479–80
Emerson, Ralph Waldo, 241
Enfield rifles, 436
England, *see* Great Britain
Epps, Master (slaveowner), 211–12
Equiano, Olaudah, 22, 67
Erie Canal, *226*, 227–28, 236, 239, 249
Erie Railroad, 228, 554
ethnic relations:
  of working class, 358
  see also immigrants, nativist attitude toward
Europe:
  plague in, 17
  political and economic crises, 16–17, 37, 262–65
  voyages of discovery from, 17
Evangelicalism, 76–77, 165, 270, 293, 301–8
  doctrines, 301–2, 304–6, 309
  growth, 301–2
  planters and, 311–12, 314–15
  politics of, 306–8
  slavery and, 311–17, 368, 369
Evans, George Henry, 311, 332, 352, 354, 384, 305–86, 388, 390–91, 405
Everett, Edward, 265

factories:
  in North, 238, 240, 242, 355, 422, 440, 443
  in South, 213, 458
Fale and Jenks spinning frame, *338*
families, 270–89
  of artisans, 271
  of ex-slaves, 466, 467, 469, 474
  farm, 233, 252, 271, 278–79, 284–85, 443
  middle-class, 271–77
  slave, 183, 184, 198–99, 207–8, 287–89, 396, 433
  in South, 284–89
  working-class, 277–84

famine:
  in China, 529
  in Europe, 17
  in Ireland, 238, 255, 258–59, *262*, 310
farmers:
  Civil War and, 425, 443
  communities of, 233
  economics and, 234–38
  families of, 233, 252, 271, 278–79, 284–85, 443
  immigrant, 262, 263, 264
  independence of, 232–33, 234–35
  migration, 231
  northern, 80, 94, 96–97, 120, 146, 148, 157, 175, 202, 205, 223, 224, 231–38
  politics and, 552
  Reconstruction and, 466, 495–96
  southern, 193, 195, 201, 231
  tenant, 204, 352
farm implements, 215, 442
Fawkes, Guy, 105
Federalist papers, 168
Federalist Party, 320, 375
Ferral, John, 338, 353, 396
Fessenden, William Pitt, 484
feudalism:
  in colonies, 82, 84
  decline of, 8–9, 16–17, 27–35
Field Order Number 15, 461, 478, 480
Fifteenth Amendment, 504–5, 511
Fillmore, Millard, 406
Finch, John, 332
Fincher's Trades Review, 444, 540
Finney, Charles Grandison, 301, 302, 304
fishing industry, 14, 81, 99
Fisk, Jim, 523
Fitzhugh, George, 197, 198, 379, 380
Florida, 62, 64, 510
  acquisition of, 221, 370
  Reconstruction and, 497, 508
  secession of, 419
  Seminole Wars in, 371–72
flour, 238, 343–45
Flournoy, J. J., 374
Floyd County, Ga., 456
Forbes, John M., 226
Ford, Ebenezer, 327
Forrest, Edwin, 295, 296
Fort Pillow, Tenn., 453
Fortress Monroe, Va., 428, 429, 430
Fort Sumter, S.C., 424
Fort Wagner, S.C., 454
Fourier, Charles, 349
Fourteenth Amendment, 487–89, 490, 511

France, 117, 127, 154, 177, 229, 368, 539
    colonies established by, 27, 81
    slavery and, 18
Frank Leslie's Illustrated Newspaper, 361, *431*, 452, *515, 532*
Franklin, Benjamin, 103–4, 105, 117, 275
    American Revolution and, *126*, 128, *131*, 148–49, 157
Frazier, William, 248
Fredericksburg, Va., battle of, 435
Free African Society, 165
free blacks, *201*, 206, *287*, 366, 376, 377, *382, 393*, 405
    in labor force, 214, 215, 384
    population of, 185, 190, 204, 375
    religion of, 314
    underground railroad and, 394–95
    white fear of, 208–9, 216–17, 312, 378, 382, 384–85, 446
    see also African-Americans; slaves
Freedman's Second Reader, 475
Freedmen's Bureau, *see* Bureau of Freedmen, Refugees, and Abandoned Lands
"Freedom Fort," 428, 429
Free Enquirer, 348
free-soil clubs, 391
free-soil issue, 389–407, 419, 422–24
Free-Soil Party, 392–93, 396, 404, 405, 406
Free State General Committee, 471–72
freethinkers, 310–11
Frémont, John C., 406, 427
French and Indian War, 129
Frethorne, Richard, 44
Friend, Isaac, 56–57
Front Street Methodist Church, 475
Fugitive-Slave Law, 394, 395, 396–97
funerals:
    of slaves, *299*
    wakes and, 310
fur trade, 14–15, 87–88, 90

Gage, Thomas, 134, 146, 151–52
Gallatin, Albert, 222, 223, 264
Galloway, Joseph, 148–49
Galveston, Tex., 556
Gama, Vasco da, 17
gang violence, *247*
Garner, Margaret, *398*
Garnet, Henry Highland, 393
Garrett, John, 554
Garrison, William Lloyd, 377–78, 383, 385
Gaspée, 138
Generall Historie of Virginia (Smith), 46

General Society of Mechanics and Tradesmen, 321
General Trades Union, 332, 335, 342, 357
General Workers' League, 356–57
Genoa, 17
George III, king of England, 127, 135, 156, 158
Georgia, 138
    agriculture of, 71, 185–86, 201, 210
    Civil War and, 450, 547, 460–61, 478
    exports of, 71–72
    politics of, 496, 497, 511
    population of, 71
    Reconstruction and, 466
    secession of, 419
    setting of, 60, *61*, 64
    slavery in, 64, 204, 207, 210, 211, 283–84
    voting rights in, 373
Germany, 156, 539
    immigrants from, 61, 64, 73, 214, 217, 223, 257, 261–63, 353, 405, 425, 442, 471, 528, 537
    revolution in, 261–62
Gettysburg, Pa., *438*, 440, 447–48
Ghana, Kingdom of, 21, 22
Ghost Dance religion, 520
Giddings, Joshua, 398
Gilbert, Sir Humphrey, 81
Gillray, James, *177*
Glennan family, *282*
Godey's Lady's Book, 275
Godkin, E. L., 539, 547–48
gold, 8, 442, 552
    in Aztec society, 10, *11*, 15
    in California, 238, 390, 393, 518
    European lust for, 15–16, 17–18
    in pre-colonial Africa, 21, 22
Goodkin, Daniel, 13
Gordon, George, 432
Gordon, N. B., 252
Gordon (slave), *197*
Gould, George, 210
Gould, Jay, 523
government subsidies, 226–27
Gowen, Franklin, 550
grain, 202, 236, 238, 456
Grange (Patrons of Husbandry), 538
Grant, Jehu, 164–65
Grant, Ulysses S.:
    Civil War and, 431, 448, 449, 453, 455, 460, 462–63
    as president, 502, 504, 506, 507, 509–10
Gray, Richard, 509
Gray, Samuel, 141
Grayson, William J., 380

Great Awakening, 76, 120–21, 377
    see also Evangelicalism
Great Britain, 27–37, 117, 229, 387
    church vs. state in, 29, 33, 35
    Civil War and, *427*, 434
    colonization by, 36–37, 81
    governments of colonies and, 116
    growth of capitalism in, 8–9, 27–36
    immigrants from, 214, 223, 257, 263, 405, 442, 528
    Ireland and, *31*
    Parliament of, 130, 131, 132, 133, 134–35, 136
    Revolution of, 32–34, 81
    rise of power of, 35–36, 127
    slavery and, 18, 25, 60
    textile industry, 29–30, 144, 184–85, 191, 195, 215, 218, 434
    trade with colonies, 54–55, 80–81, 107–8, 129–30
    War of 1812 and, 231
Great Lakes region, 228–31
Great Uprising of 1877, 516, 549, 553–59, 560–61
    aims, 557–58
    background, 554
    legacy, 559
    spread, 554–57
Greeley, Horace, 427, 501, 507
Greenback Party, 552, 553, 558
greenbacks, 442, 444, 552
Green Mountain Boys, 122–24, 159
Grenville, George, 130–31, 135, 137
Grimké, Angelina, 277, 316
Grimké, Sarah, 316
Guamán Poma de Ayala, Felipe, 8, *10, 11, 12*
Gullah, 67
Gunpowder Plot, 104
Guy Fawkes Day, *see* Pope's Day

Haiti, 369
Hale, John P., 396–97
Hale, Sarah Josepha, 275, 276
Hamilton, Alexander, 164, 166, 168–69, 176
Hammond, James H., 216–17, 315, 381
Hancock, John, 133, 140, 149, 163
hardtack, 438
Harpers Ferry, Va., raid on, 407–9, 411, 419, 420
Harper's New Monthly Magazine, 218
Harper's Weekly, 241, 255, 274, 288, 408, 431, 449, 491, 498
Harrison, William Henry, 231
Hart, Eli, 344
Hart and Company, 344–45
Harvard College, 84

Hat Act (1732), 129, 135
Hatton, George W., 450
Hawkes, James, 139
Hayes, Rutherford B., 510–11, 553, 554
Heath, Moses, 512
Heath, Rev. S., 512
Heighton, William, 327–28
Helper, Hinton, 407
hemp, 204
Henry, Patrick, 148, 369
Henry VII, king of England, 29, 35
Heroes of America, 460
Hervieu, August, *193, 352*
Hewes, George Robert Twelves, 103, 104, 105, 129, 139, 140
Hicks, Edward, *234*
Highlander (ship), 260–61
Hill, Edward, 52
Hill, Richard, 485
"Hireling and the Slave," (Grayson), 380
Hispaniola, 14
Hobbes, Thomas, 28
Hogan, Thomas, 338
holidays, 254, 298
Holland, 25, 55
  colonies established by, 27, 81
Holt, Elizabeth, 113
Homer, Winslow, *255*
Homestead Act (1862), 517–18
homesteads, 329, 352, 353, 373, 391, 407, 498
Hone, Philip, 393, 396
Hood, John Bell, 460
Hooker, Joseph, 440
Hopedale, 348
Hopi Indians, 11
hospitals, 443
household manufacture, decline of, 234–35, 238, 240
House of Burgesses (Virginia), 45, 46, 53, 54, 58, 135, 136
House of Commons (Britain), 29, 104, 134–35
House of Lords (Britain), 29
House of Representatives, U.S., 169, 348, 376, 387, 388, 390
housing, 359, 543–44
  in pre-Civil War North, 244–45, 250–51, 254
  of slaves, *64*
Houston, George, 493
Houston, Sam, 387
Howard, Josephine, 367
Howard, Oliver O., 479
Hudson, Henry, 81
Hughes, John, 310
Huldah (slave), 183, 184, 199, 287
Huntington, Collis P., 523

"Huswifery" (Taylor), 112
Hutchinson, Anne, 114
Hutchinson, Thomas, 109, 117, 134, 138
Hutchinson family, 362

iceboxes, 273, 281
Idaho, 518
Illinois, 374
  American Indians of, 229, 231
  coal industry, 525
  labor disputes, 532–35
  land ownership, 352
  race laws, 450
illiteracy:
  slavery and, 208, 382, 475
Illustrated London News, 259, 431
Illustrated Temperance Tales (Arthur), 236
Imbert, Anthony, *226*
immigrants:
  labor of, 216–17, 237, 241, 250, 255, 257–58, 259–67, 280, 311, 340–41, 355, 528–30, 542–43
  nativist attitudes toward, 264–67, *304, 305,* 306, 335, 358–59, 406, 407
  politics of, 405–6, 445
immigration:
  Civil War and, 442
  to North, 83, 223, 232, 237, 241, 255, 257–58, 261–63, 442, 527–28
  to South, 61, 64, 73, 217–18, 257
  to West, 527–28
Impending Crisis of the South (Helper), 407
impressment, 456–57, 459
Incas, 8, 10, *11,* 14
Incidents in the Life of a Slave Girl (Jacobs), 396
indentured servants, 44–45, 48–49, 60, 239, 375
  conditions of, 44, 50–53, 62
  in northern colonies, 80, 83, 95–96, 105
  rebellions by, 53, 54, 56–58
  women as, 51, 52, 73
Indiana, 231, *347,* 374
Indians, American:
  agriculture of, 10–11, 13
  alcohol and, 86, 88, 229, 230
  American Revolution and, 151, 175, 187, 220
  Asian origin of, 9
  assimilation of, 187–89, 229–30
  displacement of, 185, 188–89, 218, 228–31, 371
  diverse societies of, 8, 9–10

European diseases and, 8, 13–14, 37, 85, 86
  "Five Civilized Tribes" of, 187
  kinship and tribal ties, 11–12, 187, 229
  land taken from, 80, 82, 85–92, 122, 185, 187–89, 228–31, 516, 519
  northern colonists and, 80, 82, 83, 85–92, 122
  pre-Columbian population, 9
  religion, 12, 229–30, 520
  reservation system, 519, 520
  as slaveholders, 187, 371
  as slaves, 62, 88
  southern colonists and, 37, 41–42, 43, 45, 48, 50, 53, 56, 57–58, 77
  war among, 12–13, 15
  women, 10, 11, 13, 15, 86, 89, 112
  see also specific tribes
industrial revolution, 240
  effect of, on artisans, 243–48
  in Europe, 258, 263
  in United States, 222, 223, 238
inflation:
  in American Revolution, 161, 171
  in Civil War, 444–45, 459
  in colonies, 130
  in pre-Civil War era, 334, 359
Inness, George, *225*
Interesting Narrative of the Life of Olaudah Equiano (Equiano), 22, 67
International Workingmen's Association, 537
Intolerable Acts (1773), 134, 145
Iowa, 349, 352
Ireland:
  English subjugation of, *31,* 258–59
  famine, 238, 255, 258–59, *262,* 310
  immigrants from, 61, 64, 73, 214, 215, 217, 223, 240, 242, 255, 257–59, 280, 340–41, 358, 406, 425, 446–47, 471, 528, 549–50
Ireton, Commissary-General, 32
Iron Act (1750), 129–30, 135
iron industry, 215
  production levels, 130, 222, 441, 525
  unions and, 360–61, 532–34, 538
Iron Molders' Journal, 551–52
Iron Teeth, 520
Iroquois Confederacy, 12–13, 88–89, 91, 175
Irving, Washington, 294–95

Jackson, Andrew, *257,* 377, 407
  abolitionism and, 383
  American Indians and, 185, *187,* 188–89

Jackson, Andrew (*continued*)
  labor and, 341, *343*
  monopolies and, 330–31
Jackson, Miss., 458
Jackson, Thomas "Stonewall," 429,
  432
Jacobs, Harriet Brent, 396
Jamaica, 131
James I, king of England, 40, 45, 81
James II, king of England, 147
Jamestown, Va., 41–42, 44, 58
Jay Cooke and Company, 545
Jefferson, Thomas, 136, 239, 242
  American Indians and, 187
  American Revolution and, 149, 151
  Declaration of Independence and,
    128, 156–57
  as president, 375
  slavery and, 157, 164, 165, 375
Jess, Mary, 210
Jessup, Thomas Sidney, 372
Jesuits, 89
Jewett, B. E., 543
João III, king of Portugal, 25
Jocelyn, Nathaniel, *370*
"John Brown's Body," 411, *461*,
  462–63, 540
Johnson, Andrew:
  impeachment, 501
  Reconstruction and, 480–90
Johnson, Anthony, 52
Johnson, Guy, 155
Johnson, Sir William, 94, 95, 116
Johnson, David Claypoole, *187, 266*
Journal of Commerce, 334, 340, 343
"Jubilee of Freedom," 462–63
Julian, George, 397, 518
July Fourth holiday, 254, 298, 307, 321,
  492
juries, racial discrimination and, 450,
  498

Kabes, Johnny, 25
Kansas:
  African-American migration to, 512
  American Indians of, 231
  free-soil issue and, 397–404, 406,
    411
  settlement, 510
Kansas-Nebraska Act (1854), 397–99,
  400, 403
Keckley, Elizabeth, 198
Keith, Sir William, 117
Kendall, Amos, 383
Kentucky:
  Civil War and, 427, 453
  religion in, 302–3, 311
  settlement, 190, 374
  slavery in, 204, 208, 374, *398*

King, Edward, *479*
King, Rufus, 376
King Philip's War, 88, 113
Kirkland, Samuel, 89
Kirkwood, Samuel, 452
Knights of St. Crispin, 535, 536
Know-Nothing Party, 358, 404, 405,
  410
Kreige, Hermann, 353, 354
Ku Klux Klan, 503–5, 506
Ku Klux Klan Act (1871), 506

labor:
  change in employer-employee
    relations, with, 282–83, 320
  child, 242, 246, 251, 252
  convict, 356, 512
  factory, 251–56
  growth of, 223, 239, 523
  home, 248, 249–51, 335–36, 337
  immigrant, 216–17, 237, 241, 250,
    255, 257–58, 259–67, 280, 311,
    340–41, 355, 528–30, 542–43
  mechanization of, 223, 248, 263,
    283, 362, 384
  skilled, 243–48, 444
  unskilled, 240–42, 340–42, 356–57,
    444, *445*, 446
  urban vs. rural, 214–15
  of women, 113, 242, 246, 247,
    249–50, 252–56, 259–60, 264,
    384, *441*, 443, 458, 525–26, 536
  see also artisans: indentured
    servants; slavery; slaves
Labor League, 540
labor movement, 319–60, 531–38
  African-Americans and, 538,
    540–41, 551, 560
  Civil War and, 425, 442, 459
  demonstrations, *318, 332*, 335, 362
  depression and, 549
  length of workday and, 307, 324–25,
    335, 342, 355, 393, 531, 533–34,
    539–40
  male-female relations in, 338–39
  political affiliations, 552
  socialism and, 537–38, 547, 557
  in South, 372–74, 459
  strikes, 307, 323, 332, 334, 335,
    336–37, 341–42, 356, 357, 358,
    362–63, 444, 459, 516, 532–37,
    543, 549–50, 551, 553–59
  unions, 321, 323, 325, 327–29,
    331–35, 342–43, 354, 355–58,
    360–63, 442, 444, 531, 532–45
  unskilled workers and, 340–42
  violence and, 549–51
  women and, 335–40, 351, 356, *361*,

362–63, 488, 536, 538, 543–44,
  560
Labor Reform Party Convention, 534
Labor Standard, 537
*Lady's Magazine and Repository of
  Entertaining Knowledge,* 170
laissez-faire economics, 529, 530, 548,
  553, 560
Lamb, John, 140
land reform, 351–54, 391–93
  ex-slaves and, 466, 467, 478–81,
    487, 489–90, 511
Lanman, Thomas, 375
Larcom, Lucy, 254
Latrobe, Benjamin Henry, *70, 72, 76*
Laud, William, 81
laundry work, 543
Lawrence, Amos, 399
Lawrence *Courier,* 266
LeCount, Adam, 210
Lee, Robert E., 408, 411
  Civil War and, 432, 433–34, 440,
    447, 460, 462–63
leisure:
  increase of, 270, 274
  rural activities of, 289–91
  of slaves, 299–301
  urban activities of, 291–99
Lesueur, Charles-Alexandre, *350*
Levelers, 124
Leyden, Ann, 44
Liberal Republicans, 507
Liberator, 377, 378, 379
Liberty Party, 392
Liberty Poles, 138
Liberty Trees, 137, 138
lien laws, 497
life expectancy:
  in colonies, 48, 84–85, 111
  in Medieval Europe, 28
  in pre-Civil War North, 248
limited-liability corporation, 521
Lincoln, Abraham, 409, 481
  assassination of, 463, 472, 480
  Civil War and, 428, 431, 450, 461
  election of, 410, 417, 418–19
  Emancipation Proclamation and,
    434–35, 452
  family of, 202, 374
  free-soil issue and, 404, 405, 417,
    422–24
  labor and, 444
  political beliefs of, 331
  slaveholders and, 469, 470, 471, 472
Lincoln, Benjamin, 163
Lincoln, Thomas, 374
Lind, Jenny, 290
Little Big Horn, battle of, 520
Livingston, Ala., 491

Livingston, Robert, 97, 157
Lloyd, David, 117
lobbyists, 523
Locke, John, 34, 36, 61
London, 31
London Magazine, 147
Long Strike, 549–50
Louisiana, 62, 240, 452, 466, 510
  purchase of, 186, 221
  Reconstruction and, 469–73, 497,
    508
  secession, 419
  slavery, 184, 199–200, 206–7, 211,
    434, 470
  sugar-cane industry, 184, 186, 190,
    469
Louisiana Purchase, 186, 221, 397
Lowe, Jonathon, *533*
Lowell, Francis Cabot, 251
Lowell, Mass., 307
  textile industry of, 215, 252, 253,
    254, 255, 336–38, 351, 355, 356
Loyal League, *see* Union League
Loyal Nine, 137, 138, 139
Lucy Ann (mill worker), 279
Lutheran Church, 405
lynchings, 420, 446, *447*
Lynn, Mass., shoe industry, 244,
    247–48, 256, 336, 351, 353, *361,*
    390, 391, 393, 405, 426–27,
    535–36
McClellan, George B., 432, 450
McCormick reaper works, 532–33, 557
McDonnell, Joseph, 537
McDougall, Alexander, 140
McFealing, John, 242
MacIntosh, Ebenezer, 138, 140
McKay stitcher, 527
Macon, Ga., 457
McParlan, James, 550–51
Macready, William Charles, 296
Madison, James, 166
  political beliefs, 167–68
  slavery and, 169–70
Maine:
  statehood, 376
  textile industry, *339*
malaria, 438–39
Malcolm, John, *149*
Mali Empire, 21, 22
Manassas, Va., battle of, 438
Manigault, Peter, *71*
Mann, Thomas, 255
manufacturing:
  growth of, 238–40, 256–57, 440, 523
Manumission Society, 164
Marines, U.S., 371, 408
"maroons," 371
marriage:

of ex-slaves, 469, 474
  in northern colonies, 110–11
  in pre-Civil War North, 276, 280
  of slaves, 287
Marshall, James, 353
Martin, Joseph Plumb, 154
Marvin, William, 481–82
Marx, Karl, 537
Maryland, 51, 53, 71, 185
  Civil War and, 427, 453
  constitution, 159–60, 162
  founding, 46, 84
  labor struggles, 341
  population, 71, 185
  religion in, 312
  slavery in, 66, 69, 203–4, 211, 215,
    394
  voting rights in, 373
Mason, George, 173–74, 217
Massachusetts, 79, 80, 81, 120, 167,
    388
  constitution, 159–60, 162
  founding, 83–84
  industries, *99*
  land ownership in, 92–93
  race laws, 450
  slavery abolished in, 164
  textile industry, 251–56
Massachusetts Bay Company, 83–84
Massachusetts General Colored
    Association, 378
Massachusetts Government Act
    (1774), 146, 147, 148
*Materials Towards a History of the
    American Baptists, 121*
Matsell, George W., 283
Maverick, Samuel, 142
Mayas, 10
Mayflower, 83
Meagher, Thomas Francis, 259
Mechanics' Free Press, 327–28
Mechanics' Union of Trade
    Associations, 325
Melville, Herman, 260–61
Memphis, Tenn., 489
mercantilism, 36, 50, 62, 225
merchant class:
  abolitionism and, 404–5
  American Revolution and, 136,
    143–45, 161–63, 166
  conservatism of, 223
  in North, 99–100, 118, 202, 224,
    226, 236–37, 422, 425
  Reconstruction and, 467, 468
  rise of, 29–30, 33
Meridian, Miss., 491, 505–6
Metacom, 88
Methodist Church, 301, 302, 312,
    315–16, 368, 374, 475

Mexican War, 387–89, 391, 393, 397,
    435, 437
Michigan, 349
  American Indians of, 229, 231
Micmac Indians, 12, 87–88, 90
middle class, 271–77
  home life, 272–77
  rise, 273
militia, *330,* 341–42, *361*
Miller, Lewis, *191*
Milliken's Bend, La., 453
Milwaukee, Wis., 527
Miner's National Association, 535
mining, 518–19
Minnesota:
  land ownership, 352
Mississippi, 452, 458
  agriculture, 190
  desegregation, 497
  Ku Klux Klan, 506
  lynchings, 420
  politics, 494, 495, 508
  secession, 419
  slavery in, 184, 204
  voting rights in, 373
"Mississippi Plan," 508
Mississippi Valley, 449, 479
Missouri
  Civil War and, 426–27, 453
  politics, *326,* 489
  settlement, 190, 195, 374
  slavery, 204, 376, *401*
Missouri Compromise, 398, 422
Mitchell, Moses, 467
Mobile, Ala., 457, 458, 491
Mobile Commercial Register, 364
Mohawk Indians, 88–89, 175
Mohegan Indians, 86
molasses, 130, 131
Molasses Act (1733), 130
Molly Maguires, 550–51, *551,* 553
monopoly, 227, 327–31, *333,* 352
Monroe, Sarah, 336
Montana, 518
Montezuma, 15
Montgomery, Lizzie W., 290
Moody, Paul, 251
Morgan, Albert T., 495
Morris, Gouverneur, 145, 150, 170
Morris, Robert, 162, 166
Morrison, Toni, *398*
music, of slaves, 300

Nairne, Thomas, 63
Nantucket Indians, 86
Narragansett Indians, 91
Nashoba, *350, 352*
Nashville, Tenn., 460

Nast, Thomas, *288, 423, 465, 486, 498, 499*
Natchez, Miss., 458
Nation, 490, 501, 507, 547
National Emigration Aid Society, 512
National Industrial Congress, 396
National Labor Tribune, 546
National Labor Union (NLU), 538–45
National Molders' Union, 361, 532–34
National Trades Union, 332–33, 339–40, 353, 538
nativism, 264–67, *304, 305,* 306, 335, 358–59, 406, 407
Navigation Acts, 60, 107, 108, 131, 133, 136
Nebraska, free-soil issue and, 397–400, 403–4, 406
"Negro Dogs," 397
Negro Election Day, 106–7
Nevada, 518–19
Newark, N.J., 332
New England:
    abolitionism in, 390
    decline of agriculture, 236–37
    religion, 302
    rise of manufacturing, 238–40, 440, 441
    utopian communities, 348
    see also specific states; northern colonies
New England Farmer, 232, 234, 236, 237
New England Girlhod (Larcom), 254
New England Primer, 96
New Hampshire, 83, 120, 159, 238
    slaves in, 165
    textile industry of, *220*
New Harmony, *347, 349, 352*
New Jersey, 82, 84, 410
New Mexico:
    annexation of, 389
    slavery in, 394
New Orleans, La., 458, 491
    anti-black riot, *486,* 489
    Civil War and, 431, 466, 469
    nightlife, 297
    as port, 190, 469
    slaves in, 204, 471–73, 475
New Orleans *Daily Picayune,* 216
newspapers, growth of, 228, 298–99
New World:
    colonization, 7–9, 37
    pre-Columbian societies, 9–15
    riches, 15–16, 17–18
New York, 83, 84
    constitution, 159–60, 161
    land ownership, 94–95
    religious revival, 301

slaves in, 83, 106
voting rights in, 501
New York, N.Y., 80, 118, 243, 244, 288, 298, 388
    abolitionists, 383–84, 385–86, 393
    American Revolution and, 137, 154
    Bowery district, *291,* 297–98
    Civil War and, *423,* 425
    clothing industry, 249, 335–36, 337, 525–26
    Common Council, 334
    draft riots, 445–47
    Five Points neighborhood, *304,* 309
    growth, 97–98, 239, 527
    labor movements in, 321, 325–27, 332, 334–36, 338, 341–42, 356, 359, 537–38, 547, 549
    newspapers, 298–99
    politics, 109, 116–17
    poverty, *241, 269, 282,* 546–47
    race laws, 450
    riots, 296, 343–45, *547*
    slavery in, 83, 106, 109, 396
    theater, 293–96
    underground railroad and, 395
    unemployment, 256
New York *Abendzeitung,* 351
New York *Arbeiter-Union,* 537
New York Central Railroad, 228, 554
New York *Champion of American Labor,* 359
New York *Courier and Enquirer,* 385
New York *Daily Graphic, 499,* 546, *558*
New York *Daily Plebian,* 359
New York *Daily Sentinel,* 384
New York *Daily Tribune,* 250–51, 363, 462–63
New York *Herald,* 423–24
New York Illustrated News, 282
New York Journal, 113, 141
New York Laborers' Union Benevolent Association, 356
New York *Morning Chronicle,* 294–95
New York *Packet,* 172
New York State Agricultural Society, 235
New York State Mechanic, 246
New York Stock Exchange, 546
New York *Sun,* 443, 528
New York Tailoresses' Society, 336
New York *Times,* 216, 531
New York *Tribune,* 244–45
New York Workingmen's Movement, 327
Nicaragua, 387, *403*
Noble, Thomas S., *398*
North Adams, Mass., 536

North Carolina, 60, 62, 71, 84, 166, 478
    agriculture, 185–86
    Civil War and, 457, 460, 462
    Ku Klux Klan, 506
    population, 71
    Reconstruction and, 466
    secession, 426
    slavery in, 75, 383
    voting rights in, 373
northern colonies, 79–125
    cities, 97–99, 137, 139, 171
    currency, 129–30
    early settlement, 81
    England and, 80, 81, 107–8, 116, 129–35
    English army and, 118–19, 132–33, 140–41
    European rivalry in, 82–83, 89
    governments, 115–17, 132, 136, 146
    immigration, 83, 95–96
    laboring classes, 101–5, 144–45
    land ownership in, 91–95, 121–25
    merchant class, 99–100, 118, 136, 143–45, 161–63, 166, 202
    population, 95, 117
    pre-American Revolution, 117–25
    professional class, 100
    slavery, 80, 83, 99, 105–7, 109
    social unrest, 115, 118, 121–25
    southern colonies compard with, 84–85, 135
    taxation, 129–35, 142–43, 146
    trade goods of, 99
    uprisings, 108–9, 138, 141
    women in, 109–15
North-South relations:
    economics, 214–15, 421, 425
    politics, 375–77, 387, 417–24
Northup, Solomon, 200, 206–7, 211–12, 300
Northwest Ordinance, 171
Northwest Territory, 190, 228
Norway, 263
Noyes, John Humphrey, 346
Nueva corónica y buen gobierno (Guamán Poma), *8, 10, 11, 14*
nurses, 443
Nzinga Mbemba (Affonso I), king of Congo, 25

Oak Lawn plantation, *194*
Offering, 336
Ohio, 349, 374
    American Indians of, 229, 231
    race laws of, 450
oil industry, 524
Oklahoma, 519
    Cherokees moved to, 189

"Old Plantation," 68
Oliver, Andrew, 137, 138
Olmecs, 10
Olmsted, Frederick Law, 216
Onoogwandikha, 89
Opechancanough, Chief, 41
Oregon, acquisition of, 221, 387–88
orphans, forced labor of, 50
Orton, Lewis, 183, 199, 287
Osborne, Aaron, 154
Osborne, Sarah, 154
Osceola, 189, 371
Overseers, 70
Owen, Robert, 347, 348
Owen, Robert Dale, 311, 348

Paine, Thomas, 136–37, 140, 151, 263
    political beliefs of, 158–59, 160, 161,
      177, 310
pamphleteers, 96, 136, 144
paper money, 329, 444
Paris Commune, 538
Parker, Theodore, 394
Park Theater, 293, 294, 296
Parrott arms factory, 444
Parsons, Albert, 556
Paterson, N.J., 527
Patsy (slave), 212
Paul, Jeremiah, 302
Paul, Mary, 253, 349–50
Pawtucket, R.I., 251, 335
Paxton Boys, 121–22, 123, 124
Pearce, Charles, 476
peasants, 16, 27–33
    emigration by, 35
    revolts by, 16, 31–32
Pease, Louis M., 309
Penn, William, 82
Pennington, James, 200
Pennsylvania, 82, 95–96, 116, 349
    constitution of, 159, 160, 162
    industries of, 441, 444, 524–25,
      534–35, 549–50
    religion in, 301
Pennsylvania Canal, 341
Pennsylvania Gazette, 126
Pennsylvania Journal and Weekly
    Advertiser, 136
Pennsylvania Railroad, 228, 521, 554
"penny press," 298–99
Pequot Indians, 86
Perkins, Maria, 199
Philadelphia, Pa., 80
    artisans, 243
    economy, 104
    founding, 82
    general strike, 307
    growth, 97, 98–99, 239
    labor movements, 322, 323, 327–29,

332, 338–39, 342, 348, 356,
  360–61, 422
mummers, 298
oil and, 524
politics, 109, 137, 157–58
slaves in, 106
underground railroad and, 395
unemployment, 256
Philadelphia House of Refuge, 279
Philadelphia Society for Promoting
    Agriculture, 233
Philbrick, Edward, 468, 501
Philipse, Frederick, 95
photography, 297
    in Civil War, 438, 449
Pierce, Franklin, 398
pigs, 91
Pilgrims, 81, 83, 90
Pinkerton, Allan, 551
Pinkerton National Detective Agency,
    550
Pinkster festival, 106
Pitt, William, 130
Pittsburgh, Pa., 238, 357, 396, 524,
    554–55
plantations, 194, 205
    economics, 201
    family life, 285–86
    size, 63, 204–5
planters, 160, 166, 169, 196–98, 202,
    204
    amnesty for, 481, 482
    definition, 185
    draft exemption, 455
    Evangelicalism and, 311–12, 314–15
    hierarchy of, 196–97
    investments by, 214
    northern merchants compared with,
      197, 224
    Reconstruction and, 465, 467, 481,
      482, 490, 493, 496, 497, 500
    "redemption" of South and, 502
    resistance to industrialization,
      216–17, 218
Pocahontas, 46
political parties, 320, 404–5
    see also specific parties
Polk, James, 388, 390, 391
Polo, Marco, 17
polygyny, 20
Poole, Morton, 275
Poor Richard's Almanac (Franklin),
    103, 104, 275
Pope's Day, 104, 138
population:
    of free blacks, 185, 204
    of Great Lakes region, 231
    of immigrants, 257–58, 442
    of northern colonies, 95, 117

rural, 239
of slaves, 63, 70, 185, 186, 204, 451
of southern colonies, 71
of southern states, 184, 185, 195,
  204, 426, 457–58
of United States, 221, 231, 426, 429
urban, 239, 256, 527
Port Hudson, La., 452, 453, 471
Portugal:
    colonization by, 8
    exploration by, 17, 22
    slave trade and, 18, 23, 24–25
poverty:
    crime and, 242
    disease and, 242, 282
    of immigrants, 260–61
Power, Tyrone, 240, 296
Powhatan, Chief, 36, 41, 47
Powhatan Indians, 50
Pownall, Thomas, 119
Prendergast, William, 122–23, 124
Presbyterian Church, 33, 85, 301, 303
"press gangs," 102
price controls, 459
primogeniture, 54
printers, 311, 323, 351, 372, 384, 545
printing, 228
Proclamation of Amnesty and
    Reconstruction, 472
Promontory Point, Utah, 516
Prophetstown, Ind., 231
prospectors, 518–19
Prosser, Gabriel, 368–69, 371, 382, 401
prostitution, 250, 284, 293, 306
Protestantism, 29, 100, 258, 310
    see also Evangelicalism
Providence, R.I., 251
Pryor, Hubbard, 449
public water systems, 273, 281
Punch, 389
Puritans, 32, 85, 93, 114, 148
    American Indians and, 86, 88–89
    arrival of, 81–84
Pynchon, John, 93, 97
Pynchon, William, 93
Pyne, James T., 353

Quakers, 82, 85, 95, 96, 124, 277, 368,
    374

race relations:
    in North during Reconstruction,
      500–501, 510
    in northern colonies, 106
    in southern colonies, 58–60, 64, 66,
      70, 77
    between whites and free blacks,
      208–9, 216–17, 454–55, 477–78,
      479, 486, 489

race relations (*continued*)
  of working class, 374–75, 384,
    445–47, 538, 541, 551, 560
Radical Clubs, 493
Radical Republicans, 431, 484,
  486–90, 501, 507
railroads, 190, 201, 214, 215, *225*, 226,
  227, 238, 240, 340–41, 456,
  516–23
  Civil War and, 440, 441, 444
  expansion, 516, 524–25
  rate wars, 522
  Robber Barons, 523
  in South, 511
  strikes against, 516, 549, 553–59,
    560
  subsidies for, 516–17, 521
  territorial expansion and, 228, 352,
    516, 559
Raleigh, N.C., 476
Randolph, John, 368
Reading Railroad, 550
Reconstruction, 485–513, 539
  amnesty in, 481, 482
  beginnings, 466–69
  carpetbaggers, 494–95
  Congress and, 483–90
  education and, 470, *471*, 490, 497
  legacy and failure, 513
  new state governments during,
    481–83
  protests during, 491
  radical era, 490–500, 551, 559
  retreat from, 500–13
  scalawags of, 495
  state constitutional conventions of,
    492
Reconstruction Act (1867), 490–91,
  534
Redbank, N.J., 349
Redburn (Melville), 260–61
Reed, John C., 200
Regulators, 75–76, 159
Reierson, Johan, 263
Relief and Aid Society, 548
religion, 301–17
  of American Indians, 12, 229–30,
    520
  of ex-slaves, 466, 475–76
  in North, 286, 301–8
  in northern colonies, 120–21
  in precolonial Africa, 21, 313
  radicalism in, 33, 85, 114, 301,
    306–8
  slavery and, 198, *205*, 287, 311–17
  in South, 301–3, 311–17
  in southern colonies, 42, 46, 72,
    76–77
Remond, Charles L., 393

Republican Clubs, 493
republicanism, 166–69, 321, 325, 334,
  368, 531, 539
Republican Party:
  Civil War and, 441
  Democratic Party compared with,
    552
  free-soil issue and, 366, 404–6, 410,
    419, 421, 422–23
  Ku Klux Klan violence against,
    503–4
  labor and, 444, 530, 533, 534, 539,
    541, 544, 552–53
  Reconstruction and, 465, 466, 484–90,
    492–500
  retreat and destruction of, in South,
    507, 509, 511
Revenue (Sugar) Act (1764), 131, 132,
  134, 135
Revere, Paul, 102–4, *103*, 105, *126*,
  142, *147*, 152, 172
Rhode Island, 81, 116, 166
  slaves in, 165
  textile industry, 251, 252
rice, 135, 184, 190, 195
  increasing importance, 63, 64,
    185–86
  slavery and, 63–65, 210–11
Rice, Sally, 253–54
Richardson, Ebenezer, 141
Richmond, Va.:
  Civil War and, 432, 456–57, 458,
    459, 460
  after emancipation, 474, 491
  slaves in, 213, 368
Richmond *Enquirer*, 390
Richmond *Whig*, 371
rifles, 436
Right of Man to Property (Skidmore),
  326
Rights of Man (Paine), 177
Ripley, George, 348–49
"River Gods," 93, 115
Robber Barons, 523
Robin Hood, 16
Robinson, Beverly, 95
Rochester, N.Y., 304
Rockefeller, John D., 524
Roman Catholicism, *see* Catholic
  Chuch
Rowlandson, Mary, *90*
Royal African Company, 60
Ryland, Robert, 315

Sabbath, 298, 306
St. Louis, Mo., 444, 527, 557
St. Mary's Parish, La., 493
St. Patrick's Day, *288*

saloons, 296–97, *304, 305*
  see also alcohol
San Francisco, Calif., 450, 527, 556,
  557
San Francisco Illustrated Wasp, 542
Santa Anna, Antonio López de, 387
Savannah, Ga., *421*, 460–61
  race relations in, 217, 475, 491
Savannah Education Association, 475
scalawags, 495
Scandinavia, immigrants from, 257,
  263–64, 405
Schell, F. H., *437*
Schole, Christopher, 515
Scientific American, 442
Scotland, 33, 61, 73, 96, 263, 523
Scott, Dred, 407, 409, 485
Scott, Tom, 553, 554
Sears, Isaac, 140
Second Great Awakening, 301,
  311–317
  see also Evangelicalism, Great
    Awakening
Sedalia, Mo., 519
segregation:
  in North, 293
  during Reconstruction, 497
Seider, Christopher, 141
Selma, Ala., 458
Seminole Indians, 187, 189, 371–72
Seminole Wars, 189, 371–72
Senate, U.S., 169, 376, 388, 389, 390
Seneca Falls, N.Y., 276, 277
Seneca Indians, 89, 175
servants, 242, 259–60, 264, 273,
  280–81, 497
Seven Days' campaign, 432
Seward, William, 397, 423
sewing machines, 250, 257, 362, 526
sexual harassment, 250
Seybert, Adam, 225
Shakers, 348
Shakespeare, William, 295, 298
sharecropping, 499, 502, 511
Shawnee Indians, 187, 228–31
Shays, Daniel, 162–63
Shays' Rebellion, 162–63, 166
Shenandoah Valley, Va., 430
Sherburne, Joseph, *100*
Sherman, William T., 450, 460–61,
  462, 475, 478
Shiloh, Tenn., battle of, 431, 439
shipping, 224–25
  cost of, 224, 226, 228, 235
shipyards, 244, 440
Shirley, William, 102
shoe industry, 244–45, 247–48, 274,
  440, 442, 458, 426–27

abolitionism and, 384, 390, 391, 393, 405
labor movement and, 323, 336, 342, 351, 353, *361*, 535–36, 538
silk, 64
silver, 8, 10, 15, 17–18, 442, 518
Siney, John, 535, 552
Singletary, Amos, 173
"Sinners in the Hands of an Angry God" (Edwards), 120
Sioux Indians, 520
Sitting Bull, 520
Skidmore, Thomas, 326–27, 346
Slater, Samuel, 251, 252
slave-hunters, *395, 397, 398, 399*
"Slave-Mother's Reply," 208
slaveowners, 164, 183–85, 193, 195–201, 365–66
  Declaration of Independence and, 157, 165
  Democratic Party and, 354
  number of slaves owned by, 196, 204
  numbers of, 195–96, 386, 420
  philosophy of, 379–83
  sexual relations with female slaves of, 286, 289
  social views of, 284–86
  treatment of slaves by, 65, *197*, 199–200, 206–7, 212, 288–89, 367
  see also planters
slavery, 8, 18–27, 37, 44, 50–55, 58–65, 74, 183–219, 224, 363, 364–411
  abolition, 463
  abolition, in Massachusetts, 164
  American Revolution and, 151, 155–56, 164–65, 169–71, 174, 175
  banning, in Northwest Territory, 190
  cotton and, 183–86, 189–90, 204–5, *209*, 211–19, 375
  decline, 129, 203, 204
  destabilizing effects, in Africa, 25
  gang labor system, 210, 211, 212, 468
  illiteracy and, 208, 382, 475
  legal sanction of, 60, 63, 64
  in northern colonies, 80, 83, 99, 105–7, 109
  precolonial history, 18–19, 21
  Republican Party and, 366, 404–6, 410, 419, 421, 422–23, 463
  rice and, 63–65, 210–11
  roots, 18–19
  in South America, 200
  spread, 60–65, 184–85
  sugar and, 8, 18, 24, 26, 52, 59, 61, 204, 212
  task system, 210, 468–69

tobacco and, 50–55, 59–65, 203–4, 211
in West Indies, 24–25, 52, 60, 200
Westward expansion and, 386–93
slaves:
  ban on importation, 186, 200, 203, 206
  capture and transport, 26–27, *38*, 66–67, *186*
  children as, 207, 288, 376, 483
  in cities, 83, 106, 109, 204, 213, 214, 215–16
  cost, 200, 203, 206–7, 208
  escapes, 216, *364, 366, 371*, 394–95, *398, 399*, 428, 430, 432, 433, 448, 469
  families, 183, 184, 198–99, 207–8, 287–89, 396, 433
  funerals, *299*
  leisure activities, 299–301
  mortality rate, 210–11
  population, 63, 70, 185, 186, 204, 451
  as property, 183–85, 198, 284–86, 288–89, 367
  rebellions, 69–70, 366–72, 382–83, 406
  religion, 198, *205*, 287, 311–17, 368, 369
  as servants, 212–13
  treatment of, 65, *197*, 199–200, 206–7, 212, 288–89, 367
  women as, 183, 207, 210, 211, 212, 213, 287–89, 367, *395, 396*
  work done by, 106, 204, 209–10, 213
slave trade, 60, 407
  banning, 186, 200, 203, 206, 394
  rise, 23–27, 60
  West Africa and, 19–27
Smith, Adam, 108, 161, 168
Smith, Elizabeth Murray, 113
Smith, Gerrit, 392, 398
Smith, John, 36, *46, 47*
Social Darwinism, 530–31, 543, 548, 560
socialism, 531, 537–38, 547, 557
Society for the Protection and Promotion of Female Industry, 340
Sons of Liberty, 139–40, 144, 150
Sons of Temperance, 308
Sorge, Friedrich, 537
South America:
  slavery in, 200
Southampton, Va., 371
South Carolina, 84, 159, 478, 491
  agriculture, 60, 61, 210, 456
  Civil War and, 462
  Ku Klux Klan, 506
  politics, 494, 497, 508, 510–11

population, 71, 497–98
religion, 312
secession, 419, 420
slavery in, 60, 62–63, 67, 199, 200–201, 210, 376–77
South Carolina Gazette, 69
South Carolina Sea Islands, 466–69, 472–73, 480
southern colonies, 39–77
  agriculture, 8, 18, 37, 54, 60–65, 71, 135, 165
  frontier, 73–75
  governments, 72
  population, 71
  religion in, 76–77
  social structure, 72–73
  uprisings in, 75–76
  women in, 72
Southern Commercial Convention, 214, 215
Southern Cultivator, 202
Southern Quarterly Review, 285
southern states, 183–219
  agriculture, 184–87, 189–95, 201–19, 456
  cities, 214, 215, 457–58
  clothing market, 249, 458
  economy, 184, 186, 190–95, 196, 202, 213–19, 224, 420–21, 508
  effect of Civil War, 455–60
  industrialization, 458
  population, 184, 185, 195, 204, 426, 429, 457–58
  secession, 407, 417, 418–24, 426
  westward migration in, 186, 190, 195, 198–99, 202, 218, 374
  see also Confederate States of America; Reconstruction
Spain, 16
  decline, 27
  slavery and, 18, 24, 25
Spaulding, Washington, 208
Spencer, Herbert, 530
spice trade, 17, 22
Sprigs, Elizabeth, 73
Springfield rifles, 436
Squanto, 90
Stamp Act (1765), 109, *126*, 131–32, 134, 135, 136, 137, 138, 146, 147
Stamp Act Congress, 136
Standard Oil Company, 524
Stanton, Edwin, 461, 462, 501
Stanton, Elizabeth Cady, 277, 487–88, 544
Statute of Artificers, 30, 52
steamboats, 190, 226
Stephens, Alexander H., 419
stereographs, 555

Stevens, Thaddeus, 397, 404, 484, 486, 487, 489, 500, 507
Steward, Ira, 539, 552–53
Stiles, Joseph, 485
Still, Peter, 287
Stirpium Adversaria Nova, 40
Stone, Barton, 303
Stone, Lucy, 277
Stono Rebellion, 69
Stowe, Harriet Beecher, *272*, 397
streetcars, desegregation of, 450, 497
strikes, *see* labor movement
Stuart, J. E. B., 408
sugar:
    in Brazil, 8, 18
    cane, 184, 186, 190, 195, 212, 469
    slavery and, 8, 18, 24, 26, 52, 59, 61, 204, 212
    in West Indies, 8, 24, 26, 52, 59, 61, 130, 135, 205
Sugar (Revenue) Act (1764), 131, 132
Sumner, Charles, 397, 398, 431, 484, 486, 487, 500, 507
Sumner, William Graham, 530–31
Supreme Court, North Carolina, 197
Supreme Court, U.S., slavery and, 407
Sweden, 81, 263, 528
Swift, Gustavus, 523
Swinton, John, 543
Sylvis, William H., 360–61, 425, 532, 534, 538, 540, 543

tailors, 334, 351, 355, 358, 525, 537
Tallmadge, James, Jr., 376
Taney, Roger B., 407, 409
tariffs, 331
    of 1816, 249
    of 1828, 376–77
    of 1863–64, 441
    in Ireland, 258
tarring and feathering, *149*
Taylor, Edward, 112
Taylor, Zachary, 404
tea, 133–34, 135, 144
teachers, 443
    African-Americans as, 475, 476
    women as, 443
Tecumseh, 187–88, 230–31
telegraph, 228, 515
telephone, 515
temperance movement, 305–6, 307, 308, 348
temperance plays, 295
Tennent, Gilbert, 120, 121
Tennessee:
    agriculture, 190, 456
    Civil War and, 460
    politics, 489, 497, 500

religion, 311
secession, 426
settlement, 190, 374
slavery in, 406, 434
voting rights in, 373, 488
Tenskwatawa, 187–88, 229–31
Texas:
    agriculture, 195
    annexation, 221, 387–89
    schools, 497
    secession, 419, 420
    slavery in, 184, 204, 387
textile industry:
    cotton and, 184–85, 191, 195, 214–15, 218, 440
    in Great Britain, 29–30, 144, 184–85, 191, 195, 215, 218
    mechanization of, 251–56, *338*
    in North, 215, 218, *220*, 226, 251–56, 335–39, 351, 422, 440
    in South, 214–15, 218
Thanksgiving Day, 254
Thayendanegea, *155*
theater, 292, 293–98
Thirteenth Amendment, 418, 463, 482
Thomas, George H., 449
Thoughts on Government (Adams), 159
Thrane, Marcus, 263–64
Tilden, Samuel J., 510
Tilley, James, *101*
Timbuktu, 21
Tippecanoe River, 231
tobacco, 8, 18, 24, 26, 37, 44–65, 135, 165, 190, 456
    declining importance, 184, 195
    economics, 54–56, 186
    growth of industry, 40, 44–46, 48
    slavery and, 50–55, 59–65, 203–4, 211
Tocqueville, Alexis de, 317
Toltecs, 10
Towerson, William, 22
Townshend, Charles, 132, 135
trade, 16, 17, 224–26
    Africa and, 22–23
    East-West, 224, 226, 234–36, 238–39
    between England and colonies, 54–55, 80–81, 107–8, 129–30
    North-South, 201, 238
    regulations, 55–56, 107
    routes, 17
Trail of Tears, 189
Trainman's Union, 554
tramps, 546, *548*
Transfiguration Church, 309–10
transportation, 224–28, 243–44, 340
    see also railroads; shipping

Trask, Sarah, 274, 280
Treanor, B. S., 351, 355
Treaty of Fort Jackson, 188
Treaty of Greenville, 229
Treaty of Paris, 162, 229
Tredegar ironworks, 213, 458
Trevellick, Richard, 540, 543, 552
"trickster" tales, 300
Trollope, Frances, *193*, 294, 295
Trumbull, Lyman, 484
Truth, Sojourner, 281
Tubman, Harriet, 394–95, 451
Turkey, 17
Turnbull, Robert J., 377
Turner, Henry M., 493
Turner, Nat, 354, 370–71, 382, 384, 402
Tuscarora Indians, 89
Tuskegee, Ala., 491
Twain, Mark, 290–91
Twelve Years a Slave (Northrup), 206–7
Two Treatises of Government (Locke), 34
Tyler, Wat, 16
typewriter, 515

Uncle Tom's Cabin (Stowe), 397
underground railroad, 394–95
unemployment:
    in 1870s, 515, 546
    pre-Civil War, 241–42, 256, 342–43, 355, 359,422
Union, 332
Union Army, 428
    African-American troops, *449*, 452–55, *471*
    composition, 425, *446*
    "Corps d'Afrique" of, *471*
    destruction by, 458, 462
    Fifty-Fifth Massachusetts Colored Regiment, 461
    Irish Brigade, 425, 447
    morale, 439–40
    Sixty-Ninth Regiment, 425
    slaves and, 428–35, 450–52, 460–61, 478
    turning point, 447–49
Union League, 491–92, 494, 495, *496*, 499, 503, 504, 506, 511
Union Pacific Railroad, 516
unions, *see* labor movement
Unitarian Church, 348
United States:
    China and, 225, 226
    economy, 222, 256, 342–45, 347, 440–45, 508, 515–16, 523
    federal budget, 442
    federal bureaucracy, 442